The Voodoo Encyclopedia

The Voodoo Encyclopedia
Magic, Ritual, and Religion

JEFFREY E. ANDERSON, EDITOR

BLOOMSBURY ACADEMIC
NEW YORK • LONDON • OXFORD • NEW DELHI • SYDNEY

BLOOMSBURY ACADEMIC
Bloomsbury Publishing Inc
1385 Broadway, New York, NY 10018, USA
50 Bedford Square, London, WC1B 3DP, UK
29 Earlsfort Terrace, Dublin 2, Ireland

BLOOMSBURY, BLOOMSBURY ACADEMIC and the Diana logo
are trademarks of Bloomsbury Publishing Plc

First published in the United States of America by ABC-CLIO 2015
Paperback edition published by Bloomsbury Academic 2024

Copyright © Bloomsbury Publishing Inc, 2024

Cover design by Silverander Communications
Cover photo: Voodoo. (MARKA/Alamy)

All rights reserved. No part of this publication may be reproduced or
transmitted in any form or by any means, electronic or mechanical,
including photocopying, recording, or any information storage or retrieval
system, without prior permission in writing from the publishers.

Bloomsbury Publishing Inc does not have any control over, or responsibility for,
any third-party websites referred to or in this book. All internet addresses given
in this book were correct at the time of going to press. The author and publisher
regret any inconvenience caused if addresses have changed or sites have
ceased to exist, but can accept no responsibility for any such changes.

Library of Congress Cataloging-in-Publication Data
The Voodoo encyclopedia: magic, ritual, and religion / Jeffrey E. Anderson, editor.
pages cm
Includes bibliographical references and index.
ISBN 978-1-61069-208-3 (print)—ISBN 978-1-61069-209-0 (e-book)
1. Vodou—Encyclopedias. I. Anderson, Jeffrey E., 1974–editor.
BL2490.V656 2015
299.6'7503—dc23 2015008081

ISBN: HB: 978-1-6106-9208-3
PB: 979-8-7651-1474-2
ePDF: 978-1-6106-9209-0
eBook: 979-8-2161-6274-2

To find out more about our authors and books visit www.bloomsbury.com
and sign up for our newsletters.

To my wife, Lynn; children, Michael and David;
parents; and parents-in-law

Contents

Alphabetical List of Entries	ix
List of Entries by Topic	xiii
Preface	xvii
A–Z Entries	1
Visual Representations of Vodou and Voodoo	327
Primary Documents	337
Bibliography	393
About the Editor and Contributors	415
Index	421

Alphabetical List of Entries

Agassu/Agoussou
Agwe Ta'Woyo
Aizan-Veleteke
Alexander, Jim
Altars
Ancestral Spirits
Anti-Vodou Campaigns
Art, Vodou/Voodoo in
Ason
Ayida Wedo
Azaka

Baron Samedi
Bayou St. Jean
Beauvoir, Max Gesner
Bellegarde-Smith, Patrick
Bight of Benin
Black Cat Bone
Blanc Dani
Bòkò
Bondye
Books
Boukman, Dutty
Brown, Karen McCarthy

Cable, George Washington
Candles
Candomblé
Catholicism and Vodou/Voodoo
Cemeteries
Ceremonies
Chango
Charlo
Code Noir
Congo Square
Congress of Santa Barbara (KOSANBA)
Conjure
Cosmogram
Courlander, Harold

Creoles of Louisiana
Creolization
Cultural Politics

Dahomey
Danbala
Dances
Davis, Wade
Death
Dédé, Sanité
Desmangles, Leslie
Divination
Dolls
Dorsainvil, Justin Chrysostome (J. C.)
Drapo
Drugstores
Drums

Ellis, Alfred Burdon
Entertainment, Voodoo as
Espiritismo
Ewe
Ezili

Federal Writers' Project
Féraille, Joe
Film, Vodou/Voodoo in

Gede
Ginen
Grand Zombi
Graveyard Dirt
Gris-gris

Haiti
Haitian Immigration to the United States
Haitian Revolution
Hand

Healing
Hoodoo
Hopkins, Laura
Hurston, Zora Neale
Hyatt, Harry Middleton

Ifá
Initiations
Interventionism by the United States in Haiti

Kanzo
Konesans
Kongo
Kreyòl

Lakou
Langaj
Laplas
Lasiren
Lave Tèt
Laveau, Marie
Legba
Legislation against Vodou/Voodoo
Literature, Vodou/Voodoo in
Loederer, Richard A.
Long, Carolyn Morrow
Lwa

Macouloumba, Jean
Magic
Makandal
Mambo
Manje-yanm (Eating of the Yams)
Maroon
Maryaj Lwa (Marriage to Lwa)
Métraux, Alfred
Michel, Claudine
Modern Voodoo/Vodou and Hoodoo Businesses
Mojo
Montanée, Jean
Moreau de Saint-Méry, Médéric Louis-Élie
Music and Haitian Vodou
Myalism

Nanchons
Nation Sack
National Confederation of Haitian Vodou

Native American Influences on Voodoo
New Age and Neopaganism and Voodoo/Vodou
New Orleans
Nzambi a Mpungu

Obeah
Ogou
Opening
Ossange/Assonquer
Ounfò
Oungan
Oungenikon
Ounsi
Owen, Mary Alicia

Paket Kongo
Papa LaBas
Parterre
Petwo
Pilgrimages
Possession
Prèt Savann
Price-Mars, Jean
Pris de Je
Pythons

Rada
Rootwork
Rosenthal, Judy

Sacrifice
Saint John's Eve
Saints
Santería
Scrubs
Seabrook, William Buehler
Secret Societies
Senegambia
Simbi
The Sixth and Seventh Books of Moses
Slavery and the Slave Trade
Snakes
Souls
Spiritual Churches
Spiritualism
St. John, Sir Spenser
Swords
Syncretism

ALPHABETICAL LIST OF ENTRIES

Tallant, Robert
Terminology
Thompson, Robert Farris
'Tit Albert
Toledano, Betsy
Tourism
Twins
Two Head

Vèvè
The Vodou Church in Haiti
Vodou in Haiti

Vodu in West Africa
Voodoo in the Mississippi Valley

Wanga
Ward, Martha
West Central Africa
Worker

Yoruba

Zombi

List of Entries by Topic

CEREMONIES

Ceremonies
Dances
Divination
Initiations
Kanzo
Langaj
Lave Tèt
Manje-yanm (Eating of the Yams)
Maryaj Lwa (Marriage to Lwa)
Opening
Parterre
Pilgrimages
Possession
Pris de Je
Sacrifice
Saint John's Eve

CONCEPTS

Creolization
Death
Konesans
Syncretism
Terminology

CULTURE

Art, Vodou/Voodoo in
Catholicism and Vodou/Voodoo
Cultural Politics
Entertainment, Voodoo as
Film, Vodou/Voodoo in
Kreyòl
Literature, Vodou/Voodoo in
Music and Haitian Vodou
Native American Influences on Voodoo
New Age and Neopaganism and Voodoo/Vodou
Tourism

EVENTS AND OTHER HISTORICAL DEVELOPMENTS

Anti-Vodou Campaigns
Code Noir
Haitian Immigration to the United States
Haitian Revolution
Interventionism by the United States in Haiti
Legislation against Vodou/Voodoo
Slavery and the Slave Trade

GENERAL

Vodou in Haiti
Vodu in West Africa
Voodoo in the Mississippi Valley

INDIVIDUALS

Alexander, Jim
Beauvoir, Max Gesner
Bellegarde-Smith, Patrick
Boukman, Dutty

Brown, Karen McCarthy
Cable, George Washington
Courlander, Harold
Davis, Wade
Dédé, Sanité
Desmangles, Leslie
Dorsainvil, Justin Chrysostome (J. C.)
Ellis, Alfred Burdon
Hopkins, Laura
Hurston, Zora Neale
Hyatt, Harry Middleton
Laveau, Marie
Loederer, Richard A.
Long, Carolyn Morrow
Makandal
Métraux, Alfred
Michel, Claudine
Montanée, Jean
Moreau de Saint-Méry, Médéric Louis-Élie
Owen, Mary Alicia
Price-Mars, Jean
Rosenthal, Judy
Seabrook, William Buehler
St. John, Sir Spenser
Tallant, Robert
Thompson, Robert Farris
Toledano, Betsy
Ward, Martha

LWA AND SPIRITS

Agassu/Agoussou
Agwe Ta'Woyo
Aizan-Veleteke
Ancestral Spirits
Ayida Wedo
Azaka
Baron Samedi
Blanc Dani
Bondye
Chango
Charlo
Danbala
Ezili
Féraille, Joe
Gede
Grand Zombi
Lasiren
Legba
Lwa
Macouloumba, Jean
Nanchons
Nzambi a Mpungu
Ogou
Ossange/Assonquer
Papa LaBas
Petwo
Rada
Saints
Simbi
Souls
Twins
Zombi

OFFICES

Bòkò
Laplas
Mambo
Oungan
Oungenikon
Ounsi
Prèt Savann
Two Head
Worker

ORGANIZATIONS

Congress of Santa Barbara (KOSANBA)
Drugstores
Federal Writers' Project
Modern Voodoo/Vodou and Hoodoo Businesses
National Confederation of Haitian Vodou
Ounfò
Secret Societies
The Vodou Church in Haiti

LIST OF ENTRIES BY TOPIC

PEOPLE GROUPS

Creoles of Louisiana
Ewe
Kongo
Maroon
Yoruba

PLACES

Bayou St. Jean
Bight of Benin
Cemeteries
Congo Square
Dahomey
Ginen
Haiti
Lakou
New Orleans
Senegambia
West Central Africa

PRACTICES RELATED TO VOODOO AND VODOU

Candomblé
Conjure
Espiritismo
Healing
Hoodoo
Ifá
Magic
Myalism
Obeah
Rootwork
Santería
Spiritual Churches
Spiritualism

THINGS

Altars
Ason
Black Cat Bone
Books
Candles
Cosmogram
Dolls
Drapo
Drums
Graveyard Dirt
Gris-gris
Hand
Mojo
Nation Sack
Paket Kongo
Scrubs
The Sixth and Seventh Books of Moses
Snakes
Swords
'Tit Albert
Vèvè
Wanga

Preface

The word *Voodoo* is very much a part of Americans' vocabulary, but few understand what it means. Most likely to come to mind are images of dolls pierced with pins or groups of the walking dead laboring in the fields or perhaps eating those unable to powerwalk away from them with sufficient speed. Those who have studied the meaning behind the term and its misuse eschew such notions and envision complex, long-lived religious traditions. *The Voodoo Encyclopedia* aims to help readers fit into the second category by exploring the theology, religious ritual, and cultural impact of Haitian Vodou and Mississippi Valley Voodoo.

Voodoo is a tricky subject. For one thing, the word itself suggests a variety of meanings, depending on the audience. The average American typically assumes that Voodoo is a form of evil magic associated with New Orleans. Those who are a bit more informed may also connect Voodoo to Haiti. To scholars of Haitian religion, however, *Voodoo* is a pejorative term because of the negative associations connected with it. They prefer to use *Vodou*, which also more accurately reflects the island nation's pronunciation of the term. In the past, writers sometimes used the word *Vodun* to avoid employing *Voodoo* in a Haitian context. When referring to the religion once found in the Mississippi River Valley and associated with New Orleans, *Voodoo* is by no means inaccurate, though there is some debate among historians and other social scientists about whether it has attracted too many negative connotations to continue in use. Those in favor of scrapping the traditional form prefer adopting either the Haitian spelling or *Voudou*, one of several versions of the word popular during the 19th century.

There is more to definitions of Vodou and Voodoo than fleeing stereotypes, however. For one, Vodou is a full-fledged religion, complete with initiatory rituals, communal ceremonies, priesthood, and places of worship. Though it contains magical elements, it is certainly not limited to them. By no means is it a faith dedicated to working evil. The same was once true of Voodoo, though our knowledge of the faith is fragmentary. In the United States, scholars tend to draw a distinction between Voodoo and magical traditions such as hoodoo and conjure, with most stating their views by saying something like, "Voodoo is a religion, and hoodoo is magic." Historically, this distinction is inaccurate. New Orleans's Voodoo practitioners, for instance, once referred to their religion with the term *hoodoo*, while calling themselves *Voodoos*. Knowledge of this distinction appears to have gradually faded from popular understanding during the first several decades of the 20th century.

Yet another issue that confronts anyone wanting a deeper understanding of Voodoo and Vodou is the connection between them. In the simplest terms, Vodou is a religion of Haiti, while Voodoo was a faith found in a portion of the Mississippi River Valley stretching from southern Louisiana to northern Missouri. While Voodoo largely died out during the 1940s, Vodou remains vibrant in Haiti and its diaspora. Despite the generally clear-cut geographic distinction, there is some disagreement over whether the religions were always separate entities. Some writers, most notably Zora Neale Hurston, have contended that Voodoo entered New Orleans when large numbers of Haitian refugees migrated there during the early 1800s. While this event, which approximately doubled the population of the city, almost certainly shaped the Voodoo of the 19th century, documentary evidence of the period prior to the migration demonstrates that some form of Voodoo was already being practiced in the region. Moreover, the Haitian influx does not adequately explain the presence of Voodoo in places hundreds of miles to the north.

A final misconception that must be cleared up is the connection between Vodou and Voodoo and other African and African Diasporic religions. It is not at all uncommon to find Cuban Santería, for example, described as a form of Voodoo. Such is not the case. Voodoo, Vodou, and the many other faiths of Africa and the Caribbean have distinct histories that have led them to develop their own theologies, pantheons, and ritual practices. Santería derives heavily from the religion of the Yoruba people group of modern Nigeria. Vodou and Voodoo incorporate some Yoruba beliefs as well but are much more indebted to the Fon and Ewe of modern Benin, Togo, and Ghana, and to the Kongo people of West Central Africa. Voodoo also contains significant contributions from the Senegambian region of extreme West Africa. The extensive mixing of elements from distinct regional and ethnic traditional religions is characteristic of Vodou and Voodoo but rarely as pronounced elsewhere. In Cuba, for instance, beliefs drawn from West Central Africa have their own spiritual tradition known as Palo Mayombe, which is separate from Santería.

With firmly established definitions in place, you are ready to explore the encyclopedia. Following each entry's title is a brief essay that ranges in extent from a few hundred to a few thousand words. Following the bodies of the essays are lists of related articles, the names of the essays' authors, and lists of sources the writers consulted while preparing the articles. The essays' subjects were selected with the goal of presenting well-rounded descriptions of Vodou and Voodoo. The authors are experts from a variety of backgrounds. While most are scholars, some are also practitioners of Vodou or other African Diasporic Religions.

In addition to a wide array of topical articles, several special features will help guide readers to knowledge they can use. At the beginning of the encyclopedia are two lists of entries, one alphabetical and the other topical. The former gives a quick overview of the topics covered in the book; the latter helps readers concentrate on specific aspects of Vodou, Voodoo, and related subjects. A brief essay on visual representations is provided to help those perusing this volume "read" the images it contains. The index at the end of the encyclopedia is of invaluable aid in this respect as well. For those who crave in-depth treatments, the bibliography provides a thorough list of highly regarded books on the faiths and related topics. Of course, not all readers are interested in deep study. For those of a browsing persuasion, the encyclopedia includes fifty brief sidebars with tidbits of information on Vodou and Voodoo's history, popular misconceptions about the religions, issues debated among scholars of the faiths, and interesting trivia.

Religions like Voodoo and Vodou have been so misunderstood and, consequently, mischaracterized that works like this encyclopedia have a purpose beyond relaying information. The authors hope that this work will demystify Vodou and Voodoo, freeing them from the stereotypes that have surrounded them since colonial times.

A

AGASSU/AGOUSSOU

Agassu/Agoussou began his existence among the Fon of Dahomey. According to legend, a prince known as Agassu was born from a relationship between a woman and a leopard. He would go on to become the founder of the royal line of Dahomey. By the late 19th century, the worship of Agassu was localized in the Fon capital of Abomey. Despite the limited geographic extent of the veneration of Agassu, he was a very important spirit in the city. According to A. B. Ellis, worship was linked to the high priest, known as the Agasun-no, who was second in power only to the king.

Agassu (the Haitian name for the spirit of the onetime prince) is linked with water deities and can sometimes take the form of a crab. Unsurprisingly, considering his origins, Agassu is a member of the Rada nanchon. He is also one of several lwa believed to be Freemasons. When possessed by Agassu, devotees shape their fingers into rigid, clawlike shapes. Alfred Métraux once saw a woman possessed by the deity stretch out her arms in the form of a cross.

In Louisiana, this deity went by the name Agoussou or Vert Agoussou. During Voodoo's heyday in the 19th century, writers who recorded details of its practice were far more concerned with entertaining audiences than accurately documenting the faith. As a result, only two works written during a period when Voodoo was already in decline preserve significant details about the deity. The first of these, George Washington Cable's *The Grandissimes* (1880), described Agoussou as the spirit "upon whom the voudous call in matters of love" and went on to state that the deity loved the color red. Helen Pitkin, author of *An Angel by Brevet* (1904), added further details about Agoussou, whom she called Vert Agoussou, meaning "Green Agoussou." In Pitkin's account, the spirit is the patron of Pastonair, a Voodoo practitioner, and as a result, the deity was the focus of great respect. When Agoussou arrived in the presence of the Voodoo priest and his congregation, Pastonair picked up a bottle of gin and sprayed it from his mouth over the attendees. Carolyn Morrow Long suggests that a deity called Yon Sue, known only from a brief reference in the records of the Federal Writers' Project, was identical to Agoussou. If so, then he was identified with the Catholic St. Anthony. Long also describes Agoussou as a defeater of enemies.

See also: Ancestral Spirits; Dahomey; Entertainment, Voodoo as; Federal Writers' Project; Lwa; Nanchons; Saints

Jeffrey E. Anderson

Further Reading

Ellis, A. B. 1890. *The Ewe-Speaking Peoples of the Slave Coast of West Africa: Their Religion, Manners, Customs, Laws, Languages, &c*. London: Chapman and Hall.

Long, Carolyn Morrow. 2006. *A New Orleans Voudou Priestess: The Legend and Reality of Marie Laveau*. Gainesville, FL: University Press of Florida.

Métraux, Alfred. 1972. *Voodoo in Haiti*. Translated by Hugo Charteris and with an Introduction by Sidney W. Mintz. New York: Schocken.

Rigaud, Milo. 1985 [1969]. *Secrets of Voodoo*. Translated by Robert B. Cross. New York: Arco; reprint, San Francisco: City Lights.

AGWE TA'WOYO

Agwe Ta'Woyo is a mystery of the Rada nation and possibly comes from the city-state of Allada in Old Dahomey, where he is called by the name Agbé. He is related to Sogbo and Gbade, who are called Sobo and Bade in Haiti. Agwe may also have some roots in the West African spirits Hu and Adantohoe, both of whom have characteristics and areas of influence similar to those of Agwe. He is said to be the son of Mawu-Lisa and brother to Naété. Agwe's home is in the sea, specifically "the islands" known as *Twa Zile*. This is believed to be an island under the water's surface. There Agwe has a fabulous palace, without doors or windows, in a conch shell. Only people who occupy a position in the Vodou hierarchy can access it. This allusion to the shell resonates in all of Agwe's attributes, from the horn blown to call him forth in service to his sacred name to offerings made in his honor.

In Haiti, Agwe is considered to be the master of the world's oceans, ruling all things in the water as well as the ships that sail upon it. By virtue of his association with the lwa Sobo and Badé, he also has command over the winds that blow over the oceans of the world and the thunderstorms that flash above the waves. Agwe is further associated with the dark depths of the ocean and the mysteries that may be found there. This includes sunken ships, oil, and minerals as well as anyone who has died at sea. As the patron of people who make their living on or by the sea, he answers their call of "Koki Lanmè," meaning "Koki lan Mer" or "Shell of the Sea."

Agwe is often visualized as a master and commander in the navy. Ounfòs keep an admiral hat, naval coat, and rowing oar handy for Agwe's appearance during ceremonies. Agwe is also the head of a large escort of spirits that includes his wife Lasiren, Agassu, Silibo Nouvavou, Klemezin Klermel, Ogou Balindjo, Ogou Badagris, and others. Agwe is said to be one of the principal lovers of the lwa Ezili Freda Dahomey.

A conch shell horn is blown to signal or call to Agwe during a Vodou service. Upon his arrival, he is greeted with cool water to keep him refreshed. In possession, Agwe does not speak nor does he stand or dance. Rather, he sails on his "boat," a small chair with a cane for an oar, rowing around the peristil to greet those present. Agwe's annual service is properly done by starting in the ounfò and then moving the ceremony onto a sailing ship and heading out to sea. Once out of sight of land, the celebrants place a small boat or tray, called a *bak Agwe*, filled with offerings into the water, accompanied by songs and drum beats. The sinking of the *bak* signals Agwe's acceptance of their gift.

Agwe's services resemble high teas, with fancy table cloths, china plates, and fine crystal. As one of the big white or cool Rada spirits, his offerings lean toward sweet pastries and fine drinks instead of meats and vegetables. Agwe accepts champagne, white wine, and coffee with both sugar and cream as offerings. Sweet oils, such as olive or almond, along with cane syrup round out the liquid offerings. Fancy finger foods such as melon, rice cooked in coconut milk, boiled or fried ripe banana (the small, sweet, yellow kind), and frosted cakes in blue and white are also appropriate offerings. Agwe can also be given perfume, mirrors, naval uniforms, nautical medals, painted rowing oars, and model boats/ships.

Agwe's colors are white, blue, and in some lineages green. His sacred day of the week is Thursday, and he can be feasted annually any time between June 1 and mid-August and again between December 12 and14. His Catholic saint association is with the chromolithograph of St. Ulrich, because of its image of the wise old man holding a fish.

See also: Ezili; Lasiren; Lwa

Patricia Scheu (Mambo Vye Zo Komande LaMenfo)

Further Reading

Ackermann, Hans-Wolfgang, Maryse Gautier, and Michel-Ange Momplaisir. 2011. *Les Esprits du Vodou Haïtien.* Coconut Creek, FL: Educa Vision, Inc.

Blier, Suzanne Preston. 1995. *African Vodun: Art, Psychology, and Power.* Chicago and London: University of Chicago Press.

Burton, Richard F. 1864. *A Mission to Gelele, King of Dahome.* London: Tinsley Brothers.

Guigard, Mercedes Foucard. 2006. *Répertoire Pratique des Loa du Vodou Haïtien - Practical Directory of the Loa of Haitian Vodou.* Port-au-Prince, Haiti: Reme Art Publishing.

Thompson, Robert Farris. 1983. *Flash of the Spirit: African and Afro-American Art and Philosophy.* New York: Random House.

AIZAN-VELETEKE

Aizan-Veleteke is a female lwa that is not only depicted as an elderly woman, but also considered one of the oldest lwa in the Vodou pantheon. Despite her aged physical appearance and advanced age, Aizan-Veleteke is responsible for several different facets of Vodou life. On the practical side of life, Aizan-Veleteke is associated with mercantilism, markets, and the public sphere. On the more spiritual side, Aizan-Veleteke is regarded as the universe's original mambo or priestess and thus is tasked with overseeing the initiation rites of new priestesses and protecting sacred spaces. Some Vodou houses assert that Aizan-Veleteke is the wife of Legba, while others claim the lwa Loko as her husband. In the latter case, Loko's spiritual and ritualistic duties run parallel with those of his female counterpart. In addition to her role as the patroness of priestesses, Aizan-Veleteke is a defender, preventing malicious magical spells, curses, and even other lwa from harming her devotees. The symbol most representative of Aizan-Veleteke is the palm leaf. Those seeking to gain Aizan-Veleteke's favor will present her with simple fruits and vegetables, including bananas, yams, and, of course, palm leaves. Her devotees do not offer her alcohol, as she abstains from this type of beverage. Aizan-Veleteke's critical function in both the spiritual and practical lives of Vodouists will ensure that she remains an influential figure in the faith. In New Orleans Voodoo, a spirit similar to Aizan-Veleteke goes by the name Vériquité.

See also: Legba; Lwa

John Cappucci

Further Reading

Alvarado, Denise. 2011. *The Voodoo Hoodoo Spellbook*. Foreword by Doktor Snake. San Francisco: Red Wheel/Weiser.

Deren, Maya. 1970. *Divine Horsemen: Voodoo Gods of Haiti*. Preface by Joseph Campbell. New York: Chelsea House Publishers.

Filan, Kenaz. 2011. *The Haitian Vodou Handbook: Protocols for Riding with the Lwa*. Rochester, VT: Destiny Books.

Long, Carolyn Morrow. 2006. "New Orleans Voudou and Haitian Vodou." In *Revolutionary Freedoms: A History of Survival, Strength and Immigration in Haiti*, edited by Cécile Accilien, Jessica Adams, and Elmide Méléance, 105–112. Illustrated by Ulrick Jean-Pierre. Coconut Creek, FL: Caribbean Studies Press.

Métraux, Alfred. 1972. *Voodoo in Haiti*. Translated by Hugo Charteris. New Introduction by Sidney W. Mintz. New York: Schocken Books.

Polk, Patrick Arthur. 1997. *Haitian Vodou Flags*. Jackson: University Press of Mississippi.

Tann, Mambo Chita. 2012. *Haitian Vodou: An Introduction to Haiti's Indigenous Spiritual Tradition*. Woodbury, MN: Llewellyn Publications.

ALEXANDER, JIM

Doctor Jim Alexander was a spiritual advisor and healer active in New Orleans from the 1870s until his death in 1890. Archival records show that he was born Charles Lafontaine in Hancock County on the Mississippi Gulf Coast between 1836 and 1840. Also called "Indian Jim," he was said to have a mixture of Choctaw, European, and African ancestry. Sources described him as "fine looking, very straight and about three-quarters Indian and the other colored, with reddish skin and high cheekbones."

Doctor Jim was not the religious leader of a Voudou congregation in the manner of Marie Laveau and Betsy Toledano. He did, however conduct healing ceremonies at his home at the corner of Orleans and Johnson streets that attracted a large, interracial, and mostly female following. In the temple room was an altar decorated with an image of the Virgin Mary, candles, fruit, and bottles of brandy. While his devotees sat or knelt in a circle, Doctor Jim would perform a dance that grew in intensity. As the excitement rose in the room, he would ignite brandy in a basin and continue to dance with the flaming vessel on his head. Believers came forward one by one for treatment. Doctor Jim would scrub their heads with the flaming brandy, grasp their hands, twirl them around, lift them on his back, and dance. After he set them on their feet, dizzy and shaken, they considered themselves cured. This was said to be particularly effective in cases of apoplexy. Doctor Jim is also reported to have rented a pair of barges and conducted ceremonies on Lake Pontchartrain during the annual St. John's Eve (June 23) celebrations.

During his lifetime Doctor Jim was the subject of derogatory articles in the New Orleans newspapers, where he was derided as a "quack," and his ceremonies, when raided by the police, were characterized as "orgies." Newspaper reporters ranted vehemently against the presence of "respectable" white women alongside "low negro laborers." A more sympathetic piece by the journalist Charles Dudley Warner, titled "A Voudoo Dance," appeared in the June 25, 1887, issue of *Harper's Weekly*. Here Warner described a healing ceremony conducted by an unidentified "doctor" that was obviously Jim Alexander. Several elderly informants interviewed by the Louisiana Writers' Project in the late 1930s also provided descriptions of Doctor Jim's ceremonies.

Later writers imagined a relationship between Doctor Jim and Marie Laveau. Henry Castellanos (*New Orleans as It Was*, 1895), Zora Neale Hurston (*Mules and Men*, 1935), and Robert Tallant (*Voodoo in New Orleans*, 1946) make him Marie Laveau's mentor, her rival, or her successor. Although Doctor Jim was considerably younger than Laveau (1801–1881), they were contemporaries during her old age. There is no evidence of any association between Marie Laveau and Doctor Jim.

Doctor Jim Alexander—legally Charles Lafontaine—died on August 18, 1890. The cause of death was given as "general erysipelas." Erysipelas seems to have been a catch-all term for any infection, although it specifically refers to one caused by the streptococcus virus. There was no funeral notice. According to the *New Orleans Daily States* article of August 20, "Death of the Voodoo Doctor," Doctor Jim Alexander had been "practicing his particular medical profession among the superstitious and ignorant for nineteen years, and had acquired a reputation among them for extraordinary cures and for success in the multifarious occult pursuits which charlatans usually follow." On the same day another derisive article, "The Voudou Doctor—Death of a Notorious Negro Who Throve on the Superstitions of His Kind," appeared in the *New Orleans Daily Picayune*.

Doctor Jim Alexander was married to a white Frenchwoman named Clemence Abadie. While very rare in the American South during the 19th century, interracial marriages were legal in Louisiana from 1870 to 1894. Their three children, Pauline, Antoinette, and Joseph, were born between 1884 and 1889 and were designated as legitimate on their birth records. Ten years after Doctor Jim's death, his widow settled his estate. She and the children gained legal possession of the family home at the corner of Orleans and Johnson, two other nearby lots, and Jim Alexander's movable property. The total value was around $5,000, approximately $250,000 today.

See also: Laveau, Marie

Carolyn Morrow Long

Further Reading

Long, Carolyn Morrow. 2006. *A New Orleans Voudou Priestess: The Legend and Reality of Marie Laveau*. Gainesville: University Press of Florida.

Warner, Charles Dudley. 1887. "A Voudoo Dance." *Harper's Weekly Magazine* 31, no. 1592 (June 25), 454–55.

ALTARS

An altar is any arrangement of items relating to a specific spirit or nation of spirits in Haitian Vodou. Altars can be simple tables with just a candle, a natural formation in nature such as a cave or tree, or a collection of buildings on a family *lakou*, or compound. Altars have been created from stone, wood, clay, living trees, streams, and water falls. There is an altar at Sodo in the north of Haiti that is found beneath the waterfalls on the upper level of a river. A large fig tree with a hollow in the center, a cave with ancient glyphs, a cemetery tomb, a bottle, a chair, or a stone could also be an altar. Altars in Haitian Vodou are alive. They can reveal much to those with the knowledge and eyes to read them. An altar, as Karen McCarthy Brown has written, is where the living and the divine meet. At the altar, one finds the power and ability to facilitate communication between the divine and the human servitor. But more importantly, one finds the ability to create healing by connecting with that divine surge of power.

There are three main elements that form a Haitian Vodou altar. They are candles, a cross, and water. At outdoor altars, such as caves and natural formations, a candle and water are easily carried to be presented on the altar. The cross is made through a physical gesture. Indoors, most altars are topped with clean cloth to delineate them as sacred space, separate from the mundane world. Sometimes the cloth is the color of the spirit/nation being served. In these cases, the cross is set in the middle of this surface, with two candles placed to each side and a container of clean water before it. This simple setup signifies divine energy piercing the manifest world and allowing the spirits to travel via the water.

Altars reflect the powers, spirits, practices, and interests of their makers. Altars can be dedicated to a single spirit or a single nation or multiple ones. Often, each spirit/nation's altar is designed and set up to best represent in physical form its internal meaning in the religion of Vodou. For example, an altar to Legba is often found at the crossroads or the intersection of two pathways, since Legba is seen as the guardian of the crossroads. The Rada nation is said to be cool, royal, and beneficent. Rada altars reflect this by being assemblages that incorporate white satin coverings, white candles, and clear vessels of glass or china for offerings—these items being representative of royalty, respect, and honor in Haiti. The Petwo nation is often described as colorful, fast paced, and island born. Petwo altars can be decorated in bright Caribbean colors with metal vessels for offerings that are often clanged with metal utensils, a reminder of the slave chains of plantation-era Haiti. The Gede group is funereal in tone and morbid in expression. Gede altars can be placed on the floor or tucked away beneath the main altar to demonstrate the nature of death and dissolution as separate from the living. They are decorated in colors associated with funerals—black, purple, and white, which is the color of the ancestors in Africa—and feature skulls and other mortuary décor.

Altars in Haiti are very dependent on available space. Small alcoves, rooftops, trees, and rocks are the most prevalent. In the Haitian Diaspora, altars have been created inside closets, set up high on shelving, or tucked beneath sinks, hidden from profane eyes.

See also: Gede; Nanchons; Petwo; Rada

Patricia Scheu (Mambo Vye Zo Komande LaMenfo)

Further Reading

Brown, Karen McCarthy. 1996. "Altars Happen." *African Arts* Vol. 29:2, Special Issue: Arts of Vodou (Spring): 67.

Cosentino, Donald J. 1996. "On Looking at a Vodou Altar." *African Arts* Vol. 29:2, Special Issue: Arts of Vodou (Spring): 67–70.

ANCESTRAL SPIRITS

An ancestral spirit is the spirit of a deceased elder of a family or community. However, it is not every dead person that becomes an ancestor. An ancestor is a dead person who led a morally worthy life, died a good death, and received proper funeral rites. There is no gender differentiation in elevation of the dead to ancestor status; both males and females can become ancestors. Nevertheless, the physically disabled, lepers, and those who died by lightning or strange diseases are not regarded as ancestors in most African societies. Members of this group are not accorded proper burial rites and so do not enjoy the privilege of being recognized as ancestors. In this sense, it is the living who actually create ancestors.

The veneration of ancestral spirits is an important component of Haitian Vodou as well as African traditional religion. This practice developed in Haiti as a result of the effort of African slaves to revive their African cultural and religious heritage. It was a response to the violent dislocation of the slaves from their roots in West Africa and the imposition of Christianity by European slave owners. The slaves in Haiti secretly invoked and celebrated the spirits of their ancestors, as had been done in African societies. Whereas slavery and the forced imposition of Christianity called into question the personhood and dignity of the slaves in the slaveholding societies, reverence for spirits of ancestors was an effort to rediscover and reassert the personhood and dignity of the slaves who still felt spiritually connected to their African ancestors. African slaves in Haiti also used ancestral spirits to fight against oppression. They usually called on the spirits of their ancestors for vengeance and to mediate in their affairs.

The belief in ancestral spirits in Africa and Haiti was born out of the feeling that life does not end with the death of the physical body. Death is only a transition from the human world to the spirit world. This worldview explains why the dead are venerated by Vodouisants. The dead are given proper burials to ensure a smooth journey of their spirits to the ancestral world and to reintegrate them to the family or community as potential protectors. Funeral rites are organized in stages among the practitioners of Vodou, and the rites can also be elaborate depending on the status of the deceased in the religion. Just like title holders in African societies, burial rites are organized in terms of first, second, and third burials, and these could be expensive. In Haiti, for instance, people spend their last pennies and even borrow to give proper burials to their dead. Followers of Vodou believe that the nature of the burial given to the dead determines the state of the spirit and its relationship with the living. If the deceased is given worthy burial rites, his or her spirit rests in the ancestral world and begins to play a guardianship role for the family. In this position, the ancestral spirit ensures the continued fertility of the family and that no calamity befalls it. The ancestor appears to family members in dreams to warn of imminent dangers and to reveal secrets about vital issues in the family. Sometimes, it mediates in family disputes, especially those involving land. If, on the other hand, the deceased is not given proper burial rites, the spirit wanders in anguish as an evil spirit and often haunts family members in dreams. In that state, the spirit belongs to neither the living nor the ancestral world. Such wandering spirits sometimes strike their family members with sickness and mysterious deaths for not giving them rest through proper burial. Africans as well as Haitians believe that the invisible spirits of the dead acquire powers that transcend the natural. This is why burial in some African societies and Haiti means much more than simply putting the dead body in the grave. It also explains why, in their world view, the dead are not really dead. They are better described as the living-dead, given that they continue to play vital roles in their families and communities.

Nonetheless, the culture of elaborate burial also has a sociological explanation. While proper burials are intended to ensure smooth journeys of the dead to the spirit world, people also spend much money to show their communities how much they care about the spirits of their deceased relations. People are concerned about what their neighbors or communities would say if they do not give proper burials to their dead. This has made funeral rites a heavy burden for the living in Haiti and in some African societies. The financial implication of providing a befitting burial for the dead is sometimes a burden to people who are advanced in age. This is so especially when people are in doubt as to whether or not they would be given proper burials by their family members. Those who are not sure of the ability of their children to give them proper burials plan ahead of time by providing basic burial items, such as coffins and money to buy other necessary items. Such people entrust money to the care of reliable friends who make it available when they die. This is to ensure that all the necessary burial rites are fulfilled. Hence the saying among the Igbo, "The journey of the spirit of a wealthy dead person to the ancestral world is usually fast." This is true because preparation for the burial sometimes starts even before the person dies. Once the burial rites are completed, the spirit of the deceased is recognized among the living and in the ancestral world.

During the performance of the burial rites, family members address the spirit of the deceased by making requests or wishing it well in its journey. Those who need children request the deceased to come back quickly. The belief in reincarnation among Africans shows that the spirits of ancestors pass through the afterlife and return to their families as children. Fertility is one of the ways of maintaining a continuous dialogue between the spirits of the ancestors and their descendants. The belief in reincarnation has remained a subject of debate even among the traditionalists. There is an account of a wealthy Igbo woman, Eleya Okwara, who killed a cow to honour the spirit of her ancestors. While she danced to the village where her late father and mother were buried—as the tradition demanded—her elder brother confronted her with the question, "How many children have your dead father and mother given you since you killed the first cow for them?" This question is very relevant and open to different interpretations. It could be interpreted that Eleya's elder brother was blaming the ancestors for failing to perform their duty by returning to his sister in the form of children or that he was questioning their ability to give children. That confrontation spoilt Eleya's joy of venerating her ancestors. Although the cow sacrifice went on, Eleya never had any other child outside the two she already had. The Igbo concept was much like the Biblical perspective that God, though merciful, does not answer all prayers in the way believers would like. For instance, Moses prayed to enter the Promised Land but God refused the request. Likewise, the ancestors were also at liberty to choose what requests to grant.

In social gatherings, the ancestors come first in recognition. The eldest person in the family or village pours libations and sometimes makes food sacrifices, inviting the spirits of the ancestors to have their portion. Sometimes, family or community members make food sacrifices at designated places, such as small huts believed to house ancestral spirits, or crossroads where ancestral spirits are thought to meet. The recognition of ancestral spirits during sacrifices is usually done in order of seniority, with the oldest ancestor being mentioned first. People believe that ancestors also need food and drink. When ancestors feel neglected by the living regarding sacrifices, they make the living remember them by inflicting diseases. When someone contracts an uncommon disease or dies unexpectedly, the rest of his or her family consults a diviner, who invokes the spirit of the ancestors. The spirit explains the reason for such unusual occurrences and proffers solutions, which are often sacrifices offered to placate the angry spirits. Some ancestral spirits have become so powerful that they are elevated to the status of gods. The Yoruba god of thunder, for instance, is believed to have been the fourth king of Oyo.

Belief in ancestral spirits is also a means of uniting family members and maintaining social order. Sacrifices in family shrines sometimes require the presence of family members. On such occasions, family members who live in faraway places come together for the sacrifices and have the opportunity to reunite with each other.

See also: Baron Samedi; Cemeteries; Death; Gede; Ginen; Lwa; Saints; Simbi; Souls

Arua Oko Omaka

Further Reading

Bellegarde-Smith, Patrick and Claudine Michel, eds. 2006. *Haitian Vodou: Spirit, Myth, Reality.* Bloomington: University of Indiana Press.
Hurbon, Laënnec. 1995. *Voodoo: Truth and Fantasy.* London: Thames and Hudson.
Métraux, Alfred. 1972. *Voodoo in Haiti.* Translated by Hugo Charteris and with an Introduction by Sidney W. Mintz. New York: Schocken.
Olupona, Jacob K., ed. 2000. *African Spirituality: Forms, Meanings and Expressions.* With a Foreword by Charles Long. New York: Crossroad.
Parrinder, E. G. 1962. *African Traditional Religion.* London: S. P. C. K..
Sundermeier, Theo. 1998. *The Individual and Community in African Traditional Religions.* Hamburg: Lit Verlag.

ANTI-VODOU CAMPAIGNS

Haiti was the first black republic in the Western Hemisphere and had achieved independence through the struggle, leadership, and revolt of slaves. As Vodou was a major part of these events, it was seen by the white world as something that needed to be initially suppressed and ultimately eradicated. The Catholic Church and the Haitian government joined forces and began a series of campaigns against Vodou that were known as the anti-Vodou, or antisuperstition campaigns.

The anti-Vodou campaigns are suspected to have started as early as 1860 following the fall of Haitian President Emperor Faustin Soulouque, who was a black leader of Haiti from 1847, declaring himself Emperor in 1849 and ruling until he was overthrown in 1859. He was known to be a follower of Vodou. In 1860 Haiti signed an agreement with the Vatican to recognize and establish Catholicism as the country's official religion. Vodou had been driven into secrecy through slavery and then, in the late 19th century, by the Catholic Church. Many contemporary publications offered sensationalized accounts of Vodou, adding to the impetus of the persecution of Vodou with tales of cannibalism and human sacrifice. It was known that in the 1860s, despite the signed concordat with Rome, Haitians were still attending Vodou ceremonies and turning to Vodou for spiritual guidance. There were attempts at anti-Vodou campaigns in the 1860s and again in the 1890s when the Church and Haitian government gathered Vodou-related artefacts and burned them. These attempts failed to eradicate Vodou.

Although not deemed an anti-Vodou campaign, there are many accounts of the destruction of Vodou idols and temples by marines during the American occupation of Haiti from 1915–1934. More alarming are the references to the number of "hats" collected by soldiers, as each represented a Haitian killed. Faustin Wirkus gave an account in which he describes the number of hats and a collection of Vodou objects that had been amassed by the American occupiers in his book *The White King of La Gonave*, which was published in 1931. Although items were being collected and destroyed at an alarming rate during the American occupation, the suppression of Vodou would continue with even more ferocity during the anti-Vodou campaign of 1940.

The Suppression of Voodoo/Vodou

Both Vodou and Voodoo have experienced attempted suppression. French authorities required that enslaved Africans be baptized and instructed in Catholicism, inadvertently contributing to the creolization of the two faiths. After independence, various Haitian regimes struggled to eliminate Vodou from Haitian society, often through what were known as antisuperstition or anti-Vodou campaigns. In the Mississippi Valley, colonial and antebellum authorities used laws against gatherings of slaves to halt ceremonies. Since emancipation, laws against practicing medicine without a license, mail fraud, the production of charms, and fortunetelling have all been deployed against Voodoo. By the late 20th century, however, both Haiti and the U.S. had largely abandoned attempts at suppression.

In 1940 the Catholic Church set out to eradicate Vodou from Haiti, as it believed that Haitians were not denouncing the spirits. The Church took a radical step. It insisted that all faithful followers of Catholicism take an anti-superstition oath, which included a promise not to attend Vodou ceremonies and to destroy all Vodou objects. There were severe punishments for anyone found to be persisting in so-called superstitious practices. These punishments became more severe when Haitian President Lescot ordered the army to assist church representatives with hunting down Vodou items. Thousands of items were seized, piled high, and set on fire as a symbolic victory of the church over Satan. Irreparable damage was inflicted on Vodou. The government, increasingly aware of the international condemnation of its actions, withdrew its support for this campaign in 1942.

This severe anti-Vodou campaign lasted for just under two years, and yet, despite this attack on Haitian beliefs, the people still turned to their spirits. In 1946 Haitian President Estimé was at the forefront of a new era for the country. Many intellectuals supported the authenticity of their spiritual heritage, and there was a Vodou revival.

See also: Haitian Revolution; Legislation against Vodou/Voodoo

Louise Fenton

Further Reading

Greene, Anne. 1993. *The Catholic Church in Haiti: Political and Social Change.* East Lansing, MI: Michigan State University Press.

Métraux, Alfred. 1972. *Voodoo in Haiti.* Translated by Hugo Charteris and with an Introduction by Sidney W. Mintz. New York: Schocken.

Nicholls, David. 1970. "Politics and Religion in Haiti." *Canadian Journal of Political Science/ Revue Canadienne de Science Politique* 3: 400–414.

Wirkus, Faustin. 1931. *The White King of La Gonave.* New York: Garden City.

ART, VODOU/VOODOO IN

While little record of the art associated with historical Mississippi Valley Voodoo has survived, the vibrant art of Haitian Vodou continues to be a unique combination of history and tradition inspired by the spirits. Artistic production is evident throughout Haiti and its diaspora. There is no written text in Vodou. Because so much of the religion is visual, the religion can transcend cultural boundaries, making the visual arts appeal to a wider audience. Much of the art from Haiti also incorporates Catholic iconography, which originated during the days of slavery. In an attempt to eradicate West African religions, the Catholic Church and France required slave owners to baptize and instruct their workers in the faith. The degree to which masters complied varied greatly. Regardless of slave owners' sincerity, Christian symbolism abounds in modern Vodou and the art associated with it.

The visual arts in Haiti fall into two categories: the sacred art, which includes the ritualistic and ceremonial works that are part of Vodou, and Haitian art, which includes paintings and sculptures based on the history and culture of the country. The form of sacred art most familiar to those outside Haiti are the vèvè, transient images drawn on the ground in preparation for Vodou ceremonies. The vèvè are generally drawn in white powder or flour on the ground by priests or priestesses. These are intricate patterns that are specific to individual spirits and contain elements sacred to the Vodouisants. They clearly demonstrate the importance of aesthetics within Haiti's cultural heritage. During ceremonies the vèvè must be drawn on the floor to act as doorways to the spirits. Once the spirit has been invoked, the vèvè are no longer required and usually are erased throughout the ceremony. The temporality of the ceremonial vèvè means that they are often not seen by the outside world. Their very fragility leads to their disappearance. Purely decorative vèvè may be seen drawn on walls, made in iron, or included in paintings.

The blending of African and European cultures in Haiti contributed to the development of ritualistic flags known as *drapo Vodou*. These are made from thousands of individually sewn sequins and images of syncretized Catholic saints. The use of flags to express relationships with authority and power has transferred to the Vodou flags, which show affiliation to particular spirits. The *drapo* Vodou use a format similar to that of vèvè, and any of the lwa may be represented on them. Popular demand for the flags as a commodity has led to two distinctive styles: those made for ceremonial purposes and others manufactured for tourists, galleries, and museums. The former are still known as drapo Vodou, but the latter, commonly called art flags, allow for more artistic expression. The artists, however, remain true to their culture by representing the saints and the lwa.

Vodou altars are often highly artistic as well. Most hold at least one bottle covered in sequins, fabric, or beads that is used as an offering. They are coded to honour a particular lwa and are also used as protection or for divination. The other item often found on altars in Haiti is the *pakèt Kongo*, which has its origins in Africa. The bottles and *pakèts* are artistic creations and have components similar to those of the vèvè and the flags, mainly because they are made to honour the lwa. Many bottles and *pakèts* are also wangas. Such objects become wangas when oungans, mambos, or bòkòs place magic on them for religious purposes. The wangas contain powerful supernatural forces and are believed to be alive, filled with living souls that are directed to provide good fortune—or if created for evil, bad luck or worse.

Vodou altars are unique and individual works of art in their own right. Some are small shrines with a few offerings to a specific lwa for public or private use. They can be found in Haiti and throughout the diaspora. Many priests and priestesses have their own rooms housing altars and shrines to numerous lwa, from small tabletop affairs to ceiling-high altars. The altar is not the focus for ceremonial ritual as in Christianity, however. In Vodou it is where offerings are made and placed. Altar rooms are seen as a doorway between the spiritual world and this world.

International recognition of nonsacred Haitian art can be traced to the 1940s, when an American named DeWitt Peters was in Haiti on a wartime assignment. As a painter himself, he wished to set up a school of art to teach Haitians. It was at this point that he discovered the untrained art of Hector Hyppolite, Philomé Obin, and Rigaud Benoit. These artists are commonly referred to as the first generation. Although this discovery of Haitian art happened in the 1940s, there is evidence that well before this time Haitians were painting on the walls around their communities and on flags, bottles, and ceremonial drums.

To raise awareness of the arts in Haiti, a demand for the work had to be created, and this happened with the opening of the Centre d'Art in the 1940s. The Centre offered "primitive"-style paintings for sale. The term *primitive* causes much debate. It is a term used to define a style of Haitian painting produced by artists without formal training, but for many it has connotations of colonialism. Many prefer the word *naïve*. The work of Haitian artists is devoid of rules, which has provided a freedom of expression.

The Centre's directors, Selden Rodman and DeWitt Peters, encouraged artists to work on large pieces for public buildings. This "Renaissance in Haiti" attracted worldwide interest, and it was this international response that arguably made Haitian painting what it is today. The attention attracted financial stimulation, which encouraged additional Haitians to paint. This commercialization has faced criticism, but it also provided a great incentive for Haitians to produce artwork. The second and third generations of Haitian artists feature Vodou more than their predecessors, especially the Saint-Soleil artists, who are in constant contact with their lwa.

The subject matter of the artists is influenced by their culture and offers a unique perspective on the views of the Haitian community about historical events. The first generation of artists had a variety of inspirations for their work. Hector Hyppolite's work is predominantly influenced by Vodou. Philomé Obin documented history, including scenes of the American occupation, and Rigaud Benoit portrayed Haitian life. The generations of artists that followed were more influenced by Vodou, and painters such as André Pierre and Lafortune Félix depicted their religious visions embellished with flowers and foliage. Artists like Levoy Exil and the late Prosper Pierre Louis emphasize lwa within works celebrating Haiti and its culture.

Hector Hyppolite (1894–1948), an oungan and painter, was particularly known for his aesthetically complex portrayals of Vodou. His paintings were directly influenced by his dreams and contact with the spiritual world. Little is known of his life, but many view him as Haiti's most important and influential artist. His work was collected by the Museum of Modern Art in New York, following the raised profile of all of the Haitian artists with the development of the Centre d'Art.

André Pierre's work is more intricate than Hyppolite's, and he symbolized Vodou across the canvas. There are many images within his paintings that relate directly to the Haitian community and Vodou. The reading of these symbols depends on an understanding of the language of the religion, but even without in-depth knowledge of the faith, one can appreciate the images as decorative naïve paintings.

Haitian paintings have been affected by the political climate. The American occupation, for instance, was painted frequently, especially by Philomé Obin. He had witnessed many battles during this time, including those between the Cacos and the Marines. During the regime of "Papa Doc" Duvalier there were no paintings portraying the President or his family. Although the painters were not restricted by style, they were influenced by the powers of the government and feared incarceration. On the ascent of "Baby Doc" Duvalier, artists began to paint politically fuelled images. One painter who evaded prosecution was Yosephat Tissaint, who painted a picture of Haiti being held up by Baby Doc Duvalier, assisted by white hands, an obvious criticism of Haitian politics. He painted it just before the outbreak of revolution in 1986.

Sculpture is also an important part of Haitian art. The beauty of Haitian sculpture is that it has a sense of immediacy to it, with artworks fashioned from materials one can easily find on the streets. It was during the 1950s that the most enduring and wide-ranging phase of Haitian sculpture began. Before this time there were artists creating pieces for the tourists as well as gift shops that sold carved "African" masks, something that no reputable Haitian artist has ever made.

One of the most highly acclaimed sculptors, and the first to gain an international reputation, was Georges Liautaud (1899–1971), an artist who worked in iron and who was led by the lwa. He had several phases. He started by making distinctive crosses and then moved to more figurative work, creating free-standing pieces. Old oil drums were his primary material, and he cut pieces from them, which he shaped in his forge. His imagination was limitless. Liautaud's work involved the simplification of complex images that would appeal to anyone. This is very much the case with Vodou; it is never quite what it seems to be, as it has an ambivalent characteristic. Sadly, many of Liautaud's original crosses, which could be found in the graveyards around Haiti, have been stolen, possibly by tourists as his fame grew. He taught other artists his trade, and they have continued with the tradition of metal sculpture. Their works are widely available.

Another sculptural form found in Haiti is papier-mâché. One of the leading exponents of this craft has been Michel Sinvil. He is known for his carnival masks but has honed the craft further to make sculptural pieces. Sinvil's sculptures are painted in bright colours and are inspired by the lwa and demons. His technique relies on sand to contain paper and glue. It was adopted by a pupil of his, Léonel Simonis.

There have been developments in contemporary Haitian sculpture, and the work of Pierrot Barra and Marie Cassaise uniquely expresses the Vodou aesthetic. Their pieces are made from material available in Port-au-Prince and include the iconography of Catholicism recognized in Vodou as the lwa. Their work is not traditional. It is a fresh approach to Vodou, and they make pieces reflective of the altars and shrines found in the ounfò. Barra started by making Vodou flags but then felt that the lwa wished him to make what he called "Vodou Things." He was an oungan and president of a Bizango group, a secret society with a reputation of social enforcement through the practice of zombification. There are Bizango symbols in his work, including coffins, skulls, and crucifixes, which create a dark spiritual link. One of the startling elements to Barra's work is the inclusion of doll parts; this is an ironic appellation for the Voodoo doll so frequently featured in American and British stereotypes of Haiti and Vodou. Barra's dolls have no link with the fabric dolls used for spiritual purposes or any other historical source.

Vodou art and the art of Vodou are integral parts of Haitian society. The arts of Haiti all have a sacred element. They are inspired by Vodou, and the artists are directed by the lwa. Vodou arts are created on a low budget, recycling any objects that appear. Although the materials in isolation are not sacred and are not art, by being used for the lwa they take on a new meaning and become sacred. The arts reflect the impulse of Vodou. In the history of Haitian art there have been outside influences, but the artists have remained true to their cultural heritage. The many years of invasion and persecution have provided an influence, but the overriding inspiration comes from the lwa and the religion of Vodou. There is a dynamic cultural synthesis taking place.

See also: Altars; Drapo; Lwa; Vèvè

Louise Fenton

Further Reading

Cosentino, Donald. 1995. *Sacred Arts of Haitian Vodou*. Los Angeles: UCLA Fowler Museum of Cultural History.

Rodman, Selden. 1988. *Where Art is Joy: Haitian Art: The First Forty Years*. New York: Ruggles de Latour.

Russell, Candice. 2013. *Masterpieces of Haitian Art: Seven Decades of Unique Visual Heritage*. Atglen, PA: Schiffer Publishing.

ASON

The Ason is a calabash rattle that is the symbol of office for an oungan or mambo in Haitian Vodou. In Haiti, this rattle is created from a gourd known as the *calebassier ordinaire*. It is a tropical gourd that exhibits luxuriant growth, hence the Kreyòl nickname *kalbas kouran* or running gourd.

The *kalbas kouran* is round with a longish neck that can be seen as a sort of handle. The gourd is picked off the vine dry and a small hole made in the stem to allow the seeds to escape. The hollowed gourd is then filled with small stones and the exterior netted with glass or clay beads, giving it a distinct sound when rattled continuously. This sound is said to be the voice of the ancestors and, when correctly produced by an experienced Vodou priest, calls forth the mysteries of Haitian Vodou. The ason's netting of beads is tied in such a way as to end in a long braided tail at the head of the ason. This braid is referred to as "Danbala's tongue." When the ason is used in ritual movement, the braid spins round, resembling a serpent's tongue flashing outward.

The use of a rattle to call or control spirits has its root in Dahomey of West Africa, now known as Benin. In his expedition narrative *A Mission to Gelele, King of Dahome*, Sir Richard Burton recounted seeing the court priests use a rattle to herald the coming of the king. They then invoked the deities of Dahomey by rattling before the image of the gods. When the deities arrived in possession, the priests used the rattle to control the gods' movements as well as send to them away when their tasks were complete.

The word *ason* has an interesting etymology. Due to the institution of slavery in the Caribbean and the millions of men and women brought out of Africa in bondage, the word has changed meaning and form over the centuries. In West Africa, *asogwe* meant both the rattle itself and the manner in which it was netted with beads and bones. In the New World, *asogwe* came to mean a leader who has knowledge of the ancestors. The rattle itself became known simply as *ason*, the symbol of priests from Africa and in the New World.

Asons are also seen in Brazil, specifically in Bahia and in Rio de Janeiro. There, priests lead large troupes of people with a rattle, directing the energy of the crowd and the spirits in long parades of singing and dancing during the Lenten season. This has remarkable similarities to the parades of Rara in Lenten Haiti, where oungans with asons take troops of performers on the roads from lakou, or Vodou yard, to lakou, singing for the spirits and making offerings along the way.

Oungan and mambo asogwes receive their asons from Papa Loko Attisou during their kanzo ceremonies. There are many references in songs to this act. Oungan and mambo su pwens are said to "borrow" the ason from their kanzo or initiatory parents. They receive their ason during a special service at their batèm.

See also: Ancestral Spirits; Ceremonies; Dahomey; Kanzo; Mambo; Ounfò; Oungan

Patricia Scheu (Mambo Vye Zo Komande LaMenfo)

Further Reading

Burton, Richard F. 1864. *A Mission to Gelele, King of Dahome.* London: Tinsley Brothers.
Scheu, Patricia (Mambo Vye Zo Komande LaMenfo). 2011. *Serving the Spirits: The Religion of Vodou.* Philadelphia: Published by author.

AYIDA WEDO

In Haitian belief, Ayida Wedo is a member of the Rada nanchon and the wife of Danbala Wedo. In religious artwork and vèvès, the two often appear as intertwined serpents. They are also envisioned as together forming the rainbow, and folklore claims that whoever can take hold of the rainbow will attain wealth. Like her husband, Ayida Wedo's favorite color is white. The Voodoo of the Mississippi Valley does not appear to have honored Ayida Wedo, though her absence from history may well be a product of the incomplete nature of the documentary record.

Ayida Wedo has clear roots in the Bight of Benin region of West Africa. Curiously, among the Fon of Dahomey, this spirit was male. Many observers and modern scholars considered the Fon deity to be the same as the Da, Dan, Dangbe, or Dan Bada from which Danbala developed. According to one Dahomean tale, Ayida Wedo upholds the earth, forming a supporting ring by biting his own tale. Earthquakes result from his movements, and he appears as a rainbow whenever he emerges to drink after rain. On earth, small constrictors are his messengers, and as with the pythons associated with Da, these were often protected from harm. Like in Haiti, Ayida Wedo can bring wealth to his African followers.

The Haitian concept of complementary male and female lwas likely has its origin in the Fon deity Mawu-Lisa. Mawu, understood as female, was the moon. The male, Lisa, was the sun. Scholar Robert Farris Thompson argues that the Dahomean Da also possessed these male and female attributes and occasionally appeared as twins rather than as a single spirit. While it is possible that Da provided the model of the male/female pairing of Danbala and Ayida Wedo, Mawu-Lisa would certainly serve as an excellent model as Danbala and his wife ascended to the top of the pantheon in Haiti.

Following suggestions proposed by Wyatt MacGaffey, Robert Farris Thompson has also suggested that both Danbala and Ayida Wedo can also trace their lineage to the Kongo people of West Central Africa. There, rainbow serpents known as *ndambas* supposedly intertwine around a palm tree to mate, an image very similar to the vèvès and artwork depicting the cosmic serpents in Haitian hounforts.

See also: Bight of Benin; Blanc Dani; Dahomey; Danbala; Lwa; Nanchons; Rada; Vèvè

Jeffrey E. Anderson

Further Reading

Courlander, Harold. 1960. *The Drum and the Hoe: Life and Lore of the Haitian People.* Berkeley: University of California Press.
Desmangles, Leslie G. 1992. *Faces of the Gods: Vodou and Roman Catholicism in Haiti.* Chapel Hill: University of North Carolina Press.
Ellis, A. B. 1890. *The Ewe-Speaking Peoples of the Slave Coast of West Africa: Their Religion, Manners, Customs, Laws, Languages, &c.* London: Chapman and Hall.
Métraux, Alfred. 1972. *Voodoo in Haiti.* Translated by Hugo Charteris and with an Introduction by Sidney W. Mintz. New York: Schocken.
Olmos, Margarite Fernández, and Lizbeth Paravisini-Gebert. 2003. *Creole Religions of the Caribbean: An Introduction from Vodou and Santería to Obeah and Espiritismo.* New York University Press.
Thompson, Robert Farris. 1983. *Flash of the Spirit: African and Afro-American Art and Philosophy.* New York: Random House.

AZAKA

Azaka Mede is an agricultural spirit who hails from the Djouba nation. He is very popular in Haiti, where Azaka rules both subsistence farming and small commerce. Most servitors in Haiti address him familiarly as *kouzen* (cousin). Azaka (or simply Zaka) ties people to their roots in the land, making him a lwa of memory and ancestry. Zaka has many avatars, including Minis Azaka, who is the oldest of the Azakas, along with Azaka Gweliye and Azaka Tonè. Some servitors say he is married to Clairmesine, while others favor Kouzin Azaka, or Manbo Azaka-si, who sells the food that Azaka grows.

Zaka came to Haiti from Savalou Mayi of Dahomey, in current-day Benin. He was honored there as simply Azaka, and his attributes were farming, agriculture, and produce. He was later linked to the Mende people of Sierra Leone, Liberia, and the Ivory Coast. In Haiti, *Mende* is pronounced as Mede, and in recognition of the Mede's skills in agriculture, they became a part of Azaka's history. Hence, today the appellation *Azaka Mede* is a praise name for this hard working Lwa.

Azaka traditionally dresses in denim blue, with a straw hat and a type of sack known as a *djakout* over his shoulder. His style of dress can also be traced to the Native Taino culture of the Hispaniola's early period. Azaka is one of the most native of all the lwa and holds frequent congress with other native spirits, many of whom walk with him as escorts.

Azaka is generally good-natured, but is known to be shy, suspicious, and at times even jealous. He assumes people will make fun of him for his country-bumpkin manners and tries hard to keep people from taking what he perceives as his food or money. A hard negotiator, he will loan money to congregations but will want exorbitant fees for the lending. One must be very alert when negotiating with Azaka! The society must also be conscious of Azaka's greed. Otherwise, he will take all the offerings given him, without providing any blessings to the community in return.

Azaka loves his food but is rude and voracious in his eating habits. Eating out of calabash bowls (known as *kwis*) on the floor with his hands, he consumes startling amounts of corn, rice, and beans, only to complain there is not enough. His favorite dishes to eat are country recipes, such as boiled maize, bread soaked in oil, and slices of fried small intestine with the attached fatty membrane. His favorite drink is white rum, and his tree is the avocado.

Azaka, like a farmer, is watchful of details. He takes notes of everything going on around him. When he mounts someone, he will freely share all the local gossip, much to the embarrassment and amusement of all. He does not take kindly to being embarrassed, and he does not forgive easily. It is rumored that Azaka often appears in manifest form, dressed in his peasant outfit and sporting a limp. He begs for rum or food, punishing those who refuse him a handout.

Colors for Azaka Mede are dark blue (as denim) and white; colors for the Djouba mysteries in general are dark blue, red, green, and in some cases, all colors. His sacred day of the week is Friday, and his feast day is held between May 10 and May 25, most often on or about May 15. He is universally associated with the Catholic St. Isidore.

See also: Nanchons; Saints

Patricia Scheu (Mambo Vye Zo Komande LaMenfo)

Further Reading

Ackermann, Hans-Wolfgang, Maryse Gautier, and Michel-Ange Momplaisir. 2011. *Les Esprits du Vodou Haïtien*. Coconut Creek, FL: Educa Vision, Inc..

Gilles, Jerry M., and Yvrose S. 2009. *Remembrance: Roots, Rituals and Reverence in Vodou*. Davie, FL: Bookmanlit Publishers.

Guigard, Mercedes Foucard. 2006. *Répertoire Pratique des Loa du Vodou Haïtien - Practical Directory of the Loa of Haitian Vodou*. Port-au-Prince, Haiti: Reme Art Publishing.

Illes, Judith. 2009. *Encyclopedia of Spirits: The Ultimate Guide to the Magic of Fairies, Genies, Demons, Ghosts, Gods and Goddesses*. New York, NY: HarperCollins.

B

BARON SAMEDI

Baron Samedi is one of a multiple set of spirits who go by the title baron. Alongside Baron Samedi, the most prominent are Baron LaCroix and Baron Simitye. They are considered to be brothers, each responsible for his own operations, his own work, and his own spirits. Baron Simitye is said to own the perimeter of the cemetery, and Baron LaCroix owns the graves within the cemetery. Baron Samedi owns the entire place.

Each Baron encapsulates a theurgic idea or truth relating to death or dying. Simitye (Cemetery) on its own is not a lwa at all, but rather a concept represented by the lwa known as Baron Simitye. Simitye is the place where the bones of the ancestral dead lie. It is the place of roots, the point at which life and death blur. Baron LaCroix (the cross, the physical symbol of two things intersecting, such as life and death) is the physical resting place, the "cross" through which all the dead must pass from this life to the next. Baron Samedi is the overseer, the great grave digger who resides within the gates of the cemetery, the bones of the dead, and the earth that holds the dead within it. Some esotericists have said that his name is a conjunction of *sa m'di*, a creole phrase meaning to impede speech or choice. But it can also be translated as "Grip, seize, take by force, pronounce incantations and bury." In French, his name translates as "Saturday," the day on which is his service is held.

Samedi's work is of darkness, death, and dying. He can induce possession, is the first dead in any cemetery, and is a necromancer by trade as well as a healer by function. It is said it takes one hundred and fifty years to become Baron. When that time is complete, the dead person becomes a small black butterfly who can go anywhere and forgets his family. But there is a caveat. The individual must be an oungan who wishes to become the first dead person buried in the cemetery in order to actually become Baron. If a mambo is buried first, then she becomes Guesdesine, the female version of Gede Nibo.

Baron Samedi is a busy spirit. In Haiti, Samedi reigns over all cemeteries. He is the head of the Gede family and rules them with an iron fist. In service, Samedi is called forth at the end of the night to collect his unruly children before departing the premises. He is the lwa in charge of buying and selling souls; making *wanga*, or acts of magic; and selling protective spells, known as *gads*. One must ask the Baron permission before taking a soul to make into a zombi. He controls the souls of those who have died by black magic and must be informed about the nature of the death of each newcomer in his domain in order for there to be peace in his kingdom.

Sorcerers and necromancers depend on Baron Samedi for an *expedisyon*, also called an *envoi mort* or sending the dead. The sorcerer goes to the cemetery under cover of night and, lighting a black candle, makes an invocation to Baron. With proper offerings and propitiation, Baron Samedi will oblige the sorcerer's request. Baron Samedi also searches for souls of the dead who are lost and forgotten so he can turn them into Gedes. And yet, for all this death, it is Baron Samedi who can be appealed to for cases of infertility. The one who claims the dead can also release them back into the world.

The Baron is one of the three mystical lwa who preside over the initiatory rites of kanzo. The Baron is also the spirit who can be appealed to for healing. It is believed that no one can die without the Baron's explicit permission. Therefore, the Baron is often called upon to offer intercession for someone who is sick or dying.

The Baron is not to be approached casually. In a place like Haiti, where death is close to families, the Baron is a spirit one does not trifle with. In Haitian Vodou, some sosyetes will not serve the Baron unless a person is specifically chosen by the Baron to be his servitor. It is said that anyone born on his feast day (November 2) is his chosen child.

Baron Samedi can be syncretized with St. Expedite, Saint Martin de Porres, and Mary Magdalene in Sepulchre. He likes fiery rum laced with hot peppers, unfiltered cigarettes, and ancestral foods like strong cold coffee, white bread, and grilled peanuts. His vèvè is comprised of the cross, the coffin, and the spade, all symbols of the dead and of graveyards.

See also: Ceremonies; Death; Gede; Kanzo; Wanga

Patricia Scheu (Mambo Vye Zo Komande LaMenfo)

Further Reading

Ackermann, Hans-Wolfgang, Maryse Gautier, and Michel-Ange Momplaisir. 2011. *Les Esprits du Vodou Haïtien*. Coconut Creek, FL: Educa Vision, Inc.

Guigard, Mercedes Foucard. 2006. *Répertoire Pratique des Loa du Vodou Haïtien - Practical Directory of the Loa of Haitian Vodou*. Port-au-Prince, Haiti: Reme Art Publishing.

BAYOU ST. JEAN

Bayou St. Jean is a significant waterway located in New Orleans, Louisiana. Referred to today as Bayou St. John, the bayou runs for approximately four miles from its mouth on Lake Pontchartrain southward through the city. Bayou St. Jean has served as a home for Native Americans, an important commercial transportation route, a Confederate shipbuilding site during the Civil War, and a famed location of Voodoo ceremonies in New Orleans.

Before the Europeans' arrival, Native Americans resided along the banks of what they referred to as *Bayouk Choupic*. Occupied by the Chapitoulas nation and later by the Choctaw, the waterway provided a means of efficient transportation and travel. An overland path also connected the bayou to the Mississippi River. Native Americans subsequently constructed a trading village at the intersection of the bayou and the path to the Mississippi.

The Choctaw introduced the French to Bayou St. Jean in the spring of 1699. At the time, a French expedition headed by Pierre Le Moyne d'Iberville was exploring the area in search of a suitable settlement site. Initially, the area's prospects failed to impress Le Moyne's group. Excitement increased, however, with the realization of the area's connection to both the Mississippi River by the overland path and Lake Pontchartrain via the bayou. The site offered the possibility of easy overland portage to the Mississippi River and a water link to the Gulf of Mexico via Lake Pontchartrain. French settlement soon followed this realization, with the official founding of the city occurring in 1718 by Pierre's brother, Jean-Baptiste Le Moyne d'Bienville.

The French quickly established the bayou as the primary transit route into and out of the young city. Christened Bayou St. Jean, it offered the safest and most efficient transportation option. Both the French and Spanish colonial rulers attested to the bayou's significance by constructing forts at its entrance into Lake Pontchartrain. The bayou remained the city's main port and primary water transportation route until well into the 19th century.

In the 19th century, Bayou St. Jean received attention for activities other than transportation. During the early Civil War, for example, the Confederacy commissioned locals to build gunships along the waterway. One such vessel was the 800-ton *Bienville*. The bayou, however, became better known for its role in ceremonial activities related to the practice of Voodoo in New Orleans.

Bayou St. Jean played a significant role in the practice of Voodoo in 19th-century New Orleans. The bayou assumed great importance in the ceremonies of famed priestess Marie Laveau and her supposed daughter Marie the Second. The elder Marie often bought herbs and other supplies needed for rituals from Native Americans who resided around the bayou. The bayou also served as a favored location for Voodoo ceremonies following the prohibition of such activities at Congo Square. The banks of Bayou St. Jean thus became home to various gatherings aimed at health, good luck, and celebration. These gatherings varied greatly in size and activity, and often included large bonfires, spirited dance, loud music, and feasts. The largest annual ceremony took place on St. John's Eve (June 23) near the Lake Pontchartrain mouth of the bayou. By the last decades of the century, the St. John's Eve ceremony sometimes attracted thousands of interested onlookers.

Throughout the 20th century, Bayou St. Jean fell out of use as both a transportation avenue and ceremonial site. Today, the bayou is largely unnavigable and protected as a historic and scenic river.

See also: Saint John's Eve

Jonathan Foster

Further Reading

Campbell, Edna F. 1920. "New Orleans in Early Days." *Geographical Review* 10 (July 1920): 31–36.

Carll, Angela. 1985. "Bayou St. John is the Reason for New Orleans." *Times Picayune*, November 15, 1985. Available at http://fsjna.org/happy-birthday-grand-route/.

Fortier, Alcee. "Customs and Superstitions in Louisiana." *The Journal of American Folklore* 1 (July–September 1888): 136–40.
Greater New Orleans Nonprofit Knowledge Works. 2014. "Bayou St. John Neighborhood Snapshot," January 10, 2014. Available at http://www.gnocdc.org/orleans/4/43/snapshot.html.
Hilton, Spud. 2013. "Paddling through New Orleans on Bayou St. John." *San Francisco Chronicle*, July 5, 2013. Available at http://www.sfgate.com/travel/article/Paddling-through-New-Orleans-on-Bayou-St-John-4648862.php.
Long, Carolynn Morrow. 2007. *A New Orleans Voudou Priestess: The Legend and Reality of Marie Laveau*. Gainesville: University Press of Florida.
Merrill, James M. 1962. "Confederate Shipbuilding at New Orleans." *The Journal of Southern History* 28 (February 1962): 87–93.
"A Voodoo Festival near New Orleans." 1897. *The Journal of American Folklore* 10 (January–March, 1897): 76.
Ward, Martha. 2004. *Voodoo Queen: The Spirited Life of Marie Laveau*. Oxford: University of Mississippi Press.

BEAUVOIR, MAX GESNER

Max G. Beauvoir is a Sorbonne-educated biochemist and the first supreme leader of Haitian Vodou. He is best known for founding the Peristyle de Mariani on the outskirts of Port-au-Prince, the Temple of Yehwe in Washington, DC, and the Groupe d'Etudes et de Recherches Traditionelles (G.E.R.T.) or Group for Studies and Research on the African Tradition. In recent years, he has become an outspoken advocate in defense of Vodou and its revival in Haiti.

Beauvoir was born on August 25, 1939, in Port-au-Prince, Haiti. In 1956, he left Haiti to pursue an education abroad. After graduating from the City College of New York with a degree in chemistry, he continued his education at the Sorbonne in Paris. Between 1963 and 1973, Beauvoir had several jobs in the United States, including supervising the synthesizing of metabolic steroids at Cornell Medical Center.

It was his interest in steroids that led him back to Haiti in 1973. While in Haiti, Beauvoir's life work took a turn away from science and into the world of Vodou. This process began in 1974 at the deathbed of his grandfather, Brun Icart, who was a Vodou priest. Icart named Beauvoir as his successor. Initially, Beauvoir approached Vodou as a scientific interest, but as he studied more about the religion, he became fascinated with it. Eventually the intimate ceremonies that Beauvoir held for his friends and family grew in popularity, and he founded the Vodou temple Peristyle de Mariani.

From 1974 through 1994, Beauvoir conducted numerous ceremonies and initiations at the Peristyle de Mariani and became the most respected and well-known priest on the island. It was during this period that he founded G.E.R.T. and the Bode Nasyonal for the purpose of protecting Vodou and its followers. Beauvoir did not support former Catholic priest President Jean-Bertrand Aristide, and some have accused Beauvoir of having ties to the Duvalier dictatorship, perhaps because of their common connection to Vodou. Beauvoir denies the suggestion he had any connection to the Duvaliers and has referred to them as horrible and abusers of Vodou for personal aggrandizement. Nevertheless, in May 1986 the Peristyle de Mariani was attacked as part of a wider assault, the Dechoukaj, on Vodou priests across Haiti.

Due to increased opposition to Vodou, Beauvoir decided to flee Haiti in 1994. He made his home in Washington, DC, where he founded the Temple of Yehwe in 1996. It is an offshoot of the Peristyle de Mariani and was founded for the promotion and understanding of Haitian Vodou.

After more than ten years in America, Beauvoir felt safe enough to return to Haiti and to reinstate the Peristyle de Mariani. In 2008, the Vodou priests of Haiti met and named Beauvoir their first supreme leader or *Ati*. He has proven to be an effective ambassador for the religion, which he feels could play a powerful role in resolving the problems of Haiti.

See also: Ounfò; Oungan; Vodou in Haiti

N. Lynn Anderson

Further Reading

Lacey, Marc. 2008. "A U.S.-Trained Entrepreneur Becomes Voodoo's Pope." *The New York Times*, April 5, 2008. Accessed November 7, 2014: http://www.nytimes.com/2008/04/05/world/americas/05beauvoir.html.

Large, Tim. 2011. "One Day in Port-au-Prince: The Voodoo Priest." Thomson Reuters Foundation, January 10, 2011. Accessed November 12, 2014: http://www.trust.org/item/20110110000000-ylarg/.

Tapper, Jake. 1998. "The Witch Doctor Is In." *Washington City Paper*, June 26, 1998. Accessed November 7, 2014, http:www.washingtoncitypaper.com/articles/15309/the-witch-doctor-is-in.

Temple of Yehwe. 2005. "What Is the Temple of Yehwe." Accessed November 7, 2014, http://www.vodou.org/whatis.htm.

Wilentz, Amy. 1989. *The Rainy Season: Haiti since Duvalier*. New York: Simon and Schuster.

BELLEGARDE-SMITH, PATRICK

Patrick Bellegarde-Smith (born 1947) is a Haitian scholar and Vodou Priest. More particularly, he is an oungan asogwe, the highest ranking in the Haitian Vodou priesthood. He is the grandson of the prominent Haitian diplomat, educator, and social philosopher Dantès Bellegarde—the nemesis of Jean Price-Mars (though they remained friends throughout their lives). He is Professor Emeritus of Africology at the University of Wisconsin-Milwaukee and author of many books on the Vodou religion. He holds a PhD in international relations, comparative politics, and history from the American University. He is a founding member and President of Congress of Santa Barbara (KOSANBA), a scholarly association founded in April 1997 at the University of California-Santa Barbara and dedicated to the study of Haitian Vodou and its impact on Haitian society and the international community. Bellegarde-Smith believes that the Vodou religion is an indispensable cultural resource in the process of regenerating and rebuilding Haiti. In the same line of thought, the Congress affirms that "Vodou plays, and shall continue to play, a major role in the grand scheme of Haitian development and in the socio-economic, political, and cultural arenas. Development, when real and successful, always comes from the modernization of ancestral traditions, anchored in the rich cultural expressions of a people."

Bellegarde-Smith has been a frequent guest speaker in various radio programs in the United States to discuss Haitian culture, politics, and the Afro-Haitian Religion. He has also appeared on television and had countless newspaper and magazine interviews as well. On January 9, 2014, he was interviewed by Krista Tippett for her prestigious radio program *On Being* about the topic "Living Vodou." In *Haiti: The Breached Citadel*, Bellegarde defined Vodou "as a coherent and comprehensive belief system and world view in which every person and every thing is sacred and must be treated accordingly . . . . This unity of all things translates into an overarching belief in the sanctity of life, not so much for the *thing* as for the spirit of the thing." He contends that not only did Vodou contribute enormously to Haitian freedom as the African slaves struggled for independence and decolonization from France, but that it remains a vital force in Haitian politics and culture and has helped to define the country's nationality and ethos. Vodou is a living faith that responds to people's spiritual, existential, and temporal needs. As such it also provides for the physical and psychological health of the majority of the Haitian population by amalgamating rituals from West, West Central, and South Central Africa.

See also: Congress of Santa Barbara (KOSANBA); Haitian Revolution; Vodou in Haiti

Celucien L. Joseph

Further Reading

Bellegarde-Smith, Patrick. 2004. *Haiti: The Breached Citadel*. 2nd ed. Totonto: Canadian Scholars' Press.

Bellegarde-Smith, Patrick. 2014. Interview by Krista Tippett, January 9, 2014. "Living Vodou." Audio podcast. *On Being with Krista Tippett*. Accessed March 3, 2014: http://www.onbeing.org/program/living-vodou/128.

Bellegarde-Smith, Patrick, ed. 2005. *Fragments of Bone: Neo-African Religions in a New World*. Urbana: University of Illinois Press.

Bellegarde-Smith, Patrick, and Claudine Michel, eds. 2006. *Haitian Vodou: Spirit, Myth, Reality*. Bloomington: University of Indiana Press.

Bellegarde-Smith, Patrick, and Claudine Michel, eds. 2006. *Vodou in Haitian Life and Culture: Invisible Powers*. New York: Palgrave/Macmillan.

KOSANBA: The Congress of Santa Barbara. 2014. "Declaration," March 3, 2014. Center for Black Studies Research—The Congress of Santa Barbara. Available at http://www.research.ucsb.edu/cbs/projects/haiti/kosanba/declaration.html.

BIGHT OF BENIN

The Bight of Benin is a broad bay of the Atlantic Ocean on the western coast of Africa. It lies within the Gulf of Guinea and is bordered by southern Ghana, Togo, Republic of Benin (formerly Dahomey), and southwestern Nigeria. To the east lies another important bay known as the Bight of Biafra, the second largest exit point of

West African slaves after the Bight of Benin. A British Consul named the Bight after the Benin Kingdom in the 19th century. The Bight of Benin played a significant role during the trans-Atlantic slave trade between the 17th and 19th centuries. The region supplied many of the slaves that were exported to the Americas, earning it the epithet "the Slave Coast," in contrast to the Gold Coast (modern Ghana) to the West, which until the 18th century was a major exporter of gold. The volume of slaves exported from the Bight of Benin rivalled that of West Central Africa. About 22 percent of the slaves exported to the Americas came from the Bight. It is estimated that the Bight of Benin exported about 1.3 million slaves in the 18th century alone and about 500,000 slaves in the 19th century. Despite the abolition of the slave trade by some European countries at the beginning of the 19th century, the Bight continued to supply slaves to some European merchants until the 1860s. The slave trade at the Bight of Benin was mainly coordinated by the Kingdoms of Dahomey and Oyo, while Lagos in what is now Nigeria and Ouidah in Dahomey served as the major export centers. Other slave ports along the Bight of Benin included Badagry, Port-Novo, Ekpè, Cotonou, Offra/Jakin (Godomey), Grand-Popo, Agoué, Little Popo (Aného), Porto-Seguro, Lomé, and Keta.

Ouidah was the most important of the slave ports along the Bight of Benin. It supplied about half of the total number of slaves that were exported from the Bight between the 1670s and 1860s. This shows that Ouidah alone supplied over a million slaves out of the 11 million slaves exported from Africa during the slave trade. The dominance of Ouidah in the trans-Atlantic slave trade is evident in the survival of the culture and religion of the people of Dahomey in the Americas. For instance, there is a village known as Widah in Jamaica. A large number of slaves exported from Ouidah were settled in that part of Jamaica. In Haiti, Vodou, a dominant religious practice that originated in Ouidah, took root. In the Republic of Benin, ethnic groups, villages, and families continue to maintain their vodun, which are ancestral and guardian deities. Ezili, the Haitian goddess, is believed to be a prototype of the female river goddess Ezili in Ouidah. Although one scholar recently argued that Ezili was a Haitian creation, an Ezili shrine exists in Ouidah even today. The survival of some elements of the Ouidah culture supports the known fact that cultural practices are easily retained in an area where there is a relatively large number of people to sustain the practice. The retention of some elements of the Ouidah culture in the Americas suggests that a large number of slaves were exported from Ouidah and neighbouring regions. The European slave dealers demonstrated the prominence of Ouidah in the trans-Atlantic slave trade by naming some of their slave ships *Whydah*, after the slave port.

Although Ouidah was an important point of embarkation for the slaves at the Bight of Benin, many of the slaves were organized in regions outside of the port. Within the second half of the 18th century, the Yoruba Oyo Empire provided most of the slaves that were exported through Ouidah. A large number of these slaves were settled in Brazil, making the country the largest recipient of slaves from the Bight of Benin, followed by the French colonies. This explains why some aspects of the Yoruba culture survived in Brazil. Brazilians with Yoruba ancestry are still making conscious efforts to sustain the shared cultural heritage with the Yoruba of Nigeria through cultural visits and seminars.

Available evidence on the Atlantic slave trade shows, however, that the great expansion of the slave trade at the Bight of Benin was not initially connected to the powerful Kingdom of Benin, a historical state with no connection to the modern Republic of Benin or its predecessor, the Kingdom of Dahomey. Intriguingly, the Benin Kingdom imposed a policy that prohibited the export of male slaves from its kingdom as early as 1516 and shifted from being a major exporter of slaves to trading commodity goods, such as pepper, beads, and ivory. The embargo on the sale of male slaves to European traders remained active until the 18th century. When the Benin Kingdom, known to the Portuguese as Rio dos Escravos (meaning "Slave Rivers"), could no longer meet the increasing demand for slaves, the European merchants shifted west along the coast in search of more supplies. Subsequently, the application of the name Slave Coast also shifted westward. This explains why the coastal portions of southeastern Ghana, the republics of Togo and Benin (formerly Dahomey), and the southwestern part of Nigeria are collectively described as the Slave Coast.

While many of the slaves who were settled in Haiti were exported from the Bight of Benin, a large number of them were also shipped from the Bight of Biafra. The common belief that the African slaves who were exported to Haiti and other neighbouring islands originated from the Bight of Benin considerably underestimates the role of Britain in supplying slaves to the Spanish colonies under the *Asiento*. The *Asiento* was an agreement in which the Spanish government gave permission to other European countries to ship slaves to its colonies. Britain benefitted from this pact. Until Britain abolished the slave trade in 1807, slaves from the Bight of Biafra and Central Africa dominated the African population of the British Caribbean. Many of the slaves from the Bight of Biafra were transhipped and smuggled from their first landing within the Caribbean islands to different destinations. In some cases, slaves were re-exported from the Caribbean islands to North American colonies. The role of Britain in supplying slaves to Spanish colonies under the *Asiento* Agreement and the transhipment of slaves within the Caribbean islands explains why some elements of the Igbo culture have also survived in Haiti.

There is abundant cultural evidence to show that a large number of slaves of Igbo origin were exported from the Bight of Biafra to Haiti and other Caribbean islands. The pattern of new yam celebration in Haiti suggests a connection with the Igbo of Eastern Nigeria. The new yam festival is the single most important cultural festival celebrated in all parts of Igboland. Another connection between the Igbo people and Haiti is a shared disdain for authoritarian leadership. The Igbo, unlike the Yoruba and Hausa, did not evolve a large and centrally organized political administration before the European conquest. With the exceptions of Onitsha, Oguta, Asaba, and Agbo, most other parts of Igboland operated as village republics that gave equal opportunity in decision making to every male adult. Although the society was somewhat stratified, decisions on vital issues were reached by consensus. No one individual imposed his authority on the people. Political power belonged to the people and was given by the people. This political culture posed a huge challenge to the colonial authorities when indirect rule was introduced in Nigeria. The Igbo were the only group that gave the fiercest challenge to the colonial authority in Nigeria. The famous Aba Women's Revolt of 1929 that challenged the colonial policy on taxation in Eastern Nigeria was led by Igbo women. The independence struggle in Nigeria was mainly championed by Igbo leaders. This tendency to challenge an unpopular and dictatorial regime in Nigeria strongly resembles the revolt of African slaves against their brutal European masters in Haiti. The Igbo-Haiti connection was corroborated by President Duvalier of Haiti when he made a case for the secession of Biafra from Nigeria in 1969. Haiti was the only non-African country that recognized Biafra as a sovereign state. President Duvalier stated that Haiti supported Biafra because of its historical connection with the Igbo. While the historical connection between the Igbo and Haiti was a reason for the recognition of Biafra, President Duvalier might have had other secret reasons. Haiti may have recognized Biafra to spite Britain, which strongly supported the Federal Military Government of Nigeria against Biafra.

See also: Dahomey; Ewe; Manje-yanm (Eating of the Yams); Yoruba

Arua Oko Omaka

Further Reading

Higman, B. W. 1984. *Slaves Populations of the British Caribbean, 1807–1834.* Baltimore: Johns Hopkins University Press.
Hurbon, Laënnec. 1995. *Voodoo: Truth and Fantasy.* London: Thames and Hudson.
Isichei, Elizabeth. 1976. *A History of the Igbo People.* London: Macmillan Press.
Klein, Herbert S. 1999. *The Atlantic Slave Trade.* Cambridge, UK: Cambridge University Press.
Law, Robin. 2004. *Ouidah: The Social History of a West African Slaving 'Port', 1727–1892.* Athens: Ohio University Press.
Lovejoy, Paul E. 1983. *Transformations in Slavery: A History of Slavery in Africa.* Cambridge, UK: Cambridge University Press.
Postma, Johannes. 2003. *The Atlantic Slave Trade.* Westport, CT: Greenwood Press.
Rediker, Marcus. 2007. *The Slave Ship.* New York: Penguin.

BLACK CAT BONE

The black cat bone is a lucky charm typically used by hoodoo and conjure practitioners. Its origin is rooted in African and European culture. Characteristically, Europeans viewed black cats as unlucky, whereas African American hoodoo and conjure practitioners considered black cats to possess useful supernatural power. Popular African American authors, such as renowned Harlem Renaissance writer and cultural anthropologist Zora Neale Hurston, and blues musicians, including Gertrude "Ma" Rainey and McKinley "Muddy Waters" Morganfield, attested to black cat bones' power and their effect on those who carry them. The black cat bone reputedly gives possessors the power to become invisible and the ability to fly. It is also widely believed to protect its owners from black magic, to bring good luck and romantic success, to effect rebirth after death, and to cure sickness.

Different rituals are performed to obtain the cat's potent bone. One folkloric tradition involves boiling a cat in a cemetery, discarding its bones in running water, and observing the bone that goes upstream against the current. Another practice entails boiling a cat's flesh from the bones and picking each bone up one at a time. Once the correct bone is touched the cat will scream. In her classic 1935 book, *Mules and Men*, Zora Neale Hurston posited that obtaining a Black Cat Bone involved a period of fasting, catching, and boiling the cat. After cooking the feline, the magic practitioner consumed each bone and selected the first bitter tasting one, which would be the one possessed of supernatural power.

See also: Conjure; Hoodoo; Hurston, Zora Neale; Mojo

LaShawn Harris

Further Reading

Anderson, Jeffrey E. 2005. *Conjure in African American Society*. Baton Rouge: Louisiana State University Press.

Federal Writers' Project. 2006. *Georgia Slave Narratives from the Federal Writers' Project, 1936–1938*. Carlisle, MA: Applewood Books.

Georgia Writers' Project, Savannah Unit. 1986. *Drums and Shadows: Survival Studies among the Coastal Negroes*. With an Introduction by Charles Joyner and photographs by Muriel and Malcolm Bell, Jr. Athens and London: University of Georgia Press.

Long, Carolyn Morrow. 2001. *Spiritual Merchants: Religion, Magic and Commerce*. Knoxville: University of Tennessee Press.

Young, Jason R. 2011. *Rituals of Resistance: African Atlantic Religion in Kongo and the Lowcounty South in the Era of Slavery*. Baton Rouge: Louisiana State University Press.

BLANC DANI

Blanc Dani, also referred to as Blanc Danny, was a serpent god who also presided over storms. Though primarily worshipped in and around New Orleans, he appears to have been manifested in Missouri by a spirit known as Grandfather Rattlesnake. Associated with whiteness, wisdom, and peace, Dani served as a positive force in the Voodoo pantheon. The snake of preference for the Dahomey people was the python, but due to the absence of this serpent in the American South, followers of Dani in and around New Orleans substituted other snakes. According to some accounts, these were released by Voodoo queens on special occasions to signal both a time to worship and possession by Dani.

Dani was frequently equated with Michael the Archangel. In Catholic art, Saint Michael is often depicted with his foot on the head of a serpent-like Satan. Another interesting aspect of the Saint Michael pictures is that the angel regularly appears holding scales in one hand, giving the viewer the idea that Michael or Dani is there to administer justice or equity. This would have been an important theme for African Americans who felt the weight of injustice and prejudice—adding to the appeal of such images as representations of Blanc Dani. A similar use of Catholic art by Haitian Vodou practitioners is covered by Robert Farris Thompson in *Flash of the Spirit: African and Afro-American Art and Philosophy*. In Haiti, the deity Danbala—a rough equivalent of the Mississippi Valley's Blanc Dani—corresponds to Saint Patrick. In Catholic iconography, Patrick, the patron saint of Ireland, often appears chasing snakes out of Ireland. Some followers viewed the snakes as coming out of Saint Patrick's cloak, giving him the appearance of being a snake god.

Although many brought to the American South by the slave trade would convert to Catholicism or Protestantism, others in and around New Orleans maintained religious traditions embodied in gods such as Blanc Dani. Places such as Congo Square, allowed African Americans spaces to dance, sing, and worship. It was in such areas of limited freedom that Blanc Dani developed from the West African deity, Da or Dangbe, worshipped by the Fon-speaking people of Dahomey. Dani along with Lébat and other African deities were celebrated on the Catholic day of remembrance, Saint John's Eve. Christians in Europe celebrated the holiday with bonfires, a practice adopted by the Voodoo faithful who adapted this celebration in order to honor their gods. These celebrations, along with other aspects of worship and ritual, provided African Americans a way to express the religious traditions of their home lands.

Unfortunately, sources describing Blanc Dani are sparse. Helen Pitkin's 1904 novel, *An Angel by Brevet*, preserves songs in honor of Dani that survived well into the 19th century. Voodoo Magnian, possibly another title for Blanc Dani, also appears in literature. George Washington Cable's *Creole Slave Songs* (1880) mentions this deity.

See also: Dahomey; Literature, Vodou/Voodoo in; Vodu in West Africa; Voodoo in the Mississippi Valley

Tom Riser

Further Reading

Anderson, Jeffrey E. 2005. *Conjure in African American Society*. Baton Rouge: Louisiana State University Press.
Anderson, Jeffrey E. 2008. *Hoodoo, Voodoo, and Conjure: A Handbook*. Westport, CT: Greenwood Press.
Cable, George Washington. 1880. *Creole Slave Songs*. New York: Charles Scribner's Sons.
Glaude, Eddie S., and Cornel West. 2003. *African American Religious Thought: An Anthology*. Westminster: John Knox Press.
Hall, Gwendolyn Midlo. 1995. *Africans in Colonial Louisiana: The Development of Afro-Creole Culture in the Eighteenth Century*. Baton Rouge: Louisiana State University Press.
Jacobs, Claude F., and Andrew J. Kaslow. 2001. *The Spiritual Churches of New Orleans: Origins, Beliefs, and Rituals of an African American Religion*. Knoxville: University of Tennessee Press.
Pitkin, Helen. 1904. *An Angel by Brevet: A Story of Modern New Orleans*. Philadelphia and London: J. B. Lippincott Company.
Raboteau, Albert J. 2004. *Slave Religion: The "Invisible Institution" in the Antebellum South*. Oxford: Oxford University Press.
Thompson, Robert Farris. 2010. *Flash of the Spirit: African and Afro-American Art and Philosophy*. New York: Random House.

BÒKÒ

Bòkò has different meanings based on the context in which it appears. For instance, according to Patrick Bellegarde-Smith, the term refers to a Vodou priest in the north of Haiti. Elsewhere in the country, however, it more commonly describes an herbalist or sorcerer. *Bòkò* can also mean a priest who practices magic. According to some popular authors, the distinguishing feature that sets a bòkò apart from mambos and oungans is that while the last two have undergone initiation into the faith, the first has not. Despite the lack of proper initiation, bòkòs sometimes operate their own peristils and perform other tasks associated with oungans and mambos.

Many practitioners of Vodou look upon bòkòs as potentially dangerous individuals. Both popular and scholarly writers describe them as people who "work with both hands," which refers to their practice of serving the lwa while also using one or more of them to inflict harm through sorcery. A typical explanation for how one becomes a bòkò is that a would-be oungan or mambo was either unable or unwilling to win acceptance by a benevolent lwa. Having failed to enter the Vodou clergy by the standard method, the aspiring priest buys the assistance of such lwas as Ezili Je Wouj and Ti-Jean. The Petwo nanchon is particularly associated with magic, though not all of its lwa are willing to participate in the harmful work undertaken by some bòkòs.

The reputed harmful works of bòkòs are of many types. Among popular audiences their supposed ability to make zombis is the best known of their doings, but the raising of the dead is but a small part of their purported repertoire. One form of sorcery that is particularly associated with them is the infliction of illness and potential death on victims, described in many cases as being caused by spirits of the dead under the command of the sorcerers. The symptoms are rapid weight loss and the spitting of blood. Fortunately for those so afflicted, oungans can drive the spirit away if sought out in timely manner. Unless they invoke the aid of the Vodou priesthood, however, victims die. Moreover, the attacks of the dead can be directed at livestock as well as people.

Bòkòs can also cause harm through the use of wangas. In Haiti, this term, used interchangeably with *poison*, refers to any item given supernatural powers through magic. Such items vary greatly in form, ranging from powders to collections of several materials, often including hair, nail clippings, or other objects associated with their intended targets. In general, wangas are less deadly than attacks by the dead, but they can nonetheless inflict significant harm, usually by causing illness. There have even been cases in which bòkòs placed wangas around ounfò in order to render the beneficial work of their oungans and mambos ineffective.

Folklore links bòkò with a variety of secret societies, most commonly known as *zobops* outside of Haiti. Haitian beliefs claim that these are essentially criminal bodies. Among their reputed activities is kidnapping for the purpose of recruiting new members or obtaining sacrificial victims. Many members supposedly have shape-shifting powers. These can be used by the bòkòs themselves to take on the appearance of another or, if possessing the power of a *lougarou*, or werewolf, to change into animals. Some reports claim that they transform their captives into animals prior to sacrifice.

> ### Paying Spirits
>
> Payment for the spirits is a common aspect of Mississippi Valley Voodoo and of hoodoo. In various ceremonies, especially those geared toward the working of magic, spirits expect compensation for their services. For instance, testimony collected during the early 20th century indicates that it was normal to add a 15 cent fee to the payment charged by hoodoo and Voodoo workers. This additional charge was then given to the spirits who helped work the magic. In Haiti, the idea of bought lwa can be negative and is often associated with bòkòs.

Outside of their actual existence and supposed abilities, bòkòs influence perceptions of Vodou. For instance, evil bòkòs frequently appear in Haitian fiction. Carrol F. Coates, a contributor to *Vodou in Haitian Life and Culture: Invisible Powers* (2006), has identified multiple cases of authors depicting them as inhibitors of social betterment and even supporters of oppressive regimes. Outside of Haiti, popular authors and filmmakers have tended to depict bòkòs and their sorcery as the embodiment of Vodou—a gross misrepresentation. Although such portrayals have declined in recent years, largely because of scholars' efforts to provide a more complete and accurate depiction of Haitian spirituality, the misinformation they spread remains at the heart of how the western world thinks about Vodou.

The term *bòkò* most likely derives from the Ewe and Fon word for diviner, *bokono*. In West African, their function is much more restricted than in Haiti, almost exclusively consisting of the divination with which they are associated. There are, however, several different traditions in which a *bokono* may practice, including Ewe Dzisa, Yoruba-derived Nago, and Fon Fa. These and other traditions are known to the scholarly community as Afa or Ifá. Regardless of the specific form, Afa relies on the grasping of palm nuts or casting of an *agumaga*, a chain made of eight seed pods interspersed with beads. Unlike Haitian bòkòs, *bokonos* are highly respected individuals in their communities, and one cannot enter their ranks without extensive apprenticeship to a *tobokono*, or teaching *bokono*.

While the concept of the bokono/bòkò survived in Haiti to describe a distinct position within the worldview of Vodou, the documentary record does record it in the Mississippi Valley. The same is true for oungans and mambos, however. It is perhaps telling that Voodoo priests and priestesses in the region sometimes went by the titles *wangateur* and *wangateuse*, respectively. The terms obviously refer to their power to make the wangas so commonly associated with Haitian bòkòs. This fact may imply that Mississippi Valley believers considered all of their priests and priestesses to be bòkòs or that some distinction among the priesthood survived without being recorded by observers. On the other hand, it is just as likely to be one of the many differences that set the area's Voodoo apart from Haitian Vodou.

See also: Divination; Ifá; Initiations; Mambo; Obeah; Oungan; Petwo; Secret Societies; Terminology; Wanga; Zombi

Jeffrey E. Anderson

Further Reading

Anderson, Jeffrey E. 2008. *Hoodoo, Voodoo, and Conjure: A Handbook*. Westport, CT: Greenwood Press.

Métraux, Alfred. 1972. *Voodoo in Haiti*. Translated by Hugo Charteris and with an Introduction by Sidney W. Mintz. New York: Schocken.

Michel, Claudine, and Patrick Bellegarde-Smith, eds. 2006. *Vodou in Haitian Life and Culture: Invisible Powers*. New York: Palgrave Macmillan.

Olmos, Margarite Fernández, and Lizbeth Paravisini-Gebert. 2003. *Creole Religions of the Caribbean: An Introduction from Vodou and Santería to Obeah and Espiritismo*. New York University Press.

Rosenthal, Judy. 1998. *Possession, Ecstasy, and Law in Ewe Voodoo*. Charlottesville and London: University Press of Virginia.

Scheu, Patricia (Mambo Vye Zo Komande LaMenfo). 2011. *Serving the Spirits: The Religion of Vodou*. Philadelphia: Published by author.

Siuda, Tamara L. (Mambo Chita Tann). 2012. *Haitian Vodou: An Introduction to Haiti's Indigenous Spiritual Tradition*. Woodbury, MN: Llewellyn.

BONDYE

Bondye is the Kreyòl derivative of the French *Bon Dieu*, which translates in English as "Good God," and is the generic name for God in Haitian Vodou. Vodouists also use the term *Gran Met-la*, meaning the "Great Master," a derivative of the French *le Grand Maître* to refer to a supreme, all-powerful, but transcendent and remote deity. Bondye is the first principle and great architect of the universe; he is creator and sustainer of everything that exists and from whom life originated. In this respect Bondye is similar to Nzambi of the religion of the Kongo people. Nzambi is said to be creator of life and of all things; he is omniscient and his knowledge is comprehensive. He gears history according to his will and purpose, and he is master over life and death. Bondye, like Nzambi, has direct access simultaneously to every possible world and geographical space, both in heaven and on earth.

Bondye is also the chief administrator. He commands, rules, and judges his creation. In the Afro-Haitian Vodou cosmology, Bondye is uninvolved in the personal, day-to-day affairs of men; because of his uttermost distance and otherness, he created the lwa/orishas (spirits) to serve as intermediaries between him and human beings. The lwa represent the manifold aspects of his character and communicate his will and attributes to Vodou adepts. Through their interventions in worldly affairs, the Good God provides all good things, including life, freedom, children, prosperity, happiness, success, and the like. While the lwa and humans have weaknesses and change, the Good God is perfect, constant, and unchanged.

Bondye is not only the supreme judge but also the king of the universe. He is above all things, and the *lwa* are subject to him. He rewards those who do good things and punishes individuals who do wicked things. As it is with the Supreme Being of Yoruba theology, Bondye is majestic and splendid, and it is said that his presence fills the entire sky and stretches out over the earth. His hegemony over the universe is unchallenged, and his will is absolute. He has complete control over

> **Is Vodou Monotheistic?**
>
> In recent years, it has become popular to refer to Vodou as a monotheistic religion. Believers do recognize a distant supreme being, Bondye, who created the universe, as do many of the African religions that contributed to the development of Vodou. On the other hand, most scholars treat the lwa as lesser gods, whose role in Vodou resembles that of the gods of other polytheistic faiths, including the religion of ancient Greece. The issue is largely a semantic one. The side to which one adheres may well depend on presuppositions about the relative value of monotheism and polytheism.

human destiny. Hence, Vodou adepts could say that the Good God has created some rich and others poor. Before Haitians embark on a new project or plan a trip, they frequently repeat the phrases "si Bondye vle," meaning "if the Good God is willing," and "si Bondye pemet," if the Good God gives his permission. Both mean that the speaker will do this or that or will go here or there if Bondye allows it, affirming the absolute sovereignty of Bondye the Great Master. As one writer affirms, there is not eventuality outside of God's will. The Vodouist knows that she or he cannot do anything without the Good God. Making plans without seeking the Great Master's advice is asking for failure.

See also: Grand Zombi; Kongo; Lwa; Nzambi a Mpungu; Simbi; Yoruba

Celucien L. Joseph

Further Reading

Casseus, Jules. 2013. *Toward a Contextual Haitian Theology*. Port-au-Prince: Media-Texte.
Desmangles, Leslie G. 1992. *The Faces of the Gods: Vodou and Roman Catholicism in Haiti*. Chapel Hill: The University of North Carolina Press.
Fick, Carolyn E. 1990. *The Making of Haiti: The Saint Domingue Revolution from Below*. Knoxville: The University of Tennessee Press.
Hurbon, Laennec. 2002. *Dieu dans le Vaudou haitien*. Paris: Maisonneuve et Larose.

BOOKS

Vodou and Voodoo have long been subjects of popular fascination, beginning with the publication of Médéric Louis-Élie Moreau de Saint-Méry's *Description Topographique, Physique, Civile, Politique et Historique de la Partie Française de l'île de Saint-Domingue* (1797), which included an oft-repeated description of a Vodou ceremony. Le Page du Pratz's *Histoire de la Louisiane* (1758) first introduced elements of Mississippi Valley Voodoo to the world. Since the time of Moreau de Saint-Méry and du Pratz, many other authors have taken up the pen to recount their encounters with Vodou and Voodoo. Spenser Saint John introduced English speakers to Vodou with the publication of *Hayti; or the Black Republic* (1884). Sadly, Saint John shaped many of the stereotypes that continue to inform public perceptions of Vodou, including the idea that human sacrifice was a common aspect of the faith. Among the more popular first-hand accounts to follow in the footsteps of Saint John have been William B. Seabrook's *The Magic Island* (1929), Richard A. Loederer's *Voodoo Fire in Haiti* (1936), and Zora Neale Hurston's *Tell My Horse: Voodoo and Life in Haiti and Jamaica* (1938). As with *Hayti*, these works have tended to emphasize the sensational, lessening their value for serious researchers. Mississippi Valley Voodoo, however, attracted relatively little attention, with only short accounts by George Washington Cable and others appearing prior to the 20th century. In 1935, however, Zora Neale Hurston published a lengthy account of Voodoo ceremonies she supposedly witnessed as part of a book entitled *Mules and Men*.

Fortunately, popular authors were not the only ones to record information about Vodou and Voodoo. Scholars such as Jean Price-Mars, Justin Chrysostome Dorsainvil, and Alfred Métraux produced significant works for French-speaking audiences. Among the more important English language authors have been Melville J. Herskovits, Maya Deren, Harold Courlander, Karen McCarthy Brown, Claudine Michel, Leslie Desmangles, and Patrick Bellegarde-Smith. In regard to Mississippi Valley Voodoo, the scholarship is relatively sparse. Newbell Niles Puckett dedicated an extensive portion of his *Folk Beliefs of the Southern Negro* (1926) to the history of Voodoo, making it the first sizable scholarly contribution to the literature. Five years later, Zora Neale Hurston published "Hoodoo in America" (1931), a lengthy article, in the *Journal of American Folklore*, but its veracity is questioned by some scholars. Over the last two decades, more solid scholarship has appeared in the works of Carolyn Morrow Long, Yvonne Chireau, and Jeffrey E. Anderson.

As one might expect, however, how-to manuals are by far the most readily available category of books, at least in English. These can be found through online companies, in bookstores of all sizes, and in the many tourist shops lining Bourbon Street in New Orleans. Not all such works address the same audiences, however. Many are intended for those seeking introductory knowledge about the theology and practice of Haitian Vodou. Some authors have themselves been initiated into the faith, two of the more prominent of whom are Mambo Chita Tann (Tamara Siuda) and Mambo Vye Zo Komande LaMenfo (Patricia Scheu). Their books, *Haitian Vodou: An Introduction to Haiti's Indigenous Spiritual Tradition* (2012) and *Serving the Spirits* (2011), respectively, are designed to convey basic knowledge of the faith to the newly initiated and interested seekers. Another option for those seeking accurate information on the Haitian faith is Shannon R. Turlington's *Complete Idiot's Guide® to Voodoo* (2002). To some extent, Milo Rigaud's *Secrets of Voodoo* (1969) could be classed with such works, though it is more geared toward revealing the esoteric meaning behind Vodou symbols and ceremonies than serving as a practical reference. While these and many other works provide readers with basic knowledge on Haitian Vodou, there are few that do the same for Mississippi Valley Voodoo, mainly because of the relative difficulty involved in gathering accurate knowledge about the historical faith. One of the few is Kenaz Filan's *New Orleans Voodoo Handbook* (2011).

Closely related to works on Vodou and Voodoo are many hoodoo spellbooks, some of which claim a direct connection to Voodoo. The oldest print work associated with the magic connected to Voodoo and Vodou is the *Petit Albert*, commonly known as *'Tit Albert* but properly as *Les Secrets Merveilleux de la Magie Naturelle du Petit Albert*. An early modern French grimoire, it was being used by practitioners in Haiti and New Orleans by the late 1800s and had probably reached both areas during the French colonial period. In time, New Orleans's Voodoo entrepreneurs developed their own magical manuals. Among those most closely associated with the Crescent City was *The Life and Works of Marie Laveau*, which appeared no later than 1927. It is unlikely that Laveau had anything to do with its production, but by the early 20th century, several of her spiritual successors embraced the supposed connection with the Voodoo Queen.

Several other works gained wide acceptance among conjurers across the American South. The most popular of all has been *The Sixth and Seventh Books of Moses*, originally a German book reportedly based on Jewish magical texts. The first English edition saw print in 1910, and it has continued to be a popular item in hoodoo supply shops across the South. Books that predict the future by interpreting dreams have likewise demonstrated great longevity. One of the first by an African American author was Chloe Russell's *Complete Fortune Teller and Dream Book* (1824), now a very rare item. *Aunt Sally's Policy Players Dream Book* (1889) has proven more enduring, remaining in print well over a century since its initial publication. Part of its attraction is that it attached lucky numbers to the dreams it explicated, rendering it useful to those involved in lotteries and similar games of chance. Among other standard works of the how-to hoodoo genre are Herman Rucker's *Black Herman's Secrets of Magic, Mystery, and Legerdemain* (1938), Lewis de Claremont's *Legends of Incense, Herb, and Oil Magic* (1938), Henri Gamache's *Master Book of Candle Burning* (1942), and a host of other works, old and new.

See also: Laveau, Marie; Literature, Vodou/Voodoo in; Modern Voodoo/Vodou and Hoodoo Businesses; *Sixth and Seventh Books of Moses*; *'Tit Albert*

Jeffrey E. Anderson

Further Reading

Anderson, Jeffrey E. 2011. "Voodoo in Black and White." In *Southern Character: Essays in Honor of Bertram Wyatt-Brown*, edited by Lisa Tendrich Frank and Daniel Kilbride, 143–159. Gainesville: University Press of Florida.

Long, Carolyn Morrow. 2001. *Spiritual Merchants: Religion, Magic, and Commerce*. Knoxville: University of Tennessee Press.

Long, Carolyn Morrow. 2006. *A New Orleans Voudou Priestess: The Legend and Reality of Marie Laveau*. Gainesville: University Press of Florida.

BOUKMAN, DUTTY

Born in the island of Jamaica, Dutty Boukman or Boukman Dutty was one of the most charismatic and radical early leaders of the Haitian Revolution. He was also a leader of maroon bands, a committed Vodou priest (oungan), and a practitioner of Islam. Hence, it is conceivable that he had practiced a form of religious syncretism, which constituted an amalgamation of traditional African religion, Islam, and Christianity. In Haitian history, Boukman is notably known for mobilizing

> **Revolt or Revolution?**
>
> Until recent years, many have understood the Haitian Revolution as simply a slave revolt. While a successful revolt of bondspersons is certainly nothing to look down upon, such conceptions miss important aspects of the event. Rather than simply an uprising of slaves fighting for freedom—which happened on a smaller scale many times and arguably with success in the case of some maroon communities—it was truly a revolution. At a basic level, it fundamentally altered the labor and hierarchical structures of a society. Moreover, it established the second-oldest postcolonial nation in the Western Hemisphere.

the slaves and organizing a Vodou ceremony with the Vodou priestess (mambo) Cecile Fatiman at Bois Caïman, which sparked the slave rebellion in the island of Saint-Domingue. The exact date of his birth is unknown; he was beheaded in November 1791, only four months after he initiated the slave uprising.

Boukman's British master had sold him to a French planter in Saint-Domingue. According to various sources, Boukman was forcibly exiled to the island of Saint-Domingue because he attempted to teach African slaves in Jamaica to read and mobilize themselves for resistance and attempts to gain freedom. The maroon and religious leader entered the epic of Haitian history the night he summoned to a nocturnal ceremony a group of slave coachmen who formed the core of this freedom movement to plan their liberty. Among them were Jean-François, Georges Biassou, and Jeannot Bullet.

Boukman had previously worked as a slave driver, then a coachman on the plantation of Clement, in the Northern region of the island. An enormous man, he was known as a charismatic leader and had an incredible influence on the various work gangs on the plantations in the region. His followers knew him as "Zamba" Boukman. Not only was he deeply involved in the unfolding political events in Saint-Domingue, he was a central figure in inaugurating the general revolt. Like François Makandal, his predecessor, who in 1757 had murdered 6,000 individuals in the colony by means of poisoning and magic, he was able to gain the trust of many slave communities and established a network of slave followers in Le Cap-Français, a major city in Northern Haiti. After judicious planning, the insurgent leader, his followers, and other revolutionaries teamed up to challenge French colonial rule in a series of brutal wars and radical revolts, which would last for thirteen years from 1791 to 1804.

On the night of August 14 or 22, 1791, at Bois Caïman (Alligator Woods), the high priest Boukman gathered a gang of slaves and uttered these important words in the form of a prayer:

> *Bon Dié qui fai soleil qui clairé nou en haut;*
> *Qui soulevé la mer, qui fait gronder l'orage;*
> *Bon Dié, zottes tendé, caché nan youn nuage;*
> *La li gadé nou, li ouè tout ça blan fait;*

> ### The 2010 Haitian Earthquake
> The Island of Hispaniola, occupied by the nations of Haiti and the Dominican Republic, is prone to devastating earthquakes. In 2010, a particularly deadly one struck the southern portion of Haiti with its epicenter near the city of Léogâne. Among the structures damaged were the Presidential Palace and other governmental buildings in Port-au-Prince, numerous schools and hospitals, and perhaps as many as 1,000,000 homes. The exact number killed is unknown, though estimates range from as low as 46,000 to a high of 316,000.

Bon Dié blan mandé crime, et pa nous vlé bienfait;
Mais Dié la qui si bon ordonné nous veangeance;
Li va conduit bra ou, ba nou assistance;
Jeté pòtrait Dié blan qui soif dlo nan zies;
Couté la liberté qui parlé nan cœur nou tous.

In translation, the words mean:

> God who makes the sun which gives us light,
> Who rouses the waves and makes the storm,
> Though hidden in the clouds, he watches us.
> He sees all that the whites are doing.
> The God of the whites orders crime,
> But our God calls upon us to do good works.
> Our God who is good to us orders us to avenge our wrongs.
> He will direct our arms and aid us.
> Throw away the symbol of the god of the whites
> Who has so often caused us to weep,
> And listen to the voice of liberty,
> Which speaks in the hearts of us all.

The Bois Caïman experience was both a religious and political event, which sought the liberation of an enslaved community through a functional speech that can be understood as a form of rhetoric of resistance. The protest orator embodies the accompanying communal plight and existential conditions of the masses in chains and in quest for emancipation. The prayer embodies the historical tyranny of oppression and suffering and the collective cry for justice, freedom, and human dignity of the enslaved Africans at Saint-Domingue. Boukman's invocation registers the collective desire for justice and an urgency for human liberation. Most importantly, it symbolizes the determination of the members of an oppressed community to fight together for their total liberation. What is more remarkable about the text is the stated belief that ultimate liberty will come through divine assistance. The slaves believed their God was the author of their freedom. This is explicit in the call for divine vindication embedded in this phrase, "Our God who is good to us orders us to revenge our wrongs; He will direct our arms and aid us." The phrase indicates a sense of divine closeness. The God of the slaves is not a distant deity. The God who is near the most oppressed is a warrior and a vengeful being. He will fight for and with them because *He is the God of the oppressed*. God's act of executing justice and vindicating the cause of the slaves revealed that he was in solidarity with the most vulnerable and exploited group in the colonial hierarchy. Conversely, Boukman believed that the God of the whites, who inspires injustice and crime, was the oppressor; that is to say, he is not the God of the oppressed, the slaves.

On August 22—within a week of this politico-religious gathering—the revolutionaries went forth to put slavery and all of the tears it caused behind them. The terrorizing and controlling mechanisms of the institution were also left behind. In the early stage of the revolt, more than 2,000 insurgents went from one plantation to another murdering their oppressors, setting fire to their houses and to the cane fields. The damage was horrendous, as many historians register. It is observed that the slaves destroyed seven parishes and demolished 184 sugar plantations and 1,200 coffee plantations in the northern plain alone.

Finally, the Bois Caïman moment is a historic example of the use of religion in the interest of politics and communal emancipation. The leadership of Zamba Boukman was instrumental in the unfolding events leading to Haitian freedom and the founding of postcolonial Haiti in 1804.

See also: Haitian Revolution; Makandal; Mambo; Maroon; Oungan; Slavery and the Slave Trade

Celucien L. Joseph

Further Reading

Fick, Carolyn E. 1990. *The Making of Haiti: The Saint Domingue Revolution from Below*. Knoxville: The University of Tennessee Press.

Geggus, David Patrick. 2002. *Haitian Revolutionary Studies*. Bloomington: Indiana University Press.

Joseph, Celucien L. 2013. *Haitian Modernity and Liberative Interruptions: Disourse on Race, Religion, and Freedom*. Lanham: University Press of America, Inc.

BROWN, KAREN MCCARTHY

Karen McCarthy Brown is a feminist anthropologist who specializes in the study of Vodou. Her most celebrated work, *Mama Lola: A Vodou Priestess in Brooklyn* (1991), tells the life story of Marie Thérèse Alourdes Macena Margaux Kowalski, better known as Mama Lola. Mama Lola grew up in Haiti but moved to Brooklyn in her twenties. She temporarily returned to Haiti to be initiated as a mambo but currently practices in the United States. Today, she is one of the best known Vodou priestesses in the country. In addition to making its subject into a celebrity, *Mama Lola* has received high praise from the scholarly community for the quality of its writing, its insight into Vodou, and its feminist anthropological outlook. It won the Victor Turner Prize in Ethnographic Writing from the American Anthropological Association and the American Academy of Religion Award for the Best First Book in the History of Religion.

Jeffrey E. Anderson

Further Reading

Brown, Karen McCarthy. 2001. *Mama Lola: A Vodou Priestess in Brooklyn*. Updated and expanded ed. Berkeley: University of California Press.

CABLE, GEORGE WASHINGTON

George Washington Cable, a native of New Orleans, lived from 1844 to 1925. He is best known for his many local color works about New Orleans's Creoles, black, white, and mixed. Cable was unusual in the post–Civil War era in that he loved his region but was adamantly opposed to its racial mores. Perhaps his most important work in this regard was *The Grandissimes* (1880), a fictional account of a young Protestant white man's relocation to 1803 New Orleans and his navigation of the community's complex and often hypocritical social hierarchy.

Cable was one of the American South's greatest critical interpreters and a relevant literary source for the study of Voodoo. Specifically, *The Grandissimes* touched on aspects of Mississippi Valley Voodoo. Although the degree to which Cable took literary license with his subject is open to debate, he does give testimony to the presence of Voodoo practices in the New Orleans area. In this novel, Cable describes a quartet of "voodoo charms" left on the four corners of one Agricola Fusilier's pillow. Cable goes into some detail in describing these charms, and discusses the paranoia and fear of the Grandissime family upon discovering them. Cable's characterization seems to be a fair assessment of how many New Orleans citizens viewed the practice of Voodoo, or at least what they understood as Voodoo in and around the area. Although Cable moved out of New Orleans long before his career as a writer ended, he remained familiar with the culture of New Orleans and, to a certain extent, the practice of Voodoo.

Cable's interest in Voodoo went beyond the references in *The Grandissimes*. His two 1886 articles for the *Century Magazine*, "Creole Slave Songs" and "The Dance in Place Congo," give some details on Voodoo ritual and other aspects of New Orleans's African American history and culture. Though Cable witnessed some of what he described, he derived part of his description of Voodoo from the writings of Médéric Louis-Élie Moreau de Saint-Méry, a writer from colonial Saint-Domingue. In many of his writings, Cable directly or indirectly exposes the apparent gap between two cultures—black and white—in New Orleans. At the same time, he linked Voodoo to Creoles of all races, using its practice by whites to call into question their claim to racial supremacy.

See also: Moreau de Saint-Méry, Médéric Louis-Élie; New Orleans; Voodoo in the Mississippi Valley

Tom Riser

Further Reading

Anderson, Jeffrey E. 2005. *Conjure in African American Society*. Baton Rouge: Louisiana State University Press.

Anderson, Jeffrey E. 2008. *Hoodoo, Voodoo, and Conjure: A Handbook*. Westport, CT: Greenwood Press.

Cable, George Washington. 1886. "Creole Slave Songs." With illustrations by E. W. Kemble. *The Century Magazine* 31: 807–828.

Cable, George Washington. 1886. "The Dance in Place Congo." With illustrations by E. W. Kemble. *The Century Magazine* 31: 517–532.

Cable, George Washington. 1880. *The Grandissimes*. New York: Charles Scribner's Sons.

Long, Carolyn Morrow. 2006. *A New Orleans Voudou Priestess: The Legend and Reality of Marie Laveau*. Gainesville: University Press of Florida.

Turner, Arlin. 1956. *George Washington Cable: A Biography*. Durham, NC: Duke University Press.

CANDLES

Candles are one item of a variety of other objects used in rituals and altar arrangements associated with Vodou, Voodoo, hoodoo, and conjure. In the Mississippi Valley, their initial incorporation and use may have originated within New Orleans Voodoo, which incorporated candle burning into a wide range of ceremonies, including initiations, ritual dances, and magic. Candles later became a part of hoodoo as a consequence of the religion's prestige among African American hoodoo doctors. In recent decades, the growing influence of folk religions from Latin America furthered the incorporation of candles into hoodoo. Additionally, the publication of several literary works, including of Henri Gamache's 1942 *Master Book of Candle Burning*, popularized the use of candles, as well as contributed to the breadth of symbolic meaning associated with their use. Such meaning may be noted with regard to the color of the candle itself. For example, the color red is associated with life and love, while black is linked to hate or death. In some commercial cases, candles are accompanied by printed labels that provide instructions for their magical functions, inclusive of how to arrange, interact with, and even burn the candles themselves.

Scholars have also attributed the use of candles to the overall syncretic relationship between Catholicism and the practices of Vodou, Voodoo, hoodoo, and conjure. This relationship is perhaps most apparent through the illustrative depictions of Catholic saints and other objects printed on both the candles and the glass that they are often encased in.

See also: Catholicism and Vodou/Voodoo; Ceremonies; Saints

Salvador Jimenez Murguia

Further Reading

Anderson, Jeffrey E. 2008. *Hoodoo, Voodoo, and Conjure: A Handbook*. Westport, CT: Greenwood Press.

Gamache, Henri. 1998. *The Master Book of Candle Burning*. Revised ed. Plainview, NY: Original Publications.

CANDOMBLÉ

Candomblé is the name applied to a complex of religious practices, originating primarily in the area of Bahia, in North East Brazil in the 19th century. It has come to be associated in the popular mind with traditions of Yoruba origin, largely due to the attention given to those forms by academics. Candomblé also has varieties that are focused upon Congo, Angolan, Dahomean, and Native American traditions. These forms are known by the terms *Candomblé de Congo, Candomblé de Angola, Candomblé Jejé,* and *Candomblé de Cabocló,* respectively.

As a generalization, Candomblé is centered around houses, which are usually referred to in Portuguese as *Teirreros*. Terreiro means "yard" and describes the physical layout of the temple. There are parallels to this in another part of the Afro-diasporic world, Haiti. *Lakou*, the Kreyòl word for "yard," represents a similar idea of sacred space in Haitian Vodou, and such a comparison may reflect Dahomean influences from West Africa in Candomblé, which have been noted in relation to other practices within the religion, including the character of the pantheon itself. The name *Candomblé* has been claimed by some to mean "dance in honor of the gods," and is related to the musical term *Candombé* found in both Brazil and Argentina. Regardless, music and dance are integral to Candomblé ceremonies. Sonic patterns created by distinct drum rhythms are thought to instigate trance and possession.

In Brazil, where Catholicism remains the dominant popular religious affiliation in spite of the growth of Evangelicalism in recent years, adherents of Candomblé recognize in the saints of the church a striking parallel with the spiritual entities found within various African traditions. Many of the Bantu cultures of Angola and Kongo, of course, came to Brazil as already practicing Catholics.

While various Brazilian scholars published studies on Candomblé previously, notably including Edison Carneiro, the study that brought Candomblé perhaps the most attention in North American anthropology was Ruth Landes's *City of Women*. The issues debated in both their works tended to privilege Nago, or Yoruba, forms of Candomblé over forms such as Candomblé de Angola and Candomblé de Caboclo, which raised the perceived esteem of Yoruba traditions, especially in the public sphere. This scholarship, in turn, had real impact on how traditions evolved over the course of the 20th century.

Afro-Brazilian traditions in Northeast Brazil and Bahia, in particular before 1830, were often known by the term *Calundú*, reflecting the earlier predominance of Angolan traditions. With the establishment of the religious house known as Casa Blanca, the term gradually adopted for African religious institutions in Bahia became *Candomblés*. Interestingly, although the Nago and Jéjé houses gained prominence at roughly the same time, the name for the faith appears to be of Bantu rather than Yoruba origin.

Carneiro and Landes, committed to the understandings of their day, saw the Candomblés of Yoruba origin as more "intact," applying subjective views of purity versus degeneration. They did not ascribe a positive value to cultural evolution. They noted, however, the continued existence, still encountered today, of assertions of national origin, and noted that these were tied to various traits of dance, music, song, and ritual forms. Candomblés of Angolan origin reflect language retentions related to that area of Africa, as Candomblé de Congo does in a similar fashion. The spirits associated with those traditions, such as Kisimbi and Tempo, were also indicative of these origins.

The Candomblé de Male, or "Mohammedan" Candomble, one house of which still functioned at the time Carneiro wrote, had cultural elements related to the Hausas, Nagos, and Tapas of West Africa. Islam had been a potent force in Bahia early in the 19th century, but was significantly weakened by the failed Malé Revolt of 1835. This series of events might explain how the remnants of Islam were reconfigured into a small branch of Candomblé by the end of that century.

Candomblé de Caboclo was constructed around entities seen as representative of the indigenous tribes of Brazil, with dress and dances that reflected popular visions of what they were like. Its spirits included one with names like Tupan, and Tupinamba, seen as Native American. The ritual language retained or appropriated elements of the by-then dead language of the Tupi Indians of the coastal areas, who had mostly been driven to extinction or absorbed into mainstream culture.

Significantly, many elements of ritual, ritual space, and costume, while retaining or developing unique variations, appear to have shared elements across all of the nations. Gradually—and this change was in full force between the end of the 19th century and the end of the Brazilian dictatorships—even songs and rituals were being appropriated and blended. Thus, by the 1970s, it was not unusual to find Candomblés de Congo and Angola who would use songs that referenced the Yoruba orixás.

Contemporary anthropology sees traditions such as Candomblé—with a measure of good reason—as social constructions. In the case of Afro-Brazilian traditions, scholars argue that they formed through a process of reinventing African social and spiritual contexts in the new environments their practitioners encountered in slave and post-slave societies. The structural forms that exist across the divisions within Candomblé suggest that this is at least partially true. While different nations exist in what amounts to ethnic denominations within the complex of Candomblé, each possesses unique traditions, including but not limited to elements such as ritual language, song and liturgy, national pantheons, styles of clothing or vestments, offices or ritual personnel, and variations in ritual timing and space. At the same time, they share many similarities across these areas.

These commonalities reflect the process of social evolution. Over time, the range of entities selected for devotion evolved. Among Bantu, Dahomean, and Nago peoples in Africa, the nkisi, vodun, and orixás—the spiritual entities in each of these cultures, respectively—numbered in the hundreds at least. In Brazil, they have been reduced to approximately fifteen to twenty in most forms of Candomblé, with the primary popular focus resting on seven major ones.

While each nation of Candomblé has its own pantheon, the spirits or deities revered by their followers today tend to be identified as parallel to the main ones of all the others. There are a few exceptions, such as Tempo in Angola or Logunede in Nago, who are not found in all variants. Most, however, are identified as similar spirits in distinct national guises. In Candomblé Keto, for example, a few of the more popular orixás are Exú, Ogum, Oxóssi, Xangó, Obaluaye, Oxum, Iemanja, and Oxalá. In Angola, these are identified with Aluvaiá or Bomba Njila, Nkosi, Mutalembo, Nzazi, Dandelunda, Kissimbi, and Lembá. Among the followers of Candomblé Jejé, their names are identified as Legba, Gu, Agué, Hevioso, Sakpatá, Averekete, Aziri, and Dan.

Similar parallels occur in the area of ritual vestments and the food given as offerings for spiritual entities. At the current time, it is likely that all terreiros except those consciously engaged in overt re-Africanization, will display great similarities in dress, so that when a priestess becomes possessed by Iemanja, Kissimbi, or Aziri, she will be dressed in the characteristic blue and white or blue and silver traditionally associated with the Orixá Iemanja. Where one finds the greatest retention of distinction among nations is in the specific drumbeats used for the invocation of possession. In this area, the rhythms are more likely to derive from the respective African traditions than are elements such as food and clothing.

The Catholic Church has traditionally taken a stance of opposition to Candomblé, and followers of the faith were persecuted violently with both government campaigns and police action, often with the cooperation of church authorities. Persecution officially ended with the removal of laws requiring police permission to hold ceremonies in the 1970s. In recent years, the religion has gained in popularity in Brazil, and as many as two million people are said by some sources to be following the faith. Its center remains in Salvador da Bahia, in the northeast of Brazil.

For many followers Candomblé is not just a matter of religious belief but a way of reclaiming cultural and historical identities prohibited during slavery. Along these lines, there is a movement to remove Catholic imagery from worship services in an attempt to return the faith to its origins by those who view elements of other than African origin as incidental. Interestingly, these efforts, associated with what has been a called the re-Africanization movement, have gained considerable popularity among white, middle-class adherents of the faith, while the majority of black working-class followers are more likely to retain church-related imagery in their practice. Much of this debate has cultural and political facets and relates to issues such as economic mobility and attempts to forget or avoid the nation's historic involvement with slavery. Positions on these issues do not always follow the trajectory that outsiders might expect.

See also: Catholicism and Vodou/Voodoo; Creoles of Louisiana; Creolization; Dahomey; Kongo; Yoruba

Eoghan Craig Ballard

Further Reading
Carneiro, Edison. 1961. *Candomblés da Bahia*. Rio de Janeiro: Conquista.
Landes, Ruth. 1994. *The City of Women*. Albuquerque: University of New Mexico Press.
Sweet, James H. 2003. *Recreating Africa: Culture, Kinship, and Religion in the African-Portuguese World, 1441–1770*. Chapel Hill: University of North Carolina Press.
Thompson, Robert Farris. 1993. *Face of the Gods: Art and Altars of Africa and the African Americas*. New York: The Museum for African Art.

CATHOLICISM AND VODOU/VOODOO

Among practitioners of Vodou in Haiti, those who serve the spirits are typically practicing Catholics. These practitioners seemingly spend very little time dwelling on the inherent contradiction in practicing a variant of Christianity that condemns the sacrifices and spiritual possession by the lwa as affronts to monotheism. Because of a lack of doctrinal unity or ritual uniformity among practitioners in Haiti or the United States, the relationship between practitioners of Voodoo as it developed in and around New Orleans, Vodou as practiced in Haiti, and Roman Catholicism varies by region and even individually by practitioner. Lwa and the ancestors, the beings that populate the spiritual world of Vodou in Haiti, are frequently paired with and represented by images and names of Catholic saints. That pairing is often determined by associations between some aspect of the lwa, and the pictographic representations of the corresponding Catholic saints. For example, the association of the spirit Danbala—represented by both the rainbow and the serpent in Vodou theology—with St. Patrick—represented in Catholic iconography crushing a snake underfoot—is apparently due to the prominence of the serpent to both figures. The lwa most frequently maintain their character as determined by the local practitioners and derived from West and Central African counterparts. But rather than the saint simply serving to mask the lwa, as some earlier scholars have suggested, the powers of the saint and the lwa are additive, apparently incorporating aspects from their distinct religious geneses. This is undoubtedly partly explained by the notion among many Haitian Vodou practitioners that in order to serve the spirits one must also be a practicing Catholic. In addition, the spiritual power associated with Catholic rituals, prayers, sites, and paraphernalia is frequently used in the rituals of Vodou practitioners. There is a great deal of variation, however, as many practitioners do make attempts to keep their relationships with the spirits and the Catholic Church separate.

What those who serve the spirits most frequently share with the church seems to center on the stated use of Catholic iconography and the use of the implicit power of Catholic sites, emblems, and prayers to call upon the spirits for aid. Rites for the spirits frequently begin with traditional Catholic prayers, occur at Catholic Churches and cemeteries, and employ Catholic images of saints and the Virgin Mary. Vodou practitioners do not see any contradiction between the Catholic concept of a singular God—whom they often associate with Bondye, a deity of the Vodou pantheon—and their entreaties and offerings to the spirits, any more than traditional Catholics would see a contradiction between monotheism and the intercession of the saints. Haitian Catholics may frequently be more interested in the miraculous power of Catholicism and Catholic ritual then they are in Catholic dogma. At the same time they are often baptized Catholics who practice sacramental rituals and have their morality and ethics shaped by the standards of Roman Catholicism.

The Catholic Church in Haiti has largely been tolerant of those who serve the lwa, with the exception of periodic "anti-superstition" campaigns and instances when Vodou practitioners have co-opted Catholic sites. In the face of the repression of Vodou in Haiti, which has come and gone depending on the cultural politics of the regime in power, the association with Catholicism has served as a cover to deflect unwanted persecution of Vodou practitioners. Vodou as practiced in Haiti and by Haitian-style practitioners in the United States gets a great deal of its structure from the Catholic Church, performing its religious rituals on or around the Catholic feast days for saints. During the colonial period, Catholicism was the sole legal religion both in Haiti and Louisiana. Bondspersons, in particular, were forbidden to practice any other religion by the *Code Noir*, which codified acceptable behavior for the enslaved. With Haitian independence, the refusal of Rome to acknowledge the legitimacy of the Haitian state or to send priests to the island nation also led to a break with the church and the human and economic resources attached to it. The break weakened the hold of Catholicism on the populace and created opportunities for Vodou to grow. Some scholars of Vodou note that the prèt savann—a stand-in for a Catholic priest employed in Haitian temples when a male is needed—became necessary because of this disconnect during the period.

In Louisiana, the purchase of the formerly French territory by the United States and the influx of Americans also challenged the dominance of Roman Catholicism in that territory and introduced Protestant varieties of Christianity, which by the beginning of the 20th century had also begun to see their forms and rituals picked up by Voodoo practitioners and vice versa. In the United States, specifically in areas of the country like New Orleans where Voodoo survived, it has frequently succumbed to cultural pressures to conform to a set of values that defines Christianity, specifically the variants most popular among white, Anglo-Saxon Protestants, as the norm. Frequently by consequence, the standard for what religion should look like is determined by this normative majority and results in negative judgments on the legitimacy of Voodoo. That pressure, however, has frequently led to a more effective blending of Voodoo with Christian traditions. The sparse outsider accounts of 19th-century Voodoo in New Orleans and surrounding areas of Louisiana suggest that there, where the history of Catholic dominance has made the saints part of the popular religious culture, the blending of *lwa* and the Catholic saints has favored the saints. Practitioners who reported performing Voodoo ceremonies used the images of the saints, and their understanding of who those spirits were held more closely to Catholic interpretations of saints' histories and personalities than those of Haitian lwa or West African deities so dominant in the Caribbean. The dynamic nature of Voodoo also saw practitioners adjusting the histories and mythology of the saints to meet their contemporary needs, but with the Catholic hagiography providing the map for that departure. The saints of New Orleans Voodoo are frequently thought to derive their power and purpose from things that happened to them before their corporeal deaths. It is upon dying that they take on the miraculous powers that make them a help to the living who call on them for assistance with their problems.

Since the Haitian Revolution at the turn of the 19th century, Vodou has frequently become part and parcel of nativist movements aimed at accentuating Haitian cultural pride. The hold of the Catholic Church on the Haitian population weakened between 1804 and 1860, when Rome broke with Haiti. The Church saw a resurgence during the American occupation of the island from

> **Christianity and Voodoo**
>
> As with the Haitian Vodou faithful, practitioners of Voodoo have tended to simultaneously consider themselves Catholics, a situation that developed during colonial times out of legal requirements that masters convert and instruct slaves in the faith. Unlike in Haiti, which has a long Catholic history, the Catholics of the lower Mississippi Valley have been a minority since the antebellum era. One consequence has been that Voodoo and hoodoo practitioners have come to identify with Protestant churches as well as Catholicism. Some have even argued that the Spiritual Churches of New Orleans are simply a further Christianized form of Voodoo.

1915–1934. By contrast, during the 20th-century dictatorship of François Duvalier, the head of state embraced Vodou as Haiti's national heritage and used it as a liaison to the masses of his citizens. Duvalier granted Vodou state protection and used powerful priests as state advisors, informants, and militia commanders and Vodou temples as political headquarters. In turn, Duvalier also managed to indigenize the Catholic Church. By signing a concordat with Rome granting the Haitian dictator the right to advise on the appointment of Church officials in the nation, after 1957, the Haitian Catholic Church would see an influx of local priests and bishops, further facilitating acceptance of Vodou practitioners and tolerance by the Church.

By contrast, in and around New Orleans, the incorporation and acceptance of Voodoo as a part of local culture has been characterized both by the subsuming of Voodoo in some spaces and its marginalization and accentuation in others. Local religious culture has seen rituals common to Voodoo practitioners incorporated into other spiritual practices developed in the city, most notably the Spiritual Church movement of the early 20th century whose practitioners frequently adopted Voodoo-style rituals while simultaneously eschewing what had become a racialized and demonized subculture. Even more recognizably, Voodoo has been foregrounded by the tourist culture, which has used the distinct aspects of Louisiana culture like Mardi Gras and Voodoo to represent New Orleans as a foreign and exotic destination for travelers from the largely Anglo-Protestant United States. Catholic cemeteries and church yard statues, also frequent sites of Voodoo rituals, have accordingly become sites for the sellers of culture to peddle to tourists.

See also: Cultural Politics; Haitian Revolution; Lwa; Prèt Savann; Saints

Kodi Roberts

Further Reading

Brown, Karen McCarthy. 2001. *Mama Lola: A Vodou Priestess in Brooklyn.* Updated and expanded ed. Berkeley: University of California Press.

Desmangles, Leslie G. 1992. *Faces of the Gods: Vodou and Roman Catholicism in Haiti.* Chapel Hill: University of North Carolina Press.

CEMETERIES

Cemeteries in the Haitian Vodou religion reflect West and Central African and Roman Catholic cultures. Altars are often placed on top of tombs. Each is in honor of the deceased and can hold a picture, candles, water, money, and personal items of the dead. Food and gifts are brought in respect to the dead. The living are expected to worship the ancestors and respect their elders as well as the deceased. As in many African cultures, practitioners believe the dead will need these items in the next life so that the spirit will be at peace and not prone to wander. The idea of wearing white, not black, as the symbol for death likewise comes from Central Africa. From the Roman Catholic tradition is the practice of the living visiting the grave sites on birthdays, anniversaries, and religious holidays, such as All Saints Day and All Souls Day. Additionally, black veils are sometimes draped over the headstones.

In the United States, altars were placed not only in proximity to graves but also in houses. In a typical home altar, a picture of the loved one is placed alongside candles (sometimes kept lit), dried or silk flowers, a picture of a saint, favorite items of the dead, and sometimes money. During the development of New Orleans, African culture thrived alongside French Creole culture. Part of this influence passed over into cemeteries with the idea of respecting the dead. When masters forced enslaved Africans to assimilate French culture in Saint-Domingue (modern Haiti) and Louisiana, the ritual calendar of African Traditional Religions followed suit, adopting some aspects of what Roman Catholics believed. In both Haitian Vodou and Mississippi Valley Voodoo, there are a number of gods, called *lwa* in Haiti, that are associated with cemeteries. The most widely recognized of these is Baron Samedi, typically considered the head of the Gede family of lwa that preside over death and its accouterments. Closely related to the Baron is Papa Gede, also a leader among the lwa as well as the protector of the cemetery, the grave, and death itself. He is a curer of diseases and stands between the living and the dead. He takes souls at the crossroads after he is given food, candles, and other gifts as offerings. He is honored through the *banda*, music and dance performed in his name.

There were several other important lwa of the Gede family. The wife of Samedi, Maman Brijit, is the mother of cemeteries. She presides over money and death. Brave Gede is the one who watches the graveyard, while Gede Masaka is the androgynous gravedigger. Papa Legba—equated by some scholars with Br'er Rabbit or Compair Lapin in a North American context—stands at the spiritual crossroads and either allows or denies the living the ability to speak to the spirits.

Death is not seen as an end to the cycle of life but rather as a continuation of it in African and African Diasporic cultures. The spirits of the dead remain important to the living. In Vodou, for example, the first male to be buried in the cemetery is referred to as *Baron* and protects other family members who will be buried thereafter. Offensive souls, on the other hand, could be kept as zombis or slaves in the afterlife. Some Haitians believe such souls stay as zombis forever. In some instances, sorcerers have also reportedly raised bodies of the dead to perform manual labor.

> ### Christianity and Vodou
>
> Historically, it has been common for practitioners of Vodou to also consider themselves Christians. In part this dual adherence arose from the colonial French Code Noir, which among other things required masters to baptize and instruct their slaves in Catholicism. Moreover, the nature of Catholicism, which honors both God as the Supreme Being and a host of saints, made it easy for enslaved Africans to draw parallels between the new faith and African traditions. On the other hand, many Haitians consider it impossible to be both a Protestant and Vodouisant.

A number of Roman Catholic Creoles are buried at the St. Louis Cemeteries of New Orleans. The custom of the cemeteries, where old tombs are surrounded by arched brick wall vaults or ovens, came from French and Spanish colonists. One example of an honored gravesite is Voodoo priestess Marie Laveau's tomb at St. Louis Cemetery No. 1. A series of three X's are written on the front and sides of the tomb with offerings of food, money, Mardi Gras beads, and other small gifts as decor. It is believed that one should write three X's on Marie Laveau's grave, turn around three times, and make a request. If the request is granted, one is expected to return to Marie Laveau's grave and leave an offering.

See also: Ancestral Spirits; Baron Samedi; Cosmogram; Gede; Kongo; Laveau, Marie; Legba; Zombi

Tina N. Mullone

Further Reading

Antippas, A. P. 1988. *A Brief History of Voodoo: Slavery & the Survival of the African Gods.* New Orleans: Marie Laveau's House of Voodoo.

Hebblethwaite, Benjamin. 2012. *Vodou Songs in Haitian Creole and English.* Philadelphia: Temple University Press.

Huber, Leonard Victor. 1982. *Clasped Hands: Symbolism in New Orleans Cemeteries.* Lafayette, LA: Center for Louisiana Studies.

Long, Carolyn Morrow. 2006. *A New Orleans Voudou Priestess: The Legend and Reality of Marie Laveau.* Gainesville: University Press of Florida.

McMickle, Marvin Andrew. 2002. *An Encyclopedia of African American Christian Heritage.* Valley Forge, PA: Judson Press.

Rigaud, Milo. 1985 [1969]. *Secrets of Voodoo.* Translated by Robert B. Cross. New York: Arco; reprint, San Francisco: City Lights.

CEREMONIES

The ceremonies of Vodou are many and complex. For specific information on some of the more prominent of them, see the individual entries listed below. American Vodou priestess Patricia Scheu identifies several central ceremonies in her book *Serving the Spirits.* The first of these is the *lave tèt*, a washing of the head that is often the first ritual new converts to the faith experience. The kanzo cycle of ceremonies, which begins with a lave tèt, is Vodou's multi-step initiation. Another ritual, the *maryaj lwa*, unites a believer in spiritual marriage with a lwa that requests it. At the end of life comes a series of death ceremonies, *dessounen*, *anba dlo* or *bohoun*, and *retire mo nan dlo*. A fourth death ritual, known as *casa canari*, is rare in modern Haiti and was always uncommon outside the north of the country. Additional common ceremonies include a baptism known as *batèm* conducted a few months after a child's birth; the festivals of Roman Catholic saints and their corresponding lwa; and those involving divination and magic. In Haiti and the United States, ceremonies differ from region to region and sometimes among individual ounfòs.

The Voodoo of the Mississippi Valley included its own ceremonies. Though they were considerably less well documented than their Haitian counterparts, several distinct rituals can be identified. The first of these were initiations, known as *openings* by the 20th century, which were understood as conferring spiritual power and the ability to work magic. While openings generally took place in secret, the most visible Voodoo rite was the annual St. John's Eve ceremony, held during the second half of the 19th century along the shores of Lake Pontchartrain. Priestesses also held weekly ceremonies in private homes. These rituals were most commonly known as *parterres*, a term referring to the practice of laying out offerings to the spirits. Such laying out was a part of openings as well as weekly ceremonies, however, and the term *parterre* was likely a general one describing Voodoo ceremonies in a broad sense. Marie Laveau also reportedly held rituals called *rehearsals*, though the function of these is unknown. As was true with Haitian Vodou, magic also included important ceremonial aspects, which varied enormously depending upon the sort of work being done.

See also: Altars; Dances; Death; Divination; Drums; Ifá; Initiations; Kanzo; Lave Tèt; Laveau, Marie; Magic; Manje-yanm (Eating of the Yams); Maryaj Lwa (Marriage to Lwa); Music and Haitian Vodou; Opening; Ounfò; Parterre; Pris de Je; Saint John's Eve

Jeffrey E. Anderson

Further Reading

Anderson, Jeffrey E. 2008. *Hoodoo, Voodoo, and Conjure: A Handbook*. Greenwood Folklore Handbooks. Westport, CT: Greenwood Press.

Federal Writers' Project. 1935–1943. Northwestern State University of Louisiana, Watson Memorial Library, Cammie G. Henry Research Center, Natchitoches, Louisiana.

Long, Carolyn Morrow. 2006. *A New Orleans Voudou Priestess: The Legend and Reality of Marie Laveau*. Gainesville: University Press of Florida.

Métraux, Alfred. 1972. *Voodoo in Haiti*. Translated by Hugo Charteris and with an Introduction by Sidney W. Mintz. New York: Schocken.

Olmos, Margarite Fernández, and Lizbeth Paravisini-Gebert. 2003. *Creole Religions of the Caribbean: An Introduction from Vodou and Santería to Obeah and Espiritismo*. New York: New York University Press.

Scheu, Patricia (Mambo Vye Zo Komande LaMenfo). 2011. *Serving the Spirits: The Religion of Vodou*. Philadelphia: Published by author.

CHANGO

Chango (also spelled Sàngo, Shango, or Xangô) began as a West African god of lightning, often associated with both fire and thunder. According to African mythology, before his deification Chango was human and ruled as the fourth king of the Oyo Empire in what is now present-day Nigeria. Often depicted as a physically strong and prominent figure, Chango bears a crown, is shrouded in red and white gowns, and brandishes a double-headed axe.

Regarded as one of the more important and popular orishas among the African Diasporic religions, Chango is found in a number of Caribbean and Atlantic South American religions inclusive of Candomblé, Santería, Trinidad Orisha, and Vodou. Despite his vast presence among these religions, Chango's symbolic and practical significances are not universal. Rather, deference and veneration of Chango are based upon several attributes ranging from the defender of morality and protector of royalty to a symbol of virility, power, masculinity, and even vengeance.

Chango emerged in the Americas between the early 16th and late 19th centuries with the arrival of enslaved Africans—in particular those originating from the West African tribes of the Yoruba-Lucumí. Chango is one of several African-originating deities to have been synchronized with Catholic and Native American beliefs and practices, forming a pantheon of spirit manifestations.

As a syncretic figure, Chango has been associated with calendric events correlating with St. John and St. Peter, as well as iconographic and metaphoric characteristics aligned with Saint Barbara and Saint Jeremy.

See also: Candomblé; Ceremonies; Lwa; Saints; Santería

Salvador Jimenez Murguia

Further Reading

Olmos, Margarite Fernandez, and Lizabeth Paravisini-Gebert. 2011. *Creole Religions of the Caribbean: An Introduction from Vodou and Santería to Obeah and Espiritismo.* New York: New York University Press.

Parés, Luis Nicolau. 2006. "Shango in Afro-Brazilian Religion: 'Aristocracy' and 'Syncretic' Interactions." *Religioni e Società* 54: 20–39.

Tishken, Joel E. *Sàngó in Africa and the African Diaspora.* Bloomington, IN: Indiana University Press, 2009.

CHARLO

Charlo was a deity found in the variety of Voodoo practiced in the New Orleans area near the turn of the 20th century. All scholars know about this spirit is contained in a single account that appeared in Helen Pitkin's *An Angel by Brevet* (1904). This description of a ceremony during which Charlo appeared depicts him as arriving at the door of the room in which the ritual took place immediately after participants heard the cry of a screech owl. The spirit was invisible, but the Voodoo priest treated it as a small child, bending down to shake its hand and stroking its hair. He also offered it a drink of sugar water and a type of ginger bread known as stage planks or *l'estomac mulatte*. Before the ceremony ended, Charlo possessed the

> ### Voodoo and Civil Rights
>
> Many scholars understand Voodoo and Vodou, in part, as expressions of a yearning for equality. The Haitian Revolution, for instance, incorporated Vodou, and traditional accounts state that the revolt was instigated by an oungan. Some scholars claim that Marie Laveau fought for equality by freeing slaves, though Carolyn Morrow Long has disputed this assertion. At the very least, the magic associated with both religions often supported the cause of civil rights. History records spells designed to help slaves escape brutal masters, to prevent abuse, to win court cases, and to otherwise alleviate the injustices of slavery and racism.

priest in order to give instructions on healing a Voodoo-induced ailment. According to one of the participants in the ceremony, it was important to provide anything Charlo requested. Moreover, if one encountered a little boy who asked for something, one should always do as asked because the child might be Charlo. When unsatisfied, Charlo would reveal the secrets of the offending household.

See also: Blanc Dani; Macouloumba, Jean; Voodoo in the Mississippi Valley

Jeffrey E. Anderson

Further Reading

Pitkin, Helen. 1904. *An Angel by Brevet: A Story of Modern New Orleans.* Philadelphia and London: J. B. Lippincott Company.

CODE NOIR

The Code Noir, commonly known as the Black Code, consisted of French laws designed to govern the relations between enslaved Africans and free black and white inhabitants of French colonies and to safeguard France's socioeconomic and political interests in its overseas possessions. Code Noir laws were drafted by Jean Baptiste Colbert in 1683 and enacted by French monarch Louis XIV in 1685. Revised in 1716, 1738, 1763, 1777, and 1778, they were adopted in French settlements in Saint-Domingue in 1687, in Guyana in 1704, and in Louisiana in 1724. Composed of sixty articles, the Code Noir outlined relations between slaves and slave owners and underscored the French Empire's sensibilities concerning non-Catholics.

Several of the Code Noir's articles emphasized the French's strong ties to the Catholic Church and its intolerance of non-Catholics, particularly practitioners of Judaism. Article 1 banned all non-Catholics from residing in French colonies. Article 2 required slave owners to teach their slaves Catholicism. Article 3 prohibited the public practice of any religion other than Catholicism. Article 8 also stipulated that only Catholic marriages were legally valid and defined children produced by non-Catholic marriage unions as bastards.

French statutes created a legal framework for regulating the treatment of enslaved Africans. While the Code Noir considered slaves moveable property, laws guaranteed some rights to the enslaved population. Slaves were excused from laboring on Sundays and during holidays. Slave owners that forced slaves to work on the Sabbath or on holidays faced having their property confiscated by officials. Enslaved Africans were permitted to marry, providing they had permission from their owners. Owners could neither separate slave families for sale nor force their slaves to enter into marriage. Article 26 provided enslaved Africans with legal recourse when infractions were committed against them. Masters could be prosecuted if they killed or tortured their slaves.

Slave owners' obligations to their slaves were outlined in Code Noir statutes as well. Masters were legally required to regularly feed and clothe their property and were responsible for the welfare of disabled and infirm slaves. Additionally, the law stipulated that slave owners had to baptize slaves in the Catholic faith within a week of their arrival in the colony.

On the other hand, like slave statutes in other European and American colonies, the Code Noir laws denied enslaved Africans all socioeconomic and political rights. Slaves were forbidden from owning property, carrying weapons, suing in court, and congregating in crowds. Slaves were likewise prohibited from physically assaulting whites. Acts of violence against whites were punishable by death. Slaves accused of other illegal infractions, including theft and running away, faced public whippings, dismemberment, branding, and capital punishment.

While the Code Noir made slave owners legally responsible for their property, such laws also controlled certain aspects of white colonists' lives. In an effort to prohibit interracial marriages and sexual relationships, white colonists were prohibited from marrying enslaved Africans, free blacks, or racially mixed individuals. Moreover, religious clergy were forbidden from sanctioning interracial unions. Violators were subject to a monetary fine.

Various sections of Code Noir acknowledged the status of free blacks. Codes maintained that free black persons held many of the same basic privileges as white French citizens, including the rights to own property and to sue in court. Nevertheless, because the presence of free blacks in French colonies created anxiety for whites, aspects of the law restricted their physical, socioeconomic, and political mobility and created a racial hierarchy. Article 58 stated that all manumitted slaves demonstrate gratitude and "singular respect" toward their former owners' families for giving them liberation. Under French law, free blacks were subject to re-enslavement if they were convicted for a number of crimes, including theft, harboring a fugitive slave, and licentious conduct.

The Code Noir briefly ended with the abolition of slavery in the French empire in 1794 but was restored in 1802 under Napoleon Bonaparte. Under French monarch Louis-Philippe, Code Noir statutes as well as slavery were finally abolished in 1848.

See also: Legislation against Vodou/Voodoo

LaShawn Harris

Further Reading

Blackburn, Robin. 1998. *Making of New World Slavery: From the Baroque to the Modern, 1492–1800*. New York: Verso.

Gaspar, David Barry, and Darlene Clark Hine. 1996. *More than Chattel: Black Women and Slavery in the Americas*. Bloomington, IN: Indiana University Press.

CONGO SQUARE

Congo Square is in an area slightly north of the French Quarter in the city of New Orleans, Louisiana. It is now a cobbled stone open space that is part of the Louis Armstrong Memorial Park. During the antebellum era, it was a major gathering place for slaves.

There was a more laid-back treatment of the slaves by the French and Spanish in New Orleans than in the British colonies. During the 18th century slaves were sometimes given time off and allowed to gather. They met on the edge of what was once the Tremé plantation, an area where they could trade, play music, and dance. In 1817 the City Council of New Orleans passed legislation that allowed the slaves to meet for dancing on Sunday afternoons. The mayor of the city decided on the location, and he assigned Congo Square for this purpose. It was previously known as Place des Negres or Place Publique before it became informally known as Place Congo or Congo Square.

Locals and a growing number of visitors in the city went to Congo Square to watch the dancing and listen to the black music. The site was becoming an attraction, while still providing a space where the slaves could serve the spirits in plain view. There was little opposition to the presence of African religions, primarily because the city was Catholic and African Americans assimilated their deities with the saints. In New Orleans the practice known in Haiti as Vodou became widely known and accepted as Voodoo, as it is still referred to today.

Not all of the dances performed in Congo Square were religious in nature. Among the popular dances, one of the most frequently mentioned was the Bamboula. Another was the lesser-known Calinda. Onlookers observed that slaves were also allowed to gather in groups, and it was not uncommon for bondspersons to seek out others from their nations of origin. This led to the employment of a variety of music and instruments, as there could be as many as six hundred people in Congo Square at a time. They beat drums, some of which had been previously banned by the whites, and they struck triangles and played jawbones. There were also instruments that would be the early precursors to banjos. This music was to permeate the city of New Orleans, and over time would spread to the rest of the United States of America, gain global recognition, and become known as jazz.

The gatherings in Congo Square continued during the early decades of the 19th century before declining in the 1840s. By the beginning of the Civil War in 1861 the Congo Square gatherings had ended. There was an attempt to rename the area Beauregard Square, but this was not sustained as locals continued to refer to it as Congo Square. Eventually, it was officially designated as part of the Louis Armstrong Memorial Park. It is an area that is symbolic to all African Americans because of its contribution to the musical heritage and the cultural history of the people of New Orleans.

See also: Bayou St. Jean; New Orleans

Louise Fenton

Further Reading

Donaldson, Gary A. 1984. "A Window on Slave Culture: Dances at Congo Square in New Orleans, 1800–1862." *Journal of Negro History* 69: 63–72.
Evans, Freddi Williams. 2011. *Congo Square: African Roots in New Orleans.* With a foreword by J. H. Kwabena 'Neketia. Lafayette, LA: University of Louisiana at Lafayette.
Joyce, John. 1995. *Congo Square in New Orleans.* New Orleans: Louisiana Landmarks Society.
McKinney, Louise. 2006. *New Orleans: A Cultural History.* New York and Oxford: Oxford University Press.
Saxon, Lyle. 2004 [1928]. *Fabulous New Orleans.* New York: Century; reprint, Gretna, LA: Pelican Publishing.
Sublette, Ned. 2008. *The World That Made New Orleans: From Spanish Silver to Congo Square.* Chicago: Lawrence Hill Books.

CONGRESS OF SANTA BARBARA (KOSANBA)

KOSANBA was founded by a group of thirteen scholars in 1997 following a conference on Haitian Vodou organized by the University of California at Santa Barbara's Center for Black Studies Research (CBS). The Congress is part of the CBS' Indigenous Religion Project. KOSANBA's goals are to promote research on Vodou and to make this research available to the scholarly community. At the heart of the organization's mission is its founders' belief that Vodou has been and will continue to be central to Haitian culture and society. Its desire is to work through Vodou to help Haiti to a better future, and it encourages its members to actively take up this cause.

The Congress is an exceptionally active organization. It holds an academic conference most years, which has met in cities across the United States, in Puerto Rico, and in Haiti. In addition, KOSANBA has produced five books edited by Patrick Bellegarde-Smith and/or Claudine Michel.

See also: Vodou in Haiti

Jeffrey E. Anderson

Further Reading

Bellegarde-Smith, Patrick, LeGrace Benson, and Claudine Michel. 2013. "KOSANBA: A Scholarly Association for the Study of Haitian Vodou." Center for Black Studies Research: The Congress of Santa Barbara. Accessed on April 15, 2013: http://www.research.ucsb.edu/cbs/projects/haiti/kosanba/index.html

CONJURE

Conjure and such variations as *conjuring* and *conjuration* designate the magical traditions of African Americans. At one time, *conjure* was the most common word used to refer to black American magical practices in most of the United States. A variety of other terms served as regional synonyms and near-synonyms, however. For example, *tricking* and *cunning* were terms employed in 19th-century Virginia and Maryland. Similarly, *rootwork* was preferred in the Georgia and South Carolina Lowcountry. Magical practices similar to conjure were subsumed in the words *hoodoo* and *Voodoo* in parts of the Mississippi Valley. Since the early 20th century, the usage of *conjure* has gradually declined and has now virtually disappeared from popular usage. Near-synonyms, such as *hoodoo*, have largely taken its place among knowledgeable nonscholars. Many scholars, however, continue to use the word *conjure* because of its historical relevance and broad applicability to African American magical practices across the United States.

During the settlement of North America by the British and their African slaves, the term *conjure* did not reference specifically African or African American supernatural traditions. On the contrary, it could just as easily designate any practice of calling up and controlling demons or other spiritual forces, a practice long associated with European witches and other sorcerers. As the age-old fear of witchcraft—though not necessarily belief in it—faded throughout the 18th and 19th centuries, the use of *conjure* to refer to the magical practices of whites declined proportionally. On the other hand, the term continued in common usage to designate African American supernaturalism. Whites' assumption that blacks were inferior to them and slaves by nature assured that terminology associated predominantly with African Americans could only infrequently apply to whites.

Of course, conjure has always been more than simply a name. It embraces a wide-ranging collection of supernatural practices that have evolved over time. During the antebellum era, spells designed to kill masters were common, as were charms and powders that supposedly protected their users from whippings and other forms of brutality. At least one magical powder protected runaway slaves from the dogs used to track them. Following emancipation, conjure adapted to match the changing needs of those who believed in its power. One notable example of the change was the appearance of numerous examples of court case spells, designed to protect accused criminals from the legal system. The profound bias of the post-Reconstruction Jim Crow system likely helped spur such developments. At the same time, charms and spells to acquire jobs and attract money likewise proliferated as former slaves and their descendants found it necessary to work in exchange for money instead of under coercion.

To be sure, many conjure formulae have remained staples of the practice throughout its existence. Simple charms for luck, such as the well-known rabbit's foot, were as potentially useful to slaves as they were to free workers. The search for love was likewise an ever-present aspect of conjure, and items designed to win the affections of a desired lover have always been in high demand. Healing, often through the use of herbal remedies, likewise remained popular throughout much of the practice's history.

The physical items used in conjure are legion and depend heavily upon what one intends to accomplish. For instance, John the Conqueror Root, which had become the best known of all conjure items by the early 20th century, brought power to its possessor. Black cat bones, supposedly acquired by boiling unfortunate felines alive, could supposedly render their possessors' invisible. The most popular of all items was graveyard dirt, sometimes known as *goopher dust*. Those using the dirt frequently took it from specific graves, believing that the spirits of those buried there would imbue the dirt with powers related to their personalities. For instance, a gambler's grave would be a good place to collect soil for use in a charm prepared to aid someone in games of chance. That of a soldier, meanwhile, could bring one protection.

Historically, the working of conjure relied upon the skills of conjure men and women, also known as *workers*. In most cases, these were professionals who charged for their services. Before emancipation, conjurers typically collected small sums, and some accepted goods as a form of payment. Following emancipation, prices skyrocketed, with some of the more difficult spells going for hundreds of dollars by the time of the Great Depression in the 1930s. Interestingly, as prices rose, the prevalence of individual practitioners waned. In part, the decline was a result of the rise of spiritual supply shops that sold the botanical and zoological items used by professional conjurers as well as an ever-increasing line of manufactured items that have gradually displaced many traditional charms. To avoid potentially expensive client-conjurer relationships, those seeking magical assistance could perform their own magic following the advice of store clerks who pointed out the moderately priced items customers needed and gave instructions for their use. Even those conjurers who continued to practice professionally increasingly purchased their supplies from such shops.

The connection between Voodoo and conjure varies by locale. In the Mississippi Valley, Voodoo and hoodoo were not generally thought of as separate practices until the 20th century. In recent years, however, scholars and some laypeople have redefined the terms, designating Voodoo as the proper name for the religion and hoodoo as magical practices with little link to the ceremonies and deities of Voodoo. Outside of the Mississippi Valley, conjure has existed since at least the 19th century without links to a living African Diasporic religion. When explaining its spiritual basis, practitioners have historically been more apt to credit Jesus Christ or God the Father as the source of their power than any other spiritual force. Despite the lack of direct connection between the religion of Voodoo and the supernaturalism of conjure outside the Mississippi Valley, many people, black and white, describe all African American magical practices as Voodoo.

See also: Graveyard Dirt; Hoodoo; Magic; Modern Voodoo/Vodou and Hoodoo Businesses; Mojo; Rootwork; Voodoo in the Mississippi Valley

Jeffrey E. Anderson

Further Reading

Anderson, Jeffrey E. 2005. *Conjure in African American Society*. Baton Rouge, LA: Louisiana State University Press.

Chireau, Yvonne. 2003. *Black Magic: Religion and the African American Conjuring Tradition.* Berkeley: University of California Press.
Gomez, Michael A. 1998. *Exchanging Our Country Marks: The Transformation of African Identities in the Colonial and Antebellum South.* Chapel Hill: University of North Carolina Press.
Hyatt, Harry Middleton. 1970–1978. *Hoodoo-Conjuration-Witchcraft-Rootwork.* 5 vols. Memoirs of the Alma Egan Hyatt Foundation. Hannibal: Western.
Long, Carolyn Morrow. 2001. *Spiritual Merchants: Religion, Magic, and Commerce.* Knoxville, TN: University of Tennessee Press.

COSMOGRAM

The term *cosmogram* denotes a cross, appearing in traditional ritual contexts among the Kongo, in which a horizontal line, representing the boundary between the worlds of the living and the dead, is traversed by a vertical line, the path from one to the other. The cross may be inscribed in a circle, also representing cyclical movement between the worlds. For example, a woman quarreling with her neighbor might draw such a cross on the ground, stand on it, and swear to the truth of her assertion, inviting her own death should she be in the wrong. Another example is the point where a path crosses a village boundary, where twins and albinos, deemed to partake of both worlds, were buried. Other such marginal sites include the edge of the forest; the forest itself, containing the local cemetery, was thought of as the village of the dead, although it was said that, from the point of view of the dead themselves, "the forest was their village, and we the living were in the forest." The land of the dead was also thought of as lying across any stream, the Congo River, or (after the development of the slave trade) the Atlantic. The cosmogram was thus a shorthand reference to, or diagram of, the cosmos as a whole. It was never abstracted from its ritual uses and elaborated as a system until André Fu-kiau, after working with the anthropologist J. M. Janzen, published a version of it in Kinshasa in 1969. It was subsequently popularized by him and by the art historian Robert Farris Thompson in public lectures in the United States. *Cosmogram* has since been adopted for use in many other contexts, for example, as a term for Tibetan mandalas. Of course, in Kongo as elsewhere in the world, circles and crosses often occur as design elements with no cosmological significance.

See also: Ginen; Kongo; Nzambi a Mpungu

Wyatt MacGaffey

Further Reading
Fukiau, André. 1974. "Man in His World." In *An Anthology of Kongo Religion*, edited by John M. Janzen and Wyatt MacGaffey. Lawrence, KS: University of Kansas Press.

COURLANDER, HAROLD

Harold Courlander (1908–1996) was a folklorist, anthropologist, and prolific author who studied a host of belief systems ranging from those of the American

Southwest's Hopi to the peoples of Indonesia. His most famous works, however, addressed African, Afro-Caribbean, and African American folklore. These included specific studies of various African peoples and regions as well as two major treasuries of African and African American folklore. His most important work in relation to Vodou was *The Drum and the Hoe: Life and Lore of the Haitian People* (1960). Courlander's work resembles that of Alfred Métraux in that both authors sought to provide extensive in-depth looks at the religion as a whole. *Drum and Hoe* is particularly useful for its inclusion of a glossary of Kreyòl terms, a lengthy annotated list of the major Vodou deities, and over one hundred pages of music connected to the religion.

In addition to his well-known folklore research and writing, Courlander was best known for his claim that Alex Haley plagiarized his novel *The African* (1967) to write *Roots* (1976). The case was settled in Courlander's favor but garnered considerable attention because of the latter work's popularity.

See also: Métraux, Alfred

Jeffrey E. Anderson

Further Reading
Courlander, Harold. 1960. *The Drum and the Hoe: Life and Lore of the Haitian People*. Berkeley: University of California Press.
Courlander, Harold. 1973. *Haiti Singing*. New York: Cooper Square Publishers.
Courlander, Harold. 1975. *A Treasury of African Folklore: The Oral Literature, Traditions, Myths, Legends, Epics, Tales, Recollections, Wisdom, Sayings, and Humor of Africa*. New York: Crown.
Courlander, Harold. 1976. *A Treasury of Afro-American Folklore: The Oral Literature, Traditions, Recollections, Legends, Tales, Songs, Religious Beliefs, Customs, Sayings, and Humor of Peoples of African Descent in the Americas*. New York: Crown Publishers.
Jaffe, Nina. 1997. *A Voice for the People: The Life and Work of Harold Courlander*. New York: Henry Holt and Company.

CREOLES OF LOUISIANA

The term *Creole* can be very confusing to define, but the best way to start is at the beginning. Creoles were first defined as the descendants of Old World settlers in Louisiana. Eventually the term evolved to designate primarily French Creoles and those of African descent, who were known as Creoles of Color. The free members of the latter group often adopted the term to distinguish themselves from slaves. Creoles traditionally practiced Roman Catholicism and spoke French or Creole French. In the United States, most of those who have called themselves Creoles have lived in the vicinity of New Orleans. There is another population of Creoles that developed in Cane River, a community eleven miles south of Natchitoches, Louisiana. Today, the term most often refers to someone of mixed heritage of African, French, Spanish, and/or Native American descent born in Louisiana.

Louisiana was founded as a free colony in 1699 with Mobile (now in Alabama) becoming its first capital in 1702, a distinction claimed by New Orleans in 1718.

New Orleans became an important port and trade city for a number of significant ethnicities. Such ethnicities have included Native Americans, such as Choctaws, Colapissas, Houmas, and Tunicas; French and Spanish colonists; and free people of color (those of enslaved African descent).

Director General of the French Louisiana colony, Jean Baptiste Le Moyne, Sieur de Bienville, decided to turn New Orleans into a settlement with the help of about fifty white men and several hundred enslaved Africans. An overwhelming majority of the slaves came from West Africa, mostly Senegambia (Senegal and Gambia areas). Native Americans sometimes found themselves enslaved alongside Africans. While many American Indians could escape to their homelands, however, Africans could not. Those Africans and their descendants stayed in New Orleans, building levees, ships, streets, ironworks, shops, and farms. Though most were slaves, there are records of free people of color living in New Orleans, operating as business owners and as servants to families from France or the Caribbean, especially the French colony of Saint-Domingue (now Haiti) and Cuba.

The French legal code for slaves allowed them the right to obtain education, own property, operate businesses, marry one another, keep their families together, and be hired out for wages. Slaves could receive freedom in several ways, including a grant from their masters, fighting alongside the French during wartime, or self-purchase. The code for free people of color allowed even more rights. They could even own slaves.

By the mid-18th century, the term *free people of color* referred to second-generation people born free, living in Louisiana, or to people from the Caribbean who came to New Orleans free. During the period of Spanish rule in Louisiana (1763–1802), the enslaved population was more liberated than when the area became part of the young United States. Similar to the French laws, the Spanish code allowed enslaved peoples to petition for their freedom after living independent of their masters for ten years or more, serving in the Spanish military, performing in important capacities for the crown, becoming priests, buying their freedom, or marrying free blacks.

Throughout the development of New Orleans, it was common for free women of color and white men to have intimate relationships. What developed was an accepted societal system called *plaçage,* in which white men had children by free women of color in addition to marrying a white woman. Interracial marriage, however, was looked down upon and sometimes illegal. In return for the relationship, the male provided financial security for his concubine and any children born to the couple. Biracial male children were expected to go to school, whereas the biracial females were to follow in their mothers' footsteps by finding white suitors to take care of them. These children were sometimes designated as their fathers' heirs. A similar system was also in place in Cane River during the 1700s.

Under Spanish rule, free people of color established themselves as a population between whites and enslaved African blacks. The term *Creole* evolved into a way for them to identify themselves as neither black nor white. Free people of color married other free people of color to keep their social status and to accumulate businesses, real estate, and education. Many had the same rights as their white counterparts.

French Emperor Napoleon Bonaparte reacquired Louisiana and in 1803 sold it to the United States. Knowing something of the more rigid racial definitions found in the United States, Creoles were afraid of their rights being taken away. A number of them left for Paris or sold their property. Others stayed in New Orleans and continued their lifestyle, fighting for the right to vote and to be recognized as freed people. During the early 20th century, many states instituted the binary rule, also known as "the one-drop rule," meaning that if there was one black ancestor in one's family tree, that person was legally defined as black. In other words, no matter how white a person appeared, if there was one black ancestor in the family line, the person was labeled as black. The rule remained in place until 1970, when Louisiana passed legislation that anyone with 1/32 Negro ancestry or more was legally black.

Creoles felt threatened by the one-drop rule, knowing they could lose the in-between status that had taken them so long to establish. As a result of such measures, the term *passé en blanc* evolved. In English, the words mean "passing for white," and they referred to those who attempted to hide their African ancestry. Incidents of not claiming the darker side of the family reportedly led mothers to give away their darker offspring to avoid the stigma of being "colored." To be labeled as black would be to become a second-class citizen.

In addition to the value placed on Old World heritage and in most cases mixed race, self-identified Creoles have continued to point to several other aspects of their lives that have long made them what they were. Many associate the term with close-knit families, pride in one's heritage, and having strong values. For some, *Creole* refers to very fair blacks who could *passé en blanc*. Words like *mulatto, octoroon, brickee,* and *quadroon,* which designate degrees of racial mixture and were common during the colonial and antebellum eras, continue to come up during discussions even today.

Some believe that Voodoo is a Creole religion that is strongly associated with those of Haitian descent in New Orleans. Most modern Creoles are not aware of their people practicing the faith today or during previous generations. However, evidence does show Vodou was practiced by Haitians in New Orleans and was either introduced to Creoles or already practiced by them. Marie Laveau was a Creole woman born of a white father and a free woman of color. Her first husband, Jacques Paris, was a Haitian immigrant, who arrived with a large influx of Haitians in 1809. It is possible she became very familiar with Vodou practices during her marriage to Paris and kept learning the religion after his death. There was also a very strong relationship between Catholicism and Voodoo, and Laveau was a practicing Catholic as well as a Voodoo priestess.

This association of Voodoo with Creoles also traveled northwest to Cane River. A significant number of Creoles in Cane River made special herbs to cure illnesses in ways similar to Native Americans or any indigenous people who respected the land they used. This practice may also have had much to do with the dearth of doctors in the area during the late 19th and early 20th centuries. Creoles had to create their own cures for diseases and any other ailments, though doing so does not necessarily prove involvement in the Voodoo faith.

See also: Code Noir; Haitian Immigration to the United States; Laveau, Marie; New Orleans; Senegambia

Tina N. Mullone

Further Reading

Gehman, Mary, and Lloyd Dennis. 1994. *The Free People of Color of New Orleans: An Introduction.* New Orleans: Margaret Media.

Hirsch, Arnold R., and Joseph Logsdon, eds. 1992. *Creole New Orleans: Race and Americanization.* Baton Rouge: Louisiana State University Press.

Kein, Sybil, ed. 2000. *Creole: The History and Legacy of Louisiana's Free People of Color.* Baton Rouge: Louisiana State University Press.

Sweet, Frank W. 2005. *Legal History of the Color Line: The Rise and Triumph of the One-Drop Rule.* Palm Coast, FL: Backintyme.

Young, A. S. "Doc." 1953. "Are Creoles Negroes?" *JET Magazine*, June 25, 12–15.

CREOLIZATION

Creolization refers to the process by which a population combines selected elements of multiple traditions to yield new forms. The term *creole* refers to practices or forms influenced by more than one heritage. Populations referred to as creole peoples exist worldwide, with the most researched merging features from African, Amerindian, European, and East Indian cultures.

Initial theories regarding creolization drew on linguistic models, designed to explain how spoken languages reflect the politics of contact between cultures. Researchers approach creoles as new forms rather than as modifications of existing ones. That is, a creole language is neither a subordinate version nor a pidgin of the standard tongue. Subsequent theories about creolization have taken cues from a wide range of academic disciplines. As part of their research on creole peoples, scholars strive to learn about the formation, structure, and status of their societies. Any aspect of culture may demonstrate the interculturalism associated with creoles.

Close contact among cultural groups, whether it is marked by cooperation or conflict, proves instrumental to the establishment of linguistic or cultural creoles. Frequently, the formation of creoles began with sociopolitical experiences of trauma connected to globalization, such as colonization, conquest, enslavement, and oppression. On this basis, creole forms may be born of necessity and pain as much as of innovation. Forced migrations and involuntary relationships contributed to the diasporic diffusion of culture. These hybrids may represent voluntary blending or involuntary appropriation of cultural practices. Consequently, expressive domains including music, material culture, oral literature, folk medicine, or religion map the interstices of these diverse cultural sources, their complicated associations, and their embattled histories.

In the United States, some communities are particularly closely associated in the public imagination with the term *creole*. In the southern United States, most notably in Louisiana, creole culture incorporates elements of African, French, and indigenous practices. In this regard, it is widely acknowledged that such foodways

> ### Adaptability
> One of the most notable features of Vodou and related faiths is their adaptability. Believers have been displaced from their homelands and faith communities, but they have held fast to their religions, simply altering them to fit their new environments. Africa has always been a land of many faiths, and the interchange of rituals, deities, and the like is evident from earliest times. Enslaved Africans, encountering foreign faiths like Catholicism for the first time, would be apt to fit them into their existing notions of religion, allowing them to continue the creative adaptation they had long practiced in their homelands.

as Cajun cuisine, musical forms as zydeco, and holiday celebrations as Mardi Gras reflect interplay among cultural legacies.

Creolization characterizes many faith communities, including Brazil's Candomblé, Cuba's Santería, Haiti's Vodou, and Trinidad's Orisha. These syncretic religions blend West African cultural survivals with beliefs and behaviors associated with other locations and faiths, notably Roman Catholicism. The conduct of each faith, including its rituals, ceremonies, and healing practices, reveals cross-cultural borrowing.

An example may serve to illustrate how creolization shapes religious views and activities. During the 1930s, ethnographic research conducted by Zora Neale Hurston probed Voodoo practices in the southern United States and their origins abroad. She pursued this inquiry in part by functioning as an initiate or participant-observer. Hurston devoted particular attention to rituals associated with Haitian Vodou. Hurston's work examined how Vodou traveled to and underwent transformation in the New World. For instance, she researched how a figure from the 19th century, Marie Laveau of New Orleans, popularized a version of Voodoo that syncretized its cultural sources. Additionally, Hurston examined hoodoo, a related conjure tradition.

Creole societies take shape over time, forged through a series of intercultural encounters. Creolization describes the outcome of cross-cultural communication, not always sought but nonetheless wrought in resulting cultural systems, including religion. Unlike simple border-crossings, creolization denotes a more complex phenomenon. For these reasons, creole societies function as crossroads, locations of ongoing exploration and eclecticism.

See also: Conjure; Creoles of Louisiana; Hurston, Zora Neale; Syncretism

Linda S. Watts

Further Reading

Balutansky, Kathleen M., and Sourieau, Marie-Agnes, eds. 1998. *Caribbean Creolization: Reflections on the Cultural Dynamics of Language, Literature, and* Identity. Gainesville, FL: University Press of Florida.

Chaudenson, Robert. 2001. *Creolization of Language and Culture.* New York: Routledge.

Gundaker, Grey. 1998. *Signs of Diaspora, Diaspora of Signs: Literacies, Creolization, and Vernacular Practice in African America.* New York: Oxford University Press.

Holloway, Joseph E., ed. 2005. *Africanisms in American Culture.* 2nd ed. Bloomington, IN: Indiana University Press.

Stewart, Charles. 2007. *Creolization: History, Ethnography, Theory*. Walnut Creek, CA: Left Coast Press.
Woolford, Ellen, and Washabaugh, William, eds. 1983. *The Social Context of Creolization*. Ann Arbor, MI: Karoma Publishers, Inc.

CULTURAL POLITICS

Prominent members of Haitian society who prefer to associate themselves with the cultural capital perceived to flow from speaking French as opposed to Kreyòl and practicing Roman Catholicism as opposed to practicing Vodou have frequently eschewed practices associated with serving the lwa/spirits. In Haiti, where the majority of the population is of African descent—and thus those attempting to order and value or devalue cultural traditions have to cope with that demographic reality—it has proven difficult to demonize Vodou in a way that would permanently marginalize the religious practices by virtue of their purported African roots. Since the Haitian Revolution at the dawn of the 19th century, Vodou has taken on special meaning for those who wish to associate themselves with a separatist stance vis-à-vis colonial political authority and European cultural norms, viewed as synonymous with that authority. Vodou has frequently become part and parcel of nativist movements aimed at accentuating Haitian cultural pride, especially in resistance to the cultural dominance of French-speaking Catholic elites. The 20th-century dictatorship of François Duvalier embraced Vodou as Haiti's national heritage and used it as a liaison to the masses of his citizens. Duvalier granted Vodou state protection and employed powerful priests as state advisors, informants, and militia commanders and used Vodou temples as political headquarters.

In the United States, specifically in areas of the country like New Orleans where Voodoo survives, it has frequently succumbed to cultural pressures to conform to a set of cultural values that equates Christianity—specifically the variants most popular among white Anglo-Saxon Protestants—as the norm. That pressure has frequently led to a blend of Voodoo with Christian traditions that favors Christianity. The sparse outsider accounts of 19th-century New Orleans, where the history of Catholic dominance had made the saints part of the popular religious culture, support the notion that the blending of Voodoo spirits and the Catholic saints has favored the saints, making their back stories and presence more prominent among Voodoo practitioners in the late 19th and early 20th centuries. Practitioners who reported performing Voodoo ceremonies in these periods used the images of the saints, and their reading of those spirits held more closely to Catholic interpretations of the saints' histories and personalities. The dynamic nature of the practice of Voodoo also saw practitioners adjusting Catholic hagiography to meet contemporary needs, but with the hagiography itself providing the map for those departures.

By the end of the 20th century, however, a movement of African cultural pride frequently led to a re-Africanization of Voodoo in both Haiti and the United States. Haitian mambo and oungan began traveling to West Africa to be trained and initiated by practitioners of the Yoruba religion from which Vodou is said to have been derived, attempting to maintain or to re-create the African authenticity of

> ### Cultural Misappropriation
>
> In recent years, large numbers of whites have gravitated to Vodou. This demographic shift has raised the issue of cultural appropriation. Many Haitian and African American believers accept that nonblacks can possess genuine faith. Others reject them, seeing nonblack believers as stealing practices that rightfully belong to others and devaluing those practices in the process. While this viewpoint holds some merit in the case of those who pick and choose aspects of the faiths that serve their whims, it is difficult to justify with regard to sincere believers, regardless of their race.

their work. Similarly, travel to Haiti or training by Haitian mambo and oungan has become desirable among American practitioners of Voodoo.

In both Haiti and the United States, practitioners of Vodou and Voodoo have frequently been persecuted by law enforcement. For much of its history, Vodou in Haiti did not have the official sanction of the state. Similarly, in the United States, practitioners of Voodoo have frequently been prosecuted for fraud or, in the antebellum era, for illegal gatherings of slaves and free people. Thus, in both the Caribbean and the United States, African Diasporic religion has been a tool in the marginalization of people of African descent and their push for positive cultural identity.

See also: Congress of Santa Barbara (KOSANBA); Legislation against Vodou/Voodoo

Kodi Roberts

Further Reading

Roberts, Kodi. In press. *Voodoo and the Promise of Power: The Racial, Gender & Economic Politics of Religion in New Orleans, 1881–1940*. Baton Rouge: Louisiana State University Press.

D

DAHOMEY

Dahomey, the predecessor of modern Benin, was a creation of the Fon ethnic group. During the early 17th century, the Fon were a relatively disorganized ethnicity subject to raids from the Yoruba state of Oyo, which used the Fon as a source of income in the form of tribute, slaves, and other goods captured during military incursions. Oyo also claimed and sometimes exerted political control over the area. In addition to the threat from Oyo, the Fon had to survive economic hardships inflicted by their lack of access to the coast. The coastal area to the south was controlled by a collection of small city-states, increasing the cost of imported items and limiting the landlocked ethnicity's access to European goods, such as firearms. To make matters worse, many of the slaves traded from the coast were themselves Fon. Under such pressure, the Fon organized themselves into a kingdom during the early to mid-1600s, which eventually became centered on the city of Abomey.

Political centralization brought some blessing for the Fon. On one hand, it allowed the kingdom to rapidly develop as a military power. As Dahomey grew in strength, the might of Oyo and the cities to the south diminished. Women also benefitted, holding unusually exalted positions within the government. For instance, the king appointed individual women to monitor the actions of state officials. The Dahomean military also enlisted women in all-female combat units.

Organization was not an entirely positive development, however. The kings of the Fon, for example, were absolute monarchs who appointed all government officials. Their rule could also be quite harsh, and those who angered the monarch could expect to suffer. The most unpleasant feature of Dahomean culture was the extent to which the state participated in human sacrifice. Though many African peoples practiced occasional human sacrifice, the number killed by the Dahomeans was much more extensive than the norm. Chief occasions for the sacrifices were what Europeans designated the Annual Customs, when criminals and other captives were beheaded. During those held following the death of a king, hundreds of victims might be killed. The Fon officials who conducted the sacrifices believed that the dead would serve their deceased leader in the afterlife. The state also performed sacrifices of thanksgiving to the gods following significant military victories.

As Dahomey's military might increased, it gradually freed itself from outside control. Oyo, the chief enemy of the Fon, struggled to slow the kingdom's growing power, inflicting a serious defeat on Dahomey in 1726 and continuing attacks throughout the century. Nevertheless, the kingdom had largely freed itself from the power of Oyo by the end of the 18th century and officially declared itself

> ### Where Did Voodoo Originate?
>
> It is common for scholars to describe Mississippi Valley Voodoo as a Haitian import. Others say it developed from the religion of the Fon people of the Bight of Benin. Still others suggest it has Senegambian or West Central African origins, basing their arguments on similarities in languages, rituals, and other areas between Voodoo and the traditional faiths of these regions. Voodoo, however, has no single origin. Though its vocabulary was heavily influenced by the Fon, it also contains elements from the Mande, Kongo, and Yoruba cultures as well as European and Native American aspects.

fully independent in 1818. During its wars with Oyo, Dahomey also overcame the smaller coastal cities to the south. In 1716, Weme fell to Dahomean forces. The greater prizes of Allada and Whydah (now Ouidah) fell in 1724 and 1727, respectively, to Agaja, one of Dahomey's greatest warrior kings.

In part, Agaja and his predecessors' military efforts aimed to prevent the enslavement and exportation of his people and possibly of slaves in general, but capture of the coastal cities would prove problematic. Ports like Whydah were already important slave export centers, and the trade only increased under the rule of the Fon kings. The impetus for the embrace of the slave trade was twofold: profit and military necessity. On the one hand, Dahomey lacked some of the valuable natural resources possessed by nearby nations and therefore found it difficult to obtain European goods. Trade in humans was a way to address the shortage. In addition, the military threat presented by Oyo required the Fon to acquire the guns necessary to fight back. Whydah quickly became one of Africa's most important slave ports and continued in that capacity until near the end of the 19th century, despite the fact that the British, in particular, had been actively suppressing the Atlantic trade above the equator since 1807.

Dahomey's decline began as the British antislavery efforts intensified, and New World societies gradually ended slavery. When Brazil abolished it in 1888, the Atlantic trade disappeared. Though its overseas trade was significantly curtailed, Dahomey survived until 1893. Both the British and French competed for influence in the kingdom, but ultimately it would be France that prevailed, conquering the nation in 1893. Dahomey would remain a European colony until it regained its independence in 1960. It would later change its name to Benin.

The flow of slaves out of Whydah and the numerous wars between Dahomey and its neighbors helped make the Fon one of the most visible components of the African Diaspora. In Haiti, for instance, the important Rada nanchon of deities was named after the Dahomean city, Allada. Its deities include recognizable spirits from the area, including Danbala (called Da, Segbo, or Da Segbo in Dahomey) and Legba, two of the most important of the Vodou spirits. Similar deities, going by the names Blanc Dani and Lébat, existed in the Voodoo practiced in the New Orleans area as well. In both cases, the survival of aspects of Dahomean religion was a consequence of heavy and early importation of members of the nation and the closely-related Ewe and other speakers of the the Gbe language group into the French colonies. The strong group identity of the Fon ethnicity likewise contributed to the survival of their religious beliefs.

See also: Bight of Benin; Blanc Dani; Danbala; Ewe; Nanchons; Yoruba

Jeffrey E. Anderson

Further Reading

Belcher, Stephen. 2005. *African Myths of Origin*. London: Penguin.
Courlander, Harold. 1975. *A Treasury of African Folklore: The Oral Literature, Traditions, Myths, Legends, Epics, Tales, Recollections, Wisdom, Sayings, and Humor of Africa*. New York: Crown.
Ellis, A. B. 1890. *The Ewe-Speaking Peoples of the Slave Coast of West Africa: Their Religion, Manners, Customs, Laws, Languages, &c*. London: Chapman and Hall.
Gomez, Michael A. 1998. *Exchanging Our Country Marks: The Transformation of African Identities in the Colonial and Antebellum South*. Chapel Hill and London: University of North Carolina Press.
Harris, Joseph E. 1987. *Africans and Their History*. Revised ed. New York: Penguin Group.
Herskovits, Melville J. 1938. *Dahomey: An Ancient West African Kingdom*. 2 vols. New York: J. J. Augustin.
Oliver, Roland, and J. D. Fage. 1988. *A Short History of Africa*. 6th ed. London: Penguin Group.

DANBALA

Danbala, also called Dan and Odan, is the creator serpent of the Vodou pantheon. Danbala is thought to carry the ancestors for their proscribed sixteen stays on earth. He is said to carry even older ancestors as well as strangers whose names have been forgotten. In this manner, Danbala is seen as the most ancient and respected of all the Vodou spirits.

At the height of the Dahomean empire, the lwa now called Danbala, or Dan-Ayida Wedo, had two sources. The first was Ayida Wedo from Abomey. This spirit was represented as a sky deity, travelling with thunder bolts, which can be seen on the brass plaques of the royal palace at Abomey even today. The second was Dangbe from the town of Whydah. This spirit was also seen as both male and female, although when speaking of Dangbe, male-gendered pronouns were used. Both shared the same attributes we recognize today as Danbala: whiteness, wisdom, fecundity, abundance, fertility, and rain. These two spirits held similar positions but with one very important distinction. Dangbe was the repository of the "common" ancestors, those spirits who were the descendants of nonroyal families. Ayida Wedo was the repository of royal ancestors. Tradition dictated that these two classes never mix. The majority of Africans who were sold into bondage during the days of the Atlantic slave trade were common, not royal. It stands to reason that royal female prisoners of war would be placed in the kings' harems and royal males would be killed. Priests were kept alive in order to control the gods they served. This left the common people—militia, farmers, and others—for export to the New World. Thus, Dangbe seems to have been the source for the lwa called Danbala in Haiti, while Ayida came to reference his female aspect.

Danbala can be thought of as the original astronomer or astrologer. Numerous stories speak of his passage across the night sky, leaving a trail of scales that shine like stars. Danbala is said to have perfect knowledge of the heavens, having learned this from the African tradition called *Na-Go Oyyo*. Danbala personifies fire and water. Fire represents his serpent powers of regeneration and creation. Water represents his deep knowledge or konesans of the world and its people. In keeping with this analogy, he is served both in Rada and in Petwo rites. There is scholarship citing instances of older oungans referring to Danbala as the Feather Serpent. These are not feathers like those of a bird but a descriptive reference to the feathery trail of flames he carries as he moves into the world.

Danbala is served with white satin pakets, white liquors, and white offerings, as white is the color of the ancestors in Africa. His pakets are decorated with heavy embellishments of crystals and pearls, with a crucifix sticking out of the top to represent a tree or possibly the potomitan he travels down to have egress into the physical world. In the ever-dizzying set of relationships that make up the theology of Vodou, Danbala is paired with Ayida, but is often thought of as married to Ezili Freda. Servitors are taught to place Danbala's paket with Maitresse Ezili Freda's, as he is one of Freda's three husbands.

Danbala's day of service is Thursday, while Monday and Tuesday are Ayida's days. Servitors take white foods as offerings. They present the lwa with white chickens, white eggs, white rice, saucers of milk, eggs on mounds of white flour, anisette liquor, white cakes and pastries, white wine, rice pudding, meringue cookies, bananas, white grapes, champagne, corn meal dumplings, and coconut meal. Before services for Danbala, oungans will drop raw eggs and corn syrup at the potomitan as offerings to the great serpent. He never fails to arrive in possession of his servitor or *chwal* (horse in Creole) and lick it up, shells and all.

When Danbala arrives in possession, servitors quickly cover the *chwal* with a white sheet. He is considered too holy to be seen by profane eyes, and therefore must be hidden. Danbala is also one of the cool Rada spirits. To keep him cool, servitors offer sheets to shade him from the sun or heat.

Danbala's Catholic image is Saint Patrick because of the snakes that often appear at the feet of the saint in popular lithographs or Moses because of the story of his staff turning into a serpent in front of Pharaoh. Our Lady of the Immaculate Conception is used for Ayida because of the frequent appearance of multicolored cherubs in pictures of her.

See also: Blanc Dani; Dahomey; Konesans; Lwa

Patricia Scheu (Mambo Vye Zo Komande LaMenfo)

Further Reading

Ackermann, Hans-Wolfgang, Maryse Gautier, and Michel-Ange Momplaisir. 2011. *Les Esprits du Vodou Haïtien.* Coconut Creek, FL: Educa Vision, Inc.

Hutton, Catherine. 1819–1821. *The Tour of Africa: Containing a Concise Account of All the Countries in that Quarter of the Globe Hitherto Visited by Europeans.* London: Baldwin, Cradock, and Joy.

Spring, Christopher. 1993. *African Arms and Armor*. Washington, DC: Smithsonian Institute Press.

Wills, John E. 2001. *1688: A Global History*. New York: W.W. Norton.

DANCES

In Vodou, dance is integral to the religion's music, songs/chants, and practices. In fact, Vodou is often referred to as the dancing religion. Vodou is a New World religion blended with African beliefs, Native American traditions, and Catholic practices, and the dancing itself also altered once it left Africa and entered the New World during the institution of slavery. Many enslaved peoples from various parts of Africa were forced to stop practicing their original religions, to be grouped with other enslaved peoples outside their own societies, and to take on Christianity, particularly Catholicism. By hiding their traditional African beliefs under Catholicism, enslaved peoples were able to stay connected to their culture, and thus their identity.

Ritual dances are extremely sacred and open only to those who are either born into the religion or chosen by the practitioners, who are very protective of what goes on. One cannot blame practitioners with such an attitude, considering how mainstream society reacts to hearing the word *Voodoo*. Blood sacrifices, animalistic orgies, zombis, and cannibalistic gatherings leap into the minds of the uninformed.

Since the beginning of humankind, dance's main purpose has been religious. Ritual dance has numerous paths, and within those paths are many spirit pantheons. Within Vodou, the body acts as a vessel for the spirit to connect with the intangible lwa. Each lwa is connected to an element of nature: wind, sun, rain, water, trees, animals, and so on. A few examples of the lwa thus served are Agwe, spirit of the sea; Danbala (or Damballah Wedo), the serpent deity; and Ogou, spirit of war, iron, and steel.

In a ceremony, there is a meeting place, usually open ground or a temple. An altar is set up depending on which lwa is to be honored. Normally, it is decorated with candles, a picture of a saint, and symbolic items connected to the lwa. A feast is served before the ceremony. Then a vèvè, a specific pattern representing the lwa, is formed on the sacred place using flour, cornmeal, or some other powder. Next, the dancing of priests, priestesses, and students continues until possession by the lwa is obtained.

All ritual dance, no matter what the faith or religion, has a similar purpose. Dancers who release their spirits during their movement are said to succumb to the calling spirit and become one, a process sometimes referred to as "spirit possession." As anthropologist Wade Davis put it, "the soul of the living has been momentarily replaced by God." Therefore, the person becomes the god he or she is dancing for. Once the dancer is possessed, the lwa speaks through him or her. There is no set time as to when the spirit will present itself to the dancer, nor release her or him. It simply happens. The dancer will follow the spirit as long as the lwa wants him or her to do so. Often, one does not remember what happens during possession.

No matter which lwa is honored by the ceremony, the dance will resemble other Vodou rituals through a series of common features drawn from African cultural aesthetics. Robert Farris Thompson has identified these shared features as follows:

- Dancers have soft or bent knees.
- Participants tilt at the waist.
- Steps are flat footed.
- Movements are according to a propulsive rhythm.
- Dancers move their hips in a centrifugal or outward motion.
- Participants imitate animals.
- Dances are grounded in nature.
- Rituals incorporate drums and chanting/singing.

Nevertheless, there are distinctive features of each dance. Dancers wear distinct attire and colored beads depending on which lwa is called upon. Each lwa has a specific dance, set of drums, rhythms, chants, dress, and symbols. For example, if Baron Samedi, head of the ancestral lwa and protector of the cemetery, the grave, and death itself, is called upon, devotees offer the lwa's favorite items: cigars, rum, black coffee, bread, and grilled peanuts. The dance itself depends on which lwa is called upon as well. Samedi's dance, *banda*, is performed in his honor.

In general, a ceremony begins with a prayer to those who are deceased and any sacred instruments including drums that are no longer used or forgotten. This prayer is led by a priest (oungan) or priestess (mambo) and is another way to prepare participants for the ceremony. Chants follow the prayer, sometimes in a call-and-response matter. Specific instruments, such as the flattened bell, triangle, and drums, are utilized according to which particular rites are performed. Vodou dances rely on specialized drums. Before the ceremony, the drums must undergo their own rituals, which involve offerings of food and liquor and sacrifice to renew their strength. During the dances, participants are frequently arranged in a circle with the drummer(s) inside it. The drums control the rhythm of the dance. They also call the lwa and create the opportunity for someone to be possessed. Sacrifice is often part of the ritual as well. The animal is then cooked and eaten by the participants. Vodou dances may continue until complete possession by the lwa or indefinitely.

See also: Congo Square; Drums; Music and Haitian Vodou; Possession

Tina N. Mullone

Further Reading

Anderson, Stacey. 2014. "Voodoo Is Rebounding in New Orleans After Hurricane Katrina." *Newsweek*, August 25. Accessed December 9, 2014 at: http://www.newsweek.com/2014/09/05/voodoo-rebounding-new-orleans-after-hurricane-katrina-266340.html.

Daniel, Yvonne. 2005. *Dancing Wisdom: Embodied Knowledge in Haitian Vodou, Cuban Yoruba, and Bahian Candomblé*. Urbana, IL: University of Illinois Press.

Davis, Wade. 1986. *The Serpent and the Rainbow: A Harvard Scientist's Astonishing Journey into the Secret Societies of Haitian Voodoo, Zombis, and Magic*. New York: Simon and Schuster.

Murphy, Joseph M. 1994. *Working the Spirit: Ceremonies of the African Diaspora.* Boston: Beacon Press.

Thompson, Robert Farris. 1983. *Flash of the Spirit: African and Afro-American Art and Philosophy.* New York: Random House.

DAVIS, WADE

Davis is an anthropologist, prolific author and speaker, and adventurer. His best known work, *The Serpent and the Rainbow* (1986), primarily describes his search for the facts behind the legends of Haitian zombis. He began field work on possible ethnopharmacological explanations for the phenomenon in 1982 after being introduced to a series of supposed cases of zombification, including the celebrated case of Clairvius Narcisse. Narcisse supposedly died in 1962 but reappeared alive eighteen years later. After considerable research, much of which led nowhere, Davis concluded that zombification is a genuine practice that can be explained in part by the workings of tetrodotoxin, a powerful natural poison produced by puffer fish, which bòkòs secretly administered to victims. Tetrodotoxin causes paralysis, which can sometimes be mistaken for death. To complete the process, a sorcerer force feeds the seemingly dead body a mixture of ingredients that includes *Datura stramonium*, also known as the *zombi cucumber*, which both revives the victim and keeps him or her in a compliant, trance-like state. In addition to his claims regarding the scientific explanations for zombis, Davis also argues that zombification can be a judgment inflicted on wrongdoers by Vodou societies rather than random, self-serving crime. His work was well received, especially by popular audiences, and inspired the 1988 horror movie, also named *The Serpent and the Rainbow*.

Davis has worked on many projects in addition to Haitian Vodou. Currently he has thirteen books in print and has produced several documentary films. His subjects range from Greenland Inuit to the inhabitants of Borneo.

See also: Bòkò; Secret Societies; Zombi

Jeffrey E. Anderson

Further Reading

Davis, Wade. 1988. *Passages of Darkness: The Ethnobiology of the Haitian Zombie.* Chapel Hill: University of North Carolina Press.

Davis, Wade. 1986. *The Serpent and the Rainbow: A Harvard Scientist's Astonishing Journey into the Secret Societies of Haitian Voodoo, Zombis, and Magic.* New York: Simon and Schuster.

Davis, Wade. 2013. *"About Wade." Wade Davis: Anthropologist Author Explorer.* Accessed April 17, 2013 at: http://www.daviswade.com/.

DEATH

In African and African creole societies, death is not the end of life. It is, instead, a change in the form of life. New Orleans's Voodoo priests and priestesses, for instance, call on spirits of deceased practitioners, doctors, and others to aid them in their practice of magic. In Haiti, the ancestors are similarly important, aiding their families and communities when they receive the proper burial rites and are treated with respect. If neglected, however, they can bring harm. In some African societies gods are believed to have once been humans who gradually arose to the godhead through the devotion of their followers. Vodou practitioners express comparable beliefs upon occasion, and the deification of Marie Laveau present in early 20th-century New Orleans Voodoo points to a similar understanding of spiritual mobility in the afterlife.

Both New World religions possess deities who preside over death and the realm of the dead. In Haiti, the Gede family of lwa is associated with both death and fertility. Its members are unpredictable and are given to irreverence and obscenity. Believers typically think of the Gede as spirits of the dead themselves. The Voodoo practiced in New Orleans had its own deity associated with death known as Monsieur d'Embarass, who was probably identical to a deity called Dambarra Soutons. The personal characteristics of d'Embarass, sadly, remain obscure.

See also: Ancestral Spirits; Baron Samedi; Cemeteries; Gede; Ginen; Zombi

Jeffrey E. Anderson

Further Reading

Anderson, Jeffrey E. 2008. *Hoodoo, Voodoo, and Conjure: A Handbook*. Westport, CT: Greenwood Press.

Desmangles, Leslie G. 1992. *Faces of the Gods: Vodou and Roman Catholicism in Haiti*. Chapel Hill, NC: University of North Carolina Press.

Thompson, Robert Farris. 1983. *Flash of the Spirit: African and Afro-American Art and Philosophy*. New York: Random House.

DÉDÉ, SANITÉ

Sanité Dédé, possibly a fictitious character, is said to have been an early 19th-century Voudou priestess. She was first mentioned in Marie B. Williams's article, "A Night with the Voudous," published in the *Appleton's Journal* of March 27, 1875. Williams' article was presented as the narrative of "Professor D----- of New Orleans," who relates how in 1822, as a young teenager, he was taken to a meeting in an abandoned brickyard on the Eve of St. John (June 23). By the light of bonfires and torches, the youth could see about sixty people dressed in white, "males and females, old and young, negroes and negresses, handsome mulatresses and quadroons, and half a dozen white men and two white women."A black woman called Sanité Dédé, in everyday life a street vendor, was the presiding priestess. There was a makeshift altar, in the center of which was a cypress sapling surmounted by "a black doll with a dress variegated by cabalistic signs and emblems, and a necklace of the vertebrae of snakes around her neck." The altar was flanked by a pair of stuffed cats. An old man named Zozo sat astride a "cylinder made of thin cypress staves hooped with brass and headed by a sheepskin." With two sticks Zozo "droned away a monotonous ra-ta-ta." Others beat an accompaniment with "sheep shank bones and the leg bones of a buzzard or turkey," and "a young negro vigorously twirled a long calabash . . . filled with pebbles."

Four initiates were being received that night. Sanité Dédé "made cabalistic signs over them and sprinkled them vigorously with some liquid from a calabash in her hand." The drummer Zozo "drew forth an immense black snake, which he brandished wildly aloft. . . . He talked and whispered to it . . . [and] passed the snake over the heads and around the necks of the initiates, repeating . . . the words . . . Voudou Magnian." Then, twirling the snake around his head, he cast it into the blazing fire. "Such a yell arose no words can describe. The rude instruments took up their discords. . . . A tall, lithe black woman . . . began to sway . . . [and] gradually the undulating motion was imparted to her body from the ankles to the hips. Then she tore the white handkerchief from her forehead. . . . This was a signal for the whole assembly to . . . enter the dance."

The narrator then lapsed into the sensationalism that was typical of white reporters' depictions of Voudou: "Under the passion of the hour, the women tore off their garments, and entirely nude, went on dancing. . . . The orgies became frightful. . . . I had grown sick from heat [and] from an indescribable horror that took possession of me. With one bound I was out of the shed, and with all speed traversed the yard. . . . If ever I have realized a sense of the real and visible presence of his majesty, the devil, it was that night among his Voudou-worshipers."

Since the publication of Marie Williams's 1875 article, Sanité Dédé has become a fixture of New Orleans Voudou lore. In Herbert Asbury's *The French Quarter* (1936) and Robert Tallant's *Voodoo in New Orleans* (1946), she is portrayed as the mentor of the great priestess Marie Laveau, who later usurps her position as Queen of the Voudous. The name of Sanité Dédé appears nowhere in the archival record. She may be the invention of Marie Williams, or Williams's portrayal might be based on an actual person of a different name.

See also: Laveau, Marie; New Orleans; Saint John's Eve

Carolyn Morrow Long

Further Reading

Long, Carolyn Morrow. 2006. *A New Orleans Voudou Priestess: The Legend and Reality of Marie Laveau.* Gainesville, FL: University Press of Florida.

Williams, Marie B. 1875. "A Night with the Voudous." *Appleton's Journal* 13 (March 27), 403–404.

DESMANGLES, LESLIE

Leslie Desmangles, currently Professor of Religion and International studies at Trinity College of Hartford, Connecticut, has spent more than forty years conducting field research in Togo, Benin, Nigeria, Haiti, and Jamaica. His work most notably includes *The Faces of the Gods: Vodou and Roman Catholicism in Haiti* (1992), which *Choice* named an Outstanding Academic Book in 1994.

Faces of the Gods is one of a host of books that have appeared in English since the 1950s that refute the sensationalist accounts of Haitian Vodou composed by the likes of Spenser St. John and William B. Seabrook. Unlike authors, such as Harold Courlander and Alfred Métraux, who sought to describe the religion as a whole, Desmangles focused specifically on the symbiosis between Vodou and Catholicism throughout Haitian history. As part of his analysis, he details the Catholic beliefs that have made their way into what began as a collection of African religions and vice versa, analyzes the areas of life that Haitians understand each religion to properly address, and looks at ways in which Vodou has become dependent on Catholicism. In addition to providing a detailed account of the interaction between Vodou and Catholicism, *Faces of the Gods* is useful in that it emphasizes changes within the religion over time, beginning with a lengthy examination of the historical settings in which the faith developed that stretches back to the earliest days of European exploration.

See also: Courlander, Harold; Métraux, Alfred; Seabrook, William Buehler; St. John, Sir Spenser; Vodou in Haiti

Jeffrey E. Anderson

Further Reading

Deren, Maya. 1953. *Divine Horsemen: The Living Gods of Haiti*. London and New York: Thames and Hudson.

Desmangles, Leslie G. 1992. *Faces of the Gods: Vodou and Roman Catholicism in Haiti*. Chapel Hill, NC: University of North Carolina Press.

"Leslie Desmangles." 2013. Trinity College. Accessed April 10, 2013 at: http://internet2.trincoll.edu/facProfiles/Default.aspx?fid=1000566.

St. John, Spenser. 1884. *Hayti or the Black Republic*. London: Smith, Elder, and Company.

DIVINATION

Divination (also called *leson*) in Haitian Vodou is regarded as a method of seeking *balanse*, a Kreyòl word that means "to bring about equilibrium and harmony." It implies metaphysical meanings that are not rendered by the English word *balance*. The moral life of those who serve the spirits in Vodou revolves around five perspectives: communal emphasis, respect for the elders, wholeness of being, healing, and coping strategies. Divination is one tool used by mambos and oungans to explore these avenues as paths to *balanse*.

Divination begins with an inquiry about a situation, an individual, or a condition and serves as a method of determining how to cure illness, seek information about a scenario, or ask for help from the spirit world. As the spirits are believed to be intimately involved in the lives of their practitioners, it is natural to seek their aid when difficulties arise. This involvement of the spirits also extends to situations that are reflected in illness of the body, mind, or soul. This is referred to as *mal*, meaning a spiritual sickness manifesting as a body illness. Divination is employed to discover information about the illness as well as cure or correct it.

Divination can be done via card reading, throwing objects onto the floor and interpreting the pattern, or using a pendulum. Card divination is well known throughout Haitian Vodou and North American Voodoo, hoodoo, and conjure traditions. In Haiti, it is performed by all competent mambos and oungans as a method of determining how a problem should be solved. Vodou priests employ a standard deck of playing cards as their oracle of choice. A small ritual is performed that varies according to reader. In most instances, prayers are offered to Legba, the patron of communications, to help open the way between the client and the spirits or lwas. The mambo or oungan may begin to use their ason to call the spirits forth. He or she then pours out water three times to signify the road to Ginen that the lwas must travel to arrive at the reading and lights a candle as a beacon or call sign for the spirits. Once these preliminary offerings are complete, the reading commences.

The cards are shuffled by the priest and then laid out in a grid pattern, generally seven cards across and seven cards down. The center is considered the crossroads. The card that is revealed there is said to be the lwa who is overseeing the reading. From there, the cards that fall above the center line are said to be spiritual influences, while the cards below are physical. As the rows progress across the layout from left to right, they represent future, present, and past. The interpretation is subjective, with each reader having his or her own style and methodology of reading.

There are some general agreements. For instance, queens are generally female lwa, while kings are male. Black spades look like shovels; therefore, all the spades relate to the Gede family of spirits. The king of the suite is seen as the Baron, the queen as Mama Brijit. Court cards in the cups suite are sometimes interpreted as marine lwa, with the king of cups as Agwe and the queen as Lasiren.

There are some challenges in reading relating to language differences. *Deuce*, for example, sounds like *dous*, meaning "sweet" in Haitian Kreyòl. Any card featuring a number two can be interpreted as sweetening a scenario. The word *ke*, which is "heart" in Kreyòl, can also sound like *ko*, which is "cadaver" or "body." The suit of hearts can then mean spiritual love (the body in thought), physical love (the body in action), or something in between (the body as spirit). Card readings take on many subtle meanings when the language of Kreyòl is involved.

Readers will divine which lwa is willing to work for each client. They also suggest the offerings or sacrifices required to alleviate the situation being addressed, and the clients are free to make their own determinations on what they are willing to do or pay for. Often, the mambo or oungan performing divination for a client will undertake the required work for a fee.

Throwing objects and interpreting the patterns formed when they land is also a popular method of divining in Haiti. Any collection of items can be employed, from a set of stones or bones to coins, dice, and everything in between. Generally, the diviner makes a cross on the floor and tosses his or her items onto it. Where the items land in relation to one another and the cross convey meaning to the diviner, who then interprets it for the client. This method of reading harks back to the Yoruban system of Ifá or the Fon system of Fa. Although there are no Ifá readers in Haiti, very early in plantation culture, there were readers of Fa, and in some small corners of Haiti, this method of divining is still employed.

Divination by pendulum is done over an ailing client's body by a medsin fey. The pendulum is often a small sack holding objects, such as special stones, plants, or seeds. The manner in which it swings—left to right, up or down—indicates to the medsin fey what part of the body was experiencing illness. The medsin fey then retrieves the appropriate herbs for treatment. As with the interpretation of cards, this method of divination was known to North American conjure and hoodoo practitioners, who used it for a variety of purposes in addition to medical diagnosis.

See also: Conjure; Healing; Hoodoo; Ifá

Patricia Scheu (Mambo Vye Zo Komande LaMenfo)

Further Reading

Anderson, Jeffrey E. 2005. *Conjure in African American Society.* Baton Rouge, LA: Louisiana State University Press.

Brown, David H. 2003. *Santería Enthroned: Art, Ritual, and Innovation in an Afro-Cuban Religion.* Chicago: University of Chicago Press.

Daniels, Yvonne. 2005. *Dancing Wisdom: Embodied Knowledge in Haitian Vodou, Cuban Yoruba, and Bahian Candomblé.* Urbana: University of Illinois Press.

Michel, Claudine. 2001. "Women's Moral and Spiritual Leadership in Haitian Vodou: The Voice of Mama Lola and Karen McCarthy Brown." *Journal of Feminist Studies in Religion* 17:2 (Fall): 61–87.

DOLLS

So-called "Voodoo dolls" are one of the most common symbols associated with Vodou and Voodoo in the popular mind. According to a host of books, movies, and television shows, these dolls allow sorcerers to instantaneously harm the victims they represent. Common means of inflicting such torture are holding the figures close to blazing fires or thrusting pins into them. In keeping with such stereotypical understandings, New Orleans tourist shops carry a wide range of colorful dolls tailored to crudely resemble human figures and designed to lure customers into purchasing a bit of alleged Voodoo culture.

As with so many images of Vodou and Voodoo, however, the role of dolls has been overblown. First, the use of dolls is by no means unique to religions of Africa and the African Diaspora. Similar items appear in European accounts of witchcraft as well. Some authors have even argued that Voodoo dolls were never a part of the

Are Voodoo Dolls a Common Part of Voodoo?

According to popular stereotypes, dolls used to magically harm victims are an ever-present aspect of Vodou and Voodoo. As with so many other aspects of the religion, this conception is greatly overblown. While dolls sometimes appear as part of magical rituals intended to harm others, they are rare. In addition, the idea of sticking pins into a doll and causing instant harm to the one for whom it is intended more strongly resembles ideas associated with European witchcraft than those of the African Diaspora.

belief systems of Haiti and the Mississippi Valley. At any rate, dolls are by no means a central feature in the beliefs of Vodou and Voodoo. The mythology of the Voodoo doll is bound to the uninformed belief that the faiths they supposedly represent are little more than sorcery designed to harm enemies rather than full-fledged religions with their own pantheon of deities and religious ceremonies.

On the other hand, dolls are not wholly unknown in the magical systems associated with Voodoo and Vodou. They sometimes are part of Haitian Vodou ceremonies, for instance, when they represent the lwa. Dolls even appear in both Haitian and North American contexts as parts of magical rituals to harm enemies, break up relationships, or otherwise affect people for good or ill. Mirroring popular understandings, the figures usually represent specific people. Rarely, however, are the actions performed on the dolls expected to immediately affect the person whom they denote.

See also: Tourism; Zombi

Jeffrey E. Anderson

Further Reading

Hyatt, Harry Middleton. 1970–1978. *Hoodoo-Conjuration-Witchcraft-Rootwork.* 5 vols. Memoirs of the Alma Egan Hyatt Foundation. Hannibal: Western.

Long, Carolyn Morrow. 2001. *Spiritual Merchants: Religion, Magic and Commerce.* Knoxville, TN: University of Tennessee Press.

Turlington, Shannon R. 2002. *The Complete Idiot's Guide® to Voodoo.* Indianapolis, IN: Alpha.

DORSAINVIL, JUSTIN CHRYSOSTOME (J. C.)

Born in Port-au-Prince, J. C. Dorsainvil (December 20, 1880–September 8, 1942) was a notable Haitian psychiatrist, teacher, historian, and a religious scholar of the Vodou religion. Dorsainvil produced a series of rigorous scientific studies on the Vodou faith: *Vodou et Nevrose* (1913), *Une Explication Philologique du Vodou* (1924), and *Psychologie Haitienne: Vodou et Magie* (1937). He was the first scholar to have employed Freudian psychoanalytic theory in the research of the nature and crisis of spirit possession in the Afro-Haitian religion.

Dorsainvil affirmed that Vodou was a monotheistic religion whose origin is Dahomean, from the tribal beliefs of the Fons. He argued that Vodou was not the practice of black magic or sorcery, or unorganized pathological hysteria, as it is traditionally depicted. Dorsainvil put forth the idea that the religion of Vodou is a catalyst for understanding and penetrating the mentality of the Haitian people and discovering the driving force and motive for their actions and qualities as well as reasons for their defects. He asserted that the ancestral and "hybrid" cult had been a significant symbiosis in unifying the Haitian nation and strengthening Haitian families throughout the ages. The Vodou morality and worldview, he suggested, had helped develop an original culture in Haiti as well as shaped the moral life and identity of the nation.

While Dorsainvil challenged the prevalent notions that Vodou was a dark mystery of magic and zombis, leading to uncontrollable ecstasy, he suggested that the Vodouist mentality is a set of beliefs that overlaps much with Vodou practices. In *Vodou et Nevrose*, he observed that for denigrators of Vodou, the religion symbolized Haitian inferiority and racial stigmatization and the country's inevitable decline. On the other hand, employing the Freudian notion of the unconscious, he interpreted the Vodou trance as a form of hypnosis. Accordingly, the crisis of possession is not supernatural as traditionally conceived by Vodou adepts but should rather be understood as a psycho-neurosis phenomenon—that is, a nervous system disease. J. C. Dorsainvil pathologized the Haitian mind as split personality during the course of divine possession.

See also: Price-Mars, Jean

Celucien L. Joseph

Further Reading
Dorsainvil, J. C. 1931. *Vodou et Névrose*. Port-au-Prince: La Presse.
Dorsainvil, J. C. 1937. *Vodou et Magie: Psychologie Haïtienne*. Port-au-Prince: Imprimerie Nemours Telhomme.
Dorsainvil, J. C. 1924. *Une Explication Philologique du Vaudou*. Port-au-Prince: V. Pierre-Noel.

DRAPO

Drapo—both singular and plural in Kreyòl—means "flag" and refers to the heavily embellished flags used to decorate temples and peristils throughout Haiti. Religious drapos are sometimes designed by oungans and mambos under the direction of their familiar lwa. These flags represent the spirits that are served in the temples that house them. Drapos are also created for the consumer market.

The history of the drapo comes directly from the French who participated in the Haitian Revolution. Due to the vast spaces and mountains of Haiti, it was not possible to easily communicate verbally among multiple bodies of troops. Flags of varying colors and meanings were used to help move artillery, men, and animals across the plains and open areas. The use of flags was reinterpreted in Vodou as the drapo, which are used to help direct and call forth the mysteries of a temple. In peristils today, sequin drapo are used to open ceremonies, signaling the spirits that they are invited to come down for a dance or fet in their honor.

Drapos are hand sewn on a variety of fabrics, then heavily embellished with sequins, beads, pearls, and even buttons. The images that appear on drapo run the gamut from vèvès—ground drawings used to call the spirits forth—to scenes that illustrate the various tenets of the Vodou faith. Early flags were designed for specific lwa, using only their vèvès as the main decoration. Over time, the vèvès evolved into actual images of the lwa. Today's flags are often enigmatically rendered, encoded with secret meaning and hidden innuendo.

Popular artists such as Antoine Oleyant and George Valris sell their drapo design-filled notebooks to other artists who do not share a talent for drawing. This image sharing often leads to multiple flags of the same image, prepared by different artists in their own styles and palettes of color. A popular image, such as the

Marasa, can be rendered in browns and greens at one house, pinks and purple at another, and in all beads by a third.

From 1930 to 1940, Vodou flags were hand sewn on a remnant piece of cloth, with a modest sprinkling of sequins and a fringe border. These flags were the product of seamstresses who worked in the fancy bridal shops and high-end ateliers of Petionville. They would bring home the remnant fabrics (often velvet or satin) and leftover sequins that their clients had ordered for their clothing. These thrown-away bits of secular finery were then refashioned into consecrated sacred flags that were employed in Vodou services. Eventually, an entire cottage industry grew up around the creation of flags.

Drapos are said to be imbued with the power of their spiritual image. A drapo for Ogou is said to be the lwa named Ogou. Therefore, temple flags are accorded great respect and honor. No one is permitted to touch these flags, except initiates, out of a concern that the lwa of the flag might be insulted. There is even a special office in Vodou congregations called *ren drapo*, or flag queen. This person is consecrated to the flag, and is charged with carrying it before ceremonies in the sosyete. Current flag makers, such as Mirlande Courant and Yves Telemaque, make flags for Vodou temples as well as for the tourist industry. Telemaque actually embroiders the word *arte* onto his flags, just to emphasize that the product is not consecrated. Careful study of a particular artist's styles and color palette allows the buyer to purchase a true piece of art and not a poor copy.

See also: Laplas; Ounfò

Patricia Scheu (Mambo Vye Zo Komande LaMenfo)

Further Reading

Josephson, Nancy. 2007. *Spirits in Sequins: Vodou Flags of Haiti.* Atglen, PA: Schiffer Publishing.

Polk, Patrick. 1997. *Haitian Vodou Flags.* Oxford, MS: University Press of Mississippi.

DRUGSTORES

Until the end of the 19th century, conjurers, root workers, and hoodoo doctors made their own magical power objects, or charms, from natural ingredients and common household substances. By the turn of the 20th century, all of these wares could be easily purchased at the so-called "hoodoo drugstores." These establishments were found in the African American neighborhoods of most southern cities and towns, and with the exodus of blacks to the North during the Great Migration of 1915 to 1940, hoodoo drugstores also appeared in northern cities. The hoodoo drugstore usually began as an ordinary pharmacy operated by a white, professionally trained pharmacist.

Old-fashioned drugstores stocked "botanicals"—dried roots, leaves, barks, flowers, berries, seeds, and resins—as well as the drugs, oils, herbal essences, flavorings, and other raw materials from which healing preparations were formulated. Drugstores also sold toiletries, patent medicines, and common household preservatives and cleansers such as sulfur, alum, saltpeter, ammonia, laundry bluing, and lye. Sometimes hoodoo practitioners purchased botanicals and other perfectly mundane items for the formulation of charms, and sometimes botanicals and common household substances were actually marketed as charms by the druggists themselves.

As hoodooists made the transition from homemade charms to prefabricated "spiritual products," they began to ask for magical powders, waters, and oils. Pharmacists who had a predominantly black clientele simply responded to the demands of their patrons and gradually found themselves formulating charms more often than filling prescriptions. Harmless concoctions of butyric ether, bisulfide of carbon, powdered chalk, boric acid, magnesium carbonate, zinc oxide, alcohol, water, or oil, to which coloring and herbal essences had been added, were marketed as Love Powder, Hot Foot Powder, War Water, John the Conqueror Bath and Floor Wash, Lucky Dog Oil, or Oil of Bend-Over. Potions meant to cause strife and bad luck were concocted to have a disagreeable odor, and those meant for attraction and good luck had a pleasant smell.

Eventually the hoodoo drugstores, along with similar businesses called candle shops and "religious stores," were selling dried herbs; minerals such as lodestones and crystals; animal teeth, claws, bones, and other body parts; and manufactured incense, candles, oils, perfumes, powders, and soaps that were alleged to have supernatural properties. They also sold occult books, books of dream interpretation and lucky numbers, and books of magical formulae.

The African American anthropologist Zora Neale Hurston characterized New Orleans as the "Hoodoo Capital of America," and it may be that the hoodoo drugstore first emerged in this city. On display at the New Orleans Pharmacy Museum is a collection of historic artifacts: a little notebook open to a handwritten recipe for "Hoodoo Mixture" (containing gum olibanum, grains of paradise, steel dust, lodestone, and cayenne pepper) and brown glass bottles with hand-lettered labels bearing names like Controlling, Flying Devil, Lucky, Get Away Powder, Come to Me, Goddess of Evil, Love Drawing Powder, Goofer Dust, and Family Powder.

New Orleans's South Rampart Street area was the primary black commercial and entertainment district. Hoodoo drugstores tended to cluster there. Their presence is documented in the correspondence of Zora Neale Hurston, in town to conduct the hoodoo research that would later be published in *Mules and Men*. In an October 15, 1928, letter, Hurston thanked her colleague Langston Hughes for directing her to "the drugstore on [South] Rampart." The hoodoo drugstores are also mentioned in interviews by the Louisiana Writers' Project and Harry Middleton Hyatt in the late 1930s and early 1940s.

The most famous and longest-running of these businesses was the Cracker Jack Drug Store. The Cracker Jack, located at 435 South Rampart, was founded in 1897 by trained pharmacist George Andre Thomas. Thomas was born in New Orleans in 1877 to Belgian parents. He was later joined by his French-born wife, Alice Armande Vibert. Originally called George A. Thomas Drugs, the Cracker Jack eventually became a source of hoodoo supplies for practitioners all over the South through its retail and mail-order trade.

The Cracker Jack also sold a small, paper-bound booklet called *The Life and Works of Marie Laveau*, possibly written by George and Alice Thomas. Despite its title, *The Life and Works of Marie Laveau* bears no relation to the famous 19th-century Voodoo priestess of that name. It consists of a series of petitions, each related to a specific problem, followed by instructions for a ritual to alleviate the difficulty. The booklet was probably created as a sales vehicle for the Cracker Jack, which sold all the ingredients required to carry out the rituals.

"Doctor" Thomas died in 1940. The business was taken over by his widow, who later married another South Rampart Street merchant, Morris Karno. Mrs. Karno, aided by her son and an African American staff, continued to operate the Cracker Jack until 1974.

New Orleans's other famous hoodoo drugstore was the Dixie, at 1240 Simon Bolivar Avenue, a street that runs parallel to South Rampart. The Dixie opened about 1935 under the management of a white pharmacist named John C. Coleman. Francis Hendrick, a registered pharmacist with a degree from Tulane University, bought the store in 1963. Hendrick, who was white, was assisted by his wife Ellen, their teenaged sons, and Joseph "Buddy" Bush, a long-time black employee at the store. The Dixie closed in 1984.

All of the original hoodoo drugstores in New Orleans have disappeared. South Rampart Street's once-vibrant black commercial district and the surrounding neighborhoods have been devastated by poverty, "urban renewal," and the building of elevated highways. Their memories live on. The Cracker Jack was immortalized in 1950 by the great bluesman Champion Jack Dupree, when he sang: "Think I'll stroll on down to New Orleans, Go by that Cracker Jack Drug Store, Get myself some of that goofer dust." In 1993, rock and roller Grant Lee Buffalo recorded the hit song "Dixie Drugstore."

Other towns, of course, had their own hoodoo drugstores, and some of these still survive. Houston's famous Stanley Drug Company, 2718 Lyons Avenue, was opened by Stanley Hollenbeck in 1923 and operated by the Hollenbeck family until the late 1940s. The store has since had a series of proprietors. The original drugstore building is no longer standing. Stanley Drug, located on the outskirts of Houston, now occupies a modern, corrugated-metal structure about the size of a small supermarket, set in the middle of a parking lot enclosed by chain link fence and razor wire. There is a small retail outlet, but most of the building is devoted to manufacturing and warehouse space and to Stanley's large mail-order and online business. Stanley Drug Company carries roots and herbs, the largest inventory of animal parts offered by any mail-order house, and their own brand of baths, oils, perfumes, powders, sprinkling salts, yard dressing granules, and incense. Stanley's also sells ouija boards, Tarot decks, and crystal balls for fortune telling; an extensive collection of occult books in English and Spanish; seals from the *Sixth and Seventh Books of Moses*; holy cards and medals; and statues of the saints "for home, business, or car."

The most interesting offerings are what are categorized as "miscellaneous" products. Special lucky hands and tobies are offered for gambling and protection. A number of old-fashioned drugstore and household items used in traditional charms are available at Stanley's: herbal essences and flavorings, asafetida gum, camphor, benzoin resin, copperas, alum, powdered sulfur, ammonia, saltpeter, turpentine, laundry bluing, and Red Devil lye.

Atlanta also has a hoodoo drugstore that is still in business. Donald "Doc" Miller, a registered pharmacist with a degree from the University of Georgia, opened Miller's Dixie Hills Pharmacy in northwest Atlanta in 1960. In 1965 the business moved to 87 Broad Street SW, in Atlanta's predominantly black downtown business district, and the name changed to Miller's Rexall Drug. Doc Miller's nephew, Richard, began helping in the Broad Street store when he was twelve years old. According to Richard Miller, "We didn't know anything about spiritual products when we started, but people kept asking for these things, so we learned." Miller Drug serves mail-order and online patrons all over the world. Like Stanley Drug in Houston, Miller's catalog lists some of the preservatives, cleansers, and other household items commonly used in charm formulation.

The Corner Drugstore at 1123 South Washington Street, Vicksburg, Mississippi, was founded by Joseph Gerache, a graduate of Loyola University School of Pharmacy in New Orleans. While a student at Loyola, he became interested in the folklore of hoodoo, especially as it related to pharmacy, and visited old-time drugstores like the Cracker Jack and Dixie. In 1959 Gerache bought the Corner Drugstore and began to carry spiritual products from large manufacturers like Valmor and Sonny Boy. Gerache did not give consultations or offer advice, nor did he formulate his own spiritual products. People in need of help would visit one of the local hoodoo doctors, who phoned in the "prescription" and sent the client to the drugstore to pick it up. The Corner Drugstore is a clean, modern pharmacy, now run by Joseph Gerache, Jr. Unlike other hoodoo drugstores, the Corner Drugstore does not display the spiritual merchandise openly. Instead, these products are kept in a back room, where customers select the needed merchandise. According to Gerache, they prefer the privacy afforded by this system. The Corner Drugstore does not have a mail-order catalog or a website.

See also: Conjure; Hoodoo; Modern Voodoo/Vodou and Hoodoo Businesses; Rootwork; Voodoo in the Mississippi Valley

Carolyn Morrow Long

Further Reading

Anderson, Jeffrey E. 2005. *Conjure in African American Society*. Baton Rouge, LA: Louisiana State University Press, 115–17.

Kaplan, Carla, ed. 2003. *Zora Neale Hurston: A Life in Letters*. New York: Anchor Books. Hurston to Langston Hughes, October 15, 1928, p. 127.

Long, Carolyn Morrow. 2001. *Spiritual Merchants: Religion, Magic, and Commerce*. Knoxville, TN: University of Tennessee Press.

DRUMS

Drumming, along with song, is a primary musical accompaniment to Vodou ritual activities in both Africa and the Americas. The instruments and rhythmic patterns themselves are considered sacred objects and expressions, often associated with specific deities and ritual elements, depending on the origin of the practitioners. Master drummers typically develop a repertoire of hundreds of rhythms with precise meanings and because of this knowledge are integral figures in spiritual life.

Traditional drums employed in the western hemisphere are essentially identical to their African predecessors and are still manufactured in the Caribbean by hollowing out a log (usually a hardwood, such as mahogany) and stretching an animal skin over one end. Each individual drum is part of a set, or battery, and is typically played in consort. These batteries are then associated with specific spirits, and this association becomes the primary means for classifying drums. In Haiti and elsewhere in the Americas, most drums are a part of either the Rada battery or the Petwo, or Petro, battery.

The Rada battery comprises three conical drums of varying heights and pitches, played for spirits of the Rada nanchon. These instruments originated with Arada and Yoruba practices and are very similar to the drums of modern Nigeria, Benin, and Togo. The Petwo battery is a set of two taller high-pitched drums for playing to spirits of the Petwo branch, originating from Haitian, Ibo, and Djouba practices. Petwo drums use a thinner head than their Rada counterparts and are more often played with hands instead of sticks. Additionally, because of their lighter weight, Petwo drums are more frequently seen strapped to the drummers for increased mobility during ceremonies.

Other important instruments in Vodou drum ensembles include the Kongo timbal, the ogan, and the sacred rattles. The timbal is a double-headed drum, usually played horizontally and in conjunction with the Petwo battery. Historically, a distinct Kongo battery with various sizes of similar drums may have been more common in distinct ceremonies for spirits of the Kongo nation. The ogan, or iron gong, is a metallophone similar to the African gankogui or Western cowbell. It is struck rhythmically in a strong, repetitive pattern that establishes the chief pulse for the other musicians and dancers and therefore plays a crucial role, despite its seeming simplicity. Although most closely associated with the Rada battery, the ogan is increasingly present in rites for all spirits.

The ason and the tcha-tcha are the principal rattles in Vodou music, found in Rada and Petwo batteries, respectively. The ason is made from a hollow gourd, covered with a mesh that was historically laced with small bones, although modern makers substitute small plastic beads. The ason is often played by priests and is used to give tempo and signal the ensemble to stop playing. The tcha-tcha has a similar role but is constructed by filling the gourd with seeds or pebbles. Many other instruments make occasional appearances in Vodou ceremonies, including Yoruba batá drums, conga drums, whistles, and even Western instruments, like the violin. These inclusions are infrequent, however, compared with the main batteries and are often emergency substitutions when traditional instruments are not available.

See also: Ason; Dances; Music and Haitian Vodou; Nanchons

Patrick R. Bigsby

Further Reading

Deren, Maya. 1970. *Divine Horsemen: Voodoo Gods of Haiti*. With a Foreword by Joseph Campbell. New York: Chelsea House.

Rodriguez, Domingo Aragú. 1995. *Los Instrumentos de Percusion*. La Habana: Editorial Música Mundana.

Wilcken, Lois. 1992. *The Drums of Vodou*. Tempe, AZ: White Cliffs Media.

ELLIS, ALFRED BURDON

Ellis, who lived from 1852 to 1894, was an officer in the British Army as well as a prolific author who devoted much of his research to the religions and cultures of West Africa. His three most important works were *The Tshi-Speaking Peoples of the Gold Coast of West Africa* (1887), *The Ewe-Speaking Peoples of the Slave Coast of West Africa* (1890), and *The Yoruba-Speaking Peoples of the Slave Coast of West Africa* (1894). Ellis intended his works to be an examination of the evolution of religion, and he believed that each of the ethnic groups he described fell within a spectrum of civilization. The Tshi speakers, he believed, were the least civilized and the Yoruba were the most, while the Ewe (in his conception constituting what many modern scholars refer to as Gbe speakers) fell between the two extremes.

Despite the fact that the theories embraced by Ellis are no longer in favor with scholars, his works remain exceptionally valuable. Each book goes into considerable depth describing the culture of the ethnicity under examination, with religion and supernaturalism occupying the center of each book. The details Ellis provided are particularly valuable in the cases of the Yoruba and Ewe, who made significant contributions to the development of Haitian Vodou and Mississippi Valley Voodoo. In addition, Ellis's three major ethnic studies have a roughly parallel structure, allowing for easy comparisons among the different ethnicities.

See also: Bight of Benin; Dahomey; Ewe; Vodu in West Africa; Yoruba

Jeffrey E. Anderson

Further Reading

Ellis, A. B. 1890. *The Ewe-Speaking Peoples of the Slave Coast of West Africa: Their Religion, Manners, Customs, Laws, Languages, &c*. London: Chapman and Hall.
Ellis, A. B. 1883. *The Land of Fetish*. London: Chapman and Hall.
Ellis, A. B. 1887. *The Tshi-Speaking Peoples of the Gold Coast of West Africa: Their Religion, Manners, Customs, Laws, Language, Etc*. London: Chapman and Hall.
Ellis, A. B. 1891. "On Vōdu Worship." *The Popular Science Monthly* 38: 651–663.
Ellis, A. B. 1894. *The Yoruba-Speaking Peoples of the Slave Coast of West Africa: Their Religion, Manners, Customs, Laws, Language, Etc*. London: Chapman and Hall.

ENTERTAINMENT, VOODOO AS

Against its true nature as slave religion, consisting of both a complex system of African beliefs and elements of Catholicism, Haitian Vodou has fallen victim to Western popular culture that has sensationalized it for the purpose of entertainment. On the one hand, this form of cultural exploitation benefits the entertainment industry financially, as it sells the Haitian folk religion as a commodity to the general Western public; on the other, it satisfies the long-standing fantasy of Western societies, which found and still finds pleasure in the desire for the unknown. While Spenser St. John was the first person to elaborate on various fetishized images of Vodou in his memoir *Hayti or the Black Republic* (1884), they were revisited during the U.S. occupation of Haiti between 1915 and 1934. At this time, several writers, such as members of the U.S. Marine corps and travel journalists, reintroduced Vodou as primitive cult to the West. Based on their testimony, the entertainment industry of the 20th and 21st centuries has equated Vodou with black magic, Satanism, cannibalism, and sexual deviance. Even the international tourist industry has embraced the diasporic religion as a spectacle of entertainment.

The association of Vodou with the demonic manifests itself in the zombi. In Haitian folklore, the zombi is a dead person that has been artificially revived and turned into an unconscious slave—also known as the living dead in common parlance—although it is important to stress that it never poses a threat to the living. While anthropologist Alfred Métraux contends that a *bòkò*, or sorcerer, uses folk magic for the process of zombification, ethnobiologist Wade Davis believes himself to have discovered a biological neurotoxin responsible for the characteristics associated with zombis. The Western entertainment industry, however, fabricates the inanimate creature as an evil, flesh-devouring monster that hides in dark corners and chases innocent victims. This misrepresentation dates back to the U.S. occupation of Haiti. The writer William B. Seabrook first reported on senseless creatures roaming the streets of Haiti in his travelogue *The Magic Island* (1929). The popularity and financial success of his blood-curdling, pseudo-scientific account provided the story for the first zombi motion picture, the horror film *White Zombie* (1932). The movie, directed by Victor Halperin, revolves around the plotline of a young man who hires an evil witchdoctor on a fictitious island in order to lure a woman away from her fiancé. Instead of obeying his order, the witchdoctor turns her into an abulic creature, a zombi. The image of the zombi gradually began to gain momentum as a monstrous creature after the Marines returned to the United States and brought back home their fantasies, which mirror the storylines of movies such as *The King and the Zombie* (1941), *I Walked with a Zombie* (1943), *Revenge of the Zombie* (1943), *Zombies of Mora Tau* (1957), *Voodoo Woman* (1957), *Orgy of the Dead* (1965), and *The Plague of the Zombies* (1966).

When the postcolonial horror cinema began to fade toward the end of the 20th century, the Haitian zombi was muted, and his postmodern counterpart rose as a result from an era marked by genetic engineering, viral diseases, global capitalism, terrorism, interethnic conflicts, and weapons of mass destruction. Horror movies such as *28 Days Later* (2002), its sequel *28 Weeks Later* (2007), the *Resident Evil* film series, as well as *World War Z* (2013), depict the ongoing fight between post-apocalyptic zombis, which have retained their capacity as bloodthirsty monsters despite the shift in time and space—that is, from exotic islands to chaotic urban environments—and the last humans living in a dystopic world, beset by the eradication of ethical boundaries and driven by the collective endeavor to survive.

Apart from shocking and arousing disgust, cinematic zombis also entertain their audience by causing it to laugh. This development is equally inherent in the postmodern age, which is known to conflate the lines of different genres and thus create a frightening monster that simultaneously induces liberating laughter. According to critics, the British motion picture *Shaun of the Dead* (2004) was the inauguration of the zombi horror comedy and is therefore arguably the most notable film of this newly emerging hybrid genre. It parodies the living dead in general and their characteristics as well as the various possibilities of zombification in particular. Later zombi horror comedies such as Canadian Anagram production *Fido* (2006) and American Hollywood movie *Zombieland* (2009) followed in the wake of *Shaun of the Dead* by representing a similar pattern of amusement.

Another form of Hollywood's popular exploitation, which was heralded by imperial writers, is the association of Vodou with Satanism and cannibalism. The false relationship between Vodou and Satanism primarily emerges from animal sacrifices that serve as a practice to appease Vodou deities during a possession ceremony. Because this particular ritual requires the quick slitting of an animal's throat and the devotee to drink the gushing blood, it runs counter to the biblical experience and thus leaves Vodou ceremonies as an act of devil worship in the understanding of Westerners. As opposed to animal sacrifices, human sacrifices and cannibalism are fully detached from the cultural reality of Vodou and therefore relate to the sheer sensation mongering of colonial authors such as Faustin E. Wirkus. In his memoir *The White King of La Gonave* (1932), ghost-written by Taney Dudley, the U.S. Marine lieutenant chronicles human sacrifices in conjunction with cannibalism during his experience with ten thousand inhabitants of La Gonâve, an island located forty-two miles off the cost of Port-au-Prince. Similar to *The Magic Island* and its impact on *White Zombie*, *The White King of La Gonave* set the tone for an array of films that tie in with this distorted reality, ranging from pictures such as *Voodoo Tiger* (1952), *Macumba Love* (1960), *Live and Let Die* (1973), and *Angel Heart* (1987) to more recent productions like *Hoodoo for Voodoo* (2006) and *Voodoo Possession* (2014), to name a few.

The assumption that Vodou was a primitive cult also led the Western public to believe that worshippers engage in deviant sexual acts. In *Black Bagdad* (1933), the author and U.S. Marine Captain John Craige render the Haitian folk religion as a carnal faith full of obscenity. This particular image of Vodou was not limited to American fantasies but equally met the European imagination. In 1932, the Austrian traveler, writer, and illustrator Richard A. Loederer produced an image of orgiastic possession performances for a German-speaking audience, which was later translated into English as *Voodoo Fire in Haiti* (1935). Ever since, Vodou has been associated with wielding sexual power over others, although it is mostly Voodoo, the Mississippi Delta faith, rather than Haitian Vodou that comes to the fore in Western popular literature. Voodoo is known to incorporate material objects such as *gris-gris*, small pouches containing herbs, stones, and hair that are designed to bring good luck and ward off harm, as well as little dolls for attraction spells. Love and sex magic find expression in romances such as *Voodoo Love and the Curse of Jean Lafitte's Treasure* (2012), *Voodoo for Two* (2013), *Oxford Shadows* (2013), and *Voodoo Dreams* (2013) as well as erotic motion pictures like *Voodoo Lagoon* (2006), *Voodoo Academy 2* (2012), and *The Tale of the Voodoo Prostitute* (2012).

Equally, musicians picked up on the intersection of Vodou/Voodoo, love magic, and sexuality. For instance, LaVern Baker's "Voodoo Voodoo," produced by Atlantic in 1958 but not released until 1961, revolves around a girl who is enchanted by a Vodou practitioner and his supernatural love magic. In order to make her surrender to his love, he casts a spell on her by combining one of her teeth and a strand of her hair with various animal body parts and features, all contained in a little box, an item that resembles a *gris-gris*. The doo-wop bands the Silhouettes and the Del Vikings also draw on love as a central theme in their 1958 songs "Voodoo Eyes" and "The Voodoo Man," respectively. "Voodoo Eyes" tells the story of a man who is enamored by a woman's eyes. Being unable to resist her charismatic gaze, he consequently falls for her. Yet, to him, it is not a regular moment of love at first sight but an uncanny feeling, which he has no explanation for because he no longer has the power to control his mind and body. As opposed to "Voodoo Eyes," the Del Vikings sing about a mysterious "voodoo man." In order to win his beloved, the male Vodou practitioner casts a spell on a piece of clay replicating the person and reminding one of a Voodoo doll.

In addition to an element of entertainment in film, music, and literature, the religion of African descent also serves as a tourist sensation in both Haiti and the United States. Despite the earthquake of 2010 in Haiti, Vodou has remained intact and still lures visitors to the "Voodoo Night" at the Hotel Oloffson, an old and ramshackle Victorian hotel, where they can experience a Vodou ceremony conducted by an allegedly initiated priest, or oungan, all the while surrounded by paintings and little statutes representing deities. Unlike a nontourist ceremony, which commonly relies on the playing of musical instruments, such as African drums, the show at the Oloffson draws on modern technology such as speakers that fill the air with loud and eerie noises in order to turn the invocation of spirits, or lwa, into a spectacle. The background music does not, however, address spirits from different pantheons, as is the case with authentic ceremonies, but reduces it to one deity only: Baron Samedi. Responsible for the crossroads between life and afterlife in Vodou, devotees describe Baron Samedi as a spirit in a black tailcoat wearing a top hat and thick-framed glasses. His relation to death, however, typically renders him a skeleton within the framework of tourism and thus appeals to Western stereotypes insofar as this image satisfies their fetishized fantasies about the unknown.

After the Louisiana Purchase in 1804, the fabrication and promotion of Voodoo as tourist attraction spilled over to the United States, first and foremost New Orleans, where the system of African descent has become an integral part of the local culture due to its history of slavery and migration from Haiti. Nowadays, guides offer walking tours to Saint Louis Cemetery No. 1, where tourists can visit the tomb of Marie Laveau, the infamous and legendary Voodoo Queen, who lived in the

Crescent City between 1801 and 1881. Along the way through the French Quarter and epicenter of Voodoo, visitors to New Orleans find numerous stores such as Marie Laveau's House of Voodoo and Reverend Zombie's Voodoo Shop that sell items mass produced for commercial purposes, such as herbs, dolls, and incense sticks, and also clothes that advertise Voodoo as dark cult to tourists.

The Historic Voodoo Museum not only sells similar items as souvenirs to its visitors but also entertains the public by displaying various relics. Even though the exhibition features a relatively large collection of artifacts from Haiti and Louisiana, including a replica of a Vodou altar (at least that is what the proprietor claims), the setting inside the museum decontextualizes and thus simplifies the meaning of these relics. This is mostly due to the very fact that the museum sensationalizes the display of artifacts by intentionally accentuating grotesque drawings and paintings of dolls resembling skeletons and scantily dressed women dancing with snakes, images that remind the culturally conditioned Westerner of the diabolic. That the Historic Voodoo Museum, along with most of the shops, is located near Bourbon Street, the entertainment district of New Orleans, further indicates that its primary intention is to entertain the public as a tourist attraction.

Overall, Vodou and Voodoo have been exploited as an element of entertainment in mass media and tourism throughout the 20th and 21st centuries and, most likely, will remain stigmatized as such.

See also: Film, Vodou/Voodoo in; Haiti; Laveau, Marie; New Orleans; Seabrook, William Buehler; St. John, Sir Spenser

Christian Remse

Further Reading

Anderson, Jeffrey E. 2005. *Conjure in African American Society*. Baton Rouge, LA: Louisiana State University Press.

Fanthorpe, R. Lionel and Patricia. 2008. *Mysteries and Secrets of Voodoo, Santeria, and Obeah*. Toronto: Dundurn Press.

Gordon, Leah. 2011. "Took My Heart to a Vodou Priest, I Said, 'What Can You Do Papa?' It's All Screwed up." In *Haiti Rising: Haitian History, Culture and the Earthquake of 2010*, edited by Martin Munro, 183–185. University of the West Indies Press.

Lewis, James R. 2001. "Vodoun (also Voodoo; Vodun)." *Satanism Today: An Encyclopedia of Religion, Folklore, and Popular Culture*. Ed. James R. Lewis. Santa Barbara, CA: ABC-CLIO.

Murrell, Nathaniel S. 2010. *Afro-Caribbean Religions: An Introduction to Their Historical, Cultural, and Sacred Traditions*. Philadelphia: Temple University Press.

Ramsey, Kate. 2011. *Vodou and the Power in Haiti: The Spirits and the Law*. Chicago: University of Chicago Press.

Rushton, Cory J., and Christopher M. Moreman. 2011. "Introduction: Race, Colonialism, and Evolution of the 'Zombie'." In *Race, Oppression and the Zombie: Essays on Cross-Cultural Appropriations of the Caribbean Tradition*, edited by Cory J. Rushton and Christopher M. Moreman, 1–14. Jefferson, NC: McFarland.

Sulikowski, Ulrike. 2000. "Hollywoodzombie: Vodou and the Caribbean in Mainstream Cinema." In *Ay Bobo: Afro-Karibische Religionen, African-Caribbean Religions, Band 2*, edited by Manfred Kremser, 77–96. Wien: WUV-Universitätsverlag.

Sutler-Cohen, Sara. 2011. "Plans Are Pointless; Staying Alive Is as Good as It Gets: Zombie Sociology and the Politics of Survival." In *Zombies are Us: Essays on the Humanity of the Walking Dead*, edited by Cory J. Rushton and Christopher M. Moreman, 1–10. Jefferson, NC: McFarland.

Waligora-Davis, Nicole A. 2011. *Sanctuary: African Americans and Empire*. Oxford, UK: Oxford University Press.

ESPIRITISMO

The range of practices designated by the term *Espiritismo*, as practiced in the Caribbean and the broader Latin American world, is diverse but generally originated from the work of Allan Kardec. Allan Kardec was the pen name of the French educator Hippolyte Léon Denizard Rivail, who lived between 1804 and 1869. He is best known for having systematized modern spiritism. The major points of his doctrine included a belief in the existence of God, in spirits who are in a process of enlightenment, and in communication between spirits and the living. In keeping with Kardec's vision, Latin American Espiritismo is a doctrine emphasizing the importance of spiritual evolution. Mediums have the ability to communicate with spirits and interact with them by means of listening to, seeing, and hearing disincarnate spirits.

Kardec's Spiritism and its derivatives have adherents in many countries throughout the world, including Spain, the United States, Canada, Japan, Germany, France, England, Argentina, and Portugal. It is in Latin American countries, such as Cuba, Puerto Rico, Jamaica, and Brazil, where one finds the greatest number of followers. In most of Latin America, Espiritismo is the formal religion of Kardec, but in a number of countries in both the Caribbean and South America, it exists in a range of other forms, most of which have blended with African Diasporic religious practices.

Among the formal adherents of Kardec's Spiritism, the Africanized forms are greeted with a variety of reactions, ranging from a cool acceptance to outright disdain. Espiritismo may be found in some form in Puerto Rico; the Dominican Republic, where it has influenced some Dominican forms of Vudú; and in Venezuela, where it has influenced Maria Lionza, a syncretic tradition with much African influence. It is in Cuba and Brazil that it has grown most dramatically. Perhaps not surprisingly, Espiritismo demonstrates its greatest variety in these two nations. In Brazil the movement became widely accepted. Today, the country's official Spiritist community has about 20 million adepts. Because of the religion's influence upon other Afro-Brazilian religions, however, it is accepted and practiced in some form by as many as three times that number.

In Brazil, Espiritismo is widespread and strong. Adherents of the formal Kardecian faith refer to themselves as Espiritistas. A greater number, who are strongly influenced by the doctrines of Espiritismo, tend to self-identify with one of the many forms of Umbanda. Umbanda is an Afro-Brazilian faith that developed in the southern Brazilian city of Rio de Janeiro out of older Afro-Brazilian religions, such as Macumba and Omoloco, in which Bantu influence figured prominently.

Because of the strong presence of classic Kardecian Espiritismo, those who follow Kardec's original teachings tend to disparage even the forms of Umbanda that appear extremely close to traditional Espiritismo. These forms incorporate Pretos Velhos and Caboclos, old black slave spirits and Indian spirits common in other forms of Umbanda but generally absent in Kardecian Espiritismo. The ritual practices leading to the incorporation of spirit possession and the use of Umbanda styles of liturgy as well as necklaces and elaborate meals prepared for the possession spirits are anathema to Brazilian followers of Kardec. As a result, while some who have been strongly influenced by Kardec may be found within the complex loosely known as Umbanda, they tend to identify themselves more with Umbanda than with Espiritismo, a viewpoint with which most Kardecian Spiritists would concur.

In Cuba, a very different situation prevails. While the practice of orthodox Kardecian Espiritismo is healthy, it is not the form of Espiritismo that is dominant in the country. Whatever the leaders of Espiritismo Cientifico, as it is called in Cuba, may think of the other variants of Espiritismo privately, they have not taken as hard a line concerning what the Brazilians call Espiritismo Mistico or Religioso. This may be due to the relative minority status of Espiritismo Cientifico or simply a different cultural response.

Other forms of Espiritismo have developed in Cuba, which to a large degree have adopted significant elements of the various Afro-Cuban faiths. While these forms have been given names by academics and are often recognized as denominations, loosely speaking, by practitioners themselves, they should not be thought of as rigidly delineated. Practices, while generally consistent, may vary dramatically from community to community, and none of the variants have authorities who can designate what is orthodoxy. As a result, ritual and liturgy may vary in each established temple, and many practitioners do not resort to any formally established place of meeting, using homes of its followers instead. Added to this independence of form, many Misas Espirituales, or Spiritual Masses, are convened by and for the practitioners of the various Afro-Cuban religions in the service of their own religious communities. Both La Regla de Ocha (Santería) and Palo (the Congo Religion of Cuba) often require Spiritual Masses as part of their initiation practices.

There are three more or less clearly defined variants of Espiritismo in Cuba. These include:

- Espiritismo Cientifico (Scientific or Kardecist Spiritism)
- Espiritismo de Cordón (Cordón Spiritism or Oríle)
- Espiritismo Cruzado (Crossed or Cruzao)

Espiritismo Cruzado or Cruzao is perhaps the most widely practiced form of Espiritismo in Cuba and is simultaneously the most fluid in form. Services may take the form of a misa, in which a table is prepared with a white cloth, flowers, and candles. The table may also hold statues or pictures of saints or dead members of the community—the latter if the ceremony is for a particular person. The misa begins with prayers, usually taken from the works of Kardec, as well as prayers that are part of the popular repertoire influenced by Kardec, the Catholic Church, or folk belief. After lengthy prayers, the congregation switches to songs that belong specifically to the Cuban spiritual tradition. Many of these relate to specific spirits or deities and entities of Afro-Cuban belief. A large percentage of them describe Congo spirits and others as the orishas of Santería. At some point, the leader of the group or another member will become possessed. He or she will begin to speak, and after requesting a drink or a cigar, the spirit will begin to address problems that members of the community or other attendees may have. Additional people may become possessed, or individuals may speak of information they are receiving telepathically from the spirits. This will continue, interspersed with cleansing that may take a range of forms, but often includes asperging (despoyos) with herbs, tobacco smoke, and sprays of rum. Holy water may be used as well. Eventually the spirits depart, and a final song and prayer end the session.

In addition to such Cuban spirits as Babalu aye or San Lazaro, Yemaya, and many Congo spirits, the pantheon of Espiritismo Cruzado includes several additional classes of spiritual beings. These generally include, with local variation, Mariners, Gypsies, Congos, Africans, Spaniards, Indios, and perhaps several others. Each group, or corriente (meaning "current"), has unique characteristics, skills, and forms of working. Some heal, while others work materially, using objects like coconuts, herbs, plants, rum, and cigars to remove curses or help with work or financial problems.

While such ceremonies are typical of Espiritismo Cruzado rituals, less structured forms are known to occur. The altar may even be dispensed with, and a limited number of prayers and songs may induce more rapid possession. These possessions, depending on the spirits involved, may appear much more like those of Afro-Cuban religions, especially Palo, the Congo religious complex of Cuba.

Espiritismo de Cordón is perhaps the least widely distributed form, being restricted to several localities in the largely rural areas of eastern Cuba. It is distinguished by the formation of a chain dance by the devotees intended to raise a current of spiritual energy to produce spirit possession. It is from this practice that they receive their name, and the alternate name Oríle comes from a word participants often exclaim in their chants and songs. Their cosmological model is otherwise similar to that of Espiritismo Cruzado.

While the preceding describes practices in Cuba, it should be noted that these practices, mostly Cruzado and to a lesser degree Cientifico, can be found in many North American cities, especially in areas where large Cuban communities exist.

See also: Candomblé; Santería

Eoghan Craig Ballard

Further Reading

Fernández Olmos, Margarite, and Lizabeth Paravisini-Gerbert. 2011. *Creole Religions of the Caribbean: An Introduction from Vodou and Santería to Obeah and Espiritismo*. New York: New York University Press.

Kardec, Allan. 2005. *The Spirits' Book*. New York: Cosmos Classics.

Millet, José. 1996. *El Espiritismo Varientes Cubanas*. Santiago de Cuba: Editorial Oriente.

Millet Batista, José, and Jualynne E. Dodson. 2008. *Sacred Spaces and Religious Traditions in Oriente Cuba*. Albuquerque, NM: University of New Mexico Press.

Román, Reinaldo L. 2007. *Governing Spirits: Religion, Miracles, and Spectacles in Cuba and Puerto Rico, 1898–1956*. Chapel Hill, NC: University of North Carolina Press.

EWE

The Ewe—or Evhe as they are sometimes known—are an Africa people group who live primarily in the modern countries of Togo and Ghana. There is also a small population residing within Benin. The literature on African peoples has tended to disregard the Ewe, focusing instead on their better-known neighbors. Among the groups receiving an arguably undue share of attention has been the Fon, onetime rulers of the Kingdom of Dahomey. The Ewe and Fon, however, are closely related. Some authors, including Alfred Burdon Ellis, have treated the Fon, Aja, and other peoples as subgroups within a broader Ewe ethnicity that included all speakers of Gbe languages, which predominated over much of the Bight of Benin region of West Africa.

By the time Europeans began to encounter the Ewe on a regular basis, they had developed a strong sense of ethnicity. Despite being divided into well over one hundred independent states by this period, they recognized a shared cultural and historical heritage, claiming common descent from the town of Tado. From this reputed point of origin, the Ewe expanded to their present homelands. If one accepts the broader ethnic definition of Ellis and other authors, they also settled what developed into the Fon Kingdom of Dahomey, the Aja city-state of Allada, and other regions along the Bight of Benin. It is likely that the differences between the Fon, Ewe, Aja, and related groups arose in part as a result of the conflicts between the powerful Kingdom of Dahomey and its weaker neighbors. Even today, some aspects of these cultures remain identical or nearly so. For instance, when art historian and theorist Suzanne Preston Blier visited a major market in Lome, Togo, which catered to a largely Ewe clientele, she found that many of the magical and religious items for sale there were the work of Fon artisans. Moreover, many of the sellers of these items were themselves Fon.

As was true with other African peoples, the Ewe contributed to the culture of the Atlantic World because of their role in the slave trade. During the 18th century, Akan peoples from the west began to enslave Ewe peoples in large numbers, selling them to European traders who sought such captives to serve as laborers on New World plantations. During this same period, the expansive Fon of Dahomey also began to prey upon the Ewe. Unfortunately for historians, it is unclear precisely how many Ewe found themselves enslaved in the New World. Fortunately, the number of Africans taken from the Bight of Benin region is much clearer and provides some useful data. The importation of slaves from the area was especially high during the first half of the 18th century. During the period between 1725 and 1755, for instance, 39.4 percent of all slave trade voyages to Saint-Domingue—the colonial name for modern Haiti—originated from the Bight of Benin region. In French Louisiana, meanwhile, slave imports from the Bight of Benin were second only in number to those from Senegambia between 1719 and 1743, accounting for approximately 29.4 percent of all captives. Though the late 18th century would see these numbers eclipsed by later arrivals from elsewhere in Africa, slaves from the Bight of Benin, which doubtless included a large number of Ewe, were part of the foundational population of both Saint-Domingue and Louisiana.

The Ewe, along with their ethnic kin, were central to the creation of both Haitian Vodou and Louisiana Voodoo. For one, it was from Gbe languages that the words *Vodou* and *Voodoo* derive. Both came from the word *Vodu*, or *Vodun*, which referred to the gods or the religions of the region. *Hoodoo*, a term for magic commonly associated with the Mississippi Valley, almost certainly originated among the Ewe and other Gbe speakers as well. In Vodou, the Rada nanchon of spirits can be understood as of Ewe origin if one treats the Aja of Allada as a historical part of the former ethnicity. The secret societies connected with Haitian Vodou likewise have predecessors that can be traced in part to the Ewe. In the Mississippi Valley, the tendency of whites to see Voodoo itself as a secret society and believers' practice of referring to themselves as "voodoos" likewise has roots in the West African practices of the Ewe and their kin.

As one might expect, the deities of the Ewe also appear in the New World. For example, Haiti's Ogou, a spirit of war, was originally the Ewe Egu, god of iron and the harm that can accompany its use. The vitally important Legba was also present among the Ewe before he ever appeared in Saint-Domingue. Even the supreme being of Haitian belief, Bondye, shows clear affinities with the Ewe deity Mawu-Lisa, who rules over the other deities. The deities of Mississippi Valley Voodoo were equally well represented among their Ewe forebears. In Louisiana, Legba was known as Lébat or Liba. There he was joined by the Ewe deity Avrikiti, known as Vériquité in Louisiana, and a spirit known as the great Voodoo or Voodoo Magnian.

See also: Bight of Benin; Dahomey; Hoodoo; Legba; Nanchons; Rada; Secret Societies; Senegambia; Vodu in West Africa

Jeffrey E. Anderson

Further Reading

Anderson, Jeffrey E. 2005. *Conjure in African American Society*. Baton Rouge, LA: Louisiana State University Press.

Blier, Suzanne Preston. 1995. *African Vodun: Art, Psychology, and Power*. Chicago and London: University of Chicago Press.

Desmangles, Leslie G. 1992. *Faces of the Gods: Vodou and Roman Catholicism in Haiti*. Chapel Hill, NC: University of North Carolina Press.

Ellis, A. B. 1890. *The Ewe-Speaking Peoples of the Slave Coast of West Africa: Their Religion, Manners, Customs, Laws, Languages, &c.* London: Chapman and Hall.

Gomez, Michael A. 1998. *Exchanging Our Country Marks: The Transformation of African Identities in the Colonial and Antebellum South*. Chapel Hill and London: University of North Carolina Press.

Hall, Gwendolyn Midlo. 2005. *Slavery and African Ethnicities in the Americas: Restoring the Links*. Chapel Hill, NC: University of North Carolina Press.

Haskins, James, and Joann Biondi. 1995. *From Afar to Zulu: A Dictionary of African Cultures.* New York: Walker and Company.

Rosenthal, Judy. 1998. *Possession, Ecstasy, and Law in Ewe Voodoo.* Charlottesville and London: UP of Virginia.

EZILI

Maitresse Ezili Freda Dahomey is one of the best known of the Vodou lwa and one of the most difficult to understand. She is powerful and beneficial, as well as terrifying and demanding. Freda is the leading lwa of a group of water spirits from West Africa that include Lasiren, Klermizine, and Gran Ezili to name but a few.

Ezili is distinct from other lwa in many ways. Some of these lwa rule the more metaphysical arenas. As an example, Legba rules paths and doorways; Gede rules death. Some lwa represent natural phenomena, for example, Sobo for storms, Danbala for fertility, and Agwe for the seas. Others have a more physical presence in the world. They interact with men and women in the social arena, using their energies to bring resolution to the requests made of them. The social arena is a very diverse universe, and so the lwa reflect this diversity themselves. Ogou is a very good example. His many avatars cover the gamut of responsibilities, ranging from the occupation of military strategist to simple working man. Ezili also falls into this social arena of energy. Her avatars are mothers, wives, single working women, and "working girls."

Ezili has no specific mate, though she is often placed with Danbala, Ogou, and Agwe as husbands. Oungan Max Beauvoir has said that she is the "female energy of Legba." If Legba is the primal male force of creative fire, then his complement would be Ezili, as the primal female force. As this primal force, Ezili is every woman and no one's mate, making her truly alone in the pantheon of spirits.

Ezili Freda has tremendous power and is feared as much as she is loved. She has several different roles. She is the lwa of the word, again linking her to Legba here. She is also seen as the prime spirit of love, help, goodwill, health, beauty, and fortune, as well as being the lwa of jealousy, vengeance, and discord. She is sometimes thought of as a serpent that coiled upon itself, living on water and bananas. This image correlates with her African origins, where she was the spirit of the River Eziri, and her devotees fry bananas in cinnamon and sugar for her to eat.

Vodou has a most special place for Ezili as the lwa who is so uniquely human because she is the differentiating force between humans and all other creation. Ezili is the ability to conceptualize, the ability to dream, the artistic ability to create. She is the lwa of perfection. Qabalistically she is Binah, the great sorrowful mother who brings everything into fruition but cries nonetheless for the lack of perfection in the dream.

Ezili is fastidiously clean and will not arrive in possession unless the temple is spotless and refreshed with copious amounts of perfume and toilet water. When she does mount someone, the first thing she does is to accomplish her elaborate toilette, applying makeup and fixing her hair and nails. Servitors mounted by her can accomplish this without a mirror, using just their hands as a reflective surface. As soon as

> ### Why Did Voodoo in the Mississippi Valley Outlive African Religions Elsewhere in the United States?
>
> Most historians say that African religions had largely died out in the United States by the time of the Civil War. The Mississippi Valley—especially New Orleans—was the exception. Voodoo's tenacity can be traced to several causes. For one, the population density of African Americans in New Orleans was high, and slave smuggling helped keep it that way. A massive influx of Haitian practitioners of Vodou in 1809–1810 helped revitalize the existing religion as well. The area's Catholicism likewise benefitted African religion by providing a spiritual hierarchy of God and saints with which Voodoo practitioners equated their own pantheon.

someone is possessed by her, he or she is also washed and dressed in finery. Ezili will demand that the room be sprinkled with perfume or scented water to freshen it, and she will douse everyone with perfume to sweeten their presence for herself.

Oungans and mambos always keep fresh clothing, new toiletries, beautiful jewelry, and the lwa's favorite perfume, Anais-Anais, ready for her. They set tables laden with her favorite finger foods, fine wines, and pink champagne, all on china plates. Yet despite all the finery and food, no visit is ever completely satisfying for Ezili. She will accept all that is offered but begins to weep over the perceived imperfections of the ceremony, the offerings, or even the audience. It is this tearful, sad side of her that endears her to the women present. She is the lwa who takes on the burden of the world's sorrows.

Ezili can be compared to Aphrodite, a beautiful but haughty woman who loves men but mistrusts women as rivals. As a master of coquetry, Ezili will hug, kiss, and flirt outrageously with the men but offer only her pinky finger to the women present. Despite this outward expression of libertine character, Ezili is closely associated with the Blessed Virgin Mary, and her symbol is the heart, usually one broken with a blade in the same way the Mater Dolorosa is depicted.

Freda's colors are pink and white or pale blue and white. One should serve her cakes with white and pink icing on white china plates. Pink roses, basil, and mint in bouquets should rest on her altar. She accepts lacey hankies to dab at her weeping eyes and can be offered fried bananas in cinnamon sugar along with pink champagne.

See also: Legba; Lwa; Saints

Patricia Scheu (Mambo Vye Zo Komande LaMenfo)

Further Reading

Ackermann, Hans-Wolfgang, Maryse Gautier, and Michel-Ange Momplaisir. 2011. *Les Esprits du Vodou Haïtien.* Coconut Creek, FL: Educa Vision, Inc..

Guigard, Mercedes Foucard. 2006. *Répertoire Pratique des Loa du Vodou Haïtien - Practical Directory of the Loa of Haitian Vodou.* Port-au-Prince, Haiti: Reme Art Publishing.

Scheu, Patricia (Mambo Vye Zo Komande LaMenfo). 2011. *Serving the Spirits: The Religion of Vodou.* Philadelphia: Published by author.

F

FEDERAL WRITERS' PROJECT

The Federal Writers' Project (FWP) and the state writers' projects that operated from 1935 to 1943 provided important data on U.S. history and folklore. The project was a part of the Great Depression-era Works Progress Administration, one of Franklin D. Roosevelt's New Deal Programs, which aimed to provide work relief to America's white-collar population. The FWP, in particular, hired authors to produce what scholar Monty Noam Penkower has termed a "literature of nationhood" to celebrate the country's ethnic, racial, and regional diversity, with an emphasis on history and folklore. The project's primary goal was to produce a guidebook for each state, but several other works also resulted.

Without the efforts of the FWP, scholars' ability to study African American folk beliefs would be much more limited. Several works important to the study of Voodoo and hoodoo owe their existence to the program. In Florida, for instance, FWP research—some of it conducted by Harlem Renaissance author Zora Neale Hurston—informed Stetson Kennedy's classic *Palmetto Country* (1942), which includes valuable information on the conjure of Florida's African American community. The Writers' Project contributed even more to the literature of Voodoo. Lyle Saxon, Robert Tallant, and Edward Dreyer's *Gumbo Ya-Ya: A Collection of Louisiana Folk Tales* (1945), which contains information on Voodoo, was based on interviews collected by the FWP and written by some of its former employees. Robert Tallant's *Voodoo in New Orleans* (1946) and *Voodoo Queen* (1956) are likewise indebted to research conducted by the project.

Though the Federal Writers' Project died just after the end of the Great Depression, it remains an important source of information to scholars. Though much of the research made its way into print, even more did not. A striking example of in-depth research that did not make it to the public was Catherine Dillon's massive "Voodoo" manuscript, an exhaustive study of the religion and its practitioners in preparation for the FWP when it ceased operation. Thousands of additional records of interviews, observations of ceremonies, and the like are housed in archives across the nation. Major collections relevant to the study of Mississippi Valley Voodoo can be found in the Cammie G. Henry Research Center of Northwestern State University of Natchitoches, Louisiana; the City Archives and Special Collections of the New Orleans Public Library; and the Library of Congress in Washington, DC. These collections have become vital sources of information for modern researchers, most notably Martha Ward and Carolyn Morrow Long.

See also: Hurston, Zora Neale; Long, Carolyn Morrow; New Orleans; Spiritual Churches; Tallant, Robert; Voodoo in the Mississippi Valley; Ward, Martha

Jeffrey E. Anderson

Further Reading

Long, Carolyn Morrow. 2006. *A New Orleans Voudou Priestess: The Legend and Reality of Marie Laveau.* Gainesville, FL: University Press of Florida.

Mangione, Jerre. 1972. *The Dream and the Deal: The Federal Writers' Project, 1935–1943.* Boston: Little, Brown.

Penkower, Monty Noam. 1977. *The Federal Writers Project: A Study in Government Patronage of the Arts.* Urbana, IL: University of Illinois Press.

Ward, Martha. 2004. *Voodoo Queen: The Spirited Lives of Marie Laveau.* Jackson, MS: University Press of Mississippi.

FÉRAILLE, JOE

Joe Féraille, a character who appears in a number of early field recordings made in rural south central Louisiana, represents a fusion of the Yoruban deity of iron and iron-technology, Ogun, and Casey Jones, the popular folk and folksong hero of the American railroad. Although evidence for the precise manner in which Féraille might or might not have been worshipped or venerated in lower Louisiana remains scant, evidence from the songs suggests that the Féraille figure retained certain characteristics and associations tied to the figure of Ogun in West Africa and throughout the Yoruban diaspora.

In West Africa, Ogun coalesced as a deity in concert with the growth and spread of iron technology, and he came to embody beliefs and ideas about the dangers, benefits, and significance of iron and its use in society. The worship of Ogun was centered in (and originates from) eastern Yorubaland, in modern-day Nigeria, particularly in areas associated with iron smelting and among ironworkers such as blacksmiths.

During the transatlantic slave trade, Yorubans were transported to various parts of the New World, and Ogun emerged and was retained in many places that saw significant concentrations of Yoruban slaves. In many such locations, songs about and in veneration of Ogun appeared prominently in the resultant Afro-Creole musical traditions. This was the case in the Candomblé religion of Bahia, Brazil, in the Shango of Granada, in Cuban Santería, and in Haitian Vodou. In all of these instances, devotees associated Ogun with beliefs surrounding iron and iron technology. In many cases, as part of the broader syncretisms at work in respective Afro-Creole religions, Ogun fused with other figures from popular culture and from European religious systems. In Haiti, for instance, he became identified with the more pugnacious aspects of St. James the Greater.

In southern Louisiana, Ogun appears to have merged, at least in some folk songs, with the figure of Casey Jones, the historic Illinois Central Railroad engineer (born John Luther "Cayce" Jones) who died on April 29, 1900, when his locomotive rear-ended another train. Though Jones died, everyone else onboard survived the crash, and Jones became a revered folk hero of the American railroad, largely through the popularity of "The Ballad of Casey Jones," a song glorifying the event that went on to become a national sensation and to persist as a standard in the American folk song bag.

In songs about Joe Féraille, Ogun and Casey Jones intersect in various ways. Cajun French and Creole versions of the song "Casey Jones," to begin with, employ the melody of the "Casey Jones" song, but feature a character who behaves like Joe Féraille. Féraille always appears to be extremely hungry to the degree that he barters his wife for various foodstuffs in some songs, echoing lyrics concerning the propitiation of tutelary spirits in Vodou and other Afro-Creole traditions, as well as the marital difficulties of Ogun in his various aspects.

Songs about Joe Féraille almost always include lines about a dog named Fido, who is or has been killed by a train. Dog meat has a long history as Ogun's favored sacrifice in both Nigeria and in his New World incarnations, and in many cases Ogun is associated specifically with animals killed by iron vehicles. In addition, Ogun's association with iron and iron technology evolved into an association with long-distance transportation and its dangers. In particular, he came to be associated with trains, and devotees of Ogun, to this day (in the Santería practices of Cuban-Americans, for instance), typically include railroad ties and spikes in shrines consecrated to Ogun.

In short, although the widespread worship or reverence of Joe Féraille as a deity in Louisiana Voodoo has not been documented, Cajun and Creole oral literature contains echoes of a syncretic figure of the sort that arose throughout the Afro-Creole world. In this case, Ogun as a god of iron and technology as well as their dangers and benefits fused with America's most famous folk hero of the American railroad, the engineer Casey Jones, who himself embodied the promise and the peril of iron, iron technology, and American industry.

See also: Creolization; Music and Haitian Vodou; Ogou; Saints; Syncretism

Joshua Clegg Caffery

Further Reading

Barnes, Sandra T., ed. 1989. *Africa's Ogun: Old World and New.* African Systems of Thought Series. Bloomington, IN: Indiana University Press.

Caffery, Joshua Clegg. 2013. *Traditional Music in Coastal Louisiana: The 1934 Lomax Recordings.* Baton Rouge, LA: Louisiana State University Press.

Cohen, Norm. 1973. "'Casey Jones': At the Crossroads of Two Ballad Traditions." *Western Folklore* 32:2: 77–103.

Dew, Lee A. 1977. "The Locomotive Engineer: Folk Hero of the 19th Century." *Studies in Popular Culture* 1:1, 45–55.

Falola, Toyin, and Matt D. Childs, eds. 2005. *The Yoruba Diaspora in the Atlantic World.* Bloomington, IN: Indiana University Press.

Gomez, Michael Angelo. 1998. *Exchanging Our Country Marks: The Transformation of African Identities in the Colonial and Antebellum South.* Chapel Hill, NC: University of North Carolina Press.

FILM, VODOU/VOODOO IN

The publication of *The Magic Island* by William Seabrook in 1929 and its subsequent success provided inspiration to filmmakers and an opportunity for Vodou and Voodoo to appear on the silver screen during the Golden Age of Hollywood. The first mention in a talking movie of *Voodoo*—almost invariably the term used, whether addressing the Haitian or Mississippi Valley religion—came in the 1930 production of *The Sea Bat,* directed by Wesley Ruggles. The Voodoo content is minimal, and the film's emphasis is on sponge diving and the dangers of a giant manta ray. Voodoo provides a backdrop, and an evil from which the main female character can be rescued at the conclusion to the film.

The first full-length Voodoo film to be produced was *White Zombie* (1932, directed by Victor Halperin). It gave the religion some credibility, even though it did represent it as an evil and harmful practice. Curiously, the word *Voodoo* did not appear in the film. *White Zombie* was a box office success and is widely considered one of the best movies about Voodoo. It was also one of the few movies to place the religion in Haiti. It also explicitly linked zombis with Haiti and Voodoo.

The 1930s offered a number of films that were described as containing Voodoo, such as *Black Moon* (1934, directed by Roy William Neill), *Ouanga* (1935, directed by George Terwilliger), and a remake of the same film a few years later called *The Devil's Daughter* (1939, directed by Arthur Leonard). *Black Moon* represents Voodoo not as a religion but as a practice of frenzied dancing and human sacrifice. Predictably, it did nothing to portray Voodoo as anything other than a negative stereotype. The story in *Ouanga* is based around a plantation owner who is also a Voodoo priestess. The zombis are not menacing in any way, and Voodoo-related dialogue is limited. There is an attempt to link the depiction of Voodoo in *Ouanga* with Haiti, however. This film was remade for the race movie circuit under the title *The Devil's Daughter*. It had an all-black cast, and yet, sadly, it failed to improve on *Ouanga*. In many ways, it misrepresented Voodoo more than the original, dismissing the religion as superstition and fraud.

During the 1940s, several films involving Voodoo appeared. There was a comedic take on Voodoo in 1940 called *The Ghost Breakers,* directed by George Marshall and featuring the comic talents of Bob Hope. Zombis became increasingly central to Hollywood's version of Voodoo during this decade as well. The wartime movie *King of the Zombies* (1941, directed by Jean Yarbrough) tells the tale of a Nazi attempting to create a zombi army, only to be thwarted by the British. *Voodoo Man* (1944, directed by William Beaudine) continued with the zombi premise. Its narrative revolves around a mad doctor (Bela Lugosi) who kidnaps young women in an attempt to restore life to his zombified wife. *The Face of Marble* (1946, directed by William Beaudine) combines science and Voodoo in a story about experimental ways of raising the dead.

The 1940s were important for the quality as well as number of Voodoo-related films. Often compared with *White Zombie,* *I Walked with a Zombie* (1943, directed by Jacques Tourneur) illustrated the potential for this genre of horror. Val Lewton, the producer, based the film on Charlotte Brontë's *Jane Eyre,* thinking this would give some integrity to his film. Although based on the Brontë novel, the story was reworked extensively and bears little resemblance to its inspiration. The narrative of *I Walked with a Zombie* is based around the arrival on a Caribbean island of a nurse, Betsy, who has been employed to take care of a plantation owner's wife, Jessica, who has been zombified. Voodoo is an integral part of the story from the outset. Betsy is encouraged to seek help at a Voodoo ceremony. She does so, taking Jessica with her. The journey itself features visual Voodoo elements. At the ceremony Betsy finds Jessica's mother-in-law exploiting the beliefs of the locals by posing as one of the Voodoo spirits and determines that the imposter had caused her daughter-in-law's condition. The Voodoo practitioners attempt to end the zombi curse on Jessica by using the now-iconic Voodoo doll. At one point, the doll appears with a string around it, and as it is pulled, Jessica rises and heads back to the Voodooists. The curse is finally itself broken when a bòkò pierces the doll with a needle and Jessica is simultaneously stabbed to death. This is one of the most atmospheric films made in the horror genre and undoubtedly one of the strongest movies on Voodoo. The religion is treated sensitively for the most part. The faith appears as integral to the lives of the inhabitants of the island. This film had good intentions and put the mechanisms in place to present a serious representation of Voodoo. One of the first reactions to *I Walked with a Zombie* was a 1945 parody entitled *Zombies on Broadway* (directed by Gordon Douglas), which introduced audiences to the comedy duo of Alan Carney and Wally Brown.

By the mid-1940s cinematic horror productions were in decline, and few representations of Voodoo appeared between 1946 and 1960. The four produced were of markedly lower quality than their predecessors. *Voodoo Tiger* (1957, directed by Spencer G. Bennet) was a Jungle Jim adventure featuring head-hunters, a Voodoo tiger god, a witch-doctor, and a German war criminal. The other three "Voodoo" films were made in 1957 and did little to improve on *Voodoo Tiger*. *Voodoo Island* (directed by Reginald Le Borg), *Voodoo Woman* (directed by Edward L. Cahn), and *The Disembodied* (directed by Walter Grauman) all moved away from the Haitian religion and zombis in an attempt to integrate current trends with a Voodoo element. *Voodoo Island* represents Voodoo in a superficial manner. There are visuals that link it to older representations of Voodoo, such as dolls, but the film concentrates on killer plants. *Voodoo Woman* tells of an attempt to use Voodoo and science to make an indestructible creature. The film starts with a Voodoo ceremony and sets a promising tone, but this is brief and quickly degenerates to stereotype. *The Disembodied* features a white Voodoo queen who has the power to inflict pain by using a Voodoo doll. At one point, she sacrifices a girl and takes her heart. Ultimately this is not a Voodoo film. It is cinematic Voodoo cliché.

The 1960s saw a steady return to this genre of horror film, and popular images of Voodoo supplied material. A British film released in America as *The Curse of Simba* (1965, directed by Lindsay Shonteff) features lion-worshipping Africans and curses. There is an adaptation of the Voodoo doll in this film, but instead of a small effigy the Voodooists use a doll tied to a wooden frame to inflict pain on their enemies.

A 1965 novel helped create an exceptionally high-quality film during the era. Author Graham Greene set his novel, *The Comedians*, in Haiti. Voodoo—properly

Vodou in this case—is described accurately and shown as an integral part of the lives of Haitians. Greene went further, contending that people can be good Catholics as well as Voodooists. It was the first novel to really explore Voodoo and how it is entwined within Haitian culture and society. This book was translated onto the screen in 1967 with the same title, and the written narrative was faithfully portrayed in visual form, largely because Greene wrote the screenplay and Peter Glenville provided excellent direction. The Voodoo on the screen was as subtle as it was in the novel. There was no sensationalism, and intelligent questions about faith and belief appear throughout the film.

The first full-fledged British Voodoo zombi horror film came from Hammer productions in 1966 and was entitled *The Plague of the Zombies* (directed by John Gilling). A spate of mysterious deaths within a Cornish village provokes one of the inhabitants to contact his former professor, Sir James Forbes, asking him to visit in an effort to help. After discovering an empty coffin and hearing a tale of a zombi carrying a dead body, Forbes familiarizes himself with Voodoo. He links a local squire with zombis after learning he had visited Haiti. Later, Forbes discovers a series of small coffins and dolls. The zombi in this film was one of the most distinctive and terrifying to be seen in cinematic representations.

One of the most iconic films of the decade, and arguably the most influential zombi film ever made, was *Night of the Living Dead* (1968, directed by George A. Romero). This was the film that transformed the walking dead into flesh-eating monsters. *Night of the Living Dead* was a pivotal point in cinematic horror as it would separate zombis from Voodoo.

The 1973 screen adaptation of Ian Fleming's James Bond novel, *Live and Let Die*, featured Voodoo prominently. It was the eighth in the Bond series and was directed by Guy Hamilton. The film's version of Voodoo is confused and fails to connect the religion with Haiti. The novel had done a better job. The Voodoo spirit of Baron Samedi, played by Geoffrey Holder, made a memorable appearance onscreen and became one of the most iconic characters of Voodoo cinema.

Race was represented in some of the movies of the 1970s in a new genre known as Blaxploitation. Such films were products of white writers, studios, and directors but featured predominantly African American casts. This targeting of black audiences began with films that primarily focused on violent urban thrillers but were soon followed with horror, and more specifically Voodoo horror, including *Scream Blacula Scream* (1973, directed by Bob Kelljan) and *Sugar Hill* (1974, directed by Paul Maslansky). The Voodoo in *Scream Blacula Scream* was introduced to add a new twist to an already successful franchise. This film starts with a supposed Voodoo ceremony to resurrect a vampire and ends with a Voodoo doll being repetitively stabbed with a wooden weapon to destroy him. Otherwise, the film has little to do with Voodoo. *Sugar Hill* provided a more serious attempt at Voodoo horror because the writer had a keen interest in Haiti. This film is a tale of revenge. After her fiancé is killed, Diana "Sugar" Hill asks Baron Samedi for help, and the spirit raises an army of the dead to assist her. Voodoo dolls are used to inflict pain and death as well. This was the first of the blaxploitation movies to feature zombis, but it attempted to contextualize Voodoo in a less exploitative way.

In the 1980s, big budget investments raised the profile of Voodoo and moved the subject into mainstream cinema. The first of this new generation of Voodoo horror was arguably *Angel Heart* (1987). The story is set in 1955, and director Alan Parker recreated the steamy atmosphere of New Orleans impeccably. The basis of the story is that Louis Cyphre (Robert De Niro) hires Harry Angel (Mickey Rourke) to find a musician called Johnny Favorite with whom he has a contract. The narrative twists and turns between New York and New Orleans to a powerful, unforgettable ending. The film integrates Voodoo and Satanism throughout the narrative, but they remain identifiable as separate entities. The Voodoo in this film is a backdrop, but it has been treated predominantly realistically. Clichés were avoided, despite the underlying narrative focusing on a character selling his soul to the Devil. Moreover, while most see *Angel Heart* as a Voodoo film, the Voodoo content is secondary to the Satanist element. The sacrificial element and the soul transference are carried out by the Satanists and not the Voodooists. The directors maintain a clear distinction between the two, a detour from the historical perspective promoted by other shapers of popular perception.

When Wes Craven read *The Serpent and the Rainbow*, he was fascinated by Wade Davis's tale of Voodoo and zombis in Haiti. In 1988 the scientific account of the Haitian religion was given the Hollywood treatment in a film of the same name. *The Serpent and the Rainbow* represents Voodoo, Haiti, and zombis in as culturally accurate a way as can be expected in a fictional Voodoo film. The vèvè that appear are accurate, and the ceremonies depicted are based on actual ones in order to enhance the impression of authenticity. *The Serpent and the Rainbow* stands as one of the most accurate, atmospheric, and enjoyable films of the Voodoo horror genre.

Voodoo has continued to be incorporated into a number of major Hollywood productions as a minor element to the narrative. In *Child's Play* (1988, directed by Tom Holland) Voodoo appears intermittently, mainly at the start and end, and is used to perform a soul transference ceremony. The word *Damballah* is used, and there is an obligatory Voodoo doll. There is, however, nothing to link Voodoo to the ceremony or the characters, and the word *Voodoo* does not appear until the sequel, *Child's Play 2* (1990, directed by John Lafia). There were others in the same vein that continued into the 1990s. In *Major League* (1989, directed by David S. Ward), a Cuban player sets up an altar. His religion, identified as Voodoo, is ridiculed and proven ineffective. In *Weekend at Bernie's II* (1993, directed by Robert Klane) a Voodoo priest re-animates Bernie as a zombi with no other reference to Voodoo. *Predator 2* (1990, directed by Stephen Hopkins) features a group of drug lords known as the Voodoo Kings, though the religion itself makes no appearance.

In the 1990s the inclusion of Voodoo into films became more subtle, and the religion was used as an integral element in narratives in genres other than horror. In both *Eve's Bayou* (1997, directed by Kasi Lemmons) and *Midnight in the Garden of Good and Evil* (1997, directed by Clint Eastwood) Voodoo and hoodoo are not sensationalized. They are represented as part of the lives of the characters. The faith is not doubted, ridiculed, or dismissed. It is accepted. These films are set in the American South and depict the region's steamy atmosphere. *Eve's Bayou* is fictional and portrays the complexities of life; the Voodoo element is minimal but gives a glimpse of the belief within southern communities. *Midnight in the Garden of Good and Evil* was based on the true story of Jim Williams, who was accused of the murder of Billy Hanson. The film features the character of Minerva, described as a spiritualist. She performs graveyard rituals devoid of the sensationalism once linked to such practices.

The Skeleton Key (2005, directed by Iain Softly) focuses on hoodoo, a type of magical practice within the South that is rooted in African American folk belief. Caroline Ellis (Kate Hudson) is employed to care for a man at a former plantation house, and while there, she discovers a secret room containing bones, blood, and herbs used to practice hoodoo. Ellis eventually discovers that the room once belonged to hoodoo practitioners who had been lynched for their practice.

Throughout its history, cinema has blended the facts of Vodou and Voodoo with Hollywood fantasy. Vodou still faces misrepresentation, but there is an increasing interest in the religion that continues to fight oppression and misunderstanding. As the 21st century progresses, perhaps filmmakers will respond to audiences' fascination with Vodou with more substantial fare than that provided by the majority of Voodoo films.

Louise Fenton

Further Reading

Rhodes, Gary Don. 2001. *White Zombie: Anatomy of a Horror Film.* Jefferson, NC: McFarland Press.

Russell, Jamie. 2005. *Book of the Dead: The Complete History of Zombie Cinema.* Godalming, UK: FAB Press.

Senn, Brian. 1998. *Drums of Terror: Voodoo in the Cinema.* Baltimore: Midnight Marquee Press.

Worland, Rick. 2007. *The Horror Film: An Introduction.* Malden, MA: Blackwell.

G

GEDE

Gede (also written as Guédé and Ghédé) is the surname of a large and rambunctious family of spirits who are served throughout the Haitian countryside. The word *Gede* means "dead" in Kreyòl, and Gede are generally the spirits of people who have died. Scholar Kathy Smith states that Gede originally was a group of lwa known for healing. The ills of Haitian society soon gave birth to a much broader definition of healing, and thus today we find Gede served by everyone. The Gede are not a nanchon like the Nago or the Djouba. They are called a "family" of spirits, and this name relates to the idea of relations that are made through life and even in death for those not related by blood or family lineage.

The origins of the Gede spirits are obscure. Emmanuel C. Paul wrote in *Panorama du Folklore Haïtien*, "According to oral tradition from Africa, the Guede-vi were the original inhabitants of the Abomey plateau. The area and its people were conquered by the Fon who came from Allada" in old Dahomey (what is today modern Benin). Historical texts indicate that once the Fon had prevailed, they made the Guede-vi people the grave-digging caste in order to shame them. This placed them at the bottom of the society and gives a reasonable explanation for their association with tombs and graves. True to Fon religious ideals, the Guede-vi ancestors were incorporated into their theology as the "Lords of the Earth," and therefore were also seen as rulers of those dead who are buried within the earth. The Guede-vi were sold to the Portuguese as slaves because the Fon feared their power as necromancers. Scholar Roger Bastide says that Gede were a category of divinities that the enslaved Guede-vi people brought into Haiti. As many of the Guede-vi were taken to Haiti during the Middle Passage, it is not hard to see how the Gede family could have attained its position in the Haitian Vodou hierarchy. Beside Haiti, remnants of the Guede-vi culture can also be found in parts of Brazil. Elsewhere, their numbers were small, and they appear to have been completely absorbed into the New World cultures that held them in bondage.

The Gede family embodies the powers of death and fertility. Irreverent spirits who love ribaldry, obscenity, and sex, they adore exposing hypocrisy and the sanctimonious. Foul mouthed, filthy in dress yet truth loving and funny, they are adored by the people of Haiti because they can say anything and get away with it. After all, they are dead, so what can be done to them?

Some of the more popular Gede spirits include Gede Nibo, Gede Masaka (Nibo's helper and escort), Gede Ti Malis (Little Mischief), and Gede Zaranye (the Spider).

The Gede are all associated with the *banda*, which designates both a drum rhythm and a hip-gyrating dance. In possession, they will drink Haitian *gazolin*—an extremely fiery concoction consisting of raw rum called *klerin* in which twenty-one habanero peppers have been marinated. To test the truth of a Gede possession, the possessed person, known as a *chwal*, will often rub his or her eyes or genitals with this mixture, demonstrating that Gede is truly dead and beyond sensation in the body.

Three Gede are very prevalent in Vodou services, and make up a special trio of brothers who assist the head of their family, Papa Gede, in his work. The first is Gede Nibo, said to be the son of Baron and Maman Brijit. Legends speak of Ogou Badagris finding him as a white stone, wrapped in a cloth. Ogou Badagris brought the stone to the houmfort of Papa Loko, who blessed it and named it Nibo. Ogou Badagris agreed to be the child's godfather. Gede Nibo sails as part of Badagris' escort on Agwe's ship. He does not like to get his feet wet because of all the dead that reside in the waters beneath the ship. Nibo is said to be in love with Ezili Freda, but she rejects his advances due to his licentious behavior and foul mouth. Nibo also acts as an intermediary between the living and the dead, allowing the spirits to communicate with the living. And Nibo can also participate in mystical marriages between the living and the dead. A very magical spirit, Gede Nibo brings healing and understanding to those who petition his help.

Assisting Gede Nibo is Gede Masaka, who possesses both male and female characteristics. He wears a white headscarf and a white jacket over a black shirt. Gede Masaka carries a bag that has poisonous leaves and an umbilical cord in it, allusions to his work as a healer and a guardian to the gates of life. Gede Masaka sometimes appears as the companion of Gede Oussou, and both are understood to be bisexual. Gede Oussou wears a black or mauve jacket with a matching headscarf. On the back of his jacket is a white cross. *Oussou* means "tipsy," alluding to his fondness for white rum. His drinking is seen as an allegory of letting go of the material world and allowing oneself to be honest—as drunks generally do not have any inhibitions prohibiting them from speaking the truth. All Gede tell the truth—painfully so.

Papa Gede is not Nibo but another Gede altogether and is understood to be the corpse of the first man to ever die. He is a short, dark man who wears a high hat, grips a cigar in his mouth, and holds an apple in his left hand. A serious yet wry man, Papa Gede is the supernatural manager of Baron Samedi's world and waits at the crossroads to transport souls into the afterlife. Believers hold that that Papa will not take a life before its time. He is particularly protective of children and can be prayed to in cases where children are dying. Papa Gede has a very crass sense of humor, can read minds, and knows everything that takes place among the living and the dead. Although he is often envisioned as a tramp, he is a powerful and volatile spirit. When one visits a cemetery, it is best to let Papa Gede know. He likes cigarettes, and it would be wise to bring him some, whenever one visits the graveyard.

As one might expect, the Gede associate closely with the lwa named Baron. Depending on the tradition followed, Baron is seen as one of the Gede; their spiritual protector, who has raised them from the dead with the help of Maman Brijit; or an aspect of the Gede family. In many temples, the Baron is believed to be the anthropomorphic being called Death as well as the means by which death comes to the human population. In any of these configurations, Baron, Maman Brijit, and the Gede control death, the cemetery, and the graves.

See also: Baron Samedi; Death; Healing; Kreyòl; Lwa

Patricia Scheu (Mambo Vye Zo Komande LaMenfo)

Further Reading

Ackermann, Hans-Wolfgang, Maryse Gautier, and Michel-Ange Momplaisir. 2011. *Les Esprits du Vodou Haïtien.* Coconut Creek, FL: Educa Vision LLC.

Bastide, Roger. 1971. *African Civilisations in the New World.* Trans. by Peter Green, with a foreword by Geoffrey Parrinder. New York: Harper and Row.

Guigard, Mercedes Foucard. 2006. *Répertoire Pratique des Loa du Vodou Haïtien - Practical Directory of the Loa of Haitian Vodou.* Port-au-Prince, Haiti: Reme Art Publishing.

Paul, Emmanuel Casséus. 1962. *Panorama du Folklore Haïtien: Présence Africaine en Haïti.* Port-au-Prince, Haiti: Impr. De l'État.

Scheu, Patricia (Mambo Vye Zo Komande LaMenfo). 2011. *Serving the Spirits: The Religion of Vodou.* Philadelphia: Published by the author.

Smith, Katherine. 2010. "Gede Rising: Haiti in the Age of Vagabondaj." PhD dissertation, University of California Los Angeles.

GINEN

In Haitian belief, Ginen is the home of the lwa, who reportedly dwell in a city known as Vilokan, or Ville-au-Camps in older literature on the subject. The word Ginen derives from Guinea, a term prevalent during the colonial era to describe large swaths of West Africa. Though some modern Vodou practitioners consider Ginen to be an ancestral African homeland, most think of it as a place outside of normal geographical designations. Though opinions about this spiritual realm's location differ, one of the more common views is that it is beneath the sea.

Ginen is also what Leslie Desmangles has referred to as "the world of the ancestral spirits." In this latter capacity, it is a central focus of the desounen death ritual. Central to the ceremony are the *gwo-bon-anj*, or "big good angel," and the *mèt tèt*, or "master of the head." The former is one of two or more souls that coexist within each human during life. The mèt tèt is conceived of as a guardian angel or a third portion of the humanity's spiritual makeup. At death, another soul, known as the *ti-bon-anj*, departs the body for heaven and has no more dealings with the living world. The gwo-bon-anj and mèt tèt, meanwhile, must be separated from the body so that they can enter Ginen. Once in Ginen, the gwo-bon-anj returns to the form it possessed before taking on a human body. After a year and a day, the gwo-bon-anj can leave Ginen to be absorbed into the Gede family of lwa. Like them, it can then interact with the living world.

North America saw similar beliefs embodied in the folklore and beliefs of some African slaves. Historian Michael Gomez, for instance, has noted the existence

> ### Flying Africans
>
> The Federal Writers' Project and other sources recorded tales of slaves escaping bondage by flying to Africa. The gift of flight was possessed only by those born in Africa, or so folklore held. Seemingly upbeat tales of slaves' flight, however, apparently refer to instances of suicide. As historian Michael Gomez has noted, the Igbo people, who have been linked to such supposed flights, believed that upon death, their souls would fly back to their homeland. Thus, suicide meant a flight to freedom. The concept parallels the Vodou belief in souls passing through the water to Ginen.

of plentiful stories that maintain African-born slaves had the ability to fly back to Africa. On the surface, these tales may appear unconnected to Vodou, but as Gomez has noted, these stories appear to have developed as sanitized accounts of slave suicides. A common belief among slaves born in Africa was that after death their souls would return to their homeland to be reunited with their lost friends and family. To believers in this Ginen-like concept, suicide was a way to both escape slavery and fly back to one's home. Many but not all such accounts involved peoples of the Igbo ethnicity, who were also present in colonial Saint-Domingue.

See also: Ceremonies; Death; Gede; Lwa; Souls

Jeffrey E. Anderson

Further Reading

Desmangles, Leslie G. 1992. *Faces of the Gods: Vodou and Roman Catholicism in Haiti.* Chapel Hill, NC: University of North Carolina Press.

Gomez, Michael A. 1998. *Exchanging Our Country Marks: The Transformation of African Identities in the Colonial and Antebellum South.* Chapel Hill and London: University of North Carolina Press.

Métraux, Alfred. 1972. *Voodoo in Haiti.* Translated by Hugo Charteris and with an Introduction by Sidney W. Mintz. New York: Schocken.

Siuda, Tamara L. (Mambo Chita Tann). 2012. *Haitian Vodou: An Introduction to Haiti's Indigenous Spiritual Tradition.* Woodbury, MN: Llewellyn.

GRAND ZOMBI

Grand Zombi was a prominent deity of New Orleans Voodoo. Unfortunately, the being's precise role within the religion's pantheon is unclear. The name, a combination of French and at least one African language, roughly means "Great Spirit." According to a chant recorded in Helen Pitkin's *An Angel by Brevet* (1904), however, it was associated with the working of Voodoo magic, known as *gris-gris*. Other than this tidbit, little else is known about this deity. The lack of information was significant enough by the end of the 19th century that literary mythmakers began to claim that the name belonged to a pet snake that Voodoo Queen Marie Laveau kept as a pet and incorporated into her rituals. It is in this at least somewhat fictionalized guise that Grand Zombi is best remembered today.

Though there has been some speculation that Grand Zombi could have been the invention of late 19th- or early 20th-century writers promoting the exoticism of New Orleans, the deity was likely a genuine part of Mississippi Valley Voodoo. While mentions of a specific being known as Grand Zombi are sparse, the word *zombi* was certainly a part of the Creole French of Louisiana. According to Albert Valdman and Kevin J. Rottet's definitive *Dictionary of Louisiana French: As Spoken in Cajun, Creole, and American Indian Communities* (2010), the word can mean "ghost," "phantom," "apparition," "tooth fairy," or "anything big or grotesquely out of proportion." As evident from the majority of the term's meanings, it typically designated spiritual beings, often of the dead. George Washington Cable used the word to mean "spirit" in his novel *The Grandissimes* (1880). In some cases, *zombi* could also mean a practitioner of magic. Alcée Fortier's *Louisiana Folk-Tales* (1895), for example, includes a Creole French tale entitled "Ein Vié Zombi Malin," which the author translated as "The Cunning Old Wizard."

More telling than simple word usage, however, was an article published in the French-language newspaper *L'Union* on August 1, 1863. The article described a Voodoo ceremony broken up by the police. At the time of the incident, New Orleans was an occupied city, having fallen to northern troops the year before. The ceremony, reported *L'Union*, was held in support of the Confederacy. Attendees called upon a spirit known as Simbé to aid the cause of southern independence. *Simbé* and *Zombi* are very likely the same term, written differently depending on whether the author was a French or English speaker.

Grand Zombi's origin is as mysterious as the spirit itself. Unlike most other Mississippi Valley deities, it appears to have no Haitian equivalent. The prevailing opinion holds that Grand Zombi derives from the name of the Kongo Nzambi a Mpungu. Words similar to *zombi*, however, can be found throughout much of West and West Central Africa. For example, the Ewe speak of a night monster called *zan bibi* or *zan bii*, and the Mitsogho people of Gabon use *ndzumbi* to refer to a corpse. Even among the Kongo people, the common noun *nzambi* can refer to a deceased person's spirit. It is even possible—though unlikely—that Grand Zombi was a creation of the Mississippi Valley.

See also: Gris-gris; Laveau, Marie; Nzambi a Mpungu; Voodoo in the Mississippi Valley; Zombi

Jeffrey E. Anderson

Further Reading

Ackermann, Hans-W., and Jeanine Gauthier. 1991. "The Ways and Nature of the Zombi." *Journal of American Folklore* 104: 466–494.

Cable, George Washington. 1891. *The Grandissimes: A Story of Creole Life*. New York: Charles Scribner's Sons.

Fortier, Alcée. 2011. *Louisiana Folktales: Lupin, Bouki, and Other Creole Stories in French Dialect and English Translation*. With an Introduction by Russell Desmond. Lafayette: University of Louisiana at Lafayette Press.

Long, Carolyn Morrow. 2006. *A New Orleans Voudou Priestess: The Legend and Reality of Marie Laveau*. Gainesville, FL: University Press of Florida.

Pitkin, Helen. 1904. *An Angel by Brevet: A Story of Modern New Orleans*. Philadelphia and London: J. B. Lippincott Company.
"Tribulations des Voudous." *L'Union*. August 1, 1863, 1.

GRAVEYARD DIRT

Graveyard dirt was a common ingredient in the formulation of hoodoo charms. Soil dug from a grave—also called *goofer dust*, a name possibly derived from the Kongo word *kufwa* (to die)—evoked the power of the dead. The personal attributes of the deceased—virtue, strength, virility, or malice—were thought to permeate the dirt from his or her grave, and the use of that dirt endowed a charm with those qualities.

The utilization of graveyard dirt was especially prevalent among conjurers and rootworkers from the Mid-Atlantic coastal region, where many enslaved Africans and people of African descent were of Kongo origin. The charm assemblages made by these practitioners bore a strong resemblance to Kongo *minkisi* in their use of symbolic ingredients. In addition to graveyard dirt, human remains, or slivers from the wooden grave marker, practitioners used some combination of roots and herbs, reptiles and insects, human bodily products, unwashed clothing, salt, pepper, sulfur, pins, needles, and iron nails contained in glass bottles, jars, snuff cans, or cloth bags.

The use of graveyard dirt was documented in the late 1930s by the Savannah Unit of Georgia Writers' Project and by Harry Middleton Hyatt, who interviewed residents of the Florida, Georgia, and South Carolina Low Country for his study, *Hoodoo-Conjuration-Witchcraft-Rootwork*. One woman told Georgia Writers' Project fieldworkers that "most of the folks carry something for protection [to] keep other folks from workin' conjure on 'em. They's made of hair, and nails, and graveyard dirt . . . [and] pieces of cloth and string. They tie 'em all up in a li'l bag."

Hyatt's informants considered the power of the dead to be the most important element in rootwork. Obtaining their assistance necessitated a trip to the cemetery at some specified hour, usually midnight, to negotiate with the spirits. The rootworker chose the appropriate grave for the task at hand, using the burial place of a good Christian or an innocent child for beneficent magic and the grave of a sinner or a wicked person—"drunkards, whore mongers, gamblers, and murderers"—for evil intentions. It was sometimes specified that a spoonful of salt should be carried for protection against the spirits. The rootworker would call the name of the person buried in the chosen sepulcher, ask his or her assistance in solving the problem, and take slivers from the wooden marker, a bone or a tooth, or a handful of dirt. It was of utmost importance to pay the dead with pennies or silver coins, or occasionally with rice. These offerings were usually buried, although they sometimes were placed on top of the grave. Nobody would dare remove them.

By the later 20th century, the manufacturers of spiritual products were marketing powders alleged to be graveyard dirt—actually made from colored talc—in hoodoo drugstores, candle shops, and religious stores and by mail order. Calling upon earlier traditions, one mail-order catalog advertised "dirt from the grave of a suicide, an unbaptized infant, or a murder victim."

See also: Ancestral Spirits; Cemeteries; Kongo

Carolyn Morrow Long

Further Reading

Anderson, Jeffrey E. 2005. *Conjure in African American Society.* Baton Rouge, LA: Louisiana State University Press.

Georgia Writers' Project. 1940 [1986]. *Drums and Shadows: Survival Studies among the Georgia Coastal Negroes*; reprint, Athens, GA: University of Georgia Press.

Hyatt, Harry Middleton. 1970. *Hoodoo-Conjuration-Witchcraft-Rootwork.* Hannibal, MO: Western Publishing Company.

Long, Carolyn Morrow. 2001. *Spiritual Merchants: Religion, Magic, and Commerce.* Knoxville: University of Tennessee Press.

GRIS-GRIS

Gris-gris was a word for magic in the Mississippi Valley, roughly equivalent to the terms *conjure* and *rootwork* used elsewhere in the American South. While other words from the area, such as *wanga* and *zinzin*, had specifically negative and positive connotations, *gris-gris* was a general word for any sort of Voodoo magic and was probably a synonym for *hoodoo* before the second half of the 20th century.

The precise origin of the term is not known with certainty. Similar words have long been common throughout West Africa from Senegambia to the Bight of Benin. The weight of the evidence, however, suggests that the term was likely of Senegambian origin. Slave trader Nicholas Owen, for instance, reported seeing "gregory bag" charms during his travels in Senegambia and Sierra Leone. In basic form, these resembled the mojo bags of the American South. Beyond the similarity in form, the fact that the Mississippi Valley's earliest slave imports were heavily Senegambian in origin suggests that the region was likely the source of the word.

Interestingly, while the word *gris-gris* was once common in the lower Mississippi Valley, it was uncommon in Haiti, despite the presence of numerous Africans who would have been familiar with the prototypes of the word. In the New Orleans area, the term was in use by at least the mid-1700s, making it the oldest Voodoo-specific term recorded in the region. This development supports the likelihood that the word's prevalence in Mississippi Valley Voodoo was a consequence of the heavy and early importation of slaves from the Senegambian region of West Africa.

Gris-gris once differed substantially from conjure and hoodoo outside the Mississippi Valley. For one thing, it was long linked specifically to the Voodoo religion. Outside the area, African religions had largely died out by the early 19th century. Moreover, the materials used in fashioning gris-gris charms were distinctive. Beef hearts, for example, figured prominently in the magic of the region but were uncommon elsewhere. Other regionally prominent characteristics originated in folk Catholicism. Candles, altars, and saint images played a central role in a host of gris-gris rituals. As late as the 1940s, Harry Middleton Hyatt was able to speak of the uniqueness of the magical practices of the New Orleans area. Recently, such distinctness has become increasingly muted, as what had once been regionally

> ### Gris-gris in Africa
>
> Next to the term *Voodoo* itself, *gris-gris* is probably the most well-known word associated with Voodoo. Variations of the term are well known across West Africa and can be found as far apart as the Wolof and Fulbe of Senegal to the Ewe of the Bight of Benin. In Senegambia as in the Mississippi Valley, it continues to be a general word used to describe charms of many sorts, including bags holding verses from the Koran, strings tied around injured limbs, powders to bring about either good or ill, and a host of other items.

specific practices spread beyond the Mississippi Valley because of the prestige associated with Voodoo supernaturalism. At the same time, the proliferation of how-to books and hoodoo drugstores has inadvertently promoted the homogenization of African American magic across the nation.

See also: Conjure; Hoodoo; Magic; Mojo; Rootwork; Senegambia; Voodoo in the Mississippi Valley; Wanga

Jeffrey E. Anderson

Further Reading

Anderson, Jeffrey E. 2005. *Conjure in African American Society*. Baton Rouge, LA: Louisiana State Univerity Press.

Du Pratz, Le Page. 1763. *The History of Louisiana or of the Western Parts of Virginia and Carolina*. 2 vols. Translation. London: Becket and De Hondt.

Hall, Gwendolyn Midlo. 1992. *Africans in Colonial Louisiana: The Development of Afro-Creole Culture in the Eighteenth Century*. Baton Rouge, LA: Louisiana State University Press.

Hyatt, Harry Middleton. 1970–1978. *Hoodoo-Conjuration-Witchcraft-Rootwork*. 5 vols. Memoirs of the Alma Egan Hyatt Foundation. Hannibal: Western.

Long, Carolyn Morrow. 2001. *Spiritual Merchants: Religion, Magic, and Commerce*. Knoxville, TN: University of Tennessee Press.

Owen, Nicholas. 1930. *Journal of a Slave Dealer: A View of Some Remarkable Axcedents in the Life of Nics. Owen on the Coast of Africa and America from the Year 1746 to the Year 1757*. Edited and with an Introduction by Eveline Martin. London: George Routledge and Sons, Ltd.

Rosenthal, Judy. 1998. *Possession, Ecstasy, and Law in Ewe Voodoo*. Charlottesville and London: UP of Virginia.

H

HAITI

Haiti has one of the longest histories in the western hemisphere. The first European to sight the island was Christopher Columbus. At that time, Hispaniola was home to the Taino people, a Native American population. They had largely succumbed to disease and Spanish colonialism by the middle of the 16th century. Though the Spanish maintained control in the portion of the island that would later become the Dominican Republic, they gradually lost their hold on the western side to French buccaneers and planters. By the late 17th century France had effectively established the colony of Saint-Domingue, but the Spanish refused to recognize that fact until the 1697 Treaty of Ryswick. Under French dominion, the colony gradually developed into an enormously prosperous plantation society, built on the production of coffee, sugar, cotton, and indigo. By the 1780s, it accounted for as much as 40 percent of France's overseas trade.

There was a dark side to the prosperity, however. It relied on a particularly brutal system that enslaved Africans for their labor. Whites made up less than ten percent of the population but dominated the island politically and economically. Between the blacks and whites was a middle caste of mixed race, known as *affranchis* or *mulattoes*. The tensions one would expect to find in such a society exploded in the Haitian Revolution in 1791. By 1804, Haiti had become the second-oldest country in the Americas. Foreign interference, oppressive government, natural disasters, and endemic poverty have made it difficult for Haiti to recover its pre-Revolution wealth. Nevertheless, Haiti has had periods of relative prosperity and at one time controlled all of Hispaniola.

Today, Haiti is a republic with a population of about ten million. Roughly 95 percent of Haitians are African in descent. Population growth is low, largely because of out migration, with many leaving the country in search of economic betterment. Most Haitians profess Catholicism, but many are also devotees of Vodou. Estimates of the percentage of Vodou practitioners range from a low of 50 percent to a high of near 100 percent.

See also: Haitian Revolution; Slavery and the Slave Trade

Jeffrey E. Anderson

Further Reading

Central Intelligence Agency. 2014. "The World Fact Book: Haiti." Accessed December 10, 2014: https://www.cia.gov/library/publications/the-world-factbook/geos/ha.html.

Desmangles, Leslie G. 1992. *Faces of the Gods: Vodou and Roman Catholicism in Haiti*. Chapel Hill, NC: University of North Carolina Press.

Ott, Thomas O. 1973. *The Haitian Revolution, 1789–1804*. Knoxville, TN: University of Tennessee Press.

HAITIAN IMMIGRATION TO THE UNITED STATES

Haitian migration has been a long-standing tradition since the 18th century. Aside from a large group of Haitians who went to the Dominican Republic for jobs, much of the Haitian immigration has been directed to the United States. In 2010, there were 535,000 immigrants from Haiti who were living in the United States. 54 percent of those were female, and 46 percent were male. While Florida and New York are the main targets of immigrants from the island, there are also large communities in New Jersey and Massachusetts. The group of Haitian immigrants in the United States is the fourth largest group of emigrants from the Caribbean. Due to these numbers, the United States became a global center of the Haitian Diaspora during the 20th and 21st centuries. The fact that the United States became a favored target for Haitian people leaving their country was a consequence of economic as well as political developments in the Caribbean area.

Haiti—or St.-Domingue, as it was called before the successful revolution in the aftermath of the French Revolution and the island's independence in 1804—has a history that has almost always been tied to immigration of one sort or another. Its colonial population was defined by forced immigration because the majority of the population was African slaves brought to the island in the late 18th century. The first large wave of immigrants to the United States arrived with planters fleeing the Haitian Revolution. A large number settled in what is now South Louisiana, causing many even today to link Haitian immigration with Voodoo, zombis, and New Orleans. As a consequence of its formerly enslaved population and revolutionary history, Haiti became an area isolated from the rest of world, remaining relatively uninfluenced by outsiders for almost a century. During the 20th century, however, Haitian immigration increased with large numbers of men immigrating to Cuba to work in the sugar industry. Together with Jamaicans, they

---

Was Mississippi Valley Voodoo a Haitian Import to the United States?

Most scholars who discuss Voodoo assume that it was an import from Haiti. The influx of refugees immediately after the Haitian Revolution and similarities between the deities and ceremonies of Voodoo and Vodou support this claim. On the other hand, Voodoo certainly existed in some form before the arrival of the Haitian immigrants, as attested by a few colonial documents. Moreover, different names for the gods and the fact that the Mississippi Valley religion was historically known as *hoodoo* to practitioners indicate that while Haitian Vodou almost certainly influenced Voodoo, the two are not identical.

made up the bulk of the 600,000 migrant workers immigrating to Cuba in the first three decades of the century, when the Cuban sugar industry became the world trade leader. During the same decades, the urban middle class of Haiti sent its children to France to be educated; the European country did not become the main target of Haitian immigration, however. More poor people went to the neighboring Dominican Republic, where they provided cheap labor for the growing industries in this country, especially new factories built with U.S. investments.

The emigration of the Haitian population received a new drive due to the terroristic regime of François "Papa Doc" Duvalier, who ruled Haiti as a despot using brute force. Next to the oppressive regime, economic hardships were the leading factors in many families' decisions to immigrate to the United States. Due to this, many Haitians decided to leave their home country between 1958 and 1971. Poverty and corruption became the decisive forces of the Duvalier years, which, at first instance, forced the upper class to leave the island. The urban middle class then began to long for new perspectives and immigrated to the United States, primarily to New York. For the poorer population, this option was not available. They began immigrating to Florida, which was just 720 miles away. This distance could be surmounted by boat, leading American commentators to term the immigrants "boat people." Since 1972, more and more individuals have tried to reach the Promised Land in the north in search of a better future.

Despite the cruel aspects of the Haitian regime that was led by François Duvalier and, after his death, by his son, Jean-Claude "Baby Doc" Duvalier, the United States had a rigid immigration policy, and the "boat people" were usually sent back to Haiti, unable to be granted asylum. The Reagan administration even tried to prevent further Haitian immigration to the United States by sending ships to intercept the boats in the strait on the route between their island and the Bahamas. This, however, could not stop the growing numbers of Haitians who were willing to risk a great deal for a new life in the United States.

As a consequence of heavy discussions about asylum rights, immigration became easier for the victims of the Haitian regime. Despite the end of the Duvalier era in the late 1980s, the immigration of Haitian people to the United States increased, with most of the new arrivals heading to Florida. These men and women were fleeing a Haitian economy that remains one of the island's problems to this day. As such, it is not surprising that the number of Haitian immigrations to the United States increased in the following two decades, when the number of immigrants quadrupled from 92,000 to 419,000 people. The number of immigrants has further increased since 2000, as almost a fourth of all Haitians living in the United States today reached the country since that year.

See also: Haiti; Haitian Revolution

Frank Jacob

Further Reading

Bremer, Thomas, ed. 2001. *History and Histories in the Caribbean.* Frankfurt am Main: Vervuert.

Bulmer-Thomas, Victor. 2012. *The Economic History of the Caribbean since the Napoleonic Wars.* Cambridge, UK: Cambridge University Press.

Dessens, Nathalie. 2007. *From Saint-Domingue to New Orleans: Migration and Influences*. Gainesville, FL: University Press of Florida.
Müller, Gesine. 2012. *Die Koloniale Karibik. Transferprozesse in Hispanophonen und Frankophonen Literaturen*. Berlin: De Gruyter.
Ojo, Olatunji and Nadine Hunt, eds. 2012. *Slavery in Africa and the Caribbean: A History of Enslavement and Identity since the Eighteenth Century*. London: I. B. Tauris.
Stepick, Alex, and Dale Frederick Swartz. 1982. *Haitian Refugees in the U.S.* London: Minority Rights Group.
USA / Subcommittee on International Law, Immigration, and Refugees. 1991. Cuban and Haitian Immigration: Hearing before the Subcommittee on International Law, Immigration, and Refugees of the Committee on the Judiciary, House of Representatives, One Hundred Second Congress, first session, November 20, 1991. Washington: US Government Print Office.

HAITIAN REVOLUTION

The Haitian Revolution (1791–1804) was a war for freedom in the French colony of Saint-Domingue and is widely considered to be the first successful slave rebellion in the Western Hemisphere. It ended slavery on the island of Hispaniola and founded the free Republic of Haiti. It is said to have begun with a Vodou ceremony at Bois Caïman in August of 1791 and ended with the Declaration of Independence for Haiti in 1804. The commitment of the Africans to their freedom was fueled in part by their belief that the spirits of Vodou rode in their heads, protecting them from both the plantation masters and the superior weapons of European armies.

The island of Hispaniola was originally colonized by Spain and treated much like Britain's American colonies. Plantations sold their goods to the Spanish crown at a loss while buying supplies at a premium. This left the colony at the mercy of the ruling elites in Europe. Colonists tried to offset their losses by creating a free market on the western half of the island. Independent colonists, buccaneers, French pirates, and the few remaining Native Americans soon made the market a thriving business. When Spain discovered this, it ordered the colonists to return

---

The 1804 Massacre

Having suffered under slavery and through years of war, Governor-General Jean-Jacques Dessalines in 1804 ordered Haiti's whites of French descent killed on the grounds that they threatened the nation's security. Though Dessalines' henchmen spared many of non-French ancestry as well as others who had shown kindness to black Haitians, few whites survived. Many Haitians opposed these actions, which helped further the perception that Dessalines was a tyrant. Two years later, Dessalines was assassinated. The massacre, however, badly damaged Haiti's relations with the outside world and continues to shape outsiders' view of the Haitian Revolution.

to the capital. As the plantation owners began to comply, Spain decided to consolidate its more profitable plantations by selling the western half of the island to France through the Treaty of Ryswick in 1697.

The French would make sugar their primary export, producing it through the labor of African slaves. In 1681, there were approximately 2,000 African slaves on the entire island. By 1789, there were nearly half a million in French Saint-Domingue alone. So cruel was the form of slavery practiced on the island's sugar plantations that black laborers experienced a negative natural population growth rate. To maintain the labor force in the face of staggering mortality, new arrivals were necessary.

The French portion of the island continued to be a location of freewheeling markets, buccaneers, and the remaining native Arawaks. They were soon joined by the maroons—African slaves who had escaped the yoke of bondage. Many of these men and women were newly imported from their African homeland and were not broken by the cruelty of the plantation culture. They would play a pivotal role in the revolution. These maroon Africans held fast to their ancestral practices, making offerings to their gods for safety and security. To them, the practice of Vodou was what helped them remain free, hidden from the white plantation masters and the French military. Their belief in the gods of Vodou would be the fuel that gave others the courage to fight.

The most important of the maroons was a man named François Makandal. Some books say he was Muslim, but in Haiti he is remembered as an oungan with a great knowledge of plants and poisons. He was said to be very charismatic, uniting the different maroon groups into a secret network of organizations that raided the plantations at night, burning property and poisoning owners. He was eventually taken prisoner and publicly burned to death in 1758 in the public square of Cap-Français (what is now Cap-Haïtien).

Makandal's death would not stop the Africans from rebelling against the masters. According to traditional accounts of the beginning of the Haitian Revolution, his death opened the way for a second important person to emerge from the slave population. It has been written that Boukman Dutty was thought to be a free Jamaican man, though he may well have been a slave. His name is interpreted as meaning he was book learned or someone who could read. His large size, warrior-like

---

Toussaint L'Ouverture: Hero of the Haitian Revolution

Toussaint L'Ouverture rose to prominence as a military and political leader during the Haitian Revolution. He initially served the rebels as an herbalist, later rising through the ranks to become the ruler of a *de facto* independent country. Despite considerable military success, the French eventually captured him by promising a negotiated settlement. He died in a French prison in 1803. Despite believing in the power of Vodou, L'Ouverture did not embrace it. Instead, he discouraged its practice in favor of Catholicism.

appearance, and fearsome temper made him an effective figure in guerilla warfare. Boukman is thought to have presided as oungan over the Vodou ceremony that heralded attacks on the Northern Plains plantations. On August 14, 1791, a secret meeting was held in the area of woods outside Cap-Haïtien known as Bois Caïman. There, Boukman and his fellow revolutionaries met with slave leaders to plan their strategy of attack on the big plantations. He was aided by a mambo named Cecile Fatiman—the same woman who would sew the new Haitian flag from pieces of the old French one. Fatiman is said to have urged the gathering of slaves to "[c]ast aside the image of the God of the oppressors." It is an interesting turn of phrase as it alludes to the Africans keeping to their own spiritual practices. A pig was sacrificed as a meal and a pact sworn by everyone present that freedom would be had for all. Fatiman was overcome by the lwa Dantor, and it was she who killed the pig, offering its blood as a sacrament of the covenant they swore to free Saint-Domingue from the French. A week later, every plantation in the Northern Plains was in flames, as the rebelling slaves violently burned, pillaged, and killed across the region. So great was the conflagration that it could be seen for miles out to sea by approaching ships.

Although the story of Bois Caïman is taken as the *de facto* start of the revolution, modern scholarship has shown that there were possibly two meetings. The first took place at the Normand de Mezy plantation. Whites learned of it by torturing the slaves there. Little is known about the second, more secretive one at Bois Caïman. Some of the previously accepted details of the Bois Caïman meeting have also been discovered to be a fiction created by Antoine Dalmas in his *Histoire de la Révolution de Saint-Domingue* (1814) in order to portray the gathering as a bloodthirsty assembly of wild Africans.

Whether a pig was slaughtered or Vodou invoked, the events that followed these meetings were precipitous. The week following the purported Vodou ceremony at Bois Caïman, 180 plantations on the Northern Plains outside Cap-Haïtien were burnt to the ground. Reports showed that over one thousand slaveholders were dead, and the fighting had barely started. Boukman was captured and beheaded in November 1791. His head was publicly displayed by the French to dispel the aura of invincibility he had cultivated. It did not have the intended effect.

Within weeks, the number of slaves who joined the revolt had reached 100,000. Two weeks later, the slaves controlled fully one-third of the island. Using Vodou drums to speak over long distances, they were well organized and ready to strike at a moment's notice. A free slave named Toussaint L'Ouverture rose to lead the slaves in the rebellion. He was intelligent, organized, and articulate. As the events of the revolution unfolded, he was aided by a strange turn of events.

In 1793, France declared war on Britain, which had threatened to invade Haiti. France freed all the African slaves and then enlisted them to fight the British. L'Ouverture saw his chance and brought the slaves over to France's side in 1795. Overcoming a succession of rivals, he eventually defeated the British in 1798. He then went on to lead an invasion of Spanish Santo Domingo, freeing the slaves there in early 1801. By late 1801, L'Ouverture had secured the entire island and declared himself governor for life over a nation of free Africans.

Napoleon refused to recognize L'Ouverture as governor and sent a large expeditionary force led by his brother-in-law, LeClerc, to restore French rule. Some of L'Ouverture's closest allies defected to the French. In May 1802, he was seized and taken to France, where he died in prison. Jean-Jacques Dessalines, a former subordinate of L'Ouverture, continued to lead the rebellion until its completion, when the Haitians defeated the French in the Battle of Vertières. On January 1, 1804, Dessalines proclaimed Haiti a free republic.

See also: Boukman, Dutty; Interventionism by the United States in Haiti; Makandal

Patricia Scheu (Mambo Vye Zo Komande LaMenfo)

Further Reading

Arthur, Charles, and Michael Dash, eds. 1999. *A Haitian Anthology: Libète*. Princeton, NJ: Markus Wiener Publishers.

Dalmas, Antoine. 1814. *Histoire de la Révolution de Saint-Domingue: Depuis le Commencement des Troubles, jusqu'à la Prise de Jérémie et du Môle S. Nicolas par les Anglais; suivie d'un Mémoire sur le Rétablissement de cette Colonie*. Paris: Mame frères.

Dayan, Joan. 1998. *Haiti, History, and the Gods*. Berkeley, CA: University of California Press.

Diouf, Sylviane A. 1998. *Servants of Allah: African Muslims Enslaved in the Americas*. New York: New York University Press.

Esser, Dominique. 2012. "The Character Assassination of Samba Boukman." *Haiti Analysis*, March 10, 2012. Accessed February 7, 2014: http://haitianalysis.blogspot.com/2012/03/character-assassination-of-samba.html.

Ferguson, James. 1988. *Papa Doc, Baby Doc: Haiti and the Duvaliers*. Oxford: Blackwell.

Fick, Carolyn E. 1990. *The Making of Haiti: The Saint-Domingue Revolution from Below*. Knoxville, TN: University of Tennessee Press.

Juang, Richard M., and Noelle Morrissette, eds. 2008. *Africa and the Americas: Culture, Politics, and History*. Santa Barbara, CA: ABC-CLIO.

Reinhardt, Catherine A. 2006. *Claims to Memory: Beyond Slavery and Emancipation in the French Caribbean*. New York: Berghahn Books.

Thornton, John K. 1993. "'I Am the Subject of the King of Congo': African Political Ideology and the Haitian Revolution." *Journal of World History* 4:2: 181–214.

HAND

Hand is a term used in African American hoodoo and conjure practice to refer to a magical item, usually of a positive nature. Several words have been used as synonyms for *hand*—among them *luck ball*, *toby*, *mojo*, and *root*—though whether these words carry exactly the same meaning depends heavily upon the time and region of the United States under investigation. According to Harry Middleton Hyatt, a clergyman and amateur folklorist who collected thousands of pages of hoodoo lore between the 1930s and 1970s, *hand* frequently had a more precise meaning. In Hyatt's definition, hands are not simple good luck charms that could be used by any person who acquired them. On the contrary, each is unique to its intended user and is empowered for a specific purpose.

The composition of hands varied widely, as reported by Hyatt, but there were some commonalities. Among the materials in use during the 1930s and 1940s were crosses, buckeyes, severed hands of dead men, eggs, and a variety of roots. Many hands—but by no means all of them—were constituted of materials held together in a bag. An even more common feature of hands was the belief that their power came from spiritual forces dwelling within the material or materials that composed it. This belief was most apparent with what Hyatt named "battery hands." These needed periodic feeding with specific liquids, such as perfume or whiskey, to maintain their power. If denied sustenance, the spirit would leave, rendering the hand useless.

See also: Conjure; Gris-gris; Hoodoo; Mojo; Nation Sack; Paket Kongo; Rootwork

Jeffrey E. Anderson

Further Reading

Hyatt, Harry Middleton. 1970–1978. *Hoodoo-Conjuration-Witchcraft-Rootwork*. 5 vols. Memoirs of the Alma Egan Hyatt Foundation. Hannibal: Western.

Long, Carolyn Morrow. 2001. *Spiritual Merchants: Religion, Magic, and Commerce*. Knoxville, TN: University of Tennessee Press.

Owen, Mary Alicia. 1893 [2003]. *Old Rabbit, the Voodoo and Other Sorcerers*. With an Introduction by Charles Godfrey Leland and illustrations by Juliette A. Owen and Louis Wain. London: T. Fisher Unwin; reprint, Whitefish, MT: Kessinger Publishing.

HEALING

Healing is a significant part of both Vodou and Voodoo. In a Haitian context, not all ailments are open to treatment within the Vodou system. Those that oungans and mambos describe as "from God" are considered natural ailments and/or misfortunes that are beyond their power to heal. Others, however, come from supernatural causes and can be addressed through healing rituals. The sorts of problems treated by oungans and mambos include physical and mental illness, strained relationships, bad luck, and a host of other factors that many European and American readers would exclude from their definitions of healing.

Treatment of ailments can take many forms. The first step toward healing often involves some sort of diagnosis. Divination with playing cards is one of the more common sorts. Once the problem is determined, the healing can begin. In some cases, treatment can take the form of ingestions of botanical items or baths infused with herbs. At other times, it can involve rituals designed to free ill persons from effects of sorcery. In still other instances, healing can consist of soothing words administered over long periods to a victim of mental distress.

Haitian priests usually earn much of their income from their healing work, rendering herbalism a potentially prosperous trade. In most cases, those seeking aid provide any materials that healers need, helping oungans and mambos minimize their expenses. After the healing has been performed, clients provide the healers with gifts of money or the like. Despite the earning potential of healing, oungans and mambos typically treat it as a sacred duty, not a way to get rich. Many of the most sought-after healers are, in fact, poverty stricken.

Healing in Mississippi Valley Voodoo is a bit more difficult to fully describe than in Haiti. That healing was a part of Voodoo is undeniable. Several collections of remedies from New Orleans and elsewhere in Louisiana attest to this fact. On the other hand, the degree to which Mississippi Valley Voodoo can be distinguished from the hoodoo and conjure found elsewhere in North America is difficult to determine because of the intermingling of the two by the mid-19th century. Along similar lines, Marie Laveau, Voodoo's best known practitioner, was well known for healing work during the periodic epidemics that struck New Orleans. What remains unclear is the degree to which her knowledge of Voodoo played a role in her healing work. Moreover, since the late 19th century, Voodoo and hoodoo performed for medicinal purposes has drastically declined. Aggressive enforcement of laws against practicing medicine without a license rendered herbalism a risky endeavor, especially during the era of Jim Crow. Those who continue to engage in such healing often do so quietly for their families and friends, avoiding attracting too much attention.

If one considers healing in the sense embraced by Haitians—that it involves addressing personal ills in general, not just medical ailments—then Laveau and the rest of the Voodoo clergy were certainly healers. Across North America, diagnosis of ailments frequently began the healing process. Once the ailment was discovered, various botanical, mineral, zoological, and/or magical treatments followed. A common but by no means universal North American finale to the treatment process for those afflicted by evil magic was sending the ailment back on the one who initially laid the curse. The New Orleans area was distinctive in that much of its healing relied on the use of candles, altars, saints, and beef hearts, rarities outside the city. As in Haiti, healing financially benefited the healer. Several Mississippi Valley practitioners gained considerable fame and significant incomes from their trade.

According to James Sweet, author of *Domingos Álvares, African Healing, and the Intellectual History of the Atlantic World*, healing can be much broader than simply treating individuals' ailments. It can, he claims, include what American and European readers would typically define as evil magic. As Sweet explains it, African religions and their New World heirs thought of healing as a communal endeavor. Maintaining proper relationships with the spirit world was a key to group health. Within such a worldview, simply adhering to a faith that oppressive African rulers, New World slave masters, or modern society frowned upon could be a means to spiritual health. Likewise, attacking power structures that undermined community well-being could be understood as a healing process. Even spells designed to kill cruel masters, though harmful to individuals, could very well serve the interests of communities. Although Sweet focuses his examination on a case study of a single enslaved African taken from the Bight of Benin region to Brazil, the principles he elucidates are widely applicable across African Diasporic religions, including Vodou and Voodoo. This outlook has allowed scholar Carrol F. Coates to state that Vodou is at its heart a religion of healing in which the lwa aid those who treat them properly.

See also: Conjure; Hoodoo; Laveau, Marie; Rootwork; Vodu in West Africa

Jeffrey E. Anderson

Further Reading

Anderson, Jeffrey E. 2005. *Conjure in African American Society*. Baton Rouge, LA: Louisiana State University Press.

Coates, Carrol F. 2006. "Vodou in Haitian Literature." In *Vodou in Haitian Life and Culture: Invisible Powers*, edited by Patrick Bellegarde-Smith and Claudine Michel, 181–198. New York: Palgrave Macmillan.

Hurston, Zora Neale. 1931. "Hoodoo in America." *Journal of American Folklore* 44: 317–417.

Long, Carolyn Morrow. 2006. *A New Orleans Voudou Priestess: The Legend and Reality of Marie Laveau*. Gainesville, FL: University Press of Florida.

McCarthy-Brown, Karen. 2006. "Afro-Caribbean Spirituality: A Haitian Case Study." In *Vodou in Haitian Life and Culture: Invisible Powers*, edited by Patrick Bellegarde-Smith and Claudine Michel, 1–26. New York: Palgrave Macmillan.

Métraux, Alfred. 1972. *Voodoo in Haiti*. Translated by Hugo Charteris and with an Introduction by Sidney W. Mintz. New York: Schocken.

Sweet, James H. 2011. *Domingoes Álvares, African Healing, and the Intellectual History of the Atlantic World*. Chapel Hill, NC: University of North Carolina Press.

HOODOO

Hoodoo is a form of African American folk magic partially derived from West Africa and originally practiced in the Mississippi Valley. While the meaning of *hoodoo* has changed throughout its existence, it typically includes supernatural beliefs and practices that have been performed predominantly by African Americans. Common hoodoo practices include the acts of telling fortunes, casting spells, and creating charms. Scholar Michael Edward Bell argues that the basis of hoodoo rests on five intended results: punishment, diagnosis and divination, curing and redressing, protection from hoodoo or evil forces, and good fortune.

For many years hoodoo was mislabeled in the United States as a form of devil worship. As a result of this falsity, hoodoo was maligned as a backward and primitive religion practiced by African Americans who had not fully accepted Christianity. This idea has remained in American popular culture despite the fact that since the late 19th century a majority of hoodoo practitioners have identified themselves as Christians.

Scholars debate the origin of the word *hoodoo*. By examining linguistic similarities, most scholars trace the word to the Bight of Benin as part of the West African *Vodu* faith. In Togo, the Ewe words *hu* and *do*, when used together, can mean spirit work. Scholar Judy Rosenthal claims that the term could possibly be derived from *hudu*, a ceremonial ritual observed by the Mina that involves eating kola nuts covered in the blood of sacrificial animals. Elements of the West African faith were transplanted to the United States during the Atlantic slave trade. As a result of the slave trade, Voodoo was practiced by many enslaved blacks in the lower Mississippi Valley, Gulf Coast, and along the Atlantic Coast, most notably in Louisiana, where the first enslaved Africans that were transplanted to the area were originally uprooted from the Bight of Benin. During the 19th century the term *hoodoo* was

> ### Hoodoo and Voodoo
> Most modern scholars draw a distinction between hoodoo and Voodoo and Vodou, using *hoodoo* to describe African American magical practices across North America and *Voodoo*, *Vodou*, or some variation thereof to describe Mississippi Valley Voodoo and/or Haitian Vodou. While *hoodoo* is never properly used to refer to the Haitian religion, it was historically accurate to refer to what modern scholars call *Voodoo* as *hoodoo*. Some 19th- and early 20th-century sources state that while whites referred to the religion as *Voodoo*, African Americans called it *hoodoo*. The sharp distinction between the two terms gradually developed over the last century.

used synonymously with *Voodoo*. However, modern-day hoodoo practitioners distinguish themselves from Voodoo by not subscribing to the gods and religious ceremonies that are associated with the religion.

Throughout its existence in the United States hoodoo has been referred to by several different names. Outside the Mississippi River Valley, African American folk magic was generally designated by the English term *conjure* in reference to the act of calling up spirits. The names *jomo* and *mojo*, which are commonly used in Mississippi and Tennessee, may have originated in West Central Africa. During the late 19th century and early 20th century, the name *hoodoo* was associated largely with the Mississippi River Valley. One of the earliest print mentions of the term *hoodoo* appeared in the 1860s in reference to practitioners in Memphis, Tennessee. By the early 20th century use of the term *hoodoo* became widely accepted among African Americans due in part to the growing popularity of blues music, which regularly made references to the term. In the 21st century *hoodoo* is used synonymously with *conjure*.

Hoodoo practitioners are typically recognized by names such as *conjure men* and *conjure women*. Other historically common titles include *rootworker*, *trick doctor*, *ober man*, *witch*, or *double-headed doctor*. In the 21st century there has been a growing schism in how hoodoo practitioners identify themselves. In an effort to distance themselves from popular culture's association of hoodoo with devil worship, some have opted to identify themselves as *spiritual advisors*, *mediums*, or *psychics*. Conversely, some African Americans seeking to reconnect with their past have rejected stereotypes by maintaining the original titles associated with *hoodoo*.

Hoodoo practitioners vary in understanding and ability. Most amateur practitioners have a simple understanding of some of the charms associated with hoodoo, while professional conjurers typically have a more specialized knowledge. Historian Jeffrey Anderson explains that at one time many professional conjurers were selected because of their physical traits. Deformities such as bloodshot eyes, discolored skin, and misshapen jaws were indications of supernatural power. The perceived supernatural abilities of hoodoo practitioners made them highly respected members of the African American community.

Conjurers rely upon a variety of resources to create charms and other paraphernalia. Historically, most of these items were constructed of materials chosen from a vast array of natural materials, such as plants, animals, and minerals. High John the Conqueror, black cat bones, and goofer dust are among the most well-known items used in hoodoo practices. High John the Conqueror is a charm used to produce positive outcomes. By the 20th century it took the form of a dried root of a jalap plant. Some of its more common uses are to bring luck in games of chance, to increase personal power, or to hurt an enemy. A black cat bone is a charm used to make one invisible (typically for criminal behavior) or to return a lost lover. It is essentially a special bone that every black cat is believed to possess. According to one formula to obtain this bone, a practitioner boils a black cat at midnight until the cat's flesh falls off of the bones. The bone that rises on top of the other bones is believed to contain supernatural powers that can be activated once the person places the bone under his or her tongue. Goofer (also commonly spelled goopher) dust is used to trouble, harm, or kill enemies. The dust can be composed of several mixed ingredients, but it usually includes dirt from a graveyard.

In addition to natural materials, conjurers also use manmade items. The Bible, candles, and perfumes are common tools used in hoodoo. Bible verses may be written or recited as part of spells or during the creation of charms. The charms could be intended for negative or positive outcomes. Candles also have a wide range of uses in hoodoo. For example, some candles are used to help obtain employment. Perfumes, such as the Jockey Club Cologne, have been mostly used in the creation of love-drawing spells or for good luck in gambling games. It is difficult to compose a comprehensive list of hoodoo charms and other paraphernalia because each item could serve several different purposes.

Rootworkers combine materials with rituals that range from simple to highly complex. Some rituals can be as straightforward as placing an item in one's pocket, while others require several different steps that have to be performed in a specific sequence in order to be effective. In fact, the efficacy of certain spells can be influenced by intangible factors such as the time of day and location. According to some hoodoo doctors, sunrise and sunset are potent times for particular spells. Sites with spiritual associations, such as graveyards and churches, are also significant in hoodoo. In addition to these sites, some practitioners create sacred altars in their own households. Hoodoo rituals can be complex and filled with variety, but they have an underlying logic. Jeffrey Anderson explains that most of the magical practices in hoodoo are based on two concepts: similarity and contagion. Similarity refers to the idea that workers of magic can obtain a goal by employing objects that resemble the result they want to produce or by manipulating items in a manner that evokes the desired objective. Contagion is the principle that items once in contact can continue to influence each other. Practices relying on this concept usually entail incorporating portions of the intended victim's body or items that have touched his or her body, such as hair, fingernail clippings, or clothing.

While hoodoo has attracted more scholarly attention in the 21st century, historically there was a paucity of studies on hoodoo and its practitioners. Before 1940, several writers, both white and black, held condescending views about the practice, characterizing it as primitive, backward, and charlatanry. A few African American writers challenged these negative depictions of hoodoo. The slave narratives of Fredrick Douglass, Henry Bibb, and William Wells Brown contained some of the first written African American testimonies about it. In these texts, these newly freed men detailed how essential hoodoo was to helping members of the enslaved African American community contend with their living conditions. Zora Neale Hurston also countered the dominant discourse on hoodoo. She began researching hoodoo during the late 1920s in the midst of the Harlem Renaissance, an African American literary and artistic movement that emphasized racial and cultural pride. In a 1931 article entitled "Hoodoo in America," Hurston celebrated hoodoo for being a part of African American folk culture that endured through centuries of persecution. A majority of the early 20th-century authors did not share Hurston's appreciation of hoodoo. In fact, Anderson acknowledges that most scholars did not change their views until around 1970. Changes in American society brought on by multiculturalism and postmodernism made it more acceptable for scholars to examine the practice on its own merits.

Throughout history, some African Americans relied on hoodoo to help combat the harsh realities of American racism. Practitioners provided physical and mental health benefits to the African American community. Their medical services were often available for less expense than those of most physicians, and they created a space for African Americans to release their mental stress and receive hope for their future in the form of supernatural remedies. During the antebellum period, hoodoo doctors concocted magical powders to help enslaved African Americans avoid being flogged. In his autobiography, abolitionist Frederick Douglass acknowledged that slaves often carried roots on them to prevent slaveholders from whipping them. After the Civil War, newly freed men and women continued to seek the counsel of hoodoo doctors as emancipation came with a new set of harsh realities for African Americans. For them, hoodoo provided a way to contend with the inequities of segregation, poverty, the convict-lease system, and the overt violence of the Ku Klux Klan that plagued the era of the late 19th and early 20th centuries. For instance, hoodoo doctors had supernatural remedies that were designed to prevent incarceration and help gain employment.

African Americans who practiced hoodoo before emancipation continued to do so during the postbellum era. Some black American leaders during the late 19th century, however, encouraged their adherents to dissociate themselves from folk magic. These leaders proposed that blacks curtail aspects of their culture that were deemed inferior by white Americans. By denouncing hoodoo and other aspects of black culture that were judged primitive and unsophisticated, these leaders sought to demonstrate that their race was prepared for equal citizenship. This strategy, coined the "politics of respectability" by historian Evelyn Brooks Higginbotham, would persist among black leaders until the Black Power Era. The development of Black Studies in the late 1960s facilitated a greater appreciation of African American culture. Artists, intellectuals, and journalists gave more attention to indigenous religions in Africa and African American supernaturalism. Black writers also played

> ### Hoodoo Curses
>
> Hoodoo is a collection of spells for all purposes and should not be understood as evil magic. Nevertheless, curses have always been a part of hoodoo. Among the afflictions supposedly caused by such spells have been insanity, illness, or death. Two of the more popular methods of inflicting death were causing living creatures—most commonly insects, amphibians, or reptiles—to grow within the bodies of targeted individuals or by locking victims' bowels. While the latter was often considered incurable, hoodoo doctors could remove other curses, often by turning them back on the one who initially performed the curse.

a significant role in countering the negative stereotypes associated with hoodoo. For example, African American writers Zora Neale Hurston, Ishmael Reed, Alice Walker, and Toni Morrison have all incorporated a celebration of hoodoo as a positive part of black culture in their works.

In the 21st century several developments have helped hoodoo gain more visibility in the United States. Manufacturers have been mass producing products solely for the use of hoodoo practitioners since at least the early 20th century, but their visibility has increased in recent years. There continue to be several spiritual supply shops across the United States, and others, like the Lucky Mojo Curio Company, have been able to develop a strong presence online. The Internet has also been essential in cultivating more interest in hoodoo by bringing people throughout the world in contact with one another. Since 2003, Catherine Yronwode has also offered the "Hoodoo Rootwork Correspondence Course." The course lasts a year and contains a series of 52 weekly lessons. As of January 2014, nearly 2,000 people had enrolled in the course. The acceptance of supernaturalism and increased tolerance for different religions in the 21st century is best exhibited by the number of white Americans who practice hoodoo. Despite these advancements, scholars are uncertain that this new interest in hoodoo will be sustained. Hoodoo, however, has proven to be resilient, surviving throughout centuries of challenges. Its practitioners have embraced changes introduced by other cultures while maintaining many of hoodoo's original principles.

See also: Bight of Benin; Black Cat Bone; Conjure; Graveyard Dirt; Hurston, Zora Neale; Mojo; Rootwork; Slavery and the Slave Trade; Two Head; West Central Africa

Ronald Jackson II

Further Reading

Anderson, Jeffrey E. 2008. *Hoodoo, Voodoo, and Conjure: A Handbook.* Westport, CT: Greenwood Press.

Bell, Michael E. 1980. "Pattern, Structure, and Logic in Afro-American Hoodoo Performance." PhD dissertation, Indiana University.

Hazzard-Donald, Katrina. 2013. *Mojo Workin': The Old African American Hoodoo System.* Urbana, IL: University of Illinois Press.

Higginbotham, Evelyn Brooks. 1993. *Righteous Discontent: The Women's Movement in the Black Baptist Church, 1880–1920*. Cambridge, MA: Harvard University Press.

Hurston, Zora Neale. 1931. "Hoodoo in America." *Journal of American Folklore* 44: 317–417.

Lucky Mojo Curio Company. Copyright 1994–2014. Accessed February 21, 2014: http://www.luckymojo.com.

HOPKINS, LAURA

Laura Hopkins, known as Lala to her acquaintances in the 1930s, was one of the last New Orleans practitioners of Mississippi Valley Voodoo. While she was not particularly influential on the religion, she has proven important to scholars because she was among a handful of practitioners who supplied Federal Writers' Project (FWP) workers with important details about what had become a rapidly declining faith by the early 20th century.

Despite the fact that the FWP workers held Lala in low regard, they were diligent enough to preserve personal details about her as well as information she provided about the Voodoo practice of her day. Hopkins was a small woman of about eighty-five pounds, standing five feet and one inch tall. Her diminutive size belied her reputation. According to another practitioner, Lala was notorious for her "bad work," though Hopkins herself claimed to eschew "devil's work." The FWP workers described her as "the most famous present day hoodoo queen."

Lala's most notable action when in contact with the FWP workers was to conduct openings. One of these, a black cat opening, immediately followed a St. Peter opening conducted by a small group of practitioners that did not include Hopkins. The experiences of two representatives of *Life* magazine, accompanying the workers and posing as figures of the New York underworld, provide some insight into Lala's success. The two men treated the preceding St. Peter opening as a farce, going so far as to laugh aloud during the ceremony. In contrast, they were astounded by some of Lala's apparent powers, which included successfully commanding a candle flame to form five points and emit smoke. Hopkins also amazed them by preparing a divination device consisting of a broom straw placed on top of an egg resting on a piece of paper inside a glass. She ordered the straw to point to those who would become successful workers of evil magic. The straw complied, pointing at each initiate in turn. Later, Lala would also perform an uncrossing opening for another FWP worker, whom Hopkins claimed was cursed. Unlike the black cat opening, which had many hallmarks of an initiation, the purpose of the uncrossing opening appears to have been simply to remove the effects of malevolent magic.

Much of Lala's practice centered on the working of hoodoo. While instructing the newly initiated FWP workers, for instance, she taught them a variety of spells, which ranged in purpose from bringing luck to killing enemies. While she generally gave her interviewers little information about the theory behind her magic, she clearly relied on the power of the dead for at least some of her work, a practice attested by other practitioners interviewed by the FWP. In particular, Lala relied on several deceased Voodoo practitioners, including Marie Laveau,

> **What Was a Voodoo Queen?**
>
> Scholars and laypersons alike commonly refer to female practitioners of New Orleans Voodoo as *queens*. Originally, the term was connected with the annual St. John's Eve festivities and probably designated a specific woman elected to fill the role. Such elective offices with royal titles were common across the African Diaspora. The New Orleans term may also have had connections with the Haitian term *ren drapo* or "flag queen."

whose spirits supposedly aided her work. She also sometimes called upon the spirit of Black Hawk, a Native American spirit associated with New Orleans's Spiritual Churches.

See also: Federal Writers' Project; Initiations; New Orleans; Opening; Spiritual Churches; Voodoo in the Mississippi Valley

Jeffrey E. Anderson

Further Reading

Federal Writers Project. 1935–1943. Northwestern State University of Louisiana, Watson Memorial Library, Cammie G. Henry Research Center, Natchitoches, Louisiana.

Penkower, Monty Noam. 1977. *The Federal Writers' Project: A Study in Government Patronage of the Arts.* Urbana, IL: University of Illinois Press.

HURSTON, ZORA NEALE

Zora Neale Hurston was an anthropologist, folklorist, and novelist. Hurston authored several books, including *Their Eyes Were Watching God* (1937); published over seventy short stories, essays, articles, and plays; and wrote numerous unpublished materials. Considered by scholars to be one of most important voices to emerge from Harlem's literary movement of the 1920s, Hurston's work is most known for its use of African American folk idioms and its imagery of southern black life.

Hurston was born in Notasugla, Alabama, to John and Lucy Ann Hurston on January 7, 1891, and raised in Eatonville, Florida. In 1918, Hurston graduated from Morgan Academy, the college preparatory division of Morgan State University in Baltimore, Maryland. From 1923–1924, Hurston studied at Howard University and transferred to Barnard College in New York City in 1925. In 1928, Hurston received her undergraduate degree in anthropology from Barnard, and later did graduate work at Columbia University. Hurston's writing career began at Howard University. In 1921, Hurston published her first short story, "John Redding Goes to Sea," in *Stylus,* a college magazine created by Howard University professors Alain Locke and T. Montgomery Gregory. Throughout the 1920s, Hurston became part of an emerging group of talented New York City writers, publishing short stories

> ### Zora Neale Hurston's Reliability
>
> Scholars generally consider the writings of Zora Neale Hurston, famous for her involvement in the Harlem Renaissance, one of their most important sources on Mississippi Valley Voodoo. Some writers—notably Carolyn Morrow Long—have questioned the reliability of her accounts. Long, for instance, pointed out that much of Hurston's lengthy 1931 article "Hoodoo in America" is plagiarized from a popular how-to magical text of the time. Jeffrey E. Anderson noted that Hurston admittedly made up some of what she described as folklore. It seems that Hurston's reputation rests more on her positive treatment of Voodoo than on her reliability.

in *The New Negro* (1925) and *Fire* (1926) and winning prominent literary contests, including the Urban League's *Opportunity* prize.

Following two failed marriages and employment positions at the Library of Congress and North Carolina College for Negroes, Hurston traveled extensively throughout the American South and the Caribbean during the 1920s and 1930s. Hurston collected folklore in Florida, Louisiana, Haiti, Bermuda, and Honduras, immersing herself in local cultural rituals and collecting jokes, tales, and front porch banter. Hurston's anthropological work was published in her 1931 *Journal of American Folklore* essay entitled "Hoodoo in America." Her 1935 *Mules and Men,* considered a folklore classic, and *Tell My Horse* (1939) were also based on her anthropological research in the South and the Caribbean. *Mules and Men* is a compilation of songs, stories, and sermons from Hurston's hometown of Eatonville and includes a travelogue and treatment of New Orleans's hoodoo culture and its practitioners.

By the 1950s, Hurston migrated from New York City to Florida after a highly publicized scandal, in which accusers claimed she sexually molested a young boy. While living in Florida, Hurston spent the remainder of her life working as a schoolteacher and freelance writer and criticizing the Civil Rights Movement. After suffering a stroke in 1959, a poverty-stricken Hurston died in Fort Pierce, Florida, on January 28, 1960. Hurston was buried in an unmarked grave in the segregated section of the Garden of the Heavenly Rest Cemetery. In 1973, famed novelist Alice Walker honored Hurston with a headstone that read "Zora Neale Hurston—A Genius of the South." In 2002, historian Molefi Kete Asante placed Hurston on his list of 100 Greatest African Americans, and in 2005 Oprah Winfrey's Harpo Productions produced a film adaptation of Hurston's *Their Eyes Were Watching God.*

See also: New Orleans; Tallant, Robert

LaShawn Harris

Further Reading

Boyd, Valerie. 2003.*Wrapped in Rainbows: The Life of Zora Neale Hurston.* New York, NY: Scribner.

Hurston, Zora Neale. 1942. *Dust Tracks on a Road.* New York: Lippincott.

Hurston, Zora Neale. 1995. *Folklore, Memoirs, and other Writings*, selected and annotated by Cheryl A. Wall. The Library of America. New York: Literary Classics of the United States, Inc.

Hurston, Zora Neale. 1931. "Hoodoo in America." *Journal of American Folklore* 44: 317–417.

Walker, Alice, ed. 1979. *I Love Myself When I Am Laughing and Then Again When I Am Looking Mean and Impressive: A Zora Neale Hurston Reader*. With an Introduction by Mary Helen Washington. New York: The Feminist Press at CUNY.

HYATT, HARRY MIDDLETON

Harry Middleton Hyatt (1896–1978) was an Episcopal clergyman from Quincy, Illinois. In addition to his duties as an ordained priest, Hyatt was an amateur folklorist. Between 1936 and 1941 he undertook an ambitious study of African American hoodoo beliefs that was published years later as *Hoodoo-Conjuration-Witchcraft-Rootwork*.

Using personal funds and his own vacation time, Hyatt made several trips, interviewing practitioners in New Orleans, where remnants of Voodoo still survived; along the Gulf Coast in Mobile and St. Petersburg; in the Mississippi Delta cities of Vicksburg, Little Rock, and Memphis; in the Atlantic coastal Low Country from Jacksonville, Florida, to Wilmington, North Carolina; and in Virginia, Maryland, and Washington, DC. He did not venture far into the interior of the South, and he never visited Texas.

As a white northerner, Hyatt found it useful to have a "contact man" in the black community who would seek out conjurers, rootworkers, hoodoo doctors, and spiritual advisors. Hyatt conducted his interviews at hotels, social halls, and private homes owned by African Americans. He considered his informants to be professionals who should be paid for their time. He never asked their names or addresses, feeling that such questions were likely to frighten and inhibit them, and sometimes he did not even note the gender of an interviewee. Each is identified only by a number and a descriptive nickname. During his five-year odyssey, Hyatt recorded interviews with 1,606 informants, using a Telediphone machine and wax cylinders. He concealed the microphone in an old black hat that was left casually lying on the table; it is unclear whether the informants were aware that they were being recorded. In 1970 he conducted more interviews in Florida, this time using a tape recorder, which were published as volume 5 in 1978. The wax cylinders have not survived, although Hyatt had a few transferred to 78 rpm vinyl records. The cassette tapes of the 1970 Florida interviews have been preserved.

Late in his life, Hyatt finally was able to hire typists to transcribe the interviews. The transcriptions, accompanied by Hyatt's comments, were published in five massive volumes (4,754 pages altogether). The transcribers rendered the speakers' pronunciation phonetically, resulting in a valuable record of the speech patterns of African Americans from different regions of the South. The book's pages faithfully reproduce the single-spaced typed sheets, and the idiosyncratic phonetic spelling, along with Hyatt's liberal use of brackets, underlining, italics, and capitalization, results in a text that is extremely challenging to the reader. Despite its difficulty, *Hoodoo-Conjuration-Witchcraft-Rootwork* is an essential source of information on the magical and spiritual beliefs of black southerners in the mid-20th century.

Unfortunately, only a small number of five-volume sets were printed. They are now hard to find, even in libraries, and any that come on the market sell for exorbitant prices.

See also: Conjure; Federal Writers' Project; Hoodoo; Hurston, Zora Neale

Carolyn Morrow Long

Further Reading

Anderson, Jeffrey E. 2005. *Conjure in African American Society*. Baton Rouge, LA: Louisiana State University Press.

Bell, Michael E. 1979. "Harry Middleton Hyatt's Quest for the Essence of Human Spirit." *Journal of the Folklore Institute* 1, no. 1–2: 1–27.

Bell, Michael E. 1980. *Pattern, Structure, and Logic in Afro-American Hoodoo Performance*. PhD dissertation, Department of Folklore, Indiana University, Bloomington.

Hyatt, Harry Middleton. 1970–1978. *Hoodoo-Conjuration-Witchcraft-Rootwork*. 5 Volumes. Hannibal, MO: Western Publishing Company.

Long, Carolyn Morrow. 2001. *Spiritual Merchants: Religion, Magic, and Commerce*. Knoxville, TN: University of Tennessee Press.

Yronwode, Catherine. 2010. "*Hoodoo-Conjuration-Witchcraft-Rootwork* by Harry Middleton Hyatt." In *Hoodoo in Theory and Practice*, Lucky Mojo Curio Company. Accessed March 12, 2014: http://www.luckymojo.com/hyatt.html.

IFÁ

Ifá is both object and subject. Ifá serves as deity and as a method of divination. It is often a word used to describe the deity of wisdom known as Orunmila. Ifá is also the corpus of wisdom in the form of *oríkì* praise songs that are believed to be the cumulative past of all mankind, which can be consulted to reveal what has been forgotten. To consult Ifá, a devotee must consult a *babalawo*, or "father of secrets," a trained priest of Ifá. As scholar William Bascom succinctly put it, Ifá is "a system of divination based on sixteen basic and 256 derivative figures known as Odu, obtained either by the manipulation of sixteen palm nuts, (ikin), or by the toss of a chain (opele) of eight half seed shells." The sixteen major *odu* (Ogbe, Oyeku, Iwori, Edi, Obabra, Okanran, Irosun, Owonrin, Ogunda, Osa, Irete, Otura, Otrupon, Ika, Ose, Ofun) are multiplied by sixteen to comprise the full number of *odu*. Ifá is a system that employs the recounting of mythological tales as a tool to convey meaning, and each of the signs is connected with a particular story.

Although Ifá is dominated by men, it is a system predicated upon the most ancient of wisdoms—that of female powers. Many of the words used to describe Ifá are female centered—the greatest example being that of *odu*, which means womb. *Odu* are the voice of Ifá. When Ifá falls on the mat on which the nuts or chain is cast, an *odu* is revealed.

Bascom notes that the divination tool known as an *opele* carries similar connotations in neighboring ethnic groups, suggesting that the binary system employed in Ifá is related to other African systems. For example, the Yoruba refer to the Ifá divining chain of kola nuts used to cast *odu* as *opele*, while the Nupe of Nigeria call it *eba* and the Jukun use the term *noko*. The Yagba Yoruba dialect, meanwhile, gives this device the name *agbigba*. Bascom further notes that of "all the methods of divination employed by the Yoruba, Ifá is regarded as the most important and the most reliable." Here Bascom is referencing the system of using sixteen cowry shells. The use of the mẹrindínlógún system of cowry shells is specific to the deity the diviner serves and is not an open system as is Ifá, which performs interrelational communication within and among the full pantheon of otherworldly deities far beyond those of the Yoruba tradition.

Traditionally Ifá devotees sought divination on a five-day cycle so that he or she could retain connection with his or her destiny. It is believed among the Yoruba and supported with the liturgy of *odu* that humans select their destiny in the birthing process; the knowledge of destiny is not fully retained, however. Hence, it becomes necessary to consult Ifá—the one who knows yesterday, today, and tomorrow—in order to stay on course and a live a full life.

See also: Bight of Benin; Divination; Yoruba

Phoenix Savage

Further Reading
Bascom, William. 1969. *Ifá Divination: Communication between the Gods and Men in West Africa*. Bloomington, IN: Indiana University Press.

INITIATIONS

Ceremonies to induct members into so-called secret societies, the priesthood, and other important roles are central aspects of many African and African Diasporic religions, including Vodou and Voodoo. In the Haitian faith, the simplest form of initiation is a lave tèt, or head washing, which opens believers to the lwa. Those who wish to advance further in the faith embark on a cycle of ceremonies known as *kanzo*. These rituals can be a grueling and expensive ordeal, but according to Vodou belief, the end result will be a stronger alliance with the lwa. Moreover, such spiritual relationships confer luck, protection, health, and a route to economic advancement. Servitors of the lwa who wish to enter the priesthood undertake a final ceremony, the *pris des je*, or opening of the eyes. *Maryaj lwa*, or marriage to a lwa, can also be understood as something of an initiation in that it enters a person into a special relationship with a specific spirit.

Initiations were also a part of Voodoo, especially in the area around New Orleans. Zora Neale Hurston claimed to have undergone several while conducting research in the city. Some of them were exceptionally elaborate affairs that resemble Haitian kanzo cycles. In recent years, historians have cast doubt on much of Hurston's scholarship, rendering her descriptions of initiations problematic as sources. That initiations took place, however, is not in doubt. Several accounts of them survive, with the most valuable being collected by the Federal Writers' Project (FWP) during the 1930s. According to FWP documents, they were known as *openings* and were simpler affairs than those described by Hurston.

Outside the Louisiana context, full-fledged initiations were rare and often took the form of self-initiations during which those seeking stronger relationships with the spirit world undertook ritual tasks or ordeals. The end result was typically the acquisition of supernatural powers. The best known form of self-initiation was selling oneself to the devil, a bargain supposedly struck at a crossroads at midnight. Although diabolic pacts feature prominently in folklore, they have been uncommon—though not unknown—in fact.

See also: Federal Writers' Project; Kanzo; Lave Tèt; Maryaj Lwa (Marriage to Lwa); Opening; Pris de Je; Secret Societies

Jeffrey E. Anderson

Further Reading
Anderson, Jeffrey E. 2005. *Conjure in African American Society*. Baton Rouge, LA: Louisiana State University Press.

Anderson, Jeffrey E. 2011. "Voodoo in Black and White." In *Southern Character: Essays in Honor of Bertram Wyatt-Brown*, edited by Lisa Tendrich Frank and Daniel Kilbride, 143–159. Gainesville, FL: University Press of Florida.

Hurston, Zora Neale. 1931. "Hoodoo in America." *Journal of American Folklore* 44: 317–417.

Long, Carolyn Morrow. 2001. *Spiritual Merchants: Religion, Magic, and Commerce*. Knoxville, TN: University of Tennessee Press.

Métraux, Alfred. 1972. *Voodoo in Haiti*. Translated by Hugo Charteris and with an Introduction by Sidney W. Mintz. New York: Schocken.

Murphy, Joseph M. 1994. *Working the Spirit: Ceremonies of the Africa Diaspora*. Boston: Beacon Press.

INTERVENTIONISM BY THE UNITED STATES IN HAITI

The relationship between Haiti and the United States was established in the 18th century through trade. However, the Haitian Revolution (1791–1804) was the beginning of U.S. intervention in Haiti's political affairs. The United States contributed to the success of the largest slave revolt in the Western Hemisphere by providing arms and ammunition for Haitian rebels as a ploy to weaken France's colonial power. Subsequently, the U.S. government realized that the establishment of the first black republic could impact its own plantation economy. It would take more than a decade after the revolt for Haiti to be officially proclaimed an independent state; yet, stakeholders in the American South immediately recognized its freedom as a threat. A temporary trade embargo placed upon Haiti in 1804 after pressure from France was also a measure taken to prevent the compromise of slave labor in Louisiana and other slave states. Haiti's status as a liberated country would be tested time and time again as the United States enforced political sanctions in exchange for international aid.

From 1915–1934, the United States gained military control of Haiti, establishing a paternalistic relationship that still exists today. Through political rhetoric, the American government expressed urgency in steering the people of Haiti toward "civility" and "progress." Early 20th-century Haiti was marred by military coups, the overthrow of several presidents, assassinations, and other forms of violence and intimidation. Thus, the U.S. occupation of Haiti was premised on bringing peace and stability to the country's tumultuous social climate. In reality, it was a political tactic implemented to protect North American interests as evidenced by the Wilson administration's takeover of customs and the country's financial institutions.

The influx of American agricultural companies dispossessed peasant farmers of their lands and placed heavy tariffs on homegrown crops. Through cooperation from the Haitian elite and the governing body put in place by President Woodrow Wilson, the U.S. military allocated fertile lands for use by the American government and various U.S. corporations, while masses of Haitian peasants were forced to migrate in order to earn income. The arrival of U.S. Marines also signified institutionalized racism similar to Jim Crow and forced labor likened to modern-day slavery. Although many fought against the invasion, including the rebel Cacos through armed resistance, over 11,000 Haitians were killed during this period. In effect, the nearly twenty years of occupation immobilized Haiti's local government and its citizens. Even after the military's departure from Haiti in 1934, the United States protected its interests by giving the mulatto male elite control and by installing the Gendarmerie, the Haitian military regime trained by and fashioned after the Marine Corps. The centralization of political and economic power set the tone for a more repressive government when Dr. François "Papa Doc" Duvalier took office twenty-three years later.

In 1957, the United States government declared Duvalier the winner of the presidential election. Favored by the United States for his middle-class status and his professional ties to American organizations, Duvalier used his newly-acquired political position to his advantage. His acquiescence with U.S. foreign policy guaranteed the flow of economic aid and continued military support. Although the Kennedy administration temporarily suspended aid in response to human rights violations by Duvalier, the need for the Haitian government's vote at the Organization of American States (OAS) meeting to expel Cuba from the organization and at the United Nation's meeting in support of the 1965 U.S. invasion of the Dominican Republic led to the reinstatement of financial assistance. Over the next thirty years, Duvalier and his son, Jean-Claude "Baby Doc" Duvalier, who became president following his father's death, ruled Haiti under a brutal dictatorship that, despite opposition from some U.S. officials, provided a labor market that proved to be profitable for the United States and international corporations. During the Duvalier era, foreign investors were drawn to Haiti through the production of copper and other natural resources, a burgeoning manufacturing industry that provided cheap labor, tax incentives, and huge returns on their investments.

The overthrow of Jean-Claude Duvalier in 1986 signaled growing dissension among the largely impoverished black population and the elite and a shift in American interests in Haiti. Once a political ally, the United States now viewed the junior Duvalier as a liability. In an attempt to quell anti-American sentiment within the international community, U.S. officials orchestrated a coup d'etat to expel Duvalier. The election of Jean-Bertrand Aristide five years later was a short-lived victory for Haiti. Popular for his humble beginnings as a Catholic priest and his push for democracy, Aristide was ousted only eight months after his election. During his absence, the United States placed an embargo on Haiti that ultimately deepened the country's economic crisis. Aristide returned to office in 1994, backed by President Bill Clinton and a U.S.-led multinational military force of 20,000 soldiers in what came to be known as the second occupation of Haiti. However, the United States counted Aristide's time in exile as part of his presidential term and pressured him to leave office in 1996. By his second presidential run, the United States made it clear that it no longer supported Aristide through its refusal to provide military support and by forcing him into exile once again.

On January 12, 2010, a major earthquake in Haiti exposed the country's complicated relationship with the United States that has spanned over two centuries. The American government's response to the disaster painfully reminded Haitian citizens of earlier interventions by the United States. On that fateful day, Secretary of State Hillary Clinton's meeting to reevaluate U.S. policy in Haiti immediately became a disaster response effort. In turn, Bill Clinton's arrival in Port-au-Prince shortly thereafter underscored the impotence of the Haitian government. While Clinton was there to survey the damage and to advise the government about rebuilding, his role as co-chair of Haiti's international commission gave him political power greater than then-president, René Préval. Clinton, along with the UN, established the terms for disaster aid distribution, reaffirming how Western imperialism has historically held Haiti in a state of dependency.

See also: Haitian Revolution

Angela Watkins

Further Reading

Bellegarde-Smith, Patrick. 2004. *Haiti: The Breached Citadel.* Toronto: Canadian Scholars' Press.

Danticat, Edwidge. 2009. Introduction. In *Love, Anger, Madness*, by Marie Vieux-Chauvet. Trans. Rose-Myriam Rejouis. New York: Modern Library.

Dubois, Laurent. 2012. *Haiti: The Aftershocks of History.* New York: Metropolitan Books.

Dupuy, Alex. 2007. *The Prophet and the Power: Jean-Bertrand Aristide, the International Community, and Haiti.* Lanham, MD: Rowman and Littlefield.

Katz, Jonathan M. 2013. *The Big Truck that Went By: How the World Came to Save Haiti and Left Behind a Disaster.* New York: Palgrave Macmillan.

Renda, Mary A. 2001. *Taking Haiti: Military Occupation & the Culture of U.S. Imperialism.* Chapel Hill, NC: The University of North Carolina Press.

K

KANZO

Kanzo is the name for the initiatory rites of Haitian Vodou. Comprised of five elements over a series of days and nights, the sacred rituals confer the titles of ounsi kanzo for both men and women, oungan su pwen and oungan asogwe for men, or mambo su pwen and mambo asogwe for women. *Oungan* and *mambo* denote priesthood and designate initiates as priests of Vodou for life.

The five elements of kanzo are lave tèt, chire Ayizan, mange tet, brule zin, and batèm. Each sosyete in Haitian Vodou embellishes the work as they see fit, but all sosyetes must employ these five rites to ensure a true kanzo takes place. Lave tèt, or head washing, is the first element and is seen as preparing the candidate for a long seclusion ahead of them. This is more than a simple head washing. The candidate is bathed head to foot, cleansing them for the journey ahead. Various herbs are mixed into water and the person's head is literally washed clean then bound with a white cloth. The candidate is now a hunyo, or spirit child, and sits silently in meditation before the next rite is performed.

The chire Ayizan is the purifying dance that cleanses the initiatory chamber, known as a *djevo*, making it ready for the candidates to enter. Believers regard the djevo as the symbolic womb of the Lwa Ayizan Velekete, the mother of the hunyos. Only those individuals who are prepared to make a commitment to Ayizan for life may enter this room. *Chire* in Kreyòl means to tear or rend. Palm trees and palm fronds are sacred to Ayizan. As a symbol of her ability to rip down old patterns and tear open new pathways, an unfurled palm frond is symbolically *chired* or shredded into a huge plume. The plume is then swept across the djevo, cleansing and imbuing it with Ayizan's energy. A beautiful ceremony, the chire Ayizan is performed with pomp and circumstance as the candidates are brought in and bedded down for their kouche, or ritual sleep. What takes place within the djevo is secret and cannot be divulged. Participants perform rituals, take oaths, and learn many secret teachings to empower them for their new lives as priests.

On the final night in the djevo, the hunyos take part in the brule zin, or fire walk, of the ancestors. Having been spiritually reborn in Ayizan's womb, they are ready to prove they are protected by the spirits. Small metal pots known as *zins* are heated and set ablaze with oil. With the zins burning hot and high, the hunyos must place their hands and sometimes feet into the fires to prove they are immune to the flames. Some call this the "fire of the bones," and it symbolically demonstrates the hunyos' power over the elements.

The morning after the brule zin is the batèm, or baptismal rites. Hunyos rise with the dawn and are baptized with new names. They are assigned godparents to help mentor them through their new lives and are given all the tools required to live as Vodou initiates, practicing their faith and serving their spirits.

See also: Ceremonies; Initiations; Kreyòl; Lave Tèt; Mambo; Oungan

Patricia Scheu (Mambo Vye Zo Komande LaMenfo)

Further Reading

Scheu, Patricia (Mambo Vye Zo Komande LaMenfo). 2011. *Serving the Spirits: The Religion of Vodou.* Philadelphia: Published by author.

KONESANS

Konesans, pronounced similarly to the French word *connaissance*, is a central concept in Vodou. It has a positive meaning, akin to knowledge or insight, particularly of rituals and the spirit world and carries the connotations of both wisdom and experience. Konesans also allows some followers to understand people, including the causes of their suffering, and to heal them. Followers of Vodou may gain more konesans through several practices, including studying the use of herbs or partaking in the lave tèt, or head washing, ceremony. It can also be developed through attendance and participation in ritual practices or initiation into the priesthood.

As followers gain konesans, they can progress from being pititt-caye, or followers of the lwa, to ounsi, or spouses of the lwa, and later to oungan and mambo. Vodou teachers who have achieved the status of oungan and mambo are able to assist others, transmit konesans to other followers, and even heal others. During this journey, followers may participate in ceremonies to assist their development and demonstrate their progress.

Konesans also enables followers to communicate more effectively with lwa. Lwa are said to have access to a level of konesans unavailable to the living, as their experiences and initiations after death contribute to their sacred knowledge. They are also able to pass konesans on to the living.

See also: Ceremonies; Initiations; Lwa; Mambo; Oungan; Ounsi

Kevin Hogg

Further Reading

Brown, Karen McCarthy. 2001. *Mama Lola: A Vodou Priestess in Brooklyn.* Berkeley: University of California Press.

Murphy, Joseph M. 1994. *Working the Spirit: Ceremonies of the African Diaspora.* Boston: Beacon.

KONGO

The Kikongo-speaking peoples of West Central Africa, now numbering perhaps twelve million, are located on either side of the Congo River between the Atlantic coast and the capital cities of Brazzaville and Kinshasa. They are called Kongo, or Bakongo, and call themselves *bisi Kongo*, but such collective terms are modern designations. Kongo was never, and is not now, politically united. Bakongo usually identify themselves by some local term such as *bisi* Mayombe, Bavili, BaLari, or BaNtandu. Kikongo, a Bantu language, is divided into dialects that may not be interintelligible, but missionary publications and translations of the Bible have done much to standardize it.

At the end of the 15th century, Portuguese sailors arrived at the mouth of the great river that the people called Nzadi, which became Zaire in Portuguese and is now the Congo. They made contact in what is now northern Angola with Mbanza Kongo, the capital of the Kingdom of Kongo. The king, the Mani Kongo, was receptive to the Gospel as he understood it and converted to Catholic Christianity; Mbanza Kongo became São Salvador. The letters of the celebrated King Afonso I Mvemba Nzinga (ca. 1506–1542), a vigorous modernizer, survive. Although members of the aristocracy were literate and educated, it is clear that the majority of the population understood Christianity in indigenous terms. As a Christian kingdom, Kongo formed a missionary, commercial, and military alliance with Portugal.

From the beginning, the Portuguese, and later the Dutch and French, sought to acquire slaves for their new plantations in the Americas. Reaching its peak in the late 18th century, the slave trade exported millions of Africans from the Kongo-Angolan coast, mostly to Brazil and the Caribbean. Some of the slaves were from coastal areas, but the majority came from inland, where captives from local wars were sold to coastal traders. Because the traders preferred men to women, Kongo demography showed a marked imbalance in favor of women. Slaves from Kongo, already familiar with Catholicism, are believed to have helped spread Christianity among slaves in the Americas. They also took with them elements of their traditional skills, and in Haiti they recreated the north Kongo Lemba cult.

In the 16th century, Kongo was ruled by a king and provincial governors chosen from noble families. Although the nobility were themselves active participants in slaving, the trade eventually destroyed the old political system. After a battle with Portuguese forces in 1675, the king's control over outlying provinces, particularly those on the coast, lapsed; in Angola the Atlantic trade fell into the hands of highly organized business partnerships among ship captains, resident Europeans, and local entrepreneurs. In the mountainous north, where movement was difficult, local chiefs derived wealth from the trade in slaves exchanged at the coastal principalities of Ngoyo and Loango for alcohol, textiles, pottery, and guns. After 1895, the Kongo were divided among the former French, Belgian, and Angolan colonies now called the Republic of the Congo, the Democratic Republic of the Congo, and the Republic of Angola.

Because elsewhere in West Africa Europeans were restricted to the coast, the Kongo-Portuguese alliance generated a uniquely detailed account of a part of the African interior from the 16th to the 18th centuries. European reports, however, tended to read African institutions in European terms, so that it is often difficult to know what Bakongo were in fact doing and thinking. We are much better informed about Kongo in the late 19th century, when imperial powers began to take over.

By that time, chieftaincy was in decline. For the maintenance of order, to regulate commerce, and to correct and avenge misfortunes believed to have been caused by witches, BaKongo relied heavily on a wide range of *minkisi*, either those acquired to protect one's person, house, and property, or more powerful ones mobilized by their owner-operators, the *banganga*. *Minkisi* were complex material composites built in or around a bag, an animal horn, a pot, a basket, a wooden figure, or some other container. *Minkisi* were believed to be empowered by *simbi* spirits abiding in the waters; the ingredients they contained were chosen to represent, by visual or verbal puns, the service they were supposed to provide. In addition to the physical object, a *nkisi* required the performance of songs and verbal formulae, and it imposed rules of behavior on participants. Performances followed by the death of someone, who was thereby deemed to have been at fault, or by improvement in a patient's health, were considered to have been successful. A *nkisi* thought to be ineffective would be thrown away, its place taken by another, revealed to its *nganga* by a *simbi*. Efforts to predict and control successful outcomes by means of *minkisi* therefore constituted a field of constant creative activity. Similar devices were and are employed all over West and Central Africa. Though originally collected by Europeans as evidence of barbarism, hundreds of *minkisi*, particularly those based on sculpted figures, are now regarded as important works of art.

As Bakongo under colonial rule reconverted to Christianity, Catholic or Protestant, *minkisi* were reduced to hidden personal charms. In 1921, a Protestant catechist, Simon Kimbangu, declaring himself inspired by God, announced that a new divine dispensation made it possible for Bakongo to receive the benefits of spiritual healing that had been denied to them by the missionaries. The Kimbanguist movement was repressed as anticolonial, but persisted clandestinely; it reemerged in the 1950s as the Church of Christ on Earth by the Prophet Simon Kimbangu, together with other such movements including the explicitly nationalist Black Church of Simon Mpadi and the Amicale of André Matsoua. These are among the best-known independent African religious movements.

In French and Belgian Congos, but not Angola, KiKongo speakers, educated by missionaries and inducted into the colonial labor force, became relatively prosperous. As such, they were among the leaders of the independence movement that led to national independence in 1960, under the first President of the Democratic Republic of Congo, Joseph Kasa-Vubu, and the first President of the Republic of Congo, Fulbert Youlou.

See also: Mojo; Nzambi a Mpungu; Papa LaBas; Simbi; West Central Africa

Wyatt MacGaffey

Further Reading

Hilton, Anne. 1982. *The Kingdom of Kongo*. Oxford: Oxford University Press.
Janzen, John M. 1982. *Lemba, 1650–1932: A Drum of Affliction in Africa and the New World*. New York: Garland.
MacGaffey, Wyatt. 1986. *Religion and Society in Central Africa: The BaKongo of Lower Zaire*. Chicago: University of Chicago Press.

MacGaffey, Wyatt, Michael D. Harris, Sylvia H. Williams, and David C. Driskell. 1993. *Astonishment and Power: The Eyes of Understanding: Kongo Minkisi / The Art of Renée Stout.* Washington, DC: Smithsonian Institution Press.

Thompson, Robert Farris. 1983. *Flash of the Spirit.* New York: Random House.

Thornton, John. 1983. *The Kingdom of Kongo: Civil War and Transition, 1641–1718.* Madison, WI: University of Wisconsin Press.

KREYÒL

Kreyòl, or Creole as it is also commonly known, is the language of the Haitian people. While early authors tended to treat Kreyòl as improperly spoken French, modern scholars have rejected this approach. The abandonment of this understanding was well underway by the middle of the 20th century, when Alfred Métraux accurately observed that although the vocabulary of Kreyòl was nearly completely French, its pronunciation and structure were largely West African and resembled that of the languages of Dahomey and Nigeria.

Today, scholars treat Kreyòl as a full-fledged language rather than a dialect of French. In part, this shift in understanding is due to an artistic movement that began during the later 1940s, which emphasized the importance of Haiti's language and culture. In an effort to accentuate distinctiveness and distance themselves from older interpretations that depicted Kreyòl as a dialect, some writers have adopted a strongly nationalistic interpretation of the language's origins. Scholar Patrick Bellegarde-Smith, for instance, argues that it must be understood as a creation of the Haitian people rather than a syncretic blend of French words and West African syntax. To him, Kreyòl developed as an invention of Saint-Domingue slaves and their Haitian descendants, a language of resistance that united disparate African peoples, while also allowing communication with the Europeans who dominated their land.

For almost all of its history, Kreyòl was predominantly a spoken language. Previous generations who sought to record it in writing varied considerably in how they did so. Among scholars, French spellings were the norm until the late 20th century. In keeping with the nationalistic reinterpretation of the language, French spelling has been abandoned in favor of constructions that emphasize the language's distinctive phonetics and history. The term *Kreyòl*, which is gradually supplanting *Creole* as the language's preferred name, is a prime example. Another is the use of *Vilokan* in place of *Ville-au-Camps* for the name of the home of the lwa. The list could go on indefinitely.

African Americans from southern Louisiana have their own dialect of French historically referred to as *Gombo* and more commonly known as Louisiana Creole today. Unlike with Haitian Kreyòl, the concept of Louisiana Creole as a distinct language has not gained widespread acceptance, despite a longstanding scholarly interest in the state's Creoles of Color. The difference in viewpoint is in large part a consequence of the distinctive histories of the two areas. Put simply, unlike Haiti, Louisiana has had no history of independence. The states' inhabitants have generally embraced their French heritage as a mark of distinction, rather than rejected it as a symbol of colonial domination.

See also: Creoles of Louisiana; Creolization; Dahomey; Langaj

Jeffrey E. Anderson

Further Reading

Michel, Claudine, and Patrick Bellegarde-Smith. 2006. *Vodou in Haitian Life and Culture: Invisible Powers.* New York: Palgrave Macmillan.

Hebblethwaite, Benjamin. 2012. *Vodou Songs in Haitian Creole and English.* Philadelphia: Temple University Press.

Métraux, Alfred. 1972. *Voodoo in Haiti.* Translated by Hugo Charteris and with an Introduction by Sidney W. Mintz. New York: Schocken.

Valdman, Albert et al. 2010. *Dictionary of Louisiana French as Spoken in Cajun, Creole, and American Indian Communities.* Jackson: University Press of Mississippi.

LAKOU

Lakou is the Kreyòl term given to a family compound that houses the members of a family group, as well as the peristil where they serve their ancestral spirits. Following the Haitian Revolution for Independence, extended families in rural Haiti have organized themselves into clusters of homes. These buildings generally surround a shared courtyard or space, where communal activities are held. In the Caribbean, such outdoor spaces are used as living rooms, areas where food is served and eaten, spots for family meetings and community get-togethers, and gathering places for religious observances. These family compounds represented a sharp break from the plantation order and the family instability that it fostered. Moreover, as Duke University's Law and Housing in Haiti website puts it, the lakou served as "grassroots opposition to any state action tending to reinstate the plantation order."

A second major contributing factor to the development of the lakou was the rise of Vodou in Haiti following the war for independence in 1804. For a century—years after the defeat of the French and British armies—Haiti faced total neglect on the part of the Catholic Church. The plantation culture had ingrained Christianity as the religion of the masters, but without priests, there was no organized body of worship available to the Africans. Vodou, rooted in West African traditions rose to fill the void. The emergence of Vodou brought back the West African tradition of a compound system loosely organized around both families and intimate associates. It was this structure of family compound intimately linked to Vodou practice that became the foundation for the lakou system.

A lakou that offers annual religious functions has a leader called a *sèvitè* or servant of the spirits who is in charge of the lakou's celebrations. This individual is elected from the families that live within the lakou and serves in the role for life. Upon his or her death, a new *sèvitè* is chosen who continues the work of the lakou. He or she also performs other work for the community such as spiritual healing and medical services.

There are many active lakous, but the most well known are in the Gonaïves region of western Haiti. There are three known for their adherence to specific African traditions in Vodou. Lakou Souvenance celebrates the lwas from Dahomey (modern-day Benin). Lakou Soukri Danach celebrates the Kongo tradition, and Lakou Badjo is considered Nago (from Yoruba). Souvenance has had the same family as *sèvitè* for over five generations. Each lakou has an annual celebration of its ancestral spirits, and observers from urban Haiti as well as the diaspora are drawn by the beauty and authenticity of the services. Souvenance has the largest and longest celebration, beginning the Saturday evening before Easter Sunday and lasting all week until Friday.

See also: Ancestral Spirits; Lwa; Ounfò

Patricia Scheu (Mambo Vye Zo Komande LaMenfo)

Further Reading

Dubois, Laurent. 2012. *Haiti: The Aftershocks of History.* New York: Metropolitan.

Haiti Lab 2012 ~ Law and Development Project. "Lakou Model." Law and Housing Haiti of Duke University. 2012. Accessed March 4, 2014: http://sites.duke.edu/lawandhousinginhaiti/historical-background/lakou-model/.

Nesbitt, Nick. 2008. "Turning the Tide: The Problem of Popular Insurgency in Haitian Revolutionary Historiography." *Small Axe: A Caribbean Platform of Criticism.* March 4, 2014: http://smallaxe.net/repository/file/sx%2027/3-SA27%2520Nesbitt%2520%2814-31%29.pdf.

Stevens, Alta Mae. 1998. "Haitian Women's Food Networks in Haiti and Oldtown, U.S.A." PhD dissertation, Brown University.

LANGAJ

In Haitian Kreyòl, *langaj* or *langay* is the equivalent of the English word *language*, but in the context of Vodou, the term specifically refers to the language of the lwa. In many cases, songs and other words used in rituals are spoken in langaj. The exact origin of the language is debatable. Typically, participants identify this language as African in origin. According to Harold Courlander, langaj is sometimes identified as Greek, Arabic, Hebrew, or Spanish. Elsewhere, he described it as "the 'tongues' spoken by the houngan or possessed persons during Vodoun rites," implying that it need have no identifiable geographic origin.

Most authors, scholarly and popular, focus on the concept of langaj as a survival of one or more African languages. Scholars have identified fragments from the languages of the Fon, Kongo, and Yoruba peoples. Knowledge of the meanings of these survivals, however, has been lost. Popular author Patricia Sheu, known as Mambo Vye Zo Komande LaMenfo in her role as a Vodou priestess, strikingly describes langaj as "words of power and enchantment that were spoken over and over again, but never understood." She goes on to state, "Three hundred years of recitation, like an extended game of Whisper down the Lane, has left us bereft of their meaning, but not of their power."

An experience of Ina Fandrich in her effort to translate a single Vodou chant illustrates the difficulty of tracking the development of langaj from any particular African tongue. The chant in question, recorded by Médéric Louis-Élie Moreau de Saint-Méry during the late 18th century, went as follows:

Eh! Eh! Bomba, hen, hen!
Canga bafio te
Canga moune de le
Canga do ki la!
Canga li!

Fandrich began by consulting with an expert on Senegambian languages, who determined that it was of Malinke origin. According to the scholar, those reciting the chant were proclaiming the goodness and power of *Canga*, a Malinke word that can mean "spirit," "magic," or "witchcraft." A second scholar informed Fandrich, however, that the song was more likely of Kongo origin. His alternative translation called on the chanters to seize various people, presumably some sort of enemies. As this case illustrates, a definitive account of the origins and development of langaj will require much more research.

The documentary record of Mississippi Valley Voodoo is problematic when it comes to langaj. A key barrier in determining the prevalence of such communication is the shortage of reliable descriptions of Voodoo songs. Though several chants have been recorded, most show little sign of langaj apart from a few words and some personal names of spirits. The origin of those that do appear to incorporate langaj is often unclear. The tendency of early authors to uncritically assume that Haitian Vodou and Mississippi Valley Voodoo were essentially the same thing renders it possible that some songs reportedly belonging to the Mississippi Valley may actually have been Haitian.

See also: Dahomey; Kongo; Kreyòl; Senegambia; West Central Africa; Yoruba

Jeffrey E. Anderson

Further Reading

Courlander, Harold. 1960. *The Drum and the Hoe: Life and Lore of the Haitian People.* Berkeley, CA: University of California Press.

Fandrich, Ina Johanna. 2005. *The Mysterious Voodoo Queen, Marie Laveaux: A Study of Powerful Female Leadership in Nineteenth-Century New Orleans.* Studies in African American History and Culture. New York: Routledge.

Hebblethwaite, Benjamin. 2012. *Vodou Songs in Haitian Creole and English.* Philadelphia: Temple University Press.

Moreau de Saint-Méry, Médéric-Louis-Élie. 1797. *Description Topographique, Physique, Civile, Politique et Historique de la Partie Française de l'Ile de Saint-Domingue.* 2 vols. Philadelphia.

Scheu, Patricia (Mambo Vye Zo Komande LaMenfo). 2011. *Serving the Spirits: The Religion of Vodou.* Philadelphia: Published by author.

LAPLAS

The laplas is one of several roles, such as oungenikon and tamboye, that can be held by members of a Vodou sosyete. While each sosyete is led by a mambo or oungan asogwe, there are many other functional roles that help the group run smoothly. One of the more important is the laplas. The name *laplas* comes from the French for "commandant-general de la place." This person, generally male, is the master of ceremonies, and bears a sword at the beginning of a Vodou ceremony. Along with the ren drapo, or flag queens, his job is to cut the metaphysical roads of the lwa, so they may come into the peristil and make their presence known through the state of possession. A laplas often, though not always, holds the rank just below oungan or mambo asogwe, known as *oungan su pwen*—priest "on the point"—in a Vodou sosyete.

The laplas is also an assistant to the presiding mambo or oungan of the house. Seen as a priest in training, a laplas serves in many different capacities and functions for a sosyete. A laplas can carry the sacred emblems of priesthood, such as the ason, the embellished gourd rattles that mark their owners as oungans or mambos asogwe. As the laplas is often of the rank of su pwen, he is learning how to work with an ason. The laplas can also carry the kanzo kolyes, the sacred necklaces of the initiates; maintain and care for the kanzo pot tets of initiates; and assist in making herbal baths, pakets, and other magical items for his sosyete. Finally, it is the laplas who draws out the sacred vèvès of the lwa in cornmeal and chalk dust, creating the right mix of decoration and sacred symbology for the ceremony that evening.

The ceremonies for the rank of laplas are a secret part of the ceremonies called *kanzo*. A person who is foretold to be a laplas seeks out a life of service and remains in that role for a long time. The laplas receives a working ason from the hand of the mama or papa kanzo, the person who initiated the laplas into the priesthood. It is said that the su pwen rank is borrowing the ason and therefore cannot own the actual piece until he or she is ready to carry it fully as a priest of the faith.

The laplas can hold additional ranks as well. For instance, a laplas can also be an oungenikon. The oungenikon is the choir master and has an encyclopedic knowledge of Vodou songs. Depending on how the energy of a particular ceremony is flowing, the oungenikon can start songs of power, songs of pathos, or songs of prayer with the choir—the singers of which are often, though not always, of the rank of ounsi—directing the energy and pulse of a service in coordination with the tamboye, or drummer. The laplas can also be a tamboye, though that combination is rare in Haiti. In the United States, where one does not find large groups of family working during services, participants sometimes are called upon to do double or even triple duty. In such cases, serving as tamboye can become part of the role of the laplas.

The laplas is simultaneously a servant of the spirits, a leader of the people, and a supporter of the sosyete. In this manner, the laplas learns all the roles of the sosyete, making him or her fit to become a priest of the Vodou faith.

See also: Kanzo; Mambo; Ounfò; Oungan; Oungenikon; Swords; Vèvè

Patricia Scheu (Mambo Vye Zo Komande LaMenfo)

Further Reading

Métraux, Alfred. 1972. *Voodoo in Haiti*. Translated by Hugo Charteris and with an Introduction by Sidney W. Mintz. New York: Schocken.

Scheu, Patricia (Mambo Vye Zo Komande LaMenfo). 2011. *Serving the Spirits: The Religion of Vodou*. Philadelphia: Published by author.

LASIREN

Lasiren is a female lwa or spirit who is known as the queen of the ocean and the maritime manifestation of Ezili, the lwa of love and beauty. Lasiren is traditionally represented as an enchanting, fair-skinned, black-haired mermaid seated on a rock and admiring her reflection. Lasiren is renowned for her incomparable beauty with her symbols appropriately being the hand mirror and the hair brush. These two symbols reveal two other characteristics about Lasiren, namely her constant concern with her physical appearance and her sheer vanity. In addition to her attractive physical attributes and self-love, Lasiren is also associated with music; in fact, her presence is known by the trumpeting of a conch shell. Lasiren's association with music provides her with the ability to enchant and seduce individuals, much in the same fashion as the sirens of Greek mythology. However, despite her seductress persona, Lasiren is also a considered a guardian of children as they are in or near water. Her temperament vacillates from moments of pure kindness to instances of intense fury. In order to gain her favor or render thanksgiving for her assistance, the devotees of Lasiren offer her white wine, champagne, doves, syrup, seashells, and fragrances. In some cities, such as New Orleans, Lasiren is presented with seafood offerings. This type of ritualistic offering is not entirely accepted by other devotees, considering that Lasiren is queen of the sea and thus mother of all marine life. In other words, it would be inappropriate for a mother to eat her children. In response to these offerings, Lasiren is known for granting her devotees wealth, good fortune, sexual prowess, and ability to attract others. In reference to associated lwa, Lasiren is the consort of Agwe, a male lwa and king of the ocean. In addition to her consort, Lasiren is also known to have an ongoing affair with Ogou, the lwa of war and power. The relationship between Lasiren and Ogou is not approved by Agwe, who is locked in an eternal conflict with Ogou. The third *lwa* that Lasiren is associated with is Labalen or the Whale. The precise nature of their relationship is a matter of debate, with some stating that Lasiren is the daughter of Labalen while others believe that Lasiren and Labalen are interchangeable. The unique personality of Lasiren will not only preserve her popularity among Vodouists, but also keep her a point of interest for scholars seeking to understand one of the more important lwa in the Vodou pantheon.

See also: Agwe Ta'Woyo; Ezili

John Cappucci

Further Reading

Alvarado, Denise. 2011. *The Voodoo Hoodoo Spellbook*. Forward by Doktor Snake. San Francisco: Red Wheel/Weiser.

Deren, Maya. 1970. *Divine Horsemen: Voodoo Gods of Haiti*. Preface by Joseph Campbell. New York: Chelsea House Publishers.

Houlberg, Marilyn. 1996. "Sirens and Snakes: Water Spirits in the Arts of Haitian Vodou." *African Arts* 29, no. 2: 30–35, 101.

Métraux, Alfred. 1972. *Voodoo in Haiti*. Translated by Hugo Charteris. New Introduction by Sidney W. Mintz. New York: Schocken Books.

Olmos, Margarite Fernández, and Lizabeth Paravisini-Gebert. 2011. *Creole Religions of the Caribbean: An Introduction from Vodou and Santeria to Obeah and Espiritismo*. 2nd ed. Foreword by Joseph M. Murphy. New York: New York University Press.

Pelton, Robert W. 1972. *The Complete Book of Voodoo*. New York: G.P. Putnam's Sons.

Polk, Patrick Arthur. 1997. *Haitian Vodou Flags.* Jackson, MS: University Press of Mississippi.
Siuda, Tamara L. (Mambo Chita Tann). 2012. *Haitian Vodou: An Introduction to Haiti's Indigenous Spiritual Tradition.* Woodbury, MN: Llewellyn.

LAVE TÈT

Lave tèt, from the French for "head washing," is the most widely performed ritual of Haitian Vodou. The head is believed to be the metaphysical center of the body, the seat of reason, and home of the spirits. A cool head is preferable; a hot head is regarded as unbalanced and easily manipulated. Head washings are the manner in which Vodou creates balance for the individual and for his or her spiritual entourage.

Lave tèts can be given as standalone events, as part of a larger ritual cycle such as kanzo, or as introductory rituals into a given Vodou sosyete's membership. The reason for the lave tèt is based on a divinatory reading performed first, to see what the client needs. Lave tèt formulas are the secret knowledge of mambos and oungans. The herbs, perfumes, and oils added to a bath mixture are closely guarded by their makers. Successful formulas are never given out but are handed down from priest to initiate as the inner knowledge of the temple. Lave tèts can be received while clothed or nude, depending on the presiding priest's recipe and rules. After the physical lave is performed, the participants are bedded down with the material and liquids from the lave on their skin and heads. The head is often wrapped tightly with material as an offering to the initiate's particular set of spirits—his or her mèt tèt or spiritual constellation. In the morning, the initiate may shower, dress, and go about his or her business.

A properly done lave tèt should be an overnight event. The participant is confined to the peristil proper, where he or she will receive treatment and then sleep or kouche. This is facilitated with prayers, songs, and drum beats. In some temples, modern practices such as meditation or pathworking have begun to be employed as tools to help facilitate the correct state of being for the participant.

The standalone lave tèt is the prevalent form of the ceremony in both Haiti and the United States. A reading is done to see what is needed for the client. Often one or more lwa will come forward to be the pwen, or point, of the bath. A basic bath is composed of clean water with fresh herbs that are pertinent to the desired result. The client has his or her head washed with this mixture, while the presiding mambo or oungan sings for the lwa. Sometimes, the lwa themselves arrive via possession and perform the ritual. Once the lave is completed, the client has his or her head wrapped in a clean cloth and is given final instructions. The client is then free to go home with some simple caveats, such as no sex for twenty-four hours and avoidance of crowds.

Lave tèts are also performed as an introduction to a Vodou house. Some people do not wish to make a deep connection until they have had time to process the many changes they will experience in service. For these folks, a lave tèt is a good way to commit in a more personal manner, allowing them time to get acclimated to the house, its membership, and its method of working.

The biggest lave tèt is given as part of the kanzo cycle of initiation. Twenty-one individual baths are administered at the beginning of the kanzo to facilitate a deep change in both mind and body. This lave tèt is called the bath of dissolution and is prepared in a large drum of water, with bushels of herbs brought in and hand shredded (*pile'd*). Old-time priests would conduct this lave tèt at the edge of a river or by the ocean, utilizing the water from such sources as a material element in the baths. This particular lave tèt begins a seven-day kouche cycle that culminates in the individual's crowning as an initiate of the sosyete.

See also: Ceremonies; Divination; Kanzo

Patricia Scheu (Mambo Vye Zo Komande LaMenfo)

Further Reading

Scheu, Patricia (Mambo Vye Zo Komande LaMenfo). 2011. *Serving the Spirits: The Religion of Vodou*. Philadelphia: Published by author.

LAVEAU, MARIE

The mere mention of the name Marie Laveau still strikes fear in the minds of people over a century after her death. Was she the Voodoo Queen who had supernatural powers or a benevolent woman of faith who asserted her power and compassion to help the members of her community? One of the reasons for this fear is the mystery surrounding her life and death. Another reason stems from the conflicting stories about her life, ranging from the credible to the incredible, even ludicrous. Additionally, the lack of available records perpetuates the mystique that surrounds her life. There is even the question of whether there were two Maries, a mother and a daughter, or just one. It appears as if her life is shrouded in a veil of mystery that only intensifies as the years pass.

Even some of the most basic information about Marie cannot be verified. One bit of information that is questionable is the year of her birth. Despite the lack of detailed records, it is the general consensus that she was born in 1801. By some accounts her mother, Marguerite, was involved in Voodoo. According to others she was not. Marie was a Creole of French and African descent. The identity of her father presents another question. Some say her father was Charles Laveau, but there is debate as to whether he was white or black. Some claim her father was someone else. Other questions arise concerning the children of Marie, including how many she had, who their fathers were, and what happened to them. Even her death is surrounded by uncertainty. There are questions concerning when she died and where exactly she is buried. Once again the lack of records contributes to the uncertainties as well as the mystery.

Even Marie's role in Voodoo is uncertain. Some individuals claim she was the head of Voodoo in New Orleans, while others claim she was not a participant. Although it is not a provable fact, most believe she was involved and even the leader for several years. There are stories of her power and the abilities she had. Some people even claimed to be witnesses of her Voodoo magic. Assuming that she did practice magic,

> ### How Important Was Marie Laveau?
>
> Marie Laveau has developed into a legend. During her lifetime, however, she made only occasional appearances in the documentary record, often appearing in a less-than-impressive light. That she was nevertheless a respected personage is clear from the multiple lengthy obituaries that appeared upon her death. By the early 20th century, it was common for practitioners to claim connections with her in order to legitimate their own practice. At least one Voodoo adept of the early 20th century treated Laveau as a minor deity.

> ### How Many Marie Laveaus Were There?
>
> Since the early 20th century, most authors have stated that there were two Marie Laveaus, one the daughter of the other. Some scholars, however, have cast some doubt on the claim. Zora Neale Hurston at one time stated that there were three Marie Laveaus but later claimed that there had only been one. Carolyn Morrow Long, the most thorough Laveau biographer, states that some of the primary sources seem to describe more than one person when speaking of Laveau, but notes that just who the second might have been is unclear. In short, the jury is still out.

there are even conflicting stories of how powerful she was. Did she have supernatural abilities or was she simply a religious woman who practiced Voodoo? This question may never be answered but it adds to the mystery surrounding her.

One thing that is certain about Laveau was her charity. She helped with the invalids of New Orleans. Those in the hospital or prison were recipients of her care and concern. She tended to those whom most of society had forgotten or never cared about to begin with. She sat with individuals, read to and fed them, and prayed for them. She was even there with some as they took their last breaths. Her compassion crossed racial and social lines.

In recent years, some scholars have argued that Laveau was a covert civil rights activist. According to Martha Ward, Laveau's desire for abolition and belief that all should be free fed her actions, especially when she manipulated the legal system to help other people of color. She did not shy away from issues because of her lineage. Her belief in the rights of all individuals propelled her to stand up for individuals of all colors, especially those of Creole and/or African descent. Marie used her power and social standing to help those who could not help themselves. Laveau thrust herself into personal and legal situations when she felt an injustice had been done. Her status as a free woman of color allowed her to insinuate herself into situations where she could make a difference. Some, including Carolyn Morrow Long, dispute this interpretation of Laveau, arguing that she was, in fact, a supporter of slavery.

Marie Laveau led a colorful life that is full of mystery. Regardless of the mystique surrounding her life, her impact on New Orleans is still felt today. People still travel to the Crescent City to visit her grave and seek her guidance. They trek to her tomb, make a cross mark, and leave a gift, hoping that Marie will show favor to them. The souvenir shops sell items concerning Laveau and Voodoo. For those who believe, Marie will always be the Queen of Voodoo as well as an important figure in the history of New Orleans.

See also: Alexander, Jim; Montanée, Jean; New Orleans

Sandra Marshall

Further Reading

Long, Carolyn Morrow. 2006. *A New Orleans Voudou Priestess: The Legend and Reality of Marie Laveau.* Gainesville, FL: University Press of Florida.

Tallant, Robert. 1946 [1998]. *Voodoo in New Orleans.* New York: Macmillan; reprint, Gretna, LA: Pelican.

Ward, Martha. 2004. *Voodoo Queen: The Spirited Lives of Marie Laveau.* Jackson, MS: University Press of Mississippi.

LEGBA

Legba Atibon, or Papa Legba as he is called in Haiti and LaBas as he was known in the New Orleans area, began as an African phallic spirit who has roots among the Fon and Yoruba nations of West Africa. When Legba came to the New World, he dropped his sexual identity and become a guardian spirit of junctions, crossroads, and openings. Legba is considered an oungan and gives knowledge or clairvoyance to those he feels worthy of the gift.

In West Africa, Papa Legba is known as Alegba, the seventh and youngest son of the sky gods Mawu and Lisa. He is considered the spokesman and interpreter for all the Vodu spirits and is thought of as a spontaneous and unpredictable character, who loves to play tricks on humankind to show their weaknesses and foibles. Alegba is envisioned as a sexual spirit; those possessed in his dance carry a phallus-tipped staff, with which they chase the younger women of the audience. Alegba is also associated with fertilization, creation, and communication, attributes he carried into the New World via the Middle Passage.

In Haiti, Alegba morphed into Atibon Legba, a guardian of the gates for houses, villages, and temples. His favorite animal is the dog. The Yoruban origin of the word *Legba* means "lame," an allusion to Legba's limping walk and broken feet. Unlike the young and highly sexual Alegba of Dahomey, Papa Legba in Haiti is seen as an old bent-over man dressed in rags, limping or walking with crutches and accompanied by two dogs that lick his sores and keep him company. This appearance of ancient age only conceals his great powers. Though his virility is gone, servitors in Haiti still know Papa Legba as the cosmic phallus, and a twisted cane is kept by his altar as a visual reminder of his power of regeneration. Legba is often invoked in matters of sex, and mediates between the sexes, harking back to his hypersexualized avatar Alegba of West Africa. Despite the seriousness of his duties and given his great age, Legba is typically amicable and friendly. He is much loved by the people, who greet him as "Papa."

Legba is the head of the lwa, invoked first and honored the most. Because of his dominion over communication, Legba is the first lwa served in a Vodou ceremony. Legba controls both the gates of Ginen and the manifest world. He facilitates communication between the lwa and their servitors. No spirit can arrive in service without Legba's express permission. Conversely, a servitor who has offended Legba will find that he or she is unable to communicate with any lwa. Without communication, there are no blessings, benefits, and protections. His association with traffic, transport, and travel makes Legba the master of doors and gateways, highways and crossroads, points of intersection, and crossings of power.

Many of the songs sung for Legba speak of being on the road, of opening passages, and of passing through gates. One of his praise names is Gran Chemin or "Big Road." It is a mystery that the road walked upon at the beginning of a Vodou ceremony is also the spirit who opens the passage between worlds for the road to appear. This dual functionality is the mark of Legba in action. He is the idea and the form, the transformative crossroad that everyone must pass through when working with spirit.

Legba is also considered the linguist of the spirit world. He is the interlocutor, interpreter, and polyglot who translates the supplications of the servitor to the respective lwa for whom they are intended. Only Legba knows all the languages of both the manifest world and the spirit world. Oungans and mambos must address Legba first in order to have him carry their prayers and demands to the appropriate lwa. Legba must also be invoked to speak with spirits in a special relationship with a person, known as one's *mèt tèt*.

Given his position in service and his talents, it is no surprise that Legba is also the master of individual fate, the lwa of divination and oracles, the source of all choices and actions. This attribute is reimagined from his African origin, where he was partnered with Fa, the spirit of divination. While Fa represented fate, Legba represented change. Through Legba, fate could be thwarted and the future altered. Legba would report what Fa saw differently to each individual, offering multiple choices of events that are not all beneficial in order to serve the spiritual evolution and growth of mankind. In Haitian Vodou, Fa and Legba combined in the one personality of Papa Legba.

Though having many important avatars such as Avadra Bowa (who sweeps clear the path before Legba), Katawoulo, Vye Legba, Legba Gran Chemin, and Legba Gwetò, in Haiti he is most commonly called by the name Atibon Legba (also called Legba Se). It is this manifestation that stands before the gate of Ginen, controlling all traffic to and from both sides. The word *Atibon* is of Fon origin, and translates roughly as "the wood of justice." This is an allusion to the potomitan or center post, another symbol of Legba that is found in every Vodou temple. The potomitan is the avenue by which the lwa enter the ounfò. Often this post is simply referred to as the *poto Legba*. Legba is the guardian of this center post, as well as the temple grounds themselves. The avatar Legba Bitayson is the guardian of houses and historically is found seated by the front door in the form of a small cairn of stones, or else a mound of earth. Offerings, such as almond oil, coffee, and water, are poured on this mound daily to ask Legba to open the way for the people of the house to have a good day, no matter what they may be doing.

Legba has other symbols besides the potomitan. One is the cross, the metaphysical meeting of two planes of existence. Here between the physical realm and the spiritual is where Legba stands, opening and closing the way according to the plans of Bondye, the only authority Legba will answer to. He is also represented by a cane, thrust downward into a cross. The symbolic meaning is Legba's ability to move across multiple universes simultaneously. Another of his symbols is the sun, a source of regeneration and life. Many songs speak of him as a solar phallus, a poto of the sun that the lwa travel on, another allusion to the road the spirits move upon.

Several other characteristics define Legba. The lwa's best known attribute is his baton or crutch. He carries a clay pipe and a special bag called a *Legba djakout* to differentiate it from Azaka's peasant bag, also known as a *djakout*. Legba dresses in blue jeans, a work shirt, and a big hat. He is often accompanied by dogs and walks the byways of the world continuously, which brings to mind the lwa's baton or crutch. Legba is syncretized with St. Anthony of Padua due to the stories of the saint being able to find lost things; St. Lazarus for the crutches and sores on the his legs; St. Peter for the keys to the kingdom of heaven; and St. Roch—sometimes known as the little Legba—for the sores on his legs.

Legba's *reposoir* or tree altar is the medecinier beni or belly ache bush. He also likes the Caribbean calabash and oak. His djakout is hung in the branches of the tree altar to receive offerings from his servitors. Legba can be offered various grilled foods: cassava bread, rice, green bananas, potatoes, yams, malanga, kazoos, ears of corn, giraumons, and the flesh and bones of animal sacrifices. His sacrificial animals include roosters or hens and male goats. According to written sources, he likes black, mottled, or multicolored cocks and hens of white, black, or mottled plumage. Sacrificed fowls should be opened from the back. Their head, wings, and feet may be placed in djakout Legba as offerings. Legba also drinks strong black coffee, alcohol, "cola," and orgeat syrup. He can be offered tobacco with a pipe when honored from the Rada perspective and cigars from the Petro side.

Legba's days are Thursdays, but he can also be served on Tuesday, Friday, and Saturday. His annual feast days are June 13, which he shares with St. Anthony, and January 1 because he opens the New Year for everyone. Depending on the preferences of the oungan or mambo leading a particular sosyete, Legba's colors may vary from white on the Rada side and red on the Petro side to purple and gold or white and green. Color choices sometimes echo the images of the saints with whom he is syncretized. Legba's dances are the yanvalou, the mayi, and krabiye. All dances are appropriate for Legba, though, as he is first among the lwa.

See also: Azaka; Blanc Dani; Bondye; Dahomey; Divination; Ginen; Haitian Immigration to the United States; Lwa; Ounfò; Oungan; Papa LaBas; Slavery and the Slave Trade; Syncretism; Yoruba

Patricia Scheu (Mambo Vye Zo Komande LaMenfo)

Further Reading

Ackermann, Hans-Wolfgang, Maryse Gautier, and Michel-Ange Momplaisir. 2011. *Les Esprits du Vodou Haïtien*. Coconut Creek, FL: Educa Vision, Inc.

Anderson, Jeffrey E. 2005. *Conjure in African American Society*. Baton Rouge, LA: Louisiana State University Press.
Desmangles, Leslie G. 1993. *The Faces of the Gods: Vodou and Roman Catholicism in Haiti*. Chapel Hill, NC: University of North Carolina at Chapel Hill Press.
Guigard, Mercedes Foucard. 2006. *Répertoire Pratique des Loa du Vodou Haïtien - Practical Directory of the Loa of Haitian Vodou*. Port-au-Prince, Haiti: Reme Art Publishing.
Hyatt, Harry Middleton. 1970–1978. *Hoodoo-Conjuration-Witchcraft-Rootwork*. 5 vols. Memoirs of the Alma Egan Hyatt Foundation. Hannibal, MO: Western.
Leeming, David Adams. 1992. *The World of Myth*. Oxford: Oxford University Press.
Marcelin, Milo. 1936. *Mythologie Vodou (Rite Arada)*. Vol. 1. Port-au-Prince: Les Éditions Haitiennes.
Scheu, Patricia (Mambo Vye Zo Komande LaMenfo). 2011. *Serving the Spirits: The Religion of Vodou*. Philadelphia: Published by author.

LEGISLATION AGAINST VODOU/VOODOO

Laws affecting the practice of Vodou and Voodoo were present from the early days of the colonial period. The French Code Noir, meaning "Black Code," defined the rights of slaves beginning during the 18th century. Of the 1724 version's fifty-four articles, three established Roman Catholicism as the legal faith of the colonies. Another required masters to baptize their bondspersons and instruct them in Catholicism. Colonial officials were lax in their enforcement of the Code Noir, however, allowing for the survival of African religious beliefs in the New World while also encouraging syncretism and creolization. Local Haitian restrictions banning the sale of magical charms were just as ineffective at halting the practice of the magic associated with Vodou.

Following the Haitian Revolution, the standing of Vodou within the nation fluctuated wildly. For most of its history, the religion was tolerated if not exactly embraced by the church and state. On the other hand, there were times when sentiment against the faith became so strong within the government and Catholic priesthood that their relationship to Vodou became openly hostile. The high points of suppression of the religion were the many antisuperstition campaigns, the most notable of which took place in 1896, 1913, and 1941. Such actions continued to

---

Voodoo as Crime

Historically, observers of Mississippi Valley Voodoo have linked it with crime. Among the most common malfeasances linked to the faith were murder in the form of human sacrifice and prostitution. Of course, there is no solid evidence that anyone was sacrificed in the Mississippi Valley. Some Voodoo practitioners, however, were linked to prostitution, though there is no evidence that this was the norm. It would be surprising had the 19th- and early 20th-century press not picked up on isolated connections between the world's oldest profession and Voodoo to demonize the latter.

recur as late as 1986. During these drives, the church destroyed ounfò and religious items and increased its outreach efforts. Although these drives were initiated by the Roman Catholic Church, the government often lent support to its efforts. Along with church-initiated actions, many of Haiti's leaders, including Toussaint L'Ouverture, frowned upon Vodou and discouraged its practice. Some portions of Haiti required Vodouisants to obtain permission from the police before holding any communal ceremonies well into the second half of the 20th century. The frequent recurrence of disapproval and sometimes open hostility made Vodou's position within Haiti somewhat precarious but never really threatened its existence.

Legal prohibitions affected Mississippi Valley Voodoo well into the 20th century. Sometimes the laws directly assaulted spiritual and supernatural practices. The New Orleans city government, for instance, made it illegal to sell charms or tell fortunes. More important than laws aimed directly at Voodoo were more general items of legislation used by law enforcement officials to suppress the faith or aspects of it. During colonial times, for example, restrictions on slave gatherings gave whites the legal grounds to break up Voodoo ceremonies. Following emancipation, laws against disturbing the peace could be similarly deployed against those practicing communal rituals. Licensing laws, most notably those affecting the practice of medicine, resulted in prosecutions of those dispensing herbal and magical remedies. Even more common were allegations of fraud, made possible in a society in which the majority questioned the efficacy of Voodoo-related magic. Jean Montanée was among those charged on these grounds. Along similar lines, federal laws against mail fraud allowed authorities to pursue those who used the postal system to market or sell their wares.

Practitioners of Vodou and Voodoo did not simply acquiesce in the suppression of their faith. In both Haiti and the Mississippi Valley, they became more secretive. Outsiders came to see the religions themselves as mysterious. In the United States, practitioners of hoodoo and conjure and spiritual supply shops began to attach labels to their products that discounted any claims to actual power. It became commonplace to see items with "sold as a curio only" printed at the bottom of labels or with "alleged" as part of the product name. After all, those who made no promises could not be prosecuted for fraud.

Some believers went to much greater lengths to overcome actions against their religion. Haitian peasants violently resisted a 1941 antisuperstition campaign. So great was their opposition to the attempt to suppress Vodou that the government recognized defeat the following year, effectively ending the campaign. One extraordinary case from New Orleans involved a free woman of color and priestess known as Betsy Toledano. In 1850, a New Orleans police force broke up a Voodoo gathering she led and arrested some of the participants. Rather than simply bowing to the imposition, she protested on the grounds that law enforcement had interfered with her right to freely practice her religion. Ultimately, Toledano's challenge failed on the ground that the disruption of her gathering was to break up a meeting of slaves and free blacks, not to stop her from practicing her religion.

According to scholar Kodi Roberts, other believers in Voodoo surrounded themselves with the trappings of Christianity in order to legitimize their practices in the eyes of the broader society. Leafy Anderson took the lead in this development when she arrived in the Crescent City during the early 20th century. Though many observers considered her and/or her followers as practitioners of Voodoo, she described herself as a spiritualist and went on to found a series of what came to be known as Spiritual Churches. These bodies held to many concepts associated with Voodoo, including a belief in an invisible world of spirits, supernatural healing, and what outsiders would identify with magic. On the other hand, ministers in the churches asked for donations rather than requiring payment, and their congregations met in buildings that resembled those used by Catholics and Protestants. The trappings of Christianity, argues Roberts, allowed Voodoo to survive under another name.

See also: Anti-Vodou Campaigns; Catholicism and Vodou/Voodoo; Code Noir; Espiritismo; Montanée, Jean; Spiritual Churches; Toledano, Betsy

Jeffrey E. Anderson

Further Reading

Desmangles, Leslie G. 1992. *Faces of the Gods: Vodou and Roman Catholicism in Haiti.* Chapel Hill, NC: University of North Carolina Press.

Long, Carolyn Morrow. 2006. *A New Orleans Voudou Priestess: The Legend and Reality of Marie Laveau.* Gainesville, FL: University Press of Florida.

Long, Carolyn Morrow. 2001. *Spiritual Merchants: Religion, Magic, and Commerce.* Knoxville, TN: University of Tennessee Press.

Roberts, Kodi. In press. *Voodoo and the Promise of Power: The Racial, Gender & Economic Politics of Religion in New Orleans, 1881–1940.* Baton Rouge, LA: Louisiana State University Press.

Turlington, Shannon R. 2002. *The Complete Idiot's Guide® to Voodoo.* Indianapolis, IN: Alpha.

LITERATURE, VODOU/VOODOO IN

From gradual, comparatively recent appearances in Francophone and then Creole Haitian literature, Voodoo has grown to occupy an increasingly large space in the Anglophone literature of North America, especially that written by African Americans. Its value to literature has been partly thematic, initially as an illustration of the superstitions and ignorance of the lower classes, thanks to its status as the religion of the poor, illiterate Haitian peasant (a religion that subsequently informed the beliefs of slaves in the United States and elsewhere). But there has also been an increasing use of Voodoo imagery as a literary trope, thanks to symbolism suggesting subversion, intersection, and transformation.

Haitian literature until the 20th century was essentially regarded as a minor subdivision of French literature, and writers (Oswald Durand, Justin Lhérisson, and Frédéric Marcelin, for instance) who incorporated indigenous themes or imagery such as Vodou-related material were the exceptions. The American occupation of 1915–1934, however, prompted the indigéniste movement, outlined by Jean-Price Mars in his seminal *Ainsi Parla l'Oncle* (1928), which encouraged Haitian writers to take pride in their own national heritage. The major work to come out of this

> ### Racism and Vodou/Voodoo
>
> Many whites once saw Vodou and Voodoo as indicators of black inferiority. During the antebellum era in the United States, writers frequently used the existence of Voodoo and hoodoo among blacks as proof of white superiority. Similar attitudes existed in accounts of Haitian Vodou. These softened during the late 19th century, though whites were prone to view Vodou and Voodoo as either sinister or exotically amusing. These attitudes testify to assumptions that defined anything of black origin as suspect, a fact illustrated by the relatively positive reception whites gave the Asian faiths that were gaining visibility at around the same time.

period was probably Jacques Romaine's *Gouverneurs de la Rosée* (1944), which contained scenes of Vodou ceremonies. By the 1940s, Haitian literature was also being influenced by surrealism, thanks to a visit by Andre Breton, and later by Alejo Carpentier's magical realist writing, especially *The Kingdom of This World* (1957), which described the rise and fall of the infamous Haitian King Henri Christophe in a vivid Vodou context. Writers went on to use Vodou symbolism to make socio-political points, as in the work of René Depestre, Jacques Stéphen Alexis, Gerald Blancour, and the first Haitian novel in Creole, Frankétienne's *Défazi* (1975).

For the most part, however, literary expression was largely repressed during the Duvalier years (1957–1986), and most later writers who have incorporated Vodou thematically and symbolically into their work have done so from exile. Notable examples are Dany Laferrière and Émile Ollivier, both Francophone writers living in Canada, and probably Haiti's best-known contemporary writer, Edwidge Danticat, who writes in English and lives in the United States. In the short-story collection *Krik? Krak!* (1995), for example, she explores the wisdom that underlies "superstitious" indigenous beliefs and stories denigrated by the Haitian elite. Vodou has also often appeared in literature elsewhere in the Caribbean. In Jean Rhys's *Wide Sargasso Sea* (1966), a retelling of *Jane Eyre* from Mrs. Rochester's perspective and set largely in Jamaica, obeah features extensively and is explicitly paralleled with Haitian Vodou. Maryse Condé's *I, Tituba, Black Witch of Salem* (1986), set in Barbados and Salem, Massachusetts, explores the magical practices of a historical figure accused of practicing hoodoo.

Voodoo's presence in the Anglophone literature of North America from the 19th century onward took two initial forms, although it has recently been perceived in a more complex and nuanced way. Most commonly, it was associated with the folk magic and beliefs of slaves and ex-slaves, beliefs imported originally from West Africa and transmuted into the forms of conjure, hoodoo, rootwork, and so on. In this form, 19th-century white writers often used it to illustrate the ignorance of former slaves, and coupled the theme with nostalgia for a "simpler" antebellum era when blacks knew their place. This is the case with writers like Thomas Nelson Page, whose Dr. Moses in *Red Rock: A Chronicle of Reconstruction* (1898) is a conjurer but an obvious charlatan. Such works reinforced feelings of superiority in white readers. For African American writers, however, the Old South was hardly a site of nostalgia, and, although they tended to depict characters who used folk magic in a similar light to that of white writers, their purpose was more to consign such a worldview to the benighted past and to emphasize advances in education and enlightenment in the black community. William Wells Brown, author of the first African American novel, *Clotel, or the President's Daughter* (1853), took this approach with Uncle Dinkie, another charlatan, in *My Southern Home* (1880). Mark Twain, in turn, exploited the theme for humor, but he also deconstructed the inherent racial superiority implied by writers like Page, making it instead a class issue. Jim, in *Adventures of Huckleberry Finn* (1885), claims to have been bewitched and ridden by witches—language evocative of Voodoo possession—and to have received an all-powerful charm from the Devil's hand. The reader is aware, however, that Jim is fantasizing because of a Tom Sawyer trick, and Jim's beliefs (in signs, for example) are presented throughout the book as superstition—but then most of them are shared by the untutored Huck Finn. This association of Voodoo with the superstitions of the lower or uneducated classes is typical of 19th-century literature, although late in the century, when African American writers turned to fiction in greater numbers, a more complex picture emerged.

The other form in which Voodoo appeared in 19th- and early-20th-century American literature was in connection with the Voodoo culture of New Orleans, a subject that intrigued both black and white writers. White authors tended to stress the mystery of the imperfectly known and to hint at dangerous and dramatic powers; in Helen Pitkin's *An Angel By Brevet: A Story of Modern New Orleans* (1904), for example, the well-born heroine's involvement in Voodoo rituals, while trying to remove a family curse, nearly proves disastrous. In *The Grandissimes: A Story of Creole Life* (1880), a novel by George Washington Cable, the Voodoo practitioners (one of whom is a major character) are of the servant class, but it is also established early in the book that many upper-class Creoles consult what the book terms "voudou horses." The degree of their belief remains ambiguous, but the attraction of white Americans to Voodoo beliefs, combined with the "desegregated spectacles" accompanying some public Voodoo rites, can be seen to be at the heart of contemporaneous unease and fear surrounding the religion. When Jim Crow entrenched the color lines, alleviating some of this anxiety, New Orleans Voodoo began to appear in narratives by white writers more as what scholar Michelle Y. Gordon calls "a relic of New Orleans's wild past and Reconstruction's failings." However, the Voodoo culture of New Orleans and southern Louisiana has continued to preoccupy writers until the present day. The "Voodoo Queen," Marie Laveau, in particular, has featured as the central character in a number of novels, including Robert Tallent's *The Voodoo Queen* (1956), Francine Prose's *Marie Laveau* (1977), and Jewell Parker Rhodes's *Voodoo Dreams: A Novel of Marie Laveau* (1993). All these novels stress Marie's mixed racial heritage, suggesting both the ambiguity and the strength of power derived from two ancient traditions. The more sensationalist approach to this aspect of New Orleans culture is represented by L. D. Sledge's novel about one of Marie's descendants, *Dawn's Revenge* (1998), described on its dust jacket as featuring "[d]anger, biracial love interest, mystery and VOODOO."

In African American literature, Voodoo began to be treated increasingly seriously in the 20th century. Charles W. Chesnutt's collection of stories, *The Conjure Woman* (1899), was narrated by the ex-slave Uncle Julius, and featured characters whose powers of conjuration and goophering are treated with amused disbelief by the white northern narrator of the frame tale; his more sympathetic wife, however, recognizes at least a symbolic truth in the tales. Chesnutt was hedging his bets—although he wanted the folk magic he described to be treated with respect, he also wanted to leave enough ambiguity to protect the newly-emerging African American literate classes from the potential scorn of his predominantly white audience. It would nevertheless be clear to them that Uncle Julius was describing and manipulating a subversive kind of power that could be used to undermine their own—part of that power being its embodiment in language. As a result of telling each story to the northerner, Uncle Julius subtly orchestrates an outcome that works to his benefit. Conjuring fiction continued to be written throughout the 20th century, often in the form of romances involving blues musicians—examples are J. J. Phillips's *Mojo Hand: An Orphic Tale* (1966) and Arthur Flowers's *Another Good Loving Blues* (1992).

In 1938, Zora Neale Hurston, one of the American writers most closely associated with Vodou, published *Tell My Horse*, drawing in many respects from Charles Seabrook's earlier and widely popular *The Magic Island* (1929), but based on her original anthropological research in Haiti. The book was not aimed at an academic audience, and did not focus exclusively on Vodou; these factors, taken with a stylistic approach more appropriate to fiction than to anthropology and its subjective viewpoint, caused the book to be considered of limited value as a study of Vodou. But it did provide Hurston with material that she used increasingly explicitly in her later fiction, notably *Moses, A Man of the Mountain* (1939). Here she invoked in turn Moses's association in Haiti with Damballah, and Damballah's origin in Dahomey, so that her Moses becomes symbolically African American, described according to African American folk idiom.

Increasingly as the 20th century progressed, African American writers explored the symbolic applicability of Voodoo imagery to the African American experience, especially the metaphor of the crossroads (which permeates blues lyrics, also), presided over by Esu-Elegba. This liminal position between two worlds, coupled with the eclecticism of Voodoo mythology and tradition—and their covert resistance to and reinscription of the dominant culture, as when Catholic iconography is visually reinterpreted in terms of images of lwa—has been found by many writers to be a potent reflection of the position of African Americans in American society. Thus, for example, Ishmael Reed uses what he terms a Neo-HooDoo Aesthetic, transforming the literary forms of mainstream American culture in novels like *Mumbo Jumbo* (1972), which incorporates much Voodoo imagery and focuses on a metaphysical detective called PaPa LaBas. His investigation into a missing text does not lead to the text itself, but to the revelation of a written text's capacity for infinite regeneration and reinterpretation—a literary application of the transformative process performed

> **Voodoo's Influence**
>
> Scholars have always thought of Voodoo in the Mississippi Valley as something distinctive. Conjure, which was present throughout the American South, resembled the magical aspects of Voodoo but lacked its gods and communal ceremonies. Over the years, however, Voodoo has helped shape practices outside its home. For instance, candles, which appear to have entered Voodoo by way of Catholicism, are now ubiquitous features of spiritual supply shops across the nation. Some of the first how-to conjure books appear to have gained popularity in New Orleans. Even such words as *hoodoo* appear to have originally gained popularity in the Mississippi Valley.

in iconographical reinterpretation. Esu-Elegba himself—or Papa Legba, LaBas, Labat, or various other permutations—becomes a representative trickster, transformative figure, or general change agent in many novels, such as the chameleon-like Lebert Joseph in *Praisesong for the Widow* (1983) by Paule Marshall, an American novelist of Caribbean heritage, or Legba in William Gibson's *Count Zero* (2006), in which as Lord of the Crossroads he presides over all lines of communication, including the Internet. He even appears in Tim Powers's *On Stranger Tides* (1987), which gave birth to a *Pirates of the Caribbean* movie. Michael Gruber's novel *Tropic of Night* (2003) revolves around the African origins not just of Legba and other lwa, but of magic and religious practices generally, in New World religions such as Voodoo and Santería.

At the same time, Esu-Elegba has also frequently been used by literary critics as a means of characterizing aspects of a text that deal with crossings, transformations, and intersections, as in Heather Russell's *Legba's Crossing: Narratology in the African Atlantic* (2009), while Henry Louis Gates, Jr.,'s *The Signifying Monkey: A Theory of African-American Literary Criticism* (1988) uses him extensively as a model for the process of interpretation and the manipulation of language. Other lwa have also appeared in fiction in symbolic fashion, as in the title story of John Edgar Wideman's collection *Damballah* (1981), which evokes the lwa as an originary figure following an epigraph from Maya Deren's *Divine Horsemen: The Voodoo Gods of Haiti* (1970). Even the zombi has taken on a metaphorical dimension, symbolic of the Other or sometimes (as flesh-eater) consumerism, but this is primarily a cinematic phenomenon, and the predatory zombis of film and contemporary graphic novels have little to do with the Haitian originals.

See also: Art, Vodou/Voodoo in; Danbala; Entertainment, Voodoo as; Film, Vodou/Voodoo in; Legba

Helen Lock

Further Reading

Assélin, Charles. 1980. "Voodoo Myths in Haitian Literature." *Comparative Literature Studies* 17(4): 391–98.

Gordon, Michelle Y. 2012. "'Midnight Scenes and Orgies': Public Narratives in New Orleans and Nineteenth Century Discourses of White Supremacy." *American Quarterly* 64(4): 767–86.

Munro, Martin. 2013. *Exile and Post-1946 Haitian Literature: Alexis, Depestre, Ollivier, Danticat.* Liverpool, UK: Liverpool University Press.
Wilson, Edmund. 1954. "Voodoo in Literature." *Tomorrow* 3(1) (Autumn).

LOEDERER, RICHARD A.

Loederer was born in Vienna, Austria, in 1894, but immigrated to the United States during the Great Depression. He returned to his birth city late in life, dying there in 1981. Loederer is best known for texts and illustrations he produced in the 1930s and 1940s, one of which was *Voodoo Fire in Haiti*. The book, unlike most of its sort, appeared first in German in 1932 and three years later in an English translation. As with his other writings, the text was accompanied by woodcuts of his own design.

Like other writers of his day, Loederer travelled in Haiti, reporting on the Vodou beliefs he encountered there with an eye toward the sensational. He was certainly familiar with Spenser St. John, who helped introduce the world to the now stereotypical image of Vodou as an orgiastic, violent faith that was almost completely foreign to Western culture. As is true of many other works on Vodou produced for a popular audience during the first half of the 20th century, *Voodoo Fire in Haiti* is most valuable for its representation of white European understandings of African Diasporic religion. Along with writers such as William B. Seabrook and Zora Neale Hurston, Loederer's depiction of Vodou would help inspire works on Mississippi Valley Voodoo, notably Robert Tallant's *Voodoo in New Orleans* (1946).

See also: Hurston, Zora Neale; St. John, Sir Spenser; Seabrook, William Buehler; Tallant, Robert

Jeffrey E. Anderson

Further Reading

Hurston, Zora Neale. 1990. *Tell My Horse: Voodoo and Life in Haiti and Jamaica.* With a Foreword by Ishmael Reed and Afterword by Henry Louis Gates, Jr. New York: Harper and Row.
Loederer, Richard A. 1935. *Voodoo Fire in Haiti.* Translated by Desmond Ivo Vesey. New York: Literary Guild.
Seabrook, William Buehler. 1929. *The Magic Island.* New York: Harcourt, Brace.
Tallant, Robert. 1946. *Voodoo in New Orleans.* New York: Macmillan.

LONG, CAROLYN MORROW

Carolyn Morrow Long, a retired preservation specialist and conservator who worked for the Smithsonian Institution's National Museum of American History, has written extensively on hoodoo and Voodoo. Her two most important works on the subject are *Spiritual Merchants: Religion, Magic, and Commerce* (2001) and *A New Orleans Voudou Priestess: The Legend and Reality of Marie Laveau* (2006). Both works broke new ground and remain among the best researched studies of African American supernaturalism and traditional religion.

> **The Feeding of Spirits**
>
> In the worlds of Vodou and Voodoo, spirits like to receive and sometimes require feeding. In Haiti, for example, many ceremonies include offerings of food to the lwa. Moreover, each lwa has its own food and drink preferences. The same was once true in the Mississippi Valley. The spirits that empower charms in hoodoo often require feeding as well, most commonly in the form of liquids with which they were sprinkled or in which they were soaked. Whiskey, urine, blood, and other substances served this purpose. Today, oils sometimes are used.

Long's *Spiritual Merchants* was the first book to explore the world of hoodoo drugstores, manufacturing companies, and related businesses that produced and marketed supernatural items intended for a largely African American clientele. In addition to examining the development and operation of such businesses, Long includes short histories of many of the United States' most prominent supply shops and manufacturers and provides extensive background information on the development of hoodoo in two major cultural regions of the American South.

A New Orleans Voudou Priestess is a biography of New Orleans's most famous practitioner, Marie Laveau. Unlike most authors—scholarly and popular—to write on the "Voodoo Queen," Long seeks to demythologize her subject, freeing her from both the negative stereotypes constructed by Robert Tallant and his predecessors as well as the more recent mythology that asserts Laveau should be understood as a civil rights activist. In addition to her examination of Laveau, Long also includes material on Jim Alexander, Jean Montanée, St. John's Eve, and other aspects of New Orleans Voodoo.

See also: Alexander, Jim; Drugstores; Hurston, Zora Neale; Laveau, Marie; Montanée, Jean; Tallant, Robert; Ward, Martha

Jeffrey E. Anderson

Further Reading

Long, Carolyn Morrow. 1997. "John the Conqueror: From Root-Charm to Commercial Product." *Pharmacy in History* 39: 47–53.

Long, Carolyn Morrow. 2001. *Spiritual Merchants: Religion, Magic, and Commerce.* Knoxville, TN: University of Tennessee Press.

Long, Carolyn Morrow. 2006. *A New Orleans Voudou Priestess: The Legend and Reality of Marie Laveau.* Gainesville, FL: University Press of Florida.

LWA

Some scholars believe the term *lwa*, also rendered as *loa*, to have originated from the Fon words *lo*, meaning "mystery," and *lon*, meaning "the heavens." Patrick Bellegarde-Smith traces the word to the Yoruba culture. He states that *lwa* is related to the word *oluwa*, meaning "lord." The derivation of the term and the conflicting information about its origins reflect the confluence and survival of various African belief systems. The practice of Vodou, in which lwas are an essential aspect, can be traced back to the Fon of Dahomey (present-day Benin) and to the Ewe, Dagara, Yoruba, and Bakongo peoples of West and Central Africa. In general, lwas are spirits or lesser gods that exist in nature and the larger universe. They manifest in people and objects, and influence changes in the life cycle. In essence, lwas serve as intermediaries between humans and Bondye, the Supreme Being (God); they are the nexus between the physical and metaphysical worlds.

During Vodou ceremonies, the mambo or oungan calls upon the lwa through songs, dances, prayers, drumming, offerings, and the drawing of vèvès (spiritual symbols). The lwa then manifests in one of the devotees, usually the Vodou priestess or priest. When a lwa "mounts" an individual, it takes possession of the mind and physical body, using it as a conduit through which the spirit communicates with the living. Identified through certain behaviors, style of dress, spiritual symbols, days of the week, food offerings, and even favorite colors, the lwa materializes, sometimes performing humanly impossible feats. The lwa also gives devotees the opportunity to make requests or ask for advice. Thus, the ounsi becomes a vessel through which the lwa reveals its unique persona and cosmic knowledge.

The pantheons of lwas, also referred to as *nanchons* or nations, are categorized according to specific characteristics and African regions. There are over seventeen pantheons, the more commonly encountered ones being the Rada, Petwo or Petro, Kongo, Wangol, Nago, Ginen, and Ibo. While Haitian Vodouisants might be familiar with the different pantheons, they typically group lwas under the Rada and Petwo categories. These two categories represent the lwas' duality, with Rada being a symbol of benevolence and Petwo, a symbol of malevolence. Generally, Rada lwas are characterized as protective and loving whereas Petwo lwas are vengeful, aggressive, and dangerous. However, the dichotomous attributes between Rada and Petwo lwas are more complex than they seem.

While the distinction between Rada and Petwo lwas is thought to be based on morality, a "good" spirit is just as capable of causing harm as a "bad" one, and vice versa. For example, Papa Legba can either guide (as a Rada spirit) or hinder (as a Petwo spirit) Man's destiny. As the guardian of the crossroads, Legba holds the key to the spiritual world, and proper supplications must be made in order for the devotee to pass. Similarly, La Marassa, the divine twins, represent innocence, childhood, and the newness of life; they also represent the first death. In Haitian Vodou, Les Morts (ancestors or the dead), Les Mysteres (lwas), and La Marassa are entities that act as one in the creation and sustenance of mankind. As with other lwas, failure to properly honor the divine twins can have dire consequences.

Of the more than one thousand lwas that have been identified in the Vodou religion, a hierarchy has been established. In addition to Papa Legba, Danbala or Damballah (the serpent), Ezili (goddess of love), Lasiren (the mermaid), Agwe (god of the sea), Ogou (god of war), and Gede (god of death) are especially revered. Danbala is an ancient, benevolent father who helped Bondye create the universe, reinforcing it by intertwining himself around the four pillars that support it. As the patron of the waters and the heavens, Danbala arches his body across the sky

> **Baka and Diab**
>
> According to Vodouisants, among the forces present in the world are spirits known as *baka* and *diab*. The former is a shape-shifting being that can take the form of a dwarf or an animal. Summoned or created by bòkò, baka may serve as guardians for a locale or may be sent to harm victims. Diab can serve much the same purpose as baka, being sent out by sorcerers to attack others. While both spirits are bought by bòkò to serve them, the spirits are difficult to master and can turn against the person seeking to control them.

alongside Ayida, his female counterpart, who forms the rainbow. He is the life force that ensures the flow of motion of the earth and the ocean and the cycle of life and death. Within this context, Ezili is a symbol of fertility through the cosmic womb, of which divinity and humanity are conceived. She coexists and copulates with her male counterparts to ensure the continuity of life. In contrast, Gede, also known as Baron Samedi, Baron Cimitière, and Baron Piquant, represents the end of the physical life. Although crude and vulgar, Gede is also considered very wise. For fishermen and other seafarers in Haiti, the sea is an integral part of life. Therefore, devotees look to Agwe and his wife, Lasiren, for survival and safe passage. As the god of war, Ogou symbolizes power and strength. During the Haitian Revolution, the people called upon Ogou to defeat the French and put an end to slavery.

Today, as in the past, the merging of lwas and Catholic saints reflects the reinvention of African traditions, a necessary modification to religious practices deemed primitive in Western cultures. Catholicism, then, was used as a veil for the enslaved to practice their religious customs. The substitution of saints for lwas also reflects shared religious principles between two seemingly dissimilar faiths. Leslie Desmangles notes that the use of ritual objects, the veneration of both saints and lwas, and the incorporation of Catholic liturgy in Vodou ceremonies reflect a symbiosis between the two religions. Yet, he emphasizes that "such correspondences were not based upon the life of the saints, but upon certain symbolic accoutrements associated with them which corresponded to those found in the myths about the African deities." For example, Danbala is associated with St. Patrick because, according to Catholic hagiography, he drove all of the snakes out of Ireland. Danbala is also associated with Aaron, whose staff transformed into a snake when he threw it down before the Pharoah. Ezili is associated with the Virgin Mary as a symbol of motherhood, beauty, purity, and spiritual transcendence. Because the Catholic faith and Vodou share similar spiritual tenets, Catholic saints continue to be substituted for lwas.

See also: Agwe Ta'Woyo; Ancestral Spirits; Ayida Wedo; Bight of Benin; Bondye; Catholicism and Vodou/Voodoo; Dahomey; Danbala; Ewe; Gede; Lasiren; Legba; Nanchons; Ogou; Ounfò; Petwo; Rada; Saints; Twins; Vèvè; Yoruba

Angela Watkins

Further Reading

Bellegarde-Smith, Patrick, and Claudine Michel, eds. 2006. *Haitian Vodou: Spirit, Myth, and Reality*. Bloomington, IN: Indiana University Press.

Deren, Maya. 1983. *Divine Horsemen: The Living Gods of Haiti*. Kingston, NY: McPherson.

Desmangles, Leslie G. 1992. *The Faces of the Gods: Vodou and Roman Catholicism in Haiti*. Chapel Hill, NC: The University of North Carolina Press.

Galembo, Phyllis. 1998. *Vodou: Visions and Voices of Haiti*. Berkeley, CA: Ten Speed Press.

McCarthy-Brown, Karen. 2006. "Afro-Caribbean Spirituality: A Haitian Case Study." In *Vodou in Haitian Life and Culture: Invisible Powers*, edited by Patrick Bellegarde-Smith and Claudine Michel, 1–26. New York: Palgrave Macmillan.

MACOULOUMBA, JEAN

Jean Macouloumba, also known simply as Caloumba or Colombo, was a deity present in the version of Mississippi Valley Voodoo practiced in the New Orleans area. Unfortunately, little is known of this spirit. The deity was reportedly mentioned under the name Colombo during an 1893 St. John's Eve ceremony, but the account gave little indication of his role or purpose. It seems, however, that he was associated with alligators. Helen Pitkin's 1904 novel, *An Angel by Brevet*, gave a somewhat lengthier account of the spirit. Pitkin's work, reportedly based on eyewitness accounts of Voodoo, aspects of which can be verified from independent sources, depicts Jean Macouloumba as a being on whom participants called during a healing ceremony. Jean Macouloumba first appeared in the account shortly after another little-known spirit named Charlo made his presence known. Unlike Charlo, who was welcomed and provided healing, Macouloumba appears to have been an honored but ominous presence.

See also: Blanc Dani; Charlo; Saint John's Eve; Voodoo in the Mississippi Valley

Jeffrey E. Anderson

Further Reading

Dillon, Catherine. "Voodoo, 1937–1941." Louisiana Writers' Project, folders 118, 317, and 319. Federal Writers' Project. Cammie G. Henry Research Center, Watson Memorial Library, Northwestern State University, Natchitoches, LA.

Pitkin, Helen. 1904. *An Angel by Brevet: A Story of Modern New Orleans*. Philadelphia and London: J. B. Lippincott Company.

MAGIC

One defining feature of magic is a belief that spirits and/or other supernatural phenomena affect earthly matters. Scholars suggest that underlying all magical practices are the principles of similarity and contagion. The principle of similarity holds that in order to supernaturally affect a target object, the magical expert acts upon a representative object, which leads to corresponding change in the target object. This idea is illustrated by the idea of the so-called Voodoo doll, into which a magician sticks pins in order to harm the person it represents. The principle of contagion refers to the idea that objects, after they touch, continue to influence each other. This can be seen in the use of body by-products, such as hair, in spells and charms desired to affect from afar those to whom they once belonged.

> ### Does Magic Work?
>
> Practitioners of hoodoo and other forms of the supernaturalism would, of course, say it did. Even those lacking faith, however, have recognized that it can work. Many medicinal spells rely on herbal remedies, which can sometimes provide relief for ailments. In cases where psychosomatic ailments are evident, the intervention of a skilled supernaturalist can produce a cure by persuading those who believe themselves afflicted that they have been released from whatever is harming them. In still other cases, scholars have noted that communities tend to harm or help those they believe to be affected by positive or negative magic, respectively.

Magic, or using supernatural forces to improve people's daily lives, has been a part of African American culture since colonial times and is still very much alive today, especially in cities with large black populations. African American magic is a mixture of different cultures and magical traditions and goes by a variety of names, including *conjure, hoodoo, mojo, fixing, rootwork,* or *tricking,* depending on the region and historical era. *Hoodoo,* for example, was most commonly used to reference the brand of African American magic found in the Mississippi Valley, whereas *conjure* was the common name for magical practices found outside the Mississippi Valley until the early 20th century. In modern times, however, *hoodoo* and *conjure* are used interchangeably. *Rootwork* is an alternative name adopted because of the prevalence of roots in the practices.

Hoodoo can be a noun or a verb (to *hoodoo* someone), and is also used to describe practitioners of magic (*hoodoo* doctor). Hoodoo is frequently confused with Voodoo, the Mississippi Valley faith, and with Vodou, the Haitian religion, both of which developed in part from *Vodu,* a religion of West Africa. Magical practice in itself is not religion because it does not aim to please deities and differs from practitioner to practitioner. *Hoodoo* technically describes a "body of magical belief" and does not refer to any particular religion or worship of spirits. The main practices of *hoodoo* are fortunetelling and spell casting. Hoodoo rituals did, however, play a part in the Voodoo religion, which is why *Voodoo* and *hoodoo* are often, especially historically, used as synonyms. For instance, Voodoo had female ministers, called *queens,* and male ministers, called *doctors,* who presided over certain ceremonies, told fortunes, and cast spells. Some scholars suggest that the use of specific magical items, such as altars and candles, in African American hoodoo started with the Voodoo faith. Vodou, a mix of traditional African religion and Catholicism imported to the United States from Haiti, also contains elements of magic, particularly a belief in spirits, who are the workers of magic.

Conjure is an important part of African American culture, particularly in the South. African American conjure has its roots in slavery and includes European, Native American, and African elements. During the 19th century, it was used by slaves as a way of helping them deal with their awful circumstances, but it was seen as a form of devil worship and a threat to the *status quo* by Christian whites. Even though many whites claimed not to believe in magic, they were still afraid of slaves casting spells on their masters and often forbade magical practices. After emancipation, whites saw conjure not as a threat, but as charlatanry that allowed the unprincipled to prey on simple-minded blacks.

Overall, the most common view of hoodoo throughout the ages has been that it was mere superstition, a sign of being backward. Many whites came to view hoodoo as central to black identity, which helped them support their beliefs in African American inferiority. Educated blacks also removed themselves from hoodoo, as many were ashamed of it. This notion of magic has decreased since the 1970s and has been replaced by a view of conjure as an important expression of black culture. To a large extent the embrace of hoodoo has been a function of the rise of postmodernism, the development of New Age/Neopagan spirituality, and the consequent formulation of multicultural ideologies. A rising acceptance and appreciation of supernaturalism has attracted both blacks and whites to hoodoo. There is currently a strong interest in hoodoo among scholars and the public alike—a stark contrast to how African American magic has been neglected in the past.

Even though lay people can easily use simple charms, such as carrying a rabbit's foot for good luck, professional conjurers are relied upon for specialized magical expertise. Such career practitioners of magic are known as *conjurers*, *rootworkers*, or *trick doctors*, reflecting the magical practices that these individuals partake in. Sometimes, believers refer to such people as *two-headed* or *double-headed doctors*, names that may refer to their knowledge of both physical and spiritual realities. Some modern-day conjurers choose to call themselves names such as *spiritual advisor* or *healer* to avoid the negative connotations associated with the more traditional terminology. Conjurers are divided by scholars into roughly three groups: healers (who heal natural ailments), readers (fortune tellers), and hoodoo doctors (who perform both helpful and harmful magic, such as curing or cursing victims, respectively). These distinctions, however, are not clear cut, as many conjurers work across all three divisions.

African American magical practitioners reportedly acquire their abilities in multiple ways. Some conjurers gain their powers through initiations performed by other hoodooists. Others are said to inherit the gift from their parents or are given their powers as a gift from a god. In the past, especially in the United States, gifting was often indicated by having physical abnormalities or odd features, such as albinism or blue gums.

There are five predominant intended results of magical practices: punishment, diagnosis and fortunetelling, healing, protection from evil forces, and good luck. The specific materials and spells used for each purpose are based on the conjurer's preferences. Curing cursed individuals is one of the most popular actions performed by conjurers. Court case spells are also common; these are intended to sway court proceedings, such as silencing witnesses or influencing jury decisions. Working magic designed to win love, money, or luck is also popular.

Magical items and actions have unique names in different regions. The supernatural milieu of New Orleans provides several examples. There, positive charms are *zinzin*. Harmful charms, meanwhile, are known as *wangas*, a word also found in Haitian Vodou. A general term for both magic and the items it produces is *gris-gris*.

Throughout the United States, magic items, such as charms and magical poisons, are sometimes called *hands* or *mojos*. The phrase *feeding the hand* refers to the common practice of "feeding" a charm with whiskey or oils in order for it to retain its power. *Fixing* is a term for placing a curse on someone, with insanity, illness, or death being common desired outcomes. Cross marks, on the other hand, are powerful symbols used for protection against such actions.

Materials used in magic are traditionally items found in nature, such as plants, minerals, and animal parts. Animal bones are frequently employed for spells, and High John the Conqueror Root is one of the most well-known plants used for positive magic. Many conjurers use graveyard dirt or goopher dust for harmful spells or hexes. Everyday manmade objects can also be used for spells and charms. For example, the Bible, perfumes, and candles are all common conjure tools. Different times of day, such as midnight, and specific places, such as graveyards, also have magical powers. Charms and spells vary from the very simple, such as placing a High John the Conqueror Root in one's pocket for protection, to intricate rituals that use many materials and consist of elaborate steps that must be followed closely in order for the magic to work.

Conjure has evolved over the years, becoming commercialized and consumer-oriented with a modern rise in spiritual supply stores that sell mass-produced hoodoo goods. This development has increased uniformity in the practice of hoodoo, erasing regional variations. Items like special candles encased in glass are manufactured specifically for magical uses. There is also an increasing popularity in self-help books of magic and do-it-yourself hoodoo manuals, which teach various spells and charms, as well as dreambooks that are used to help pick winning lottery numbers.

People often turn to hoodoo and other forms of magic when circumstances are difficult, which is why belief in them is popular among poor and oppressed populations. People consult conjurers because of their hope that magic can help with their troubles. Despite its spiritual basis, magic has efficacy beyond beliefs in the supernatural. It can, for example, bring healing though the use of medicinal plants, because of the psychological benefits of having an attentive listener for one's troubles, or through the placebo effect of thinking one has been magically cured of an ailment. Fear can also bring about the deaths or psychosomatic illnesses of enemies. In addition, conjurers often just give good, common-sense advice under the guise of magical instructions. No matter how the results happen, magic has often been shown to be effective.

See also: Conjure; Gris-gris; Hoodoo; Laveau, Marie; Modern Voodoo/Vodou and Hoodoo Businesses; Mojo; New Age and Neopaganism and Voodoo/Vodou; Rootwork; Vodou in Haiti; Voodoo in the Mississippi Valley

Urszula Pruchniewska

Further Reading

Anderson, Jeffrey E. 2005. *Conjure in African American Society*. Baton Rouge, LA: Louisiana State University Press.

Anderson, Jeffrey E. 2008. *Hoodoo, Voodoo, and Conjure: A Handbook*. Greenwood Folklore Handbooks. Westport, CT: Greenwood Press.

Bellegarde-Smith, Patrick. Interview by Krista Tippett. January 9, 2014. "Living Vodou." Audio podcast. *On Being with Krista Tippett*. Accessed February 21, 2014: http://www.onbeing.org/program/living-vodou/128.

Brown, Karen McCarthy. 2001. *Mama Lola: A Vodou Priestess in Brooklyn*. Updated and expanded ed. Berkeley: University of California Press.

Greenwood, Susan. 2005. *The Nature of Magic: An Anthropology of Consciousness*. New York: Berg.

Hoodoo Muse: The Worldwide Web of Conjure. 2013. Accessed February 21, 2014: http://hoodoomuse.blogspot.com/.

Lucky Mojo Curio Company. 1994–2014. Accessed February 21, 2014: http://www.luckymojo.com.

Ward, Martha. 2004. *Voodoo Queen: The Spirited Lives of Marie Laveau*. Jackson, MS: UP of Mississippi.

MAKANDAL

François Makandal, often known simply as Makandal, was an opponent of French rule in Saint-Domingue. Reportedly a native African, Makandal was enslaved and forced to work on a plantation. Following an accident that left him maimed, he escaped and became a maroon leader. He gathered about him followers who supposedly considered him an immortal mouthpiece for God. As such, they believed he could foretell the future. In 1757, Makandal began a campaign to disrupt white rule in the island, reportedly with the goal of completely driving the French from Saint-Domingue. Among his tactics were raids and vandalism, but he became most famous for killing slave masters by poisoning wells. Some sources claim that as many as 6,000 were poisoned in this manner, though scholar Pierre Pluchon has argued that the number was far lower. Whatever the number killed, Makandal struck fear into the hearts of the French colonists.

The rebel leader met a gruesome end the year after beginning his campaign. The French, who desperately wanted to suppress the poisoning, captured him when he unwisely visited a plantation in order to attend a dance. He was condemned to die by being burned at the stake. Though many slaves believed that he would use magic to avoid execution, he proved unable to do so, though he did manage to briefly escape the flames when he ripped from the soil the stake to which he was bound. Those supervising the burning quickly returned him to the fire, however.

Despite his short career, Makandal made a lasting impact on the culture and history of Saint-Domingue, which would become the nation of Haiti approximately two generations after his death. Modern authors, in fact, often present him as a freedom fighter and forerunner of the Haitian Revolution. He certainly inspired his followers to oppose the oppression of the French. His reputation for spiritual power was so great that many slaves refused to believe that he had died. Although his body was destroyed by the flames, his name lived on as a word meaning "poison for enemies."

There is some disagreement about Makandal's background. According to LeGrace Benson, a contributor to the 2006 book *Invisible Powers*, he was a Muslim who spent time in Jamaica before being transported to Saint-Domingue. On the other hand, Hein Vanhee argued in an essay appearing in *Central Africans and Cultural Transformation in the American Diaspora* (2002) that Makandal was of Kongo origin. According to Vanhee, the name *Makandal* is strikingly similar to Kongo terms referring to herbalists, those who administer ritual poisons, and spiritual specialists in general.

See also: Haitian Revolution; Kongo; Maroon; Vodou in Haiti

Jeffrey E. Anderson

Further Reading

Heywood, Linda M., ed. 2002. *Central Africans and Cultural Transformations in the American Diaspora*. Cambridge, UK: Cambridge University Press.

Métraux, Alfred. 1972. *Voodoo in Haiti*. Translated by Hugo Charteris and with an Introduction by Sidney W. Mintz. New York: Schocken.

Michel, Claudine, and Patrick Bellegarde-Smith, eds. 2006. *Vodou in Haitian Life and Culture: Invisible Powers*. New York: Palgrave Macmillan.

Pluchon, Pierre. 1987. *Vaudou, Sorciers, Empoissoneurs: De Saint-Domingue à Haïti*. Paris: Karthala.

MAMBO

Mambo, or *manbo*, is a class of female clergy in the religion of Haitian Vodou. They are leaders of their societies, give service to the spirits, and act in accordance with the reglemen of Haitian Vodou. The word *mambo* is derived from the Fon name *nana* or mother. Combined with the word *bo* for spirit, *mambo* can be translated as "Mother of the spirit," an accurate description of the work performed by a mambo. Mambos in Haitian Vodou are required by their vows of ordination to serve their own family spirits, their immediate society's needs, and their community at large. The ever-expanding religious and secular nature of a Vodou society requires the mambo to be many things at the same time.

A Vodou mambo can be one of two ranks, su pwen or asogwe. The lower of the two is mambo su pwen or mambo "on point." A mambo su pwen is said to be "borrowing" the ason from her mambo or oungan asogwe. This is a veiled reference to the work she must do to earn the rank of asogwe. Mambo su pwen is the position where one learns how to become the leader of a Vodou society, called a *sosyete*. She can hold different positions in the sosyete such as ren drapo or flag queen. She is often the oungenikon, or song mistress, of the sosyete, building an encyclopedic knowledge of the songs for service. A mambo su pwen acts as the helper for the asogwe, learning alongside the asogwe. By shadowing the asogwe, a mambo su pwen learns the reglemen of the house: how to perform a successful ceremony for the lwa; what is entailed in the various rituals such as lave tèts and kanzo; and, most importantly, how to facilitate healing for the various segments of the community who come to the sosyete for help. Not all healing takes place within a service.

> ### Voodoo and Women
>
> Both Haitian Vodou and Mississippi Valley Voodoo are unusual among world religions in that they allow women to enter the priesthood. In Haiti, female priests, known as *mambos*, are highly respected individuals, operating their own ounfòs much as would men in their positions. Many deities are also female, including among their number Ezili Freda, among the most beloved of all lwa. In North America, women historically were even more prominent than in the Caribbean nation. Although female deities do not appear to have been as common as male ones, women composed a substantial majority of the priesthood.

Skills such as divination, dream analysis, medical knowledge, and common sense all play a role in the development of a mambo su pwen.

Mambo asogwe is the top rank in Vodou. Women receiving this rank have demonstrated their konesans, or spiritual knowledge, of the reglemen and their ability to facilitate communion between the congregation and the spirits. This is the rank of selfless service to everyone—her immediate family, the sosyete she leads, and the community in which she lives.

On the religious level, a mambo asogwe has demonstrated her konesans of service. She knows the prayers, invocations, and secret names of the lwa. She has demonstrated her grasp of the musicality required to bring about communion with the divine and has shown herself to be a skilled negotiator by facilitating contracts between the spirits and the congregation. Moreover, she has shown the talent, skill, and energy needed to lead a multilevel service to the spirits long into the night.

Mambo asogwes are not only skilled leaders, but they are empowered by Papa Loko to ordain other initiates, including priests. No other rank in Haitian Vodou may do that. Having received her ason directly from the hand of Papa Loko Attissou, she is fully empowered to raise initiates, ordain priests, and lead a sosyete on her own.

On a secular level, mambo asogwes are also healers and are called upon for many things within the community. Marital counseling, bereavement consolation, birthing ceremonies, and arbitration are just some of the many talents required of asogwes. They provide whatever is needed for their hunyos, or spirit children: meals, school supplies, or places to sleep for the night for those who have no place of their own. People understand that when a large service such as a multiday kanzo is being held, there will be food offered as part of the ceremonies. Feeding the membership and guests is how an asogwe demonstrates her konesans to the community. A strong asogwe has the power to care for everyone because her lwa provide for her to do so. Furthermore, asogwes are required to perform acts of charity, such as organizing food drives and providing medical assistance and clothing for the less fortunate of their communities. It is understood that a mambo asogwe's konesans will enable her to do the work required of her by the community. Mambo asogwes' time and talent belong to the community, and they are forever in service to the lwa, the sosyete, and the congregation at large. Service is the hallmark of a mambo asogwe in Haitian Vodou.

See also: Divination; Kanzo; Konesans; Lave Tèt; Ounfò; Oungan

Patricia Scheu (Mambo Vye Zo Komande LaMenfo)

Further Reading

Blier, Suzanne Preston. 1995. *African Vodoun: Art, Psychology, and Power.* Chicago: University of Chicago Press.

Scheu, Patricia (Mambo Vye Zo Komande LaMenfo). 2011. *Serving the Spirits: The Religion of Vodou.* Philadelphia: Published by author.

MANJE-YANM (EATING OF THE YAMS)

Yam culture is an ancient tradition that developed among the Igbo many centuries before they had contact with the outside world. The practice of venerating the yam spirit is a cultural event that marks the beginning of the harvest season. Among the Igbo, yam is the king of all crops and enjoys primacy in their social and religious life. Yam is believed to have a spirit-force known as *ahajioku* or *njoku*. The African slaves rediscovered the yam feast in Haiti. Among Haitians, the yam feast is known as *manje-yanm*. It is the only public ceremony that is related to harvest in Haiti. The manje-yanm in Haiti corresponds with the new yam festival in Igboland. Among the Igbo, the new yam feast is called *Iriji* or *Ikeji*. Whereas the new yam festival is celebrated in October in Haiti, different Igbo communities celebrate it between August and September, for ecological reasons. Just as in Haiti, the new yam festival is an occasion in which farmers give thanks to the earth goddess, the spirit of fertility, for a good yield and successful harvest in the farming season. It also marks the end and beginning of a new year in Igbo society.

There are minor variations in the way different Igbo communities celebrate the new yam. In some places, the feast starts on an *Afor* market day. On this day, various communities alert their members of the commencement of the festival by sounding the *ikoro*, a big cylindrical drum with a carved human head. By this alert, farmers are formally informed to go to their farms and harvest the new yam for the first time after planting. The harvest usually takes place the following market day (*Nkwo*). On the succeeding market day, *Eke*, the yam priest, known as *Elomji* or *Ezeji*, offers a sacrifice of fowl or goat to the yam spirit. Other family heads offer similar sacrifices to the yam spirit at their individual shrines. They pour libations, offer kola nuts, and pray to the yam spirit for a safe consumption of the new yam. After the rituals, individuals then eat the new yam. These rites are common among the Igbo and Haitians.

In Haiti, the new yam feast lasts for about two days, whereas it goes on for four days in Igboland. During the celebration, people who share the same ancestors gather together to celebrate. Those who live in distant places go back to their ancestral homes for the festival. Such a gathering offers a good opportunity for children to learn about their family history. Families also use the occasion to settle quarrels between members. It is a common belief among many Igbo communities that members of the same ancestral family do not eat the new yam at the common gathering with bitterness.

Yam culture in Igboland was so advanced that the planting, harvest, and consumption of yam were highly ritualized and guided by religious sanctions. Yam was not cooked with "inferior" crops such as cassava and maize. A woman could not throw a yam tuber in anger. Women did not quarrel or fight on a yam farm. People were also forbidden from defecating on the yam farm. These were considered desecration of the yam spirit.

In the present Igbo society, the ritualization of the new yam feast has been further advanced with the institutionalization of an annual lecture series known as Ahajioku Lecture. Ahajioku Lecture is an intellectual harvest instituted by Igbo scholars from different parts of the world to commemorate the celebration of the new yam festival. Thus, the feast of the new yam is the single most important festival that every Igbo community celebrates. The new yam festival is no longer a strictly agrarian practice. Igbos in North America and Europe who have no access to any farmland symbolically celebrate the new yam. Its survival in Haiti supports the claim that many of the slaves that were moved to Haiti were of Igbo origin.

See also: Ceremonies; Kanzo; Lave Tèt; Slavery and the Slave Trade

Arua Oko Omaka

Further Reading
Afigbo, A. E. 1981. *Ropes of Sand: Studies in Igbo History and Culture*. Ibadan, Nigeria: University Press Limited.
Métraux, Alfred. 1972. *Voodoo in Haiti*. Translated by Hugo Charteris and with an Introduction by Sidney W. Mintz. New York: Schocken.
Uchendu, V. C. 1965. *The Igbo of Southeastern Nigeria*. New York: Holt, Rinehart and Winston.

MAROON

Maroons were runaway slaves who founded settlements, typically in remote areas, beyond the control of whites. These escapees sometimes formed communities that lasted for many years. They existed in every New World society with a substantial slave population and sufficient land suitable for concealed settlements. Villages of escaped slaves began to develop during the 16th century in Spanish colonies, and they soon began to appear in the colonies of their British, French, Dutch, and Portuguese competitors. The largest of all maroon communities was Palmares, in Brazil, which had as many as 30,000 inhabitants at its height during the 17th century. Though many maroon societies eventually fell to whites, some survived into the present.

Hispaniola, the island that eventually became home to the French colony of Saint-Domingue and modern Haiti, had its own maroon communities beginning in the 16th century. In 1655, the Spanish, who then controlled the island, even authorized the existence of one such settlement of free blacks. Following the establishment of the French colony of Saint-Domingue, as many as five hundred practiced marronage in the mountains that divided the French and Spanish portions of the islands.

Maroons were a disruptive force in Hispaniola. During the 16th and 17th centuries, the former slaves conducted raids, stealing food and supplies and burning plantations. Though they were a threat to whites throughout the island, during the period of French rule in Saint-Domingue, they were most active in the northern portion of the colony. One of the most famous of all maroons in Saint-Domingue and elsewhere was Makandal, who carried out a campaign of poisoning prior to his capture and execution in 1758. Boukman, the slave who led the Vodou ceremony that reportedly sparked the Haitian Revolution can also be understood as a maroon. Though a slave at the time of the ceremony, his subsequent self-liberation and attacks on plantations were very much in keeping with the other instances of marronage.

Maroon communities also existed in North America. The Lowcountry of South Carolina and Georgia provided the dense forests, swamps, and plentiful food required by hidden settlements, and a handful sprang up during the 18th century. By 1786, a maroon village on an island in the Savannah River reportedly had over one hundred inhabitants. The Spanish colony of Florida had its own maroon settlements, a development helped by the long-term Spanish policy of granting freedom to runaways from British North America and the United States who made their way to the colony. The Spanish policy was designed to weaken their competitors to the north as well as populate their own colony with loyal subjects willing to help defend it. Just north of St. Augustine was North America's most famous maroon settlement, Gracia Real de Santa Teresa de Mose, commonly known as Fort Mose, a state-sponsored community and military outpost that played an important role in the defense of Florida between 1738 and 1763.

Louisiana had several maroon communities during the 18th century. It was a particularly easy colony in which to form runaway communities because of its numerous and inaccessible cypress swamps. Moreover, geography and French law dictated that most of the plantations that lined the Mississippi River and other waterways were long and narrow, stretching from the river to the cypress swamps in their rear. Escape for slaves and communication between maroons and multiple plantations was easy in such an environment.

Maroons and Voodoo/Vodou

The popular imagination links maroons with Voodoo and Vodou. The reasons for the ties are clear in that both the religions and the existence of maroon communities once represented resistance to slavery. In Haiti, maroons clearly took part in the struggle against bondage and doubtless contributed to the formation of Voodoo. Maroon communities also existed in colonial Louisiana, but they proved transitory. While it is reasonable to assume that some form of creole religion was a part of life in such communities, there is no way to know what its impact was on the development of Voodoo.

Maroons were a consistent presence during the colonial era. During the early 18th century, when significant numbers of Native America slaves served alongside African Americans, members of both races frequently escaped together. Over time, the enslavement of Indians declined, and many native peoples served as fugitive slave hunters rather than allies. Though blacks were left to form their maroon communities alone, they continued to do so in large numbers.

Many Louisianan slaves left in families, taking arms with them, to set up settlements that would last for years. Though early runaways lived by hunting, gathering, and raiding plantations, late 18th-century maroons generally grew crops and traded with slaves and whites for their livelihood. Even some slaveholders relied on them for goods and services, notably lumbering and the production of food and crafts.

By the 1780s, maroons controlled a large portion of the Mississippi River Delta east of New Orleans, which they called Gaillardeland. They operated from several villages and were led by an escaped slave called St. Maló. Colonial officials feared St. Maló's maroons, who maintained contacts with slaves throughout the colony. Not only did they provide refuge in the swamps to runaways, but they were a military threat to the colony. During 1783 and 1784, the Spanish rulers of Louisiana conducted a series of attacks on the Gaillardeland maroons, which eventually resulted in the capture and execution of St. Maló himself. Despite his defeat, St. Maló remained the subject of folklore until after the Civil War.

Popular interpretations link maroons with the development of Vodou and Voodoo. Desmangles argues that this was indeed the case in Saint-Domingue, where their villages preserved ethnically specific bodies of belief. While it would be surprising if African Diasporic religions were not also practiced by Louisiana maroons, there is little evidence to demonstrate a particularly strong influence on Voodoo. Maroons' small numbers compared to the enslaved population surrounding them and their communities' generally brief survival made them unlikely shapers of the faith.

See also: Boukman, Dutty; Makandal

Jeffrey E. Anderson

Further Reading

Desmangles, Leslie G. 1992. *Faces of the Gods: Vodou and Roman Catholicism in Haiti.* Chapel Hill, NC: University of North Carolina Press.

Hall, Gwendolyn Midlo. 1992. *Africans in Colonial Louisiana: The Development of Afro-Creole Culture in the Eighteenth Century.* Baton Rouge, LA: Louisiana State University Press.

Landers, Jane. 1999. *Black Society in Spanish Florida.* With a Foreword by Peter H. Wood. Urbana, IL: University of Illinois Press.

Morgan, Philip D. 1998. *Slave Counterpoint: Black Culture in the Eighteenth-Century Chesapeake and Low Country.* Chapel Hill, NC: University of North Carolina Press.

Price, Richard. 1996. *Maroon Societies: Rebel Slave Communities in the Americas.* 3rd ed. Baltimore: Johns Hopkins University Press.

Rodriguez, Junius P. 2007. *Encyclopedia of Slave Resistance and Rebellion.* 2 vols. Westport, CT: Greenwood Press.

MARYAJ LWA (MARRIAGE TO LWA)

This ceremony, found among Vodu practitioners in West Africa as well as in Haitian Vodou, centers around marriage to a lwa. It constitutes a lifelong commitment to a particular lwa but does not preclude honoring other spirits.

The lwa takes the lead in seeking out a human spouse. Moreover, the lwas can choose to marry someone of the same sex as well as the opposite sex. As Mambo Vye Zo Komande LaMenfo put it in regard to Ogou, "Ogoun is a huge spiritual dimension . . . Ogoun is everything we make of him and much, much more. Hence, he can marry anyone he pleases!" Though being married to a human partner does not usually prevent one wedding a lwa, if the person espousing the deity is not already married, he or she is sometimes barred from taking a human spouse future.

The ceremony itself strongly resembles that of an ordinary marriage. During the ritual, a person possessed by the lwa involved is the counterpart to the human seeking the union. Along with the two principal participants, rings usually appear in the festivities. In some cases, these are expected to be expensive. Ezili, for example, wants her human partner to wear a golden ring with her name and her spouse's initials engraved on it. Other lwa, such as Ogou, do not demand great expenditures, expecting simple rings of iron, representing his connection to fire and forges. Marriage contracts, often read aloud at the start of ceremonies, and wedding cake are also incorporated into the festivities.

Following the union, the human marriage partner sets aside one or more days a week to serve his or her spirit spouse. On such days, typically those already sacred to the lwa, the human partner wears the favored colors of his or her spouse. In many cases, certain activities are forbidden on these days. For instance, Ezili will not allow those married to her to dance, smoke, drink, or gamble on Tuesdays or Thursdays. At night, the earthbound spouse sleeps alone and abstains from sexual activity, even if married to a human partner. In addition to honoring one's spiritual spouse, the night alone serves as a time for the lwa to communicate through dreams.

See also: Dahomey; Ewe; Ezili; Initiations; Kanzo; Ogou; Possession; Vodu in West Africa

Jeffrey E. Anderson

Further Reading

Hebblethwaite, Benjamin. 2012. *Vodou Songs in Haitian Creole and English*. Philadelphia: Temple University Press.

McCarthy-Brown, Karen. 2006. "Afro-Caribbean Spirituality: A Haitian Case Study." In *Vodou in Haitian Life and Culture: Invisible Powers*, edited by Patrick Bellegarde-Smith and Claudine Michel, 1–26. New York: Palgrave Macmillan.

Scheu, Patricia (Mambo Vye Zo Komande LaMenfo). 2011. *Serving the Spirits: The Religion of Vodou*. Philadelphia: Published by author.

MÉTRAUX, ALFRED

Alfred Métraux was born in Lausanne, Switzerland, in 1902 and then lived most of his childhood in Argentina where his father was a well-known surgeon. He travelled extensively throughout his life and career, but sadly his body was found near the Chateaux de la Madeleine in the Vallée de Chevreuse approximately 30 km outside Paris in 1963. Here, just a few months after his sixtieth birthday, he took his own life.

Métraux is best known for his pioneering historical and cultural anthropology and ethnographical research, especially the work he undertook in South America, Easter Island, and Haiti. He also helped to establish the framework for the United Nations Declaration of Human Rights. It was his work in Haiti during the 1940s that led to his text, *Voodoo in Haiti*. The book appeared in French in 1959 and was then translated into English by Hugo Charteris. As with many of his works, the text was accompanied by drawings and photographs from his fieldwork.

Unlike previous writers, Métraux undertook fieldwork in Haiti to observe and understand the religion and culture of the Haitian people with a focus on Vodou. He was so outraged at the persecution of Vodou that he, along with the Haitian writer Jacques Roumain, was instrumental in the formation of the Bureau of Ethnology for Haiti. Métraux did not write a sensationalist account but an objective description in an attempt to redress the myths and stereotypes that had permeated the Western imagination. In contrast to the texts of the first half of the 20th century, *Voodoo in Haiti* established that Vodou is a religion and nothing more than a conglomeration of beliefs and rites of African origin and does not relate to the character it was given in previous publications. This text is invaluable for its contribution to the representation of Haitian culture. Along with writers such as Milo Rigaud, Harold Courlander, and Maya Deren, Métraux helped to dispel the myth and misrepresentation of Vodou.

See also: Courlander, Harold; Hurston, Zora Neale

Louise Fenton

Further Reading

Courlander, Harold. 1960. *The Drum and the Hoe: Life and Lore of the Haitian People*. Oakland, CA: University of California Press.

Deren, Maya. 1953. *Divine Horsemen: The Living Gods of Haiti*. London and New York: Thames and Hudson.

Hurston, Zora Neale. 1938. *Tell My Horse: Voodoo and Life in Haiti and Jamaica*. Philadelphia: J. B. Lippincott.

Métraux, Alfred. *Voodoo in Haiti*. 1972. Translated by Hugo Charteris and with an Introduction by Sidney W. Mintz. New York: Schocken.

Rigaud, Milo. 1985 [1969]. *Secrets of Voodoo*. Translated by Robert B. Cross. New York: Arco; reprint, San Francisco: City Lights.

MICHEL, CLAUDINE

Michel has had a wide and varied career. She began her professional life teaching kindergarten, secondary school, and college courses in Haiti. While doing so, she also produced two children's educational television series for Haitian audiences. At present, Michel is a professor in the Department of Black Studies at the University of California, Santa Barbara, where she served as chair of two departments and as an assistant dean.

In addition to possessing impressive credentials as an educator, Michel is also an active scholar and defender of Haitian culture and religion. Her first book-length study of Vodou was *Aspects Educatifs et Moraux du Vodou Haïtien* (1995). She has also edited several volumes of essays, among the more notable of which were two 2006 collections, *Haitian Vodou: Spirit, Myth, and Reality* and *Vodou in Haitian Life and Culture: Invisible Powers*. Her numerous other works include books and articles that address aspects of gender, education, and culture in Haiti. In addition to her writing, Michel is the editor of the peer-reviewed *Journal of Haitian Studies*. She is also a founding member of the Congress of Santa Barbara (KOSANBA), an organization of scholars devoted to the study and defense of Haitian Vodou. Professor Michel's extensive multidisciplinary work has made her one of the leading scholars of Vodou and Haitian life in general.

See also: Bellegarde-Smith, Patrick; Congress of Santa Barbara (KOSANBA); Desmangles, Leslie

Jeffrey E. Anderson

Further Reading

"Claudine Michel, Professor." 2013. Department of Black Studies, University of California, Santa Barbara. Accessed August 21, 2013: http://www.blackstudies.ucsb.edu/people/bios/michel.html.

Michel, Claudine. 1995. *Aspects Educatifs et Moraux du Vodou Haïtien*. Port-au-Prince, Haiti: Le Natal.

Michel, Claudine, and Patrick Bellegarde-Smith, eds. 2006. *Haitian Vodou: Spirit, Myth, and Reality*. Bloomington, IN: Indiana University Press.

Michel, Claudine, and Patrick Bellegarde-Smith, eds. 2006. *Vodou in Haitian Life and Culture: Invisible Powers*. New York: Palgrave Macmillan.

MODERN VOODOO/VODOU AND HOODOO BUSINESSES

In some places, Vodou, Voodoo, and hoodoo incorporate a business aspect. Vodouisants, for instance, sometimes rely on businesses known as *botanikas* that sell materials needed for communal ceremonies, personal devotion, and the performance of private rituals. Among items commonly found in these shops are images of the saints, herbs, and ceremonial attire. Some also offer divination services and may sell animals for sacrifice. Such businesses are particularly common in the Haitian Diaspora and are numerous in places like Miami, Florida, which has a large Haitian community. Owners are often—but not always—oungans or mambos. While botanikas are certainly a growing part of the United States' African Diasporic landscape, they are by no means the only businesses of their kind in the country. Similar ventures belonging to other African Diasporic religions meet the needs of American practitioners of the faith as well as those practicing hoodoo or seeking to revive Mississippi Valley Voodoo.

Scholars debate the degree to which hoodoo and Mississippi Valley Voodoo should be considered business practices. According to Kodi Roberts, author of the forthcoming *Voodoo and the Promise of Power*, New Orleans's Voodoo is properly considered a form of business endeavor through which workers, both black and white, sell access to spiritual power to their clients and customers. He includes not just individual practitioners, such as Marie Laveau, in his business-oriented concept of Voodoo but also Spiritual Churches, which he understands as having developed as a way to mask supernatural businesses behind the trappings of Christian churches. A rival understanding has been expressed by Katrina Hazzard-Donald, author of *Mojo Workin'* (2013), an examination of hoodoo. Hazzard-Donald dismisses the idea that such practices should be considered businesses and instead argues that they constitute a true religion. Those who use it primarily for profit, she argues, are illegitimate marketeers.

Tourism rather than simple faith or ritual practice has been a driving force in many modern Voodoo businesses, a fact particularly evident in New Orleans. The city's numerous ghost and supernatural tours frequently visit places associated with the faith and its notable adherents. In fact, the tomb of Marie Laveau is one of the better known sites in the area. Visitors, whether they believe in Voodoo or not, frequently leave offerings to the Voodoo Queen's spirit. Other locales frequented by tours are Congo Square and the temples of modern believers.

While the religion is a part of many tours, it takes center stage in some businesses. The New Orleans Historic Voodoo Museum is the best known of these. The museum itself plays to stereotypical images of the religion in order to attract customers while also seeking to portray it in a sympathetic manner. In addition to the museum itself, the business houses a shop selling supernatural items, offers tours, and provides Voodoo-themed entertainment. Voodoo Authentica of New Orleans Cultural Center and Collection is a similar business. Like the Historic Voodoo Museum, it contains some displays, organizes Voodoo events for groups of all sizes, and sells a variety of ritual items. It also hosts an annual Voodoofest each Halloween, which is free to the public.

In addition to businesses that memorialize or promote Voodoo, there are a variety of retail shops that seek to capitalize off the Crescent City's vast tourist trade. The best known of these is probably Marie Laveau's House of Voodoo, located in the heart of the city's chief tourist thoroughfare, Bourbon Street. Though geared primarily to attract customers by playing to stereotypes associating the faith with death, mystery, and spells, it also sells a wide variety of how-to books and items associated with both Voodoo and hoodoo. Alongside the genuine paraphernalia are tee shirts and other souvenir items as well as materials drawn from other religious traditions, such as Santería, Mexican folk Catholicism, European occultism, and Neopaganism. A similar business is Reverend Zombie's House of Voodoo. In addition to these two shops, numerous other stores in the city sell items that at least pay lip service to the religion. Shirts emblazoned with Voodoo-inspired phrases and "Voodoo dolls" are ubiquitous across the New Orleans souvenir market.

In contrast to Voodoo proper, hoodoo and conjure have contained a business component since at least the 19th century. During the days of slavery, fortunetellers and magic workers required payment for their services. Sometimes, the fees took the form of hard-to-come-by cash. On other occasions, bondspersons settled their tabs through barter. Following emancipation, the business aspect of hoodoo easily adapted to African Americans' changing circumstances.

As with many other aspects of American life, hoodoo and conjure adopted the trappings of modern industrial commercialism. At the heart of the development was a diminished role for the professional hoodoo worker–client relationship following the rise of shops selling ready-made items to customers. These businesses tended to minimize the sort of in-depth consultation and customized charm and spell work associated with 19th-century conjure and hoodoo, replacing them with advice from sales clerks on what products best suited customers' supernatural needs. The first shops to appear were probably hoodoo drugstores. Many of these began life as standard pharmacies that catered to the needs of an African American clientele. Repeated requests for herbal and magical items eventually persuaded some pharmacists to regularly carry such products. In a few cases, the magical aspect of such businesses displaced their original role as dispensers of medicines. Author George Washington Cable indicated that as early as the first decade of the 19th century, some African Americans expected New Orleans's pharmacies to carry magical items, including the 'Tit Albert. At any rate, several hoodoo drugstores have been well documented in the New Orleans area, serving both the Voodoo faithful and those whose interest extended no further than the desire for supernatural power. Among the best known were the Cracker Jack Drug Store, which operated in the city from 1897 to 1974, and Dixie Drugstore, which sold hoodoo supplies until 1984.

Not all spiritual supply businesses were connected to pharmacies, however. Conjure and hoodoo practitioners themselves sometimes opened shops. Such was the case with Jim Jordan of Como, North Carolina, who gradually transformed himself from a small-scale conjurer into the owner of a large spiritual supply shop as well as other businesses. Today, the most prominent New Orleans spiritual supply business is the F and F Candle Shop, which is located outside the portion of the city frequented by tourists. Though some sightseers manage to make their way there, it caters primarily to practitioners of supernaturalism and followers of African Diasporic faiths. Following the rise of Spiritual Churches during the early decades of the 20th century, their leaders have sometimes opened shops to cater to the needs of members. The same is true to modern-day Vodou practitioners and Voodoo revivalists in New Orleans. One example can be found in Miriam Chamani's Voodoo Spiritual Temple. It acts both as a religious organization and retails a variety of Voodoo- and Vodou-related items, some intended for tourists and others for practitioners.

The products sold by modern spiritual supply shops are a mixture of traditional items and newer products. Most shops sell biological and herbal curios that are more or less the same as what 19th-century conjurers would have gathered from nature. Alongside them are books, such as *The Sixth and Seventh Books of Moses*, that have had a place in African American supernaturalism since at least the early 20th century. Joining these old staples of conjure and hoodoo are items of modern manufacture. Some entered the practice during the early 20th century, notable examples of which are various colognes used in love spells. Other items are manufactured specifically for the magical trade and include oils, powders, incense, and aerosol sprays. Many of them bear names referencing traditional items, such as black cat bones or a root charm known as John the Conqueror. Otherwise, they have little in common with their namesakes.

The new additions to the hoodoo and conjure repertoire are largely manufactured items. Some are produced on a small scale by the shops that sell them, as in the case of the F and F Candle Shop. Others come from large-scale spiritual supply manufacturers that sell their products to multiple shops across the nation or even overseas. One of the earliest to produce items for a distinctively African American market was DeLaurence, Scott, and Company, later known as the L. W. DeLaurence Company. Though originally geared toward a largely white clientele, it had begun to market itself to black customers by the early 20th century. By the 1930s, many of its magical how-to guides had become staples of African American supernaturalism. During the first half of the 20th century, major rivals of the DeLaurence Company were Chicago's Valmor Company and Keystone Laboratories of Memphis, Tennessee. Indio Products, founded in 1991, is currently the largest manufacturer of hoodoo and conjure items.

Since the late 19th century many manufacturers and individual practitioners of Voodoo, hoodoo, and conjure have broadened their markets by making their products available by mail. Exactly who was the first to avail himself or herself of the post is unknown, but among those who certainly relied on the mail was Dr. Buzzard of Beaufort, South Carolina, who was second only to Marie Laveau in fame. Laveau herself does not appear to have engaged in mail-order Voodoo and hoodoo business, but other New Orleans workers did. Among the better known were Julius P. Caesar, who practiced around the turn of the 20th century, and Rockford Lewis, who was in business from the 1920s to the 1950s. Unfortunately for many practitioners, using the mail to conduct business was risky because it opened them to prosecution on federal charges of mail fraud. Rockford Lewis, a very well-known figure in his day, spent two years in prison after a conviction.

Some practitioners developed significant marketing acumen. Fliers, for instance, were a common feature of hoodoo and conjure businesses by the early 20th century. By the late 19th century, African American newspapers sometimes carried advertisements for magical goods that buyers could order. As African American beliefs spread into northern cities during the Great Migration of the 1910s and beyond, similar ads began to flood the pages of the *Chicago Defender*, the United States' premier African American periodical. During the 1990s, African Diasporic practice made its way online. The Lucky Mojo Curio Company has one of the most extensive websites, supplementing its mail-order business with extensive data on the practice of hoodoo and other supernatural subjects. Lucky Mojo is certainly not alone, however. Indio Products and other manufacturers also have significant online presences. Even individual shops and Voodoo and Vodou congregations tend to have their own websites.

Since the 19th century, Voodoo and hoodoo have proven quite profitable. Marie Laveau, for instance, while never rich, was certainly not poor. At times, she even possessed sufficient funds to own slaves. According to some, her contemporary, Jean Montanée, was considerably more successful, amassing a sizeable fortune. Hoodoo and conjure practitioners could also become quite well-to-do. Caroline Dye, a conjure woman from Newport, Arkansas, reportedly used the proceeds from her work to purchase eight farms. Although some older hoodoo businesses, like the Cracker Jack, have closed in recent decades, many others have appeared in their place. Rising interest in both Voodoo and hoodoo will likely keep them open for many years.

See also: Black Cat Bone; Books; Conjure; Dolls; Drugstores; Hoodoo; Laveau, Marie; Legislation against Vodou/Voodoo; Montanée, Jean; New Age and Neopaganism and Voodoo/Vodou; New Orleans; *The Sixth and Seventh Books of Moses*; Spiritual Churches; *'Tit Albert*; Tourism; Worker

Jeffrey E. Anderson

Further Reading

Anderson, Jeffrey E. 2005. *Conjure in African American Society*. Baton Rouge, LA: Louisiana State UP.

Cable, George Washington. 1891. *The Grandissimes: A Story of Creole Life*. New York: Charles Scribner's Sons.

Davis, Rod. 1999. *American Voudou: Journey into a Hidden World*. Denton, TX: University of North Texas Press.

Hazzard-Donald, Katrina. 2013. *Mojo Workin': The Old African American Hoodoo System*. Urbana, IL: University of Illinois Press.

Johnson, F. Roy. 1963. *The Fabled Doctor Jim Jordan: A Story of Conjure*. Murfreesboro, TN: Johnson.

Long, Carolyn Morrow. 2014. "The Cracker Jack: A Hoodoo Drugstore in the 'Cradle of Jazz'." *Louisiana Cultural Vistas* (Spring): 64–75.

Long, Carolyn Morrow. 2006. *A New Orleans Voudou Priestess: The Legend and Reality of Marie Laveau*. Gainesville, FL: University Press of Florida.

Long, Carolyn Morrow. 2001. *Spiritual Merchants: Religion, Magic, and Commerce*. Knoxville, TN: University of Tennessee Press.

Marie Laveau's House of Voodoo. Accessed June 5, 2014: http://www.voodooneworleans.com/.

McTeer, James Edwin. 1970. *High Sheriff of the Low Country*. With an Introduction by William L. Rhodes, Jr. Columbia, SC: JEM Company.

McTeer, James Edwin. 1976. *Fifty Years as a Low Country Witch Doctor*. Beaufort, SC: Beaufort Book Company.

New Orleans Historic Voodoo Museum. 2009. Accessed June 4, 2014: http://www.voodoomuseum.com/.

Roberts, Kodi. In press. *Voodoo and the Promise of Power: The Racial, Gender & Economic Politics of Religion in New Orleans, 1881–1940*. Baton Rouge, LA: Louisiana State University Press.

Turlington, Shannon R. 2002. *The Complete Idiot's Guide® to Voodoo*. Indianapolis: Alpha.

Voodoo Authentica. 1996–2014. Accessed June 4, 2014: http://voodooshop.com/.

Yronwode, Catherine. *Lucky Mojo*. 1994–2014. Accessed June 5, 2014: http://www.luckymojo.com/.

MOJO

The term *mojo*, which sometimes appears as *Moe Joe*, *jomo*, and other variations, most commonly identifies a bag charm associated with African American conjure and hoodoo. Other names for such items are *hands*, *tobies*, and *luck balls*. The name likely derives from the language of the Kongo people, in which *mooyo* designated the indwelling spirit of magical charms. Though found across the United States, the word *mojo* is most commonly associated with the western portions of Mississippi and Tennessee. In these areas, *mojo* is often a synonym for conjure and hoodoo as well as the name for a type of charm.

An interesting description of the powers associated with some such items appears in Mary Alicia Owen's 1893 collection of Missouri folklore *Old Rabbit, the Voodoo and Other Sorcerers*. According to the account, a woman the author called Aunt Mymee lost her mojo one morning. Owen reported that Mymee's consternation over its disappearance was so great that she abandoned all other activities in quest of it. After searching in vain, she threw herself to the floor and cried out that "she would be better off in her grave, for an enemy had stolen her luck-ball, and her soul as well as her luck was in it." Fortunately for Aunt Mymee, a child under her care found the mojo and returned it to her. The happy woman speculated that the mojo had left her in search of something to drink since she had forgotten to supply it any sustenance for a week.

There are numerous formulae and functions for such charms, depending largely on the purpose for which they are designed. For instance, a gambling mojo described in an oral history collected by Harry Middleton Hyatt during the early 20th century contained a High John the Conqueror root, a black lodestone, an Adam and Eve root, and violet incense powder enclosed in red flannel. Though the charms have historically varied widely in composition, general features included an outer shell of cloth, often but not exclusively composed of red flannel. In many cases, makers tied it with string, or sometimes wrapped the string around the mouth of the charm in order to seal in the ingredients. Upon occasion, these cloth bags were sewn shut instead. Practitioners also typically believed such charms housed spirits, which had to be fed with whiskey, cologne, or some other liquid to maintain their power.

It was once common for African Americans to carry mojos created for use by specific individuals, as illustrated by the case of Aunt Mymee. In some cases these were understood to be permanent parts of their owners' lives. Missouri luck balls described by Owen held spirits named after their owners. It was this spirit, not the simple ingredients that composed the charm, that compelled Mymee's luck ball to seek nourishment after its owner neglected to supply drink. The spirit's importance was so great that its owner wore its dwelling place suspended on a string looped over one shoulder and under the other, placing the mojo itself under her right armpit directly against her skin.

See also: Conjure; Hand; Hoodoo; Owen, Mary Alicia

Jeffrey E. Anderson

Further Reading

Anderson, Jeffrey E. 2005. *Conjure in African American Society*. Baton Rouge, LA: Louisiana State University Press.

Hyatt, Harry Middleton. 1970–1978. *Hoodoo-Conjuration-Witchcraft-Rootwork*. 5 vols. Memoirs of the Alma Egan Hyatt Foundation. Hannibal: Western.

Owen, Mary Alicia. 1893 [2003]. *Old Rabbit, the Voodoo and Other Sorcerers*. With an Introduction by Charles Godfrey Leland. With Illustrations by Juliette A. Owen and Louis Wain. London: T. Fisher Unwin; reprint, Whitefish, MT: Kessinger Publishing.

MONTANÉE, JEAN

Jean Montanée, popularly known as Doctor John, was an African-born conjurer, fortune-teller, and herbal healer active in New Orleans from the 1840s until he died in 1885. His birth date, based on census and other civil records, is variously given as being between 1800 and 1815.

The notion that Doctor John was the mentor, lover, or professional rival of the great Voodoo priestess Marie Laveau (1801–1881) was introduced by Robert Tallant in his 1946 book, *Voodoo in New Orleans*, and his 1956 novel, *The Voodoo Queen*. The story has been taken up and elaborated upon by later writers of fiction, such as Ishmael Reed (*The Last Days of Louisiana Red*, 1974), Francine Prose (*Marie Laveau*, 1977), and Jewel Parker Rhodes (*Voodoo Dreams*, 1995). Marie Laveau and Jean Montanée were indeed contemporaries, but there is no evidence that any relationship, friendly or hostile, existed between them.

Doctor John was not the leader of a Voodoo congregation in the manner of the priestesses Marie Laveau and Betsy Toledano. Rather he held consultations, gave readings, and performed cures for individual clients from his home on the Bayou Road. His method of telling fortunes by means of throwing and interpreting a handful of shells bears a striking resemblance to the cowrie shell divination performed by the Santería priesthood of Cuba. He was supposedly called upon by people of all classes and colors, from the enslaved, to working-class white and free-colored persons, to the elite of both races. His prices were high, and he amassed a fortune. He was said to have dressed elegantly, had a carriage and a comfortable house, and surrounded himself with his enslaved concubines and children. Articles about Montanée's interactions with clients and the police appeared in New Orleans newspapers of the time, in which he was characterized as a charlatan.

The most comprehensive—and sympathetic—account of Jean Montanée/Doctor John was written just after Montanée's death by the New Orleans journalist and fiction writer Lafcadio Hearn. Hearn's "The Last of the Voudoos" was published in the November 7, 1885, issue of *Harper's Weekly*. According to Hearn, Jean Montanée "was a native of Senegal, and claimed to have been a prince's son," displaying as proof parallel scars "extending in curves from the edge of either temple to the corner of the lips." These tribal scars, or "country marks," were also mentioned in several newspaper articles of the 1850s and 1860s. Later writers referred to them as "tattoos." Lafcadio Hearn described Montanée as a man "of middle height, very strongly built, with broad shoulders, well-developed muscles, and inky black skin, retreating forehead, small bright eyes, a very flat nose, and a woolly beard . . . He had a resolute voice and a very authoritative manner." Hearn declared that Jean Montanée had been sold away from his African nation and transported as a slave to Cuba. He eventually obtained his freedom, worked as a cook on Spanish vessels, and later settled in New Orleans, where he became a dock worker. He attracted a devoted clientele and grew wealthy from his spiritual and medical practice. In his later years, Hearn tells us, Montanée lost his money and property through gambling, bad investments, and debts.

Much of Hearn's article is substantiated by archival records. Notarial acts show that Jean Montanée bought many lots and houses in the Tremé, Nouvelle Marigny, and Bywater neighborhoods. Court records show that he lost some of these properties in settlement of judgements against him. He was listed in the census and city directories as a physician or "Indian doctor." The census also verifies that he was a native of Africa and that the value of his real estate and personal property was significant. Montanée owned seven enslaved women and three enslaved men. The census, civil birth certificates, and court records show that he had as many as twenty children, although some found in these documents have the same name and could have been the same person. He is known to have had eight children with Marie Armant, his only legal spouse. In 1868, when Montanée was around sixty, he married the sixteen-year-old Louisiana-born woman at St. Theresa's Catholic Church. She is listed as his wife "Armantine" in the 1870 and 1880 census. Montanée also fathered an undetermined number of children with his female slaves, and had at least one son with Matilda Griffin, a woman from Baltimore. He might be the father of two sons born to John "Montanet" or "Montaney" and Marie Populus.

Jean Montanée died of Bright's disease, a kidney ailment, on August 23, 1885. The death certificate gave his age as seventy, but he might have been as old as eighty-five. The newspapers published no obituary and no articles, positive or negative, about the passing of the famous Doctor John. He was interred in an unmarked wall vault in the Campo Santo of St. Roch's Cemetery in New Orleans.

Montanée's widow, Marie Armant, and their two surviving children, Jeanne and Edward Montanée, settled his estate in 1921, and were able to reclaim some of his property that had been declared abandoned by the state.

See also: Alexander, Jim; Conjure; Divination; Hoodoo; Ifá; Laveau, Marie; New Orleans; Senegambia

Carolyn Morrow Long

Further Reading

Long, Carolyn Morrow. 2006. *A New Orleans Voudou Priestess: The Legend and Reality of Marie Laveau*. Gainesville, FL: University Press of Florida.

Hearn, Lafcadio. 1885. "The Last of the Voudoos." *Harper's Weekly Magazine* 24, no. 1507 (November 7), 726–27.

Trevigne, Barbara. 2010. "Ball of Confusion." *New Orleans Genesis* 48, no. 192 (October), 319–23.

MOREAU DE SAINT-MÉRY, MÉDÉRIC LOUIS-ÉLIE

Médéric Louis-Élie Moreau de Saint-Méry was born at Fort Royal in Martinique in 1750. It is believed that his parents, who were from Poitou, a province in West-Central France, emigrated to Martinique in the 1600s, where they settled and became one of the most prominent families. Moreau de Saint-Méry was raised on the island. He died on January 28, 1819, in Paris at age sixty-nine.

Moreau de Saint-Méry was a Creole colonist, lawyer, and writer with a career that was based primarily in France, Martinique, and Saint-Domingue (present-day Haiti). He is most well known for his two-volume publication of 1797–1798, *Description Topographique, Physique, Civile, Politique et Historique de la Partie Françoise de l'Isle Saint Domingue: Avec des Observations Generals sur la Population, sur le Caractère & les Moeurs de ses Divers Habitans, sur son Climat, sa Culture, ses Productions, son Administration.*

At the age of nineteen, Moreau de Saint-Méry went to Paris to pursue a formal education, and after just three years he attained the rank of avocat au Parliament. In 1772, at the age of twenty-two, he returned to the French West Indies, to Saint-Domingue, where he lived in Cap Français and practiced law. Being very successful he was soon made a member of the Superior Council of the colony. The Royal Government sanctioned and assisted Moreau de Saint-Méry in his collection of information about the law, history, and other matters relating to the French in the West Indies. The reason for this collection was to rescue documents from damage due to insects and the Caribbean climate. He travelled extensively, visiting all of the French island colonies in the West Indies, and the information he collected formed the basis of his future writings. In Saint-Domingue, Moreau de Saint-Méry believed he had found the tomb of Christopher Columbus.

Moreau de Saint-Méry returned to Paris in 1784 at age thirty-four to assist in the administration of the colonies. He served in various capacities within the pre-revolutionary French Government before he was arrested for his radical views and jailed in 1793. He managed to escape and avoided death by guillotine by fleeing to New York before settling in Philadelphia in 1794. It was here that Moreau de Saint-Méry became an established author.

Moreau de Saint-Méry supported the rights of the white colonists and defended legal slavery and segregation based on race. While in Saint-Domingue he developed a system for categorizing races that broke the island's inhabitants into eleven racial groups going back seven generations, which could produce one hundred and twenty-eight combinations. Despite his strong racial beliefs, it is believed he had a mixed-race mistress with whom he had a child.

His writings were some of the earliest to mention Vodou; he studied the religion while in Saint-Domingue. He discovered its practices among the slaves on the island and concluded that the individuals were "snake-worshippers." Vodou was in colonial Saint-Domingue before Moreau de Saint-Méry was born, and the forced conversion of slaves to Catholicism syncretized African worship. Moreau de Saint-Méry observed that the altars reflective of Catholicism were there to conceal the African worship. In *Description* Moreau de Saint-Méry discusses "Vaudoux" as superstition, bizarre practices, and a dance.

Although these volumes were widely read and understood to be the findings of Saint-Méry, there is the possibility that some of his information came from second-hand sources. Interestingly, in these pre-Haitian Revolution writings, Moreau de Saint-Méry hinted at the possibility of Vodou causing a future revolt.

See also: Haitian Revolution; Snakes

Louise Fenton

Further Reading

Dubois, Laurent. 2004. *A Colony of Citizens: Revolution and Slave Emancipation in the French Caribbean, 1787–1804.* Chapel Hill, NC: University of North Carolina Press.

Fick, Carolyn E. 1991. *The Making of Haiti: The Saint Domingue Revolution from Below.* Knoxville, TN: University of Tennessee Press.

Garrigus, John D. 2011. *Before Haiti: Race and Citizenship in French Saint-Domingue.* Oxford: Palgrave Macmillan.

Moreau de Saint-Méry, Médéric-Louis-Élie. 1797. *Description Topographique, Physique, Civile, Politique et Historique de la Partie Française de l'Isle de Saint-Domingue.* 2 vols. Philadelphia: Pauteur.

MUSIC AND HAITIAN VODOU

Haitian Vodou music and ritual are synonymous with the syncretic Vodou religion that originated in Haiti during the 18th century. The birth of Haitian Vodou grew out of the French slave colony of Saint-Domingue, where many West and Central African slaves emigrated. The musical rites and practices adopted by Haitian slaves have many different sources, including the Yoruba, Bakongo, and Taino peoples and Catholicism, mysticism, Masonic orders, militarism, secret societies, spiritism, and other influences. Some escaped slaves managed to form communities in the wilderness and adopted cultural and linguistic elements from both Europeans and Africans, which formed the basis for a new language—Haitian Creole (Kreyòl). The language was used in the establishment and incorporation of Vodou and Vodou music in hundreds of locations all over Saint-Domingue. Importantly, all types of Haitian Vodou music have developed free of any standardization authority, allowing for local and regional variations in Vodou practice and musical arrangements throughout the society. Haitian Vodou music is reserved for sacred occasions honoring lwa and saints, which primarily takes place at home or in a temple, also known as an *ounfò*.

The primary subject of Haitian Vodou music surrounds sacred servitude to spirits, called *lwa*. The songs are accompanied by ason (rattle), badji (altar), and drums that are specific to each deity, and they capture the personality or power of the lwa. The ceremony may invite or send lwa away, depending on the need. The songs can present advice and philosophy, focus on enemies, or deal with current or past political and historical events. The sacred songs are believed to originate in the spirit world of Ginen. At any rate, the songs are not easily explained, and they may cover obscure deities or incorporate a spiritual language called *langaj*, which some priests may not be able to decipher. Furthermore, the point of view may change during a song performance. The songs, however, are directed to the lwa, meaning that it may not be necessary to fully understand each performance to elucidate its goal.

Haitian Vodou music contains many different rites and practices, but the most important rite is Rada. The Rada rite originates with the Fon culture of present-day Benin, a nation once known as Dahomey. Rada developed out of the plantation slavery system in the Caribbean. The specific music rituals of the Rada form stem from three conical single-headed drums of different sizes, various rattles, and a bell. The largest drum, the *manman*, produces a very low register sound. The drum is played with a bare hand and an *agida*, which is a hammer-shaped stick. The drum primarily orchestrates, leads, and choreographs the dances. The mid-sized drum, the *segon*, is played with an *abara*, a half-moon-shaped stick and a straight stick. The sound produced is somewhere in the middle register, and the performer using the *segon* mainly plays intricate patterns in dialogue with the *manman*. The smallest drum, the *boula*, is played with two straight sticks. The tone is rather high, and the regular playing pattern coincides with the short strokes of the *ogan*, or bell. The ason, or rattles, are played by priests and priestesses, oungan and mambo, respectively, or by an oungenikon, an assistant. The assistant is often the chorus leader. In some cases, a *bas*, or tambourine, accompanies the *manman*. The music of the Rada rites is the most complex, and the rhythms for the Rada lwa include *yanvalou*, *mayi*, and *zepol*. The three aforementioned rhythms are subdivided into other rhythms, such as *nago cho*, *nago gwan kou*, *twa rigol*, *kongo-rada*, *mazoun*, and *dyouba-matinik*.

The Kongo-Petwo music rite utilizes two conical single-headed drums that are smaller than the Rada drums, and each is tuned by tightening laces on the drum head. The drums are known as *gwo baka* and *ti baka* and are played in call-and-response formats. An *ogan* plays a continuous time signature, and *tcha-tcha* rattles, played by song leaders, play in counterrhythms with other instruments. Sometimes, a third, smaller drum, called a *kata*, is used. The *kata* adds more texture to the music and a brighter tone. The primary rhythms played with Kongo-Petwo rites are *kita* and *boumba*.

The third most important Vodou music rite involves the Bizango secret societies created for the protection of the community. Their musical repertoire includes a *tanbou* drum played with bare hands. A double-headed tambourine known as a *kes* is played with two sticks. The rhythm is distinctive and features a staccato sound. There are also whistles and a *fwet kach*, a cracking whip, that accompany the rite performances. The Bizango rites include the *chika* and *kongo-sosyete* rhythms.

Haitian Vodou music is also part of a public celebration known as rara. Rara is only performed in public streets, cemeteries, and other public spaces, which is different from the intimate sacred rituals of Vodou. Rara is a street celebration that begins at the onset of the Lenten season and lasts until Easter Sunday. Usually, the most active rara celebrations are near Easter, but throughout the period, partygoers roam the cities, countryside, and towns looking for audiences. The musical repertoire is provided by the *bann rara* (Rara band) on simple instruments, consisting primarily of the *vaksin* (bamboo trumpet), *tanbou* (single-headed drum), and *graj* (metal scraper), and also including the *kone* (zinc trumpet), *kes* (snare drum), *tcha-tcha* (maracas), and other assorted percussion instruments that can be easily carried. Brass instruments make up another part of the repertoire, and include trumpets, trombones, baritone horns, and saxophones. Yet, the *vaksin* plays a pivotal role in most rara groups. The *vaksin*-led groups feature different playing patterns, while allowing every player room for considerable variation and improvisation. The primary rhythm is the *raboday*, which is built around a three-note rhythmic pattern played with sticks on the side of a *kata* (drum). Interestingly, the drumming patterns closely mimic Kongo-Petwo Vodou rituals, themselves militant religious forms of expression developed during the late 18th century, shortly before independence.

The Rara performances are produced primarily by the rural class and comprise numerous throngs that cover the roads and snarl traffic with boisterous music and animated dance maneuvers. Motorists who dance in their seats are waved through the crowds, while other motorists unmoved by the music must pay a small toll to drive through the streets. The rara bands are not haphazardly structured, but rather are organized by several key members. The concept behind rara is generally a sacred promise to a lwa or group of lwa that is organized by a master or president for a certain number of years, with seven being the normal range. Rara bands perform consecratory ceremonies and extensive rehearsals in the weeks leading up to Easter Sunday to prepare for the festivities. While performing, the band leader directs his group with a whistle or whip to cajole the street marchers or dancers along. Additionally, the *majo jon*, or male dancers, dress in multicolored scarves. Their role involves entertaining the spectators, along with female dancers known as *ren* (queen). The ren engage the male audiences with their playful and somewhat suggestive dance movements. The ren also collect tolls from the audience. The master or president supplies the band members with instruments, flags, costumes, and other celebratory items for other members. The bands are modeled on military and courtly or governmental hierarchies. The rather rigid organization of musical discipline and coarse language serves both a sacred and profane purpose. In fact, rara songs tend to venerate obscene situations and/or contain references to political topics or historic events. Rara's association with lower-class roots, Vodou congregations, and secret societies has won for it a poor reputation among

---

Hoodoo, Voodoo, and Popular Music

African American magical and religious practices appear frequently in American popular music. Sometimes, the songs addressing such practices recount tales of legendary practitioners. The Memphis Jug Band, a blues group, recorded a song about Caroline Dye, a famed hoodoo practitioner from Newport, Arkansas. Jazz musician Oscar "Papa" Celestine did the same for Marie Laveau. Musician Malcolm John Rebennack, Jr., has even adopted the stage name *Dr. John* in tribute to 19th-century Voodoo doctor Jean Montanée. A host of other songs, particularly of the blues tradition, pay tribute to the power of hoodoo and Voodoo.

Christian elites and the secular middle classes of Haiti. For example, parents often instruct their children to stay away from the *diab* (devils) and women at the rara, as this would possibly earn one a reputation as a prostitute.

Haitian Vodou and pop music connections were constructed in the 1950s. The traditional Vodou rites, rituals, and sounds became diverse and syncretic with regard to popular music. Many middle-class musicians incorporated the traditional Vodou styles in commercially viable music hybrids. After World War II, Haitian contemporary music was heavily influenced by jazz and dance bands with some classical influences. Some of these performers—notably Jazz des Jeunes, Lumane Casimir, Martha Jean-Claude, and Orchestre el Saieh—were inspired by the intellectual and political movements during the first American Occupation after World War I.

However, none of the earlier music movements treated the religious beliefs of Vodou with the veneration present in the more recent roots music movement of the 1990s. The roots music, or *mizik rasin*, movement grew out of the 1970s roots, funk, and reggae sound of Jamaica. A few groups from the aforementioned era combined Afro-Haitian religious music with Vodou percussionists and transnational popular music. The predecessors of such groups as Foula, Sanba-yo, and Boukman Eksperyans all existed before François "Papa Doc" Duvalier fled Haiti, which eventually laid the groundwork for a new roots revival. An important popular group, Rara Machine, was formed by percussionist and vocalist Clifford Sylvain shortly after the overthrow of Duvalier's regime. The group incorporates actual Vodou ceremonial music in the performances.

One of the most popular music groups in Haiti is Boukman Eksperyans. The group combines *mizik rasin* with Vodou traditions and African elements. The group was founded by Lolo Beaubrun in Port-au-Prince, Haiti. The group was named after a Vodou priest, Dutty Boukman, who led the start of the Haitian Revolution around 1791. Boukman Eksperyans began music-making in the 1980s. The incorporation of electric guitar and bass instruments was a nod to Jimi Hendrix. Their 1991 Grammy-nominated album, *Vodou Adjae*, weaves a connection between a Haitian and Guinea Vodou line. Lyrically, the band is committed to the Kreyòl language, even though some elites in power prefer English, Spanish, or French as official country languages. Many *mizik rasin* groups use the language as well as Vodou traditions in their music.

See also: Dahomey; Dances; Drums; Ginen; Ounfò; Rada; Secret Societies

Matthew J. Forss

Further Reading and Listening

Averill, Gage. 1997. *A Day For the Hunter, A Day For the Prey: Popular Music and Power in Haiti*. Chicago: University of Chicago Press.

Averill, Gage. *Alan Lomax's Recordings in Haiti*. Liner notes. Harte Recordings, LLC.

Courlander, Harold. 1960. *The Drum and the Hoe: Life and Lore of the Haitian People*. Berkeley, CA: University of California Press.

Courlander, Harold. 1973. *Haiti Singing*. New York: Cooper Square Publishers.

Kershaw, Andy. *The Rough Guide to Haiti*. World Music Network RGNET 1067.
Largey, Michael. 2006. *Vodou Nation: Haitian Art, Music, and Cultural Nationalism.* Chicago: University of Chicago Press.
McAlister, Elizabeth. 2002. *Rara! Vodou, Power, and Performance in Haiti and Its Diaspora.* Berkeley, CA: University of California Press.
McAlister, Elizabeth, David Yih, Gerdes Fleurant, and Gage Averill. n.d. Liner notes. Various Artists. *Rhythms of Rapture: Sacred Musics of Haitian Vodou.* Shanachie LC 5762.

MYALISM

Myalism or Myal is an African Diasporic tradition practiced in Jamaica since the second half of the 18th century. As with many aspects of the African Diaspora, the precise origins of Myalism are difficult to determine. One of the authors to posit a solution was Joseph J. Williams, who argued in his 1932 book, *Voodoo and Obeahs*, that it was "the old tribal religion of the Ashanti." As is true with many other aspects of New World creole religions, however, such identifications are tenuous and may well be mistaken, especially in light of the many different African people groups who contributed to Jamaica's population.

Throughout its history, Myalism has been linked with the Jamaican version of Obeah. The precise relationship between the two remains a subject of considerable debate, however. Since the mid-19th century, most observers have treated Obeah as a malevolent practice devoted primarily to harming others and Myal as a positive tradition. On the other hand, the two have maintained a strong connection and cannot always be separated by sharp distinctions. During the 19th century, for instance, at least one Christian missionary on the island stated that the primary work of Myal practitioners was to counteract the evil perpetrated by Obeah men. Others noted that Obeah practitioners, like Myal-men, were known for their ability to cure ailments. Still others classified Myalism as but a variety of Obeah. Perhaps the best definition of *Myal* is one proposed by Joseph M. Murphy in *Working the Spirit* (1994). According to him, Myalism should not be understood as the antithesis of the private and secretive practice of Obeah but as a communal effort to control the improper use of Obeah.

Perhaps the most obvious distinction between Jamaican Obeah and Myalism is the latter's communal aspect. According to 18th- and 19th-century accounts, Myalism was an initiatory fraternity. Slaves found it attractive because of its proponents' claims to be able to prevent pain and death inflicted by whites. Observers claimed that initiation centered on the consumption of an herbal extract that produced a deathlike state in those who ingested it. A second concoction revived the seemingly dead bodies and completed their initiation into the society.

After initiation, believers' chief involvement in Myalism was participation in communal dances. These commonly took place under silk-cotton trees, and sacrifices of birds sometimes preceded them. Each dance had a director, who began it with a call-and-response song. At that point, dancers formed a ring, a practice similar to the ring shout of the antebellum American South. The ring would itself move in a circle, while those who formed it sang, hummed, and whistled, while keeping time with their hands and feet. Other dancers sometimes moved in a smaller ring inside the first. As the dance progressed, it would become more and more ecstatic—a shocking sight to whites, who viewed it as akin to insanity. After a time, participants would enter a trance state in which they acquired the supernatural powers of prophecy. A prime activity among participants at this point was accusing various people of practicing Obeah and identifying the hiding places of harmful charms. They might also capture the shadows—roughly equivalent to souls or spirits—of those who had died through accident and lay them to rest.

Myalism and Vodou have aspects worthy of comparison and contrast. For example, the practice of administering herbs to cause apparent death and resurrection may be related to zombification. According to Wade Davis, the Haitian practice serves the community by punishing wrongdoers—a goal not so different from Myalism as stereotypical concepts of zombis would lead one to believe. The shadows captured during Myal ceremonies also resemble Vodou concepts of *zombis astral*, envisioned as disembodied spirits under the control of bòkòs.

Unlike Vodou, Myalism appears to have possessed no African-derived pantheon. In fact, one song from the 1840s recorded by a missionary to Jamaica referenced Christ and "the Lord," presumably God the Father. Whether this song was typical, however, remains open for debate because at least some observers noted that the songs performed during such ceremonies were usually extemporaneous. The documentary record also states that many devotees of Myalism proclaimed the imminent return of Jesus and the end of the world. For at least some participants, Myal was clearly part of a Christian worldview. Despite such persuasive evidence about the mindset of Myal practitioners, it is likewise important to note that Christian prayers, saints' images, and the like appear in Vodou ceremonies. Moreover, Vodou chants and songs are much more formalized than were those of 19th-century Myal. In short, such trappings of faith do not necessarily demonstrate full-fledged conversion to Christianity on the part of slaves.

Some scholars have suggested that the trance states achieved by participants in Myal dances were spirit possessions comparable to those present within Vodou. The documentary record bears this out. During the 1840s, a Presbyterian minister who attempted to stop a dance was admonished that the dancers had "the spirit." Whether these were possessions by the Holy Spirit of Christian belief or by others left unidentified in the literature, the similarity to possessions in Vodou, various African religions, and a host of New World African Diasporic faiths is evident. Some have noted that participants in Myal dances also claimed the ability to communicate with the dead. The ability to capture shadows during ceremonies also points to this connection with the spirits of the dead.

As a communal organization and belief system, Myal functioned as a means of resistance to slavery. According to at least one colonial observer, Myalism played a role in a 1760 slave uprising. In addition, by supposedly protecting slaves from harm at the hands of whites, it acted in much the same way that some North American conjure powders and root charms purportedly guarded slaves against masters' violence. At the same time, whites were not shy about seeking out practitioners. One 19th-century observer noted that whites frequently turned out to watch Myal dances. He also stated that one member of Jamaica's colonial legislature openly welcomed the dancers to his property so that they could disclose the buried Obeah charms hidden there.

Aspects of Myalism survived under increasingly Christianized exteriors as time progressed. The Native Baptist movement, which arose after a massive influx of Christian missionaries during the late 18th and early 19th centuries, reportedly incorporated many elements of Myalism. Its adherents certainly set it apart from mainstream manifestations of the Baptist denomination by emphasizing the importance of dream visions and other distinctive features. The merging of the Myalism with a form of Baptist faith contributed to a 1831–1832 slave rebellion, which in turn advanced the antislavery cause, leading to emancipation two years later.

More recently, Myalism has contributed to the development of Zion Revivalism and Pukkumina. The impetus for this development was what was known as the Great Revival, which began in the midst of economic hardship, brought on in part by the impact of the American Civil War. Practitioners of Zion Revivalism often see themselves as breaking with non-Christian spirituality. Indeed, many of the beliefs about God, the Bible, and other aspects of the spirit world would be clearly recognizable to mainstream Christians. At the same time, as in Vodou, Zion Revivalism holds that spirits must be fed and otherwise cared for in order to obtain their support. If properly honored, they will serve as guides. As was true of Myalism, services often include dancing, which is undertaken to produce trances. Once the participants have entered trance states, spirits descend upon the congregation, allowing them to prophesy.

Pukkumina, also known as *Kumina* or by the derogatory term *Pocomania*, has been influenced by Myalism, albeit in less direct ways than the Native Baptists or Zion Revivalists. Pukkumina was a relative latecomer to Jamaica, developing among West Central African indentured laborers who arrived on the island after slavery ended. Unlike the heavily Christianized Zion Revivalists, practitioners of Pukkumina do not accept the Bible as a guide to conduct or understanding of the spirit world. In addition, they focus their worship on a deity known as Zambi or King Zambi. Like their religious cousins, however, their practice includes herbalism and calling down of spirits to aid the ill. Many of the parallels between Pukkumina and Myal can be explained by their common African ancestry. On the other hand, the word *Myal* has made its way into Pukkumina, where it refers to a trance state during which practitioners can perceive spirits and uncover Obeah. This understanding of the term would be as familiar to an 18th-century participant in a Myal dance as it is to today's adherents of Pukkumina.

See also: Bòkò; Conjure; Kongo; Obeah; Sacrifice; Spiritual Churches; Vodou in Haiti; West Central Africa; Zombi

Jeffrey E. Anderson

Further Reading

Davis, Wade. 1986. *The Serpent and the Rainbow: A Harvard Scientist's Astonishing Journey into the Secret Societies of Haitian Voodoo, Zombis, and Magic*. New York: Simon and Schuster.

Murphy, Joseph M. 1994. *Working the Spirit: Ceremonies of the African Diaspora*. Boston: Beacon Press.

Olmos, Margarite Fernández, and Lizbeth Paravisini-Gebert. 2003. *Creole Religions of the Caribbean: An Introduction from Vodou and Santería to Obeah and Espiritismo*. New York: New York University Press.

Raboteau, Albert J. 1978. *Slave Religion: The "Invisible Institution" in the Antebellum South*. Oxford and New York: Oxford University Press.

Williams, Joseph J. 2011. *Voodoo and Obeahs: Phases of West India Witchcraft*. New ed. Calgary, Canada: Theophania.

N

NANCHONS

Nanchons is the Kreyòl word for "nations" and is a reference to the many ethnic groups of African people who were brought into Haiti via the Atlantic Slave trade from 1681 to 1801. These people brought their religious ideals, spirits, and styles of religious service with them as well. In Haitian Vodou today, all of these elements gave rise to the twenty-one nanchons of Vodou, and they give the faith its distinct ceremonial characteristics.

The majority of Africans who were brought as slaves to what would become Haiti were from Central and Western Africa. The survival of their belief systems in the New World is remarkable, especially in light of the brutality of slavery. Plantation owners, desiring to keep the Africans from revolting, separated the various groups upon their arrival to the island. This separation of people gave different areas of the colony and later nation distinct ethnic styles that became incorporated into the Vodou practiced in that region. Furthering the process, the Code Noir of King Louis XIV of France forced slaveholders to convert their slaves to Catholicism within eight days of their arrival in Saint Domingue. Over the course of the 18th century, African religious practice adapted to these provisions but managed to incorporate the distinct styles of service, spirits, and musical memories that each nation of Africans retained.

Under slavery, African culture and religion were suppressed on the island. Religious lineages became broken or fragmented, and the people had to pool their collective religious knowledge. Out of these fragments of religion, culture, and ideology arose Haitian Vodou, and within its liturgy, we find the nanchons served throughout the country.

Believers say there are twenty-one nanchons of lwa, a remarkable number that cannot be verified, but is held as truth. This reference to twenty-one nanchons reflects the manner in which the slaves were broken apart. We know that there were major groups from Kongo in Central Africa and Nago (Yoruba) from Western Africa. But each of these states held many minor groupings such as Adja, Mina, and Ewe of the Bight of Benin region of West Africa. These minor groups also had religious ideas, cultural norms, and spiritual practices that would become a part of the liturgical whole known as *reglemen*. This liturgical corpus is the ordering of services, and it is here that one finds the nations of people remembered, sung for, and given praise. The Rada nanchon is the first group honored in service. The Rada were largely from the Fon and related peoples of West Africa, and here one finds the cool, beneficent spirits, such as Danbala, and Ayida Wedo, royal

> ### The Nanchons and Vodou
>
> The deities of Vodou exist in multiple nations, or nanchons, most of which are linked to a specific African region or ethnicity. As their distinct origins indicate, individual nanchons once served as pantheons for their own religions, only gradually coming to be understood as a unified Vodou religion. Haiti is unusual in this respect. For instance, the nearby island nation of Cuba has two Afro-Latin faiths, Palo Mayombe and Santería or Lucumí, of Kongo and Yoruban descent, respectively. While individuals might well believe in or even practice both, they are not seen as a single religion.

spirits who still have their own religious center in modern-day Ouidah in West Africa. They are followed in reglemen by the Djouba nanchon with Azaka Mede. The Djouba nanchon is followed by the Nago nanchon with songs and offerings made to Ogou.

Within each overall group ordering, such as Rada, are subgroups that may or may not belong to the nation with which they are honored. There are also individual spirits who fall within groups' ordering—such as a lwa named Philomen who is honored with the Rada spirits—who are not a part of the nanchon. Such specific ordering is part of a given sosyete's lineage, and may be pertinent to only that sosyete. The complexity of nanchons, the elements within the nanchons, and the groups that fall under a given nanchon are all part of reglemens localized in different portions of the island.

Similarly, while reglemen governs the order of service, that order is specific to the versions of Vodou practiced in different portions of Haiti. For example, in the south of Haiti, Legba is saluted first according to reglemen. In Sen Mark in the Artibonite Valley, however, the Marasa are first. Sen Mark and the Artibonite received many slaves from Angola, doubtless influencing the order. Jacmel saw many Kongo people brought into its coffee port as slaves. Thus, the Congo nanchon is honored proportionally. A study of the various Africans, their service styles and spiritual histories, would be an excellent roadmap to the many practices of Vodou in Haiti today.

See also: Bight of Benin; Code Noir; Dahomey; Ewe; Kongo; Lwa; Petwo; Rada; Slavery and the Slave Trade; Twins; West Central Africa; Yoruba

Patricia Scheu (Mambo Vye Zo Komande LaMenfo).

Further Reading

Gilles, Jerry M. and Yvrose S. 2009. *Remembrance: Roots, Rituals, and Reverence in Vodou.* Davie, FL: Bookmanlit.

Riguad, Milo. 1953. *La Tradition Voudoo et Le Voudoo Haitien: Son Temple, Ses Mystères, Sa Magie.* Paris: Editions Niclaus.

Scheu, Patricia (Mambo Vye Zo Komande LaMenfo). 2011. *Serving the Spirits: The Religion of Vodou.* Philadelphia: Published by author.

NATION SACK

The nation sack was a cloth bag, worn by a woman around her waist inside her clothes, in which she kept her money and various magical objects and substances. Although Harry Middleton Hyatt, in *Hoodoo-Conjuration-Witchcraft-Rootwork*, called it a *nation* sack, the correct term might have been *nature* sack, which, owing to the pronunciation of the informant, was misinterpreted by Hyatt or his transcribers. This feminine power object was used to control a man's sexuality, or "nature." A Memphis woman interviewed by Hyatt in 1939 related that her mother-in-law wore such a charm. "I know she did conjuring on [her husband] 'cause she been married to him fifty years, and she really kept him too. She had him in that bag." This informant confirmed that the nation sack was never to be touched by a man: "A man . . . goin' have some serious trouble with that old lady if he try to touch that bag . . . you'll see her every night go and lock it up in her trunk. Next mornin' you see her go there and get it." The great Delta bluesman Robert Johnson, in his classic recording "Come On in My Kitchen," confesses that he violated hoodoo tradition by rummaging in his woman's nation sack and stealing her last nickel.

See also: Mojo

Carolyn Morrow Long

Further Reading

Hazzard-Donald, Katrina. "Nation Sack—A White Fabrication?" *Hoodoo in the Old Tradition*, http://omogun.webs.com/nationsack.htm.

Hyatt, Harry Middleton. 1970. *Hoodoo-Conjuration-Witchcraft-Rootwork*. Hannibal, MO: Western Publishing Company.

NATIONAL CONFEDERATION OF HAITIAN VODOU

The National Confederation of Haitian Vodou (*Kofederasyon Nasyonal Vodouwizan Aysyen* or KNVA) is a Haiti-based organization that seeks to provide structure and support for the practice of Vodou in the country. The KNVA was officially created in 2008, and Max Beauvoir was elected as Supreme Leader. Beyond Beauvoir, KNVA is directed by a twenty-one member Secretary General, composed of oungans, or priests, from around the nation.

Before the creation of the KNVA, Haitian Vodou was decentralized and lacked structure. Beginning in the early 1980s, Beauvoir promoted the need for more structure for the religion and an increased level of input in Haitian Government from Vodou practitioners. Educated in the United States and France, Beauvoir blamed many of Haiti's social and political challenges on a governmental structure that turned away from such central national characteristics as Vodou in efforts to keep and maintain foreign aid. This, according to Beauvoir and supporters of the KNVA, is problematic, as Vodou is part of the Haitian identity and oungans have the greatest knowledge of the needs of the Haitian people. The KNVA continues to argue for Vodou's central place in Haitian identity and fights to reduce foreign influence in the country.

See also: Congress of Santa Barbars (KOSANBA); Cultural Politics; The Vodou Church in Haiti; Vodou in Haiti

Jonathan Foster

Further Reading

Beauvoir, Max. "Interview with Ati Max Beauvoir, part I." Interview by Valerio Saint-Louis. Edited by Benjamin Hebblewaite. Transcribed by Joane Buteau and Benjamin Hebblewaite, translated by Megan Raitano, Tahiri Hean-Baptiste, and Benjamin Hebblewaite. Vodou Archive, University of Florida Digital Collections, George A. Smathers Library, Gainesville, Florida. Available at http://ufdc.ufl.edu/AA00013287/00001?search=max.

Lacey, Marc. 2008. "A U.S. Trained Entrepreneur Becomes Voodoo's Pope," *New York Times,* April 5, 2008, A7.

Simons, Marlise. 1983. "Power of Voodoo, Preached by Sorbonne Scientist," *New York Times,* December 15, A2.

NATIVE AMERICAN INFLUENCES ON VOODOO

Native American religious traditions predate all others in the Western Hemisphere by some thousands of years, yet academics have only begun to investigate how these religions influenced and shaped subsequent belief systems in the New World. In Haiti, the Caribbean, Louisiana, and the Mississippi Valley, Vodou, Voodoo, and related traditions adopted and adapted ideas from Native American peoples about spirits, power, and magic, particularly from the practices of the so-called Five Civilized Tribes and other Native American groups of the Southeast. More than a cosmos was shared, however; believers also incorporated Native Americans themselves, perceiving particular power in the persons and objects of Native America.

Connections between African Americans and Native Americans were fairly common after 1492, particularly in the 17th and 18th centuries. Indeed, popular historian Charles C. Mann has called the "great encounter" of the 17th century "less a meeting of Europe and America than a meeting of Africans and Indians"— because the number of Africans forcibly brought to the New World dwarfed the number of Europeans who immigrated. In Florida, Louisiana, Brazil, and elsewhere, Indians and Africans united to push back European invaders. The relationship between Native Americans and Africans was not uniformly friendly, however; many Indian societies possessed slaves and had no interest in making common cause with enslaved people or escapees.

Specific historical moments of connection—when Native Americans directly shared their religion with African-Americans—are harder to come by. By the end of the 17th century, virtually all the Native Americans on Haiti had been exterminated by Spanish violence and European diseases; any religious syncretism there would have to have been long ago, although a small number of Natchez Indians were later forcibly relocated to the island. Another possible point of interaction could have occurred in the united maroon resistance between Native Americans and African Americans in the Bahoruco region of Hispaniola. Similarly, spiritual connections could also have been forged in the resistance of maroons and

Indians in 18th-century Louisiana. Much later, in the era of Indian Removal in the United States (1830–1839), the Five Civilized Tribes of the Southeast (Cherokee, Chickasaw, Choctaw, Creek, and Seminole) were forced from their lands and into Oklahoma, in the process passing through the cradlelands of hoodoo in the Mississippi Valley. All these moments presented opportunities for shared religious conversation.

Yet the real evidence of connection between African religions and Native American beliefs lies not in a single moment of historical connection, but in the continuity of cosmos: the parallels between Voodoo and Vodou practices and Native American religious traditions. It is impossible to generalize about Native American religious beliefs; the peoples now referred to as Native Americans comprise literally hundreds of tribes, clans, kinship groups, and legal entities, each of which possesses different concepts of history, religion, and spirituality (to say nothing of Native Americans who practice Christianity as their religion). Nevertheless, a series of assumptions regarding the spiritual world are shared among the Southeastern Indians—the cultural group most often linked to the emergence of Mississippi Valley Voodoo.

The scholar Charles Hudson refers to traditional Southeastern belief systems as a world of "supernatural justice"—a place where all events have causes, and where humans and spirits interact to create the cosmos. Indigenous American religious systems feature a broad array of spirits and other invisible natural forces that can be propitiated for aid, consulted for advice, or pacified by gifts. "Power lay at the center of all concerns," writes historian Gregory Evans Dowd, and human life was both preserved and enhanced by respecting and supplicating spirits through "rituals and ceremonies [that] had once been gifts, donated by benevolent forces." A similar sense of a living universe of invisible spirits, of propitiation and sacrifice, of aid between the living and the dead, also pervades Voodoo.

Specific parallels abound. Both Native Americans of the Southeast and practitioners of Voodoo revered and feared serpents; the great African snake god Da presumably incorporated elements of Native American snake spirits in the Americas, such as Grandfather Rattlesnake (feared and respected by several Plains tribes). Ancestor worship is common in African religions, Voodoo, and some Native American religions. Concepts of multiple souls among the Southeastern Indians also mirrored African and Voodoo beliefs; Seminoles believed that one soul stayed with the body while another journeyed outward in dreamtime, similar to the Yoruban *okan*. There was a shared belief in witchcraft, and Voodooists and Indians of multiple cultural regions affirmed the existence of "shooting magic"—the ability of witches to insert objects (pins, cloth, flint, vermin, frogs, and the like) into their victims' bodies via sorcery.

These connections are only suggestive. After all, West African religions also possess reverence for snakes, so the religious role of serpents in Voodoo cannot derive exclusively from Native American cosmologies. Rather, these are regions of commonality that perhaps suggest ways in which belief systems bled into one another. The evidence is more than coincidental, but less than definitive—as most evidence surrounding the history of syncretic religious systems is.

What is clear is that many Indian lifeways, objects, and indeed persons commanded extreme reverence from practitioners of Voodoo and Vodou. Indian arrowheads and *zémi* statuettes have been incorporated into Vodou ceremonies for their assumed magical power; *zémis* have been found among Vodou paraphernalia throughout the Caribbean. The concept of a magical bag that provides spiritual power to its owner has ancient roots among Native Americans and powerful resonance within Vodou. The famed Indian "medicine bags" were a source of spiritual strength and of power in the healing arts; they were also, as the Sauk guide Wennebea said, "indispens[a]ble to obtain success against our enemies." Many contents of Indian medicine bags could also be found in African American gris-gris bags. Indeed, some of the medicinal herbs used in hoodoo and Voodoo derived from Native American religious use, including the puffball mushroom (devil's snuff box), amaranth, and puccoon root. The ceremonies involving these plants differ among numerous Native American and African American communities, but the medical lore surrounding them is surprisingly similar and points to an incorporation of a Native American religious vocabulary. Image magic (sympathetic dolls) and the countermagical properties of salt could be found among conjure and Voodoo practitioners and some Native American groups. The use of conjure stones—such as the "singing stone" Zora Neale Hurston reported that Uncle Monday employed—has a likely antecedent in the Cherokee story of the Uktena, an underground serpent beast with crystals embedded in its body. Crystals removed from the Uktena brought luck and magical power to their possessors, though like conjure stones, the crystals from the Uktena had to be fed.

Yet it is not merely Indian artifacts or ideas that have been woven into the world of Voodoo and Vodou, but Native Americans themselves. Many Voodoo doctors past and present have claimed to possess some Indian descent and that their Native American ancestry improved the efficacy of their religious power and authority. According to Robert Tallant, both Marie Laveau and her supposed nemesis, Doctor Jim, claimed to be part Native American. Indeed, one name for a hoodoo doctor is an "Indian doctor."

One particular Native American looms above all others in the world of Voodoo and hoodoo: the Sauk leader Black Hawk (1767–1838). The historical Black Hawk led an uprising against American treaty violations in the 1832 war that bears his name. He subsequently wrote a bestselling account of his struggle and ironically found himself feted and praised in white American society. Black Hawk's spiritual place in Voodoo and other religions is less straightforward. Some practitioners view the indomitable Sauk as a saint, closely identifying him with St. Michael. Black Hawk is "a brother . . . working to save men's souls," in the words of a member of one New Orleans Spiritual Church. Alternatively, Black Hawk is understood as a "bad saint," who "never did believe in the Gospel" and possessed a powerful book with white writing on black pages. Statues of Black Hawk can be found in numerous religious contexts in New Orleans and elsewhere, a "superheroic figure, equal parts history and myth," according to filmmaker Jason Berry.

Black Hawk's status—whether good saint or bad—testifies to the complexities of connection between Native American religion and Voodoo. These connections are only beginning to be understood, in part because these religions were treated so shabbily by academics and historians for so long. White scholars conflated these faiths with superstition, and often deployed myths, half-truths, and shards of evidence to define the practices as barbarism—thereby identifying Christianity with civilization. Construction of Voodoo, Vodou, and Native American religion as "superstition" in turn justified white American intervention in Haiti and Native America in the 19th and 20th centuries. Practitioners in turn often hid their religion, with good reason. As these attitudes of superiority recede and as the academic world becomes more open to people of more diverse backgrounds, the intricate relations between Voodoo and Vodou and Native American practice may yet be known in more than their broad outlines. A full account still awaits its historian.

See also: Blanc Dani; Conjure; Danbala; Gris-gris; Hoodoo; Interventionism by the United States in Haiti; Mojo; Nation Sack; Spiritual Churches; Terminology

Adam Jortner

Further Reading

Anderson, Jeffrey. 2005. *Conjure in African-American Society*. Baton Rouge, LA: Louisiana State University.

Berry, Jason. 1995. *The Spirit of Black Hawk: A Mystery of Africans and Indians*. Jackson, MS: University Press of Mississippi.

Dowd, Greory Evans. 1992. *A Spirited Resistance: The North American Indian Struggle for Unity, 1745–1815*. Baltimore, MD: Johns Hopkins.

Hudson, Charles. 1976. *The Southeastern Indians*. Knoxville, TN: University of Tennessee.

Jacobs, Claude F., and Andrew J. Kaslow. 1991. *The Spiritual Churches of New Orleans: Origins, Beliefs, and Rituals of an African-American Tradition*. Knoxville, TN: University of Tennessee Press.

Laguerre, Michael S. 1989. *Voodoo and Politics in Haiti*. New York: St. Martin's.

Mann, Charles C. 2012. *1493: Uncovering the New World Columbus Created*. Reprint ed. New York: Vintage.

Tallant, Robert. 1946. *Voodoo in New Orleans*. New York: Macmillan.

Yronwode, Catherine. 2010. "Nation Sack." In *Hoodoo in Theory and Practice*, Lucky Mojo Curio Company. http://www.luckymojo.com/nationsack.html.

NEW AGE AND NEOPAGANISM AND VOODOO/VODOU

In recent years the New Age and Neopagan movements have significantly impacted the perception and practices of religion in much of the world. Within the United States, the New Age movement came first, growing to prominence within the counterculture of the 1960s and 1970s. Inspired initially by a variety of Eastern religions, adherents rejected the Christian faith of most Americans and embraced a concept of self-spirituality. Scholar Paul Heelas argues that this self-spirituality is defined by three broad principles embraced by most adherents of the movement. First, they believe that experience trumps belief, and that operating within a belief system can hinder one's spiritual development. Second, New Agers hold that

> ### Whites and Voodoo
> Through the years, most scholars have equated Voodoo—and for that matter Vodou—with blackness. In fact, some white New Orleanians were certainly members of Voodoo congregations by the 19th century, as attested by newspaper accounts of police raids. Author George Washington Cable even used white Creoles' involvement in the religion to critique their claims of racial superiority. In the United States, whites are increasingly attracted to both Voodoo and hoodoo, treating them as yet another option for Neopagans in search of a faith.

each person's mind is the only valid source of spiritual truth. Third, rejection of societal norms and mainstream institutions frees one to realize his or her spiritual potential, they maintain. The cumulative effect of these assumptions has been to create a highly individualistic spiritual ethos in which participants feel free to pick and choose between competing concepts of the supernatural or to reject all, creating their own private spiritualities.

Though the New Age movement peaked in the 1970s and declined thereafter, its beliefs had entered the mainstream of American culture by the 1980s. Within this milieu, which stressed the absence of barriers, Americans felt free to experiment with a host of religious and spiritual traditions. As time passed, those influenced by New Age ideology gradually moved away from the Eastern spirituality that initially helped inspire it. Instead, increasing numbers began to seek spiritual development in efforts to revive ancient religions, such as Celtic Druidism and a variety of supposed witchcraft traditions, commonly referred to as Wicca. These efforts to resuscitate lost faiths have come to be known as Neopaganism, which can be interpreted as either an aspect of the New Age movement or an offshoot that developed into a movement in its own right.

Initially, African and African American traditions were not particularly appealing to adherents of the New Age and Neopagan movements. For one, the movements' appearance during the 1960s and 1970s was too little removed from the not-so-distant Jim Crow era. It is likely that at least some of the mostly white seekers after alternative spiritualities would be uncomfortable breaking with preconceived notions of the superiority of Far Eastern and Western forms of spirituality, despite their abandonment of Christianity. Moreover, many Americans wrongly associated any faith having African roots with evil magic. Perhaps more important was the fact that Vodou remained a living communal tradition in Haiti, not a long-dead religion subject to reimagining by highly individualistic seekers after spiritual enlightenment. Meanwhile, although Mississippi Valley Voodoo had largely disappeared as an intact religion, it was a homegrown creole faith. Vodou and Voodoo were simply not countercultural enough for those attracted to New Age and Neopagan ideas.

The growing appeal of Voodoo and Vodou is evident within the modern New Age and Neopagan community. One example of their appeal is the plethora of how-to texts that have appeared in recent years. A search of the online book catalog

> ### The Reputation of New Orleans
>
> New Orleans is widely seen as a capital for magical practices, largely because of its association with Voodoo. Similar practices once existed elsewhere in the United States, including the Florida Keys, the Tampa Bay area, and the South Carolina Lowcountry. New Orleans, however, has been a city since colonial days, complete with a cosmopolitan culture, lively trade, and multiple newspapers. These together served to record tales of the religion and to spread them across the nation and eventually beyond.

of Llewellyn, a leading New Age and Neopagan press, indicates that the company currently publishes five books on some aspect of Voodoo and/or Vodou, most of them geared to the working of magic. A quick perusal of online retailer Amazon.com reveals dozens of additional books and magical kits involving the use of stereotypical "Voodoo dolls."

In keeping with the markedly individualistic nature of the New Age movement and Neopaganism, many works that address Voodoo and Vodou mix and match elements of the religions with other traditions. For one, few draw any significant distinction between Haitian Vodou and Mississippi Valley Voodoo. It is also common for how-to-works to incorporate elements from Santería and other Afro-Caribbean faiths into the practices they purport to describe. At times, such works blend aspects of Vodou and Voodoo into a broad-based mix of spiritual and/or supernatural practices with which they had little or no historical connection. A good example of this approach is Judika Illes's *Element Encyclopedia of 1000 Spells*. Intended as a catch-all collection of magic, it includes elements drawn from the practices of Haiti and Mississippi as well as from the folk beliefs of the Islamic Middle East, China, India, and other areas. On the other hand, one could correctly argue that this disparate blending of traditions is not without precedent. During the era of the Atlantic slave trade, the bondspersons who shaped the early forms of Voodoo and Vodou certainly incorporated aspects of Christian belief into what had originally been distinctly African belief systems.

While Vodou in Haiti has been relatively untouched by Neopaganism, within the United States, both Voodoo and Vodou have been subject to its influence. The individualism of Neopaganism—and increasingly of American society as a whole—has legitimized these religious and magical practices that most Americans once viewed as mere superstition or even demonic manifestations. Today, increasing numbers of Americans treat Haitian Vodou as one of many equally valid paths to spiritual growth. While significant numbers of black Americans seek out information and sometimes begin to practice Vodou because of its links to their African heritage, whites are more likely to seek it out in part because of preexisting Neopagan leanings. For instance, many Wiccans turn to Vodou or Voodoo after becoming dissatisfied practicing a religion that seeks to revive a dead faith. In particular, Vodou, unlike many Neopagan faiths, is a living tradition with a long history. Unsurprisingly, many of those entering the religion in recent years have been white.

The individualism and subjectivism common to most aspects of the New Age movement and Neopaganism also has led some to abandon it in favor of Vodou or Voodoo. Sallie Ann Glassman, arguably the best-known New Orleans practitioner of Vodou, began her involvement in alternative spirituality with New Age and occult practices. She eventually abandoned them in favor of Vodou. According to her, Vodou is much more community oriented than the often self-focused practices associated with countercultural faiths.

Most practitioners have adopted at least portions of the New Age/Neopagan mindset. Miriam Chamani, a well-known New Orleans Voodoo priestess, considers her practice to be but one of many legitimate paths to spiritual growth, a corollary of the individualism characteristic of the New Age worldview. This mindset also allows some practitioners to take part in multiple spiritual traditions, such as Christianity, Wicca, Native American religions, and the like, alongside Vodou or Voodoo without feeling any conflict between divergent and even contradictory claims of the faiths. Along the same lines is a willingness on the part of some U.S. practitioners to abandon the strict rules of Haitian Vodou. Glassman, a highly knowledgeable initiate, does not participate in the animal sacrifice that is an integral part of Haitian practice. Along more pronounced lines, the very existence of how-to guides represents a departure from the communal aspects of Vodou, in which knowledge of the spirits and their world is transmitted orally. Moreover, some of their authors explicitly advocate picking and choosing those aspects of the faith one wishes to embrace. For example, S. Jason Black and Christopher Hyatt's *Urban Voodoo* is openly suspicious of initiation into an Afro-Caribbean religion and suggests the alternative of self-initiation.

The impact of New Age and Neopagan concepts has been so great that increasing numbers of Americans think of Vodou and Voodoo as little more than options available to choose from a vast spiritual smorgasbord. How-to books and the increasing numbers of tourist-oriented shops and Voodoo-themed trinkets in places like New Orleans testify to this attitude. In response, admirers of historical Voodoo and some practitioners of Vodou have responded by condemning what they see as cultural misappropriation. Tamara Siuda, a white American who practices Vodou under the name Mambo Chita Tann, struggled with this problem while writing a recent book on her religion. Recognizing that she had grown up outside of Haiti and its religious culture and noting how frequently fellow Americans denigrated Haiti while claiming to practice the faith that so defines its culture, she considered abandoning the project. Siuda persisted with her research and writing, however, incorporating into it the argument that picking and choosing those aspects of a religion one wishes to practice based on mere personal preference is a form of bigotry. Instead of thinking oneself entitled to practice Vodou however one wants, she argues, spiritual seekers should consider themselves no more than guests in the Haitian culture. Not until they have undergone initiation into the faith do they have any claim to it.

See also: Creolization; Dolls; Initiations; Konesans; Tourism

Jeffrey E. Anderson

Further Reading

Adler, Margot. 2006. *Drawing Down the Moon: Witches, Druids, Goddess-Worshippers, and Other Pagans in America*. Revised and updated ed. London: Penguin.

Anderson, Jeffrey E. 2005. *Conjure in African American Society*. Baton Rouge, LA: Louisiana State UP.

Anderson, Jeffrey E. 2008. *Hoodoo, Voodoo, and Conjure: A Handbook*. Greenwood Folklore Handbooks. Westport, CT: Greenwood Press.

Black, S. Jason, and Christopher S. Hyatt. 1995. *Urban Voodoo: A Beginner's Guide to Afro-Caribbean Magic*. Tempe: New Falcon.

Heelas, Paul. 1996. *The New Age Movement: The Celebration of the Self and the Sacralization of Modernity*. Oxford, UK: Blackwell.

Illes, Judika. 2008. *The Element Encyclopedia of 1000 Spells*. New York: Barnes and Noble / Harper Element.

Siuda, Tamara L. (Mambo Chita Tann). 2012. *Haitian Vodou: An Introduction to Haiti's Indigenous Spiritual Tradition*. Woodbury, MN: Llewellyn.

NEW ORLEANS

Established by explorer and co-founder of Louisiana Jean Baptiste Le Moyne, Sieur de Bienville, at the behest of the French Company of the Indies, New Orleans grew rapidly from the time of its earliest construction in 1718 to become the economic, political, and cultural capital of French colonial Louisiana. Long the legendary home of Voodoo in the United States, New Orleans's history as the center of culture for French colonial Louisiana (1699–1763) and then the seat of government for Louisiana's Spanish government (1763–1803) made it a distinct and unique destination for Americans after the purchase of the Louisiana Territory by the United States. The salient linguistic, religious, and racial differences between the metropolis on the Mississippi River and the incoming American settlers that poured into the city after the purchase made New Orleans exotic and foreign to the city's new inhabitants. Cultural conflicts quickly arose between incoming Americans and the local Creoles, the American-born but culturally Latin inhabitants of Louisiana. In addition to the widespread use of French in educational facilities and cultural activities and the dominance of Roman Catholicism, the intimate relationships between European- and African-descended locals and the consequently large population of interracial inhabitants of the city were commonly cited by Americans as evidence of the backwardness and barbarism of the local Creole population.

Among the other exotic cultural products in Louisiana were the religious practices of the African-descended populations, commonly termed Voodoo. The first official record of the practice of Voodoo in Louisiana may have been documented in 1773, in what one scholar termed "The Gri-Gri Case," when Spanish authorities prosecuted a number of slaves for attempting to kill their owner and overseer using a supposedly poisonous charm. This early account marks both the racialization and criminalization of the practice of Voodoo in New Orleans that would characterize it from the 18th century until at least the mid-20th century.

As far as journalists, historians, and law enforcement in New Orleans were concerned, Voodoo was the practice of Africans brought to Louisiana—superstition and magic of a barbarous nature with harmful intent. As conflicts between Americans and Creoles in New Orleans intensified in the 19th century, local journalists began writing stories about Voodoo, some for entertainment and others geared toward racial fear mongering. The contested nature of slavery and its expansion in the United States in the decades between the Louisiana Purchase and the Civil War made these stories of barbarous African practices among the largely Creole slave population part of a national dialogue in which defenders of slavery used what they labeled as barbarous African religious practices as proof that the enslaved were unprepared for freedom and better suited to be legally and culturally controlled by whites. In New Orleans, as Creoles battled their English-speaking competitors for control of the city, these accusations of barbarism were transferred to the European-descended French-speaking population, largely in the form of accusations that the white Creole population had been mongrelized through unfettered interracial sex with the sizeable African-descended population of New Orleans.

After the Civil War, local color writers used popular images of Voodoo as a strange and exotic religion birthed in Africa to enhance the reputation of the quickly Americanizing city as exotic and foreign. As the use of French became less common at the end of the 19th century and the dominance of the Catholic Church was challenged by a huge influx of Protestant Christians, what remained culturally distinctive about New Orleans was the Afro-Creole population, which retained French language, education, and culture longer than its white counterpart. Moreover, the Afro-Creoles remained tied by race to stories of the supposedly African religion of Voodoo. While historical records of arrests of the people of African descent in connection with religious ceremonies performed in New Orleans before the Civil War almost always mention the presence of white practitioners as well, suggesting the interracial character of these mysterious and largely undocumented ceremonies, the literature coming out of New Orleans increasingly described magic, dancing, and sex as characteristics of Voodoo as practiced by largely African American participants. Authors wrote stories about the priests and priestesses of Voodoo ceremonies, termed *doctors* and *queens*, who populated the old quarters of the city. Stories about Sanité Dédé, Marie Saloppe, Marie Comtesse, Doctor Jim Alexander, Malvina Latour, Doctor John, and the most famous practitioner of Voodoo in New Orleans, the famed 19th-century Voodoo queen, Marie Laveau, populated accounts of culture in New Orleans. By the late 19th century, journalists were covering celebrations of St. John's Eve on the night of June 23 along New Orleans's Bayou St. John. At these ceremonies Voodoo had by the late 1860s apparently become a tourist attraction in the city. Local public transportation ran up to the Bayou for the ceremonies, and queens and doctors performed ceremonies for a paying public. By the end of the 19th century Voodoo had an ambiguous status in New Orleans, functioning both as a cultural attraction described salaciously by writers and journalists to enhance the exotic image of the Crescent City, while at similar periods being characterized as fraud by both local law enforcement and federal authorities, who prosecuted practitioners who sold their products and services in the city and via the mail across the country.

By the beginning of the 20th century prosecutions represented the only firsthand accounts of the practice of Voodoo in New Orleans. The criminalization of Voodoo in both the 19th and 20th centuries made practitioners reticent to record or attest to their ritual practices, leaving modern historians only with the sensationalized journalism and fictionalized historical accounts of outsiders to characterize the city's practitioners. These accounts served to mark New Orleans as the home of Voodoo in the collective imagination both of outsiders and would-be practitioners throughout the United States. In the first four decades of the 20th century, ethnographer Harry Middleton Hyatt, famed African American novelist and Columbia University–trained ethnographer Zora Neale Hurston, and agents of the Louisiana Writers' Project, a division of the Works Progress Administration's Federal Writers' Project, all gathered interview material in New Orleans. By working with self-proclaimed practitioners, recording their accounts of their rituals and their explanations of their meanings and purposes, they provided historians with firsthand evidence of what it meant to practice Voodoo in New Orleans.

Many of the practitioners who were interviewed in early 20th-century New Orleans claimed to look to 19th-century Voodoo queen Marie Laveau as a ritual exemplar of how to practice Voodoo. They held ceremonies in their homes and the homes of colleagues in imitation of rituals that practitioners who claimed to have worked with Laveau during her life recalled and replicated. Practitioners also introduced new details in these rituals to meet the needs of clientele paying for services and thus economically sustaining professional practitioners. They made offerings to the images of Catholic saints—some part of the official pantheon of the Catholic Church, others brought in from folk Catholic traditions. Unlike Haitian Vodou, which retained the names of African deities for whom the images of saints functioned as representations, in 20th-century New Orleans, practitioners made very few references to spirits of apparent African or Haitian origin. Practitioners molded and shaped the stories about the origins and predilections of saints, re-creating them to function as patrons and allies of contemporary practitioners and their clientele.

Still under the pressure of possible fraud prosecution, some professional practitioners of Voodoo also became members and spiritual heads, or *mothers* and *fathers*, in Spiritual Churches. The Spiritual Churches, a largely working-class Christian movement, was introduced to New Orleans circa 1920 by Spiritual Mother Leafy Anderson. From the beginning Anderson was known to have consulted a local worker about her practices, and she employed similar rituals imploring saints for aid, some of them traditionally associated with other Christian churches and others unique to the Spiritual Churches. The best known of the innovative variety was Black Hawk, a Native American spirit. Anderson created a network of interconnected churches that allowed her students to run their congregations independently and shape their ritual practices to their needs and the needs of their churches.

Some Spiritual mothers and fathers incorporated rites common among local practitioners of Voodoo. In other cases, workers known to be practitioners of Voodoo, such as Alonzo Rockford Lewis, who became infamous in the interwar period because of his practice and arrests related to it, simply opened Spiritual Churches of their own and integrated their prior practices into this Christian framework. The Spiritual Church movement in New Orleans remained indiscernibly intertwined with Voodoo until the years following 1937, when an association of the Spiritual Churches of the Southwest met and began to standardize the practices and theology around the Trinity of God the Father, the Son, and Holy Spirit, and in particular the figure of Jesus. The adoption of Christian church–style infrastructure and moves to accept donations rather than payment and offer disclaimers in the sale of professional services and goods related to Voodoo resulted in a legal space in which Voodoo practitioners of New Orleans could prevent their arrest, continue their practices, and help to retain the practice of Voodoo in New Orleans. Workers of Voodoo and Spiritual Church heads were joined in New Orleans's community of practitioners and entrepreneurs by a group of drug store owners who sold the paraphernalia needed for rites to get jobs, keep romantic relationships, pay rent, and harm enemies. The central role of Voodoo in this expansive community demonstrates the extent to which practitioners had made the religion an integral part of the city's cultural landscape by the 20th century.

The end of the 20th century witnessed yet another re-creation of Voodoo in New Orleans. A cultural renaissance in the practice of African Diaspora religions throughout the Americas has seen the re-Africanization of traditions like Brazilian Candomblé, Cuban Santería, and Haitian Vodou, characterized by the travel of priests and priestesses of these religions to West Africa to be trained, educated, and initiated by Yoruba practitioners of similar West African traditions. These priests and priestesses then return these ritual forms to their respective homes in the New World. Fueled by a revaluation of African identity in New World cultures that has sought to counter some of the damage of racism and the concomitant devaluation of African culture that led to the suppression of the African aspects of these faiths throughout their histories, practitioners have sought to re-Africanize their traditions. In a similar trend, the late 20th century has seen an importation of practitioners of Caribbean-style African Diasporic religious traditions, including Haitian Vodou, into New Orleans.

Practitioners in late 20th- and early 21st-century New Orleans are a combination of locally trained practitioners and those who have sought out other African Diasporic teachers. For example, Ava Kay Jones, a Louisiana local, has been initiated in Haitian Vodou and an African American variant of Cuban Santería. Voodoo in contemporary New Orleans is both religion and cultural tourism. Brandi Kelley, former employee of the Voodoo Museum and now godchild of famed Haitian priestess Mama Lola from Brooklyn, New York, runs a cultural center and collection, *Voodoo Authentica*, dedicated to both local and foreign contributions to New Orleans Voodoo in the city's most concentrated tourist district, the French Quarter.

See also: Brown, Karen McCarthy; Dédé, Sanité; Federal Writers' Project; Hurston, Zora Neale; Hyatt, Harry Middleton; Laveau, Marie; Modern Voodoo/Vodou and Hoodoo Businesses; Spiritual Churches

Kodi Roberts

Further Reading

Hirsch, Arnold, and Joseph Logsdon, ed. 1992. *Creole New Orleans: Race and Americanization*. Baton Rouge, LA: Louisiana State University Press.

Jacobs, Claude F., and Andrew J. Kaslow. 1991. *The Spiritual Churches of New Orleans: Origins, Beliefs, and Rituals of an African-American Religion*. Knoxville, TN: University of Tennessee Press.

Kelley, Brandi C. 2012.Interview with the author.

Long, Carolyn Morrow. 2001. *Spiritual Merchants: Religion, Magic, and Commerce*. Knoxville, TN: University of Tennessee Press.

Porteous, Laura L. 1934. "The Gri-Gri Case: A Criminal Trial in Louisiana during the Spanish Regime, 1773." *Louisiana Historical Quarterly* 17: 48–63.

Roberts, Kodi. 2012. "The Promise of Power: The Racial, Gender & Economic Politics of Voodoo in New Orleans, 1881–1940." PhD dissertation. University of Chicago.

Touchstone, Blake. 1972. "Voodoo in New Orleans." *Louisiana History* 13: 371–386.

Wall, Bennet H., et al. 2002. *Louisiana: A History*. Santa Ana, CA: Forum Press, Inc.

NZAMBI A MPUNGU

An expression in the Kikongo language nowadays usually translated as "God Almighty." This is certainly not what it originally meant. Catholic missionaries who arrived in Kongo at the end of the 15th century assumed that *Nzambi* was the local equivalent of *God* and embodied it as such in liturgies and prayers. Over the next four hundred years, Catholic teaching and practice profoundly affected Kongo culture, even though the active missionary presence declined. Protestant and Catholic missions resumed their evangelical activity at the end of the 19th century; most Bakongo are now at least nominally Christian. Nevertheless, 20th-century ethnography allows a tentative reconstruction of what *Nzambi* originally meant. The term *nzambi* can be respectfully applied to any dead person. It was and still is believed that after living in the visible world a person goes to live in the land of the dead (*nsi a bafwa*; see "Cosmogram"), where he lives until he "dies the second death," and becomes an anonymous *simbi* spirit in the bush or in a body of water. Succeeding deaths make him ever more remote from the living. *Nzambi a Mpungu*, "highest Nzambi," designates the most distant and featureless of the dead. Whereas a diviner may point to witches among the living, or *simbi* spirits among the dead, as the cause of misfortunes among the living that can be corrected by ritual means, his diagnosis that "Nzambi is responsible" means that the cause of the misfortune is unknown and that nothing can be done about it. Rather than "God Almighty," *Nzambi a Mpungu* was simply, in traditional thought, a residual or empty category. There was no sense of Nzambi as the creator of the world, which has always existed.

See also: Ancestral Spirits; Cosmogram; Grand Zombi; Kongo; Simbi

Wyatt MacGaffey

Further Reading

MacGaffey, Wyatt. 2006. *Religion and Society in Central Africa*. Chicago: Chicago University Press.

O

OBEAH

"If there shall be found in the possession of any slave any poisonous drugs, pounded glass, parrot's beaks, dog's teeth, alligator's teeth, or other materials notoriously used in the practice of Obeah or witchcraft, such slave upon conviction, shall be liable to suffer transportation from the island [deportation]." So read a law passed in the mid-1700s in Jamaica to address increasing demand to bring the use of obeah under control. This law speaks to obeah in a number of manners. First, it validates the actual prevalence and/or suspicion of prevalence of behaviors deemed in need of controlling, in this case Obeah. Second, it speaks to a prevailing belief in Obeah by both whites and blacks. Had blacks not maintained a belief in Obeah's efficacy then perhaps neither would whites hold a belief in its effectiveness to the point of codifying Obeah. Third, and just as interesting, is the specificity of the law in listing the "ingredients" of the trade.

Beginning with the third observation, the ingredients and "other materials notoriously used in the practice of Obeah" suggest an understanding of the acts of Obeah, an understanding that took nearly two hundred years on the part of the colonizers. The first laws to speak against the behaviors of the practice of Obeah were enacted in the late 1600s. At that time the understanding by the planter class was still very vague, but it was becoming clear that incidents of poisoning both within and among the planter class and their chattel slaves were the workings of Obeah. It is conceivable that the acts of poisoning were not malevolent behaviors via deviant slaves. They may well have been part of a larger conspiracy on the part of enslaved persons, often in consort with Obeah healers, as acts of sabotage against enslavement. One case occurring in the mid-1800s demonstrates this. An enslaved man attempted to poison his owner, who was also a preacher. The preacher often sermonized on the glory of heaven and stated that that he desired to obtain this glory. In defense of his actions, the enslaved man, claimed he was "moved to kill Massa Parson" in an effort to assist said Parson in reaching his goal of getting to heaven.

Obeah is a derivative of traditional African spirituality having commonalities with other African Diaspora spiritual systems such as Vodou, Santería, and hoodoo. Scholars state that hoodoo was not able to maintain its relations with African deities due in great part to demographic issues and the religious teachings of the planter class. This would also have been true of Obeah, but unlike slavery in many parts of North America, where enslaved populations were relatively small and thus unable to hold and disperse collective cultural traditions, Jamaica had large plantation systems very much like those of Cuba and Brazil. Nevertheless, the faith of the planter class had a great deal of influence on which African religious retentions survived on the island.

The practices of Obeah and hoodoo both developed in societies dominated by a Protestant planter class. Protestantism, unlike Catholicism, offered little opportunity to syncretize deities, effectively eliminating the connections between ingredients employed and their associative deities. In African traditional religions, particular deities govern particular body parts, as well as specific elements in the natural world in addition to their controlling arenas in the supernatural realm of the universe. Trained healers are also spiritual practitioners and honor the relations between spirit and medicine. In spite of the loss of specific spiritual beings in Jamaica, Obeah healers maintain an understanding of the connection between their herbal and magical materials and the spirit world.

Keeping this in mind, Obeah practitioners are forced to rely upon the limitation afforded by Protestant prayers and imagery. It is partly owing to this reason that the use of fauna and animal parts takes center stage in the workings of Obeah. A skilled practitioner would take the time to study the natural world around him or her. His or her studies would have revealed the behaviors of plants and animals, which they would make note of in order to determine their efficacy for the outcomes they sought.

Speaking of the influence of Obeah in Jamaica, Alexander Giraldo summarized its importance as follows:

> Modern historians believe that Obeah originated from the Ashanti and Koromantin tribes of Africa on the Gold Coast, and that imported slaves introduced it to the Caribbean as early as the mid-17th century. Regardless of its use, for "evil" or "good", the Obeah men were treated with the utmost respect and fear by all whom met him. The Obeah man and women played a prominent role in the Caribbean slave societies from the beginning of the slave trade. They functioned as community leaders and teachers of the African folk's cultural heritage.

In keeping with its leaders' exalted role, Obeah was heavily associated with rebellions, most notably Tacky's Rebellion, which took place in Jamaica in 1760. While the rebels were defeated, it took colonial forces weeks to restore order on the island. Obeah's use in resistant acts is seen far more as nefarious behaviors associative to witchcraft than behaviors of human agency enacted for the greater humanity of the enslaved population. It is important to understand that at one time or another most religions have held elements of magic and medicine as part of their epistemology. These similarities allow for systems such as Obeah to cross cultural and ethnic boundaries once the geographical boundaries of these cultural and ethnic groups have been removed as a result of slavery. Furthermore, the foundational similarities allowed for an interchange of medicinal inquiry between enslaved healers and whites who for a brief period shared similar beliefs concerning the use of herbs as curative agents.

It should not be expected that enslavement necessitated the full and complete loss of cultural mores and pathways of existence. Nor should it be assumed that

> **Vodou and Other Afro-Caribbean Religions**
>
> Americans are apt to label any Afro-Caribbean religion "Vodou." This tendency is, of course, incorrect, and rests on the misguided assumption that creole religions are all more or less the same thing. Santería or Lukumí, a Cuban religion, is the faith most commonly mistaken for Vodou. The two, however, are distinct in several ways. Santería, for instance, has only a handful of major deities of Yoruba background, while Vodou has thousands of lwas who originated among the Yoruba, Fon, BaKongo, and a host of other ethnicities. Ritual actions, terminology, and much else also differ between the two religions.

these cultures migrated with the enslaved intact and whole. Rather it should be understood that culture is porous and mutable. Obeah is but one strong example of cultural mutations that occurred as a direct result of the transatlantic slave trade.

See also: Creolization; Myalism; Syncretism

Phoenix Savage

Further Reading

Giraldo, Alexander. 2014. "Obeah: The Ultimate Resistance." Slave Resistance: A Caribbean Study. Accessed July 1, 2014: http://scholar.library.miami.edu/slaves/Religion/religion.html.

Olmos, Margarite Fernández, and Lizbeth Paravisini-Gebert. 2003. *Creole Religions of the Caribbean: An Introduction from Vodou and Santería to Obeah and Espiritismo.* New York: New York University Press.

Olmos, Margarite Fernández, and Lizbeth Paravisini-Gebert, eds. 1997. *Sacred Possessions: Vodou, Santería, Obeah, and the Caribbean.* Piscataway, NJ: Rutgers University Press.

Williams, Joseph J. 2011. *Voodoo and Obeahs: Phases of West India Witchcraft.* New ed. Calgary, Canada: Theophania.

OGOU

Most scholars consider Ogou to be Yoruba in origin. In West Africa, this spirit was known as Ogun and understood as a deity in charge of fire. Those who worked with fire or wielded items produced through its use—blacksmiths, hunters, warriors, farmers, and the like—were his special charges. Ogun made his way into multiple Latin American creole religions, including Santería, as well as Vodou. Some have argued that he survived under the name Joe Féraille in the 20th-century United States.

While retaining many of his African attributes, Haiti transformed Ogun. He maintained his traditional associations but came to be especially known for his warlike qualities because of Haiti's experience during its revolution. Believers consider him to have motivated and led the slaves and maroons who fought to overthrow the French, a successful struggle that resulted in the western hemisphere's second-oldest country. Besides his warlike associations, he has come to be associated with machinery because of its reliance of iron and steel, surgeons in consequence of their use of metal tools, and atomic energy.

Like other lwa, Ogou is associated with a variety of items and attributes. Among them are the iron and fire of blacksmith's forges and the weapons of warriors, notably machetes, swords, and sabers. Rum is Ogou's drink of choice. He is said to be able to imbibe great quantities of the liquid without getting drunk. His favored colors are blue and red, both of which signify protection from harm, and his day of the week is Wednesday.

Ogou can appear in many guises in his roles within the Rada, Petwo, and other nanchons. As the Petwo lwa, Ogou Feray, he is most often identified with St. James the Greater, especially because of the latter's frequent depiction as a mounted warrior. This concept of the warrior saint derived from medieval Spain's *reconquista* of the Iberian Peninsula from Muslims who had conquered it centuries before. According to legend, St. James fought on the side of the Christian Spaniards. The production of lithographs depicting the saint according to his fabled warlike attributes allowed his image to easily connect to preexisting notions of the West African Ogun. In addition to images showing him as a warrior entering battle, Ogou sometimes appears as a wounded soldier near death, supported by his comrades.

Possession by Ogou is reportedly an intense experience. Those chosen by the lwa dress as soldiers and act the part. Speaking loudly, they carry the machetes or swords associated with Ogou. Some of the possessed are reportedly able to handle hot iron without injury because of Ogou's power over it.

See also: Creolization; Féraille, Joe; Haitian Revolution; Lwa; Maroon; Nanchons; Saints; Santería

Jeffrey E. Anderson

Further Reading

Desmangles, Leslie G. 1992. *Faces of the Gods: Vodou and Roman Catholicism in Haiti*. Chapel Hill, NC: University of North Carolina Press.

Hebblethwaite, Benjamin. 2012. *Vodou Songs in Haitian Creole and English*. Philadelphia: Temple University Press.

Olmos, Margarite Fernández, and Lizbeth Paravisini-Gebert. 2003. *Creole Religions of the Caribbean: An Introduction from Vodou and Santería to Obeah and Espiritismo*. New York: New York University Press.

OPENING

In Haitian Vodou, the term *opening* may refer to ceremonies performed at the beginning of rites dedicated to the lwa. Frequently, St. Peter or Legba, the guardian of the crossroads between the world inhabited by people and realm inhabited by the lwa, is called upon to open the path of those seeking to contact, seek aid from, or be possessed or ridden by the lwa. They are often characterized by specific dances and music used to appeal to Legba, sacrifices, and the use of vèvè, symbolic geometric figures specific to a particular lwa, to get Legba to "open the gates" to initiate a Vodou ceremony.

An opening in the U.S. context frequently refers to an initiation performed in order to grant the power to function as a worker, or practitioner, especially as a professional practitioner of Voodoo in New Orleans. Openings were observed in the 1930s and had their proceedings documented by researchers of the Louisiana Writers' Project, supported by the Works Progress Administration (WPA). In an unfurnished room workers set up an altar on the floor. The altar was based on a white cloth the size of a table surface placed on the floor. The cloth was adorned with a picture of St. Peter, candles, and various sacrifices, including cider, soda, alcohol, sugar, and various food items—both raw fruits and spices as well as cooked dishes like beans and rice and cakes. Researchers documented that the workers performing the initiation began by knocking on the floor three times and having their guests do the same while praying in French. The worker performing the ceremony broke into dance while drinking copious amounts of alcohol. Initiations described by author and ethnographer Zora Neale Hurston also entailed covering or bathing in a variety of substances, wearing special garments and lying prone, alone, for long periods of time.

Initiates could apparently undergo several openings, designed to bring them into the practice of different kinds of work. Workers who specialized in love might perform an opening that was different from workers who specialized in causing harm or death. One of the most distinctive openings reported by researches was a "black cat opening" required to initiate a practitioner into malevolent ritual practices.

While there were a variety of openings documented in New Orleans, some workers referred potential initiates to other colleagues, suggesting that not all workers were qualified to do, or felt comfortable performing, openings. This may suggest that these initiations in and of themselves were the expertise of some workers and not a universal practice among Voodoo adherents in the Crescent City. Workers in New Orleans were paid for their participation in an opening and afterward frequently offered to aid new initiates in their future endeavors as practitioners of Voodoo, provided them with lists of necessary supplies, and connected them with suppliers and other practitioners in the city. Even though some researchers in early 20th-century New Orleans reported becoming Voodoo practitioners without the benefit of participating in an opening, the ceremony undoubtedly provided these professional connections to new practitioners, and by referring clients to other associates, practitioners might also facilitate economic prosperity within the community of Voodoo practitioners. This suggests that openings may have been as much about maintaining a community as initiating someone into it.

See also: Ceremonies; Federal Writers' Project; Hoodoo; Initiations; New Orleans; Vèvè; Worker

Kodi Roberts

Further Reading

Roberts, Kodi. In press. *Voodoo and the Promise of Power: The Racial, Gender & Economic Politics of Religion in New Orleans, 1881–1940*. Baton Rouge, LA: Louisiana State University Press.

OSSANGE/ASSONQUER

In New Orleans, this spirit was known as Monsieur Assonquer, sometimes spelled Onzoncaire or On Sa Tier. As with many Voodoo deities, characteristics of this deity are imperfectly known. The first author to mention this being was George Washington Cable, who called him a spirit of good fortune. In his 1880 novel *The Grandissimes*, a Voodoo priestess known as Palmyre Philosophe calls on the deity to win the love of a man for a white client. The ensuing ceremony consisted of offerings of pound cake and cordial and the burning of a green candle standing in a tumbler partially filled with sugarcane syrup. Palmyre also "paid the floor" with silver coins to prevent what Cable referred to as "guillons (interferences of outside imps)." Later in the book, Cable also mentions that the client continued to throw small amounts of whatever she was eating onto the floor for Assonquer in order to avoid his displeasure and thereby escape bad luck. Elsewhere in the novel, Cable uses the word *imp* to describe Voodoo deities, including Assonquer himself. While the accuracy of Cable's descriptions are open to question, Assonquer was a genuine Voodoo deity, as confirmed by interviews conducted by the Federal Writers' Project during the late 1930s and early 1940s. Other than describing Assonquer as corresponding to the Catholic St. Paul, the additional sources offer little more information than Cable. The paucity of detail is particularly unfortunate because alongside Blanc Dani and LaBas, Assonquer was the most widely mentioned deity of the religion.

Vodou includes its own version—and perhaps versions—of this spirit. Haitians know him by the name Ossange. Milo Rigaud mentions an Ossangne in *Secrets of Voodoo* (1969), but says nothing further about the spirit. Mambo Vye Zo Komande LaMenfo, a U.S.-born and Haitian-initiated mambo, describes an Ogoun Ossange as an "escort spirit" for Agwe. Ogoun Ossange, she states, is characterized by calm, direct energy and is understood as a retired warrior, sailor, and priest of Danbala who can speak for the speechless serpent spirit. He is a member of the Nago nanchon, and his colors are "the blue and azure green of the ocean."

Despite the lack of specific details about Ossange/Assonquer and his role—especially in the Mississippi Valley—his Transatlantic history is reasonably clear. The deity appears to have originated among the Yoruba of Nigeria, where he was known as Osanyin. Among the Yoruba, he was the god of herbalism, making him one of the more important deities. He may well have made his way into the religion of the neighboring Fon and Ewe peoples, as had Legba, but if so, he had become difficult to identify by the time modern scholars began to study the religions of the region. The slave trade carried him to Saint-Domingue and New Orleans, though there is no easy explanation for why his importance faded in the former. The New World descendants of Osanyin flourished elsewhere, such as Cuba, where he became Osain, deity of the forest and healing.

See also: Cable, George Washington; Federal Writers' Project; Vodou in Haiti; Voodoo in the Mississippi Valley

Jeffrey E. Anderson

Further Reading

Anderson, Jeffrey E. 2008. *Hoodoo, Voodoo, and Conjure: A Handbook*. Westport, CT: Greenwood Press.

Cable, George Washington. 1891. *The Grandissimes: A Story of Creole Life*. New York: Charles Scribner's Sons.

Federal Writers' Project. 1935–1943. Northwestern State University of Louisiana, Watson Memorial Library, Cammie G. Henry Research Center, Natchitoches, Louisiana.

Olmos, Margarite Fernández, and Lizbeth Paravisini-Gebert. 2003. *Creole Religions of the Caribbean: An Introduction from Vodou and Santería to Obeah and Espiritismo*. New York: New York University Press.

Rigaud, Milo. 1985 [1969]. *Secrets of Voodoo*. Translated by Robert B. Cross. New York: Arco; reprint, San Francisco: City Lights.

Scheu, Patricia (Mambo Vye Zo Komande LaMenfo). 2011. *Serving the Spirits: The Religion of Vodou*. Philadelphia: Published by author.

Thompson, Robert Farris. 1983. *Flash of the Spirit: African and Afro-American Art and Philosophy*. New York: Random House.

OUNFÒ

Ounfò, also spelled *hounfort*, *hounfor*, or *hounfo*, is a word that describes several elements of a Vodou society. Open to the countryside or enclosed in a city basement, ounfòs are the spiritual, religious, and secular centers of the sosyetes that work in them. The ounfò is both the physical location of the society as well as the arrangement of people and roles that make up that society's group of practitioners.

The word *ounfò* takes its root linguistically from the Dahomean word for spirit, *houn*. The word *houn* means "spirit" in Haiti as well. The source of the root *houn-* figures in terms such as *oungan* ("spirit priest") and *ounsi* ("spirit wife"). *Hounfo*, or *ounfò* as it is pronounced, likewise includes the *houn* root. The ending of ounfò, *fo*, means "place." Thus, ounfò means something akin to "where the family of the gods meets."

The spatial arrangements of many ounfò hark back to their Central and West African roots. They feature a series of rooms surrounding an open courtyard. The central focus is the peristil, or peristyle, a roofed-over dancing court. Beneath the roof, also called a *tonnel*, one finds the potomitan, the center post. This is the main axis of the ounfò, the location where the spirits descend in service, and the still point of vodou dances that are embellished with vèvès of the spirits surrounding its base. Tall, often covered in spiraling serpent designs, the potomitan is the main altar for services, healing baths, and divinatory readings performed by the oungan or mambo of the society. It is often planted into a concrete base called a *pe*, the main altar space for the peristil.

Adjoining the dance court is usually a building housing several rooms that can be opened directly onto the peristil. One or more rooms are set up as altar spaces called *bagi*, or *badjis*. These rooms house the ritual accoutrement of the spirits. They can be set up for one specific spirit (i.e., Ezili) or for a nanchon of spirits (i.e., Nago). The room usually contains an altar upon which are items relating to its occupant. Bottles of liquor; bowls of jewelry, tobacco, and candies; clothing; perfumes; and flags are all stored in the bagi, ready at a moment's notice to be brought forth for the pleasure of the occupant.

> ### The Potomitan
>
> The chief ritual space of the ounfò is the peristil, and at the center of this is the potomitan. The potomitan is a post made from a single tree trunk that stretches upward from a low base, usually of concrete, to the roof of the peristil. Believers consider it the conduit through which the lwa descend to the earth to communicate with humans. Vèvès and other symbols of the lwa surround the post, and many of the rituals of the ounfò center around it.

The ounfò also holds the initiatory chamber called a *djevo*. It is here that candidates of Haitian Vodou *kouche* ("lay down") for a period of time during which rituals are performed to make them initiates of the ounfò.

The peristil is also the location where oungan and mambo perform secular work. Divination is laid out on the pe, the base of the potomitan, to seek information for a problem. Bagis double as hospital rooms for spiritual ailments. Clients may need to kouche before the lwa's altar in the bagi, in order to bring about healing. Baths are crafted in bowls laid out on the pe to absorb its spiritual power, then poured over people who sit upon its edge and subsume themselves in the spiritual power of the place.

Ounfò also means the arrangement of people within the sosyete. Sosyetes reflect familial relationships, with the head called *Papa* or *Mama*. They are the potomitan of the group, around whom the sosyete revolves. Initiates called *ti-moun* ("children") or *ti-fey* ("little leaves") are seen as the children of the leaders. They are helpers who serve a myriad of functions from simple cleaning and serving to more complicated roles, such as laplas or oungenikon. This family arrangement is the most common legacy left from colonial times and continues to inform and uphold the idea of ounfò as family centered and community focused.

The spirits and symbols of an ounfò may change over time. New spirits arrive, making new demands, and the location of the ounfò may need to physically expand, add new members, or even divide in order to accommodate the wishes of the spirits. Additional spirits may require the bagis to be moved to the edge of the peristil proper, so that they are separate from the main building but still a part of the overall arrangement. In some compounds, the bagis surround a large natural feature, such as a mapou tree. Then the peristil is said to be *fran Ginen*, the real deal. With the mapou standing in for the potomitan and the very ground surrounding it consecrated, the servitor is transported back to Ginen and truly dances in the ounfò of the ancestors.

See also: Dahomey; Kanzo; Laplas; Mambo; Oungan; Oungenikon

Patricia Scheu (Mambo Vye Zo Komande LaMenfo)

Further Reading

Gilles, Jerry M. and Yvrose S. 2009. *Remembrance: Roots, Rituals and Reverence in Vodou.* Davie, FL: Bookmanlit Publishers.

Michel, Claudine, and Patrick Bellegarde-Smith, eds. 2006. *Vodou in Haitian Life and Culture: Invisible Powers*. New York: Palgrave Macmillan.

Scheu, Patricia (Mambo Vye Zo Komande LaMenfo). 2011. *Serving the Spirits: The Religion of Vodou*. Philadelphia: Published by author.

Thompson, Robert Farris. 1983. *Flash of the Spirit: African and Afro-American Art and Philosophy*. New York: Random House.

OUNGAN

The word *oungan*, which can also be written *hungan* or *houngan*, is the name for a Haitian Vodou priest. The term itself is of Fon and/or Ewe origin and means "master of the god" or "spirit chief," a reference to oungans' primary role as ministers to the lwas. They are sometimes known as *papalwas* or *papa-lois*—variations of a Yoruba word meaning "father of the lwas"—because of their relationship with the spirits. Other titles one sometimes encounters are *gangan* and *capla*, the former a word of Bantu origin meaning "doctor" or "conjurer" according to scholar Harold Courlander.

Oungans are often the heads of Vodou temples, known as *ounfòs*, though these may also be led by their female counterparts, known as *mambos*. Unlike many faiths, Vodou has no hierarchy beyond the individual congregation, members of which join voluntarily. On the other hand, great respect is attached to each oungan's initiation-based spiritual lineage, which helps maintain traditions and ties between what might otherwise become isolated congregations. For practical purposes, however, each ounfò acts independently, and oungans operate free from outside institutional control.

Within the ounfò, the oungan is in charge of a hierarchy of temple workers. Immediately below the oungan is often the laplas, or laplace, whose general function is to carry a sword as part of a flag corps known as the *kò drapo* and to serve as a master of ceremonies. In the absence of the oungan himself, the laplas operates the ounfò. A mambo caille is often the next most important assistant to the oungan and is herself an apprentice to him who can take over the work of the ounfò when both its head and the laplas are absent. Other officers who serve under the oungan are known as *oungenikons*, who lead songs during services, and assistants known as *ounsi*. Members of congregations who have not taken on a particular office are known as the *pittit-caye*, or "children of the house."

Becoming an oungan can be a complex process. Almost all identify a call from the lwas as the motive behind their pursuit of the priesthood. The summonses can take many forms, but the most common are verbal calls communicated by those possessed by a lwa or by dreams indicating the will of the spirits. Other indicators can be prophetic signs that suggest the lwas have chosen one as a priest and unexplained misfortunes, indicating that the lwas are unhappy with one's degree of service to them. Whatever the nature of the call to the priesthood, refusal to comply leads to punishment, which often takes the form of illness.

Those who accept the guidance of the lwa next undergo training. While some claim to have learned entirely from the lwas or to have attained a special relationship with the lwas through ownership of spiritually empowered objects, most study under established oungans or mambos. During this period of apprenticeship, they usually progress through their teacher's ounfò hierarchy as they gradually master the theological and ritual knowledge necessary to operate their own ounfòs. Part of this process includes progressing through a cycle of initiatory rituals known as *kanzo*, which begins with a ritual washing known as *lave tèt*. Those oungans who practice without undergoing the prescribed initiatory rituals are known as *bòkòs*.

Believers differentiate between oungans largely on their possession of konesans, a Kreyòl term referring to spiritual knowledge and power. To a large extent, konesans consists of understanding the lwas and their preferences. Each lwa can have its distinctive drum rhythm, corresponding saint, favorite food and color, preferred clothing, and the like, making such knowledge incredibly difficult to master. Not all the wisdom expected from oungans is strictly theological in nature. As scholar Alfred Métraux stated in *Voodoo in Haiti* (2006), a successful oungan must be "at one and the same time priest, healer, soothsayer, exorcizer, organizer of public entertainments and choirmaster." Métraux also went on to describe many of them as community counselors, political guides, and witnesses to contracts.

Despite oungans' multitude of roles and the respect most obtain, not all are trusted members of their communities. Many Haitians, for instance, judge bòkòs to be practitioners of harmful sorcery who have bought their spiritual powers from one or more less-than-savory lwas. Many also consider those oungans who have not undergone the proper training with established mambos or oungans to possess inferior knowledge and disparagingly call them *oungan-makout*, linking their claims of priestly office to the makout, the straw bag traditionally carried by Haitian peasants. Some believers even question whether certain bòkòs and oungans cooperate with each other, the former causing evil to befall the faithful so that seemingly benevolent oungans can then remove it. Nevertheless, Vodou devotees do not doubt that the lwas can and will punish those who abuse their priesthood, even going so far as to strip the worst offenders of their spiritual abilities.

The word *oungan* does not appear to have been employed in the Mississippi Valley. There Voodoo priests were known as *wangateurs*, *workers*, or *doctors*. Moreover, in the New Orleans area, most of the ministers of the faith were female, the equivalent of Haitian mambos. Despite these facts, there were certainly individuals who fulfilled the role of oungans, at least in the New Orleans area. One prominent 19th-century practitioner was Charles Lafontaine, better known as Dr. Jim Alexander. In addition, one of the last recorded members of the Voodoo priesthood was Oscar Felix, also known as Nom Felix. He continued to initiate new members into the faith until at least the 1930s.

See also: Alexander, Jim; Bòkò; Dahomey; Ewe; Kanzo; Konesans; Lave Tèt; Lwa; Mambo; Opening; Ounfò; Possession; Worker

Jeffrey E. Anderson

Further Reading

Anderson, Jeffrey E. 2005. *Conjure in African American Society*. Baton Rouge, LA: Louisiana State UP.

Anderson, Jeffrey E. 2008. *Hoodoo, Voodoo, and Conjure: A Handbook*. Greenwood Folklore Handbooks. Westport, CT: Greenwood Press.

Courlander, Harold. 1960. *The Drum and the Hoe: Life and Lore of the Haitian People*. Berkeley, CA: University of California Press.

Long, Carolyn Morrow. 2006. *A New Orleans Voudou Priestess: The Legend and Reality of Marie Laveau*. Gainesville, FL: University Press of Florida.

Métraux, Alfred. 1972. *Voodoo in Haiti*. Translated by Hugo Charteris and with an Introduction by Sidney W. Mintz. New York: Schocken.

Olmos, Margarite Fernández, and Lizbeth Paravisini-Gebert. 2003. *Creole Religions of the Caribbean: An Introduction from Vodou and Santería to Obeah and Espiritismo*. New York: New York University Press.

Scheu, Patricia (Mambo Vye Zo Komande LaMenfo). 2011. *Serving the Spirits: The Religion of Vodou*. Philadelphia: Published by author.

OUNGENIKON

The position of oungenikon is held by either a man or a woman. These individuals are song masters, leading the ounsi choir in song and dance during a Vodou fet. The title *oungenikon* is from the Fon language. *Ougeni-* has a root in *dó gbè*, meaning to greet or speak. The second part, *-kon*, can be arbitrarily assigned to any number of meanings in the Fon language, but the root for all is *–jihan*, which translates as "sing." Thus, one can deduce that *oungenikon* in Haitian Vodou means "the one who sings to greet the spirits."

Oungenikons must have an encyclopedic knowledge of Vodou services. Each nanchon of lwa has its own sets of songs, drum beats, dance rhythms, and clave. Oungenikons must know songs for all twenty-one nanchons and the appropriate drum rhythms and dances so they can appropriately string together groups of songs to follow the reglemen, or ceremonial order of service. Oungenikon must know and understand these items intimately to be able to change or call upon anything in their repertoire during the course of the service.

Songs vary from place to place. Individual ones may be rare outside of a specific area, such as southern Haiti. A song can be a common one that most houses sing, but use different melodies behind the words. They can be handed down from generation to generation, or they can be made up on the spot to fill in empty spaces. A skillful oungenikon can blend his or her knowledge of songs with that of drum beats and dances. Those who are extremely gifted are often in high demand to sing at multiple sosyetes beside their own. Like popular drummers who play at various houses, good lead singers have the power to draw together a loose group of ounsi into a power choir of the gods.

The oungenikon, together with the ounsi choir and the drummers, creates a powerful triangle of energy, sound, and rhythm. It is said that this triad of voice, hands, and feet is the power behind numinous experience in service. Understanding the meaning of a song, matching it to the correct drum rhythm, and leading the choir in singing it can bring about the arrival of the lwa in a Vodou ceremony. All three points of energy must be in sync, however, for the real magic of a Vodou service to occur.

See also: Bight of Benin; Dahomey; Ewe; Lwa; Mambo; Nanchons; Oungan

Patricia Scheu (Mambo Vye Zo Komande LaMenfo)

Further Reading

Lefebvre, Claire, and Anne-Marie Brousseau. 2002. *A Grammar of Fongbe*. Berlin: Mouton de Gruyter.

Scheu, Patricia (Mambo Vye Zo Komande LaMenfo). 2011. *Serving the Spirits: The Religion of Vodou*. Philadelphia: Published by author.

OUNSI

Ounsi is the title of a servitor in a Haitian Vodou sosyete. Ounsi takes its root in the Fon word *houn*, meaning "spirit," and *si*, meaning "wife." So, an ounsi in Vodou is a spirit wife. Men and women both can be seen as wives of the spirits, however, as the lwa make no distinction between sexes.

There are two grades or ranks of ounsi. There is ounsi bossale, which translates literally as a "wild ounsi." What is meant spiritually is that this person has not received his or her baptism into the sosyete. The wild servitor has not had services to seat their spirits in their heads. They can participate in house events, but they are limited in what they can do within a sosyete. They may not touch consecrated items, such as flags and sacred beads known as *kolyes*. They may not enter the initiatory chamber, known as a *djevo*. Often, they are relegated only to menial tasks like cleaning, sweeping, and fetching firewood. That said, bossales often make up a disproportionate number of servitors in a given Vodou sosyete.

The ounsi kanzo is the second rank and indicates a servitor who has undergone full initiatory rites and is consecrated to the lwa. Like ounsi bossale, they perform menial jobs like sweeping the peristil, preparing and serving food, and running errands for the mambo or oungan. What sets them apart is that their spirits have been formally seated in their heads, allowing them to do many things that ounsi bossale cannot. They can handle the kolyes and clean and service the sacred vessels of kanzo, the pot tets. They may enter the djevo during a kanzo to help out.

Ounsi kanzo can also be dedicated to minor roles with the larger sosyete. Female ounsi kanzo can serve as ren drapo, or flag queens. They are dedicated to specific sequin flags and are responsible for carrying them at the beginning of important ceremonies, then folding them up and putting them away when done. Ounsi also perform a myriad of smaller tasks within the ounfò. They care for the pot tèts of the initiates. They replenish offerings, clean altars, and help with children and elderly of the sosyete. Ounsi also sew sequin flags and bottles and prepare mange lwa, or food for the Lwa. Their sacred duties also includes making up the choir of singers who are called upon in service to sing for the lwa. They are the dancers, and they can switch between complicated Vodou dances, such as Kongo and Ibo, to popular ones like méringues and crabienne. Their most important job is to offer themselves up as the chwal, or horses, of the lwa during possession. Ounsi are truly the backbone of the Vodou sosyete.

See also: Kanzo; Laplas; Mambo; Ounfò; Oungan; Oungenikon; Possession

Patricia Scheu (Mambo Vye Zo Komande LaMenfo)

Further Reading

Bellegarde-Smith, Patrick, and Claudine Michel, eds. 2006. *Haitian Vodou: Spirit, Myth, and Reality*. Bloomington, IN: Indiana University Press.

Scheu, Patricia (Mambo Vye Zo Komande LaMenfo). 2011. *Serving the Spirits: The Religion of Vodou*. Philadelphia: Published by author.

OWEN, MARY ALICIA

Mary Alicia Owen was born in 1850 in St. Joseph, Missouri. She would remain a resident of the town throughout her life, passing away there in early 1935. Owen was a well-known folklorist during her lifetime. She published dozens of articles and five books, most of them addressing African American and Native American folklore. Unfortunately, Owen's work has been largely forgotten today. According to her biographer, Greg Olson, her current obscurity is a consequence of her choice of professional acquaintances, who were predominantly English, which inadvertently caused her to be overlooked by her fellow countrypersons.

The works of Mary Alicia Owen are among only a handful of sources that address Voodoo in the Mississippi Valley outside of New Orleans. Much of her work was conducted in 1890 and 1891, during which time she investigated magical practices in the area near her Missouri home. She was assisted in her investigations by a variety of conjurers, including a well-known practitioner called King Alexander. During Owen's study, she determined that although Voodoo's practice was largely decentralized and focused on the workings of hoodoo, it continued to include dances. Some prominent practitioners also gathered periodically as a group they called the Circle. There they would discuss their successes and Voodoo and hoodoo news from across the country.

See also: Voodoo in the Mississippi Valley

Jeffrey E. Anderson

Further Reading

Olson, Greg. 2012. *Voodoo Priests, Noble Savages, and Ozark Gypsies: The Life of Folklorist Mary Alicia Owen*. Columbia, MO: University of Missouri Press.

Owen, Mary Alicia. 1892. "Among the Voodoos." In *The International Folk-lore Congress 1891: Papers and Transactions*, 230-248. London: David Nutt.

Owen, Mary Alicia. 1893 [2003]. *Old Rabbit, the Voodoo and Other Sorcerers*. With an Introduction by Charles Godfrey Leland. With Illustrations by Juliette A. Owen and Louis Wain. London: T. Fisher Unwin; reprint, Whitefish, MT: Kessinger Publishing.

P

PAKET KONGO

Paket Kongo is the name given to the small bundles of herbs and other items tied for healing. The tying of a paket requires an assemblage of beads, sequins, pins, ribbons, string, thread, feathers, and mirrors. Each is a bricolage of elements that has a spiritual purpose. Pakets can be tied for healing, jobs, lost loves, health, and wealth. They are similar to *nkisi*, the Kongo bundles of power that are often tied and nailed to contain the energy of the spirits inside.

Some of the most powerful pakets are tied by the lwa during the nights of the Bat Ge service of the kanzo cycle. A square of satin is filled with charged herbs, blessed waters, perfumes, oils, sticks, and a myriad of substances specific to the purpose of the paket. The material is then gathered into a bundle, and the paket is tightly tied, while the oungan or mambo sings over the work. A candle is lit, and the paket is passed over the flames to "heat it up" and make it work faster.

The manner in which one ties a paket can often reveal its purpose. Male pakets are always tied with a round bottom, and a stiff vertical top. They are tightly wound with ribbon and topped with a feather, real or artificial. The purpose is to give the paket the power to waft its energy about. Female pakets are tied with two or more arms gently curving down and then secured to the large bottom of the paket's body. The image is of a dancing female form, with movement and energy flowing from it in a steady stream.

See also: Gris-gris; Hand; Kongo; Magic; Mojo; Nation Sack

Patricia Scheu (Mambo Vye Zo Komande LaMenfo)

Further Reading

Thompson, Robert Farris. 1983. *Flash of the Spirit: African and Afro-American Art and Philosophy.* New York: Random House.

PAPA LABAS

In Haiti, the old man at the crossroads goes by the name Papa Legba, from the African deity Alegba among the Fon and Yoruba people of the Bight of Benin region of West Africa. The Master of the Crossroad was known as LaBas, Lébat, or Liba in the form of Voodoo practiced in the New Orleans area. Though many of his attributes have been forgotten over time, he was clearly an important deity and is one of the most frequently mentioned in written sources about the religion since the late 19th century. As with his Haitian counterpart, one of his functions was to serve as the doorkeeper for the gods. Likely for this reason, he was identified with

St. Peter, keeper of the keys of heaven. The prevalence of devotion to St. Roch in the New Orleans area may also owe something to LaBas, whose Haitian counterpart was often associated with the saint. The similarities between the New Orleans deity and the Haitian Legba suggest that perhaps immigration from the island may have had greater impact on understandings of LaBas than it did on other Mississippi Valley Voodoo spirits, such as Blanc Dani.

While West Africa appears to have supplied the most direct ancestor of LaBas, other regions might have contributed as well. For example, in 1946, Robert Tallant reported that an informant had seen Marie Laveau leading a procession of people who were screaming "We are goin' to see Papa Limba!" This extant reference is the earliest and perhaps only notation of the name Limba in relation to New Orleans Voodoo. The name *Limba* takes its root from Lenba, a city in the Kongo nation, and a prestigious religious organization in the Kongo during the 1660s. Whether Limba and LaBas were the same, however, is uncertain.

In 1920 jazz recordings, "eh lá-bas" may have been a way of invoking Papa Legba in the music and energy of the period. *Eh lá-bas* roughly translates as "over there" and was often called out to the audience to engage them in a call-and-response style of entertainment. In *The Signifying Monkey*, musical scholar Henry Louis Gates has suggested that "eh lá-bas" was a code for calling Legba:

> [C]alled Papa Legba as his Haitian honorific and invoked through the phrase "eh lá-bas" in New Orleans jazz recordings of the 1920s and 1930s, Papa LaBas is the Afro-American trickster figure from black sacred tradition. His surname, of course, is French for "down" or "over there," and his presence unites "over there" (Africa) with "right here." He is indeed the messenger of the gods, the divine Pan-African interpreter, pursuing, in the language of the text, "The Work," which is not only Vaudou but also the very work (and play) of art itself.

Another mention of the phrase *eh lá-bas* comes from Ishmael Reed's 1972 book, *Mumbo Jumbo*. A wildly imagined fictional tale, it follows the exploits of a detective by the name of Papa LaBas who examines everything from the Knights Templar to the storied roles of famous figures in history. As befits a story about Legba, it is both a tale of fiction and a commentary on the story at the same time.

See also: Cable, George Washington; Kongo; Laveau, Marie; Legba; Secret Societies

Patricia Scheu (Mambo Vye Zo Komande LaMenfo)

Further Reading

Filan, Kenaz. 2011. *The New Orleans Voodoo Handbook*. Rochester, VT: Destiny Books.
Gates, Henry Louis. 1989. *The Signifying Monkey: A Theory of Afro-American Literary Criticism*. New York: Oxford University Press.
Reed, Ishmael. 1972. *Mumbo Jumbo*. Garden City: Doubleday.

PARTERRE

A *parterre*, also known as a *layout*, was the name for some of the ceremonies of Mississippi Valley Voodoo. The word describes the common practice of laying out offerings to the deities on a white cloth. These services took place in the homes of workers, as Voodoo and hoodoo practitioners were sometimes known. Though the specific sites of the ceremonies varied, they occurred predominantly in the African American suburb of New Orleans known as the Faubourg Tremé. The word *parterre* appears to some extent to be a general one. While many other distinct ceremonies existed—including a variety of openings and the annual St. John's Eve festivities—many of them incorporated parterres. Most often, however, parterres tended to be private affairs for individual Voodoo congregations or even for handfuls of individuals.

Most often the term *parterre* applied to weekly services held by Marie Laveau and other Voodoo priestesses. According to Laveau biographer Carolyn Morrow Long, who examined accounts of Voodoo ceremonies compiled by the Federal Writers' Project (FWP) during the 1930s, these had several recurring elements. For instance, they included chorus-led singing and dancing, accompanied by instrumental music. By the time of Marie Laveau, the instrument of choice was an accordion, at least for some such ceremonies. In addition to the presence of music, one account collected by the FWP maintained that certain foods always made an appearance, among their number a dish of rice and black-eyed peas or red beans known as *congris*, red peppers, apples, and oranges. These were appropriately laid out upon a white table cloth placed on the floor of the home in which the congregation met. At each corner of the cloth was a lighted candle. The clothing of Laveau and her coworkers varied, depending on the individual meetings' purposes. Laveau would herself sit in a chair while presiding over the meeting.

An illustration by Edward Windsor Kemble entitled "Voodoo Dance" appears to confirm the depictions of the rituals collected during the 1930s. The scene, which is based in part on a description given by Cable in the text, depicts an 1884 St. John's Eve parterre that reportedly took place in a fisherman's cabin along Lake Pontchartrain. Presiding over the ceremony is a seated woman, one of Marie Laveau's successors. Before her are several dancers and a combination chorus and band. Unlike the ceremonies described by the Federal Writers' Project accounts, there is no accordion present. Instead, members of the ensemble perform on small drums and an instrument that Cable described as a cross between a banjo and violin. The dancers appear to be moving around a square cloth upon which sit offerings of food. At each corner of the cloth sits a candle. Other than the choice of instruments, these accounts of ceremonies are almost identical. Kemble's illustration is particularly significant because it appeared in George Washington Cable's "Creole Slave Songs," which the *Century Magazine* published in April 1886, nearly fifty years before the creation of the FWP.

Despite a gradual decline in Voodoo practice during the late 19th and early 20th centuries, parterres continued to take place in the homes of the faithful. In fact, the most detailed accounts of any such ceremonies were recorded in 1936–1937 by employees of the FWP. Two distinct ceremonies took place in the home of a white Voodoo practitioner known as Mrs. Dereco. In each case, a man known as Oscar "Nom" Felix conducted many of the related rituals. An elderly Mrs. Robinson, who went by the name Madame Ducayielle, also presided over the first, while Laura "Lala" Hopkins, the best known Voodoo priestess of her day, took part in the second. Before the first opening and the parterre around which it centered, Madame Ducayielle explained the purpose of the ceremony, stating that it was "a drink or feed to the spirits."

The Writers' Project workers gave descriptions of both parterres but recorded the most detail about the first. According to Felix, who prepared much of the parterre with materials supplied by the FWP employees, the offerings to the spirits should always be laid on the floor. As with the ceremonies reported from earlier days, a large piece of white fabric served as an altar cloth. Felix placed a picture of St. Peter, also known as Lébat, in the center of one edge of the cloth, so that the saint could "open the way to heaven." A glass filled with a mix of gin, sugar, and water with a large sprig of basil sat before the picture. A camphor branch leaned against the portrait, and a court notice sat nearby. Two candles—one with a bag of sugar behind it—burned just off the sides of the cloth adjacent to the one graced with the image of St. Peter. Nom Felix placed a wide array of offerings upon the cloth, including cider, raspberry soda, unlit candles, a box of ginger snaps, pieces of a type of gingerbread known as stage planks, bananas, apples, two pots of congris, a bottle of olive oil, and plates of steel dust, orris root, birdseed, cloves, cinnamon, and dried basil. Prayers in French, ritual movement, washing with herbal mixtures, and distribution of spiritually powerful objects followed. Throughout the proceedings, Madame Ducayielle sat in a chair diagonally across the cloth from the picture of St. Peter.

To be sure, the parterre described by the FWP workers was not a carbon copy of the one recorded by Cable. Perhaps the ceremony had evolved. On the other hand, the differences may have resulted from the initiatory nature of the opening. Nevertheless, the similarities between this 1930s parterre and those of the previous century are evident, ranging from the foods offered to the placement of the presiding priestess. The common aspects of the ceremonies should come as no surprise, however. After all, Voodoo was very much a living tradition at the time. Moreover, Oscar Felix claimed to have personally sung as part of parterres performed by Marie Laveau during his youth, a plausible claim considering the depth of his knowledge and the similarities between his openings and 19th-century parterres.

See also: Hoodoo; Hopkins, Laura; Initiations; Laveau, Marie; Legba; Opening; Saint John's Eve; Worker

Jeffrey E. Anderson

Further Reading

Cable, George Washington. 1886. "Creole Slave Songs." With illustrations by E. W. Kemble. *The Century Magazine* 31: 807–828.

Federal Writers Project. 1935–1943. Northwestern State University of Louisiana, Watson Memorial Library, Cammie G. Henry Research Center, Natchitoches, Louisiana.

Long, Carolyn Morrow. 2006. *A New Orleans Voudou Priestess: The Legend and Reality of Marie Laveau*. Gainesville, FL: University Press of Florida.

PETWO

Haitian Vodou is a complex mixture of elements deriving from a number of distinct African cultures combined with aspects borrowed from European society. Inarguably, the foundation of Vodou and the majority of its focus is African in character. That fact does not mean that any of its components are accidental or insignificant. Much speculation has resulted from attempts to attribute origins to the components contributing to the contemporary tradition. This has been problematic and has often resulted in incomplete and sometimes incorrect conclusions. As academic reach has expanded, it has been possible for alternative and even conflicting theories to develop.

Haitian Vodou self-consciously incorporated all of the existing African traditions that survived the revolution. While there are several rites or spirit families, called *nanchons*, within the Vodou pantheon, the two dominant ones are Rada and Petwo, the latter often known as Petro. There are two main theories offered about the Petwo rite within Haitian Vodou. It is generally believed that the Petwo cult was the repository for largely Haitian, and perhaps even Native American, survivals. Most of these views need revision and are being reevaluated in some academic circles.

Petwo is usually characterized as "hotter" than the Rada, which is described as the domain of "cooler" spirits. Petwo prefers hot colors, such as red, and multi-colored attire is common in Petwo services. The rhythms are faster and more aggressive, and the lwa are typified by behaviors that are far less restrained than those of the Rada. Because many of the lwa associated with Petwo have historical connections to the Haitian Revolution and its foundational story is synonymous with the origins of Haitian independence, it is understandable that it might be considered essentially a New World phenomenon.

The now classic description of the Petwo deities, supposedly named after an otherwise unknown slave named Don Petwo, is that they are largely the semideified heroes of the Haitian Revolution. The behavior of the Petwo Lwa can be graphic and frightening; they handle flame, stab themselves, eat live coals, and drink kerosene all without injuring the person they are possessing. They are viewed less as dispensers of wisdom and advice and more as resolvers of problems, a significant benefit in a country like Haiti, with its poor infrastructure and health care and extensive economic hardship.

Don Petwo, the mythic progenitor of the Petwo Rite has been identified by some scholars as a creolization of Dom Pedro, the name borne by no less than five Kings of the Kongo. Further, significant figures in the Kongo rituals of Vodou, closely associated with the Petwo, include lwas named La Reine Congo (The Kongo Queen) and Roi Ouangol (King Angola), further confirming a Kongolese influence.

Janzen notes that "retentions and continuity alone do not assure vitality." Variations may be as significant as continuities. Just as African faiths invoked a variety of gods in different regions, it is reasonable to see Petwo, called Lemba in some areas of Northern Haiti, invoking Haitian figures of mythical and historical significance such as Jean Pétro, Toussaint L'Ouverture, Rigaud, Desslaines, Christophe, and Pétion as a reflection of these Kongolese practices.

Whatever conclusions one draws about the origins of Petwo—whether African, Haitian, or both—it is clear that in contrast to the Rada rituals within Vodou, which are concerned with stability, peace, and well-being, the Petwo address violence within the social context. Whether the violence is contemporary or historical, Petwo rites seek to make manageable and safe the lives of their participants by confronting the chaotic and attempting to control its impact upon daily life. They do so by seeking to reinforce the barriers between the domestic world and that of the undomesticated forces represented by the hot and tempestuous lwa of the Petwo division.

See also: Haitian Revolution; Kongo; Nanchons; Rada

Eoghan Craig Ballard

Further Reading
Cosentino, Donald. 1995. *Sacred Arts of Haitian Vodou*. Los Angeles: UCLA Fowler Museum of Cultural History.
Courlander, Harold. 1955. *The Loa of Haiti: New World African Deities*. Havana, Cuba: Sociedad Económica de Amigos del País.
Janzen, John M. 1982. *Lemba, 1650–1930: A Drum of Affliction in Africa and the New World*. New York: Garland.
Michel, Claudine, and Patrick Bellegarde-Smith. 2006. *Vodou in Haitian Life and Culture: Invisible Powers*. New York: Palgrave Macmillan.

PILGRIMAGES

Pilgrimages have been a part of Haitian Vodou since at least the first half of the 19th century. During the early part of that century, many Haitians traveled to Higuey on the feast day of Our Lady of Altagracia, a manifestation of the Virgin Mary. This early religious trek is noteworthy not only because it was one of the first attested Vodou pilgrimages but because it took Haitians outside their country into the Spanish-ruled eastern portion of Hispaniola.

The most famous of all Vodou pilgrim destinations is the area near the waterfall Saut-d'Eau (Sodo in Kreyòl). According to most accounts, the site became a center of religious devotion in 1849, when Our Lady of Mount Carmel appeared in a palm tree near the village of Ville-Bonheur, a few miles from the falls. The palm tree atop which the saint reportedly manifested herself has long been gone, destroyed by a Catholic priest who worried that the growing number of travelers arriving to honor the Virgin and receive physical healing were engaging in idolatry. Although the tree, including its roots, was removed, devotees continued to visit the grove in which it once stood, coming to number in the thousands. Eventually, the Catholic Church submitted to the will of the people, naming the grove an official pilgrimage site. In a slightly different interpretation, Alfred Métraux suggested that the falls were already sacred to Danbala and various water spirits and that Our Lady of Mount Carmel was a later addition to an already holy location. Though now linked with veneration of the Virgin, the falls and water surrounding them remain tied to distinctly African spirits, with the snake deity figuring prominently in the possessions that frequently occur when pilgrims bathe in the water from the waterfall.

Visitors to the holy area typically visit both the former site of the palm tree as well as the waterfall, usually on or near the feast day of Our Lady of Mount Carmel (July 16). The town itself celebrates a festival at this time, which attracts not only pilgrims but purveyors of supernatural and mundane goods to serve the needs of the visitors. As described by American author Zora Neale Hurston in 1939, a visit to the area often begins with a trip to the sacred grove—where many devotees spend a night—and the church in Ville-Bonheur built in honor of the Virgin. A short journey to Saut-d'Eau follows. There pilgrims leave offerings on the branches of a sacred fig tree, disrobe, and climb the falls.

Pilgrimages are also known in Mississippi Valley Voodoo, though they are much less prominent and sometimes motivated by forces other than religious devotion. During the 19th century, for instance, believers traveled to the mouth of Bayou St. John on Lake Pontchartrain for annual St. John's Eve ceremonies, which involved dancing, ritual bathing, feasting, and the appearance of a "queen." Although the journey to the lakeshore was not a lengthy one, it appears to have represented a sacred journey of sorts, comparable to the Haitian pilgrimage to Saut-d'Eau. Modern practitioners in the area have revived the St. John's Eve rituals, and at least one, Sallie Ann Glassman, gathers her followers along the banks of St. John's Bayou, albeit not at the spot where 19th-century Voodoo practitioners gathered.

In addition to the foregoing, new forms of pilgrimages have developed in recent years. For instance, New Orleans has become a pilgrimage spot for both tourists, whose interest in Voodoo rarely extends beyond its entertainment value, and those interested in interacting with the spiritual traditions embodied in the faith. Haiti itself fulfills a similar but much more pronounced role in Vodou. Practitioners living outside Haiti, especially those seeking initiation into the priesthood, frequently travel to the country, treating it as something of a Vodou holy land. Trips to Africa are sometimes viewed in a similar manner by practitioners.

The origins of pilgrimages in Vodou and Voodoo lie in the Old World. Pilgrimages have long been an important part of Catholicism, and the religion certainly influenced the forms taken by the religious journeys of the New World. It is no coincidence that the Saut-d'Eau pilgrimage and the St. John's Eve ceremonies are linked to Christian saints. At the same time, African religions also contributed to their development. For example, the Fon of Dahomey once practiced what outsiders described as the Annual Custom each autumn. Officials from throughout the kingdom traveled to Abomey in order to witness a series of sacrifices and other ceremonies that composed the affair. Though travelers did not undertake the journey of their own volition, it nevertheless was a largely religious trek. In an essay included in the 2002 book *Central Africans and Cultural Transformations in the American Diaspora*, Terry Rey argued that even the Catholic contributions to Vodou might have an African aspect. According to Rey, the early 19th-century origins of Haitian pilgrimages render them unlikely to have been a creation of European Catholicism. After all, the Catholic Church refused to send priests to the country from the time it achieved independence in 1804 to 1860. Rey suggests that rather than developing from European models, Vodou pilgrimages may well have grown out of Catholicism long practiced by the Kongo people of West Central Africa.

See also: Bayou St. Jean; Catholicism and Vodou/Voodoo; Dahomey; Danbala; Kongo; New Orleans; Saint John's Eve; Saints; Tourism; West Central Africa

Jeffrey E. Anderson

Further Reading

Ellis, A. B. 1890. *The Ewe-Speaking Peoples of the Slave Coast of West Africa: Their Religion, Manners, Customs, Laws, Languages, &c.* London: Chapman and Hall.

Heywood, Linda M., ed. 2002. *Central Africans and Cultural Transformations in the American Diaspora.* Cambridge, UK: Cambridge University Press.

Hurston, Zora Neale. 1995. *Folklore, Memoirs, and other Writings,* selected and annotated by Cheryl A. Wall. New York: Literary Classics of the United States, Inc.

Long, Carolyn Morrow. 2006. *A New Orleans Voudou Priestess: The Legend and Reality of Marie Laveau.* Gainesville, FL: University Press of Florida.

Métraux, Alfred. 1972. *Voodoo in Haiti.* Translated by Hugo Charteris and with an Introduction by Sidney W. Mintz. New York: Schocken.

Scheu, Patricia (Mambo Vye Zo Komande LaMenfo). 2011. *Serving the Spirits: The Religion of Vodou.* Philadelphia: Published by author.

POSSESSION

Possession, the taking control of a human body by a spirit, is a common element of African Traditional Religions and their offshoots, Voodoo (the Mississippi Valley faith) and Haitian Vodou. Some hoodooists (practitioners of African American magic) also claim to get their magical powers from spirits that possess them.

During possession the host takes on a passive role and loses his or her agency. The spirit occupies the body of the host and animates it. Possession is theoretically possible because of the psychological concept of dualism, that is, the separation of the physical and spiritual aspects that are said to reside in one person. People who are possessed report going into a trance. Individuals about to go into a possession trance may feel a blackness descending upon them. Other symptoms of possession include odd body movements, such as seizures, trembling, and writhing, and the making of incoherent sounds. Dancing for a long time can also be symptomatic of possession.

Spirit possession can be both a gift and a burden. It is a sensual experience and gives power, including the social power afforded those who are chosen by spirits to be possessed, but it is also draining. People who are possessed are not aware of what is happening to them at the time, but afterward many report feeling changed, as if they have been let in on a secret. Spirit possession is often seen as the religious calling for Vodou priests or priestesses; being possessed is part of their initiation into the faith. Possession can also be a way for spirits to communicate with the living during festivities and ceremonies.

The most well-known Voodoo ritual of the New Orleans area, the St. John's Eve gathering, is one ceremony that has been reported to have included spirit possessions. St. John's Eve was historically celebrated annually on June 23 on the Bayou St. John in New Orleans. The ceremony usually included bonfires, dancing, drumming, singing, and feasting. Participants provided offerings in the form of food, wine, and perfumes to attract spirits. The ceremony was presided over by a priest or priestess who may have been possessed by spirits during the celebrations. When a priestess or priest was possessed, he or she sometimes danced as if in a trance for a very long time and started making strange sounds.

Voodoo was a women-centered religion, and people who feel the tug of the spirit world are often women. Marie Laveau was a famous Voodoo priestess of the 19th century who presided over many ceremonies, particularly dances in New Orleans's Congo Square and the St. John's Eve gatherings. During these ceremonies, witnesses reported that Laveau danced with a snake, in a swaying movement, without her feet leaving the ground. Those who watched her often felt hypnotized and started dancing as well. Laveau would eventually go into a trance and was said to be possessed by her primary deity, the Great Serpent Spirit named Grand Zombi, which took over her body.

In Vodou there are many spirits called *lwa* or *loa*. Their role is to serve as intermediaries between humans and the supreme god, Bondye, and possession is one way in which they do so. Lwa correspond to Christian saints in some manner. For instance, St. Peter is understood as being identical or otherwise connected to Papa Legba. The lwa are not exclusively good or evil spirits, however. They have elements of both good and bad in them, much like the humans who serve them.

Possession in Vodou is considered a blessing rather than a curse; it is simply the way that the spirit world communicates with the living world. In order to manifest, spirits come down during worship ceremonies and possess a person—and sometimes multiple people—in the congregation. Offerings such as food and wine are presented during ceremonies to attract the lwa. Chanting, singing, drumming, dancing, and prayer are also important aspects of ceremonies, which call on the spirits and help place participants in trances. Any person present at a Vodou ceremony can be possessed, as possession is not indicative of a calling reserved only for priests or priestesses. Nevertheless, the spirits choose only those who are worthy of possession. A ceremony that encompasses frequent possessions is deemed successful.

Possession has been described by those who claim to have experienced it as giving up complete control of one's body. One priest described the feeling of possession as the equivalent of "handing the keys of your car to your good friend and hoping that the car doesn't come back mangled." Believers describe the soul of the person as displaced by a god during possession. This process is also called *mounting*, the idea being that the possessed serve as the horses of the spirits. Once possessed by a lwa, a human subject's body is used by the spirit, and the person unknowingly does the lwa's bidding. The deity possessing the person can make the person perform specific tasks, advise spectators, or prophesy the future. Following the trance state of possession, the possessed individual sometimes feels exhausted and does not remember what he or she experienced.

The intensity of the symptoms of possession varies depending on both the spirit and the person whose body is being possessed. The inexperienced tend to have stronger, more violent symptoms of possession, such as wild gesturing and frantic dancing, than those who have experienced it before. Gentler lwa cause gentler symptoms of possession than do more powerful lwa.

Some members of the Vodou community fake being possessed because of the high social status afforded those who are chosen to be mounted by the spirits. In order to prevent faking, those who become possessed are often asked to undergo some type of test. A common test is having the possessed one drink a potent rum and chili pepper beverage without showing any feelings of pain. Successfully doing so reputedly proves that the possession is genuine.

The phenomenon of possession also occurs in other religions, such as Christian Pentecostalism, for instance. Whereas the lwa possess worshippers in Haitian Vodou, the Holy Spirit possesses members of the congregation in Pentecostal churches. Moreover, a person who is possessed by the Holy Spirit starts speaking in tongues, which can resemble the utterances of some lwa. A common outcome of possession in Pentecostalism is conversion to the religion. Christian baptism, especially in churches with black congregations, has symptoms similar to those of possession, such as odd movements and sounds emitted from the person being baptized.

See also: Ancestral Spirits; Bondye; Grand Zombi; Hoodoo; Laveau, Marie; Lwa; Snakes; Vodou in Haiti; Vodu in West Africa; Voodoo in the Mississippi Valley

Urszula Pruchniewska

Further Reading

Anderson, Jeffrey E. 2005. *Conjure in African American Society*. Baton Rouge, LA: Louisiana State UP.

Anderson, Jeffrey E. 2008. *Hoodoo, Voodoo, and Conjure: A Handbook*. Greenwood Folklore Handbooks. Westport, CT: Greenwood Press.

Bellegarde-Smith, Patrick. Interview by Krista Tippett, January 9, 2014. "Living Vodou." Audio podcast. *On Being with Krista Tippett*. Accessed February 21, 2014: http://www.onbeing.org/program/living-vodou/128.

Brown, Karen McCarthy. 2001. *Mama Lola: A Vodou Priestess in Brooklyn*. Updated and expanded ed. Berkeley, CA: University of California Press.

Cohen, Emma. 2008. "What is Spirit Possession? Defining, Comparing, and Explaining Two Possession Forms." *Ethnos* 73:1, 101–126.

Greenwood, Susan. 2005. *The Nature of Magic: An Anthropology of Consciousness*. New York: Berg.

Handwerk, Brian. 2002. "Voodoo a Legitimate Religion, Anthropologist Says." *National Geographic News*, October 21, 2002. Accessed February 27, 2014: http://news.nationalgeographic.com/news/2002/10/1021_021021_taboovoodoo.html.

Jones, Mitchell. 2010. "Possession in Haitian Voodoo and Pentecostalism: A Cross-Cultural Analysis." *Open Anthropology Cooperative*, April 16. http://openanthcoop.ning.com/profiles/blogs/possession-in-haitian-voodoo\.

Ward, Martha. 2004. *Voodoo Queen: The Spirited Lives of Marie Laveau*. Jackson, MS: UP of Mississippi.

PRÈT SAVANN

Few aspects within the world of Haitian Vodou have engendered more speculation than the prèt savann. The term means "bush priest." One can deduce something of his role and also possibly of his origins. He is according to some, a contradictory figure because he is not an employee or priest of the church, nor does this role require initiation as a priest or oungan in Vodou.

Many authors, before this century, dismissed this role as one more example of supposed dissimulation theorized by academics and Vodouisants alike as intending to dupe an otherwise observant class of slave owners intent on eradicating African spirituality. Recently scholarship relating to the history and beliefs of Central Africa has offered other intriguing alternatives to this underscrutinized theory. While many African nations shaped the development of Haitian culture and religion, the Kongolese represent one particularly significant source of African influence.

In the thirty years preceding the Haitian Revolution, half the souls imported into Saint-Domingue as slaves originated from the Kingdom of Kongo. Due to high fatality among slaves in 18th-century Saint-Domingue, by the time of the Haitian Revolution, two-thirds of slaves on the island were born, raised, and educated in Africa. This suggests that despite the heterogeneity of the slave population, at least a significant percentage were familiar with Central African Christianity.

Christianity entered Haitian Vodou from a variety of sources. It was formerly assumed that Christianity was first encountered by newly enslaved Africans either upon departing Africa as slaves or upon arrival in the Americas. While doubtless many did encounter the faith in these ways, many others did not. While it is unlikely that the Kongo alone were the source of Christian elements in Vodou practice; the role of the Kongo needs to be recognized as a strong influence.

The Kingdom of Kongo and ultimately some of its vassal states converted to the Catholic faith as early as the last decade of the 15th century. By the time the Haitian Revolution occurred, the Bakongo (as the Kongo people are known to scholars) had been recognized as a Catholic nation for some three centuries. Even if one were to assume that baptized Christians represented a minority of the slaves brought from the Kongo to Haiti, which is unlikely, their impact would have far outweighed their numbers. For one, they would most often be picked as catechists, or teachers of Christian doctrine to other slaves, especially among their own ethnicity, and for them, Christianity had been introduced to them in their native tongue by other Kongolese.

The Haitian prèt savann may be seen as—at least in an attenuated form—a survival of the Kongolese secular catechists, also called lay priests, or *mestres* in Portuguese. It was a practice of the Kongo kings to hire or elect lay priests, men who were mostly literate or who had had significant training in the catechism and the prayers of the church. The kings drew them mainly from the noble class of Kongo society and paid them salaries in the Kongo currency of nzimbu shells (known to English speakers as cowries). The lay priests would teach literacy and the tenets of the Christian religion. Their existence explains how the elite Kongolese, at least, were able to maintain a strong hold on their Christian faith even in the absence of European clergy in remote areas. The clergy themselves, mainly Jesuits and Capuchins, worked closely with the lay teachers. These lay teachers would travel to remote areas after a clergy member had passed through to baptize mostly children, and they would provide the rudiments of religious training. Moreover, the sacrament of baptism was eagerly sought by the Kongolese according to European missionaries. In practice, the effectiveness of lay preachers was comparable to the often minimal religious education received by illiterate European Christians in remote areas. At least one missionary reported that he had baptized over 700,000 during fourteen years of work, and he was far from being the only one to report significant numbers of baptisms among the Kongolese peasantry. The result of this was that virtually all Kongolese were baptized Christians, and thousands of them would have been among the slaves who disembarked in Saint-Domingue in the years before the Revolution.

In Haiti, one can see this model fairly clearly paralleled in the role of the prèt savann. Before 1840, the lay practitioners of Catholic services provided baptisms for individuals and of door posts, boats, and houses—usually for a fee. In those days, it was often difficult to determine who was a legitimate official of the church and who was not. After all, money would often change hands regardless of the qualifications of the person performing the ceremonies. Such were the antecedents of the prèt savann of Vodou in the 20th century.

Several widespread and often violent attempts to eradicate Vodou and its priesthood, called *dechoukaj* in Kreyòl, resulted in the destruction of temples and the deaths of many religious leaders. For this reason in part, the modern prèt savann has no formal relationship with the Catholic Church—which does not necessarily mean he lacks formal religious education—and his activities are limited to services rendered to Vodou temples and communities. He appears to be found mostly among temples in the southern regions of Haiti and most commonly among those adhering to the ason traditions. They remain active even in the Haitian diaspora of the United States.

An annual prayer service in honor of the Virgin of Mount Carmel held in New York's Haitian community is led by a prèt savann. This prèt savann indicated that he had joined an order of brothers when young with the intent of becoming a monk. On the eve of his final vow, his candidacy was terminated. He was informed in a dream by the zanj, a Kreyòl word that can designate lwa or spirits of the dead, that he was being claimed for the Vodou priesthood and subsequently underwent kanzo initiation and was married to the lwas Freda and Dantor.

This prèt savann still relies heavily on his training and the paraphernalia of Catholicism. He was formally schooled in the French and Latin prayers of the church and now leads novenas, serves as priest at marriages of people to the zanj or lwa in Vodou services, and officiates at events, such as the service he was attending when interviewed. His equipment includes several prayer books, a chalice, a brass censor, and a small bucket of holy water. To perform his services, he wears a white lace chasuble and a necklace with a wooden cross. He began the prayer service in honor of the Virgin of Mount Carmel by purifying the room at the four cardinal points with cologne. Lighting incense, he censed the area and the congregation so that all were touched by the smoke. He performed Latin chants in a loud voice, while sprinkling all with holy water. Leading a mass reading from photocopies and prayer books, he introduced himself and announced they were saying Hail Marys and Our Fathers for the family, the homeless, children in the streets, and Haiti. This service included no prayers or songs for the lwa, and none came down to possess those in attendance.

While the relationship between the church and the Vodou community undoubtedly remains adversarial, at least in the eyes of the church, in the case of the prèt savann, his association, however tentative, with the church hierarchy and formal church education helps establish his credentials and presumably makes him a more effective ritualist, both spiritually and procedurally. His role may be more circumscribed than in the past, but it does not appear to have substantially changed.

See also: Catholicism and Vodou/Voodoo; Haitian Revolution; Kanzo; Kongo

Eoghan Craig Ballard

Further Reading

Desmangles, Leslie Gérard. 1992. *The Faces of the Gods: Vodou and Roman Catholicism in Haiti.* Chapel Hill: University of North Carolina Press.
Heywood, Linda M., ed. 2002. *Central Africans and Cultural Transformations in the American Diaspora.* Cambridge, UK: Cambridge University Press.
McAlister, Elizabeth. 2002. *Rara!: Vodou, Power, and Performance in Haiti and Its Diaspora.* Berkeley, CA: University of California Press.
Simpson, George Eaton. 1940. "The Vodun Service in Northern Haiti." *The American Anthropologist* 42:2 (April–June): 236–254.
Thornton, John. 1998. *Africa and Africans in the Making of the Atlantic World, 1400–1800.* Cambridge, UK: Cambridge University Press.

PRICE-MARS, JEAN

Born in Grande Rivière du Nord, Jean Price-Mars (October 15, 1876–March 1, 1969) was an eminent Haitian scholar, cultural critic, teacher, ethnologist, physician, diplomat, and senator. Known as the father of Haitian ethnology, Price-Mars was committed to researching and studying African cultural traditions and religious practices in Haiti. From a scientific perspective, in his groundbreaking 1938 text *Ainsi Parla l'Oncle* (*Thus Spoke the Uncle*), he established the relationship between Haitian folklore and Haitian cultural identity and worldview. His emphasis was given to the Afro-Haitian cosmology and the Afro-religious sensibility of the Haitian peasant majority, which Price-Mars argued are representative of the Haitian soul. Not only was Price-Mars able to establish the link between Haiti and Africa, but he also examined the persistent ancestral customs and practices in the Caribbean nation of Haiti. Nonetheless, the thrust of Price-Mars's book is concerned with the religious identity and sentiments of the Haitian masses, namely the Afro-Haitian religion of Vodou. His linkage of Vodou to Haitian culture and peasant spirituality placed the Vodou faith in the same category of thought and religiosity as monotheistic belief systems.

Among Price-Mars's chief contributions to the literature of Vodou are the following:

1. His argument that Afro-Haitian faith is a symbiosis and a process of religious *métissage* between African religions and Catholicism
2. His explanation of the constitutive elements of the Vodou faith and the Catholic tradition in the context of the Haitian culture
3. His argument, which follows from the previous two points, that Vodou and Catholicism are connected through the shared ritual of ancestral veneration (or the veneration of the saints) and a common theological worldview

While Price-Mars may not be correct in every theological aspect, he pursued his observations by establishing historical links and interweaving dynamics between the two religions. For instance, he argued that the Vodou religion paved the way to the Haitian Revolution and identified itself with the dream of slave emancipation in Saint-Domingue in the night of the general revolt in 1791. For Price-Mars, Vodou is liberating and had contributed enormously to social transformation and to the reversal of the colonial order and slave society at Saint-Domingue/Haiti.

Price-Mars brilliantly defended the authenticity of Vodou as a religion on the basis of these articulated antecedents of religiosity. As he explained, Vodou is neither superstition nor black magic as traditionally perceived. On the contrary, it has its own religious worldview and satisfies all the demands, requirements, and ideals of religion. It has, moreover, its own theology and system of morality. Price-Mars elaborated on these basic points, making several key assertions in their support. First, Vodou is a religion because all its adherents believe in the existence of spiritual beings who live in close intimacy with humans, whose activity they dominate. Second, Vodou is a religion because the cult appertaining to its gods requires a hierarchical priestly body, a society of the faithful, temples, altars, ceremonies, and finally, a whole oral tradition. Though the tradition has certainly not come down to us unaltered, the essential elements of worship have been transmitted. Third, Vodou is a religion because we can discern within it a theology, a system of representation through which Haitians' African ancestors accounted for natural phenomena and which lies dormant at the base of the anarchical beliefs upon which the hybrid Catholicism of Haiti's popular masses rests.

See also: Dorsainvil, Justin Chrysostome (J. C.)

Celucien L. Joseph

Further Reading

Joseph, Celucien L. 2012. "The Religious Philosophy of Jean Price-Mars." *Journal of Black Studies* 43:6 (September), 620–645.

Price-Mars, Jean. 1928. *Ainsi Parla l'Oncle. Essais d'Éthnographie*. New York: Parapsychology Foundation Inc.

Price-Mars, Jean. 1983. *So Spoke the Uncle*. Boulder, CO: Lynne Rienner Publishers.

Price-Mars, Jean. 1929.*Une Etape de l'Evolution Haïtienne: Etude de Socio-Psychologie*. Port-au-Prince: Imprimerie "La Presse."

PRIS DE JE

Pris de je or simply *je* means prize of the eyes. Je is understood as a way of seeing various realities in the world. It is the ability to consciously see in two worlds simultaneously—the material world and the spirit world. The spirit realm is believed to be parallel to this one, and the individual with je can see both simultaneously. All initiates in Vodou are expected to be able to develop their je, so that they may serve their communities through it. It is not just a Vodou trait, but one that can be displayed by nonpractitioners as well. For example, after a long night of service at Souvenance in the 1940s, Odette Rigaud reported seeing Gede eating food prepared for the Marasa. When told who it was, she denied the fact. A servant of the spirits at Souvenance said Odette had "good je" but did not believe in her vision.

Je is also a state of being, a spiritual attitude. It is ability to hold oneself in a void where the two worlds touch. This "place of nothing" is said to be the entrance to Ginen. The seclusion during the kanzo rites is supposed to lead to je. Erroneously, some people have written that je is the fourth initiatory rank of kanzo, following after asogwe. It is not. The development of je follows the asogwe rank, when it is seen or expressed during kanzo. Individuals who display a talent for je are given additional seclusion to see if their je improves or strengthens.

The seclusion follows a person's initiation into the Vodou faith. The individual in question would be held in seclusion for a fairly long period of time—up to a month—with no contact with family or the outside world. During this time, only the oldest priests of the sosyete have contact with them, bringing food and checking on them. The seclusion is a form of sensory deprivation and is meant to facilitate conversation with the spirits. During isolation, a person's ability to move into and out of the void would be heightened. This ability to move through trance, without the aid of drums or songs, would indicate a strong talent for je. The person would then be held in very high esteem in the community. And he or she would be considered worthy of its power and capable of carrying its great responsibility. This ability to "see" means speaking to the spirits on behalf of the community. Such a gift would not be used for selfish purposes, but for the betterment of the community at large.

See also: Ceremonies; Gede; Ginen; Initiations; Kanzo; Twins; Two Head

Patricia Scheu (Mambo Vye Zo Komande LaMenfo)

Further Reading

Beaubrun, Mimerose P. 2013. *Nan Domi: An Initiate's Journey into Haitian Vodou.* San Francisco: City Lights Books.

PYTHONS

In several parts of Africa, the python historically was an important spiritual being. According to the Kom people of Cameroon, for instance, a python guided them to the spot where they were to found their kingdom. The Venda people of South Africa also claimed a python as their founder. Pythons were even more prominent in the 18th-century city-state of Whydah (modern Ouidah) and were adopted into the religious beliefs of the Fon after their conquest of the city. One of the chief gods of the Fon, known as Dangbe, Da, or Dan, was envisioned as a python. Living pythons were honored with processions, a temple in Whydah, and other trappings of divinity. This reverence for pythons among the Fon and closely related Ewe probably explains the place snakes once held in Haitian Vodou and allegedly in Louisiana Voodoo. Even Missouri Voodoo, which included a spirit named Grandfather Rattlesnake, owed a debt to the sacred pythons of West Africa.

See also: Snakes; Vodu in West Africa

Jeffrey E. Anderson

Further Reading

Courlander, Harold. 1975. *A Treasury of African Folklore: The Oral Literature, Traditions, Myths, Legends, Epics, Tales, Recollections, Wisdom, Sayings, and Humor of Africa.* New York: Crown.

Ellis, A. B. 1890. *The Ewe-Speaking Peoples of the Slave Coast of West Africa: Their Religion, Manners, Customs, Laws, Languages, &c.* London: Chapman and Hall.

Moreau de Saint-Méry, Médéric-Louis-Élie. 1797. *Description Topographique, Physique, Civile, Politique et Historique de la Partie Française de l'Île de Saint-Domingue.* 2 vols. Philadelphia.

Owen, Mary Alicia. 1892. "Among the Voodoos." In *The International Folk-lore Congress 1891: Papers and Transactions*, 230–248. London: David Nutt.

RADA

Rada is one of the two major rites that are served under the reglemen of Haitian Vodou. *Rada* is the shortened abbreviation of *Arada*, a variant of *Allada*, which is the name of holy city and once-prominent slaving port of southern Dahomey. Although fewer than 25 percent of the Africans brought through the Middle Passage were from Dahomey, the culture informed and colored much of what is Haitian Vodou today. Nevertheless, despite the identification of the nanchon with a particular Dahomean city, many aspects of the faith have been influenced by other peoples. For instance, the Rada rite's music draws its ritual structure from the Ewe and Yoruba as well as the Fon of Dahomey. The pattern of Rada drum rhythms, dances, and songs traces its roots to the holy city of the Dahomeans, Allada. Rituals, names of deities, and offering styles can be traced to numerous peoples other than the Fon.

Rada shrines are identified by multitiered altars, covered in elaborate bowls, fabric, and effigies. This collection of seemingly random objects is a display of the altar's power as well as a statement of the presiding priest's ability to rule this miniature spirit world. Such altars are directly copied from their West African counterparts. Dahomean altars in West Africa are multilevel assemblages, with an emphasis on simultaneous assuagement via liquid offerings and exaltation through the ascending structure of altar tiers. The intermingled statuary and containers on the West African altar finds its complement in chromolithographs of Catholic saints and offertory vessels on Haitin altars.

Rada came to be the title given to the older, cooler-tempered deities from Old Dahomey—chiefly Legba, Ayizan, Loko, and Agwe. Andre Pierre, the painter and oungan, referred to the Rada lwa as "civilized," in opposition to Petwo lwa, whom he called military. Karen McCarthy Brown calls Rada lwa "family" and describes Petwo deities as foreign.

The Rada spirits are said to be cooler, sweeter, and easier to handle. They are served warm, sweet foods with clear liquid offerings, such as white rum and anisette. The ambiance of their possessions is warmer. Even those Rada spirits who are said to be awesome in their wisdom and power are treated like family, with an underlying affection that is evident in all services. They are more like family, beneficent, forgiving, and easy on their servitors. Rada spirits are said to be *fran Ginen* or African. While fidelity and respect is exercised in service with Rada lwa, these spirits are not overly strict in their dealings with the living. If promised a service that cannot be held, the Rada can be persuaded to wait for another year before receiving the promise. Unlike the Petwo, who are hot and easily agitated, the Rada nanchon is slow to anger and understands the human tendency to overstate our capabilities.

While Petwo spirits tend to be singular forces of nature, Radas often appear as balanced pairs of energy. The Priye Ginen, an opening prayer for Vodou ceremonies, lists them according to reglemen. Loko and Ayizan, the father and the mother of the initiates, appear first, followed by Marasa Dosu Dosa, the dual creation energies. Next come Danbala and Ayida Wedo, the rainbow serpent and the creator serpent. Then come Agwe and Lasiren, a marriage of talents in both the realm of emotions as well as material wealth and capabilities. As balanced spirits, the Rada bring healing, blessings, wealth, and fecundity to their servitors.

See also: Ayida Wedo; Agwe Ta'Woyo; Bight of Benin; Dahomey; Danbala; Ewe; Lasiren; Lwa; Nanchons; Petwo; Twins; Yoruba

Patricia Scheu (Mambo Vye Zo Komande LaMenfo)

Further Reading

Bellegarde-Smith, Patrick, and Claudine Michel, eds. 2006. *Vodou in Haitian Life and Culture: Invisible Powers.* New York: Palgrave Macmillan.

Bellegarde-Smith, Patrick, and Claudine Michel, eds. 2006. *Haitian Vodou: Spirit, Myth, and Reality.* Bloomington, IN: Indiana University Press.

Brown, Karen McCarthy. 2001. *Mama Lola: A Vodou Priestess in Brooklyn.* Updated and expanded ed. Berkeley, CA: University of California Press.

Gilles, Jerry M. and Yvrose S. 2009. *Remembrance: Roots, Rituals and Reverence in Vodou.* Davie, FL: Bookmanlit.

Thompson, Robert Farris. 1983. *Flash of the Spirit: African and Afro-American Art and Philosophy.* New York: Random House.

ROOTWORK

In modern usage, the term *rootwork* is a synonym for *conjure* and *hoodoo*. Rootwork has long been the preferred word for the magical practices of African Americans in the Low Country, which includes the Sea Islands and coastal areas of the Atlantic Coast from North Carolina to Florida. In that region, practitioners are known as *rootworkers* or *root doctors*. As one might surmise, these terms were inspired by the prominence of roots in forms of magic associated with African Americans. Despite the biological associations of the region's magical terminology, *root* has come to mean any magical charm to practitioners in the region.

Historically, rootwork was a distinctive Low Country version of the magical practices widely spread across the South. Carolyn Morrow Long has noted that when the first significant research on the coastal regions with which the term rootwork is associated began during the 1930s, its magical practices differed significantly from those elsewhere in the South. For one, the Catholic elements associated with Mississippi Valley Voodoo and hoodoo—such as altars and candles—were absent. Another distinction was that graveyard dirt, though important in other regions as well, was the most valued magical item in the Low Country. Its prominence likely derives from the fact that many of the slaves imported into the area came from the

Kongo ethnicity of West Central African, a people who strongly emphasized the power of the dead.

Interestingly, some of the United States' best known practitioners of African American magic came from the Low Country. These include the likes of Jim Jordan of Como, North Carolina, and Dr. Buzzard from near Beaufort, South Carolina. The only practitioners outside the Low Country to rival these two in fame were Caroline Dye of Newport, Arkansas, and Marie Laveau of New Orleans.

Anthropologist and folklorist Zora Neale Hurston drew a distinction between rootwork and hoodoo based on function rather than regional distinction, indicating that the former involved healing and that not all those who practiced rootwork dealt in hoodoo. Hurston gave a brief account of some of their formulae in an appendix to *Mules and Men* (1935). Faith Mitchell, working from both a regional and functional definition, published *Hoodoo Medicine: Gullah Herbal Remedies* (1999), a compendium of herbal folk medicines associated with the Low Country. Catherine Yronwode's *Hoodoo Herb and Root Magic: A Materia Magica of African-American Conjure and Traditional Formulary Giving the Spiritual Uses of Natural Herbs, Roots, Minerals, and Zoological Curios* (2002) also contains numerous examples of rootwork.

See also: Conjure; Healing; Hoodoo; Magic

Jeffrey E. Anderson

Further Reading

Anderson, Jeffrey E. 2005. *Conjure in African American Society*. Baton Rouge, LA: Louisiana State University Press.

Hurston, Zora Neale. 1995. *Folklore, Memoirs, and other Writings*, selected and annotated Cheryl A. Wall. The Library of America. New York: Literary Classics of the United States, Inc.

Johnson, F. Roy. 1963. *The Fabled Doctor Jim Jordan: A Story of Conjure*. Murfreesboro, NC: Johnson.

Long, Carolyn Morrow. 2001. *Spiritual Merchants: Religion, Magic, and Commerce*. Knoxville, TN: University of Tennessee Press.

McTeer, James Edwin. 1976. *Fifty Years as a Low Country Witch Doctor*. Beaufort, SC: Beaufort Book Company.

Mitchell, Faith. 1999. *Hoodoo Medicine: Gullah Herbal Remedies*. Columbia, SC: Summerhouse Press.

Yronwode, Catherine. 2002. *Hoodoo Herb and Root Magic: A Materia Magica of African-American Conjure and Traditional Formulary Giving the Spiritual Uses of Natural Herbs, Roots, Minerals, and Zoological Curios*. Forestville, CA: Lucky Mojo Curio Company.

ROSENTHAL, JUDY

Judy Rosenthal, a professor of anthropology at the University of Michigan-Flint, has produced several works on the African cousins of Haitian Vodou and Mississippi Valley Voodoo. In 1985, members of the Ewe Gorovodu Society asked her to write an ethnography of their order. Rosenthal spent the next eleven years studying the spiritual beliefs of the Ewe of Ghana, Togo, and Benin. Her most important work on the subject is her 1998 book *Possession, Ecstasy, and Law in Ewe Voodoo*. Its focus is on spirit possession within the Gorodovu and Mama Tchamba societies.

Rosenthal's research is particularly important for several reasons. First, it addresses an understudied aspect of African Traditional Religion. Many scholars have addressed the beliefs of the Yoruba, and current American historiography stresses the Kongo ancestry of Vodou and Voodoo. The Ewe, however, have remained neglected, despite the fact that many of the words associated with Vodou and Voodoo—especially the names of deities—appear to be of Ewe origin. In addition, Rosenthal's in-depth research into two West African orders is valuable for the light it shines on the ancestors of the so-called secret societies of Haitian Vodou, which have long been a favorite topic for scholars of the religion. Finally, she was the first to explicitly suggest an Ewe origin for the word *hoodoo*.

See also: Ellis, Alfred Burdon; Hoodoo; Initiations; Secret Societies; Vodu in West Africa

Jeffrey E. Anderson

Further Reading

Anderson, Jeffrey E. 2008. *Hoodoo, Voodoo, and Conjure: A Handbook*. Westport, CT: Greenwood Press.

Blier, Suzanne Preston. 1995. *African Vodun: Art, Psychology, and Power*. Chicago and London: University of Chicago Press.

Ellis, A. B. 1890. *The Ewe-Speaking Peoples of the Slave Coast of West Africa: Their Religion, Manners, Customs, Laws, Languages, &c.* London: Chapman and Hall.

Rosenthal, Judy. 1998. *Possession, Ecstasy, and Law in Ewe Voodoo*. Charlottesville and London: University Press of Virginia.

S

SACRIFICE

As with a multitude of religions throughout recorded history, Vodou involves sacrifice. The same was true for its Mississippi Valley cousin, Voodoo. The purpose of sacrifice is generally understood as providing a form of spiritual sustenance for the lwa to whom it is dedicated. For this reason, the animal sacrificed depends heavily upon the specific lwa being honored. For example, the Petwo lwas usually prefer black pigs, while members of the Ibo nanchon prefer guinea fowl. Chickens, however, are the most common sacrifices, while goats and cattle are also fairly common. The sacrifice victims' colors should also be matched to the hues preferred by the lwas being fed by each. Before its death, each animal is sanctified to the lwa in rituals that include bathing and feeding. Some lwa, on the other hand, do not require any animal sacrifices.

Vodou practitioners in the United States and Western Europe often encounter significant opposition from local communities that frown upon practices they view as cruelty to animals, which has led some scholars and practitioners to downplay the importance of sacrifice. A few even abandon it altogether. While it is true that chickens frequently have their wings broken and goats often undergo castration and the removal of their beards as part of the process of sanctification, this usually occurs just before death. The animals' suffering is doubtless less intense than that of many animals killed for human consumption. Moreover, the resultant flesh is typically consumed by the ceremonies' attendees in addition to spiritually providing for the lwas. In short, sacrifice is important not only to the theology of Vodou but to those who participate in its ceremonies.

The precise role of sacrifice in the history of Mississippi Valley Voodoo is difficult to determine. According to Zora Neale Hurston, Federal Writers' Project oral histories, and newspaper accounts, sacrifice was certainly a part of Voodoo. On the other hand, the most reliable descriptions of ceremonies either do not mention sacrifice or do not describe how it took place. A few sources do give details, but these are often problematic. An excellent example is the case of Zora Neale Hurston's supposed initiation into the Voodoo fold by Samuel Thompson. The ritual included a late-night sacrifice of a black sheep, which Hurston described in considerable detail. While the ceremony might well have taken place, Hurston's reliability has been questioned in recent years.

Much has been made of the supposed practice of sacrificing humans—known as "goats without horns"—as part of Vodou ritual. To a large extent, this perception can traced to the general belief that ritual murder and cannibalism were common parts of African and Afro-Caribbean religions, a stereotype repeated in a legion of

> ### Are Humans Sacrificed in Voodoo?
>
> The short answer is no, at least in the case of the New World. While human sacrifices were certainly part of the African religious ancestry of Vodou and Voodoo, history records only a few cases of the practice in Haiti. Many argue that there has been only one verifiable instance of the practice. Moreover, the broader Haitian Vodou community roundly condemned those who did so. There have been no verified cases of such sacrifices in Louisiana Voodoo.

books, articles, cartoons, and films from the days of the slave trade to the present. This misconception was furthered by an event recorded by Spenser St. John, who reported on two specific cases of child sacrifice. The first was the work of Congo and Jeanne Pellé, who ritually murdered and cannibalized their niece, Claircine, on New Year's Eve 1863. The couple had been acting on the advice of two oungans (or perhaps bòkòs), who had suggested the sacrifice as a method of socioeconomic advancement. The second supposedly took place in the Arcahaie Arrondissement of southern Haiti in 1869. In both instances, the perpetrators were sought out by police, and in the case of the Pellés, a total of eight people were executed by firing squad for the crime. In addition to the accounts of Spenser St. John, Haitian folklore is replete with stories of human sacrifice, usually carried out by bòkòs working with secret societies devoted to that purpose.

Stories also tell of human sacrifice in New Orleans Voodoo. According to documents collected by the Federal Writers' Project during the 1930s and early 1940s, Laveau kept the corpses of infants in her home, though at least one source suggests that these were supplied by an abortionist rather than obtained through sacrifice. Moreover, the accounts could be little more than folklore or rumor. Even the much-reviled Robert Tallant, author of *Voodoo in New Orleans* (1946), doubted the reality of such tales, stating, "There is little proof of human sacrifice ever having been used in Louisiana."

While awaiting sentencing for murder, Jeanne Pellé reportedly asked, "Why should I be put to death for observing our ancient customs?" She and her associates may well have considered themselves to be following the spiritual dictates of their ancestors. Human sacrifice did exist in parts of Africa, including Dahomey, a major supplier of slaves during the 18th and 19th centuries. Nevertheless, as the vigorous prosecution of the Pellés and the general condemnation of the practice in both Haiti and the Mississippi Valley demonstrate, human sacrifice has never been an accepted part of Vodou or Voodoo. Those few instances in which it can be proven to have occurred are best understood as the work of malevolent bòkòs hoping to buy the aid of lwas than legitimate Vodou rituals.

See also: Bight of Benin; Bòkò; Dahomey; Federal Writers' Project; Initiations; Laveau, Marie; Openings; Oungan; Petwo; Tallant, Robert; Slavery and the Slave Trade; St. John, Sir Spenser; Vodou in Haiti; Vodu in West Africa; Voodoo in the Mississippi Valley

Jeffrey E. Anderson

Further Reading

Ellis, A. B. 1890. *The Ewe-Speaking Peoples of the Slave Coast of West Africa: Their Religion, Manners, Customs, Laws, Languages, &c*. London: Chapman and Hall.

Federal Writers' Project. 1935–1943. Northwestern State University of Louisiana, Watson Memorial Library, Cammie G. Henry Research Center, Natchitoches, Louisiana.

Frank, Lisa Tendrich, and Daniel Kilbride, eds. 2011. *Southern Character: Essays in Honor of Bertram Wyatt-Brown*. Gainesville, FL: University Press of Florida.

Hurston, Zora Neale. 1931. "Hoodoo in America." *Journal of American Folklore* 44: 317–417.

Métraux, Alfred. 1972. *Voodoo in Haiti*. Translated by Hugo Charteris and with an Introduction by Sidney W. Mintz. New York: Schocken.

Scheu, Patricia (Mambo Vye Zo Komande LaMenfo). 2011. *Serving the Spirits: The Religion of Vodou*. Philadelphia: Published by author.

St. John, Spenser. 1884. *Hayti or the Black Republic*. London: Smith, Elder, and Company.

Tallant, Robert. 1946 [1998]. *Voodoo in New Orleans*. New York: Macmillan; reprint, Gretna: Pelican.

SAINT JOHN'S EVE

In much of Europe, the night before the feast of St. Jean Baptiste (St. John the Baptist in English), June 23, was a time charged with spiritual power. Also known as Midsummer Eve, it took place near the summer solstice. During the early modern period, many believed that witches and fairies were particularly dangerous on that night and should be guarded against by building bonfires and collecting plants associated with St. John. These herbs were then hung above the entrances to homes or burned in the bonfires in order to drive away the beings supposed to be lurking in the darkness, thereby protecting humans and their livelihoods. These ceremonies also once included bathing in sacred spots. Both practices made their way into the Voodoo of New Orleans, though the degree to which the religion depended on European models for St. John's Eve and the extent to which preexisting African practices attached themselves to a similar European holy day is open for debate.

St. John's Eve was a significant yearly event in both Haiti and the New Orleans area, though its importance was much greater in the latter. In Haiti, the evening is marked by the burning of bonfires, much as it had been in Europe. The bonfire and rituals connected with it were minor events, however, and most scholars have little to say about the holiday. On the other hand, the New Orleans version of St. John's Eve had developed into the most visible—and arguably most important—Voodoo ceremony of the year by the second half of the 19th century.

The location of the annual event changed over time. At least one early 19th-century St. John's Eve gathering occurred in the city. It is likely that others did as well. By the last several decades of the century, the ceremonies had moved to the shores of Lake Pontchartrain, typically near the mouth of Bayou St. John. Based on numerous accounts that appeared in 19th-century newspapers and in the records of the Great Depression-era Federal Writers' Project, the evening began with crowds numbering in the hundreds gathering along the lakeshore. Late in the evening, the queen would arrive by boat, and the activities would begin. These consisted of dancing and singing, with at least some of the participants entering the lake, and the burning of bonfires and feasting. White observers frequently described the gatherings as orgies, in part because the participants tended to be sparsely clothed, but most historians consider such accounts to be exaggerations and distortions for racist white audiences that held lasciviousness to be an innate characteristic of African Americans.

The precise purpose of the festivities has not been fully determined. That the deities of Voodoo were invoked is certain. In Haitian Vodou, St. John was himself a minor lwa, and he may well have been in Louisiana as well. One informant for the Federal Writers' Project stated that the events were celebrated by those who wanted to be like St John. Another indicated that they brought good luck. The fact that the evening often included ritual bathing suggests that another purpose may have purification. Unfortunately for future scholars, the ceremonies had become infrequent by the late 19th century, and much of their meaning gradually passed from living memory. Moreover, in their later years, the ceremonies appear to have at least partly transformed into a tourist event, which white observers paid to view.

Another aspect of St. John's Eve that warrants further research is the official capacity of the queens who presided over the ceremonies. Since the early 20th century, writers have referred to any female Voodoo priestess as a queen. During the 19th century, the title appears to have been more specific, designating the priestess who acted as mistress of each St. John's Eve ceremony. It is likely that the queenship was a North American expression of a broader African Diasporic practice of electing monarchs to preside over communal ceremonies. Such traditions once existed in almost every New World society with a significant African presence, and may also be reflected in the kings that have been associated with U.S. Gulf Coast Mardi Gras societies since the 19th century.

See also: Congo Square; Federal Writers' Project; Laveau, Marie; New Orleans; Voodoo in the Mississippi Valley

Jeffrey E. Anderson

Further Reading

Heywood, Linda M., ed. 2002. *Central Africans and Cultural Transformations in the American Diaspora.* Cambridge, UK: Cambridge University Press.
Kightly, Charles. 1987. *The Perpetual Almanack of Folklore.* London: Thames and Hudson.
Long, Carolyn Morrow. 2006. *A New Orleans Voudou Priestess: The Legend and Reality of Marie Laveau.* Gainesville, FL: University Press of Florida.
Ward, Martha. 2004. *Voodoo Queen: The Spirited Lives of Marie Laveau.* Jackson, MS: University of Mississippi Press.

SAINTS

In Haitian Vodou, the Catholic saints serve as stand-ins for the lwa, or spirits, entreated or served by practitioners of the religion. The images of the saints, generally statues or lithographs, correspond to the personas of largely

African-derived spirits. This relationship is historically the result of the suppression of African religion by French colonial authorities during the era preceding the Haitian Revolution (1791–1804). Under the French *Code Noir*, the practice of any religion other than Catholicism among enslaved Africans was criminalized. In order to continue their ritual practice, Haitian adherents to the religion that eventually became known as Vodou used the Catholic images, religious paraphernalia, and churches to practice their own religion and offer sacrifices to the spirits. Legba, lwa of the crossroads, is paired with and represented pictographically by Saint Peter. Danbala, snake lwa and co-creator of the universe, is paired with St. Patrick, and various female spirits are represented by incarnations of the Madonna. The lwa and saints are generally paired because images of the saints contain some aspects that correspond to properties associated with individual lwas. Images of St. Peter frequently depict him holding the keys to heaven, and Legba is the lwa of the crossroads between the realm of the spirits and human practitioners who unlocks a path to travel between the two. Similarly, St. Patrick is frequently depicted standing on snakes and thus has come to symbolize Danbala.

In New Orleans Voodoo, by the beginning of the 20th century, mention of the Haitian lwa was almost completely absent. The saints replaced the African deities almost completely for a time, with local practitioners making no mention of the African counterparts of these saints in their prayers or offerings. The most popular of these were St. Peter, entreated in the opening of Voodoo ceremonies, and St. Raymond, patron of money or finances. Practitioners in New Orleans, rather than pairing the saints with the lwa that would serve practitioners' needs, simply adjusted the hagiography of the saints to reflect their purpose. According to folk beliefs common in the city, St. Rita, Catholicism's patron saint of women victimized by domestic abuse, had been abused by her husbands or lovers and was thought to not only serve the needs of women but to despise men. New Orleans's practitioners also called upon saints that were derived, popularized, and re-created via folk Catholicism. Since the late 20th century, the lwa and spirits of Vodou and West African Yoruba traditions have been reimported by Caribbean-trained practitioners, with the saints now being almost as difficult to spot among Voodoo practitioners as their Caribbean and African counterparts were decades before. The re-Africanization of Vodou in Haiti and concomitantly in modern New Orleans is likely the reason for the recent prominence of Yoruba and Haitan spirits in place of the saints.

See also: Catholicism and Vodou/Voodoo; Haitian Revolution; Lwa

Kodi Roberts

Further Reading

Desmangles, Leslie G. 1992. *Faces of the Gods: Vodou and Roman Catholicism in Haiti*. Chapel Hill, NC: University of North Carolina Press.

Roberts, Kodi. In press. *Voodoo and the Promise of Power: The Racial, Gender & Economic Politics of Religion in New Orleans, 1881–1940*. Baton Rouge, LA: Louisiana State University Press.

SANTERÍA

The Afro-Cuban religion known as Santería has often been described as a syncretic combination of Roman Catholicism and an African religious tradition closely associated with Voodoo. However, this is a misrepresentation.

Santería, also known as Lukumí, Orisha Religion, and Yoruba Tradition Religion, is a version of the religious traditions of the Yoruba people of southwest Nigeria as it was reconstituted in Cuba in the 18th and 19th centuries. It was developed on the island by both enslaved peoples and the *gente de color*, free people of color, who recreated their religious tradition in Havana, Santiago de Cuba, and in the many smaller towns in between. Although there were Cubans and practitioners of Santería in the United States prior to the twentieth century, Cubans leaving the island after the Revolution in 1959 and again in 1978 during the Mariel boatlift expanded the tradition from a local cult to an international religion. Today it is estimated that as many as 100 million people practice some version of this religion worldwide, including several hundred thousand in the United States. This means that there are more practitioners of these religions than there are Jews, Sikhs, Jains, or Zoroastrians.

The focus of Santería and the reason it is often called "Orisha Religion" is the deities who form the sacred pantheon. As with other polytheistic traditions, in its Nigerian homeland Santería has an almost infinite number of gods, known as the *orisha*. Some are so ancient that they are said to have been present at creation. Others are associated with forces of nature, including rivers, oceans, wind, lightning, and particular natural locations. Some are ancestors who were deified by their descendants. Not all of these orisha survived their exile from their African homeland, so in the New World the pantheon has attenuated to about twenty well-known and widely worshipped deities. These include Eleggua, the trickster; Obatala, the great king; Shango, the younger king; Ogun, the blacksmith; Ochosi, the hunter; Orula, the diviner; Yemaya, the great mother; Oshun, the vibrant younger woman; and Oya, the warrior woman and owner of the marketplace.

Both in its homeland and throughout the world, the community of Santería practitioners is organized into households and families known as *ile* or *casas*, rather than churches and congregations. Individuals join these communities and rise in their ranks through a system of initiations. Even though a child may be born into a family of practitioners, he or she is not a part of the religion until initiated as the godchild of a priest or priestess. The most basic of these initiations is known as *elekes*, beads, or necklaces. During this ritual the individual is given a set of three to seven simple beaded necklaces representing specific orisha. Each necklace is designed around the colors and numbers associated with those orisha. Receiving these necklaces brings the individual into the family or religious household of the presiding priest or priestess and places them under the protection of the orisha represented.

Over the last fifty years several orisha communities have departed from the traditional home-based shrines to establish publicly recognized congregations. The most well-known of these communities is the Church of Babalu Aye near Miami, Florida, and Oyotunje Village in South Carolina.

Often individuals receive a second initiation known as *Los Guerreros*, or The Warriors, at the same time they receive their initial necklaces. It is this ritual that converts the individual into a practitioner of the religion. In this rite he or she receives a set of objects blessed and imbued with the presence of the orisha Eleggua, Ogun, and Ochosi, and the protector orisha, Osun. At this point, practitioners set up a shrine for these orisha in their homes and offer regular worship there.

Other common initiations include the priestly initiation known as *Asiento*, *Kariocha*, or Crowning; the initiation into the priesthood of Orula the diviner; and initiation as a drummer. All of these initiations give the practitioners certain rights and responsibilities within the religious community. The Crowning initiation is an intense week-long ritual that creates a new priest or priestess dedicated to a primary orisha as well as consecrates all the objects and icons associated with that orisha and several secondary orisha. After a year-long novitiate period and several additional ceremonies the fully-crowned priest gains the right to perform all the basic rituals including initiating others into the religion. During the novitiate period when the new priest is known as *iyawo* he or she is subject to many regulations and injunctions, including the requirement to wear all white, be inside after dark, and not to frequent certain places such as bars. At the completion of the *iyawoaje* and the requisite rituals, the new priest is known as a *santero* (male), *santera* (female), *babalocha* (male), or *iyalocha* (female).

The sacred drums used in Santería rituals are considered to be orisha in their own right. They are played by especially initiated and trained drummers. This initiation is generally limited to men, although women have been known to learn to play these drums and perform in nonreligious settings. The hourglass-shaped, two-headed drums, called *bata*, are created in sets of three. The largest drum is known as the *Iya* or mother, the middle drum is the *Itotele*, and the smallest is the *Okonkolo*. The playing of the drums is in the form of a conversation between the three drums and through them with the orisha. The drums are played both to honor the orisha and as part of rituals inviting the orisha to join the celebration through possession trance. During the possession ritual the bodies of initiated priests are taken over and controlled by the spirit of their primary orisha. In this way the orisha are able to speak directly to their devotees, and devotees are able to communicate directly with an orisha.

For many, but not all, communities of orisha practitioners, initiation into the priesthood of Orula the diviner is limited to straight men. Some communities give women this initiation, and some gay men have also been known to have been initiated. Such priests are known as *babalawo* (*iyanifa*, if women). They practice the most sophisticated form of divination using palm nuts or a special divining chain known as *opele* to communicate with their patron orisha. This form of divination performed by the priest of Orula, known as *Ifá*, is considered the highest form of divination. In addition to Ifá divination, the religion uses two other types of divination. The most basic form of divination uses four shards of coconut meat. This type of divination is commonly used during rituals and in simple cases when yes-no answers suffice. A more complex form of divination known as *Diloggun* uses a set of cowry shells to explore more complicated questions. Both Ifá and Diloggun divination use proverbs and stories to interpret the numbers or *Odu* generated by the palm nuts, *opele*, or cowry shells. These proverbs and stories are used to gain insights into an individual's current situation and provide guidance for the best way forward to bring the client's life into harmony with his or her destiny.

Practitioners of these traditions believe that each person has a destiny for this lifetime either chosen by them or given to them before birth. One's destiny includes the circumstances of one's birth, one's skills, abilities, and propensities, and the general path of one's life. When illness or other problems intrude into an individual's life, divination is used to discover how he or she may have wandered away from this destiny. Included within one's destiny is the relationship one should develop with the orisha. While typical devotees worship most of the commonly recognized orisha, many are marked to be initiated as a priest of a particular orisha. Divination is used to determine which orisha is calling the individual into its priesthood and who should be the priests to perform that initiation.

At their base all Santería ceremonies are healing rituals designed to bring individuals into harmony with their best and highest destiny. Often in order to bring an individual's life in harmony with his or her destiny, the divination priest will suggest certain rituals and sacrifices. These sacrifices can be as simple as offering a glass of water to one of the orisha or following certain short- or long-term proscriptions or prescriptions, or they can be more complex ceremonies requiring blood offerings or some type of ritual or initiation. The most controversial of the latter are the blood offerings known as *ebo eje* where the blood of animals is offered to the orisha. Animals commonly sacrificed include small birds, turtles, chickens, and other farm animals. The animals are killed as quickly and painlessly as possible, and in many cases, the meat is cooked and eaten by the community. In its 1993 case *Church of Lukumi Babalu Aye, Inc. v. Hialeah* the U.S. Supreme Court ruled that a set of ordinances passed by the city of Hialeah, Florida, forbidding such rituals was unconstitutional under the First Amendment, making it easier for devotees to practice this part of their religion.

See also: Candomblé; Myalism; Obeah

Mary Ann Clark

Further Reading

Brown, David D. 2003. *Santería Enthroned: Art, Ritual, and Innovation in an Afro-Cuban Religion*. Chicago: University of Chicago Press.

Clark, Mary Ann. 2007. *Santería: Correcting the Myths and Uncovering the Realities of a Growing Religion*. Westport, CT: Praeger Publishers.

Clark, Mary Ann. 2005. *Where Men are Wives and Women Rule: Santería Ritual Practices and Their Gender Implications*. Gainesville, FL: University of Florida Press.

Curry, Mary Cuthrell. 1997. *Making the Gods in New York: The Yoruba Religion in the African American Community*. New York: Garland Pub.

Mason, Michael Atwood. 2002. *Living Santería: Rituals and Experiences in an Afro-Cuban Religion*. Washington and London: Smithsonian Institution Press.

Murphy, Joseph M. 1994. *Working the Spirit: Ceremonies of the Africa Diaspora*. Boston: Beacon Press.

Vega, Marta Moreno. 2000. *The Altar of My Soul: The Living Traditions of Santería*. New York: One World, Ballantine Publishing Group.

Wendel, Johan. 2003. *Santería Healing: A Journey into the Afro-Cuban World of Divinities, Spirits, and Sorcery*. Gainesville, FL: University Press of Florida.

SCRUBS

By the early 20th century American conjurers and workers frequently employed liquid mixtures of water and any number of other magical and household items to clean or bathe homes or businesses, and, somewhat less frequently, people. Scrubs were most commonly used to attract luck in both personal and social affairs, as well as in economic and business matters. Common ingredients included cinnamon, honey, white and brown sugar, filé, soured smartweed, parsley, green onions, John the Conqueror powder or root, syrup, milk, rosewater, garlic, fish, ants, perfume, rainwater, and numerous other components in various combinations and permutations. The thinking behind some of the combinations was obviously to mix pleasant tasting or smelling spices and other substances in hopes of "sweetening" one's personal or business exchanges in the building or room being treated in the liquid. Because scrubs were rarely (if ever) used for negative purposes, the spiritual logic of mixtures that used less pleasant components like insects or sour substances is less obvious.

New Orleans workers prescribed scrubs for every kind of business venture, but those most frequently mentioned are small temporary economic ventures like fish fries and house parties, in addition to illicit businesses like bootlegging operations, gambling houses, and brothels. Scrubs, like many other forms of Voodoo or conjure, were most prevalent among those involved in socially or legally marginal economic projects. Some were as simple as prescriptions to scrub homes with holy water from a Catholic Church. Others required adding spiritual products like John the Conqueror or Control Powder to the liquid along with sweeteners and spices. The promised result was generally to increase the number of customers attracted to the business in question and to make existing customers more amiable and open to spending their money. In the case of a business that was not attached to the underground economy, landlords also used scrubs to attract tenants. In what is a comparatively rare case, one worker actually prescribed a scrub for sex workers that required them to bathe themselves rather than their place of business. The formula included the woman's urine and sugar. A similar rite required placing urine and bath water in front of the "spo'tin' house" to bring in johns, suggesting the same idea that water that had been in contact with the client's skin as opposed to simply placed in the business would be most effective.

See also: Conjure; Hoodoo

Kodi Roberts

Further Reading

Hyatt, Harry Middleton. 1970–1978. *Hoodoo-Conjuration-Witchcraft-Rootwork*. 5 vols. Memoirs of the Alma Egan Hyatt Foundation. Hannibal, MO: Western.

Roberts, Kodi. In press. *Voodoo and the Promise of Power: The Racial, Gender & Economic Politics of Religion in New Orleans, 1881–1940*. Baton Rouge, LA: Louisiana State University Press.

SEABROOK, WILLIAM BUEHLER

William B. Seabrook (1884–1945) was a reporter, traveler, adventurer, and writer. His many and varied experiences included living with Bedouins, flying over the Sahara, and experimenting with cannibalism. He wrote a great many books and articles about his experiences, including an autobiography. One of his best-known works is a 1929 account of his experiences with Haitian Vodou, entitled *The Magic Island*. This book helped shape 20th-century conceptions of Vodou as defined by zombis, orgies, and evil magic. Other works in this vein include Richard A. Loederer's *Voodoo Fire in Haiti* (1935) and Robert Tallant's *Voodoo in New Orleans* (1946).

The book is an entertaining read as well as a source of Vodou lore. Seabrook possessed scholarly credentials in the form of a PhD from Roanoke College. Among the useful features of *The Magic Island* are numerous formulas and accounts of Vodou ceremonies and other aspects of Haitian culture. Unfortunately, Seabrook also had an eye for the sensational and depicted the religion accordingly for an American audience interested in lurid tales of foreign lands. He was also a sexual deviant, which likely contributed to his portrayal of Vodou as highly erotic. At times, his descriptions could be rather disturbing. At one point, for instance, he described a ceremony, a significant portion of which supposedly involved sexual tension between a girl and a goat. Though the book contains some legitimate Vodou lore, it should be treated with extreme caution.

As one might suspect, Seabrook's personal life was troubled. He went through multiple wives, struggled with alcoholism, and eventually committed suicide.

See also: Loederer, Richard A.; Tallant, Robert; Vodou in Haiti

Jeffrey E. Anderson

Further Reading

Beherec, Mark A. 2015. "The Works of William Buehler Seabrook: A Chronological Annotated Further Reading." The Life and Works of William Buehler Seabrook. Accessed on April 5, 2013: http://www.geocities.com/williambseabrook/.

Graybeal, Jay A. 2010. "William Buehler Seabrook." Historical Society of Carroll Country, MD. Accessed on April 5, 2013: http://hscc.carr.org/research/yesteryears/cct2001/011028.htm.

Loederer, Richard A. 1935. *Voodoo Fire in Haiti*. Translated by Desmond Ivo Vesey. New York: Literary Guild.

Seabrook, William B. 1929. *The Magic Island*. New York: Harcourt, Brace.

Seabrook, William B. 1942. *No Hiding Place: An Autobiography*. Philadelphia: J. B. Lippincott.

Tallant, Robert. 1946. *Voodoo in New Orleans*. New York: Macmillan.

SECRET SOCIETIES

Secret societies are a global phenomenon. For Haitian history, especially, such organizations are of high relevance. Conspiracy theories tend to overestimate the role of secret societies, however, by depicting them as almighty organizations that determine the fate of people and politics all around the globe. Despite these theories, such organizations do function as social networks or ordering forces for communities. As in other countries, secret societies in Haiti underwent a transformation in their role from the independence movement on the island onward until becoming a suppressive force during the Duvalier regimes of the 20th century.

Much like Vodou, the secret societies of Haiti—the best-known of which is the Bizango—are an essential part of Haitian cultural and social history. The societies of Haiti show traceable similarities to those of Western Africa. The island's population is almost entirely descended from the hundreds of thousands of slaves brought to the French colony of Saint-Domingue to work on the island's sugar plantations, which peaked in both profitability and demand for labor in the late 18th century. For these communities of slaves, who were mainly bought in West Africa, secret societies were a normal part of social life. Many elements of African cultures continued to survive, and secret societies played a significant role in everyday life. In Africa, members had been responsible for organizing the society, and the former Africans continued to use these societies to order their world.

Fortunately, the many late arrivals to the plantations were not doomed to be slaves for an extended period. As the French Revolution's influence spread around the globe after 1789, it had a tremendous impact on the world's political and social scenery. In Haiti, it resulted in a revolution that established the second oldest independent nation in the Western Hemisphere. So great was the influence of these social upheavals that members of the secret societies later traced their origins to the revolutionary phase of the 1790s, a time when the organizations worked as centers of resistance that were responsible for anti-French actions and the emancipation of the slaves. The secret societies developed a strict organizational structure, which, due to these events, became militarily rigid. Both male and female members were allowed to enter the societies, which met at night, performing traditional dances using drums. These organizations were in control of large parts of the agrarian countryside where their members functioned as a regulating force for the community. This is a typical process for Diasporic societies in which traditional forms of organization remain active to provide a common structure for the new group of formerly African people. It is possible to trace similar developments with regard to the role of the Chinese triad societies and Chinese communities in exile. Haitian societies also played a role in the developing Diasporic communities in the United States and other parts of the world to which Haitian people emigrated.

In the case of Haiti, the role of the secret societies was not always a positive one. When the 20th century saw emergence of the Duvalier regimes in Haiti, the role of the hidden organizations underwent a transformation process. François "Papa Doc" Duvalier (1907–1971) and his son, Jean-Claude "Baby Doc" Duvalier (born 1951), established a rule of terror between 1957 and 1986. Those who were not able to leave the country suffered under a regime that employed violence and the assistance of the existing secret societies' easily corrupted leaders to control the country for years. These effects were most prevalent with regard to the agrarian countryside, which hidden organizations found easiest to dominate. During the cruel years of Papa Doc and Baby Doc's reign, the members of the organizations functioned like a secret police network, attempting to silence any form of criticism.

The role of secret societies during the centuries since the beginning of the Haitian Revolution in the late 18th century is ambivalent. It is obvious that these organizations, especially with regard to Haiti and its African heritage, were responsible for the conservation of older traditions of West African origin. Next to this, the members of these societies were responsible for keeping alive a social structure familiar to enslaved Africans. Particularly during the revolutionary period, the militarily organized societies were of high importance in providing some kind of hierarchical order to structure the society. Despite their positive role during the 18th and early 19th centuries, the societies underwent a process of transformation much like that of the Chinese triads, becoming more criminal in their forms of organization, and at times corrupted by the ruling regime. The secret societies survived this period, however, and still play a role in Haitian popular culture; their prevalence is akin to Vodou and will remain as an important aspect of the country's development, even in the Haitian societies outside the Caribbean island.

See also: Haiti; Haitian Revolution

Frank Jacob

Further Reading

Abbott, Elizabeth. 1988. *Haiti: An Insider's History of the Rise and Fall of the Duvaliers.* New York: Simon and Schuster.

Bernard, Diederich, and Al Burt. 2006. *Papa Doc and the Tontons Macoutes.* Princeton, NJ: Wiener.

Cooper, Anna Julia. 1988. *Slavery and the French Revolutionists, 1788–1805.* Translated by Freance Richardson Keller. Lewiston, NY: Mellen Press.

Geggus, David Patrick. 2001. *The Impact of the Haitian Revolution in the Atlantic World.* Columbia, SC: University of South Carolina Press.

Jacob, Frank, ed. 2013. *Secret Societies: Studies in Culture, Society and History.* Würzburg, Germany: Königshausen and Neumann.

SENEGAMBIA

In light of Africa's vast size and considerable ethnic diversity, scholars of slavery and the transatlantic slave trade divide the continent into regions based on geography and cultural similarities among the people groups who inhabit it. The term *Senegambia* designates one such area that makes up the extreme western portion of coastal Africa. The precise geographic borders of the region vary depending on whom one consults. For most, it encompasses roughly the territory occupied by the current countries of Senegal and the Gambia. Others, however, argue that a broader definition is necessary. Gwendolyn Midlo Hall, one of the leading historians of colonial Louisiana, maintains that those studying the slave trade should think of modern-day Senegal and the Gambia as but a portion of what she terms Greater Senegambia. According to her, Greater Senegambia should be understood to encompass the coastal area of West Africa between the Senegal and Sierra Leone rivers, encompassing all or part of Senegal, the Gambia, Guinea-Bissau, Guinea, and Sierra Leone.

Senegambia is home to a range of ethnicities. For example, the Fulbe or Fulani of the region are the only significant pastoral people in West Africa. They are now a presence from coastal Senegambia far into the interior of the continent. Other prominent peoples of the area are the Wolof, Malinke or Mandingo, and Bamana. Many of these peoples once controlled powerful states in the region, capitalizing off Senegambia's rich natural resources and important trade routes.

Moreover, Senegambia once composed part of the three great medieval African empires: Ghana, Mali, and Songhai. The first of these may have originated as early as the fourth century and survived until the mid-13th century. At its height during the 11th century, its king could reportedly field an army of 200,000 men. It was eventually supplanted by the Empire of Mali, which emerged in the first half of the 13th century under the leadership of the legendary ruler Sundiata. Mali would peak in power during the 14th century. One of its kings, Mansa Musa, reportedly took 80,000 companions with him when he travelled. While visiting Egypt on a pilgrimage, he distributed so much gold that it wrecked the area's economy for more than a decade. Some claim that under his reign a massive fleet set off to the west in search of new lands. Despite its great wealth, however, Mali gradually gave way to the last of the major West African empires, Songhai, during the 15th and 16th centuries. Of the three empires, Songhai was the largest. It throve off trade to North Africa in gold, slaves, and other goods until crushingly defeated by a Moroccan army in 1591.

Unlike in much of sub-Saharan Africa, Islam has been a powerful force in Senegambia since the middle ages. During the 11th century Islam began to win large numbers of converts. Initially, the conversions were peaceful and were furthered by the Kingdom of Ghana's welcoming of Muslims into its borders. As time went by, however, the spread of Islam became more violent, with Ghana suffering military defeat and eventual destruction at the hands of the Almoravids, a radical Islamic state based in Northwest Africa. The emperors of Mali and Songhai, meanwhile, would themselves embrace Islam and promote its expansion. Mansa Musa, in fact, was the first sub-Saharan West African ruler known to have undertaken a pilgrimage to Mecca, an exploit that made him the best known of the many monarchs who ruled the West African empires. In more recent times, the Fulani were among the most active jihadists, with converted populations aggressively imposing Islam on non-Muslim communities of their own ethnicity and increasingly conquering neighboring peoples. During the 18th century, such Fulani holy wars provided many of the slaves who ended up in the coastal slave markets and eventually on New World plantations.

Peoples from Senegambia were particularly influential in North America, making up a substantial percentage of the enslaved population of much of what would become the United States. According to scholar Gwendolyn Midlo Hall, Georgia and South Carolina received more slave voyages from Greater Senegambia than any other portion of Africa. Together, voyages from Greater Senegambians accounted for 44.4 percent of the trade in South Carolina and 62 percent of those to Georgia. Louisiana, the hub of Mississippi Valley Voodoo, was even more thoroughly dominated by Senegambians during its early history. From 1718 to the Spanish acquisition of the territory in 1763, as many as 64.3 percent of all slaves were of narrowly defined Senegambian origin. Even after the era of Spanish occupation, which relied heavily on imports from West Central Africa, the number of Greater Senegambians living in Louisiana composed at least 37 percent of the population, and perhaps even a slight majority. Such heavy importation of Senegambians resulted in the Malinke and Bamana becoming two of the most common ethnicities among North American slaves. The most famous of their number possibly is 18th-century poet Phillis Wheatley, who was most likely a Malinke.

Such large numbers can be explained by the fact that Senegambians were many slave buyers' most sought-after ethnicity. For one, the region was closer to most of the New World than any other portion of Africa. Slave trading voyages were therefore quicker and potentially more lucrative. Moreover, the relatively short travel time reduced the rigors associated with the perils of the Middle Passage. In addition to practical issues of transport, slaves tended to be plentiful in the region because of conflict between Senegambia's competing states and religions. In addition to jihads, military conflicts between ethnicities or even within them led to numerous captives, all of whom could be sold at a profit. In terms of physical appearance, Senegambians had a reputation for height, a marker of prowess appealing to many planters. Perhaps most importantly, many Senegambians had extensive knowledge of rice cultivation, a major boon to those regions that grew it as a major cash crop. South Carolina, Georgia, Florida, and Louisiana were prime rice growing areas and thus sought out the services of Africans with knowledge of the crop. Some have even suggested that Senegambians helped to introduce the crop to North American planters.

Islamic laborers were additionally prized among North American planters because whites considered them more intelligent than other slaves. At least some Muslim slaves also considered themselves superior to other blacks, reportedly because of their fellow slaves' adherence to traditional religions or embrace of Christianity. A few Muslim Africans from the Greater Senegambian region rose to considerable prominence in North America; for instance, Umar ben Said, known as "Prince Moro," and Lamine Kaba, were well known for their conversions to Christianity and efforts to send Arabic language Bibles to West Africa. In Georgia, Muslims were known for their leadership skills and loyalty. Two men, Silah Bilali and Bilali, served in important management roles over fellow slaves. Louisiana, meanwhile, saw the arrival of Abd al-Rahman in 1788. Al-Rahman was a particularly interesting case in that he had been a nobleman in his homeland.

The number of Muslims imported into the Americas is difficult to determine, largely because surviving records preserve little in regard to captive Africans' religion when they arrived in the New World. Nevertheless, historian Michael Gomez argued that they probably numbered in the thousands, and many continued to be particularly recognizable because of their determination to hold onto their religion. Their presence is well attested in Louisiana, Georgia, and the Carolinas. The area of Florida near St. Augustine had a particularly large Muslim community during the mid-18th century as evidenced by the fact that the third largest African ethnicity in the area was the Malinke, a largely Muslim population.

The religion of the Mississippi Valley was influenced by Senegambians from the outset. The earliest references to Voodoo evidence a clear link to the region. Le Page du Pratz briefly mentioned what were evidently the prototypes of what would later become Voodoo ceremonies in his 1758 history of the region. Though he did not specify the ethnic group or groups involved, the preponderance of Senegambians in the area renders them the most likely participants. In addition, Du Pratz later referenced slaves' possession of gris-gris, which he described as "little toys" of supposedly superstitious bondspersons. Such charms, also known throughout much of West Africa, almost certainly made their way to the Mississippi Valley in the possession of Senegambian slaves.

Du Pratz was not the only one to record the influence of Senegambian religion in the Mississippi Valley. Gris-gris made a second prominent appearance in 1773, when a group of slaves faced trial for the attempted murder of their master and an overseer through the use of magic. In this case, the link to Senegambia is clear from the fact that one of the conspirators was a Mandingo man. Another case of Senegambian influence was a person, New Orleans's Jean Montanée, better known to Anglophone audiences as Dr. John and second in fame only to Marie Laveau during his 19th-century lifetime. Montanée was a native of Senegal, and he carried on his person facial scarification or tattooing—known as country marks during his time—that many observers noted was a common adornment of those from his homeland.

Senegambian influence was much less evident in Haitian Vodou than in Louisiana Voodoo, despite the fact that slavers imported many captives from the region into Saint-Domingue, especially during its early history. Nevertheless, Senegambians possess their own nanchon among the lwas, the Siniga. Though it is far less well known than the Rada or Petwo nanchons, it remains a living part of Vodou. Among the lwas belonging to the nanchon is Mèt Senega and Ezili Seneka. Moreover the Islamic culture of Senegambia is clearly visible in the fact that Mèt Senega rejects offerings of pork and that practitioners welcome his arrival with a phrase derived from the Muslim greeting *as-salamu alaykum*. According to Harold Courlander, when a particular lwa known as Siningal possesses a man or woman, he or she speaks Arabic. Moreover, the Vodou community in a Haitian village known as Balan mixes songs in praise of the Islamic Allah with others derived from Catholicism. They also claim descent from the Mandingo people of Senegambia.

Though Senegambian influence is evident in both the Mississippi Valley and Haiti, its visibility has declined over time. The principal reason for this was that numerous later arrivals from the Bight of Benin, West Central Africa, and elsewhere ultimately reduced the numerical advantage of the Senegambian population. It is also possible that the Islamic religion of some arrivals made them less willing to contribute elements of their faith to the creole religions of Vodou and Voodoo, which were largely products of the spiritual interactions of Fon, Ewe, and Kongo peoples in their new homelands.

See also: Bight of Benin; Gris-gris; Nanchons; West Central Africa

Jeffrey E. Anderson

Further Reading

Courlander, Harold. 1960. *The Drum and the Hoe: Life and Lore of the Haitian People*. Berkeley, CA: University of California Press.

Du Pratz, Le Page. 1763. *The History of Louisiana or of the Western Parts of Virginia and Carolina*. 2 vols. Translation. London: Becket and De Hondt.

Gilles, Jerry and Yvrose Gilles. 2009. *Remembrance: Roots, Rituals, and Reverence in Vodou*. Davie, FL: Bookmanlit.

Gomez, Michael A. 1998. *Exchanging Our Country Marks: The Transformation of African Identities in the Colonial and Antebellum South*. Chapel Hill and London: University of North Carolina Press.

Hall, Gwendolyn Midlo. 1992. *Africans in Colonial Louisiana: The Development of Afro-Creole Culture in the Eighteenth Century*. Baton Rouge, LA: Louisiana State UP.

Hall, Gwendolyn Midlo. 2005. *Slavery and African Ethnicities in the Americas: Restoring the Links*. Chapel Hill, NC: University of North Carolina Press.

Harris, Joseph E. 1987. *Africans and Their History*. Revised ed. New York: Penguin Group.

Hebblethwaite, Benjamin. 2012. *Vodou Songs in Haitian Creole and English*. Philadelphia: Temple University Press.

Long, Carolyn Morrow. 2006. *A New Orleans Voudou Priestess: The Legend and Reality of Marie Laveau*. Gainesville, FL: University Press of Florida.

Michel, Claudine, and Patrick Bellegarde-Smith, eds. 2006. *Vodou in Haitian Life and Culture: Invisible Powers*. New York: Palgrave Macmillan.

Oliver, Roland, and J. D. Fage. 1988. *A Short History of Africa*. 6th ed. London: Penguin Group.

SIMBI

Simbi is the collective name for a group of spirits who are descended from the Kongo people of West Africa. There the simbi were thought to be humans who had drowned, taken their own lives by accident in water, or hung themselves. They are essentially benevolent spirits, and can give great wealth to the people they love. In both Africa and Haiti, it is believed that any structure near water houses its own simbi spirit. Uniformly imagined as serpents, they are served in Haiti as magicians, diabs or devils, and lwa. Their imagery tends toward snake or snakelike designs, with a crossroad marking the center of their vèvès. This crossroad is an allusion to the mystical crossroad they rule in Haitian Vodou magic. Simbis are considered shy and hard to connect with, a hallmark of magical spirits in Vodou who distance themselves from servitors in order to perform their feats of powers in privacy.

The simbis are synthesized with the Magi, the three Persian priest kings who came seeking the Christ child in Catholic hagiography. Their magic was of fire and alchemy, two attributes that fit simbis very well. Fire or "heat" is an expression of magic in Vodou—things are heated up metaphorically to get them charged and operating. Alchemy is not a word used in Vodou, but the alchemical process of making change in accordance to a proscribed method is very much a part of *pwen cho* (hot points), *travay* (work), and *envoye l'esprit* (the sending of spirits), all disciplines of the magician in Vodou.

Simbis have several avatars in Haitian Vodou. Three are very common and popular. There is Simbi Dlo, the father figure of the nanchon. He is imaged as

Moses and is depicted on flags as a venerable old man, dressed in a white robe with a green scarf around his neck. Simbi Andezo or Simbi "of two waters" is said to be a major magician. His colors are turquoise and red, and he is served with two fluids, as indicated by his name. Andezo likes saltwater and whiskey or fresh water and coffee. He is the master of tying *pwen* for the hunyos of kanzo. Simbi Makaya is a sorcerer and shaman, the spiritual leader of the Makaya rites. It is told that he was a runaway slave who led the maroons in the Haitian Revolution. Makaya was so powerful that his name is on a mountain (Pik Macaya) and a national park (Parc Makaya), which contains the last of Haiti's once-magnificent rain forests. A lwa of trees, leaves, and plants, it is Makaya who rules poisons, healing leaves, and the ritual of *gads*, protective talismans cut into individuals' skin.

Simbis love freshness, so they are often served by fresh water pools, under waterfalls, or in ponds. It is said their altars are the largest stone one finds in pools of water. Haitians say that simbis take young children under the waters so that they can give them the gift of clairvoyance. They are also polygamists and have many wives on all the islands of the Caribbean.

Simbis' feast day is Tuesday. Their offerings are the tools of their trade—magic lamps, packets and talismans of healing herbs, and small sacks containing powdered plant material, such as bark, stems, and leaves. They will accept offerings of potatoes, plantains, yams, peas, corn flour, rice, milk, cakes, and roasted peanuts, and they drink cola as well as white and red wine. Their sacrificial animals are red roosters, hens *zenga* (meaning ash gray and white), and all sorts of black or gray animals, including pigs, goats, or turkeys.

See also: Grand Zombi; Haitian Revolution; Kanzo; Kongo; Maroon; Nanchons; Nzambi a Mpungu

Patricia Scheu (Mambo Vye Zo Komande LaMenfo)

Further Reading

Ackermann, Hans-Wolfgang, Maryse Gautier, and Michel-Ange Momplaisir. 2011. *Les Esprits du Vodou Haïtien*. Coconut Creek, FL: Educa Vision, Inc.

Guigard, Mercedes Foucard. 2006. *Répertoire Pratique des Loa du Vodou Haïtien - Practical Directory of the Loa of Haitian Vodou*. Port-au-Prince, Haiti: Reme Art Publishing.

Illes, Judika. 2009. *Encyclopedia of Spirits: The Ultimate Guide to the Magic of Fairies, Genies, Demons, Ghosts, Gods and Goddesses*. New York: HarperCollins.

Thompson, Robert Farris. 1983. *Flash of the Spirit: African and Afro-American Art and Philosophy*. New York: Random House.

THE SIXTH AND SEVENTH BOOKS OF MOSES

The Sixth and Seventh Books of Moses is an English translation of a German occult text, originally published by Johann Scheible as *Die Sechsten und Siebten Buch Mosis* in 1849. The title refers to the fact that the first five books of the Old Testament—Genesis, Exodus, Leviticus, Numbers, and Deuteronomy—are called the five books of Moses. *Die Sechsten und Siebten Buch Mosis* was based on the Kabbalah and other Hebrew writings. The first section consists of magical seals with their accompanying uses, such as the Seal of Fortune and Long Life; the Seal of Dreams and Visions; the Seal of Good Luck, Play, and Games; and the Seal of Shemhamforas, that "brings to light the treasures of the earth." The rest of the book is a conglomeration of treatises on "The Magic of the Israelites," "Formulas of the Magical Kabbalah," an "Extract from the Genuine and True Clavicula of Solomon the King of Israel," the "Arcana Magica of Alexander," the "Citation of the Seven Great Princes," the "Magical Cures of the Old Hebrews," and the "Use of the Psalms for the Physical Welfare of Man."

The book was first introduced into the United States by the Pennsylvania German community. An inaccurate and garbled English translation, titled *The Sixth and Seventh Books of Moses*, was published in 1880 by the Vicor Company in Elizabethtown, Pennsylvania. Subsequent 20th-century reprints by mail-order merchants that catered to the spiritual trade have repeated its many errors, making the book nearly unintelligible to English-speaking readers. Despite its difficulty, *The Sixth and Seventh Books of Moses* became popular among African American conjurers, rootworkers, and hoodoo doctors. It may be its very impenetrability that gave the book its air of power and mystery, rendering it more valuable in the eyes of its users.

See also: Books; Conjure; Drugstores; Hoodoo; Rootwork; 'Tit Albert

Carolyn Morrow Long

Further Reading

Davies, Owen. 2009. *Grimoires: A History of Magical Books.* Oxford: Oxford University Press.
Long, Carolyn Morrow. 2001. *Spiritual Merchants: Religion, Magic, and Commerce.* Knoxville, TN: University of Tennessee Press.
Peterson, Joseph. 2005–2006. "Esoteric Archives." Accessed on March 14, 2014: http://www.esotericarchives.com/moses/67moses.htm.

SLAVERY AND THE SLAVE TRADE

Slavery existed as an African institution well before the arrival of Europeans, but the rise of the plantation societies of the New World transformed slavery from a slowly dying institution into a driving force behind European prosperity and forcibly displaced millions of Africans. The beginnings of what would develop into the Atlantic slave trade can be traced to 1444, when Portuguese sailors began kidnapping sub-Saharan Africans during voyages down the coast in search or gold and a route to the spice-producing Indies. Other European nationalities sometimes followed the Portuguese example, raiding the coast for captives to sell in Europe and later the New World. In this context, however, their captives often served as sources of information, curiosities, and status symbols rather than the agricultural workers characteristic of later years.

Economic opportunity coupled with a severe shortage of workers transformed slavery into a system of labor that brought prosperity and power to Western Europe and eventually helped give rise to the various nations of North and South America. Christopher Columbus's claim of the New World for Spain exposed Europeans to vast new territories from which they hoped personal wealth could be extracted. Initially, much of the economic exploitation of the new lands centered on mining. During the 16th century, plantations began to appear in Spanish- and Portuguese-controlled areas, most notably Brazil and the Caribbean Islands, including Hispaniola, now home to Haiti and the Dominican Republic. Sugar became the dominant crop. It was the rise of an agricultural economy in the New World that created a pressing need for laborers.

As early as Columbus's first voyage, the Spanish had considered enslaving Native Americans, and while many of the New World's indigenous inhabitants did experience bondage, the enslavement of American Indians proved unworkable. As late as the early 16th century, the number of the New World's indigenous inhabitants was large. Some estimates put the population of Hispaniola alone at 7 million before the arrival of the Spanish. Within two generations, the West Indies were practically devoid of population, almost entirely because of Old World diseases carried by the Spaniards and inadvertently passed to Native Americans. To make up for the absence of a native workforce, the Spanish turned to Africa for their labor needs. Africans, themselves an Old World people group, had roughly the same immunities to disease as did Europeans, leaving them relatively safe from the pandemics that decimated Native Americans.

African attitudes toward the slave trade varied widely. For example, the rulers of the Kingdom of Kongo sought to regulate and limit the Atlantic trade, although, like most African peoples, they also practiced slavery. As one might expect, their claims were ignored by the Portuguese, who were the primary enslavers in the area. Other African peoples embraced the slave trade as a route to wealth and power. Perhaps the most notorious was Dahomey, a kingdom of the Fon people that eventually became modern Benin. Not only did Dahomey permit the slave trade, it actively fostered it from the national level, with the king enriching himself through personal control of the sale of captives. The high point of the Dahomean slave trading began in 1727 with the kingdom's conquest of the much smaller coastal nation of Ouidah. The former city state became Dahomey's chief slave port, with perhaps 10,000 Africans leaving their native land from the city annually.

While raiders provided many bondspeople, the predominant method of enslavement was warfare. Throughout history, prisoners of war have frequently found themselves the slaves of their captors, a fate many Africans would expect if defeated in battle. Before the development of a New World market for captives, however, enslavement was not itself a prime motive for African warfare. The lure of wealth made battle lucrative for those who had no qualms about selling captured enemies. In West Africa, the Fon and Yoruba fought frequently, with each side selling prisoners to European slavers. To the northwest, holy wars between Muslims and practitioners of traditional religions led to additional captives. In West Central Africa, destabilization—largely created by Portuguese colonizers—led not only to wars between peoples but even within once-powerful states, such as the Kingdom of Kongo.

After capture, the newly enslaved faced an overland trip to the coast, a journey generally carried out on foot and sometimes stretching for hundreds of miles.

Many died on the route, with perhaps as few as 50 percent ever reaching the slave pens, called *barracoons*, on the coast. The slaves' confinement could last from mere days to months while their captors awaited interested buyers. As had been true of the travel to the coast, many never lived to find themselves owned by Europeans. Those who survived eventually experienced confinement on seagoing vessels, often in chains, that transported them to their future homes across the Atlantic. The unsanitary and often cramped conditions of the slave ships led to another 10 to 20 percent death toll. In the end, only a fraction of the original captives ever saw the New World.

The number of Africans transported to the Western Hemisphere was staggering. During the 16th century, the number of enslaved people rapidly increased, coming to outnumber European settlers in some areas as early as the 1560s, which was the case in Hispaniola. The total number of forced African immigrants to the Americas has never been adequately determined, but most historians accept that around 11.9 million left African ports en route for the Americas, with most of them enslaved during the period 1701 to 1850. Although the majority of captives ended up in the Caribbean or Brazil, Africans found themselves dispersed across North and South America.

The western half of Hispaniola, which gradually transformed into the French colony of Saint-Domingue, was a prime destination for bondspersons, second among the New World colonies only to the massive Portuguese colony of Brazil. By the 17th century, Saint-Domingue was an incredibly lucrative colony, and its wealth only grew with time. The colony produced 60 percent of the world's sugar by the second half of the 18th century. On the eve of the Haitian Revolution, 8,000 plantations—whose produce accounted for 40 percent of France's overseas trade—operated in the small colony.

Such extensive cultivation required a massive labor force. By 1789, approximately 20,000 new Africans arrived each year, with the numbers coming heavily from the Bight of Benin and West Central regions of Africa. This number is rendered all the more poignant by the fact that high death tolls and low birthrates among those already enslaved required this constant influx of new slaves to keep the colony's plantations in operation. Despite over two centuries of slavery in the island, Saint-Domingue's black population had only reached 452,000 in 1780. Nevertheless, the massive annual shipments resulted in an extreme disparity in the number of whites and blacks in the colony. By 1790, there were over eleven people of African descent for every one of European ancestry.

The Mississippi Valley, while also a colony of France, was an unprofitable backwater compared to Saint-Domingue. Its slave importation patterns mirror this fact. Whereas Saint-Domingue saw some 700 ships carrying bondspersons arrive each year during the height of the trade, Louisiana had just twenty-five visit the island from 1718, the beginning of its slave dealing, to 1763, the year France lost control of the colony. Moreover, after 1731, only a single slave ship arrived in the colony before the departure of the French. At the same time, white immigration also was sparse, making Africans and their descendants a slight majority during much of the colonial period. After Spain took control of the western half of the massive Louisiana colony following the defeat of its former owners during the French and Indian War (also known as the Seven Years War), slave importation increased significantly as the Spanish struggled to make Louisiana profitable. Spain's acquisition of the colony also altered importation patterns. Under the French, Louisiana was unusual among New World colonies in that the majority of its bondspersons came from Senegambia, with the Bight of Benin a distant second. The Spanish, however, acquired perhaps three-quarters of their slaves from West Central Africa.

The ethnic mix of Africans brought to Saint-Domingue and Louisiana helped to shape Vodou and Voodoo. Modern Haitian Vodou's spiritual realm is peopled by a plethora of deities, most of whom exist within a particular nanchon, or nation. These nanchons represent the places from whence the spirits originally came. The Rada nanchon, usually described as the most important to Vodou, derives from the beliefs of slaves from Allada and nearby areas conquered by Dahomey. Among the several other nanchons are the Kongo, Ibo, and Siniga, whose ethnic origins are easily recognizable in their names. Initially, the slaves of Saint-Domingue probably worshipped each nanchon within a distinct religion, but by the time the first scholars began to study the island's religion, the multiple faiths had at least partially merged into what is today called Vodou. Although nanchons do not appear to have figured prominently in Mississippi Valley beliefs, the distinct ethnicities who contributed to the region left their mark on Voodoo. For example, Blanc Dani, a prominent spirit, was of Fon and Ewe origin. Others, such as Grand Zombi, likely originated in West Central Africa.

Enslaved Africans of all ethnicities faced considerable hardship on New World plantations, but the nature of slavery varied greatly from place to place. As the greatest of the Caribbean sugar islands, Saint-Domingue became the jewel of the France's colonial empire. So great were the profits to be made that many planters worked their bondspersons to death, secure in the knowledge that they were maximizing their profits and that they could always buy more slaves. Another motive for the extreme cruelty that masters inflicted upon their slaves was fear. Whites were right to be afraid. After all, the vast and unhappy slave majority threatened to overwhelm their masters by sheer numbers. In the end, they did.

While Saint-Domingue prospered from the growing of sugar and its slaves suffered in inverse proportion, the Mississippi Valley—especially the portion of it composing the modern state of Louisiana—struggled. Early in its colonial history, no one crop dominated. Instead, tobacco, rice, sugar, trade with Native Americans, and other pursuits drove its meager economy. Under the Spanish, however, sugar gradually became the crop of choice, and the region's agricultural profits showed signs of improvement. Following the United States' acquisition of the Louisiana Territory and the arrival of tens of thousands of American settlers, the Lower Mississippi became an economic powerhouse based on the production of sugar along the coast and cotton to the north. The Mississippi River also made it a major transportation hub and contributed to it becoming the nation's largest slave-trading center. Interestingly, an 1809–1810 influx of refugees from the Haitian Revolution contributed to this economic boom.

While life for slaves was rarely easy, bondspersons in Louisiana had a better lot compared to those of Saint-Domingue. The cotton plantations of the northern portion of modern Louisiana incorporated the sunup-to-sundown gang labor common to much of the antebellum South. The sugar-growing parishes, however, had a reputation for hardship, helping to give rise to the planters' threats that they would "sell down the river" those who displeased them. Nevertheless, the United States was a notable exception among slave societies in that its black population grew under slavery. In part, this can be explained by the facts that food and space were plentiful. In some places, the climate was less disease-ridden than in the Caribbean as well.

There were some similarities between the slave systems of Louisiana and Saint-Domingue, however. In both areas, white masters freely used the whip and paddle to enforce discipline and control their laborers. Other common features were the consequence of French influence. Slaves in both Saint-Domingue and early Louisiana, for instance, were subject to various versions of the strict Code Noir, meaning "Black Code," that carefully regulated bondspersons' activities but also granted them very limited rights. It also required that slaves be baptized and instructed in Catholicism, though planters often ignored the latter stipulation. Finally, both colonies saw the rise of a large mixed-race free population that came to occupy a position between whites and blacks. In Louisiana, it was these free people of color, especially the women, who emerged as Voodoo's leadership.

African Diasporic Religions and magic sometimes functioned to help Africans and their descendants cope with slavery. African American hoodoo, which served as an aspect of Voodoo in the Mississippi Valley, included many charms and spells designed to help bondspersons resist punishment or escape from slavery. The writings of escaped slaves testify to powders designed to be sprinkled around masters to prevent whippings. Roots of various sorts could be carried in the pocket or chewed to accomplish the same purpose. Some slaves drank a concoction known as hush water to maintain their calm in the face of provocation. Still others applied powdered lizards to their feet in order to help them elude slave tracking dogs while fleeing toward safe havens in the North or Canada.

Slaves' religion sometimes had impacts on slavery that extended well beyond the individual. The Denmark Vesey Conspiracy in South Carolina, which aimed

---

Voodoo in Places Other than Haiti and the New Orleans Area

Most people strongly associate Vodou/Voodoo with only two places: Haiti and New Orleans. To say it has been confined only to these locales, however, would be incorrect. For one thing, its parent religion, Vodu or Vodun, continues to survive in Benin and its West African neighbors. Likewise, within the United States, Voodoo was once a part of African American life in Missouri and probably other areas along the Mississippi River. A few historical reports place it in coastal Texas and Florida as well. Moreover, some form of the religion also exists in other Caribbean nations, most notably the Dominican Republic.

to end slavery entirely, saw one Gullah Jack, a conjurer, serve as Vesey's lieutenant. The Haitian Revolution, the only successful slave revolt in modern history, reportedly began during a Vodou ceremony. Many scholars also interpret Makandal's poisoning activities earlier in the 18th century as an antislavery campaign linked to the religion. Recently, some scholars have argued that New Orleans's Marie Laveau used her position as a Voodoo priestess to help slaves obtain their freedom. Unfortunately, hard evidence that Laveau did so is lacking. On the other hand, some evidence suggests that not all the Louisiana practitioners opposed the system of slavery. One account of an 1863 New Orleans ceremony suggested that the participants called on the Grand Zombi to aid the Confederate cause. The participants were likely free persons of color who stood to suffer just as much as whites if the South were to lose the Civil War.

See also: Bight of Benin; Boukman, Dutty; Code Noir; Haitian Revolution; Kongo; Makandal; Nanchons; Senegambia; Vodu in West Africa; West Central Africa

Jeffrey E. Anderson

Further Reading

Anderson, Jeffrey E. 2005. *Conjure in African American Society*. Baton Rouge, LA: Louisiana State University Press.
Desmangles, Leslie G. 1992. *Faces of the Gods: Vodou and Roman Catholicism in Haiti*. Chapel Hill, NC: University of North Carolina Press.
Gomez, Michael A. 1998. *Exchanging Our Country Marks: The Transformation of African Identities in the Colonial and Antebellum South*. Chapel Hill and London: University of North Carolina Press.
Gomez, Michael A. 2005. *Reversing Sail: A History of the African Diaspora*. Cambridge, UK: Cambridge University Press.
Hall, Gwendolyn Midlo. 1992. *Africans in Colonial Louisiana: The Development of Afro-Creole Culture in the Eighteenth Century*. Baton Rouge, LA: Louisiana State University Press.
Hall, Gwendolyn Midlo. 2005. *Slavery and African Ethnicities in the Americas: Restoring the Links*. Chapel Hill, NC: University of North Carolina Press.
Kolchin, Peter. 1993. *American Slavery, 1619–1877*. New York: Hill and Wang.
Long, Carolyn Morrow. 2006. *A New Orleans Voudou Priestess: The Legend and Reality of Marie Laveau*. Gainesville, FL: University Press of Florida.
Métraux, Alfred. 1972. *Voodoo in Haiti*. Translated by Hugo Charteris and with an Introduction by Sidney W. Mintz. New York: Schocken.
"Tribulations des Voudous." *L'Union*, August 1, 1863, 1.
Ward, Martha. 2004. *Voodoo Queen: The Spirited Lives of Marie Laveau*. Jackson, MS: University Press of Mississippi.

SNAKES

Snakes were spiritually important in African Vodu and were historically a part of Haitian Vodou. Serpents figured most prominently in the beliefs of the Fon and Ewe of the Bight of Benin region. By the 19th century, these peoples understood at least two of their deities to be spiritual serpents. One of them, known as Anyi-ewe among the western Ewe and Aido-wedo among the eastern, was a

> **Do Vodouisants Worship Snakes?**
>
> One of the earliest accounts of Vodou, written by Louis-Élie Moreau de Saint-Méry, emphasized the role of a serpent in Haitian ceremonies. There may well have been truth in his description, especially in light of the serpent veneration of the old Kingdom of Dahomey. Unfortunately, a host of popular writers have seized upon Moreau de Saint-Méry's description to define Vodou as simple snake worship—a patent misrepresentation intended to exploit the image of Vodou as exotic superstition. Moreover, snakes are not prominent features of modern Vodou, unless one includes such spiritual serpents as Danbala.

rainbow serpent that generally dwelt underground but extended itself into the heavens to drink from the god Mawu's stored-up rain. The second, Dangbe or Dan, was associated with Dahomey, especially the city of Ouidah, where he was worshipped as a spirit of wisdom and humanity's benefactor, embodied as a divine python. In Dahomey, pythons were sacred, and many are still housed in a temple located in Ouidah.

Both the Ewe and Fon deities survived in Haitian Vodou, though under the altered names of Ayida Wedo and Danbala. During the religion's early days, living serpents were also part of the religion. Médéric Louis-Élie Moreau de Saint-Méry's well-known account of a late 18th-century Voodoo ceremony describes the use of a caged serpent as a representation of a deity, most likely Danbala. Sometime after Moreau de Saint-Méry penned his account, the use of living snakes in Vodou ceremonies faded away. The serpent deities, however, have remained important parts of the religion.

The exact role of snakes in Mississippi Valley Voodoo is unclear. Oral histories conducted by the Louisiana branch of the Federal Writers' Project during the 1930s and early 1940s—often one of the best sources for the study of the religion—are contradictory. Some informants described snakes as part of rituals performed by Marie Laveau, during which they represented one or more deities. Others claimed that she never used them. The situation is further complicated by the fact that since the late 19th century, many authors have paraphrased Moreau de Saint-Méry's account of a Haitian ceremony in their descriptions of Louisiana Voodoo. So widespread were such misleading depictions, that they certainly entered the folklore surrounding the faith. The elderly informants who passed their knowledge onto Writers' Project workers may have simply blended what they actually saw with what they had read or heard spoken of as fact.

On the other hand, snakes did figure in Voodoo and related practices. Zora Neale Hurston claimed to have participated in an initiation ceremony that employed several snake skins. Missouri Voodoo practitioners, meanwhile, honored a spirit known as Grandfather Rattlesnake, who appears to have occupied a position similar to that of Blanc Dani in Louisiana or Danbala in Haiti. In conjure both in the Mississippi Valley and elsewhere, snakes figure prominently, though usually as a harmful agent secretly inserted into the bodies of one's enemies to cause the victims to sicken and die.

See also: Dahomey; Danbala; Moreau de Saint-Méry, Médéric Louis-Élie; Pythons

Jeffrey E. Anderson

Further Reading

Ellis, A. B. 1890. *The Ewe-Speaking Peoples of the Slave Coast of West Africa: Their Religion, Manners, Customs, Laws, Languages, &c.* London: Chapman and Hall.
Hurston, Zora Neale. 1931. "Hoodoo in America." *Journal of American Folklore* 44: 317–417.
Hyatt, Harry Middleton. 1970–1978. *Hoodoo-Conjuration-Witchcraft-Rootwork.* 5 vols. Memoirs of the Alma Egan Hyatt Foundation. Hannibal, MO: Western.
Long, Carolyn Morrow. 2006. *A New Orleans Voudou Priestess: The Legend and Reality of Marie Laveau.* Gainesville, FL: University Press of Florida.
Moreau de Saint-Méry, Médéric-Louis-Élie. 1797. *Description Topographique, Physique, Civile, Politique et Historique de la Partie Française de l'Isle de Saint-Domingue.* 2 vols. Philadelphia.
Owen, Mary Alicia. 1892. "Among the Voodoos." In *The International Folk-lore Congress 1891: Papers and Transactions*, 230–248. London: David Nutt.

SOULS

Adherents of African Diasporic religions frequently believe that humans are composed of multiple souls or spirits. The existence of multiple souls is not well attested in Mississippi Valley Voodoo, though a few references to the belief exist in descriptions of hoodoo. In Georgia, for instance, postbellum planter Roland Steiner recorded the words of conjurer Braziel Robinson, who claimed to have two spirits. One of these remained within his body, while the other "prowled around." According to Robinson, the only people to have multiple spirits are those born with double cauls. Both of his spirits were good and helped to protect him from malevolent spirits and to keep him from becoming evil himself. He stated that at one point, he had heard his roaming spirit tell an approaching spirit to leave him alone. If Robinson had ignored his spirit's guidance, however, they would have deserted him, and evil ones would have taken their place.

Accounts of mojos collected from Missouri Voodoo practitioners by Mary Alicia Owen give some tantalizing glimpses of what may have also been multiple souls. According to Owen, mojos of the region were often effective specifically for the person for whom they were fashioned. They frequently carried the names of their intended owners. The strong link between the individual and his or her mojo clearly indicates the spiritual ties between the two, seemingly implying that a portion of the owner's soul or perhaps one of multiple souls was bound to the charm.

In contrast to the situation in North America, numerous scholars have recognized the existence of multiple souls in Haitian belief. Leslie Desmangles's *Faces of the Gods* (1992) provides an excellent summary of Vodou's concept of the immaterial portion of human beings, which the author describes as compartments of the spiritual portion of humans. Believers think of each person as possessing an espri, or spirit, which is divided into two parts, the gwo-bon-anj and ti-bon-anj, meaning "big good angel" and "little good angel," respectively. The gwo-bon-anj is the immortal life force of the individual that provides motion and is understood as a part of Bondye, the Supreme Being. The ti-bon-anj, in contrast, is the primary source of personality and morals. Although aspects of individual disposition exist within the gwo-bon-anj, it is the ti-bon-anj that manifests them in the visible world. It also acts as the conscience and allows people to feel emotions related to how well or poorly they treat others. According to Desmangles, a third part of the soul, the mèt tèt or master of the head, is a guardian lwa that protects its possessor and is the subject of possession by other lwas. Of the three portions of the soul, the gwo-bon-anj is the most important after death because it continues to interact with living humans and can eventually become a lwa in its own right.

The concept of multiple and/or multicompartmental souls almost certainly originated in Africa. Fon practitioners of Vodu, for instance, understand the spiritual portion of humans as composed of either two or four souls, with the former concept predominating. The first soul, known as the sɛ, resembles the Haitian gwo-bon-anj in that it comes from Mawu-Lisa the powerful creator deity. It is the source of each person's destiny and must will an action before a person can perform it. Mawu-Lisa also uses the sɛ to speak to humans. Like the ti-bon-anj of Vodou and Braziel Robinson's spirits, the sɛ also governs individuals' morals. The yɛ, on the other hand, links each living human to his or her ancestors, current family members, and descendants. The yɛ is associated with peoples' shadows and is understood to manifest the actions of the body, which are themselves shaped by the actions of the sɛ. Similar beliefs are well documented among the Ewe, BaKongo, Yoruba, and others.

While ideas of multiple souls probably came from Africa, blacks in the New World found plenty in surrounding cultures to support their beliefs. Native Americans, for example, frequently understood humans to be composed of two spirits. Among the aboriginal inhabitants of the American South, many accepted the existence of a bodily soul similar to the gwo-bon-anj or sɛ, which dwelled within the human body. Free souls, in contrast, could leave the body and wander about, creating dreams as their possessors slept.

Support for African and African Diasporic concepts of multiple souls also came from within Christianity. Since ancient times, western Christians have generally envisioned humanity as a dichotomy of body and soul. Some biblical texts as well as eastern churches, early church fathers, and many others have held to a tripartite division of body, soul, and spirit. In this conception, the spirit is roughly analogous to the gwo-bon-anj as a life force that links humans to God. The two differ, however, in that the spirit is also understood as directing morals, the will, and reason. The soul, in contrast, is primarily focused on the self rather than the divine and directs memory, comprehension, and imagination. Still others hold to even greater division within humanity's spiritual makeup. The degree to which African Americans encountered such relatively obscure theological concepts, however, is difficult to determine.

See also: Mojo; Two Head

Jeffrey E. Anderson

Further Reading

Anderson, Jeffrey E. 2005. *Conjure in African American Society*. Baton Rouge, LA: Louisiana State University Press.

Blier, Suzanne Preston. 1995. *African Vodun: Art, Psychology, and Power*. Chicago and London: University of Chicago Press.

Deren, Maya. 1953. *Divine Horsemen: The Living Gods of Haiti*. London and New York: Thames and Hudson.

Desmangles, Leslie G. 1992. *Faces of the Gods: Vodou and Roman Catholicism in Haiti*. Chapel Hill, NC: University of North Carolina Press.

Enns, Paul. 2008. *The Moody Handbook of Theology*. Revised and expanded ed. With a foreword by J. Dwight Pentecost. Chicago: Moody Publishers.

Hultkrantz, Åke. 1979. *The Religions of the American Indians*. Translated by Monica Setterwall. Berkeley, Los Angeles, and London: University of California Press.

Owen, Mary Alicia. 1893 [2003]. *Old Rabbit, the Voodoo and Other Sorcerers*. With an Introduction by Charles Godfrey Leland. With Illustrations by Juliette A. Owen and Louis Wain. London: T. Fisher Unwin; reprint, Whitefish, MT: Kessinger Publishing.

Steiner, Roland. 1901. "Braziel Robinson Possessed of Two Spirits." *Journal of American Folk-Lore* 14: 226–228.

SPIRITUAL CHURCHES

These compose a largely Christian community of religious institutions that date to the first decades of the 20th century. It is still debated by anthropologists and historians where the community first arose, Chicago or New Orleans. What is known is that the founder of what became a community of Spiritual Churches in New Orleans, Mother Leafy Anderson, started her own church in Chicago in 1913 and by 1920 had relocated to the Crescent City, where she founded Eternal Life Spiritual Church. Anderson's church was the first of what evidence suggests was a community of congregations that numbered over a hundred throughout the 20th century. Despite this fact, it has been maintained by some scholars that the Spiritual Church model established in Chicago was transplanted at some earlier date from New Orleans.

Spiritual Church congregations, operating largely independently for most of their early history, incorporated a variety of practices and belief structures, many of which were not shared by other Spiritual Churches. What defines and unifies the congregations across a diverse set of practices is a form of spirit possession common across various churches. The understanding of this spirit possession varies, however. Some congregations understand the inhabiting force at work during possession to be the Holy Spirit of the Christian Trinity, while others claim various supernatural guides, the most prominent of whom is a Native American spirit known as Black Hawk.

The prominence of spirit possessions has led to comparisons to both New Orleans Voodoo and 19th-century Spiritualism, popular in both New York and New Orleans. Despite the racialized stigma attached to the practice of Voodoo throughout the 19th and 20th centuries, some prominent leaders of Spiritual Churches in the first decades of its presence in the city did acknowledge infamous Voodoo

Queen Marie Laveau and practitioners of Voodoo as predecessors to the Spiritual Churches. As the 20th century progressed, however, the insistence on exclusivity and the dominance of Christian paradigms among Spiritual Church leaders increased members' reluctance to attach the history of the Spiritual Churches to Voodoo or any non-Christian influences that Christians might define as magic.

Following the precedent set by Mother Anderson, in the first decade of their proliferation in New Orleans, many Spiritual Churches had female leaders, and by the late 20th century, much of their membership was skewed toward working-class African American women. In the first two decades the earliest churches in New Orleans were reportedly interracial and welcomed both white laypersons and leaders. Leafy Anderson died in 1927, leaving behind a network of congregations she had helped to establish via a training program for ministers, who were called Spiritual Mothers and Fathers. She trained the heads of many of these churches and sometimes financially supported protégés founding their own congregations. By the mid-1930s, Spiritual Church leaders began to decrease the gap between more established forms of Christianity and the Spiritual Churches by relating the doctrines explaining spiritual possession to the most recognizable figures and doctrines of Christianity, such as Jesus, the Holy Spirit, and any number of Christian and folk saints. Even after the creation of official associations between Spiritual Churches throughout New Orleans and with others elsewhere in the United States, many Spiritual Churches still enjoyed a great deal of autonomy and variety in their beliefs and practices. Theological readings of spirit possession posited by the Southwest Conference of Spiritual Churches in 1937 that focused on Jesus and Trinitarianism deviated significantly from ideas propagated by Leafy Anderson in the 1920s, which downplayed Christ's importance as an individual to the extent that witnesses recalled that she and her congregation never mentioned him by name. While Spiritual Churches have survived in New Orleans to be documented by anthropologists, artists, and photographers, both their numbers and visibility had dwindled significantly by the end of the 20th century. By the beginning of the 21st century they had become few and far between in the city of New Orleans.

See also: Laveau, Marie; New Orleans; Voodoo in the Mississippi Valley

Kodi Roberts

Further Reading

Baer, Hans A. 2001. *The Black Spiritual Movement: A Religious Response to Racism*. 2nd ed. Knoxville, TN: University of Tennessee Press.

Berry, Jason. 1995. *The Spirit of Black Hawk: A Mystery of Africans and Indians*. Jackson, MS: University Press of Mississippi.

Jacobs, Claude F., and Andrew J. Kaslow. 1991. *The Spiritual Churches of New Orleans: Origins, Beliefs, and Rituals of an African-American Religion*. Knoxville, TN: University of Tennessee Press.

Roberts, Kodi. In press. *Voodoo and the Promise of Power: The Racial, Gender & Economic Politics of Religion in New Orleans, 1881–1940*. Baton Rouge, LA: Louisiana State University Press.

SPIRITUALISM

The American Spiritualist movement provides the theoretical foundation for many contemporary movements that engage in communication with different sorts of spiritual entities, including many so-called New Age traditions. Spiritualists believe that they can pierce the veil between the spiritual and material worlds in order to allow dead relatives, angels, saints, important public figures, and highly evolved spiritual beings to speak through them.

The American Spiritualist tradition is generally considered to have started in 1848 when a pair of young farm girls began communicating with a murdered peddler buried in the cellar of their home. In the middle of the night on March 31, the sisters Margaret (also called Maggie) and Kate (also called Katherine) Fox were frightened out of their sleep by unexplained knocking. Eventually the girls (aged 15 and 12), their parents, and neighbors determined that the noises were communications with a disembodied spirit that the girls called "Mr. Splitfoot."

The Fox family lived in Hydesville, New York, part of the area known as the Burned Over District for the great number of religious reform movements that swept though it during the early to mid-1800s, including the Second Great Awakening, the Millerist movement, Mormonism, and others. The area was also known for its thriving African American community and its social radicalism, including the women's suffrage and abolitionist movements. Hence it was fertile ground for the idea that direct, rather than mediated, communication with God, angels, and other spiritual beings was possible.

Soon the girls were sent to nearby Rochester, where the rappings followed. The girls gave performances of their abilities in both private and public séances where they were not only valorized by their adoring audiences but also scrutinized by the scientists of the day. Soon the girls were not alone, as others, especially young women, manifested the ability to serve as mediums between the living and the dead.

A typical early Spiritualist event revolved around a public lecture or sermon outlining Spiritualist principles and adding a scientific veneer to the proceedings followed by a performance by the medium, who relayed messages to the audience from the spiritual world. While most of the lecturers were men, the mediums were women, often young women, and African Americans who, according to the sensibilities of the time, were the perfect conduit for the words of the spirits because it was assumed they did not have the intellectual prowess to speak for themselves.

During its heyday in the 19th century hundreds of thousands of people consulted Spiritualist mediums or were sympathetic to their ideas, including such luminaries as Ralph Waldo Emerson, Henry Wadsworth Longfellow, and Mary Todd Lincoln, the wife of President Abraham Lincoln. Spiritualist communications were seen as proof that individual consciousness not only existed after death but that individual spiritual beings were interested in communicating with the living.

Based on the philosophical and mystical writings of Emanuel Swedenborg (1688–1772) and Andrew Jackson Davis (1830–1910) along with direct communication with their spiritual guides and conversation partners, Spiritualists developed their own vision of the afterlife independent of ministers and church hierarchy. Although Spiritualism eventually built its own church organization and association of congregations, it continued to follow a doctrine of individual liberty and responsibility led by each person's own spirit guides. Because there was no central authority, Spiritualists often disagreed on even the most important ideas about their own tradition. However, they did hold some common viewpoints including ideas about a Divine Spirit, the "universal brotherhood" of humanity, a belief in the unceasing progression of the soul after death, and a belief that hell is a condition of the mind rather than a physical place. This led Spiritualists to see the world as an organic and interconnected whole and to believe that death was not an absolute end but rather simply a change of one's state.

In many ways the afterlife envisioned by Spiritualists, often called the Summerland after the ideas of Andrew Jackson Davis, was similar to the world of the living. There spirits dwelled together with friends and relatives, working toward the spiritual growth of both the living and the dead. Drawn together by their mutual sympathy, husbands and wives, parents and children, friends and others, even beloved family pets were believed to enjoy each other's company beyond the grave.

As mediums became more and more popular they were increasingly challenged by the scientific community. Over time the "physical" manifestations of their spirits including rapping sounds, ectoplasmic displays, levitations, and the like became ever more fantastic. Although not all of these manifestations have been explained, many mediums were exposed as frauds who produced these phenomena themselves or with the help of accomplices. Eventually mental mediumship, including clairvoyance (clear seeing), clairaudience (clear hearing), clairsentience (clear feeling), crystal gazing, divination, dowsing, and the like became more popular if less verifiable.

For many, Spiritualism was dealt a death blow in 1888 when Maggie Fox claimed that she and her sisters were frauds and charlatans and that Spiritualism was evil. Less than a year later, however, Maggie recanted her claims against Spiritualism, and observers were left to wonder which of her statements held the truth. By that time Spiritualism was well beyond the control of a single individual or family, as thousands of people had already had their own experiences of talking to the "other side."

Eventually interest in Spiritualism receded, although Spiritualists and their congregations have not completely disappeared. Today Spiritualist and (African American) Spiritual Churches continue to exist, and mediums, often called *channels*, continue to relay messages from a wide range of spiritual entities.

See also: Espiritismo; Spiritual Churches

Mary Ann Clark

Further Reading

Baer, Hans A. 2001. *The Black Spiritual Movement: A Religious Response to Racism.* Knoxville, TN: The University of Tennessee Press.

Braude, Ann. 2001. *Radical Spirits: Spiritualism and Women's Rights in Nineteenth-Century America.* Bloomington, IN: Indiana University Press.

Clark, Mary Ann. 2014. "Spiritual is Universal: Development of Black Spiritualist Churches." In *Esotericism in African American Religious Experience: "There Is a Mystery"*, edited by Stephen C. Finley, Margarita Simon Guillory, and Hugh R. Page, Jr., 86-101. Leiden, The Netherlands: Brill.

Cox, Robert S. 2003. *Body and Soul: A Sympathetic History of American Spiritualism.* Charlottesville, VA: University of Virginia Press.

Leonard, Todd Jay. 2005. *Talking to the Other Side: A History of Modern Spiritualism and Mediumship.* New York: iUniverse, Inc.

Weisberg, Barbara. 2004. *Talking to the Dead: Kate and Maggie Fox and the Rise of Spiritualism.* New York: HarperSanFrancisco.

ST. JOHN, SIR SPENSER

Sir Spenser Buckingham St. John was born in London, United Kingdom, in 1826, the third of seven sons. He was educated in private schools and was then introduced to Sir James Brooke, an adventurer and explorer and friend of his father, in 1847. In 1848 Sir Spenser St. John was appointed private secretary to Sir James Brooke; this was through the patronage of Lord Palmerston and his father's friendship with Brooke.

St. John accompanied Brooke on many of his travels, including to Malaysia, Brunei, and Siam in 1850. There was an official enquiry into Brooke's conduct, which St. John is reported to have found "high-handed," and this resulted in St. John acting temporarily as Commissioner in Singapore for Brooke (1851–1855). St. John was then appointed in 1856 as British Consul-General at Brunei, and it was while there that he explored the country. These explorations penetrated further into the interior than any other traveller, and St. John's journals were the basis for his very successful text, *Life in the Forests of the Far East*, which was published in 1862. In 1863 St. John became Charge d'Affaires in Haiti. He was to remain in the West Indies for twelve years.

It was during his time in Haiti that the country was facing civil disputes and a war with neighbouring Santo Domingo, now the Dominican Republic. St. John was to take violent measures against these disturbances of peace and disorder, actions that did not go unnoticed, and he was made Charge d'Affaires in the Dominican Republic in 1871 before being promoted to Resident Minister in Haiti in 1872. It was during his time in Haiti that he wrote a description of the history of the country, *Hayti; or the Black Republic*, which was published in 1884 with a French translation. A second edition was published in 1889. This was arguably one of the most inflammatory literary works about the country. It contained chapters on Vodou and cannibalism, none of which were first-hand accounts but rather relied on sensationalized second-hand accounts and hearsay.

When his time finished in Haiti, St. John became Minister Residentiary in Peru and Consul-General at Lima from 1874 to 1883 before then being sent to Mexico. During his service in Mexico, St. John was to negotiate the resumption of diplomatic relations with Great Britain. Disputes between Mexico and the British Government were to continue, but under the guidance of St. John as Envoy Extraordinary and Minister Plenipotentiary, these long-standing disputes were terminated.

> ### What Is Pure Vodou/Voodoo?
>
> Vodou and Voodoo have roots in many cultures, among them European and Native American peoples as well as Africans. The only version of the faith that could claim some level of purity would be West African Vodu. Even it has changed over time, however, notably with the disappearance of the human sacrifices once associated with the Dahomean state. Within the United States, some have contended that practitioners of African Diasporic religions should eliminate non-African elements from their faiths. Considering Voodoo and Vodou's history of adaptation to changing circumstances, the limited success of such drives is unsurprising.

Following three years as Minister to Sweden from 1893 to 1896, St. John retired from the diplomatic service. In 1899, aged 73, St. John married 31-year-old Mary Augusta Armstrong in Paris. They settled in Surrey, where Sir Spenser St. John died in 1910, aged 83.

He was awarded the Knights Commander of St. Michael and St. George in 1881 and was then promoted to Knight of the Grand Cross of St. Michael and St. George in 1894. These are awarded by the British Monarchy to those who render very important nonmilitary service in a foreign country.

Louise Fenton

Further Reading

Deren, Maya. 1970. *Divine Horsemen: Voodoo Gods of Haiti*. Preface by Joseph Campbell. New York: Chelsea House Publishers.

Ghachem, Malick W. 2012. *The Old Regime and the Haitian Revolution*. Cambridge, UK: Cambridge University Press.

Léger, Jacques Nicolas. 1907. *Haiti: Her History and Her Detractors*. New York: Neale Publishing.

St. John, Spenser. 1884. *Hayti or the Black Republic*. London: Smith, Elder, and Company.

SWORDS

As was the case across many cultures throughout history, swords can symbolize power and authority within Haitian Vodou. The laplas, who keeps order within the ounfò and during processions, typically carries a sword or machete. It is also common for swords to rest atop altars. Some lwa—most notably Ogou—are associated with swords or similar weapons.

African and European precedents exist for the use of swords as ritual objects. After all, societies like Dahomey valued war as a tool for wealth and territorial expansion. Figures of the Dahomean Gu, god of war and metalworking, frequently appear carrying swords. As Gu's name indicates, he and his Yoruba equivalent, Ogun, would serve as the model for the Ogou of Haiti. Though Gu's sword was transformed into a machete in the iconography of Ogou, the warlike personality symbolized by the weapon remains intact. Saint images depicting armed warriors, such as St. James the Elder or St. Michael the Archangel, likely reinforced existing African concepts of warrior deities.

See also: Altars; Dahomey; Laplas; Vodu in West Africa; Yoruba

Jeffrey E. Anderson

Further Reading

Blier, Suzanne Preston. 1995. *African Vodun: Art, Psychology, and Power*. Chicago and London: University of Chicago Press.

Desmangles, Leslie G. 1992. *Faces of the Gods: Vodou and Roman Catholicism in Haiti*. Chapel Hill, NC: University of North Carolina Press.

Métraux, Alfred. 1972. *Voodoo in Haiti*. Translated by Hugo Charteris and with an Introduction by Sidney W. Mintz. New York: Schocken.

SYNCRETISM

Specifically in the study of African diaspora religious traditions, *syncretism* has been used to denote the combining of ritual forms and religious practices from West and Central Africa with those of Europe and the Middle East, especially in the greater American context. In the case of Haitian Vodou, this has generally referred to the deployment of Catholic iconography to reference perceivably West African-based lwa, as well as the use of Catholic ritual implements and infrastructure in the service of the spirits. Recent scholarship has brought into question the use of the term in that its descriptive implications focus on the disparate nature of the components and cultures that contribute to Vodou and other New World religious traditions to which the term is most frequently applied. While some researchers have begun to favor other terms, such as *symbiosis*, to steer us away from the misleading implications of the word *syncretism*, even these terms seem to be deployed to center discussions on the separation between and distinctiveness of the African, European, and New World components that make up the collages that are African Diaspora religions. Notions about the incompatibility of these cultures are invariably tied to long-held prejudices based on racial difference, especially with reference to people of African descent, which in their most contemporary expressions substitute culture for race, only to then reify ideologies that insist on the impermeability of African cultural productions. In this sense, continued use of the word *syncretism* may do more to cloud than clarify our understanding of religious practices of the Americas. Specifically, it implies a conceptual divide between practices of Roman Catholic roots and West African origin not frequently expressed or borne out by practitioners of Vodou in their reading of their practices that almost seamlessly incorporate ideas and rituals of Catholicism into a broader New World spiritual system. Most frequently, and for a long time almost exclusively, the use of *syncretism* to denote religions with traditional African components also implies a different cultural process at work with people of those diaspora communities than with the combining of diverse religious and cultural influences that have given birth to the proselytizing religions like Buddhism, Christianity, and Islam. The term *syncretism* has long been used to reify a hierarchy that confines Vodou and religions of the African Diaspora to the social margins by implying that these traditions are somehow piecemeal in comparison to world religions that are in some way more whole. It also moves our focus away from the creative aspects of African Diaspora religions that represent conceptual innovations in favor of a view of them as conglomerations of preexisting traditions. In favor of acknowledging the syncretic nature of all religious traditions in their conglomeration of diverse cultural influences into a single ordering of the spiritual universe as well as focusing on the acts of creation that are also intrinsic to originating new religious systems, it may benefit scholars of the African Diaspora religions in general, and Vodou specifically, to steer clear of *syncretism* as a descriptor.

See also: Creolization

Kodi Roberts

Further Reading

Shaw, Rosalind, and Charles Stewart. 1994. *Syncretism/Anti-Syncretism: The Politics of Religious Synthesis*. London: Routledge.

TALLANT, ROBERT

Robert Tallant (1909–1957) was a journalist and writer of popular fiction. In the 1930s he was hired as an editor by Louisiana Writers' Project (LWP) director Lyle Saxon. With Saxon and Edward Dreyer, he coauthored the LWP's 1945 collection *Gumbo Ya-Ya: Folk Tales of Louisiana*.

Tallant never pretended to be a folklorist or a historian. He was more interested in telling a good story than in presenting facts. In 1946 he completed the sensationalistic and sexually titillating *Voodoo in New Orleans*, replete with lurid tales of nudity, drunkenness, devil worship, snake handling, blood drinking, the devouring of live chickens and dead cats, and interracial sexual orgies. *Voodoo in New Orleans* was not entirely Tallant's own creation. Louisiana Writers' Project employee Catherine Dillon had already produced a factual but rather unpolished 700-page "Voodoo" manuscript based on actual interviews with black New Orleanians and archival research conducted by the LWP. Tallant reworked Dillon's manuscript, combining bits and pieces of the interviews, changing the names of informants, and concocting fictitious conversations when needed to prove some point. To this he added dubious "facts" culled from newspaper articles and other published sources and stirred it all together into a smoothly written mélange. *Voodoo in New Orleans* includes tales of Marie Laveau, Betsy Toledano, Sanité Dédé, Doctor John, and Doctor Jim Alexander, as well as reports on 20th-century practitioners and hoodoo drugstores. In 1956, Tallant published a novel about Marie Laveau, titled *The Voodoo Queen*, which was based even more loosely on the Louisiana Writers' Project materials. *Voodoo in New Orleans* and *The Voodoo Queen* have been primary vehicles for the perpetuation of misinformation about Marie Laveau and Voudou, influencing virtually everything written in the latter half of the 20th century.

In addition to *Voodoo in New Orleans* and *The Voodoo Queen*, Tallant produced seven other novels, five other works of nonfiction, plus short stories and articles. Later in life he taught English at Newcomb College and was a reporter for the *New Orleans Item*.

See also: Alexander, Jim; Dédé, Sanité; Federal Writers' Project; Laveau, Marie; Literature, Vodou/Voodoo in; Montanée, Jean; New Orleans; Voodoo in the Mississippi Valley

Carolyn Morrow Long

> **The Difficulty of Studying Mississippi Valley Voodoo**
>
> Voodoo in the Mississippi Valley is a tricky topic to research. Most published books on the religion—notably Robert Tallant's *Voodoo in New Orleans* and Zora Neale Hurston's *Mules and Men*—are sensationalistic and often unreliable. More dependable accounts were gathered by the Federal Writer's Project during the Great Depression and are held by Louisiana's Northwestern State University, but the gap between their date of production and many of the events they describe is large, rendering them less-than-pristine accounts. Moreover, almost no one has investigated the religion outside New Orleans!

Further Reading

Long, Carolyn Morrow. 2006. *A New Orleans Voudou Priestess: The Legend and Reality of Marie Laveau*. Gainesville, FL: University Press of Florida.

Tallant, Robert. 1946 [1983]. *Voodoo in New Orleans*. New York: Macmillan; reprint, Gretna, LA: Pelican.

Tallant, Robert. 1956 [1983]. *The Voodoo Queen*. New York: Putnam; reprint, Gretna, LA: Pelican.

TERMINOLOGY

The study of Vodou, Voodoo, and related practices is beset by unusual terminological problems. Prior to the mid-20th century, the vast majority of writers, both scholarly and popular, depicted the faiths as sensational topics. Both implicit and explicit racism abound in these older works. Because of the negative baggage attached to words like *Voodoo*, many scholars have sought to distance themselves from popular understandings of the religions by avoiding words and spellings of words with potentially pejorative connotations. In addition, Kreyòl, the language of Haiti, has always been a predominantly spoken language without a set orthography, historically leaving its written expression largely a matter of personal taste.

Haitian Vodou, for instance, has had several spellings preferred by scholars over the years. Many English speakers first came to hear of Haitian Vodou as *Vaudoux*, the spelling preferred by Spenser St. John in his 1884 *Hayti or the Black Republic*. The anglicized *Voodoo* became the typical word for the Haitian religion during the early 20th century, garnering much of its stereotypical image from its depiction in works like William Seabrook's *Magic Island* (1929) and Richard A. Loederer's *Voodoo Fire in Haiti* (1935). To set their works apart from those of popular authors—and often to more accurately reflect the spoken version of the faith's name—scholars have generally avoided *Voodoo*. Their alternatives include *Vodoun*, *Vaudou*, and *Vodun*. Today, scholars most commonly use *Vodou*, a spelling based on the orthography of Yves Dejean, which has been the most common method of transcribing Haitian terms since the mid-1980s.

Mississippi Valley Voodoo has seen a similar diversity of spelling. During the 19th century and before, there was little uniformity. Among the terms designating

> ### *Voodoo* versus *Vodou*
>
> A hot topic amongst scholars is the proper use of terminology. Most modern speakers of English know the religion of the Haitian people by the term *voodoo*. The very fact that older authors failed to capitalize the word indicates their disdain for the religion. Modern scholars not only capitalize the term, but most have rejected its use outright, seeing it as too tied to derogatory depictions of the faith. Most prefer to use *Vodou*, the Kreyòl term for the religion. Scholars of Mississippi Valley Voodoo, however, continue to use *Voodoo* or have adopted the creole French spelling, *Voudou*.

the religion were *Vaudoo*, *Voudou*, *Voudoo*, and *Voodoo*. Of these, *Voudou* was the most popular during the 19th century, followed by *Voodoo*. After the publication of Robert Tallant's *Voodoo in New Orleans*, most authors followed his lead. Recently, some scholars, most notably Carolyn Morrow Long, have broken with the 20th-century trend, returning to the older spelling, *Voudou*.

Other words associated with Vodou have undergone significant spelling changes. For instance, the once-common word for Haitian divinities, *loa*, is being supplanted with *lwa*. Along the same lines, the name for a male Vodou priest variously appears as *hungan*, *oungan*, or some variation of the foregoing. Their female counterparts are called either *mambos* or *manbos*. Such spelling variations typically depend on individual authors' preferred orthography more than on concerns about stereotyping.

Most modern scholars draw a sharp distinction between Voodoo and the African American magical practice known as *hoodoo*. The term *hoodoo* usually appears as a synonym for *conjure* and *rootwork*. While this distinction is arguably accurate in a 21st-century setting, it would not have been during the early 20th century and before. At least as late as the 1930s, Mississippi Valley practitioners of Voodoo referred to themselves as *Voodoos* and to their practice as *hoodoo*. In this context, *hoodoo* properly designated the religion, while *Voodoo* referred to those who practiced the religion, presumably following an initiation ritual.

See also: Hurston, Zora Neale; Initiations; Long, Carolyn Morrow; Tallant, Robert

Jeffrey E. Anderson

Further Reading

Desmangles, Leslie G. 1992. *Faces of the Gods: Vodou and Roman Catholicism in Haiti*. Chapel Hill, NC: University of North Carolina Press.

Hurston, Zora Neale. 1995. *Folklore, Memoirs, and other Writings*, selected and annotated by Cheryl A. Wall. The Library of America. New York: Literary Classics of the United States, Inc.

Métraux, Alfred. 1972. *Voodoo in Haiti*. Translated by Hugo Charteris and with an Introduction by Sidney W. Mintz. New York: Schocken.

St. John, Spenser. 1884. *Hayti or the Black Republic*. London: Smith, Elder, and Company.

THOMPSON, ROBERT FARRIS

Robert Farris Thompson is Yale University's Colonel John Trumbull Professor of Art History. A native of Texas, Thompson has been an active scholar since the 1950s. Over the course of his career, he has published numerous books and articles on the art and music of the African Diaspora. In addition to scholarly work, he has also organized exhibitions of African art at such prestigious locations as the National Gallery.

Thompson's chief contributions to the study of Vodou have been two works, *Flash of the Spirit: African and Afro-American Art and Philosophy* (1983) and *Face of the Gods: Art and Altars of Africa and the African Americas* (1993). The former, in particular, has become something of a classic in the decades since its publication. *Face of the Gods*, while not as well known as its predecessor, is especially valuable for its large number of full-color illustrations depicting a host of African and New World altars.

Both *Flash of the Spirit* and *Face of the Gods* use art, mainly of a religious nature, to examine the connections between communities of the African Diaspora. Writing from what is known as an Atlantic history perspective, Thompson examines the artistic traditions shared among various African populations and their New World descendants. Though Thompson focuses most intently on the Yoruba, the Kongo, Fon and Ewe, Mande, and Ejagham also receive significant attention in his studies. In addition to exploring the links between individual African ethnicities and their New World populations, Thompson also devotes considerable space to the examination of cultural exchanges and similarities among distinct ethnicities.

See also: Altars; Drapo

Jeffrey E. Anderson

Further Reading

Blier, Suzanne Preston. 1995. *African Vodun: Art, Psychology, and Power*. Chicago and London: University of Chicago Press.

Thompson, Robert Farris. 1993. *Face of the Gods: Art and Altars of Africa and the African Americas*. New York: The Museum of African Art.

Thompson, Robert Farris. 1983. *Flash of the Spirit: African and Afro-American Art and Philosophy*. New York: Random House.

'TIT ALBERT

The *'Tit Albert* is a French *grimoire*, or book of magic, popular among French-speaking Voodoo devotees in Louisiana and Haiti. Properly titled *Les Secrets Merveilleux de la Magie Naturelle du Petit Albert*, which can be translated *Little Albert's Marvelous Secrets of Natural Magic*, it was written by Albertus Parvus Lucius and published by Beringos Fratres of Lyon, France, in 1668. The *'Tit Albert* was one of a number of occult texts mass-produced by French publishers in the late 1600s and early 1700s. These inexpensive grimoires were collectively known as the *Bibliothèque Bleue* because of their blue paper covers. Thousands of copies were distributed by traveling peddlers. By the 19th century the books had spread to the rest of Europe and Britain and to the French New World colonies.

Elements of European magic were thus incorporated into Afro-Catholic religions such as Vodou and Voodoo.

Voodoo practitioners interviewed by the Louisiana Writers' Project in the late 1930s spoke of the *'Tit Albert* as a dangerous book to own. But unlike other French grimoires that contain instructions for calling up demons and making diabolical pacts, the *'Tit Albert* is mostly innocuous. The text gives advice on medicine, palm-reading, gardening, fishing, exterminating vermin, and formulating cosmetics, although one section deals with magical talismans. Most interesting is *Le Main de Gloire* (Hand of Glory), made from the preserved hand of a hanged criminal. An illustration shows the Hand of Glory with a magical candle inserted between the fingers; burning such a candle was supposed to throw householders into a deep sleep and allow thieves to work undetected.

The *'Tit Albert* was only recently translated into English and was not historically sold through spiritual supply stores or mail-order catalogs. It has exerted little influence in the United States beyond the French-speaking population of Louisiana.

See also: Books; New Orleans

Carolyn Morrow Long

Further Reading

Beauvoir-Dominique, Rachel. 1995. "Underground Realms of Being: Vodoun Magic," in Donald Cosentino, ed., *Sacred Arts of Haitian Vodou*. Los Angeles: University of California Fowler Museum of Cultural History.

Davies, Owen. 2009. *Grimoires: A History of Magical Books*. Oxford, UK: Oxford University Press.

TOLEDANO, BETSY

Betsy Toledano was a Voodoo priestess active in New Orleans in 1850. The only documentation of her life in civil or church records is her appearance in the 1850 census for New Orleans. Here she was listed as a forty-year-old free black female of no stated occupation, born in Louisiana around 1810. There were no other members of her household.

Betsy Toledano came to public attention in New Orleans newspaper reports during the summer of 1850, when city authorities conducted a crackdown on Voodoo. Although many would not have considered Voodoo to be a legitimate religion, it was never officially banned in New Orleans. Instead, police raided ceremonies and arrested the participants for unlawful assembly of slaves, free persons of color, and white persons. The Third Municipality Guards, charged with policing the neighborhoods below the French Quarter and the less-populated areas near Lake Pontchartrain, were particularly vigorous in this pursuit.

The Third Municipality Guards' report shows that on the night of June 27, 1850, an interracial group of enslaved and free women were arrested "for being in contravention of the law . . . dancing Voudou all together" in a remote area near the St. Bernard Canal. Their leader was Betsy Toledano. About a hundred women were reported to have been present when the police arrived, but only two white women, fifteen free women of color including Toledano, and one slave were apprehended. After the accused spent a miserable night in jail, the magistrate fined the free women ten dollars each and released them; the enslaved woman was flogged. Newspaper reports of the raid commented on the "large quantity of nonsensical paraphernalia" confiscated by the guardsmen. These "banners, wands, [and] enchanted rods" resemble the flags and sword carried in procession at the beginning of a Haitian Vodou ceremony.

On July 2, 1850, there was another Voodoo raid. An entry in the Third Municipality Guards' Book states that a group of women was arrested "at Milneburg [on Lake Pontchartrain] in a house of ill fame for being in contravention of ordinances prohibiting slaves, free people of color, and white persons assembling together."

In addition to deriding Voodoo as "the grossest superstition" and "the indulgence of depravity and licentiousness," journalists attempted to associate the practice with prostitution. According to the *New Orleans True Delta*, Betsy Toledano "pretends to possess supernatural powers, and thoughtless women are induced to visit her and participate in the ceremonies she directs, by promises of having their wishes gratified. . . . [Toledano] is one of the most noted procuresses in the city, and like the whole tribe of fortune tellers and practitioners of witchcraft, assumes supernatural knowledge and powers to bring within her toils the unsophisticated of her sex and conduct them to speedy ruin."

The ramifications of the Voodoo arrests were felt throughout the summer of 1850. On July 14, the Voodoo women took the officers of the Third Municipality Guards to civil court. Led by Betsy Toledano, they claimed they had been illegally arrested while in the performance of religious ceremonies, falsely imprisoned, improperly fined, and subject to assaults, batteries, and general ill-treatment.

On July 30, Betsy Toledano and her followers were arrested at Toledano's home on Bienville Street in the French Quarter. The charge, as usual, was unlawful assembly of free persons and slaves. Newspaper reports described Toledano's "rude chapel [with] walls hung round with colored prints of the saints," and an altar on which were found "bowls . . . containing stones varying from the size of gravel to the largest pavers" and "goblets and vases filled with unknown liquids." Betsy Toledano again defended her right to practice the religion of "the mother-land" learned from her African grandmother.

The next day's newspaper carried a warning about the danger to society engendered by "unlawful assemblies," which read, in part, as follows:

> This kind of meeting appears to be rapidly on the increase. . . . Carried on in secret, they bring the slaves into contact with disorderly free negroes and mischievous whites, and the effect cannot be otherwise than to promote discontent, inflame passions, teach them vicious practices, and indispose them to the performance of their duty to their masters. . . . The public may have learned from the recent Voudou disclosures what takes place at such meetings—the mystic ceremonies, wild orgies, dancing, singing, etc. . . . The police should have their attention continually alive to the importance of breaking up such unlawful practices.

After that, nothing more was heard of Betsy Toledano in the newspapers. She never reappeared in the census or other official records. This courageous woman, who stood up to the police and the courts and suffered the attacks of reporters who ridiculed her religion and called her a procuress, seems to have disappeared after her few months of fame in the summer of 1850.

See also: New Orleans; Vodu in West Africa; Vodou in Haiti; Voodoo in the Mississippi Valley

Carolyn Morrow Long

Further Reading
Long, Carolyn Morrow. 2006. *A New Orleans Voudou Priestess: The Legend and Reality of Marie Laveau.* Gainesville, FL: University Press of Florida.

TOURISM

Sensationalistic accounts of both Haitian Vodou and Mississippi Valley Voodoo have led to the rise of a tourist industry associated with the religions. In New Orleans, the phenomenon that Carolyn Morrow Long has termed "tourist Voodoo" began to develop at least as early as the late 19th century, a time when the faith itself was fading in prominence. Initially, locals were the proto-tourists, and the chief attractions were the annual St. John's Eve ceremonies. By the 1870s, hundreds of spectators would assemble to watch the rituals. In some cases, the presiding queen or doctor would charge admission fees. The public proved so interested in the event that the city's newspapers typically covered it for those who chose not to attend in person.

Today, Voodoo is a pervasive feature of New Orleans's tourist culture. Some businesses, which sport such colorful names as Reverend Zombie's House of Voodoo, cater predominantly to the Voodoo-themed fantasies of the city's visitors. Even catch-all tourist shops are likely to carry a line of products inspired by the religion. Tours of sites associated with the faith are legion and vary in quality from those that seek to give vacationers a genuine glimpse into the historical religion's inner workings to those that promote cheap thrills at Voodoo's expense. There is also a small museum, the Historic New Orleans Voodoo Museum, which focuses primarily on Haitian Vodou. An annual music and arts festival, called Voodoo Fest, takes place in the city each year in late October or early November. A local tourist shop, Voodoo Authentica, holds the similarly named Voodoofest each year on Halloween.

Tourist Voodoo is not confined to New Orleans, however. Haiti, home of Vodou, has long been a tourist destination. The government actively encouraged the industry from 1957 to 1986. During these years, stage productions supposedly depicting Voodoo were common fare for sightseers. Political instability and natural disasters have greatly reduced the country's appeal to foreign visitors. The West African nation of Benin, which contributed many deities and words to both Haiti and the Mississippi Valley, holds an annual festival devoted to Vodu each January in Ouidah.

Over the years, a literature of Voodoo tourism has developed. Travelogues have been the most prominent example, especially in regard to Haitian Vodou. Many of the most famous accounts of the religion are essentially the tales of travelers seeking out the exotic thrills associated in the popular mind with Afro-Caribbean faiths since the days of Spenser St. John. The best known writers to produce such works were William B. Seabrook and Richard A. Loederer. Zora Neale Hurston's *Tell My Horse* (1938) can also be understood as a travelogue, albeit one informed by the author's formal study of anthropology and folklore.

North American Voodoo and hoodoo have their own tourist literature that stretches as far back as the 19th century, much of it concentrated around the New Orleans area. George Washington Cable, best known for his critiques of white Creole society, inadvertently served as the inspiration for many of these works. Following the later publication of several brief accounts of Voodoo that appeared in New Orleans newspapers, popular periodicals, and short story collections and paralleling the writings of Seabrook, Loederer, and Hurston, two major books on the Mississippi Valley faith appeared. The first, Zora Neale Hurston's *Mules and Men* (1935), is a rare example of positive treatment of the religion that nevertheless embraces the sensationalism common for such writings. More typical of the genre—though not technically a travelogue as it was written by a native New Orleanian—was Robert Tallant's *Voodoo in New Orleans* (1946). While not wholly unsympathetic to the faith and its practitioners, Tallant nevertheless depicted Voodoo as sexually titillating and potentially dangerous. Many imitators have followed the lead of Hurston and Tallant, providing vicarious thrills to armchair sightseers.

Such tourist literature exists elsewhere in the United States, where it is typically less skewed toward the sensationalistic than is the New Orleans variety. Rod Davis's *American Voudou: Journey into a Hidden World* (1999) is an account of African Diasporic magic and religion as practiced across the American South and includes substantial information on the growing presence of Haitian Vodou in the United States. A similar work is Christine Wicker's 2005 *Not in Kansas Anymore: A Curious Tale of How Magic Is Transforming America*. While the book does not focus exclusively on Voodoo and hoodoo, much of it describes the author's encounters with atypical practitioners. The works of both Davis and Wicker have value beyond that of typical tourist literature in that they seek to situate African Diasporic faiths within the modern American spiritual milieu.

In addition, New Orleans's tourist industry has itself produced several books to satisfy the consumer demands for information. Marie Laveau's House of Voodoo, for instance, published *A Brief History of Voodoo: Slavery and the Survival of the African Gods* in 1988. The New Orleans Historic Voodoo Museum has also produced booklets for sale in its gift shop. In keeping with many recent scholarly works, these books downplay popular conceptions of Voodoo as frightening or threatening, emphasizing a new mythology of spiritual power in their place.

The impact of tourism has been problematic. For one, it has largely been inspired by the lurid and often inaccurate portrayals of the religion by authors like Seabrook, Loederer, and Tallant. In consequence, tourists seek out depictions of the religion that portray it as sexually charged black magic. The profit motive

> ### The Voodoo Economy of New Orleans
>
> By at least the late 19th century, Voodoo had developed strong economic components in the Crescent City, and the transfer of these goods and services evolved continually. Marie Laveau, for instance, acquired some of the materials she needed to work magic from Native Americans who would visit her in the city. At some point before the 1930s, spiritual supply shops, often doubling as pharmacies, had taken their place. Eventually, shops began to supplant priests, selling a wide range of do-it-yourself products to believers.

induces many entrepreneurs to perpetuate these stereotypes in order to make money. On the other hand, the misconceptions fostered by tourism keep interest in the Haitian and Mississippi Valley faiths high among the general public. Scholars are often attracted for the same reasons or because they see the need to combat misrepresentations of the religions. In addition, the tourism-driven Voodoo market of New Orleans has drawn authentic modern-day practitioners of Vodou to the city, many of whom work to promote accurate understandings of their beliefs. At any rate, whether one views it as primarily positive or negative, tourism is unlikely to disappear.

See also: Cable, George Washington; Hurston, Zora Neale; Laveau, Marie; Literature, Vodou/Voodoo in; Loederer, Richard A.; New Orleans; St. John, Sir Spenser; Seabrook, William Buehler; Tallant, Robert

Jeffrey E. Anderson

Further Reading

Anderson, Jeffrey E. 2005. *Conjure in African American Society*. Baton Rouge, LA: Louisiana State University Press.
Long, Carolyn Morrow. 2001. *Spiritual Merchants: Religion, Magic, and Commerce*. Knoxville, TN: University of Tennessee Press.
Touchstone, Blake. 1972. "Voodoo in New Orleans." *Louisiana History* 13: 371–386.

TWINS

In Haitian Vodou society, twins are considered as one soul sharing two human bodies. The presiding lwa is known as Marasa the sacred twin. The culture of twins in Haiti is very similar to that of the culture of twins among the Yoruba of Nigeria, who produce more multiple births than any other ethnic group. The following poem, recorded and translated by Moyo Okediji and known as an *oríkì*, offers an illustration of the value of twins within a Yoruba household:

M ba bejire
M ba jo
M ba bejire
M ba yo

O wole alakisa
O salakisa dalaso

If I had twins
I would dance
If I had twins
I would rejoice
They entered a household full of poverty
Transformed it into one full of wealth

In Haitian society, twins are revered and accorded considerable favor by their parents, siblings, and society as a whole. They share the tradition of having a doll carved for a deceased twin as occurs among the Yoruba with the creation of *Ibeji* dolls. These dolls personify the deceased twin and are cared for in the same manner as the surviving twin.

Twins within Haitian society come under the protection of the Marasa lwa, believed to be the sacred twin children of the Supreme Being Bondye. Twins are considered as much malevolent as benevolent, and thus, careful and considerate treatment is accorded them. In the pantheon of Haitian Vodou, the Marassa are venerated only second to Papa Legba, the one who opens the way for communication and access to the spirit realm.

In one Yoruba tradition, twins figure prominently in the founding of two city-states of Yorubaland. A wife of the Yoruba kingdoms' legendary founder, Oduduwa, bore twins. Now in those ancient days twins were killed in Yorubaland, and Oduduwa, fearing for the safety of his children and his wife, sent them away from his capital, Ife. Life proved difficult for them, however, and they wandered for many years through a forest. In time, the twins matured. The elder, a male, founded the town of Epe, and the younger, a woman named Pupupupu, founded a town called Ondo.

See also: Bondye; Legba; Lwa

Phoenix Savage

Further Reading
Okediji, Moyo. 1997. "Art of the Yoruba." *Art Institute of Chicago Museum Studies* 23:2, 164–181, 198.

TWO HEAD

The term *two head* typically refers to a practitioner of magic within an African American tradition, especially but not exclusively those credited with the power of second sight. Historically, it was a common synonym for *conjurer, hoodoo doctor*, and the like. Like many other words for conjurers, *two head* is not gender specific. Though there were many names for practitioners of conjure, *two head* has captured the imagination of scholars and popular writers largely because of its unusualness and indeterminate origin.

A few writers have attempted to explain the origins of the designation. One of the first to do so was M. S. Lea, a white, early 20th-century author of popular literature based in Washington, DC. After learning of hoodoo from a mixed-race female domestic worker, Lea inquired further and was told that practitioners were sometimes known as "two-headed doctors." Lea's informer went on to explain the reason for the name, stating, "That's because they knows two ki's o' medicine. They can see both ways." Lea failed to explain what the two types of medicine and sight were, but fortunately, Zora Neale Hurston elaborated on the subject in her 1931 article, "Hoodoo in America." According to her, two heads were familiar with both herbal remedies and magical powers. Within this definition, the two heads of a practitioner represented two bodies of knowledge.

Recent scholars have also weighed in on the matter. Carolyn Morrow Long, author of *Spiritual Merchants: Religion, Magic, and Commerce* (2001), suggests that the name parallels the Haitian Vodou concept of "working with both hands." In the Haitian context, the saying typically refers to a mambo or oungan who also practices sorcery as a bòkò. This explanation is certainly in keeping with Lea's account, which gave no explanation beyond referencing two types of medicine and sight. Moreover, Lea followed this definition by describing instances of harmful conjure and its cure, suggesting that the two types of medicine might well have been good and evil rather than herbal and magical.

A 2006 article for *The Greenwood Encyclopedia of African American Folklore* suggests that the title of *two head* might reference its possessors' ties to the second sight, which often included the purported ability to foretell the future and see ghosts. Folklore held that babies born with a membrane covering their heads possessed second sight. At least some hoodoo practitioners believed that the presence of the membrane, generally termed a *caul*, indicated that the child would have two spirits. These spirits were the power behind the conjurers' abilities. Either the multiple spirits or the caul itself could explain the origin of *two head*, an explanation that also fits the vague statements of M. S. Lea.

See also: Bòkò; Conjure; Hoodoo; Mambo; Mojo; Oungan; Voodoo

Jeffrey E. Anderson

Further Reading

Hurston, Zora Neale. 1931. "Hoodoo in America." *Journal of American Folklore* 44: 317–417.
Hyatt, Harry Middleton. 1970–1978. *Hoodoo-Conjuration-Witchcraft-Rootwork*. 5 vols. Memoirs of the Alma Egan Hyatt Foundation. Hannibal, MO: Western.
Lea, M. S. 1927. "Two-head Doctors." *The American Mercury* 12: 236–240.
Long, Carolyn Morrow. 2001. *Spiritual Merchants: Religion, Magic, and Commerce*. Knoxville, TN: University of Tennessee Press.
Prahlad, Anand ed. 2006. *The Greenwood Encyclopedia of African American Folklore*. 3 vols. Westport, CT: Greenwood Press.

V

VÈVÈ

The vèvè are drawings that represent the spirits, or lwa, in Vodou and are most frequently used for ceremonial purposes. The vèvè are transient images, symbols drawn on the ground in preparation for the Vodou ceremony, and are temporary in nature. The priest (oungan) or priestess (mambo) generally draws the vèvè in powder in preparation for the ceremony. They can be drawn in ground corn, coffee, wheat flour, talc, sand, or even gun powder, depending on which spirits are to be invoked. They consist of intricate patterns that are specific to individual lwa and have elements that are sacred to those who serve the spirits. The vèvè can be abstract or figurative, depending again on which spirit or lwa is to be invoked, and they feature many small symbols, such as stars. These small symbols may be there to indicate a rest period (such as the stars) or the end of part of the drawing, or they may be a signature of the particular oungan or mambo who created the vèvè. Some of the lwa have numerous vèvè designs attributed to them, while some of the spirits have none at all.

The role of the vèvè is not to embellish the place of the ceremony, whether that is in an ounfò or other location. They are an intrinsic part of the process to evoke the spirits and so have a religious function. The vèvè have to be drawn on the floor as they act as a doorway to the spirits and are an integral part of the ceremony. Once the spirit has been invoked, the vèvè has served its purpose and tends to be destroyed during the remainder of the ceremony by those present. Vèvè can be found in paintings, in ironwork, or on walls within villages, but these vèvè are purely decorative and do not have any ceremonial purpose. To be used for ceremonies they have to meet certain religious criteria such as ensuring the correct powder has been used and that the environment is conducive to what is about to take place.

It is understood that the vèvè have iconography that derives from Catholicism, Africa, and, according to some, pre-Columbian Native American influences. Gerard Alphonse Férère and Patricia Mohammed both agree that these are the influences. There is also a theory that European secular art may have had an influence. Alfred Métraux, for instance, attributes some of the intricacies of the vèvè to the ironwork and embroidery of the 18th century. The temporary nature of the ceremonial vèvè means that people do not see many of these images as they are so fragile and transient in nature. It is this fragility that often leads to their disappearance.

See also: Art, Vodou/Voodoo in

Louise Fenton

> ### Did Voodoo in the Mississippi Valley Die Out?
>
> Visitors to New Orleans can see stereotypical images of Voodoo plastered across storefronts all along Bourbon and Canal streets. While one might take them as evidence of Voodoo's survival, the images are misleading. The historical Voodoo of the area gradually declined after the late 1800s, probably dying out as a full-fledged religion during the 1940s. Though many aspects of the faith survive in ongoing hoodoo practices and the services of Spiritual Churches, most New Orleanians who speak of themselves as Voodoo priests and priestesses are adherents of Haitian Vodou rather than historical Mississippi Valley Voodoo.

Further Reading

Férère, Nancy Turnie. 2005. *Vèvè: L'Art Rituel du Vodou Haitien/Ritual Art of Haitian Vodou/Arte Ritual del Vodu Haitiano*. With an Introduction by Gerard Alphonse Férère. Boca Raton, FL: ReMe Art Publishing.

Métraux, Alfred. 1972. *Voodoo in Haiti*. Translated by Hugo Charteris and with an Introduction by Sidney W. Mintz. New York: Schocken.

Mohammed, Patricia. 2005. "The Sign of the Loa." *Small Axe* 18 (September). Accessed November 6, 2014: http://smallaxe.net/18

THE VODOU CHURCH IN HAITI

Since 1987, Haiti's constitution has accepted freedom of religion within the country, and Vodou has been recognized as the national religion of Haiti. This has allowed its practitioners, vodouisants, to conduct their services in a more open manner in recent years, and has added to the development of its church. This acceptance of the religion led to the establishment of the Vodou Church in Haiti in 1998, founded by Wesner Morency, a Vodou priest influential in changing Haiti's policy toward the religion. Despite this seeming mainstream attitude about the religion, it is still often practiced with great secrecy as many still hope to abolish Vodou within Haiti.

The basic principles of the Vodou ceremony focus on the lwa or loa. The lwa represent spirits comprised of both African and creole gods. The group practice of Vodou in Haiti takes place in a temple, ounfò, overseen by a priest, known as a *oungan*, or priestess, known as a *mambo*. It is within the temple that the connection between Vodouisants and the lwa is created. This is accomplished through many ceremonial practices, including dance, drumming, ritual foods, song, sacrifice of animals, and possession.

Possession is particularly important to the ceremonies within the Vodou Church in Haiti as it is through this practice that Vodouisants draw the energy and power of the lwa. The services allow a Vodouisant to connect to the lwa as spirits. Conversely, the lwa utilize the spiritual form of the people to draw stronger connections and are more able to answer questions. This connection between Vodouisants and lwa serves as the foundation of Vodou practice. This makes the

Vodou Church in Haiti of utmost importance to the religion, as it is where many of these connections are developed.

See also: National Confederation of Haitian Vodou; Vodou in Haiti

Matthew R. Blaylock

Further Reading
Edmonds, Ennis B., and Michelle A. Gonzalez. 2010. *Caribbean Religious History: An Introduction.* New York: New York University Press.
Gaelembo, Phyllis. 2005. *Vodou: Visions and Voices of Haiti.* Berkeley, CA: Ten Speed Press.
Laguerre, Michel S. 1989. *Voodoo and Politics in Haiti.* New York: St. Martin's Press.
Olmos, Margarite Fernandez, and Lizabeth Paravisini-Gerbert. 2011. *Creole Religions of the Caribbean: An Introduction from Vodou and Santeria to Obeah and Espiritismo.* New York: New York University Press.
Olmos, Margarite Fernandez, and Lizabeth Paravisini-Gerbert, eds. 1997. *Sacred Possessions: Vodou, Santeria, Obeah, and the Caribbean.* New Brunswick, NJ: Rutgers University Press.

VODOU IN HAITI

Haitian Vodou is a creole religion that was the result of the multicultural, linguistically mixed Africans who made up the slave populations during the 18th and 19th centuries on the island of Hispaniola. Brought from West and Central Africa by the Portuguese, the Africans were a mix of Dahomeans and Kongolese with a variety of other ethnicities, including the Ewe, Ibo, Senegal, Yoruba, and Djouba. Each group lent critical elements to the mix that would bloom into the faith of Haitian Vodou.

The first group is the Fon of Dahomey, from what is today Benin. Their influence on Haitian Vodou was due to their critical mass importation to the French colony of Saint-Domingue, along with their theological sophistication found throughout that region among the Yoruba, Dogon, Dagara, and other peoples. The names of spirits, dances, and liturgical practices, such as initiatory rites, can be traced back to the Dahomean people. The Fon also contributed words, such as *ounfò* (house of spirits), *ounsi* (spirit wife), and *oungan* (spirit priest).

The second most influential group was the Kongolese, who brought their magical ideologies, religious philosophy, and cultural identity into the crucible in which Vodou was blended. The Kongo lakous of Soukri, Badjo, and Souvenance still maintain the purest practices of African ritual. The Kongolese were also widely distributed in the south of Haiti, from Les Cayes through to Jacmel. The language, ritual practices, and organizational structure of ounfòs there reflect this heritage clearly

Finally, other groups added in various articles of faith and practices that are still part of the areas where their ancestors settled. The Igbo, for instance, lent the idea of jars such as canaris and govis for housing spirits, and the Ewe contributed ancestral practices such as food offerings to propitiate the dead. This inclusiveness of styles of service, ancestral traditions, and religious idioms is how the Africans were able to survive during the plantation era.

Haitian Vodou's voice became a bricolage of ideas and forms when these individual African ethnic formations met. The Africans spoke a large variety of languages and dialects. They adopted French with African syntax as their language of choice. Unlike Yoruba, which became the liturgical language in both Cuban Santería and Brazilian Candomblé, Haitian Kreyòl was the lingua franca spoken by all at the time of the Independence in 1804. This is because fully two-thirds of the slaves at that time had been born in Africa and retained knowledge of both their language and their spiritual practices. As Rachel Beauvoir-Dominique put it in an essay that appeared in Donald Cosention's *Sacred Arts of Haitian Vodou* (1995):

> Vodou emerged [from slavery and the revolution] with a fundamental vision in which religion and magic, though autonomous, nevertheless constitutes a single body . . . each temple, even the most "religious" in outlook is under the patronage of one or several . . . divinities destined to work, render service and even amass small fortunes for their possessors.

The Vodou that developed following Independence was in part the result of neglect by the Catholic Church to help its poorest members and of the Africans needing to establish a living on the island. These two streams merged in the resurgence of the lakou, an African system of family compounds with shared land. The lakou system also helped to keep the state from reinstating plantation culture and furthered the implementation of African ancestral practices. People, both blood related and nonrelated, created family compounds that still exist to this day. Within these compounds, the African practices of farming, family, and religion became the way of life for most Haitians, right up to present.

Haiti is a rural society, where the cult of ancestors serves to guard peasants' traditional values. Within these rural lakous, Haitian peasants serve the spirits daily and gather with their extended families for special occasions, such as birthdays, both biological and spiritual. People will often walk miles or even days to attend a celebration or partake of ceremonies held monthly and sometimes yearly. Celebrations are not the only reason for attending ceremonies at family compounds. Rural lakous are also where one finds a medsin fey, or leaf doctor, individuals who are known as much for their spiritual konesans (knowledge) as they are for their healing talents. With a medical system set more in the cities, rural people place their trust in the local healer, who treats both the physical illness and its spiritual causes. Medsin feys grow their healing plants within their compounds or know where the plants grow locally. Often inheriting sets of spirits and their medical knowledge from a parent or relative, a local medsin fey is commonly a priest of Vodou as well.

Vodou is the religion for most of the population in Haiti today. Although membership is not counted, there is a common saying that Haiti is 70 percent Christian and 100 percent Vodou, an allusion to the hidden nature of the latter. This is especially true of the wealthy and the upwardly mobile, who reject overt association with their African heritage. Vodou practitioners generally perceive themselves as good Christians and see no conflict with practicing Catholicism as well as serving the spirits. In fact, many ounfò mark the feast days of the lwa by following the Catholic calendar of observances.

With much of Haiti still being a rural society, Vodou is heavily linked to veneration of the ancestors, family life, and the land. In the absence of formal places of worship, Vodou can be practiced everywhere. Crossroads, cemeteries, trees, caves, waterfalls, and other natural formations become the temples of Vodou. Each location holds importance within the liturgy, whether it is a simple *reposoir* (sacred trees that house Vodou spirits) growing on the side of a family compound or a majestic waterfall pouring down the side of a mountain. This acknowledgement of the spiritual world as manifest in the physical is a possible reason why Vodou has been misinterpreted. The people looking at Vodou from the outside mistook the act of worship at the foot of a sacred mapou (silk cotton tree) as worshipping the tree, rather than acknowledgement of the spirit believed to be symbolized by the tree itself.

Monotheistic religions such as Christianity are prescriptive and use a sacred text such as the bible from which followers derive the doctrines and basic laws of the faith. Haitian Vodou offers few absolutes and does not have a prescriptive code of ethics. Followers define moral principles for themselves and are guided by life lessons, the wisdom of the ancestors, and communication with the spirits.

Vodou is central to Haitian culture and is based on a conception of reality that includes life's goals, forces that determine the fate of living things, proper social organization, balanced interpersonal relations, and practices that promote the welfare of the community. Vodou takes into account the needs of the people. Vodou sosyetes (the membership of a Vodou ounfò) will take up collections to help members, providing money for rent, clothes for children, or fees for school. A Vodou sosyete's hierarchy helps maintain order and allows each person to be respected for the level at which they can participate. The mambo or oungan is the presiding judge, jury, and, when needed, enforcer. She or he mediates arguments, provides guidance in marital discourse, comforts people after natural disasters, encourages young people in their learning, offers hope through debilitating illness, and manages the expectations of the sosyete. Leaders' public side is on display when hosting a fet for their sosyetes. Food, drink, good singers, and powerful drummers are supplied to ensure that the fet is a success for the sosyete as well as for her community at large. Mambos' and oungans' prestige as ritual leaders and their reputation as *fran Ginen manbo* (a moral and upstanding member of the community) are intimately tied to their work as priests and healers.

Urban Vodou differs from its country cousin only in being called "temple" Vodou. The concepts of communal life still revolve around the ounfò, mambo, and oungan, but the devotees must recreate the family left behind by migration to urban centers and continue their quest for religious and moral values. Urban temples can be located in houses, basements, or near churches. It is not unusual for participants of an urban Vodou temple to leave the ceremony in the morning and go directly to attend mass at church afterwards. Where urban Vodou does differ is in the liturgical structure found in temple Vodou.

The rural Vodou lakous of Souvenance, Soukri, and Badjo in the Gonaïves area of Haiti stay true to their African ideas and practices. Their liturgy is sung, and the style of worship is known as *deka*, a Kongo word that means "from the stars." Deka

> ### *Sosyete versus Ounfò*
>
> Those examining Haitian Vodou for the first time are likely to encounter several unfamiliar terms. Two that can easily confuse those unfamiliar with Kreyòl are *sosyete* and *ounfò*. English speakers sometimes use the terms interchangeably. To be precise, however, the latter refers to the temple in which a Vodou congregation meets, while the former describes the congregation itself.

services are annual celebrations tied to the astrological calendar and celebrated much as they are in Africa. Temple Vodou follows the Catholic calendar of observances for its high holy days and has elements of Freemasonry, Catholicism, and Dahomean and Kongo theology in its liturgical structure. Scholar Claudine Michel once wrote:

> While ritual variations are true throughout Haiti due to the dominating nation of Africans brought into that area of the country via slavery, each temple is its own universe. Myths and ceremonies may differ from one ounfò to another as well as from one family to another, depending on the region, types of spirits served and invoked, styles of worship, and issues specific to a given community, they also have much in common.

Today, Vodou in Haiti has developed into multiple streams that all take their inspiration from the same West African sources. There is rural Vodou which is family oriented, blood related, and found in the countryside from the Plateau Central to Cap-Haïtien. Within this style one finds leaders called *sèvitè* (servitors), who are chosen from the family to serve one spirit or one nanchon of spirits at the family compound. Then there is urban or temple Vodou, which is centered on Port-au-Prince and extends south from Jeremie to Jacmel. Within this style is the ason lineage, where nonfamily members are initiated into the sosyete and serve in the temple. These temples often serve a range of spirits or nanchons and are led by mambo and oungan asogwe, the highest rank in initiatory Vodou lineages. In the western district can be found Deka Vodou at the trio of lakous outside of Gonaïves. Harking back to their African roots, this style of service is also known as the *tcha-tcha* or *makout* lineage. Makout refers to the straw bag carried by these ritual experts that contains their sacred items, one of which is the tcha-tcha, a round gourd rattle often painted in bright colors and used in service much like an ason.

Furthermore, there are many secret societies that may or may not be part of Vodou. With names such as *Bizango*, *Chanpwel*, and *Sect Wouje*, they function outside the norms of temple or rural Vodou. They descend from the maroon and revolutionary groups of 18th-century Haiti and tend to practice mercenary, morally ambiguous forms of magic and religion. Many Vodouisants today regard them as outsiders to the faith. Whether they are or not, most regard them as *pa Gine*, meaning "not Ginen." As Oungan Herard Simon once remarked, "One cannot be Bizango and Ginen. They are mutually exclusive." There are also many Masonic and pseudo-Masonic organizations in Haiti that meet and operate within Vodou-defined paradigms but that are not religious in practice or ideals.

See also: Ason; Bight of Benin; Creolization; Dahomey; Ewe; Kongo; Kreyòl; Lakou; Mambo; Ounfò; Oungan; Secret Societies; West Central Africa; Yoruba

Patricia Scheu (Mambo Vye Zo Komande LaMenfo)

Further Reading

Bellegarde-Smith, Patrick, and Claudine Michel, eds. 2006. *Haitian Vodou: Spirit, Myth, and Reality*. Bloomington, IN: Indiana University Press.

Bentley, W. Holman. 1887. *Dictionary and Grammar of the Kongo Language*. London: Baptist Missionary Society.

Cosentino, Donald L., ed. 1995. *Sacred Arts of Haitian Vodou*. Los Angeles: University of California Fowler Museum of Cultural History.

Davis, Wade. 1986. *The Serpent and the Rainbow: A Harvard Scientist's Astonishing Journey into the Secret Societies of Haitian Voodoo, Zombis, and Magic*. New York: Simon and Schuster.

Geggus, David. 2001. "The French Slave Trade: An Overview." *The William and Mary Quarterly*. Third Series, 58, New Perspectives on the Transatlantic Slave Trade (January): 119–138.

Gilles, Jerry M. and Yvrose S. 2009. *Remembrance: Roots, Rituals, and Reverence in Vodou*. Davie, FL: Bookmanlit.

McGee, Adam M. "Whose Vodou." *Dreams of Ginen*. May 23, 2012. Accessed on March 31, 2014: http://dreamsofginen.wordpress.com/2012/05/23/whose-vodou/.

VODU IN WEST AFRICA

Vodu, also known as Vodun, is a traditional religion of a large portion of West Africa, with its center being the Bight of Benin region and including the modern nations of Benin and Togo as well as eastern Ghana. Anthropologist Judy Rosenthal defines the boundaries of Vodu as stretching from Cameroon in the east to Côte d'Ivoire in the west while also noting that one can envision New World Vodou and Voodoo as varieties of the religion. In addition to serving as a name for the religion, *vodu* can be used interchangeably with *edro* and *tro* to designate an individual spirit of the Vodu pantheon and to refer to objects representing the gods.

The vodu of the Bight of Benin are numerous. At the head of the gods is Mawu, generally thought of as the creator but understood in multiple ways among different Ewe, Fon, and related ethnicities. Some consider the deity to be male, while others say Mawu is female. Among the Fon and some Ewe, Mawu is part of a divine couple or twins known as Mawu-Lisa, with Mawu being female and Lisa male. In this interpretation, the pair represents balance. The exact position of the deity (or deities) is also subject to divergent interpretations. While many consider Mawu to be simply the most powerful among the many spirits of Vodu, others think of him or her as filling a unique role as a supreme being over all the deities. Mawu's exalted status led early Christian missionaries to adopt his name for the Christian

God, a practice that remains common today. To further complicate matters, *mawu* has also become a synonym for *vodu* and is often used as a generic term for any deity. Interestingly, direct worship of Mawu has historically been minimal, a circumstance that 19th-century author A. B. Ellis attributed to the fact that the god had little interaction with people, who therefore saw no harm in focusing their devotion on deities who were more likely to affect them for good or ill.

Among the many spirits prone to intervene in the lives of the faithful are Gu, Heviesso, and Legba. Gu, also known as Egu, is a deity of iron. By extension, he is also the patron spirit of those who work with iron as warriors, hunters, metalworkers, mechanics, and the like. In addition to aiding those who wield iron, he also protects his devotees from being harmed by it. Heviesso, sometimes spelled Hebiosso, Khebioso, or a variant thereof, is the god of lightning and thunder. He is believed to punish evil doers, and according to tradition, those killed by lightning have been struck down by the god. Legba is a trickster who enjoys stirring up discord and is also associated with sexuality and fertility.

In addition to the deities who are well known to most Fon and Ewe are a host of others connected to specific locales and Vodu societies. Among them is Avrikiti, a marine deity and patron of fishermen, who gained prominence along the seacoast. Another, Nesu, once served as the guardian of Dahomey's royal family. An example of those connected to specific societies are the gorovodus associated with the Ewe Gorovodu society, which is most popular in the coastal areas of Ghana, Togo, and Benin. Believers understand the gorovodus to be the spirits of foreigners and of slaves. Each deity, regardless of its geographic appeal, has its preferred animal sacrifices, sacred objects and images, and ceremonies in its honor.

As one might guess from the divinization of deceased slaves, humans play an important role in the spiritual cosmos. To begin with, they serve as vessels for the divine through spirit possession, a phenomenon shared with many African creole religions in the Americas. Moreover, each person is understood to possess two of what those of European descent might term souls or spirits, which A. B. Ellis conveniently termed the indwelling spirit and the soul. According to him, each living person possesses one of the former, which can leave and return to his body at will. At death, the spirit typically enters a newborn child, remaining with him or her throughout life. Some, however, enter animals or even remain disembodied. Others become protectors of their family lines, a role like that filled by Nesu in regard to the former royal family of Dahomey. The soul, on the other hand, is tied to the body and rarely leaves it before death. If it does depart from its abode, the body will take on the appearance of a corpse, remaining so unless the soul returns. Historically, family members would wait to bury bodies until they showed signs of decay, hoping that perhaps the soul had only temporarily absented itself. If permanently separated from the body, the soul proceeds to an afterlife, sometimes known as Kutome, where it exists in a land of the dead.

Among the Ewe and Fon, what westerners would call magic is rather common. It centers around obtaining personal desires, ranging from protection from injury to harming or killing enemies. Charms take the form of amulets dedicated to specific deities, animal body parts, and a variety of other natural items. Magical powders and liquids likewise are common.

In none of its homelands is Vodu practiced in a vacuum. Each country is host to multiple faiths, with Christianity claiming the largest number of adherents. The Christian prayer guide and reference work, *Operation World*, suggests that Ghana has the highest proportion, with more than 63 percent identifying themselves as Christians in 2010. In both Benin and Togo, Christianity holds a plurality of the population, with slightly under 40 percent and just over 45 percent, respectively. Islam is the second largest religion in Ghana. In each nation, Vodu and other traditional faiths remain powerful, claiming the allegiance of more than 30 percent of the population in Benin and Togo. Simple statistics, however, do not tell the full story. As was long true in the Mississippi Valley and remains the norm in Haiti, many follow both Vodu and Christianity. The same can be said for Islam and Vodu. According to one estimate for Benin, as much as 80 percent of the population can be described as practicing Vodu on its own or in combination with Christianity or Islam. Such facts blur the boundaries between the religions and call into question statistics purporting to be precise accountings of the numbers of adherents of each faith.

As is evident in its current interactions with Christianity and Islam, Vodu is subject to change, and the version now practiced in West Africa significantly differs from the form prominent during the heyday of the Atlantic slave trade. For instance, gone are the days when Fon Vodu centered around Dahomean royalty, which hosted annual customs that sometimes included the sacrifice of thousands of war prisoners. Some prominent Ewe Vodu orders, such as the Gorovodu and Mama Tchamba societies, are also considered by the faithful to have come from outsiders. While believers often describe foreign aspects of the societies as arriving from people groups to the north, Judy Rosenthal notes that they also have cultural ties to the Asante to the west. Even some of the most recognizable aspects of Vodu, such as the Fa or Afa form of divination, did not originate among the Ewe and Fon. Fa is patterned on the Yoruba Ifá and reportedly gained prominence among the Fon in the 1720s and 1730s during the reign of King Agaja. Before this time, diviners received communications from the spirit world by turning a pot upside down and either rubbing it with cowries or speaking specific ritual words to it, after which a voice could be heard speaking from under the upturned vessel. Agaja, however, considered such diviners threats to his power and worked to suppress them both by promoting Fa and by selling as slaves those who practiced competing forms of divination. Agaja took similar actions against a powerful priesthood that served Sakpata—generally thought of as the deity of smallpox during that era but also the name for a larger group of earth divinities—transforming them from influential spiritual leaders to merchandise for European slave ships.

The activities of King Agaja and his successors, which helped define Vodu in Dahomey and elsewhere in West Africa, had a similar effect on beliefs and practices elsewhere. The upturned pot form of divination, having been outlawed in Dahomey, began to appear in Brazil, apparently because of Agaja's enslavement and sale of such diviners. Sakpata made his was to Cuba, Haiti, and elsewhere for the same reason. The Gede family of spirits from Haitian Vodou may have had a similar origin. According to oral tradition, they originated with Dahomey's Guede-vi clan, the legendary founder of which was known as Ghédé. According to the traditions, members of the clan angered King Andanzan, who ruled the country during the late 18th century, by taking part in a plot against him. After the king uncovered their conspiracy, they quickly found themselves sold overseas, where they either became the Gede spirits after death or contributed their own family spirits to the developing Vodou pantheon.

The wars of the kings of Dahomey had a similar impact on Vodou and Voodoo. The best example of their influence was the introduction of Danbala to Haiti and Blanc Dani to the New Orleans area. The key event in this case was Agaja's 1727 conquest of the coastal city of Whydah, which supplied numerous captives to Atlantic slave traders. With them they carried an adherence to a serpent deity of great local power known variously as Da, Dan, Dangbe, and other, similar names. He would later become the Haitian and New Orleans deity. An earlier conquest of Allada provided Haiti with the prototype for the Rada nanchon of lwa.

See also: Bight of Benin; Creolization; Dahomey; Ewe; Ifá; Lwa; Nanchons; Rada; Vodou in Haiti; Voodoo in the Mississippi Valley; Yoruba

Jeffrey E. Anderson

Further Reading

Blier, Suzanne Preston. 1995. *African Vodun: Art, Psychology, and Power.* Chicago and London: University of Chicago Press.
Desmangles, Leslie G. 1992. *Faces of the Gods: Vodou and Roman Catholicism in Haiti.* Chapel Hill, NC: University of North Carolina Press.
Ellis, A. B. 1890. *The Ewe-Speaking Peoples of the Slave Coast of West Africa: Their Religion, Manners, Customs, Laws, Languages, &c.* London: Chapman and Hall.
Mandryk, Jason. 2010. *Operation World: The Definitive Prayer Guide to Every Nation.* 7th ed. Colorado Springs: Biblica Publishing.
Opoku, Kofi Asare. 1978. *West African Traditional Religion.* Accra, London, et al: FEP International Private Limited.
Parrinder, Geoffrey. 1961. *West African Religion: A Study of the Beliefs and Practices of Akan, Ewe, Yoruba, Ibo, and Kindred Peoples.* 2nd ed. With a Foreword by Edwin Smith. London: Epworth Press.
Rosenthal, Judy. 1998. *Possession, Ecstasy, and Law in Ewe Voodoo.* Charlottesville and London: University Press of Virginia.
Sweet, James H. 2011. *Domingoes Álvares, African Healing, and the Intellectual History of the Atlantic World.* Chapel Hill, NC: University of North Carolina Press.
Thompson, Robert Farris. 1983. *Flash of the Spirit: African and Afro-American Art and Philosophy.* New York: Random House.

VOODOO IN THE MISSISSIPPI VALLEY

Like many other areas of the New World settled by Europeans and enslaved Africans, the Mississippi River Valley developed its own creole religion, known in this case as Voodoo or Voudou, which survived as a distinct tradition until at least the 1940s. Although the majority of accounts describing the religion came from the New Orleans area, the faith also existed elsewhere along the Mississippi River, most notably in Missouri.

Though often conflated with Haitian Vodou, the two religions have never been identical. Evidence indicates that Voodoo initially developed in the Mississippi Valley and was not simply an import from Haiti. Aspects of Voodoo were present in the area near New Orleans since the early 18th century, the same time that Vodou was developing independently in what was then the French colony of Saint-Domingue. Nevertheless, the two religions interacted over the years and have much in common beyond the obviously related names. Terminology was often similar, with words like *gris-gris* being used in both the Mississippi Valley and Haiti. Likewise, some deities were shared between the faiths, though they did not always go by identical names. Initiations and other ceremonies likewise resembled each other. Moreover, the two possessed similar magical traditions. Resemblances in terminology and practice can be explained because of the similar African ethnicities brought into the two regions, notably captives from Senegambia, the Bight of Benin, and West Central Africa. Both populations then lived and developed culturally as slaves of French Catholics. Preexisting similarities doubtless strengthened, however, with large-scale immigration from Haiti to the region of New Orleans during the early 19th century following the success of the Haitian Revolution.

Members of the general public frequently but inaccurately treat Voodoo as little more than a collection of spells and charms, equating it with practices known as *conjure*, *rootwork*, or *hoodoo* elsewhere in the United States. To be sure, Voodoo possessed many magical aspects, but has never been the same thing as conjure or rootwork, which originated in the former English colonies along the Atlantic coast. The relationship between Voodoo and hoodoo, on the other hand, is a bit more problematic. Scholars frequently differentiate hoodoo from Voodoo by declaring the former to be magic and the latter to be a religion. Historically, however, practitioners of what modern historians consider to be Voodoo referred to the faith as *hoodoo*, using the term *Voodoo* to designate its practitioners.

Regardless of the terminological difficulties surrounding the faith, it was certainly a religion. As with most religions, Voodoo had its own clergy, most of whom were women. By the late 19th century, priestesses had come to be known as *queens*. Some writers indicate that men were known as *kings*, though instances of particular people operating under this title were exceedingly rare. Only one case from Missouri supports this claim. More often, male ministers were known as *doctors* in their capacity as workers of magic. Among the best-known Voodoo ministers were Marie Laveau, Jean Montanée, Jim Alexander, and Betsy Toledano, all of whom practiced in New Orleans. Missouri had its own well-known practitioner in the form of a man known as King Alexander, who was prominent in the St. Joseph area during the late 19th century. Documentary evidence collected by the Federal Writers' Project during the 1930s indicates that some Voodoo ceremonies incorporated other functionaries alongside ministers, including singers, dancers, and musicians.

The spirits served by Voodoo ministers were numerous, though the full pantheon has been lost. If frequency of appearance is any indicator of importance, some of the most popular deities in the New Orleans area were Blanc Dani, Papa LaBas, and Assonquer. The first of these was a serpent god who played a central role in the religion and was a rough equivalent of Haiti's Danbala Wedo. Papa LaBas, also known as Liba, Lébat, or Limba, corresponded to Legba from Haiti. He was an opener of communication between humans and the divine. Assonquer, also known as Onzoncaire, appears to have been similar to the Haitian Ossange. He was particularly associated with good fortune. Some other deities who appear here and there in the documentary record are Grand Zombi, Jean Macouloumba or Colomba, Maman You, Vériquité, and Monsieur d'Embarrass. In Missouri, the lone deity whose name has survived was Samunga, a being whose function remains obscure. A "Grandfather Rattlesnake" prominent in the folklore of 19th-century Missouri practitioners and envisioned as a powerful sorcerer may well have been a local manifestation of Blanc Dani.

Spirits of the dead also had a prominent place in Voodoo. The documentary record gives no limits on precisely who could be called upon by believers, but certain deceased individuals possessed a higher status in the spirit world. For examples, medical doctors figured prominently in the magical deeds of some practitioner. Deceased priests and priestesses were even more important. Marie Laveau, in particular, held high status.

As is also the case in many Caribbean nations, the religion did not exist separately from the Catholicism that characterized former French and Spanish colonies. The process of creolization resulted in a faith in which African religion blended with European Christianity. Marie Laveau, for example, was a practicing Catholic as well as a Voodoo priestess. For that reason, the Christian God and the Virgin Mary appeared in many prayers that appeared in Voodoo ceremonies. Altars and candles, adopted from Catholic practice, also played a role in worship and the workings of magic. Many of the Voodoo-specific deities even had saint equivalents. Blanc Dani, for instance, was St. Michael the Archangel, and Assonquer was St. Paul.

The ritual life of Voodoo was incompletely documented, but reliable accounts of several distinct ceremonies have survived through the years. During the 19th century, for example, numerous accounts of an annual St. John's Eve ceremony on the night of June 23–24 appeared in New Orleans newspapers. In part, these were celebrations that resembled those held by many whites on the same evening. The Voodoo gatherings, however, included ritual dance, feasting, and bathing. Next to the St. John's Eve events, initiations were the best documented type of ceremonies. They were of several sorts, at least some of which were known as *openings*. Each included offerings to the spirits, prayers, and dances. Some accounts report what seem to have been spirit possession. Other ceremonies appear occasionally in the records, though their precise purposes remain unclear.

Scholarship on Voodoo has been sparse and often inaccurate. One of the most thorough studies of the religion was produced by Catherine Dillon for the Louisiana Writers' Project, an organization that for much of its history was part of the Depression-era Federal Writers' Project. The never-published manuscript includes hundreds of pages of detailed, well-researched information.

On the other hand, the tome is marred by pervasive racism, rendering it all but unpublishable today. Those wishing to consult it can do so by visiting the Cammie G. Henry Research Center of Northwestern State University in Natchitoches, Louisiana.

Some of the information gathered by Dillon and her Writer's Project colleagues did make it into print, however, as part of Robert Tallant's perennially popular *Voodoo in New Orleans* (1946). While Tallant eliminated much of the racism expressed by Dillon, he was not careful with his sources. According to scholar Carolyn Long, he frequently combined information from more than one source into a single account and implied that he had been the one who collected the data. Moreover, in keeping with others of his era, he sensationalized the religion, treating it predominantly as an exotic, sexually charged system of magic.

Though the years, numerous scholars have taken issue with the version of Voodoo embodied in the works of Dillon and Tallant. One, Zora Neale Hurston, constructed an alternative vision that predated them. Writing during the first half of the 1930s, she depicted Voodoo, which she called *hoodoo*, as a true religion and a valuable part of African American culture. Unfortunately, she resembled Tallant in her penchant for sensationalism and less-than-scrupulous regard for accuracy. Nevertheless, Hurston provided the basic outlines of the interpretation followed by many modern scholars, most notably Martha Ward, author of the first scholarly biography of Marie Laveau, *Voodoo Queen: The Spirited Lives of Marie Laveau* (2004). One scholar who has embraced neither Tallant's nor Hurston's version of the religion is Carolyn Morrow Long. Her *New Orleans Voudou Priestess: The Legend and Reality of Marie Laveau* (2006) meticulously examines not only Laveau but other aspects of Voodoo with an eye to uncovering the historical events buried under more than a century's worth of folklore.

Voodoo has largely disappeared as a distinct living tradition. The last recorded initiations into the faith appear to have taken place during the late 1930s or 1940s. After that point, the historical record is silent. The religion had always been in a precarious position and was consistently suppressed using local, state, and national ordinances. Likewise, many Christians increasingly found their faith incompatible with the creole religion.

Though it had died as an organized faith, aspects of Voodoo survived the religion. For instance, the candles once common to New Orleans hoodoo have spread across the United States, appearing in conjure and rootwork traditions that originally made little use of them. Even the term *hoodoo* has come to be a synonym for *conjure*. Likewise, folklore continues to associate Voodoo with certain areas, principally New Orleans, preserving its memory for future generations. Perhaps the most important survival of the religion are the Spiritual Churches. These nominally Christian congregations originated as a combination of many religious traditions, including Catholicism, Pentecostalism, and Spiritualism. Voodoo figured prominently as well. Modern churches not only worship the Christian God but honor a variety of spirits, ranging from saints to angels to deceased Native Americans, and frequently employ hoodoo-style rituals that outsiders would construe as magic. One could accurately describe such congregations as refuges for Voodoo beliefs or even as descendants of the religion that simply continued the process of Christianization begun during colonial times.

Despite the fading of Voodoo, many inhabitants of New Orleans claim adherence to the religion even today. Unlike earlier generations, however, they are not participating in a living tradition of the Mississippi Valley. Instead, most practice a form of Haitian Vodou or a reconstructed version of Voodoo based on historical research. The closest one can come to the living religion of the 1940s and before are hoodoo and Spiritual Churches.

See also: Alexander, Jim; Ancestral Spirits; Blanc Dani; Federal Writers' Project; Haitian Immigration to the United States; Hoodoo; Hopkins, Laura; Laveau, Marie; Legba; Montanée, Jean; Ossange/Assonquer; Owen, Mary Alicia; Rootwork; Saint John's Eve; Spiritual Churches; Toledano, Betsy

Jeffrey E. Anderson

Further Reading

Anderson, Jeffrey E. 2005. *Conjure in African American Society*. Baton Rouge, LA: Louisiana State University Press.

Anderson, Jeffrey E. 2008. *Hoodoo, Voodoo, and Conjure: A Handbook*. Greenwood Folklore Handbooks. Westport, CT: Greenwood Press.

Anderson, Jeffrey E. 2011. "Voodoo in Black and White." In *Southern Character: Essays in Honor of Bertram Wyatt-Brown*, edited by Lisa Tendrich Frank and Daniel Kilbride, 143–159. Gainesville: University Press of Florida.

Hall, Gwendolyn Midlo. 1992. *Africans in Colonial Louisiana: The Development of Afro-Creole Culture in the Eighteenth Century*. Baton Rouge, LA: Louisiana State University Press.

Hurston, Zora Neale. 1931. "Hoodoo in America." *Journal of American Folklore* 44: 317–417.

Hurston, Zora Neale. 1995. *Folklore, Memoirs, and other Writings*, selected and annotated by Cheryl A. Wall. The Library of America. New York: Literary Classics of the United States, Inc.

Jacobs, Claude F., and Andrew J. Kaslow. 1991. *The Spiritual Churches of New Orleans: Origins, Beliefs, and Rituals of an African-American Religion*. Knoxville, TN: University of Tennessee Press.

Long, Carolyn Morrow. 2006. "New Orleans Voudou and Haitian Vodou." In *Revolutionary Freedoms: A History of Survival, Strength and Immigration in Haiti*, edited by Cécile Accilien, Jessica Adams, and Elmide Méléance, 105–112. Illustrated by Ulrick Jean-Pierre. Coconut Creek, FL: Caribbean Studies Press.

Long, Carolyn Morrow. 2006. *A New Orleans Voudou Priestess: The Legend and Reality of Marie Laveau*. Gainesville, FL: University Press of Florida.

Long, Carolyn Morrow. 2014. "The Cracker Jack: A Hoodoo Drugstore in the 'Cradle of Jazz'." *Louisiana Cultural Vistas*, Spring, 64–75.

Roberts, Kodi. In press. *Voodoo and the Promise of Power: The Racial, Gender & Economic Politics of Religion in New Orleans, 1881–1940*. Baton Rouge, LA: Louisiana State University Press.

Tallant, Robert. 1946 [1998]. *Voodoo in New Orleans*. New York: Macmillan; reprint, Gretna: Pelican.

Ward, Martha. 2004. *Voodoo Queen: The Spirited Lives of Marie Laveau*. Jackson, MS: University Press of Mississippi.

W

WANGA

These items of West Central African origin are present in both Haitian Vodou and Mississippi Valley Voodoo. According to most scholars, a common feature of wangas in both locales is that they are usually meant to harm others. Because of their malevolent nature, many refer to them as *poisons*, though their harmful effects are understood to be supernatural in origin rather than the effect of toxic substances. Some modern Vodou practitioners, on the other hand, reject the notion that such items are inherently harmful, describing *wanga* as a general term for Vodou magic or a charm designed for any purpose, positive or negative. In New Orleans, the association of Voodoo with the production of wangas—virtually always understood as harmful—was so great that workers of magic went by the designation *wangateur* if male and *wangateuse* if female.

Wangas vary widely in appearance. During the mid-20th century, Alfred Métraux described wangas taking the form of sticks designed to cause death at a blow, of thorns that killed after piercing the skin, of injurious powders, and of chickens imbued with malevolent forces through the power of bòkòs. In the New Orleans area, wangas were often collections of magical items assembled in jars, bags, tins, and other containers. Harmful powders were also common in the Mississippi Valley, though it is unusual to find them referred to as wangas in historical documents.

See also: Bòkò; Gris-gris; Hand; Mojo; Paket Kongo

Jeffrey E. Anderson

Further Reading

Hall, Gwendolyn Midlo. 1992. *Africans in Colonial Louisiana: The Development of Afro-Creole Culture in the Eighteenth Century*. Baton Rouge, LA: Louisiana State University Press.

Long, Carolyn Morrow. 2001. *Spiritual Merchants: Religion, Magic, and Commerce*. Knoxville, TN: University of Tennessee Press.

Métraux, Alfred. 1972. *Voodoo in Haiti*. Translated by Hugo Charteris and with an Introduction by Sidney W. Mintz. New York: Schocken.

Siuda, Tamara L. (Mambo Chita Tann). 2012. *Haitian Vodou: An Introduction to Haiti's Indigenous Spiritual Tradition*. Woodbury, MN: Llewellyn.

WARD, MARTHA

Martha Ward is an American cultural anthropologist and the author of the first full-length academic work focused on the life of Marie Laveau, the legendary

> ### Where Did Vodou Originate?
>
> Vodou's origin cannot be traced to a single location. Its multiple African sources are clear from the many nanchons, or nations, from which its gods hail. Most scholars agree, however, that Fon and Kongo deities are the most prominent. At the same time, European secular culture and Catholicism have contributed saints, ritual paraphernalia, and language to the religion. Some researchers have suggested that Native Americans also made significant contributions to Vodou. Perhaps the faith is best understood not as an import from Africa or elsewhere but as a creole religion unique to Haiti.

priestess—some say founder—of American Voodoo. Ward has conducted field research in Micronesia, Italy, China, and the United States. She is fluent in six languages and her specialties include the fields of sociolinguistics, urban studies, qualitative methods, women's studies, health, and fertility. Outside of academia, Ward has worked with the Social Science Research Council, the World Health Organization, and the National Institutes of Health. Ward is currently a professor emerita at the University of New Orleans.

Ward earned a PhD in cultural anthropology from Tulane University in 1969, where she grew to love the city of New Orleans. Her affection for the Crescent City inspired her to research the life of one of the city's most mythical and mysterious historical figures, Marie Laveau. In *Voodoo Queen: The Spirited Lives of Marie Laveau* (2004), Ward explained that Marie Laveau was in fact two women, a mother and daughter who shared the same name. From 1803 to 1877 both free women of color negotiated their own space within a slave and postslave society. To document the complex lives of the Laveau women, Ward took guided tours through New Orleans, attended Voodoo rituals and church services, and visited cemeteries. In addition to using legal and Federal Writers' Project documents, Ward also relied upon nontraditional sources such as rumors, dreams, and imagination.

During the mid-1990s, Ward became involved with the growing field of women's studies. She designed the first official course in women's studies in Louisiana and coauthored the textbook *A World Full of Women* in 1995. Ward's other notable books include *Nest in the Wind*, *The Hidden Life of Tirol*, *Poor Women, Powerful Men: America's Great Experiment in Family Planning*, and *Them Children: A Study*.

See also: Federal Writers' Project; Laveau, Marie

Ronald Jackson II

Further Reading

Ward, Martha. 1989. *Nest in the Wind: Adventures in Anthropology*. Long Grove, IL: Waveland Press.

Ward, Martha. 1995. *A World Full of Women*. Boston: Allyn and Bacon.

Ward, Martha. 2004. *Voodoo Queen: The Spirited Lives of Marie Laveau*. Jackson, MS: The University of Mississippi Press.

WEST CENTRAL AFRICA

Many scholars have settled on the idea of Vodou as a composite religious practice comprised of a syncretic blend of various aspects of Roman Catholicism along with traditional African religious practices. In this formulation, the West African country of Dahomey (present-day Benin) and that region's great pantheon of divine spirits loom large as a focal point for the African origin of Vodou as practiced throughout the plantation Americas. Despite the well-documented role that ritual practice in Dahomey played in the subsequent development of Vodou, the particular influence of West Central Africa, generally, and that of the Kingdom of Kongo, in particular, is also crucial, even if often overlooked. In Kongo, broad-based forms of traditional religion along with a centuries-long engagement with Catholicism helped to create in Vodou a singular ritual practice whose influences are evident throughout the plantation Americas.

Four years after the Portuguese arrived in West Central Africa in 1487, Kongo King Nzinga a Nkuwu converted to Catholicism, assuming the name João I upon his baptism. Soon after, other members of the royal court and nobility also adopted the faith. A Catholic church was constructed at *Mbanza Kongo*, capital of the country, and European missionaries arrived in Kongo in earnest, offering sacraments and conducting mass. When, in 1506, Affonso I, a devoted Catholic though royal outcast, enjoyed an unlikely defeat of his unconverted brother, Mpanzu, in a battle for the throne, Catholicism quickly became a state-sponsored religion in the country. In this way, Catholicism emerged as a part of the traditional religious landscape of West Central Africa during the late 15th century, some two hundred years before the trans-Atlantic slave trade reached its zenith in the region. As scholar John Thornton notes, "since Kongo converted to Christianity of its own free will, the shape and structure of the Church and its doctrines were determined as much by Kongo as by Europeans." Always woefully undermanned, the Church and its missionaries relied on locally trained African lay priests who worked as itinerant interpreters and catechists, travelling throughout the countryside and bearing the principal weight of Catholic instruction and conversion to the country's peasantry.

The effect of this system was that key elements of Catholicism, including central aspects of its dogma, emblems, and theology, were adapted and translated into particularly Kongolese spiritual understandings. From the earliest years of missionary activity in the country, dating to the late 15th century, the Kongolese imported numerous Catholic cult objects, including crucifixes and rosaries, which they then assimilated into Kongolese ritual understandings and uses. For example, the Kongolese referred their own notions of a high deity or first ancestor, Nzambi a Mpungu, into the Biblical God. In addition, they began to equate Christian saints with Kongo spirits, and European priests with Kongolese healers, known as *banganga*. As John K. Thornton argues, "Christianity 'conquered' Kongo peacefully—but at the cost of adapting itself almost wholly to Kongolese conceptions of religion and cosmology."

Even before the Portuguese arrival, religion in West Central Africa was based on a set of widely shared concepts that would come to play an important role in the subsequent development of Vodou practices throughout the plantation Americas.

Historian and anthropologist Jan Vansina, writing in *Paths in the Rainforest*, used linguistic data going back more than four millennia to document several longstanding features of religious belief and practice in the region. Vansina noted a longstanding belief in the duality between an apparent world that was tangible and visible and another, ethereal world inhabited and dominated by spiritual beings, including the spirits of long-deceased leaders and ancestors, "whose personalities and even whose name had been forgotten and then rediscovered when he wrought wonders." In exchange for demonstrated reverence on the part of supplicants, the spirits offered protection and the bounties of the natural world. Manifested in the construction of shrines and practiced in prayer, libations, and sacrifice, the legitimacy of the spirit was every day renewed and demonstrated by the continuous well-being of the individual and the community. Failure to properly propitiate the spirits might be met with harsh punishment, sickness, or even death.

In addition to the practice of hero/ancestor reverence, Vansina noted a longstanding acknowledgement of nature spirits who inhabited lands and waters and who controlled key aspects of the physical world. Moreover, West Central Africans referred to a higher deity who might be thought of as a first ancestor or first cause who, though far distant from mundane, earthly affairs, yet reflected the creative force that first fashioned and then animated all things. Much of Kongo's religious practice has had to do with the mediation between, on the one hand, this ultimate divine power who operates just beyond the reach of human action and comprehension and, on the other, the need to satisfy human worldly wants and desires through spiritual supplication.

Notably, the Kongolese perceived spiritual power as neither good nor bad. Instead, it could be put to positive ends as when healing the sick or for any other cause intended to contribute to the common good or to ill ends when used to harm or amass wealth, power, and influence for an individual against the larger needs of the community. Indeed, highly successful political and military leaders were thought to have owed their personal success and advancement to witchcraft, that is, to their successful usurpation of resources and power from the community, which they hoarded for personal gain.

For their part, humans could harness these various powers through several ritual intercessors, including chiefs (*mfumu*), who maintained social order, and healers (*nganga*, pl. *banganga*), whose expertise included the ability to create *minkisi* (s. *nkisi*)— specially designed ritual objects used to harness, contain, and control spiritual power—and the knowledge of the varied prescriptions, prayers, and medicines used to animate them. In contradistinction to healers, witches (*kindoki*) perpetrated and fulfilled the antisocial, even if sometimes necessary, functions of society through selfishness and greed. Lastly, prophets (*ngunza*) helped to maintain ritual order by periodically proposing both ritual and social reform.

This varied ritual world and its agents contributed to a longstanding "tradition of renewal" in Kongo religious thought, an overarching sense that the sources of otherworldly power must continually be brought to bear in the living world as a way of cleansing it of its varied and continual corruptions. Perhaps the best demonstration of this tradition in renewal is the *dikenga*, or the Kongo cosmogram, which seamlessly melded at one and the same time key features of West Central African notions of renewal and rebirth into a figural representation—the cross—that also lay at the heart of Christian iconography and belief. In this figure, the horizontal line of the cross reflects the boundary between the land of the living (above the line) and the watery world of the dead (*mpemba*), situated below the line. Human life begins at birth before circling—like the sun—counterclockwise through the various stages of life/time, including noon at the zenith of life, sunset at death, through darkness at midnight, before returning to new life at the dawning of a new day. It was into this spiritual world that the Portuguese entered when they arrived in Kongo in the late 15th century. It was to this already expansive spiritual repertoire that João I contributed when he converted to Catholicism, and it was this same repertoire that many enslaved Kongolese took with them during the Middle Passage onto the plantations of the New World.

Many enslaved Africans from West Central Africa entered the plantation Americas with a strong sense of themselves as Catholic. To be sure, their Catholicism was deeply infused with particularly Kongolese religious and ritual concepts, but they and the missionaries who attended to them in Kongo—both European and African alike—regarded them as Catholics. In spite of this, European missionaries bitterly complained, both in Kongo and in the New World, about the novel and noncanonical religious practices and interpretations of the Kongolese faithful. As scholar Hein Vanhee has pointed out, in Haiti, Brazil, Louisiana, and Florida, Catholic missionaries often excoriated enslaved Kongolese who so freely "mixed Catholicism with their pagan beliefs." In Haiti, Catholic missionaries complained that some Kongolese slaves not only practiced their own brand of the faith but also sought to spread their vision of Catholicism, acting as missionaries and priests to unconverted men and women in the slave community. It is likely that some of these enslaved missionaries served in similar capacities in Kongo, but under a new slave regime in the Americas, their doctrine would surely be seen as subverting the teachings of the Roman Catholic Church and, by extension, the slave order. Vanhee has pointed out that the earliest documentary references to "*Vaudoux*" appear in 18th-century Saint-Domingue as a "generic designation for various possession cults organized by Africans on the colonial estates." In this sense, Vodou emerged first as an amalgam of different traditions conspiring to form a new practice based on African antecedents. While this has led some scholars to argue that the search for specific African origins is a futile, if not misguided enterprise, Hein Vanhee and other scholars interested in the field see in Vodou evidence of particularly Kongolese strains of ritual thought and practice. For example, 18th-century devotees to Vodou sang ritual songs in kiKongo, a widely spoken language in West Central Africa. Moreover, several observers in Saint-Domingue noted that enslaved Kongolese of the period approached missionaries with a significant familiarity with Roman Catholicism. Indeed, Vanhee has concluded that West Central Africans in Saint-Domingue "freely drew on Catholic ritual and imagery they were already familiar with, in organizing local cults on local estates." Because Vodou practice in the Americas often included references, signs, and symbols drawn from Roman Catholicism, one must consider seriously the history of West Central Africa, generally, and the history of the Kongo kingdom, in particular, to better understand the historical origins of Vodou.

Given Kongo's long history with Catholicism, the distinction commonly drawn between Catholic ritual and traditional African religion may be overstated. As scholar Terry Rey has noted, Vodou and Catholicism in Haiti "appear somewhat indistinguishable, inter-permeating one another in their liturgy, ritual, [and] mysticism." If, as noted above, Catholicism conquered Kongo but at the cost of adapting itself almost wholly to Kongolese ritual conceptions, the same may be said of Catholic practice in the New World. It is in this sense that Alfred Métraux, a leading scholar on Vodou in Haiti, described the "veritable seizure of Catholicism by Vodou in Haiti."

Notably, Haitian Vodou crystallized as a formal religion from 1760 to 1860, a period punctuated by the 56-year period from 1804 to 1860, when the Vatican refused to send priests to the newly independent country established after the Haitian Revolution in 1804. The persistence of Catholic signs, symbols, and liturgy in the country and their easy adoption into Haitian Vodou relied on the expertise of Catholic Haitians, many of whom would have been adherents in Kongo. In this way, both Vodou and popular Catholicism developed in tandem in Haiti during the 19th century, becoming deeply connected and intertwined in the process.

If Kongolese Catholicism played a major role in the development of Haitian Vodou, it is also true, as Terry Rey has argued, that Kongolese Catholicism also affected the nature of Haitian popular Catholicism. That is to say that "the god manifest in Jesus, far from being widely perceived among the subjugated as merely 'the god of the dominant classes,' had long been embraced by the baKongo (however syncretized with Nzambi Mpungu) prior to their arrival in Saint-Domingue." In this sense, one might argue for the persistence of a transatlantic Kongo Catholic community between West Central Africa and the plantation Americas that helped to install a ritual practice devoted to Catholic saints and sacraments alongside Kongo spirits in a broad-based faith that has come down to us as Vodou in Haiti, Voodoo in North America, and a range of related belief systems throughout the New World.

See also: Bight of Benin; Cosmogram; Dahomey; Kongo; Nzambi a Mpungu; Senegambia; Simbi

Jason R. Young

Further Reading

Janzen, Jan. 2013. "Renewal and Reinterpretation in Kongo Religion." In *Kongo Across the Waters*, edited by Susan Cooksey, Robin Poynor, and Hein Vanhee, 132–142. Gainesville, FL: University of Florida Press.

Rey, Terry. 2002. "Kongolese Catholic Influences on Haitian Popular Catholicism: A Sociohistorical Exploration." In *Central Africans and Cultural Transformations in the American Diaspora*, edited by Linda M. Heywood, 265–285. New York: Cambridge University Press.

Thornton, John. 1984. "The Development of an African Catholic Church in the Kingdom of Kongo, 1491–1750." *Journal of African History* 25:2, 147–167.

Vanhee, Hein. 2002. "Central African Popular Christianity and the Making of Haitian Vodou Religion." In *Central Africans and Cultural Transformations in the American Diaspora*, edited by Linda M. Heywood, 243–264. New York: Cambridge University Press.

Vansina, Jan. 1990. *Paths in the Rainforests: Toward a Political Tradition in Equatorial Africa*. Madison, WI: University of Wisconsin Press.

WORKER

Worker is a common euphemism for practitioners of Voodoo, particularly in and around New Orleans, and in the southeastern United States more generally. Unlike some of other terms such as *hoodoos* or *Voodoos*, *worker* has been commonly used by practitioners to refer to themselves and one another and may therefore be looked at as the preferred term in some periods and locales, rather than a label imposed by hostile outsiders. The term undoubtedly comes from references to spiritual rites as "the work" both in New Orleans, and Haiti. The Haitian term *travay* has been translated as "work." Specifically, "the work" characterizes rites that deploy spiritual power to improve the material circumstances of practitioners or those on whose behalf they are working. Workers, by consequence, are those who perform such rites. Most frequently the term *worker* is employed in New Orleans to reference professional practitioners and much less frequently their clients.

Workers were called upon to do everything from curing illness, to getting jobs for the unemployed, to securing the affections of prospective lovers. Workers also performed rites to sicken, maim, or kill for their clients. Most frequently, workers in New Orleans charged a fee for services that depended on the complexity of the rites and their desired result. Practitioners seemed to have maintained networks in the city, frequently referring one another to potential clients. The term *work*, therefore, may also suggest that the pay for services and the economic aspect of these spiritual practices were thought of as integral to the process.

There appear to have been very few criteria through the mid-20th century in New Orleans to be considered a worker. When famed African American novelist and Columbia University trained ethnographer Zora Hurston studied with workers in New Orleans in order to become a Voodoo practitioner, she claimed to have been initiated several times with elaborate ceremonies in which offerings were made to the spirits by her and on her behalf, and music and dance were integral. Similarly, when researchers from the Louisiana Writers' Project sought to learn about the practice of workers in New Orleans, they had to perform an opening, an initiation rite not unlike those described by Hurston. Offerings were made to the spirits so that prospective initiates would be granted the power to do various kinds of work, some beneficent and some malevolent. There were several workers present, perceivably to provide their own expertise and lend their spiritual power to the initiation rites.

Initiation rites were by no means universal among professional practitioners of Voodoo, some of whom picked up their trade from other practitioners, magic

> ### Voodoo during the American Civil War
>
> For most of the American Civil War, Union forces controlled the southern city of New Orleans. At least some of the occupiers feared that the Voodoo practitioners were working against them, calling on their deities to grant victory to the Confederacy. Though the evidence for Voodoo-practitioners' southern sympathies is slight, that they might side with their region should not be surprising. After all, New Orleans had a large free black population, some of whom were themselves slaveholders and many of whom had served in pro-South militia units early in the war.

manuals, and even members of Spiritual Churches, suggesting that a formal initiation was not always necessary. In contrast to those initiated by preexisting practitioners, some workers seemed to simply have gleaned aspects of their craft from other practitioners and picked up supplies purchased from local drugstores that specialized in hoodoo and Voodoo paraphernalia. With this knowledge they simply began working for themselves and clients without having been initiated.

See also: Conjure; Hoodoo; New Orleans; Opening; Two Head

Kodi Roberts

Further Reading

Long, Carolyn Morrow. 2001. *Spiritual Merchants: Religion, Magic, and Commerce.* Knoxville, TN: University of Tennessee Press.

Roberts, Kodi. In press. *Voodoo and the Promise of Power: The Racial, Gender & Economic Politics of Religion in New Orleans, 1881–1940.* Baton Rouge, LA: Louisiana State University Press.

Y

YORUBA

Historically among the present-day Yoruba peoples, various ethnic groups have held to their own origin stories as well as their own names. According to Robin Law, not until these various ethnic groups had to "compete for power against other ethnic groups in Nigeria did they cosign to an origin story central to all Yoruba based upon the 'Ife-centered Oduduwa mythology.'" Other scholars, including J.D. Peel, contend that the Yoruba's coming to see themselves as an ethnic group was a means of consolidation to accommodate missionary efforts. The various views of historical origin within and among the ethnic make-up of present day Yoruba is explained in the words of Law as follows: "In an oral society, there is not so much a traditional history as a range of historical traditions, each tradition (or at least each group of traditions) with its own function and institutional context." Scholar Andrew Apter has gone a step further: "Recorded Yoruba traditions of origin almost all agree in deriving the major Yoruba kingdoms from Ife, but the circumstances of the original foundation of Ife itself are disputed. The Yoruba traditions of origin are conventionally divided into two groups: stories of creation, which claim that Ife was the ancestral cradle of all mankind rather than just of the Yoruba, and stories of migration."

The historical nature of the Yoruba people is indicated in their oral histories, known as *oríkì*, or praise poems. According to Bolanle Awe:

> Such *oríkì* can be divided into three groups, viz.:
> (1) *oríkì ìlú* (towns) which deals with the foundation of a town, its vicissitudes and its general reputation among its neighbors.
> (2) *oríkì orílẹ̀* (lineages) which gives the characteristics of a patrilineage by focusing attention on a few illustrious members of the lineage whose attributes are supposed to typify the main features of that lineage.
> (3) *oríkì ìnagijẹ* (individual personalities) which deals mainly with individuals.

The collective nature of *oríkì* offers a continual common origin for the Yoruba people, albeit one not without contention. As Andrew Apter puts it:

> Creation myths generally state that in the beginning, Olodumare, the Yoruba High God, had a son, Oduduwa, who climbed down a chain from Heaven to an uninhabited world. The world was covered with water so Oduduwa placed a handful of earth and a cock on top of it. As the cock began to scratch and kick the earth about, the land spread out over the water. According to this myth, Ile-Ife (hereafter called Ife) is the sacred spot of Oduduwa's original descent, where he became the first Yoruba

king, owner of the land, and fathered future generations of Yoruba kings through sixteen sons. This basic narrative, found with minor variations, is generally thought to express the origin of Yoruba monarchy at Ife.

Migration myths tell how Oduduwa, founder of the Yoruba people, came from somewhere in the East. Some myths are vague about where he migrated from, others cite Nupeland, Egypt, or Medina as his place of departure, in this latter, Oyo, version Oduduwa, son of a Meccan king, rebelled against his father and Islam, and fled to Ife with his children where he founded Yoruba kingship. Of his seven sons, the first six left Ife to found the kingdoms of Owu, Ketu, Benin, Ila Orangun, Sabe, and Popo, while the last born, named Oranyan (or Oranmiyan) succeeded his father at Ife. The myth finishes with an account of the founding of Old Oyo.

There are currently about 25 million Yoruba living in southwest Nigeria, where they account for over 21 percent of the population, and in Benin. The people's division is nothing new. For centuries, the Yoruba have been divided into various kingdoms. Typically, a king and council of chiefs or elders ruled each, and every kingdom had distinctive cultural and artistic features.

The dispersal of the Yoruba population occurred in two major waves. The first was the transatlantic slave trade, which exported millions of Yoruba-speaking people to Brazil, Cuba, and the Caribbean islands. Yoruba culture remains a profound influence on present-day Brazilian life. A second wave of migration was more self-imposed and resulted as political tensions in Nigeria rose in the 1970s, prompting many Yoruba to depart for the United States and Europe.

The Yoruba continue to maintain many traditional aspects of their culture. Patrilocal marriage, for instance, is still a part of the typical Yoruba lifestyle, with women keeping their lineage affiliations while moving into their husbands' compounds. Many Yorubas' approach to religion is similar. Today, the Yoruba adhere to Christianity, Islam, and Traditionalist faiths. Over 50 percent are Christian, and fewer than 40 percent are Muslim. The remainder practice Ifá, the traditional religion of the Yoruba people. As with Haiti, however, many of those who practice Christianity or Islam continue to maintain aspects of their traditional beliefs.

The Yoruba held and retain a very accomplished artistic aesthetics. Works of Yoruba art are retained the world over in museums promoting African art collections. From metal casting to textiles, Yoruba artists exhibit naturalistic styles and practices unattained in other regions of Africa.

See also: Bight of Benin; Candomblé; Ifá; Santería

Phoenix Savage

Further Reading

Apter, Andrew. 1987. "The Historiography of Yoruba Myth and Ritual." *History in Africa* 14: 1–25.

Awe, Bolanle. 1974. "Praise Poems as Historical Data: The Example of the Yoruba Oríkì." *Journal of the International African Institute* 44:4 (October), 331–349.

Law, Robin. 1976. "Early Yoruba Historiography." *History in Africa* 3, 69–89.

Lloyd, P. C. 1955. "The Yoruba Lineage." *Journal of the International African Institute* 25:3 (July), 235–251.
Okediji, Moyo. 1997. "Art of the Yoruba." *Art Institute of Chicago Museum Studies* 23:2, 164–181, 198.
Peel, J. D. Y. 2000. *Religious Encounter and the Making of the Yoruba*. Bloomington, IN: Indiana University Press.

Z

ZOMBI

Zombis, frequently known as *zonbis* in scholarly literature and *zombies* by almost everyone else, pervade popular culture's understanding of Vodou. According to folklore, they are the animated bodies of the dead, raised from the grave to serve evil sorcerers. Zombis, however, have taken on a life of their own through novels and film. If Hollywood is to be believed, a zombi apocalypse is just around the corner, and we can all look forward to a gruesome death at the hands of the walking dead. As with so much else associated with Vodou, the stereotypical zombi has little to do with the Haitian faith.

To begin with, some dispute that zombis can be properly called part of Vodou. According to scholars Carrol F. Coates and Leslie Desmangles, the concept of the zombi belongs to the realm of folk religion rather than Vodou. As such, the relationship is akin to that between Catholicism and hoodoo in the United States. While the latter frequently incorporates candles with images of saints, prayers, and Bible verses into its workings, hoodoo is not something that a Catholic priest would consider part of the faith he served. Others, however, draw no such distinctions between Vodou and the concept of the zombi. Even within this mindset, no scholar would argue that zombis are more than a small part of Vodou. They certainly do not define it.

Popular culture has so obscured the image of the zombi that some explanation is in order. First, there is more than one sort of zombi. The best known is the *zombi cadaver* or "zombi of the body," an animated but soulless corpse. Another more common form is the *zombi astral* or "zombi of the soul," the spiritual portion of a person that lingers near the grave of its deceased owner. Second, zombis do not wander in groups seeking to harm those who cross their path. Instead, they supposedly serve bòkòs acting as sorcerers. While bòkòs might indeed send them to harm others, zombis might just as easily fill the role of agricultural laborers, their prime function in much of the Haitian folklore. Finally, zombis are not cannibalistic.

Zombis have a long history. As discussed at length by folklorists Hans-W. Ackermann and Jeanine Gauthier, zombis are almost certainly of African origin. Words resembling *zombi* in both sound and definition abound along the western coast of the continent from Ghana to Angola. Moreover, a common African concept that humans possess multiple souls supports a belief system in which one spiritual aspect of a person can find itself enslaved as a *zombi astral* while a separate one enters into the afterlife. As the international slave trade carried Africans across the

> ### Werewolves
>
> Though only marginally connected to Voodoo and Vodou, werewolves, called *loup garou* or some variation thereof, are part of the folklore of both Haiti and the lower Mississippi Valley. In Haiti, werewolves more closely resemble what Americans would think of as witches or vampires, possessing the ability to fly and the desire to drink blood. To change shape, a loup garou must remove its human skin, to which it must return in a short time. The Louisiana variety possesses the same vampiric and shape-shifting features and is sometimes considered to travel by being carried through the air by a giant bat.

Atlantic, it also transported their beliefs to new lands. While Haitians developed their distinctive ideas about zombis, other societies tended to build concepts similar to that of the *zombi astral*. A prime example are the *duppies* of Jamaica and Barbados, ghostly beings that can be used by sorcerers to harm enemies.

Of course, one could well question whether or not zombis actually exist. In many instances, cases of alleged zombification—of the *zombi cadaver* variety—can be accounted for simply as persons with mental illness or disability. Some scholars, notably Wade Davis, have argued that zombis are genuine phenomena that can be explained as instances of apparent death caused by pharmacologically active ingredients administered by bòkòs who then revive the supposed corpse, thereafter keeping their victims in drug-induced stupors. The zombis are then compelled to work for their new masters. Davis's contentions, most memorably expressed in *The Serpent and the Rainbow: A Harvard Scientist's Astonishing Journey into the Secret Societies of Haitian Voodoo, Zombis, and Magic* (1985), remain controversial.

The term *zombi* can also be found in French-speaking southern Louisiana, although it historically had quite different meanings than those associated with Vodou and popular culture. In Voodoo, Grand Zombi was an important spirit, and there may have been some connection to the Kongo deity Nzambi a Mpungu. On the other hand, the word *zombi* or *zombie* appears in other contexts, where it can mean "spirit," "wizard," "ghost," or simply something extremely out of proportion. In a Francophone society, where *grand* meant "great," *Grand Zombi* could have simply meant a particular great spirit. In fact, the name could well have served as a title for a deity with a distinct personal name. References to lesser zombis may have referred to either independent spirits or something like the enslaved *zombis astral* of Haitian belief.

See also: Bòkò; Grand Zombi; Nzambi a Mpungu; Souls

Jeffrey E. Anderson

Further Reading

Ackermann, Hans-W., and Jeanine Gauthier. 1991. "The Ways and Nature of the Zombi." *Journal of American Folklore* 104: 466–494.

Cable, George Washington. 1891. *The Grandissimes: A Story of Creole Life*. New York: Charles Scribner's Sons.

Coates, Carrol F. 2006. "Vodou in Haitian Literature." In *Vodou in Haitian Life and Culture: Invisible Powers*, edited by Patrick Bellegarde-Smith and Claudine Michel, 181–198. New York: Palgrave Macmillan.

Coates, Carrol F. 2006. "'The Jew' in the Haitian Imagination: Pre-Modern Anti-Judaism in the Postmodern Caribbean." In *Vodou in Haitian Life and Culture: Invisible Powers*, edited by Patrick Bellegarde-Smith and Claudine Michel, 79–99. New York: Palgrave Macmillan.

Davis, Wade. 1988. *Passages of Darkness: The Ethnobiology of the Haitian Zombie*. Chapel Hill, NC: University of North Carolina Press.

Davis, Wade. 1986. *The Serpent and the Rainbow: A Harvard Scientist's Astonishing Journey into the Secret Societies of Haitian Voodoo, Zombis, and Magic*. New York: Simon and Schuster.

Fortier, Alcée. 2011. *Louisiana Folktales: Lupin, Bouki, and Other Creole Stories in French Dialect and English Translation*. With an Introduction by Russell Desmond. Lafayette, LA: University of Louisiana at Lafayette Press.

Long, Carolyn Morrow. 2006. *A New Orleans Voudou Priestess: The Legend and Reality of Marie Laveau*. Gainesville, FL: University Press of Florida.

Pitkin, Helen. 1904. *An Angel by Brevet: A Story of Modern New Orleans*. Philadelphia and London: J. B. Lippincott Company.

Valdman, Albert et al. 2010. *Dictionary of Louisiana French as Spoken in Cajun, Creole, and American Indian Communities*. Jackson, MS: University Press of Mississippi.

Visual Representations of Vodou and Voodoo

Throughout this volume are essays on the socio-historical development of Vodou, the role Vodou plays in contemporary African-American/Caribbean societies, the ceremonies themselves, the lwa or Vodou spirits and their roles, sacred objects used in ceremonies, and being mounted by a lwa (or spirit possession), to name but few topics. What follows differs from these texts precisely because it is not text. Once past this short essay, you will encounter a link to a portfolio of images of oungan and mambo (priests and priestesses, respectively), ceremonies, practitioners, sacred objects, and landscapes celebrating and illustrating the Vodou religion, culture, and environments where it is practiced. The photographs in this essay and on the website were funded in part by the UF-Duke National Endowment for the Humanities Collaborative Grant (RZ-51441-12), The Archive of Haitian Religion and Culture (www.dloc.com/vodou).

Photographs and text are similar in that they are both ways to communicate information. Traditionally in academic writing, the written word rules. But as Ira Jacknis has commented in his article "Franz Boas and Photography," images are more often than not used as window dressing (2). They are redundant and subservient to the written word. Sometimes the accompanying photographs have little to do with the discussion in the text. However, today there exists an ever-expanding group of visual social scientists who are trying to change this relationship. Their interests vary, but each researcher uses the communicative properties unique to photographs in a more profound manner than is typically done in academic writings—to make the image the primary message deliverer, independent of and not subservient to, the written word. This approach is becoming more widely accepted. It is not a position of favoring one medium over another but recognizing that different situations may lend themselves better to images (or text) as the choice to communicate one's message. Anthropologist Sarah Pink is one advocate for visual anthropology. In *Doing Visual Ethnography*, she makes the claim that "there is no essential hierarchy of knowledge or media for ethnographic representation" (5). This is by no means universally accepted.

I am one of those who admit to being a "visual anthropologist." In my work I have used images in different ways, trying to place them on the same or on a higher level than the text. One way I have used images in research is as primary data, illustrating and giving proof to the theoretical point I am trying to make. A second way I have attempted to make photographs more integral to the research and text in my ethnographic writing is to attempt to "put" the reader in the location in which the activities I discuss take place, such as in work I completed on political protests in the city of Buenos Aires. With the discussion and description of these political activities and their participants—the prime subject of my research—I felt it would benefit the reader if he or she had a better visual grasp of the geography, or place, on which all these actions played out.

Images can be read in different ways. There might be a single image. There may be a set of several images, much like what we see in a photojournalistic piece, often as an accompaniment to text (though integral to the piece), such as in *Life* magazine or *National Geographic*. There may also be a complete photographic monograph or photo exhibit in a museum, often with little text. In all of these scenarios, much of the meaning is gained through context. One way to "read" a large collection is to look at several images and identify a theme common to them all. Once a theme is recognized, you can then apply it while looking at the collection and better understand the message the creator is trying to communicate. As Howard Becker discusses, arrangement can be quite critical. In *Another Way of Telling*, art critic John Berger and photographer Jean Mohr discuss the unique communicative properties of the photographic image. They propose using these unique properties to tell stories in ways texts cannot. At the risk of oversimplifying their discussion, they look to the assemblage of images called *montage*. They believe that this kind of collection of images, if done right, can get to the subjective understanding of the subject. "The story narrates on behalf of this subject, appeals to it and *speaks in its voice*" (285, emphasis added). In anthropology we call this an *emic* view, an insider's view, a goal for many ethnographers. This is in opposition to an *etic* view, an outsider's view, often equated with the voice of the ethnographer.

I have discussed and adapted Berger and Mohr's belief in the power of montage to tell a narrative through images. I confess, however, that I always have had some text. Sometimes the text is integrated with the images, and sometimes an introduction to them. Unlike this essay, which is explaining how to look at photographs, the other introductions are about the theoretical discussions being made (the essays in this book are my textual accompaniment). Regardless, I enthusiastically advocate and have presented variations on a montage of images *a la* Berger and Mohr. Building on their theories and discussions, I want to add another dimension, or concept, a kind of frame of mind to further help guide the viewer in reading a body of images (again, depending on the context). This concept is what I am calling *immersion*. The 1972 edition of the *American Heritage Dictionary* defines *immerse* as, "To involve profoundly; absorb." You have read about Vodou and Voodoo, their ceremonies and sacred objects, and much more. I wish you to look at the images below, throughout the text, and those accessible through the link below, keeping this knowledge in the back of your mind, but do not let these details distract you from immersing yourself in them. Absorb them. Let them wash over you so that in their totality you can begin to sense how it feels to be at a Vodou ceremony. Later, feel free to look at individual images to see illustrations of particular ceremonies, notable personalities, and the like. But at first, just lose yourself in the moment depicted in each image. I want you, the reader, to be absorbed in the montage. Profoundly.

Vodouists display symbolic swords. (Courtesy of Richard B. Freeman)

A scene of ritual bathing, reminiscent of New Orleans's St. John's Eve Ceremonies or the bathing at Saut-d'Eau in Haiti. (Courtesy of Richard B. Freeman)

The potomitan, or center post, of an ounfò. Note the typical spiraling design around the post and the vèvès that surround it. (Courtesy of Richard B. Freeman)

A goat on the verge of being sacrificed. Note that it stands tied to the potomitan of an ounfò. (Courtesy of Richard B. Freeman)

VISUAL REPRESENTATIONS OF VODOU AND VOODOO 331

Drummers during a Vodou ceremony. Drums are common in many African Diasporic religions. In Vodou, specific rhythms summon the lwa. While the task can be enjoyable, it can also be exhausting during long ceremonies. (Courtesy of Richard B. Freeman)

Transvestites celebrate in a rara band. (Courtesy of Richard B. Freeman)

Vodou imagery abounds in this photograph of the interior of an ornate ounfò. Among the most prominent figures are images of saints along the wall and an ornate potomitan with painted serpents on all sides of the pole and the base, called a pe. Two asons rest on the pe. (Courtesy of Richard B. Freeman)

An outdoor shrine for Danbala Wedo, the serpent spirit, of the Société Linto. The wording in the basin reads "Mambo Jeanine." (Courtesy of Richard B. Freeman)

VISUAL REPRESENTATIONS OF VODOU AND VOODOO 333

Every cycle of salutation to a Vodou spirit involves greeting the drums (among other stations in the Vodou temple). The priests bow, rotate, pour libations, and make gestural signs with the ason. (Courtesy of Richard B. Freeman)

Vodou mambos and others during a ceremony. Note the beaded asons held by some participants. (Courtesy of Richard B. Freeman)

In the foreground stands a mambo with an ason and bell. To her right are drummers. Images of the lwa are in the background. (Courtesy of Richard B. Freeman)

A Vodou oungan. In his right hand in an ason. With his left he holds a bottle of Florida Water, a type of cologne incorporated into Vodou ceremonies and North American hoodoo. (Courtesy of Richard B. Freeman)

Vodou initiates have a processional with clay pots wrapped in silken cloth that represent specific spirits. (Courtesy of Richard B. Freeman)

Offering before a shrine for Azaka Mede. (Courtesy of Richard B. Freeman)

Brightly colored Vodou drums of the group "Racine Lakay." (Courtesy of Richard B. Freeman)

To further immerse yourself in a collection of images representing Vodou, visit http://ufdc.ufl.edu/AA00029509/00001/thumbs.

Richard B. Freeman

Further Reading

Becker, Howard S. 1982. "Afterword." In *Good Company*, by Douglas A. Harper, 169–172. Chicago: University of Chicago Press.
Berger, John, and Jean Mohr. 1982. *Another Way of Telling*. New York: Pantheon.
Freeman, Richard. 2001. "The City as Mise-en-Scène: A Visual Exploration of the Culture of Politics in Buenos Aires." *Visual Anthropology Review* 17(Spring-Summer): 36–59.
Freeman, Richard. 2001. "Learning to Rebel: Socialist Youth Activism in Contemporary Buenos Aires." PhD dissertation, University of Illinois at Urbana-Champaign.
Freeman, Richard. 2009. "Photography and Ethnography." In *Viewpoints: Visual Anthropologists at Work*, edited by Mary Strong and Laena Wilder, 53–75. Austin, TX: University of Texas Press.
Jacknis, Ira. 1984. "Franz Boas and Photography." *Studies in Visual Communication* 10 (Winter): 2–60.
Pink, Sarah. 2001. *Doing Visual Ethnography: Images, Media, and Representation in Research*. London: Sage.

Primary Documents

1. Early Descriptions of New Orleans Voodoo, 1763–1863   339
   From *The History of Louisiana or of the Western Parts of Virginia and Carolina*, 1763   339
   "Idolatry and Quackery," 1820   340
   "The Virgin of the Voudous," 1850   340
   "The Voudou Case Disposed Of," 1863   341

2. Two Accounts of Voodoo in Missouri, 1880s–1890s   342
   William Wells Brown, *My Southern Home: The South and Its People*, 1880   343
   Mary Alicia Owen, "Among the Voodoos," 1892   344

3. Reports of Marie Laveau's Death, 1881   350
   "Death of Marie Laveau," 1881   350
   "A Sainted Woman," 1881   352

4. Mississippi Valley Voodoo Songs, 1885 and undated   353
   "I Will Wander in the Desert," 1885   353
   Selections from Federal Writers' Project interviews, 1940

5. Spenser St. John and Vodou, 1889   359

6. A New Orleans Voodoo Ceremony, 1904   367

7. Opening Ceremony from New Orleans Voodoo/Hoodoo, 1920s–1930s   378

8. Interview of Mambo Patricia Scheu (Vye Zo Komande LaMenfo), 2013   381

9. Congress of Santa Barbara Declaration   391

10. U.S. Library of Congress Changes Subject Heading from "Voodooism" to "Vodou," 2012   391

Early Descriptions of New Orleans Voodoo, 1763–1863

The first three articles provide an outline of Voodoo as it was practiced before the Civil War. Le Page Du Pratz's short mentions of gris-gris and communal ceremonies are the first descriptions of the religion. The French edition of his book appeared in 1758 but described events of an even earlier period, indicating the presence of some form of Voodoo well before the 1809–1810 migration of Saint-Domingue refugees to New Orleans—often erroneously cited as the origin of the faith in Louisiana. The next two selections are news items that describe the breakup of Voodoo gatherings and include some interesting information on their worship, including descriptions of two images representing deities.

The fourth selection is a particularly interesting case of prosecution for practicing Voodoo that took place during the occupation of New Orleans by Union troops during the Civil War. The arrests described in the account occurred a few days before the trial, which attracted considerable attention in the local press. The gathering of free blacks with a few whites—described as "visitors" in the article—for a ceremony that allegedly incorporated nude dancing would have attracted public interest under any conditions. The accusation that the Voodooisants were appealing to the deities to liberate the city from the Yankees, however, posed a threat to northern control of the city and thus the Union's effort to conquer the South. What is perhaps most surprising is that the accused escaped any penalty. According to a brief notice in the November 26, 1863, issue of the Daily Picayune, *officer Long, who testified against the women, did not emerge unscathed. He reportedly suffered for several months under a curse that made him hear strange noises, feel pain when he walked or tried to sleep, and have nightmares. He had reportedly lost the favor of his fellow police and become an object of suspicion among the general populace.*

From The History of Louisiana or of the Western Parts of Virginia and Carolina, *1763*

The negroes must be governed differently from the *Europeans*; not because they are black, nor because they are slaves; but because they think differently from white men. . . .

They are very superstitious, and are much attached to their prejudices, and little toys which they call *gris, gris*. It would be improper therefore to take them from them, or even speak of them to them; for they would believe themselves undone, if they were stripped of those trinkets. The old negroes soon make them lose conceit of them.

. . . In a word nothing is more to be dreaded than to see the negroes assemble together on *Sundays*, since, under the pretence of *Calinda* or the dance, they sometimes get together to the number of three or four hundred, and make a kind of

Sabbath, which it is always prudent to avoid; for it is in those tumultuous meetings, that they sell what they have stolen to one another, and commit many crimes. In these likewise they plot their rebellions.

Source: Le Page Du Pratz, *The History of Louisiana or of the Western Parts of Virginia and Carolina*, 2 vols, translation (London: Becket and De Hondt, 1763), 254–255, 271.

"Idolatry and Quackery," 1820

In the middle of town, public attention was yesterday attracted, and a large crowd gathered at the Principal to see several persons who has been brought before the Mayor, on a charge of holding illegal nightly meetings.—For some time past, a House in the suburb Tremé, has been used as a kind of temple for certain occult practices and the idolatrous worship of an African deity called Vaudoo. It is said that many slaves, and some free people, repaired there of nights to practice superstitious, idolatrous rites, to dance, carouse, &c. &c. it is also suspected that the slaves carried there the fruits of their robberies, which the leaders appropriated to further their own debaucheries and villainy. The jugglers had collected some trumpery to aid their views: the image of a woman, whose lower extremities resemble a snake, and many smaller articles, were seized and bro't to the mayor's office. Among the persons arrested, there was one white man; the others were free colored people and slaves.

Source: "Idolatry and Quackery," *Louisiana Gazette*, 16 August 1820, 2.

"The Virgin of the Voudous," 1850

About 11 o'clock yesterday, the time when cits do take their lunch, Common street was in commotion. A compact crowd of sturdy Anglo-Saxons, marching in close column occupied the southern banquette, and filed in regular order into Hewlett's, to partake of his roast beef and Galphin sausages. The opposite banquette was equally crowed with Afric's daughters of every age, of every shape, and of every shade of color, from a bright yellow hue to sooty. They, in single file, wended their way up the stairs which lead to Justice Winter's court . . .

The cause we have ascertained, and shall, briefly state. It was reported in this paper some time ago, that the "vigilant" police of the Third Municipality made a descent on a party of colored people, engaged in celebrating the rites and mysteries of Voudouism. We are not among the initiated to tell what these mysteries are: but the priestesses who practice them, profess themselves to be—

> Gypsies, who ev'ry ill can cure,
> Except the ill of being poor,
> Who charms 'gainst love and agues sell,
> Who can in hen roost set a spell,
> Prepar'd by arts, to them best known
> To catch all feet except their own,
> Who as to fortune can unlock it,
> As easily as pick a pocket.

No spell or incantation which they could weave was sufficient to prevent the police from doing their duty, and so they made prisoners of the party, and seized on their paraphernalia. Among the latter—and the chief relic of reverence and veneration—was a quaintly carved wooden figure, resembling something between a Centaur and an Egyptian Mummy. This was the Voudou Virgin, so called. Of this the police retained possession for some time, and many were the devices [us]ed among the Voudous to regain the valued prize. It was finally understood that the officer of police, in whose possession it was, would restore it to those who worshipped at its shrine for $8.50, the costs, as he said, of Court. What true-believing Voudou would not [very] treble the sum to possess that which was at once the symbol and the sanctuary of their belief? The question among them was—not who would down with the dust, but who, for a sum so trivial, would be the fortunate possessor of the mysterious Voudou Virgin, possessing such supernatural powers. A young quadroon was the first to present to the officer the ransom of $8.50, for the Voudou Virgin. He accepted the offer, and she grasped the mysterious relic, more rich in her treasure than the Queen of England felt on receiving the Lahore diamond. She had not well left the presence of the police officer, when another, and another, and still another of the colored sisterhood came, presented the stipulated sum—aye, its double, and claimed the Voudou Virgin. The officer not having taken duplicates of it, could not comply with their request. He only saw he had committed an error. If he had set it up at auction, and knocked it down to the highest bidder, the speck [w]ould have told.

They left him, determined to try their right to the relic by a suit at law, and this they did yesterday, before Justice Winter. Hence the commotion on Common street. The details of the suit are too prolix, and would prove uninteresting to our readers. Suffice it to say, that the trial occupied the time of the court throughout the day— that the parties were represented by able counsel, who made learned speeches[,] that the witnesses were numerous, and that juvenile Voudouism triumphed, the Court having decided that the holder of the virgin had the right to retain it.

Source: "The Virgin of the Voudous," *Weekly Delta,* 12 August 1850, 354.

"The Voudou Case Disposed Of," 1863

The great Voudou case was yesterday disposed of by Judge Hughes in the Provost Court. There was a good deal of testimony, but none of a very positive or important character. The officers who made the arrest said that none of the women were positively naked when they entered, though some of them were very lightly dressed. A black girl, who lived in the back part of the yard, testified that as something mysterious was going on in the assembly room, curiosity prompted her to peep in through the back door, which was slightly ajar. She saw some of the women, who were naked, dancing a strange dance. The other women wore lose dresses, most of them *en chemise*, as were the witches who, (see description by Robert Burns,) had a midnight dance in "Alloway's auld haunted kirk." The girl heard her own name mysteriously pronounced, and being satisfied that it was a Voudou meeting, ran away and told the police.

Another witness, a colored girl, who lived in the upper part of the same house, testified that, as she was passing through the yard, one of the sisters offered her something to drink out of a curious, sinister looking bottle. She, however, declined to drink the infernal stuff. Afterwards another of the sisters threw after her some liquid abomination, which frightened her. She pointed out two or three of the dusky sisterhood who were entirely naked, and who were dancing strangely to a wild, weird tune that she never heard before. There was a fascination in the tune and the movements of the dancers which she could not resist. For a time she was completely spell-bound under their combined influence. The assemblage consisted altogether of free colored women and two or three white visitors. There were no slaves there, and witness confessed that considerable enmity existed between the free people of color and the slaves.

Another black slave girl testified that from a back gallery she heard the dancing and singing of the party. One of the sisters, being naked, threw on her a very nasty smelling liquid. Mr. Long asked the witness if she did not hear the accused talking about the Confederates, and the question being objected to, he stated that he was well assured that the object of the meeting was to produce spells and incantations which would restore the Confederates to power here, so that the slaves might no longer be on an equality with them—the free people of color.

This led to some sharp discussion between the prosecuting witness, Long, and the counsel engaged by the dusky sisterhood. It was contended for the defence that no law, either human or divine, had been violated by the assembly; that it was a private social reunion, that it had been grossly misrepresented by some ignorant slave women, as well as by the unfounded surmises of a special officer. We will not report the lengthy arguments offered, though they were replete with the mythological lore of Africa, and therefore greatly instructive. The result alone we give—it was the discharge of all the accused. They went their way rejoicing, some of them doubtless believing that the power of the Voudou charms had softened the judge's heart.

Source: "The Voudou Case Disposed Of," *Daily Picayune,* 2 August 1863, 3.

Two Accounts of Voodoo in Missouri, 1880s–1890s

The Mississippi Valley and Haiti were certainly not the only homes of African Diasporic religions. Moreover, the terms Vodou *and* Voodoo *describe faiths found in several other islands of the Caribbean and portions of Latin American. Within the United States, forms of Voodoo have been reported in Texas, the Florida Keys, Ohio, and elsewhere. In many cases, unknowledgeable observers misidentified conjure as Voodoo. Missouri, however, appears to have had a version of Voodoo all its own.*

Sadly, the sources addressing addressing Missouri Voodoo are exceedingly sparse. The situation resulted in part from the relatively early demise of the religion in that region. By the time that Mary Alicia Owen composed her 1891 account of the faith only two of the believers she encountered continued to refer to themselves as Voodoos, a situation comparable to that of Louisiana Voodoo during the late 1930s. In addition, Missouri's variety of Voodoo never captured the public imagination in the way that New Orleans's version did. With the latter, public awareness generated news articles and books, which in turn attracted additional interest.

The two accounts that follow come from the pens of very different authors. William Wells Brown, author of My Southern Home, *had grown up as a slave. As a child and young man, he had encountered conjure in various forms but only once saw a Voodoo ceremony, in Missouri. His description, unfortunately, did not see print for decades after it occurred, rendering it less than ideal. Mary Alicia Owen, a white amateur folklorist from St. Joseph, Missouri, was closer to the faith she described and conducted interviews with several knowledgeable individuals. As she acknowledged, however, she did not witness many of the rituals she described. Her position as a racial outsider would have made it difficult for her to do so had she desired. Together, Brown and Owen provide an interesting if incomplete description of a largely forgotten manifestation of Voodoo.*

* * *

Forty years ago, in the Southern States, superstition held an exalted place with all classes, but more especially with the blacks and uneducated, or poor, whites. This was shown more clearly in their belief in witchcraft in general, and the devil in particular. To both of these classes, the devil was a real being, sporting a club-foot, horns, tail, and a hump on his back.

The influence of the devil was far greater than that of the Lord. If one of these votaries had stolen a pig, and the fear of the Lord came over him, he would most likely ask the Lord to forgive him, but still cling to the pig. But if the fear of the devil came upon him, in all probability he would drop the pig and take to his heels.

In those days the city of St. Louis had a large number who had implicit faith in Voudooism. I once attended one of their midnight meetings. In the pale rays of the moon the dark outlines of a large assemblage was visible, gathered about a small fire, conversing in different tongues. They were negroes of all ages—women, children, and men. Finally, the noise, was hushed, and the assembled group assumed an attitude of respect. They made way for their queen, and a short, black, old negress came upon the scene, followed by two assistants, one of whom bore a cauldron, and the other, a box.

The cauldron was placed over the dying embers, the queen drew forth, from the folds of her gown, a magic wand, and the crowd formed a ring around her. Her first act was to throw some substance on the fire, the flames shot up with a lurid glare—now it writhed in serpent coils, now it darted upward in forked tongues, and then it gradually transformed itself into a veil of dusky vapors. At this stage, after a certain amount of gibberish and wild gesticulation from the queen, the box was opened, and frogs, lizards, snakes, dog liver, and beef hearts drawn forth and thrown into the cauldron. Then followed more gibberish and gesticulation, when the congregation joined hands, and began the wildest dance imaginable, keeping it up until the men and women sank to the ground from mere exhaustion.

Source: William Wells Brown, *My Southern Home: The South and Its People* (Boston: A.G. Brown, 1880), 68–69.

* * *

I have frequently been asked, "What is Voodoo worship?" frankly I answer, "I don't know." It seems to be like the old woman's recipe for fruit-cake—"a little of this, and a little of that, and a little of most anything, but a heap depends on your judgment, in mixing." "To be strong in de haid"—that is, of great strength of will—is the most important characteristic of a "Cunjerer" or "Voodoo". Never mind what you mix—blood, bones, feathers, grave-dust, herbs, saliva, or hair—it will be powerful or feeble for good or ill in proportion to the dauntless spirit infused by you, the priest or priestess, at the time you represent the god or "Old Master."

How then must we set about obtaining this "strength of head"? Alexander—"King Alexander", as he insists on being called—prescribes the following initiation:

"Go to the woods in the dimness of the morning, and search through them until you find two small saplings growing so near together that when the wind sways them the upper parts of their trunks rub against each other. Climb up to where the swaying trunks have rubbed the bark perfectly smooth. Gather two handfuls of bark, one from each tree (the higher you climb for this purpose the higher your rank in Voodoo craft is destined to be). Take this bark—from what kind of tree it comes is no matter, though it is likely to be hickory—put it into a gallon of rain-water, and boil it until there is but a quart of the decoction. Add a pint of whiskey, and drink it all at one draught if possible, at one sitting, as a necessity of the case. In the old time, in the outlandish country, or Africa, the fermented juice of some herb was used to produce ecstasy, but whiskey answers every purpose. This dram may make the novice very drunk, but no matter for that, he must hide himself and sleep off the effects of it. For nine days after taking it he must keep away from human kind, sleeping in the woods if possible, and eating little or nothing. During this time he must give his mind to a consideration of the power and strangeness of the new life upon which he is about to enter. He must sleep as much as he can, and pay great attention to his dreams. Dreams that come at this time are all fraught with meaning and prophecy. Some object he will dream of he will at once feel is his peculiar fetich or medicine. When the nine days are over he must present himself to the conjurer who is to be his teacher."

Alexander expressly states that a man's teacher should be a woman, and a woman's should be a man. His instructor was a man, but one night he dressed in woman's garb, and the next his master assumed the undivided raiment. Then begins the preparation for full membership in what Alexander, Arthur McManus, John Palmer, Aunt Stacie, Aunt Dorcas, and others call "The Circle". This preparation consists in learning the "Luck numbers" (not lucky numbers), a simple feat, "for seven is a lucky number to cunjer or hoodoo by, but nine is better; three is a good number, but five is better." Four times four is the Great Number. Neither the devil nor his still greater wife can refuse to assist in the working of a charm with that number "quoted in". "Sometimes devils are contrary, just like folks", Alexander explains, "but they can't help giving in to four times four times four." Ten is the unlucky number. At the first lesson the student receives a secret name by which he must call himself when he is working spells. Alexander's name is Eminaw.

The second initiation—the one I received from Aunt Dorcas, a little, lame, poverty-stricken old black woman, whose ability to "fetch luck" evidently did not extend to herself—was as follows:

"Go at midnight to a fallow field, go bare-footed, bare-headed, walking backward, and not looking on the ground. Stoop down in the field, reach your hand behind you, and pull up a weed by the roots. Run home, fling the weed under your bed, and leave it there until sunrise. At sunrise strip off its leaves, make them into a little packet, and wear it under your right arm for nine days. At the close of the ninth day, take the packet, separate the leaves and scatter them to the four winds of heaven, throwing them, a few at a time, over your right shoulder as you turn round and round, so as to have them fall east, south, west, and north. What dreams you have during the nine days are warnings, consequently you must carefully consider the "sign" of them. For instance, if you dream of fire you will have trouble in getting your witch education. If you dream of honey bees you will be a successful conjurer (Dorcas never said "Voodoo"), and receive money and presents. As soon as your leaves are scattered you are ready for lessons." In passing, it may be as well to state that the more leaves there are in your weed, the more exalted will be your rank in sorcery.

After the numbers are learned, a season is given to acquiring knowledge of the value of certain vegetable remedies and poisons, such as snake root, smart weed, red clover, mullein, deadly nightshade, Indian turnip or "Cunjor John", mayapple, etc., together with the proper times (all times are regulated by the moon) of gathering and administering the same. There is nothing mysterious in this much of the profession: any old woman who has an herb-bag has the same simples as a witch, and plants that which is to grow mostly under ground in the dark of the moon, that which is to go to leaves and blossoms when the moon is waxing; gathers all beneficent things when the moon is full, the same as she does.

Afterwards it is imparted that charms and tricks are of four degrees. To the first degree belong the good tricks which are hardest to perform, because it is always harder to do good than evil. Of this class are " luck balls", "jacks", and other fetiches prepared and then endowed with a "familiar or attendant spirit in the name of the Lord". For this class the formulas all begin, "The God before me, God behind me, God be with me." John Palmer said "THE God" always. Alexander said it sometimes. All close with, "I ask it in the name of the Lord or God."

Here is a complete formula as I took it from the lips of the Great Alexander when he was preparing a luck-ball for Mr. Charles G. Leland:

"The God before me, God behind me, God be with me. May this ball bring all good luck to Charles Leland. May it bind down all devils, may it bind down his enemies before him, may it bring them under his feet. May it bring him friends in plenty, may it bring him faithful friends, may it bind them to him. May it bring him honour, may it bring him riches, may it bring him his heart's desire. May it bring him success in everything he undertakes. May it bring him happiness. I call for it in the Name of God."

These kind wishes sound a good deal like a Christian prayer, but you should have seen this ancient, ill-smelling, half-naked, black sinner as he rocked himself to and fro, now muttering in a whisper, now raising his voice to its ordinary conversational pitch as he repeated the good wishes over his materials, four skeins of white yarn, four skeins of white sewing-silk, four leaves and blossoms of red clover, four bits of tinfoil, four little pinches of dust. Over and over he said the words: I couldn't keep count of the times, but he said that as he tied each knot in the yarn and silk, he carefully said his charm four times. Four skeins, four knots in each skein, four times muttered the formula for each knot. And then the whiskey and the saliva, no prayer surely ever had such an accompaniment! The king had a bottle of whiskey beside him, and filled his mouth therefrom every time he tied a knot. Half of it he swallowed, and the other half with a copious addition of saliva he sprayed through his jagged stumps of teeth upon the knots. When all were tied he spat upon the clover, the tinfoil, the dust, and declared that his own strong spirit was imparted with the spittle. When he had gathered the several components into a little ball he spat once more, violently and copiously. "Dar," said he, "dats a mighty strong spurrit. Now to keep it dataway wet it in whiskey once a week."

"Shall I spit on it, or tell Mr. Leland he must?" I asked. He looked at me with scorn, and made reply that we neither of us had any strength. We had nothing to spit out.

Last of all he breathed on the ball and shed, or pretended to shed, a tear. Then the ball was done. It had a spirit in it to work for the one for whom it was named.

"Go to the woods, Charles Leland," commanded Alexander, dangling the ball before his eyes, "for I'm going to send you a long way off, an awful long way, across big water. Go out in the woods now and 'fresh yourself. Do you hear me? Are you going, are you going 'way off? Are you climbing? Are you climbing high?" After a long pause Charles Leland was invited to return. Was asked if he had started back from the woods, if he was drawing nearer, if he was back in the ball.

To all this "Charles Leland" replied by causing the ball to dance and spin in the most delirious manner, and by a murmur sounding now far now near, something like the coo of the wood-dove, but it was oo-oo, oo-oo, not foo-ool, foo-ool, as the dove calls to those who penetrate miasmatic woods. Then there was another shower-bath of whiskey, after which the ball was wrapped, first in tinfoil then in a silk rag. I was warned at the time to tie no knots in the wrappings: such knots would tie the spirit up helpless. This thing is to be worn under the right arm. . . .

To the second class belong the bad tricks, charms and fetiches made in the name of the devil: those queer little linen, woollen, or fur bags, or tiny bottles filled with broken glass, bits of flannel, hair, ashes, alum, grave-dust, jay or whippoorwill feathers, bits of bone, parts of snakes, toads, newts, squirrels, fingers of strangled babes and frog-legs—this last component being especially necessary, because in the old time the devil made the moon to illuminate the night for the convenience of his votaries. As the Good Man had used up all the material of the universe in his creations, the devil or Bad Man took a frog, skinned it, and made it into a moon.

To the third class belong all that pertains to the body, such as nails, teeth, hair, saliva, tears, perspiration, dandruff, scabs of sores even, and garments worn next the person. These are used in conjurations and charms for good or ill, not alone, but with other things. I will illustrate their use by a story told me by Alexander. He said, "I could save or ruin you if I could get hold of so much as one eye-winker or the peeling of one freckle." Then he went on to make his meaning clear by giving a scrap of biography.

Just before the civil war, in the days when he was a slave, he lived for a short time in Southern Missouri, "nigh de big ribber." He had an enemy, a conjurer also. The enemy affected friendship, invited him to his cabin, and offered him refreshments, of which Alexander refused to partake. "Dar wuz spiders in de dumplins and hell in de cakes," he explained, "and I dassent eat 'em, but I 'greed ter stay all night."

Both men lay down on a bed on the floor. The guest pretended to fall asleep. Presently the host cautiously raised himself up and peeped into the face of the other, to see if he was asleep. There was bright firelight in the room, cast from the great open fireplace where many dry logs were burning. Alexander breathed heavily, and, as he said, held his face like a stone, though he was watching through a crack in his eyelids. The host reached a pair of scissors towards the sleeper's head. Alexander stretched out his hand and struck down the advancing arm, at the same time muttering a curse upon the musquitoes.

Both lay quiet for a while, then the scene was re-enacted. Again and again this was repeated, and all this time each man was willing with all the strength that was in him that the other should sleep. Finally Alexander prevailed. "I'd been a cunjurer longer than he had, and my will was made up strong," said the victor.

While his host slept, Alexander arose, took his (the host's shoes) and scraped the inside of the soles—they had been worn without stockings. Then he took the man's coat and scraped the collar where it had rubbed his neck at the edge of his hair. The fire was out then, and he had no light but a little grey streak of dawn coming through the chinks of the wall. He stole forth with the scrapings, put them into a gourd with red clover leaves, alum, snake root, and the leaves and stalks of a may-apple. Then he put the gourd into the river and said, "In Devil's name go, and may he whose life is in you follow you." The very next week the unfortunate "cunjered" conjurer was sold and sent down the river. "But no one could touch me," said the old man, "for I cunjered master and all of 'em."

The fourth class is composed of "commanded things", such as honey locust thorns, parts of "sticks", sand, mud from a crawfish hole, wax from a new beehive, things that are neither lucky nor unlucky in themselves, but may be made so. No charms are said over them: they are merely "commanded" to do a certain work. Take, for instance, the locust thorn, used innocently enough as a hairpin or dress-fastener, but which when "commanded" proves a terrible little engine of mischief. A small rude representation of the human figure, made of mud from a crawfish-hole or wax from a beehive, when named by a conjurer and pierced by a thorn of his implanting, is supposed to make the man for whom it is named deaf, dumb, blind, crazy, lame, consumptive, etc., according to the place pierced. Worse still, the one killed or maimed will after death "walk" till judgment day. A prolific maker of uneasy ghosts is the "commanded thorn".

After each lesson, both pupil and teacher of witchery get drunk on whiskey or by swallowing tobacco-smoke. I feel it necessary, however, to state that I was an honourable exception to the rule, although I did find it necessary to set forth spirituous refreshment for my teachers. I must add to this, that maids and bachelors do not progress very far in the degrees of Voodooism.

After the preliminaries I have mentioned, the pupil begins to make some acquaintance with Grandfather Rattlesnake and the dance held in his honour. The origin of the dance was in this wise:

In the old times Grandfather Rattlesnake and his sister lived together; so say Mymee and a dozen other darkies of my acquaintance. The sister's disposition was as sweet as his was bitter. As he was very wise, many men and animals came to him for instruction, which he gave freely; but as he took leave of a disciple he always stung him. The sister, in the goodness of her heart, immediately healed the poisoned wretch, who then went off with all the serpent wisdom he had acquired. Finally Grandfather became so enraged that he changed his sister into snakeweed. As such she still heals, but not so freely as formerly, for she cannot go to the afflicted: they must come to her.

Since that time men, warned by the sister's fate, have not willingly approached Grandfather very nearly. They find it best to dance about him, and thus absorb the shrewdness and cunning he really cannot help giving out. As a further precaution they render him almost torpid by giving him a young rat, bird, or toad just before the dance begins.

The dance itself has no method in its madness, I have been told. The participants, who are not all Voodoos by any means, have been on short rations or none for nine days; they are full of tobacco-smoke or whiskey, and their nerves are still further excited by fear of the snake and the god or devil he represents. They howl in any key, without words or rhythmic sounds, the same as they do at a religious revival or camp-meeting. Sometimes they circle wildly about, with their hands clasping those of the persons next them; sometimes they jump up and down in one spot, while they make indecent gestures or twine their arms about their own naked bodies. They keep up this exercise until the greater number of them fall exhausted, when they have a rest, followed by a feast of black dog and, Arthur McManus says, kid. Four conjurers—two men and two women—cook the meat and distribute it.

The fire-dance is for strength of body, as the snake-dance is for strength of mind. I have never heard of anything being eaten at this dance. The same ceremony, or lack of ceremony, in the dancing is observed.

Any wood may be used for the fire except sassafras or maple. During the dances to the moon they chant—what I know not—and circle round with rhythmic motion, which sometimes changes into a rapid trot. I have never seen a moon-dance, nor more than a glimpse of the others, but I am sure my information is correct. The reason I am sure, I may state in parenthesis, is because every participant in the dances denies that he has been present, but accuses his fellow-sinner, with whom he has had a quarrel, and described what the offender has stated he did: "When he wuz thes so drunk that his tongue runned off with him." The full moon is by common consent given as the time for these exercises. What the dance means I do not know, and cannot find out. . . .

The dances of the ghosts of the departed conjurers also take place at the, full moon. All I know about this is that Aunt Mymee was said by other negroes to be able to appear in two places at once, to take any shape she pleased, and to know what people were saying and doing when they were miles away. This, they said, was because she had found out where these "hants" met, had watched their exercises to their close, and had asked and received her heart's desire. Anyone as bold as she is may ask and receive aid of these shades, it is said. The snake- and fire-dances may take place any time: that is, anywhere that policemen are not likely to come. The moon-dance must be in an open space in the woods.

There is a sacrifice of a black hen to the moon. Alexander said that Arthur-McManus had no better sense than to sacrifice a black hen and white rooster, and then wait for luck when he ought to be making power for himself. I do know that all negroes, and not a few white people who have been raised with them, believe that black hens, split open and applied to the body warm, will cure typhoid or bilious fever, and stay the progress of cancer.

For sacrifice, Alexander says the way to kill the hen is to slit her side and let the entrails protrude, then turn her loose; she will run a little way, then jump up into the air, crow like a cock, and die instantly without any struggle. I asked what was then done with her. He said, "Nothing." . . .

A dance is not an initiation: that is done with leaves or bark, as I have said. I don't know what a moon-dance is for, but the other two are considered as remedies rather than ceremonies. As for getting a male friend to do anything for me, I've never found one who would entertain the suggestion for a moment. . . .

My knowledge of Voodoos began at an early age. Aunt Mymee Whitehead, or, as some called her, "Aunt Mymee Monroe", was my nurse. She has always wished it understood that she is the daughter of the devil. Her mother was a Guinea woman, a conjurer also, who inspired such fear and hatred that the people rose against her to kill her. She fled on board a slave-ship, and was brought to this country—to what part Aunt Mymee did not know. Soon after landing Mymee was born, and was sent with her mother to Kentucky. When ten or twelve years old they were brought to Missouri. I may remark here that Aunt Mymee, pure-blooded Guinea, and Alexander, half Guinea and half Cherokee Indian, are the only two conjurers I ever heard speak of themselves as Voodoos. The others, while practising the same rites, invariably speak of themselves as Witches, men or women, or conjurers. Their humble admirers, however, frequently speak of them as "Voodoos", and of their deeds as "Noodoos".

Aunt Mymee gave me the first glimpse of her secret business by importuning me to get from my grandmother some amaranth seeds. When I insisted on knowing what she wanted with them, she acknowledged she wished to make them into a little cake which would make any who ate it love the one who handed it to him. That sounded reasonable enough to anyone as fond of all sorts of sweeties as I was, so I procured the seeds, and had the cake made up.

Not long after I heard other servants of the family say that Mymee had surely conjured me, for I followed at her heels like a dog that had eaten shoebread.

Afterwards, partly by coaxing and partly by watching, I learned to make a trick or two, and came to know of the existence of some being called Samunga. When you go for mud, call out

"Minnie, no, no Samunga,
Sangee see sa soh Samunga."

Perhaps this may be the Gounja of the Hottentots.

Source: Mary Alicia Owen, "Among the Voodoos," in *The International Folk-lore Congress 1891: Papers and Transactions* (London: David Nutt, 1892), 230–239, 241–242.

Reports of Marie Laveau's Death, 1881

The death of Marie Laveau just before St. John's Eve in 1881 attracted considerable attention. New Orleans's major newspapers carried lengthy obituaries as did the New York Times. *In many cases, the press treated her kindly, lauding her good works and praising her character. Not all agreed with such approving comments. The profound contrast between the two articles that follow says much about public opinion in regard to Voodoo and its practitioners during the late 19th century.*

Inaccuracies in reporting, common enough today, were even more prevalent during the 19th century. Scholar Carolyn Morrow Long, author of A New Orleans Voudou Priestess, *conclusively refutes the first article's statements that Laveau was nearly one hundred years old and that she had fifteen children. Divergent spellings, such as* Lavaux *for* Laveau *and* Voudou *for* Voodoo, *are not mistakes but reflect a time when spelling was not quite so standardized as it is at present. In fact, several scholars prefer to use* Voudou *to describe the Mississippi Valley religion.*

"Death of Marie Laveau," 1881

A Woman with a Wonderful History, Almost a Century Old, Carried to the Tomb Yesterday Evening.

Those who have passed by the quaint old house on St. Ann, between Rampart and Burgundy streets, with the high, frail looking fence in front over which a tree or two is visible, have, till within the last few years, noticed through the upon gateway a decrepid old lady with snow white hair and a smile of peace and contentment lighting up her golden features. For a few years past, she has been missed from her accustomed place. The feeble old lady lay upon her bed with her daughter and grandchildren around her ministering to her wants.

On Wednesday, the invalid sank into the sleep which knows no waking. Those whom she had befriended crowded into the little room where she was exposed, in order to obtain a last look at the features, smiling even in death, of her who had been so kind to them.

At 5 o'clock yesterday evening Marie Laveau was buried in her family tomb in St. Louis Cemetery No. 1. Her remains were followed to the grave by a large concourse of people, the most prominent and the most humble joining in paying their last respects to the dead. Father Mignot conducted the funeral services.

Marie Laveau was born ninety-eight years ago. Her father was a rich planter, who was prominent in all publics affairs, and served in the Legislature of this State. Her mother was Marguerite Henry, and her grandmother was Marguerite Semard. All were beautiful women of color. The gift of beauty was hereditary in the family, and Marie inherited it in the fullest degree. When she was twenty-five years old she was led to the altar by Jacques Paris, a carpenter. The marriage took place at the St. Louis Cathedral, Pere Antoine, of beloved memory, conducting the services, and Mr. Mazureau, the famous lawyer, acting as witness. A year afterwards Mr. Paris disappeared, and no one knows to this day what became of him. After waiting a year for his return she married Capt. Christophe Glapion. The latter was also very prominent here, and served with distinction in the battalion of men of San Domingo, under D'Aquin, with Jackson in the war of 1815.

Fifteen children were the result of their marriage. Only one of these is now alive. Capt. Glapion died gravely regretted, on the 26th of June, 1855. Five years afterwards Marie Laveau became ill, and has been sick ever since, her indisposition becoming more pronounced and painful with the last ten years.

Besides being very beautiful Marie was also very wise. She was skillful in the practice of medicine and was acquainted with the valuable healing qualities of indigenous herbs.

She was very successful as a nurse, wonderful stories being told of her exploits at the sick bed. In yellow fever and cholera epidemics she was always called upon to nurse the sick, and always responded promptly. Her skill and knowledge earned her the friendship and approbation of those sufficiently cultivated, but the ignorant attributed her success to unnatural means, and held her in constant dread.

Notably in 1853 a committee of gentlemen, appointed at a mass meeting held at Globe Hall, waited on Marie and requested her on behalf of the people to minister to the fever-stricken. She went out and fought the pestilence where it was thickest, and many alive to-day owe their salvation to her devotion.

Not alone to the sick was Marie a blessing. To help a fellow creature in distress she considered a priceless privilege. She was born in the house where she died. Her mother lived and died there before her. The unassuming cottage has stood for a century and a half. It was built by the first French settlers of adobé, and not a brick was employed in its construction. When it was erected it was considered the handsomest building in the neighborhood. Rampart street was not then in existence, being the skirt of a wilderness, and latterly a line of entrenchment. Notwithstanding the decay of her little mansion, Marie made the sight of it pleasant to the unfortunate. At any time of night or day any one was welcome to food and lodging.

Those in trouble had but to come to her and she would make their cause her own after undergoing great sacrifices in order to assist them.

Besides being charitable, Marie was also very pious and took delight in strengthening the allegiance of souls to the church. She would sit with the condemned in their last moments and endeavor to turn their last thoughts to Jesus. Whenever a prisoner excited her pity Marie would labor incessantly to obtain his pardon, or at least a commutation of sentence, and she generally succeeded.

A few years ago, before she lost control of her memory, she was rich in interesting reminiscences of the early history of the city. She spoke often of the young American Governor Claiborne, and told how the child-wife he brought with him from Tennessee died of the yellow fever shortly after his arrival, and with the dead babe upon her bosom was buried in a corner of the old American Cemetery. She spoke sometimes of the strange little man with the wonderful bright eyes, Aaron Burr, who was so polite and so dangerous. She loved to talk of Lafayette, who visited New Orleans over half a century ago. The great Frenchman came to see her at her house and kissed her on the forehead at parting.

She remembered the old French general, Humbert, and was one of the few colored people who escorted to the tomb, long since dismantled, in the Catholic cemetery, the withered and grizzly remains of the hero of Castelbar. Probably she knew Father Antoine better than any living in those days—for he the priest and she the nurse met at the dying bedsides of hundreds of people—she to close the faded eyes in death and he to waft the soul over the river to the realms of eternal joy.

All in all Marie Laveau was a most wonderful woman. Doing good for the sake of doing good alone, she obtained no reward, oft times meeting with prejudice and loathing, she was nevertheless contented and did not flag in her work. She always had the cause of the people at heart, and was with them in all things. During the late rebellion she proved her loyalty to the South at every opportunity and freely dispensed help to those who suffered in defense of the "lost cause." Her last days were spent surrounded by sacred pictures and other evidences of religion, and she died with a firm trust in heaven. While God's sunshine plays around the little tomb where her remains are buried, by the side of her second husband, and her sons and daughters, Marie Laveau's name will not be forgotten in New Orleans.

Source: "Death of Marie Laveau," *Daily Picayune,* June 17, 1881, 8.

"A Sainted Woman," 1881

Who has been stuffing our contemporaries in the matter of the defunct voudou queen, Marie Lavaux? For they have undoubtedly been stuffed, nay crammed, by some huge practical joker. The informant for all is evidently the same, as the stories of the Picayune, Item and States consist admirably in their uniform departure from historical fact. According to the accounts of these esteemed but deluded contemporaries, Marie Lavaux was a saint, who had spent a life of self-sacrifice and abnegation in doing good to her fellow mortals, and whose immaculate spirit was all but too pure for this world.

One of them goes even so far in his enthusiasm as to publish a touching interview with the sainted woman, in which the reporter boasts of having deposited a chaste kiss on her holy forehead. We are sorry for that reporter if his story is true, for, if he really believes it all, his only consolation is in the fact that greenness is the color of hope. These fictions had one good result, for they created a vast amount of merriment among the old creole residents, and in fact among all men of mature age who knew the social history of their time in New Orleans.

The fact is that the least said about Marie Lavaux's sainted life, etc., the better. She was, up to an advanced age, the prime mover and soul of the indecent orgies of the ignoble Voudous; and to her influence may be attributed the fall of many a virtuous woman. It is true that she had redeeming traits. It is a peculiar quality of the old race of creole negroes that they are invariably kind hearted and charitable. Marie Lavaux made no exception. But talk about her morality and kiss her sainted brow—*pouah!!!*

Source: "A Sainted Woman," *Democrat*, June 18, 1881, 2.

Mississippi Valley Voodoo Songs, 1885 and undated

Music is a vital part of the ceremonies of both Vodou and Voodoo. For an excellent collection of Haitian songs, see Benjamin Hebblethwaite's Vodou Songs in Haitian Creole and English *(2012). Extant examples from Louisiana are sparse but not unknown. The following are some of them. Most were, unsurprisingly, originally performed in a local version of French. For this reason, the original words are followed by English translations.*

Sadly, the context of some of these songs has been lost, but there are others about which we have some substantial information. The first selection was performed by a male Voodooisant in the presence of Queen Malvina Latour during a St. John's Eve ceremony in about 1884. Another is the brief chant referring to dying in a lake, Pontchartrain in this case, the shores of which were a major site of Voodoo ceremonies. The invocation to St. Peter that follows is readily recognizable as the New Orleans equivalent to a Haitian chant calling on Papa Legba to open communication with the lwa. A similar song calling on Liba (the Voodoo name for St. Peter) appears in the selection from Helen Pitkin's Angel by Brevet *(1904), included in this Primary Document section).*

"I Will Wander in the Desert"

Original

 Mallé couri dan déser,
 Mallé marché dan savane,
 Mallé marché su piquan doré,
 Mallé oir ça ya di moin!

 Sangé moin dan l'abitation ci la la?
 Mo gagnain soutchien la Louisiane,
 Mallé oir ça ya di moin!

Translation

 I will wander into the desert,
 I will march through the prairie,

I will walk upon the golden thorn—
Who is there who can stop me?
To change me from this plantation?
I have the support of Louisiana—
Who is there who can resist me?

Source: Writers of the New Orleans Press, *Historical Sketch Book and Guide to New Orleans and Environs* (New York: Will H. Coleman, 1885), 231.

Original, Version 1

Yé n'a pas comme moin,
Yé n'a pas comme moin,
Yé n'a pas comme moin,
La poule a moin,
Yé n'a pas comme moin,
Yé n'a pas comme moin,
Yé n'a pas comme moin,
La poule a moin.

Allez vielle negrèsse,
Allez vielle negrèsse,
Allez vielle negrèsse,
Pour moi.

Original, Version 2

Yé ná pas com me moin,
Yé ná pas com me moin,
Yé ná pas com me moin,
La pauvre a moin.
Yé ná pas com me moin,

Yé ná pas com me moin,
Yé ná pas com me moin,
La pauvre a moin.

Al-lez vielle ne-gresse,
Al-lez vielle ne-gresse,
Al-lez vielle ne-gresse,
Pauvre moin!

Translation, Version 1

There are none like mine,
There are none like mine,

There are none like mine,
That hen of mine,
There are none like mine,
There are none like mine,
There are none like mine,
That hen of mine.

Go way old negress,
Go way old negress,
Go way old negress,
For me.

Translation, Version 2

There is none like me,
There is none like me,
There is none like me,
Poor me!
There is none like me,
There is none like me,
There is none like me,
Poor me!

Go old negress,
Go old negress,
Go old negress,
Poor me!

Source: Version 1 from Maud H. Wallace, [Lala], Federal Writers Project, 1940, Northwestern State University of Louisiana, Watson Memorial Library, Cammie G. Henry Research Center, box 3-C-1, folder 43, 6. Version 2 text and translation from Michinard and Maude H. Wallace, "Song Sung by Lala, the Voodoo Queen," Federal Writers' Project, 1940, Northwestern State University of Louisiana, Watson Memorial Library, Cammie G. Henry Research Center, folder 3, 1–2.

* * *

Original

Mo Marches sue a epigne
Mom Marchez Sur an neguille
Peut Piscon qui Moin

Translation

I am walking on a pin
I am walking on a needle,
Which one stings the least?

Source: Dauphin, interview, New Orleans, LA, Louisiana Writers' Project, folder 588, Federal Writers' Project, Cammie G. Henry Research Center, Watson Memorial Library, Northwestern State University, Natchitoches, LA, 1.

* * *

Original

> Pele moa Batis
> Lioulay oua, lioulay ous Batis
> > Seyay moa
> Ou don Batis, lioulay oua,
> Il ay bel Batis
> > Seyay moa
> Condui moa Batis
> > Seyay moa
>
> Pele moa Gustine
> Lioulay oua, lioulay oua Gustine
> > Seyay moa
> Ou don Gustine, lioulay oua,
> Il ay bel Gustine
> > Seyay moa
> Condui moa Gustine
> > Seyay moa

Translation

> Call me Baptist
> I want to see, I want to see Baptist
> > Try me
> Where is Baptist, I want to see him
> He is good looking Baptist
> > Try me
> Lead me Baptist
> > Try me
>
> Call me Gustine
> I want to see, I want to see Gustine
> > Try me
> Where is Gustine, I want to see him
> He is good looking Gustine
> > Try me
> Lead me Gustine
> > Try me

Source: Charles Raphael, interview by Hazel Breaux, New Orleans, LA, Louisiana Writers' Project, box 3-C-1, folder 25, Federal Writers' Project, Cammie G. Henry Research Center, Watson Memorial Library, Northwestern State University, Natchitoches, LA, 4.

* * *

Original

Nous allons mourrir dans ce lac, c'est vrai! Nous allons mourrir dans ce lac, c'est vrai!

Translation

We are going to die in this lake, t'is true! We are going to die in this lake, t'is true!

Source: Michinard, "Marie Laveau," Federal Writers' Project, 1940, Northwestern State University of Louisiana, Watson Memorial Library, Cammie G. Henry Research Center, box 3-C-1, folder 25, 1.

* * *

>St. Peter, St. Peter open the door
>I um callin you, come to me
>St. Peter, St. Peter (repeat)

Source: Mary Washington, "Marie Laveau," interview by Robert McKinney, New Orleans, LA, Louisiana Writers' Project, box 3-C-1, folder 25, Federal Writers' Project, Cammie G. Henry Research Center, Watson Memorial Library, Northwestern State University, Natchitoches, LA, 88.

* * *

"Chaute par les Voudou sur la place Congo"

Original

>Conduit moin la reine
>Conduit moin dans château le roi
>Conduit moin dans château le roi
>Conduit mon dans palais mo roi
>
>Si mo mourri jordi comme demain
>Voyé dit yé vini voir moin
>
>Conduit moin la reine
>Conduit moin dans château le roi
>Conduit moin dans château le roi
>Conduit mon dans palais mo roi

Si mo mourri jordi comme demain
Mouchoir madra méné moin couri

Conduit moin la reine
Conduit moin dans château le roi
Conduit moin dans château le roi
Conduit mon dans palais mo roi

Tout péche oui, que mo fait
Mo vole femme qui té pas pou moin

Conduit moin la reine
Conduit moin dans château le roi
Conduit moin dans château le roi
Conduit mon dans palais mo roi

Si vous voir nainaine zabo
Boyez dit li vini voir moin

Conduit moin la reine
Conduit moin dans château le roi
Conduit moin dans château le roi
Conduit mon dans palais mo roi

"Song of the Voudous on Congo Square"

Translation

Lead me to the Queen
Lead me to the King's Castle
Lead me to the King's Castle
Lead me to my King's Palace

Should I die to-day as to-morrow
Send tell them come see me

Lead me to the Queen
Lead me to the King's Castle
Lead me to the King's Castle
Lead me to my King's Palace

Should I die to-day as to-morrow
Bandana kerchief led me to it

Lead me to the Queen
Lead me to the King's Castle
Lead me to the King's Castle
Lead me to my King's Palace

All sins yes, that I committed—
Me stole woman that was'nt for me.

Lead me to the Queen
Lead me to the King's Castle
Lead me to the King's Castle
Lead me to my King's Palace

Should you see nainaine Zabo
Send tell her, come see me.

Lead me to the Queen
Lead me to the King's Castle
Lead me to the King's Castle
Lead me to my King's Palace

Source: Michinard, "Song of the Voudous on Congo Square," Federal Writers' Project, 1940, Northwestern State University of Louisiana, Watson Memorial Library, Cammie G. Henry Research Center, folder 3, 1–4.

Spenser St. John and Vodou, 1889

In the following selections, Spenser St. John, a 19th-century British diplomat to Haiti, gives his impressions of Vodou. His account, as one should expect, is colored by the racial and cultural assumptions of the era. St. John saw the religion as superstitious barbarism, considering it a blot upon the Haitian nation and a barrier to its betterment. Though he recognized that it was the faith of the majority of the people, he believed that the Haitian government should work diligently to suppress it.

At the heart of St. John's interpretation was his belief that Vodou sometimes involved murder and cannibalism. The centerpiece of his contention is an account of a murder involving a group of Vodouisants, including two oungans and a mambo, who reportedly sacrificed a child and fed upon the body. The killers were quickly found out. Following a trial, eight of them were executed by firing squad. To back up his assertion that this crime was not an isolated incident, St. John provided additional tales of human sacrifices. Sadly, St. John's description attracted considerable attention in the English-speaking world and has defined stereotypes about Vodou ever since.

What is one to make of such stories? On the one hand, as St. John noted, human sacrifice and cannibalism were not part of the variety of Vodou practiced by most Haitians. It is not a part of the modern faith at all. In addition, the incident on which St. John focused is the only well-documented case of its type, and aspects of the testimony on which his description was based are open to dispute. The others he addresses are based on highly suspect information or simply rumor. On the other hand, even if one considers human sacrifice a rare but real part of early Vodou, it should not be used to condemn the religion as a whole. After all, human sacrifice was once part of many religions. Peoples as diverse as the Incas, Canaanites, and Celts at one time embraced it as the highest form of worship.

* * *

When the news reached Paris of the massacres in Port-au-Prince of the mulattoes by orders of the black President Soulouque in April 1849, it is said that Louis Napoleon took the opportunity of saying at a public reception, in presence of the sable representative of Hayti, "Haïti, Haïti! pays de barbares." Had he known all the particulars relating to Vaudoux worship and cannibalism, he would have been still more justified in so expressing himself.

There is no subject of which it is more difficult to treat than Vaudoux worship and the cannibalism that too often accompanies its rites. Few living out of the Black Republic are aware of the extent to which it is carried, and if I insist at length upon the subject, it is in order to endeavour to fix attention on this frightful blot, and thus induce enlightened Haytians to take measures for its extirpation, if that be possible.*

It is certain that no people are more sensitive to foreign public opinion than the Haytians, and they therefore endeavour to conceal by every means this evidence of the barbarism of their fellow-countrymen. It is, however, but the story of the foolish ostrich over again; every foreigner in Hayti knows that cannibalism exists, and that the educated classes endeavour to ignore it instead of devising means to eradicate it.

The only Governments that endeavoured to grapple with the evil were those of President Geffrard and President Boisrond-Canal, and probably they in some measure owe their fall to this action on their part.

The first question naturally asked is, "Who is tainted by the Vaudoux worship?" I fear the answer must be, "Who is not ?" This does not necessarily imply that they are tainted with cannibalism, as I shall hereafter explain. It is notorious that the Emperor Soulouque was a firm believer, and that the mulatto general Therlonge was one of its high priests, and in his younger days used to appear in a scarlet robe performing antics in the trees. A late Prime Minister, whose bloody deeds will be an everlasting reproach to his memory, was said to be a chief priest of the sect, and many others whom I will not at present indicate.

If persons so high placed can be counted among its votaries, it may be readily believed that the masses are given up to this brutalising worship. During the reign of Soulouque, a priestess was arrested for having performed a sacrifice too openly; when about to be conducted to prison, a foreign bystander remarked aloud that

---

*One thing I wish distinctly to state, that I never heard of any mulatto, except Generals Salnave and Therlonge, who was mixed up with the cannibalism of the Vaudoux, nor of any black educated in Europe.

probably she would be shot. She laughed and said, "If I were to beat the sacred drum, and march through the city, not one, from the Emperor downwards, but would humbly follow me." She was sent to jail, but no one ever heard that she was punished. . . .

To explain the phrase of "the goat without horns," I must notice that there are two sects which follow the Vaudoux worship—those who only delight in the blood and flesh of white cocks and spotless white goats at their ceremonies, and those who are not only devoted to these, but on great occasions call for the flesh and blood of the "goat without horns," or human victims.

When Hayti was still a French colony Vaudoux worship flourished, but there is no distinct mention of human sacrifices in the accounts transmitted to us. . . .

But the incidents I am about to relate formed the subject of a trial before a criminal court, and are to be found detailed in the official journal of the period, and I was present during the two days that the inquiry lasted.

It occurred during the Presidency of General Geffrard, the most enlightened ruler that that unfortunate country possessed since the time of President Boyer; it too plainly proved that the fetish worship of the negroes of Africa had not been forgotten by their descendants, nor to be denied by any one, and the attention of the whole country was drawn to the subject of cannibalism. As the case greatly interested me, I made the most careful inquiries and followed it in its most minute particulars. It is worth while relating the whole story in its disgusting details, as it is one of the truth of which there is not a shadow of a doubt.

A couple of miles to the west of Port-au-Prince lies the village of Bizoton, in which there lived a man named Congo Pellé. He had been a labourer, a gentleman's servant, an idler, who was anxious to improve his position without any exertion on his own part. In this dilemma he addressed himself to his sister Jeanne, who had long been connected with the Vaudoux—was, in fact, the daughter of a priestess, and herself a well-known Mamanloi—and it was settled between them that about the new year some sacrifice should be offered to propitiate the serpent. A more modest man would have been satisfied with a white cock or a white goat, but on this solemn occasion it was thought better to offer a more important sacrifice. A consultation was held with two Papalois, Julien Nicolas and Floréal Apollon, and it was decided that a female child should be offered as a sacrifice, and the choice fell on Claircine, the niece of Jeanne and Congo.

This was the account given in court; but it appears also to be an undoubted fact that human sacrifices are offered at Easter, Christmas Eve, New Year's Eve, and more particularly on Twelfth Night, or *Les Fêtes des Rois*.

On the 27th December 1863, Jeanne invited her sister, the mother of Claircine, to accompany her to Port-au-Prince, and the child, a girl of about twelve years of age, was left at home with Congo. Immediate advantage was taken of the mother's absence, and Claircine was conducted to the house of Julien, and from thence to that of Floréal, where she was bound, and hidden under the altar in a neighbouring temple. In the evening, the mother, returning home, asked for her child, when her brother Congo told her it had strayed away; a pretended search was made by those in the plot, and another Papaloi was consulted. This man told the mother not to be uneasy, as the Maître d'Eau, or the spirit of the water, had taken her daughter, but that in a short time her child would be restored to her. The woman believed, or pretended to believe, this story, and, by the papa's recommendation, burnt caudles before the altar of the Virgin Mary for the prompt return of her offspring,—another proof of the strange mingling of Catholicism and Vaudoux worship.

On the evening of the 31st of December a large party assembled at the house of Jeanne to await the arrival of the child, who had remained for four days bound under the altar. When the chief members of the plot came to the temple to bring her out, she, guessing the fate reserved for her, gave two or three piercing shrieks, which were soon stifled, and, gagged and bound, she was carried to Jeanne's house, where preparations were made for the human sacrifice. She was thrown on the ground, her aunt holding her by the waist, whilst the Papaloi pressed her throat, and the others held her legs and arms; her struggles soon ceased, as Floréal had succeeded in strangling her. Then Jeanne handed him a large knife, with which he cut off Claircine's head, the assistants catching the blood in a jar; then Floréal is said to have inserted an instrument under the child's skin, and detached it from the body. Having succeeded in flaying their victim, the flesh was cut from the bones, and placed in large wooden dishes; the entrails and skin being buried near to the cottage. The whole party then started for Floréal's house, carrying the remains of their victim with them. On their arrival Jeanne rang a little bell, and a procession was formed, the head borne aloft, and a sacred song sung. Then preparations were made for a feast.

Roused by the noise caused by the arrival, a woman and girl sleeping in another chamber looked through some chinks in the wall and saw all that passed,— Jeanne cooking the flesh with Congo beans, small and rather bitter (*pois congo*), whilst Floréal put the head into a pot with yams to make some soup. Whilst the others were engaged in the kitchen, one of the women present, Roséide Sumera, urged by the fearful appetite of a cannibal, cut from the child's palm a piece of flesh and ate it raw (this I heard her avow in open court).

The cooking over, portions of the prepared dish were handed round, of which all present partook; and the soup being ready, it was divided among the assistants, who deliberately drank it. The night was passed in dancing, drinking, and debauchery. In the morning the remains of the flesh were warmed up, and the two witnesses who had watched the proceedings were invited to join in the repast: the young woman confessed that she had accepted the invitation, but the girl did not.

Not satisfied with this taste of human flesh, the priests now put the young girl, who had watched their proceedings from a neighbouring room, in the place of Claircine, and she was bound in the temple, to be sacrificed on Twelfth Night. It came out in evidence that she had been decoyed to the house for that purpose, and that the young woman who was sleeping in the same room was in reality in charge of her.

Fortunately for her, the inquiries which Claircine's mother had made on her first arrival home and the disappearance of the second girl had roused the attention of an officer of police, and a search being made, the freshly-boiled skull of the murdered girl was found among the bushes near Floréal's house, where careless impunity had induced the assassins to throw it. A further search led to the discovery of the girl bound under the altar and the other remains of Claircine.

Fourteen persons were arrested, against eight of whom sufficient evidence could be obtained, and these were sent to prison to answer for their crime before a criminal court. The trial commenced on the 4th of February 1864, and lasted two days. Incidents were related in the course of the evidence which showed how the lower classes are sunk in ignorance and barbarity, and renewed the proofs, if any fresh proofs were required, that the Vaudoux worship is associated by them with the ceremonies of the Catholic religion, even the Papalois recommending the burning of tapers in the Christian churches, and the having crosses and pictures of the Virgin Mary strangely mingled on their altars with the objects of their superstition.

In the dock we saw the eight prisoners, four men and four women, with faces of the ordinary Haytian type, neither better nor worse. Their names were: men—Julian Nicholas, a Papaloi; Floréal Apollon, another Papaloi; Guerrier François and Congo Pellé: the women—Jeanne Pellé, a Mamanloi, Roséide Sumera, Neréide François, and Beyard Prosper. Some had been servants to foreigners, others had been gardeners and washerwomen. The French procedure is observed in all trials in Hayti, and to an Englishman the procedure, as practised in that republic, is contrary to the first principles of justice. The prisoners were bullied, cajoled, cross-questioned, in order to force avowals, in fact, to make them state in open court what they were said to have confessed in their preliminary examinations. I can never forget the manner in which the youngest female prisoner turned to the public prosecutor and said, "Yes, I did confess what you assert, but remember how cruelly I was beaten before I said a word;" and it was well known that all the prisoners had at first refused to speak, thinking that the Vaudoux would protect them, and it required the frequent application of the club to drive this belief out of their heads. That prisoners are tortured to make them confess is known to be a common practice in Hayti.

However this may have been in the present case, there, on a table before the judge, was the skull of the murdered girl, and in a jar the remains of the soup and the calcined bones; and the avowals of the prisoners in court and the testimony of the witnesses were too clear and circumstantial to leave a doubt as to their criminality.

As I have remarked, I was in court during the two days' trial, and I never was present at one where the judge conducted himself with greater dignity. His name was Lallemand, and he was one of the few magistrates who had the courage to do justice, even when political passion would have condemned victims unheard.

Among those who gave their evidence was the young girl who witnessed the ceremonies, and for whom was reserved the fate of Claircine. The judge called her up to his side, and gently asked her to tell the court what she had seen; but, with a frightened look, she started and burst into tears, and the judge, looking up sharply, saw the prisoners making the most diabolical grimaces at the poor child. He then turned round to the jury and said, in view of the intimidation attempted, he would do what was not strictly regular; the child should whisper the story to him, and he would repeat it to the court. He placed her with her back to the prisoners, and putting his arm round her, drew her gently to him, and said in a soft voice, "Tell me, *chère*, what occurred." The girl, in a very low tone, began her testimony, but the silence in court was so profound, that not a word she uttered was lost, and, almost without faltering, she told her story in all its horrible details; but her nerves then gave way so completely, that she had to be taken out of court, and could not be again produced to answer some questions the jury wished to ask.

Then the young woman, her companion of that night, was called, and she confirmed the account, and confessed that in the morning she had joined in the feast; the mother's testimony followed, and that of numerous other witnesses. The guilt of the prisoners was thus fully established, when one of the female prisoners, Roséide, in the hopes perhaps of pardon, entered into every particular of the whole affair, to the evident annoyance of the others, who tried in vain to keep her silent. Her testimony was the most complete, and left not a doubt of the culpability of the whole of the prisoners. I did in consequence suggest that her life should be spared, but President Geffrard reminded me that it was she who had confessed, in open court, that she had eaten the palms of the victim's hands as a favourite morsel.

Jeanne, the old woman, though she showed the utmost coolness during the trial, did at length appeal for mercy, saying she had only been practising what had been taught her by her mother as the religion of her ancestors. "Why should I be put to death for observing our ancient customs?"

They were all found guilty of sorcery, torture, and murder, and condemned to death.

I asked the public prosecutor if he thought that the mother had been really ignorant of the fate reserved for her child. He replied, "We have not thought proper to press the inquiry too closely, for fear that we should discover that she partook of the feast; we required her testimony at the trial." After a pause, he added, "If full justice were done, there would be fifty on those benches instead of eight."

The execution took place on Saturday, February 13, 1864, the authorities wisely selecting a market-day, in order that the example might have the greater effect. The following particulars relating to it I received from the American Commissioner, Mr. Whiddon, who was present at this last scene. The prisoners, men and women, were all clothed in white robes and white headdresses, the garments reserved for parricides, and were drawn in carts to the place of execution, and all but one had a sullen look of resignation, and neither uttered a word nor a complaint, whilst the eighth, the young woman Roséide, kept up a continued conversation with the crowd around her.

Every effort was made by the Government to give solemnity to the occasion; the troops and National Guard were summoned, for even the word "rescue" had been pronounced; the principal authorities attended; and thousands of spectators gathered round the spot. The prisoners, tied in pairs, were placed in a line, and faced by five soldiers to each pair; they fired with such inaccuracy, that only six fell wounded on the first discharge. It took these untrained men fully half an hour to complete their work, and the incidents were so painful, that the horror at the prisoners' crimes was almost turned into pity at witnessing their unnecessary sufferings. As usual, the prisoners behaved with great courage, even the women standing up unflinchingly before their executioners, and receiving their fire without quailing, and when at last they fell wounded, no cry was heard, but they were seen beckoning the soldiers to approach, and Roséide held the muzzle of a musket to her bosom and called on the man to fire.

The Vaudoux priests gave out, that although the deity would permit the execution, he would only do it to prove to his votaries his power by raising them all again from the dead. To prevent their bodies being carried away during the night (they had been buried near the place of execution), picquets of troops were placed round the spot; but in the morning three of the graves were found empty, and the bodies of the two priests and the priestess had disappeared. Superstitious fear had probably prevented the soldiers from staying where they had been posted, and as most of the troops belonged to the sect of the Vaudoux, they probably connived at, rather than prevented, the exhumation.

Among those who attended the trial were the Spanish *chargé d'affaires*, Don Mariano Alvarez, and the Admiral, Mendez Nuñez, but they were so horrified by the sight of the child's remains on the judge's table and the disgusting evidence, that they had precipitately to leave the court. For years Congo beans were forbidden at our table. . . .

As late as 1878, the last year of which I propose to treat, two women were arrested in a hut near Port-au-Prince. They were caught in the act of eating the flesh of a child raw. On further examination it was found that all the blood had been sucked from the body, and that part of the flesh had been salted for later use. In 1869 the police arrested, in that beautiful valley to which I have referred in my first chapter, about a dozen cannibals, and brought them bound to La Coupe. They had been denounced by the opposing sectaries of the Vaudoux. From the time they were taken from their houses they were beaten in the most unmerciful manner, and when thrown into prison they were tortured by the thumbscrew and by tightened cords round their foreheads, and under the influence of these they made some fearful avowals, in which, however, little confidence could be placed. A French priest, with whom I was on intimate terms, hearing of their arrest, had the curiosity to go and see them. At first they would not converse with him, but when they found him protesting against the inhumanity with which they had been treated, and threatening the jailer that he would officially report him should such conduct continue, they placed more confidence in him. He visited them nearly every day, and had many conversations with them in private. They confessed to him that their avowals under torture were true; and when the priest, horrified by the details, said to a mother, "How could you eat the flesh of your own children?" she answered coolly, "And who had a better right,—est-ce que ce n'est pas moi qui les ai fait ?"*

---

* Barbot, in his account of the Aosiko kingdom, says: "That which is most inhuman is, that the father makes no difficulty to eat the son, nor the son the father, nor one brother the other; and whosoever dies, be the disease ever so contagious, yet they eat the flesh immediately as a choice dish." — Barbot, in Churchill's Collection, vol. v. p. 479.

One of these prisoners died under the torture of the cord tightened round his forehead.

Though the Haytians believe in the mythical "*loup garou,*" they have also the fullest faith in his counterpart among their fellow-countrymen. It is the *loup garou* who is employed by the Papaloi to secure a child for sacrifice in case the neighbourhood does not furnish a suitable subject; and they are supposed to hang about lonely houses at night to carry off the children. I have often heard my young Haytian servants rush into my country-house laughingly saying that they had seen a *loup garou*—their laugh, however, tinged with a sort of dread. They have often said that these human monsters prowl about the house at night, and that nothing but the presence of my dogs kept them in respect. I have occasionally seen the object of their fear in an ill-looking negro hanging about the gate, but the sight of my dogs was enough to induce him to move on. The negroes have fortunately an almost superstitious terror of dogs.

There is no doubt that these *loup garous* do carry off many children, not only for the priests, but for cannibals. They generally look only for native children, and I have only heard of one instance in which they attempted to carry off a white girl. She was snatched from the arms of her nurse, whilst walking on the Champs de Mars, by a huge negro, who ran off with her towards the woods, but being pursued by two mounted gentlemen who accidentally witnessed the occurrence, he dropped the child to save himself.

One of my Haytian friends who had studied botany informed me that the number of poisonous plants to he found on the island is very great, and that it was absolutely certain that the Papalois made use of them in their practices. I believe in some French botanical works lists of these plants have been published, and their medical value would appear to merit further study. It is not more remarkable that the Papalois should know the properties of the plants in Hayti than that the Indians of Peru and Bolivia should have discovered the properties of the cinchona bark and the coca-leaf.

If it be remembered that the republic of Hayti is not a God-forsaken region in Central Africa, but an island surrounded by civilised communities; that it possesses a Government modelled on that of France, with President, Senate, and House of Representatives; with Secretaries of State, prefects, judges, and all the paraphernalia of courts of justice and of police; with a press more or less free; and, let me add, an archbishop, bishops, and clergy, nearly all Frenchmen,—it appears incredible that sorcery, poisonings for a fee by recognised poisoners, and cannibalism, should continue to pervade the island. The truth is, that except during one year of Geffrard's Presidency, no Government has ever cared resolutely to grapple with the evil. If they have not encouraged it, they have ignored it, in order not to lose the favour of the masses.

Source: Spenser St. John, *Hayti, or the Black Republic* (London: Smith, Elder, and Company, 1889), 182–184, 185, 196–206, 225–228.

A New Orleans Voodoo Ceremony, 1904

Helen Pitkin's An Angel by Brevet *is a love story set in New Orleans around 1900. The heroine, a young white Creole named Angèlique—Angèle for short—is in love with Numa, a young man she fears prefers another woman. Much of the action of the story centers on Angèle's attempt to win Numa's heart through Voodoo magic. To that end, Pitkin provided detailed accounts of two ceremonies, one of which appears in the account below. At the point at which the selection begins, she is preparing to secretly leave her home to seek out the services of Voodooisant Ma'm Peggy.*

Even a cursory review of the selection will reveal Pitkin's negative impression of Voodoo. For one, she depicted it as primarily the workings of evil magic, although she acknowledged its religious underpinnings by recording songs and chants directed toward the non-Christian deities Liba (Papa LaBas), Blanc Dani, and Vériquité (resembling Haiti's Aizan-Veleteke). The book also describes the faith as satanic and emphasizes that Angèle has betrayed her own Catholic beliefs by turning to Voodoo. In addition to the explicit critique of the religion, An Angel by Brevet *is marred by racist assumptions about African Americans, which are used to explain their attachment to what Pitkin saw as a defective religion.*

The reliability of this source is open to some question. On the one hand, the book is a work of fiction. The author's less-than-positive view of Voodoo could also be a source of distortion. In the work's introduction, on the other hand, Pitkin claimed that her account was "lacking in adequacies rather than accuracies." Although it would be unwise to accept her claim at face value, there are reasons to think that she possessed some reliable information on Voodoo. The ceremony, for instance, resembles some later recorded by Federal Writers' Project workers. In addition, the names of deities mentioned in this selection as well as others found elsewhere in the book appear in other sources, often with different spellings, an indication that Pitkin had knowledge of these spirits from sources other than print ones.

* * *

At once Angèle sat up, throwing off the neatly-laid coverlet, and in another instant she had issued from the lacy netting and paused to listen. Reassured, she stepped lightly to the floor and sank down upon her *chauffeuse*, hastily pulling on her stockings. Within ten minutes she was dressed and stood before the eerie light. She would not kneel upon the satiny cushion; the old *prie-Dieu* was seasoned with prayer as an old violin with melody, and the inconsistency of her present service she fairly realized. "Save me, protect me, dear Blessed Mother," she appealed, stifling her conviction that her request was irreverent in view of her fixed purpose. She tiptoed out of the room, listening all the while, passing down the steps, stopping at each creak caused by her gentle foot-fall, and finally, reaching the end of the close, manipulated the lock in the street door noiselessly. Angèle breathed deep. "Toussi!" she whispered. There was a faint answer, and the girl stood outside in the shadow, her heart beating angrily and her members cold.

"Hurry," whispered Toussine. "We are already late."

Mr. O'Brien turned to look after the two women as they scurried along, but he did not recognize Miss Le Breton under such unusual circumstances. Her head was hung; her hat shaded her face and the collar of her redingote was pulled high about her cheeks. They went out to St. Ann Street and skirted Congo Square, Toussine speaking softly in explanation, preparing Angèle for all she might expect.

"W'en I lef you Sad-day, I wen' to see ooman who call Ma'm Peggy, an' give her firs' six bits and den fo' bits, because she need' money for de arrangement'. You brought yo' purse, *hein?* De leas' work dey make is fi' dollar'."

Toussine saw by an electric light that Angèle was somewhat richly, though soberly, dressed, and she frowned.

"Eh!" she said; "*to chapeau fait tapage!*"*

Angèle pulled her veil over its trimmings, and Toussine continued:

"I give up Sonny, 'cause one ooman tol' me Ma'm Peggy she alway' succeed, her. She sevent' daughter an' bawn wid caul. Me, I know she kin mek work w'enever she set a table! 'Fo I know Ma'm Peggy I was dat onlucky dat if it rain' two-bitses I'd be in jail. She change' all dat. She brought me back Antoine. His wife had him, but I got him back, *juste ciel!* She can mek good work. One *cunjer* fo' one t'ing, one fo' nudder, but Ma'm Peggy fo' all!"

"Why didn't you save your money and pray to Saint Antoine for your devil Antoine?" asked Angèlique, wise in the lore of the canonized.

Toussine grunted. "I owes him a candle right now," she said ; " but I ain't goin' to pay him. You has to stomp yo' foot at him, often,—dat's true. He's a mean saint."

Angèlique was not shocked. "It is true. I wanted to find my little diamond cross when I lost it, and I gave ten loaves to Saint Antoine's poor before I prayed. I never found my cross, do you believe it? When I wanted to dance the Carnival german I was too smart for him, and I promised him ten loaves for his poor if I was asked to dance. Of course, the invitation came, for he wanted those breads. Never pay Saint Antoine in advance."

They walked half a square further in silence.

"All de sem, I'm got de trimbles, an' you, M'amzelle L'Ange?"

There was no denying her nervousness, but the quality that lent Angèle persistence gave her courage, and she would not turn back. Instead, she asked Toussine, anxiously, if they might not be too late; if Madame Peggy would fail to await them and go to bed. Toussine assured her that Ma'm Peggy had given them the evening, and would wait a reasonable time, which did not preclude their visit so far, and they flew on together through the dense atmosphere, their shoes saturated with ground-moisture.

"It's good we go to-night to Ma'm Peggy," remarked Toussine. "She don' reciv' Sadday. She say dere's Monday, Chewsday, We'nsday, T'ursday, Friday fo' mek work, but never Sad-day. Dat's de day of *la Sainte Vierge*. An' she won' reciv' in Lent no more, neider Good Friday. Not in Lent, 'cause de saint' too busy to work wid her."

---

* Your hat is so gay it is noisy.

"You know plenty of voudous, Toussi?" asked Angèle, keeping her spirits up with a brisk step.

"*Plein!* Dy's Ma'm Bob, Sonny, Jeansin, Authuriste, Igène de Bully, Sam—he got de voudou face, I'm tellin' you, *laid à faire peur.* He wo'n reciv' negro', but you come firs' de mont'! You see lady f'om up-town in carriage', *plein, plein!* One lady give one hunderd dollar' fo' set a table! She wan' bring a sickness on a ooman 'cause she was jalous. Den dere's Jean Baptiste, an' Oscar—he's *menture,* Oscar ! Dey calls him *docteur,* an' he show me to mix salt an' pepper fo' mek troubl' w'enever I wan'. He say you t'row salt affer person an' he never will come back. Victorine know dat; she mek dat work plenty time' wid yo' comp'ny w'enever she do'n like fo' associate some man wid you."

They met scarcely a soul. The streets were deserted and uninviting for a promenade, shrouded in blue dusks under a weak luminance of stars. "But St. John' Eve—dat's de time!" exclaimed Toussine, rapturously. "Dats a feas'! All voudou has feas' *dat* night an' big time. Dey has turkey an' bile' onion' an' *congri* bean' an' all de wine you wan'. Den dey dances roun' a fiah an' swink (shrink) an' come small, small, small!" Toussine stretched her hand in the darkness, and Angèle could just discern it measuring a foot's distance from the ground.

"You *saw* that, Toussi?" asked Angèle, incredulously. The statement, positive as it seemed, was a too close correlation of the fictional and the factional to convince Angèle.

"I swear!" cried Toussine, excitedly. "Dey come small like dat, an' den dey come big again, big like giant', an' den we'n de fiah go out dey was like dead on de groun'."

Toussine felt righteously important that she could surprise her companion with her wonderful recounting of that which she believed she had seen.

"You ain' comin' see Ma'm Peggy 'bout dat coffin?" asked Toussine, curiously.

"No," said Angèle, determinedly.

"Because, me, I kin fix dat if dey put any mo'. Ef I fin' a coffin on my do'step, I would pay a boy a dime—a dollar, even—an' tek fif'een cents an' go wid him on Canal Street ferry to Algier' an' drop de coffin overbo'd jes in de middle o' de river an' t'row de fif'een cent' atter it, callin' to Grand Zombi, an' sayin' '*Dieu misericorde!*' Den I would come back St. Ann ferry. Dat mek de work pass sho'."

They had reached Roman Street, and were continuing downward. Suddenly Toussine stopped before a low cottage giving on the sidewalk, revealing even in the dim twilight of distant electric lamps a disrepair exceeding that of its neighbors. The batten doors were closed beyond any suspicion of occupancy, so that Angèle thought Toussine mistaken in the house. But the colored woman shook her head in silence, and knocked three times at longish intervals. There was quite a delay in answering the summons, so that Angèle's doubt as to their destination was revived. But Toussine placed her foot on the wooden step and held the attitude of waiting with perfect patience.

The doors parted with caution and a young mulattress, whom Toussine greeted at once as Taducine, came slowly into outline. At once the way was made clear and the young woman was obsequious in her conduct towards the guest of the evening.

"*Assite-là*," she invited in the Creole jargon, designating a hair-cloth sofa against the wall. She then left the room, and Angèle began to look around her.

As effectually as she could discern her surroundings by the infirm light of two tallow candles set upon the mantel-piece, the interior of the cottage, as the outside had premised, was rankling with decay. The flooring had been scrubbed through, apparently, with "*jaune*" as the ochre used for such purposes is termed, or perhaps by the shambling old feet of shifting generations.

There was a carved four-post bed in the opposite corner from where Angèle was sitting, and at the side of this formidable piece of furniture a square of smooth-worn carpet was placed in service as a rug. There was a table alongside the wall, and a specimen of furniture of many decades ago that caught and fastened the attention of Angèle for its degenerate magnificence. It was an *armoire*, or wardrobe, of great height and width squared just before her, a pathetic and inapposite feature in the dismal room. The wood was mahogany, its texture grimed with a damp soil, and reared upon four large globes of brass. A broad rod ran the length of the doors, and massive ornamentation of the metal, describing embossed roses and foliage, clamped either side.

Toussine noted Angèle's absorption and the cause.

"Dat was giv' Ma'm Peggy's ma by her ol' mistis dere is sixty year' now. Her ol' man sol' it once, but Ma'm Peggy got it again fo' fi' dollar'." The instance was not uncommon, Angèle knew, for members of her own family had given in the keeping of old servants, for preservation during the war or long absences abroad, their movable effects,—old glass, silver, ermine, cloaks, furniture, and, indeed, family jewels,—treasures that in the course of events had come to be hereditaments of the humble protectors and trustees.

There were vases on the narrow mantelshelf, porcelain with bisque figures and roses, and these were full of dried grasses. There was some gimcrackery on the shelf besides. Angèle was too preoccupied with fear to fix upon details. The odor of the room made her uneasy, anyway: it was the smell of age and the colored race, and of unaired effects and clothing long in use, distilled by the damp. Presently, a man attired in blue jeans, trousers, and "guinea" blouse, redolent of *carotte*, and two women, all of the negro type, entered and deferentially wished the couple on the sofa a good-evening. The faces of the three were so brown that only the balls of their eyes and the glow of their even teeth could be distinguished accurately in the awesome dusk of the room.

At this moment a woman scarcely older than Angèle herself entered from the region veiled by a limp, red calico curtain beyond, and straightway put the question to the young mademoiselle, in a request from Ma'm Peggy, as to what purpose had brought her there. The girl spoke fairly good French, as if service in a refined family had trained her tongue above those of her class. Her complexion looked like a too-floury cookie, or, as the Creoles put it in maxim, "a roach coming out of a flour-barrel."

Angèle now suffered the most strenuous embarrassment she had ever known. To confess she loved unrequitedly, to bring the name, perhaps, of the man she respected into a den of this character, to put herself in the posture of a suppliant, provoked her to a sudden anger. Then, as her position became clear to her, the exactions of the black folk about her, and the scene with its loathsome accentuations and the cause that had brought her there, she let go a notch of her self-respect, gradually, as those things happen. She swallowed hard, and refrained from looking at Toussine.

"I love where I am not loved in return," she said in a hard voice.

"You may tell me anything," murmured the young mulattress, whom Toussine addressed as Lorenza. "It is necessary. You see, Ma'm Peggy will know nothing when she is through with you—your secret will be lost."

Angèle was never logical, and it did not occur to her to ask Lorenza if she, too, would forget.

The three on the other side of the room wore mournful faces now, as Angèle discerned by the faint candle-light.

"You are afraid?" asked Angèle of Toussine.

"*Oui, mo peur*," answered the woman, looking, indeed, almost pale in the dusk.

There was another aching pause, Angèle in a fury of impatience all the while, unwilling to give herself up to the petrifying tranquillity that was apparently growing upon the watchers.

The silence was as packed with mystery as the room with malodor.

Lorenza came in again, softly, and whispered to Angèle that Ma'm Peggy had sent word she must wear nothing black.

"But my dress is black!" cried the girl. "My shoes! stockings!"

Lorenza shrugged her shoulders and smiled with importance.

"Ma'm Peggy can do nothing if there is the least black, I assure you."

"What will I do, then?" asked Angèle, despairing. I have nothing else at present."

"I will lend you my clean josey," said the woman; "and your petticoat is white, isn't it so? And you must take off your shoes, stockings also; you won't catch cold as long as you are with Ma'm Peggy."

Angèle demurred, filled with dread and shame.

The man and two women yonder in the corner were now almost totally lost to view, as the candle nearby had extinguished itself; their eyes were downcast.

"But those persons," indicated Angèle, still recalcitrant; "they wear black."

"No; it is brown and blue, *hein z'amis?* An' Bélisaire will put on a white coat."

The women were called to form a screen about Angèle while she disrobed partly and slipped on the starchy "josey" that must have been the pride of its owner, for it was of good linen, neatly tucked, and crochet lace of sea-shell pattern was inserted perpendicularly, a jabot falling half-way to the waist from the circular neck-band. A pair of slippers was tendered, but Angèle shivered at the idea, and preferred to be barefoot as an unsatisfactory alternative.

"Now all hair-pins must be taken out of the hair," announced the mulattress, raising her voice for general enlightenment. "Nothing must be crossed, neither your feet, neither your hands. For fear two pins might cross in your hair, it is best to take them out now."

Toussine rose and began to uncoif Angèle's hair, which sprang into a glittering halo; then she tied her own into a knot, and slipped her feet into Lorenza's brown gaiters. Angèle glanced at her for the first time since their entrance, and was alarmed at the suspense and earnestness of her face, which was drawn down in heavy lines, aging her and provoking new hints of character hitherto unsuspected.

Angèle felt that all tethering to her usual life had been loosed, and she was hideously solitary.

Taducine crossed the worn sill once more to whisper to Angèle not to be frightened at anything she might see in the inner chamber. "And, above all things," she said in French, "do not let go when she wheels you round; it is necessary, and there is no harm."

Angèle looked hopelessly at Toussine.

"It is going to be dreadful," she sighed. "If I had shoes on my feet I would take the door."

Toussine glared; her deference of manner vanished. "*Pchutt!* We'n you git dere once dey ain' no gittin' out no mo'. Do'n fo'git! An' de noise like *charivari!* An' it will be hot! About sev'n degree! But dat mek nuttin'. We'n dey starts rampagin' you cain git out."

The preliminaries were over. Taducine spoke to the three in the dark corner, who rose to shadowy heights and melted over the sill into the adjoining room. She then led Angèle by the hand to the portal, and, with a tragic gesture, swept aside the limp calico that had shielded the eyes from the glories within.

As Angèle stood there she emitted an exclamation of surprise.

In the furthest corner of the small room an altar was raised under a dais of velvet, from which depended lace curtains, parted and held back with cords, through which shone the tinsel gauds of cabalism.

There were ancient colored prints and paintings of the saints on the angle of the wall, and on the tiers of shelves many small statues, an altar-lamp, and three candles. The shelves were covered with immaculate cloth, which fell in outline to the floor, where a lace-bordered oblong of linen was spread smoothly upon the bare boarding. On the corners of this cloth brass candlesticks were set, in which blue tapers burned.

"The table," as it is called, was laid on the floor; plates of apples and oranges, pralines, dishes of candies, a tall nougat, a soup-tureen, and several bottles of anisette, cognac, and white wine. In the centre a saucer was set, in which were white sand, quicksilver, and molasses, apexed by a blue candle—a ritualistic plea to St. Joseph.

The altar gleamed brilliantly in contrast with the sooty walls of the room ; and on the hearth were the outlines of a clay furnace and a large black pot, from which there was the whisper of a simmer and a luscious steam. Before the altar, like a priestess of the Stoics, stood Ma'm Peggy, her back to those assembled there, her coppery face rising above her white neckerchief in startling relief.

The lines of her mouth and eyes were like gashes in the light that danced upon her, and she kept her eyes fast closed. Her dress was purplish "blue-guinea," dear to the hearts of all her race, and her tignon was saffron and white.

Taducine led Angèle to a chair that had been placed before the altar singly, and designated a seat to Toussine, who obeyed with an exaggerated reverence. The negro "singers" had slipped off their outer skirts, and were kneeling on the floor; the man sat on a bench in the dark.

When the stir of settling had subsided, Ma'm Peggy knelt on both knees at Angèle's feet, and remained thus rigidly for several moments. Then her old voice intoned the "Hail Mary" of the Roman Catholic Church. "*Salue, Marie, pleine de graces,*" she said rapidly, and "*Salue, Marie, pleine de graces,*" echoed the three women on the floor; the "*Ainsi soit il*" was the signal for all to cross themselves.

Ma'm Peggy began to snap her fingers just over the boarding, and in a moment the sharp filliping of other fingers sounded, the women leaning forward with intentness.

"Call luck," cried Ma'm Peggy; and "Call luck" echoed from divers throats, and the filliping continued till Ma'm Peggy began an unmusical recitative with weird repetitions like those of a round, her treble intonations shadowed by the rich gutturals of the negresses and the occasional bass of Bélisaire:

"*Bonjour Liba,**
Ouvert la porte,
Bon jour mon cousin."

The negresses sat about apathetically, droning the senseless sentences; now and then the clamant note from the man's throat would sound, but the chant continued as persistently and monotonously as the buzzing of mosquitoes:

"*Bon jour Liba,*
Bon jour Liba, ouvert la porte,
Ouvert la porte, Bon jour mon cousin,
Bon jour mon cousin, Bon jour Liba."

Ma'm Peggy knocked three times on the board beneath her, continuing her song, while Angèle observed Taducine rising from her sidelong sitting posture, and then lifting a small glass dish from the "table," inquiring, through the mazes of the chant, "Who has de change?"

Angèle made a sign and dropped a bill into the dish. Without looking at its denomination, Taducine knelt before the altar, slipped the money under the white cloth on the floor, and made the sign of the cross. The inconsonance of the incident, amid the devotional surroundings, did not occur to Angèle, who was now avidly interested in the proceedings.

Ma'm Peggy began another plainsong, in staccato staves, rising from her knees:

"*Blanc Dani,*†

---

* Voudou term for St. Peter.
† St. Michael.

Dans tous pays blanc
L'a commandé
Blanc Dani, Dans tous pays blanc
L'a commandé."

The aged woman's treble lowered to a hoarse bass as she sang, when she suddenly interrupted herself by diving forward and snatching the bottle of brandy from the floor-table, and threw half its contents in half-circles around Angèle, replacing it with a wide salaam. Kneeling as Mussulmen kneel, bending her forehead to the bare floor, she gave strange cries; and the others, following her example, struck their heads and then their forearms resoundingly against the planks after strange gyrations, their song moaning on monotonously all the while.

Ma'm Peggy ceased her cadencing, but the others went on repeating the sentences in minor notes like a threnody, Bélisaire yawning on his own account, accenting a syllable now and then over the wavering trebles, each striking like a bell into Angèle's awed hearing.

The obi-woman moaned, her body in a prosilient swaying, her eyes closed, and her limbs fluttering, under her lank gown, then leaning to the floor, lifted a bottle of wine to her lips, filled her cheeks with its contents, and spurted a shower upon every one, a spray falling upon Angèle's buoyant hair and inspiring an inner revolt that shrunk her with loathing.

Ma'm Peggy's gnarled form shivered and writhed and shrugged.

"*Blanc Dani,*" she shouted, grimacing horribly, with new and more fantastic contortions of her frame. "*Dans tous pays blanc*—"

The singers were on a high key, irrespective of her apostrophe, a sing-song that Angèle thought unnerving. "*L'a commandé*—" Her face grew more and more distorted, and she grinned under the influence of agony rather than of pleasure. Whirling about in a circle, she tried to kick off her *savales,* Taducine quickly assisting her. In a sort of rage she tore the fichu from her breast and the tignon from her head, the matted plaits rising as if surprised and jutting like quills over the whitened poll. She knelt and rose, and knelt again, repeating this office as if frenzied beyond self-containment, perspiration streaming down her face, glazing it like ebony.

"De sperrit's comin' strong on her," cried Lorenza, breathless from the chant, and resuming it once more.

Ma'm Peggy, in a measured shuffle, approached Angèle, who cowered; the old woman grinned with the hideous hilarity of a fiend.

"Do'n be 'fraid!" encouraged Toussine, who, in a transport, had joined in the general plaint.

"It is no mo' Ma'm Peggy," said Taducine, reverently. "It's de gret sperrit. We'n she turn you, as' w'at you wan'. Anyt'ing you wan' know you can ax her."

The woman's tone was steady, and emboldened Angèle, who rose and allowed the shrivelled hands of the witch to take her own. Peggy raised the girl's arms high above her head and pulled them down with a jerk, which was repeated twice, not without effort and pain. She then retained Angèle's left hand, and swung her in rotary motion six times, when Taducine whispered to Angèle to bow to the spirit.

Angèle tottered with dizziness, but she found herself braced by the spiggoty head placed firmly on her chest, Ma'm Peggy holding her hands, with arms extended.

Now Angèle mustered her forces sufficiently to ask her heart's desire concerning Numa.

"De young man is *coquina!*" said Ma'm Peggy, grinning still.

The women and man began to sway on their knees, making comments and iterations as the hag spoke.

"He loves brune—mo' brune dan you, *chere*. Ah—dey is anudder love you! All would be champagne wid him,—but no—you don' wan'! You prefer *coquin!* Ah, Yout'!"

Convulsions once more shook the spare body, but Ma'm Peggy recovered herself.

"He goin' mek wid brune like he mek wid you. *Mais, ef* you wan' 'im fo' true, gi' me money fo' mek *novena*. But it will be a work, yass! He love dat gal now; you can pull a hair o' dem!"

Angèle signified her willingness to go to any extent to wreak the charm. Ma'm Peggy bolted forward and grasped the bottle of whiskey, taking a deep draught, then placing it to the lips of every one present save Angèle with such vim as to half-choke them in swallowing as she poured; their chins were dripping with the fluid. A sickening smell of cheap whiskey and stale tobacco pervaded the room, mingled with the acid of perspiration. Peggy approached Angèle and spun her around again.

"Mek wish! Mek wish!" shouted the negress. Angèle desired the removal of all obstacles to her love. "*À genoux!*" they cried, and, with the rest, Angèle dropped to her knees.

Again the snapping of fingers as they bent downward with inscrutable eyes, as if seeking the mysteries of the nether world.

Ma'm Peggy moved slowly in a circle on a heel by the momentum of her other foot, spraying anisette from her mouth and sending ringlets of the sticky cordial over her head to the floor. Then she mumbled inarticulate phrases in a coarse voice. "*Guette ça!*" cried Bélisaire. "It is him, de white man himself! Look, how he is strong! It is no mo' Ma'm Peggy!"

Taducine vented an exultant "Whoop-la!" and the others droned with melancholy.

"Me, I love you w'en Ma'm Peggy mek one novena," said the coarse voice. "I co'te you six. mont', I marry wid you sev'n. I commence already fo' love you. Wait one week—you goin' see."

Ma'm Peggy placed her hands upon Angèle's arms and made a pass down the girl's sides with more vigor than seemed to be stored in her frail structure, grinning with sinful ugliness all the while. Passing along to the others she performed the same exercise, then edged off towards the gloom, her arms akimbo, shuffling her feet zigzag and yielding her shrunk body to weird flexures, her eyes closed.

The women rose one by one, each like a black phantom, growing taller and more numerous in the shadows, slow-writhing figures emitting ululations like animals from moment to moment. They circled about the furnace, which was sending out rich savors, and Ma'm Peggy lifted the lid and stood like a wraith in the mist that arose. Taducine brought bowls for the *gombo filé* and rice, which were served in generous portions, Ma'm Peggy digging her iron spoon into the mass and bringing forth a snake limply balancing upon it. There was a yell from somewhere; it sounded far away to the half-fainting Angèle, who checked the scream she would have uttered, but dared not.

The eyes of Bélisaire bulged, and the heads of the women darted from immovable bodies, their mouths open wide. Some one offered a dish to Angèle, who took it, terrified, not daring to lay it down; the others, even Toussine, ate of it with zest.

Ma'm Peggy approached the altar again, stamping her stockinged feet and working her body backward and forward wildly. Plunging to the floor, she caught up two apples and threw them into the girl's lap, she receiving them with loathing. "Mek 'im eat apple!" cried the old Sibyl; "dat will mek 'im love!" Lorenza then offered the candies, two to each. In transmission one of those to Angèle dropped to the floor, whereupon there was an immediate shout. "Dat's goin' succeed!" was the cry, at which Angèle began to sympathize with the general enthusiasm.

The cognac was placed again to the lips of the company, the anisette and white wine later, and then Angèle was asked to write her name, her lover's, and her rival's on slips of paper which only herself could see.

The slip containing Carmelite's name was placed to soak in a deep dish full of vinegar, salt, and pepper; Angèle's and Numa's were dropped into a bowl of burning whiskey that sent leaping shadows into the dark corners. Ma'm Peggy lifted the candles from the altar and those from the floor, save the one votive to "*Vériquité*" (voudou term for St. Joseph), and handed one to Angèle. It bore seven notches in the blue tallow, and Ma'm Peggy instructed her to burn it seven nights in her own bedroom, only from notch to notch, repeating three "Hail Mary's" meanwhile. The sorceress then gave Angèle a pinch of the "*poiv' guiné*" from the saucer and bade her put five grains in her mouth whenever her lover would come near her,—this to soften him towards her; also, when he would first enter the house, to make a glass of sugared water, very sweet, and with *basilique*, and throw it in the yard with her back towards the street.

"Put *poiv' guiné* an' clove in yo' mout' an' you kin git anyt'ing you wan' f'om yo' w'ite man," continued Ma'm Peggy, with the authority of a prophet. "An' put one piece o' his hair by yo' cist'en w'ere one drop o' water kin fall to a big splash. Tek dat piece loadstone—dat ambition a man. Put it near w'ere you set wid 'im. Fo' de gal, me, I fix her, yass !"

Peggy grouped the lighted candles on the floor, and lifted the brandy bottle to her head and left it there. She wriggled about in a circle, but the bottle scarcely trembled. Three hard knocks came from somewhere, and there was an excited cry from the women, who crossed themselves, and sidled into the corners and back again into the chiaroscuro of the altar. The room grew very warm and the air sourly fetid.

"*Grand Zombi!*"

Bélisaire shouted, and his voice came back, reverberating through the rafters. Ma'm Peggy with a vault landed in the midst of the burning candles, mashing out the flames that ran in the tallowy mass, muttering incomprehensible sentences and sobbing the sob that is without woe.

The murk was now alarming, for when the last wick had been overcome and expired with a slight supping sound, only the blue candle remained, and, though the room was small, the taper was almost overcast by the obscurity creeping out of the corners.

Bélisaire groaned at intervals, and set his legs in the most fantastic steps, while the women, now mere dim and blurry silhouettes, shrieked in irrational excitement.

A church steeple sounded midnight without. A cat wauled overhead, and the dancers spun around swiftly crying responsively, Ma'm Peggy's voice losing sonancy with physical fatigue and taking on brute tones like those of an animal at bay or in great pain. Angèle sat appalled by the frenzy, for Toussine had joined in the incantation, and the girl felt a danger she would not formulate. Her springy hair, unleashed, bounded in the current of air set in motion by the dancers, and her dark eyes, large and intense, were fastened upon the devilish fetichism.

Ma'm Peggy was whirling like a dervish. The orgy was upon them all. Grasping hands, they surrounded the frightened girl and whooping, threatening forward till their bodies touched hers, and then in scuffling regression widening the circle. Loosening hands, they bounded about in kangaroo fashion, their heads in independent agitation, their arms working wildly from their sockets.

"Hi! Hi! Hi! Hi! "cried the women, and Bélisaire snorted, his voice surd, finished. *Blanc Dani!*" cried Ma'm Peggy, and "*Vériquité!*" shrieked Taducine in the babel. Bélisaire made an attempt to leap in the air, but his strength was failing him. The cat wauled again, disturbing the loosened tiles overhead to a stealthy slipping. The exhausted women were revived by the sound and capered about faster and sent hoarse whispers, mere words without tones, upon the crepuscule.

Slower and slower the ghostly shapes issued from the formless shadows, growing blottesque and weird, now beginning to reel to regain their poise, striking against the walls, tottering to catch any stable article. Lorenza was the first to gain self-control, holding fast to the mantel, and steadying herself by a rigid tension of nerves.

Bélisaire fell dizzily along the bench; Toussine dropped to her knees, keeping her eyes tightly closed.

Lorenza touched Ma'm Peggy's arm, tried to keep hold of her, but to no avail; the old woman shook her off, lunging beyond her reach, wriggling and trying to free herself, apparently, of something fastened on her back. She shrugged her shoulders and vented sharp cries, more of annoyance than of pain.

"Sit down," urged Lorenza. Ma'm Peggy scowled and raised an arm as if to strike.

"*Va t'en!*" she said, angrily. "*Mais non—que diabe ça!—Tonnerre!—Ça to geignin? Laissé moin!*" She reeled about the room, her face working hideously, with sugent sounds on her lips, her arms contorting to reach her shoulder-blades.

"Mamzelle wishes to speak to Ma'm Peggy," said Taducine, pulling her to a corner.

"Ma'm Peggy, she is not there; I don't see her," answered the old woman, stumbling and writhing with the unseen discomfort.

Her body undulated with twists, and she fell against Bélisaire, who was prone upon the bench. The women lifted her, though she shook them off. Then she stretched as from sleep, yawned, and stood erect.

"I mus' tell her all about that is happen'," said Lorenza. "She don' know nottin'."

Ma'm Peggy folded her hands before her, a type of the decent negress of some decades since, and inquired, with respect, "Are you satisfied, at present, *momzelle*?"

Bélisaire rose, still in a stupor, and reseated himself on the bench. Ma'm Peggy knelt before the little shrine and began the litany of the Blessed Virgin, in which the others joined, even Angèle herself. This finished, Ma'm Peggy raised the floor-cloth slightly and extracted the money that had been placed there at the beginning of the satanic formalism, and tossed it with indifference upon the lower shelf of the altar, leaving it there inconsequently, as if for any wind to whisk it away. But the apartment was without ventilation!

Then Ma'm Peggy turned and addressed Angèle suavely, her face kind and bland. "Come," she said. "I show you who mek a work fo' you: St. Michel. He yo' saint. You see, I put a nice bride fo' you by St. Michel fo' mek novena. Ever' day fo' nineteen day' I mus' put one candle; you mus' sen' me nineteen candle, an' some honey, some holy water, an' orange-flow'r water. I mek dat fo' you fo' fi' dollar'."

Angèle extracted the remaining bill from her purse and laid it with the other on the shelf. Ma'm Peggy was pleased to give further advice with this stimulus.

"You bu'n one candle, *hein*, de firs' Monday an' Friday ever' mont', unstan'? Nex' week Friday you go at St. Roch jus' at t'ree 'clock an' mek wish. Dat sem day you mus' tek hol' sometin b'lougin' to yo' *rivale* an' you mus' cut an' sew it. She won' neber leve to wear it. Den rub dat gal pigshur wi' dis dus'. It come off de grave o' murderer-man. Wear dat pigshur capsize in yo' pocket. She die sho'."

"But I don't want her—any one—to die!" cried Angèle in consternation.

Ma'm Peggy pulled her underlip out like elastic and inserted a pinch of snuff at the roots of her yellow tushes. Then she shrugged.

"You come heah tell me fo' mek work. I mek work. I lay wanga 'ginst her. You don' need tell me nottin' now ! Dat gal got to die now, anyhow!"

Angèle felt herself growing faint, and she rose, feeling her way into the outer eclipse, Toussine following, and Taducine with a new-lighted candle. Toussine helped her to dress in silence. When they were ready to go, Taducine looked out of the door, up and down the starless night, listening for a sound in the dark. Assured, she opened the door wider and bade *mamzelle* good-night.

Angèle put her arm through Toussine's and set a quick pace through the streets in silence. A sensitive cock heard them as they passed and crowed for dawn. Then the neighbor-chanticleers took up the alarm, as if a score of Peters were afoot.

Source: Helen Pitkin, *An Angel by Brevet: A Story of Modern New Orleans* (Philadelphia: J. B. Lippincott, 1904), 175–212.

Opening Ceremony from New Orleans Voodoo/Hoodoo, 1920s–1930s

The Great Depression of the late 1920s and 1930s saw people of all walks of life out of work. To provide incomes for the unemployed, the federal government instituted a wide range of work relief programs, collectively known as the New Deal. Among them was the Works Progress Administration. One of its many branches was the Federal Writers'

Project, which employed out-of-work authors on a variety of projects designed to emphasize American culture, especially in the fields of history and folklore. Among the better known employees of the Federal Writers' Project were Voodoo researchers Zora Neale Hurston and Robert Tallant.

The following is a rare example of a detailed description of a New Orleans Voodoo ceremony, an opening, or initiation, in this instance. Robert McKinney, an aspiring African American author, composed the account, which he based upon his personal experience. Accompanying him in the ceremony was Hazel Breaux, a white woman who also worked for the Writers' Project. The opening was held in the home of white Voodoo practitioner Mrs. Dereco, and was officiated over by African Americans Oscar Felix, called "Nom" in the account, and Mrs. Robinson, called "Grandma" in the document. Robinson was also known as "Madame Ducayielle," a name that she likely adopted to hide her identity as a precaution against legal difficulties.

Please note that the author refers to Voodoo as hoodoo, *a practice in keeping with older Mississippi Valley terminology that used* hoodoo *to refer to the religion now known as* Voodoo. *The word* Voodoo *designated one of its practitioners. For comparison, note the similar distinction in Mary Alicia Owen's account of Missouri Voodoo, which appears above. That Voodoo included significant magical elements likely contributed to modern usage in which* Voodoo *references the religion while hoodoo means a form of magic.*

* * *

The purpose of this "opening" is to call upon the spirits, thus making a person a member of the sect.

This "opening" was conducted in a very secretive manner, taking place in an unfurnished room in the rear of the house with all doors, windows and blinds tightly shut. The only persons attending were "Grandma", Nom, a medicine man and high Priest at this ceremony, Miss Breaux and the writer.

Nom immediately set about preparing the altar, which according to him must always be placed on the floor. First, a clean well pressed piece of white cotton goods, about the size of an average table cloth, was spread; second, a picture of St. Peter (as he opens the way to heaven) was placed, in a leaning position, against the wall; third, one white and one green candle were lighted and placed, about mid-way, on each side of the altar, the former to the right and the latter to the left; fourth, two quart bottles, one of cider and the other of raspberry pop, were placed about mid-way on the altar; fifth, a bunch of various colored candles were placed in front of the raspberry pop; sixth, the other articles were scattered on the altar, a plate of steel dust to the right of the picture, a plate of orris root to the left, a plate of dried basile in front. In the center of the altar, to the front, was placed a plate of broken stage planks (cake) and a box of ginger snaps; to the left of the cakes was a plate of mixed bird seed and some bananas, to the right, plates of powdered cloves and cinnamon and some small apples. Two granite pans of congris (in this case it consisted of cooked red beans and rice) and a small bottle of olive oil were also used. A bag of sugar was placed behind the white candle. A camphor branch, used in the absence of a palm leaf was leaned against the picture. A tall glass containing gin, sugar, water, and a spray of large basile was placed in front of the picture, a court notice was by the picture, a bottle of Jax beer was also used.

After this arduous task was completed, Norn began undressing; first, he took off his coat, his vest, shirt and shoes. This was done in such a startling manner that we did not know what to expect next. Nom commanded the writer to take off his coat, and the two participants to take off their shoes, socks and stockings. The three pairs of shoes, (Miss Breaux's, Nom's and the writer's) were placed on both sides of the altar against the wall.

We were commanded to kneel down on our right knee, our heads in our left hands, then told to knock loudly and slowly on the floor three times with our right hands. This being done to invoke the aid of the spirits. After which, the Lord's Prayer was very slowly recited by all. Nom worked himself into a frenzy by singing and praying in French. He made all kinds of peculiar motions at the same time. He took a large drink and went into a semi-trance. Nom grunted, hollered and called on the spirits for assistance. After every drink of gin Nom acted like a man going crazy with all kinds of dances and prayers. Nom seemed to have forgotten where he was. He often spit gin in his hand and rubbed it on his face. Nom still in a trance, which lasted through the entire ceremony, went to Miss Breaux, seizing her violently, and turned her under his arm three times. The writer went through the same procedure but with more action. The writer was hit on his pocket three times and had to keep his hands there for ten minutes. Nom took the writer on his beck, turning him around three times. He returned to Miss Breaux and turned her three times on his back. During this procedure we were to ask for the power to do the kind of work desired. Next our feet and legs were worked with the mixture in the tub, which consisted of nearly everything on the altar. Nom passed the lighted candles over his face and through his mouth several times. Miss Breaux was given the lighted white candle for good luck. Miss Breaux was instructed to burn it at three different occasions, each time asking for what she desired. The writer was given a red candle, broken in three parts. He was told to burn it and ask for anything that is wanted. This candle should be used for bad work. Nom bit off the bottom of the red candle and instructed the writer to light it at the bitten end, stating, "dis will mak yo enemies upset." Nom rubbed steel dust, dry basile and cinnamon on the inside souls of our shoes. The shoes were also rubbed with the mixture that was in the tub. He spit in the shoes of the writer and washed Miss Breaux's stockings with gin. Nom next offered us gin but we refused it. However, the bottle was put to our mouths. Near the end of the "opening" Miss Breaux's hair was washed with gin.

Nom gave us some of the material that was on the altar. He was paid two dollars for the "opening", which is absolutely necessary for anyone who would like to be a hoodoo queen or doctor.

At the completion of the ceremony Nom had consumed the pint of gin and came out of his trance with no difficulty, whatsoever. He asked, "how was it, was you dissipointed?"

Source: [Robert] McKinney and [Hazel] Breaux, "Hoodoo Opening Ceremony," 1920–1930, Louisiana Writers' Project, folder 44, Federal Writers' Project, Cammie G. Henry Research Center, Watson Memorial Library, Northwestern State University, Natchitoches, LA, 1–3.

Interview of Mambo Patricia Scheu (Vye Zo Komande LaMenfo), 2013

The following is an interview with Mambo Vye Zo Komande LaMenfo conducted by the author in June 2013. Among the topics she discusses are her background, entrance into Vodou, experiences in the faith and with other believers, and the ceremonial life of a sosyete. In addition, she also discusses the similarities and differences between Vodou in Haiti and in the United States and among Vodou and other African Diasporic religions. The interview helps contextualize manifestations of Vodou within the United States and provides fascinating insight into why so many find themselves drawn to the religion.

Mambo Vye Zo is a prominent priestess who leads the Sosyete du Marche, Inc., a Vodou congregation located in Pennsylvania. Though her background as a white American is atypical, she is committed to the Vodou faith and has served the lwa for over two decades. In addition to her sosyete, she is a defender of the much-maligned Vodou faith. To this end, she spends much of her time educating those with an interest in the religion through seminars, online classes, and the website, sosyetedumarche.com. She has also written Serving the Spirits *(2011), an introduction to the religion.*

* * *

Q: What is your personal background? Let people know who you are.

A: I am American. I was born in Connecticut in 1954. I am Italian on my dad's side and Canadian on my mom's side. The Italian side of the house was a mixed lot of folks. They came from southern Italy. The towns that were mentioned when I was growing up were Benevenuto, in the southern part of the boot and the Providenza del Toro or the "Providence of the Bull." You know, the secret about southern Italians is that there is African blood mixed in with them. My family was a rainbow of colors. We never thought of it as, "oh, he's too black" or "he's too white." That was the family. Uncle Alfredo was dark as a berry nut. My dad was a redhead with blue eyes but dark skin. My cousins were a wide range of colors. I was pretty much the odd kid out because I was blond and fair skinned, but my siblings both have dark curly hair. When you grow up in a family like this, you tend to look at the world a little bit differently.

I was raised Catholic when [Vatican II] made all the changes—changed the mass into English, turned the altar around, all those kinds of things—and so I was continually challenged in school with progressive and new ideas about faith. What I really knew was that I wanted to be a priest, and that just wasn't an avenue open to a young lady growing up in the '60s. You either were a nun or you weren't. So, I walked away from the church when I was about eighteen or nineteen. That's where my religious background ended. By the time I was in college, my mother called me a *Noth-a-narian*, which was her way of saying that I didn't believe in anything but God.

In college, I was exposed to a lot of different folks. I came out of this little community in Connecticut where I knew everybody and everybody knew me. It was a big change for me at the University of Connecticut. In 1972, it had an on-campus population of 20,000 folks. It was my first experience meeting people from everywhere: from China, Japan, the Pacific, Europe. It was just an astounding time to be in school. They were experimenting with content and teaching in all the classes. I was an art student in a field in which you had to feel the yellow, breath the blue, that kind of thing. The idea of experimentation was highly encouraged. That included a literary class in which we were studying African writings. There was a lot of writing about Vodou in that class. It piqued my interest.

Parallel to meeting all these people in school was the experience of my mother's best friend. He was a high school teacher of history who used to travel. Whenever he and his wife would come home, they would have pictures from their trip. One year—probably my second or third year of college—they went to the Dominican Republic and Haiti. They brought their pictures over and I was taken by it! I was just taken by the people, by the island, and by the Vodou, by the spirits. You might say that was the first time I actually felt the calling to come to the Vodou and Haiti.

The other piece of the puzzle had to do with charity. My parents were very involved in charitable work. My dad was a volunteer baseball coach. My mom had knitting circles. They were very proactive in giving back. Here were two people who together probably never made more than $40,000 a year in their entire life, yet they felt so well cared for that we had to give back to people that were not. So I grew up in this household of philanthropy and charity in which you were expected to help those you see behind you. Moving into Haiti with its poverty seemed to blend into my personal history.

I graduate from college in 1975, and I still hadn't gone back to the church. I don't really get involved in any kind of spirituality, until I was a producer. After UConn, I did a lot of freelance work in print and ended up working in Audio-Visual (AV). I became a producer, doing what was called B-roll. You know, when you look at the news at night, there are newscasters talking about, "There was a car fire at First and Second," and then they show a picture of First and Second. I was the producer shooting that film. It was an exciting life but also lonely because that kind of shooting was usually done by men. I was an unusual crew member—a female producer out on the road with crews shooting video. But my parents had always encouraged me—particularly my mother—to have a career and not just be stuck at home. She told me to go out and make a name for myself. And so I did. I traveled across the country a lot, and it was on the West Coast when I had my first encounter with Afro-Caribbean folks.

It was the early nineties, and I was just knocking around San Francisco on a day off. I wandered into a shop in Berkeley. A woman, dressed in a very colorful dress and turban walked up to me, grabbed me by the arm and said, "Your father is waiting for you." I just kind of looked at her and said, "Really?!" She said, "Yes, he is waiting for you in Haiti and you need to get there." With that she turned and left. When I went to check out, the clerk said to me, "So, is your father in Haiti?" I said, "No, he is in Connecticut." We both laughed, but it stuck with me because the turbaned woman had said Haiti and I had this little connection with Haiti.

Now go forward a couple more years, and I am at the height of my career. I am one of the big AV producers in Philadelphia. I am working for the local ABC station. *Meetings Magazine* names me one of the five "big dogs of AV" in Philadelphia. I am producing all kinds of huge shows – Sales Incentives, Product Launches, Shareholder Meetings for the top Fortune 100s here in Philly. I get hired by Donald Trump to do the opening of his Taj Mahal Resort and Casino in Atlantic City. My husband and I were flying high. We had a Jaguar and a vacation house in Florida. We are living the high life.

On an off weekend, I return home to Connecticut and discover that my mother is deathly sick. She had been diagnosed with Alzheimer's. My dad has been diagnosed with cancer. Neither had told me anything because they did not want to forestall my career. At that point, I begin to question everything. "What planet was I on that I did not see this? How could they hide something like this from me?" What I realize is that I was on the road three weeks out of every month. I'd come home for a short break and leave again on assignment. That is how I missed it. So I resolved to get off the road and be more involved with my family. I also begin to question every little thing that happens to me. For example, if I forgot where I put my keys, I would panic thinking "Oh my God, it is happening!" Or, if I forgot the address of where I was going—"Oh my God, this is the start, I am getting Alzheimer's!" It was like having the Sword of Damocles hanging over my head.

The final straw that proved to be life changing for me is that I was scheduled to work a Goldman-Sachs meeting in New York in 2001, at the top of the World Trade Towers. I had worked this same meeting the year before, and had a great time. It was a beautiful location. We rode the mile high elevators up and down. We did the Ferris Buehler thing in the windows. The day before the 2001 meeting, I was cut from the team, which is not unusual in the AV world. They said, "Don't worry about it. We'll make it up to you next year. We'll hire you twice as often." I said, "Okay." And then, the towers came down. I can't talk to my mom. She's not there mentally any more. And I can't talk to my dad because he is in shock, trying to help my mom. Adding to my panic was the knowledge I could have been there. I lost friends who were working at Windows on the World the day the towers were attacked. But I wasn't there – God had seen fit to save me. And so that's when I made my decision to do something that would help me be more aware of the world, not just moving through it because I made a good salary.

I reduced my footprint in the AV world. And it's an interesting thing, Jeff, when you make the decision to turn to spirit; Spirit embraces you, helping you shed your mundane life. I started to become *persona non grata* in the AV because I was turning down jobs involving travel. In the AV business, once you start turning work down, you fall off the A-list.

Towards the end of 2002, one afternoon, Don said to me, "Well, that's it. I don't have any work. You don't have any work. What do you want to do?" I said, "Let's dip into the bank account. Let's go to Haiti." And that's what we did. We traveled to Haiti. I had met a woman named Mambo Racine Sans Bout on line. I had a lot of communication with her. I'd gone down to New Orleans and met her. I liked her, and so Don and I traveled to Haiti in 2003 and initiated into the priesthood. We came back, and I've been a mambo ever since.

Q: The name of the mambo that you met?
A: The mambo's name was Mambo Racine Sans Bout. She's very controversial these days, and she and I no longer have any relationship. At the time that I met her, she was working with a Haitian gentleman who became my Kanzo father. His name was Fritzner Georges, and it was Papa Fritzner's house that came together with Racine to do the actual kanzo, the ordination rites into the faith. The piece that people confuse all the time is that kanzo is a start. It is not an end-all-be-all ritual. It's a commitment to the spirits, and so when you make that commitment, you are making a life changing decision. Everything you do from that point forward, proceeds from that choice.

After my kanzo, Mambo Racine and I parted ways. I was talking to another mambo of my acquaintance recently, and she asked me why I never re-kanzoed. I said, "Because I was taught by Oungan Edgar that I could not disrespect what the spirits had given me; because in kanzo you are elevated to a rank by the spirits." There is a human facilitator who is organizing the rituals and setting things up, but the actual events that raise you to Kanzo are done by the Vodou spirits. So, to go to another house and re-kanzo would be like telling the very spirits that were raising me that they didn't know what they were doing in the first place. I couldn't do that. I felt intrinsically that I had been made correctly and that I did not need to re-kanzo.

I'm an anomaly in the American lineages here in the States because I'm recognized by the entire Haitian community as an authentic mambo. The Americans are not quite sure what to make of me because I'm not attached to a Haitian house. I'm independent with my husband.

We still have supervision. I realigned myself with a mambo here in Philadelphia. She's not around anymore, but her name was Shakmah Windrum. She was made Kanzo in Croix de Bouquet, Haiti in the '60s. I also aligned myself with Papa Edgar Jean-Louis of Belair, and I'm still aligned with a gentleman named Papa Lazireau Lerine of LaFond, Haiti. So, all of these elders, true elders, helped me grow up and helped me build my practice and gave me advice and steered me in the right direction. That is my lineage.

Q: You mentioned that you are recognized as a mambo by the Haitian community now. What is your current role within your community? Do you have a group of your own?

A: My current role in my community is that my husband and I lead a 501(c)(3) Vodou Church here in southeastern Pennsylvania. The name of the church is Sosyete du Marche, Inc. You can find us on GuideStar [an online guide to nonprofit organizations]. Within the greater Haitian community, I am called *Marriene*, which means godmother in Kreyòl, and I am tapped quite often to be the godparent to new initiates in other houses.

We have a group of people who have been working together for twenty five years or so. We ran a Masonic-style lodge for about ten or twelve years prior to going to Haiti. When we returned, the members were very interested in what we were doing. So, they just folded into what we now do to the point that we just practice Vodou. We do the Vodou work because in keeping up with the calendar of obligations, there's a lot to do. There are about twenty individuals who attend any given weekend on which we serve. One weekend a month, we have a prayer circle in which we do a rosary and the French prayers. We sing songs. It's called an Aksyon du Gras, or an "act of grace." Then, on a second weekend we serve one of the major spirits in observance of the yearly calendar.

Most people think Vodou is unorganized, undisciplined and just made up from point A to point B. That's untrue. Vodou is an extremely formal faith with a very strict hierarchy for serving a full calendar of observances. There are all kinds of obligations to be attended to; it's a busy life. When people come to me and say, "I want to do Vodou," my admonition to them is "Make sure this is really what you want, because you have no idea how big this root is or how deep it goes and how much work it is to tend it."

Our current membership is around forty people. Those forty individuals don't make every service. Most probably make around half the events that we do. We run the sosyete in true Haitian style, in that it's a family. My husband and I are the *de facto* mother and father, and then everybody downstream from us is referred to as our godkids. We treat them as such. I talk to everyone each week. I know who they're married to. I know what their parents are up to. I know what their kids are doing. I know what their grandkids are doing. It's like a big extended family with all of the things that go on in a big extended family with crises big and small. Right now, it's a big crisis because Papa Don is in the hospital. They're all hysterical because I told them not to come. There's a handful that live close by, but by and large, the house is dispersed across the country. Getting here is at least a day trip for most of them.

Q: Well, that would make it difficult.

A: I am humbled by how far the lwas have extended themselves to find servitors. Currently, I am running an online class. I am teaching the first level of Vodou to a Russian, a Ukrainian, an Uzbekistanian. There are two students are from Seattle and Massachusetts, as well as house members who want to keep refreshing themselves. One co-teacher is in New Mexico. The other is in New York. The online class has proven to be very fruitful in helping people feel like they're a part of something.

Q: That's interesting. It brings me to another question. What would you say the current state of Vodou is in the U.S. and then also in Haiti?

A: Wow. I don't know that I'm qualified to be the spokesperson on that topic because I practice Haitian Vodou. I don't practice American style. The Americans here in the United States—only a handful of us actually have houses. There's Mambo Chita Tann out in San Jose; Houngan Hector Salvo in New Jersey. There are some people in New Orleans.

I think Vodou here in the United States is still pretty underground. Fewer people are shocked when I tell them I practice Vodou. The earthquake in Haiti did a lot for bringing all of us to the forefront and proving it wasn't the demonic religion that everybody thought it was, but it's still an unusual religion to name.

Last fall, I taught a class at Millersville University. I do a lot of outreach as part of my vows, and so my drummer and I went there. Invariably there's some smart aleck in the back row who says, "Well, I have a question. How come you're white?" I always answer, "Well, that's what I popped out as this time around." What I try to tell them is, "You know, the Haitians don't see me as white." They see me as *blan*, which technically means "white" in their language, but actually implies "foreigner." So, they see me as something other than themselves, or at least, they used to. They don't anymore. Now, when I go to Haiti and I tie my head, everybody addresses me as "mambo," and nobody thinks twice about the fact that my skin's whiter than theirs. The Haitians that I work with, who come to my kanzos and to the kanzos I've done in Haiti have never questioned anything at all.

Q: That is interesting. Do you see any differences between Vodou in the U.S. *versus* in Haiti, or is it truly a transplant into America with no significant difference?

A: The differences are subtle, but they're there. There is a thing that Haitian Vodou follows called reglemen. You could call it the liturgy of Vodou. There is an organization to the way you do a ritual or you conduct a ceremony or service. There's a hierarchy that you have to work at following. We have to speak Kreyòl because the service is sung in Kreyòl. You have to memorize all the songs. It's a huge amount of work to learn how to run a service. Vodou services are not thrown together. You have to know the prayers of the lwas. You have to know their songs, drumbeats, dances. You have to know the order in which they're called. You have to know the hierarchy that's serving with you. The asogwes do one thing. The su pwens do something else. The ounsis do a third thing. Guests do a fourth thing. It's very, very regimented. The word *reglemen* means "regimentation." This liturgy has not changed. It came here from Haiti. Those of us that practice Haitian Vodou, follow the reglemen to the T.

What has changed is the make-up of people in a society because in Haiti, everybody is connected to everybody else. If they are not a blood relatives, they are usually related through marriage, cousins—things of that sort—and so, houses in Haiti generally are gathered around the family. You know, if you're a houngan, then your dad was a houngan, your mom a mambo. When you get together, it's a family thing. Even though it may look like there are forty different people there, they're all related to each other, which is not the case here in America where nuclear families are dispersed throughout the country. We create a family based on relationships and experiences together. Our sosyete is as tight as it is, because we worked under that Masonic idea for so long. We built the respect. We built the relationships. There are people in my house that I have worked with for twenty-five years, which is very comparable to what it is in Haiti. People in a Haitian Vodou house have probably been together all their lives. They started at two or three years old at their mommies' knee, learning songs and dances. As they got older, it was expected that they pick up the ason and serve. Here in the United States they haven't done it long enough, and so that kind of lineage is not in place.

It's delightful to see the young kids come back year after year and see how they know the liturgy. The adults are still struggling to get their tongues around some of the Kreyòl songs and the kids are upstairs dancing in front of the TV singing the most complicated lines effortlessly. We now have children that we have baptized into the faith. We had to establish a separate grade of initiation for the younger people who want to make a commitment to the faith but are not ready to go to kanzo. I've had to come up with a catechism to teach the younger ones. You can't use the same explanations as you do with adults. We have a Sunday School program we're trying to develop for next year so that the eight to thirteen year olds have a way of beginning to understand some of this stuff. I have a young member who's nine, and he just did a whole talk at his school about Vodou and his *Marriene*. He stood in front of the class and showed them how to do the *yanvalou*, which is the opening dance move, and he sang a song for his mèt tèt. I was so proud of him! It's one of the reasons I speak at colleges because if you can express it to young minds and demystify it, then Vodou has a chance of becoming recognized as a real faith. It is a real religion, but being recognized as such instead of always being maligned as devil worship or whatever.

Q: That's really interesting, actuallyhearing it from that standpoint because that's the kind of thing I don't come across in the books I would read about it myself.
A: Yes, there's a lot of material out there today, but it's using outdated sources, unfortunately. Métraux, Herskovits and Deren are good books, but all of them were visiting the same temple in the same place in Haiti, and they were reporting on the same services. There's not a lot about the breadth of the religion and what it looks like among the practitioners because it's new to the mainstream. I've been asked this question about how I see the differences. What I see is a family faith in Haiti, practiced by families who are related by blood. Here in the United States because it's too new, it's a faith uniting strangers. I can't speak to what's found in the Mississippi Valley and American Vodou, but certainly for Haitian Vodou.

Q: I was actually going to ask you next if you'd done any looking into the Mississippi Valley Voodoo that really kind of died out more or less in the 1940s, depending on how you define it. Not much, you say?

A: The only experience I have of what I guess you would call American Vodou is that I was the *mama hunyo* for Sallie Glassman's first kanzo in New Orleans with her papa, Edgar. That's when I met Edgar, and we aligned ourselves with him. I have her to thank for introducing me to Vodou. It was her deck that was one of the first resources available to people looking for stuff way back in the day. I think Sallie Ann's Vodou is the closest to what might be termed American Vodou.

Q: All right. My next question was the last question that I had really written out. I'm sure you're aware of this. Some years ago, you used to constantly see other African Diasporic religions referred to as *Voodoo*. Anything that came from the Caribbean that wasn't Catholic was *Voodoo*. What, would you say, is the relationship between Vodou and, say, Santería or Espiritismo or Candomblé—those kind of things?

A: What you have to remember is that all the people who came out of West Africa were dispersed across the Caribbean Basin. West Africans were introduced to Cuba, Jamaica, Haiti, and Guyana. They were brought by the Portuguese down into Brazil and up to the southern areas of the U.S. The root of their faiths comes out of West Africa, but when it landed in Haiti, it evolved into Haitian Vodou. When it landed in Brazil, it evolved into Candomblé. When it landed in Cuba, it evolved into Lucumi. The particular religion practiced in a given area had to do with the nation of the African who were enslaved there.

As example, Haiti is a melting pot. The religion of Vodou, its reglemen, is based on the ordering of four hundred nations of African people—Mandingo, Kongo, Senegal, Nago, Dahomey, Fon, Djouba. All these different nations of Africans were brought into the island. They didn't share the same language. They didn't worship the same god. They could barely communicate with one another. They developed a language that they took from the plantation masters. It becomes Kreyòl which is French with African syntax. That's the first amazing thing – that they took the language of their masters and made it their own.

There are a lot of spirits in Vodou who are reflections of the era in which they were born. Within the Priye, the foundational prayer of Vodou, we sing to all of the old Dahomey entities who come from Rada—Allarada in Dahomey. They're very royal, beneficent and cool. Following the Rada segment, we sing for the Nago nation, which is an actual section of West Africa. Then we move into the Kongo and Petwo. *Petwo* doesn't mean a hot spirit per se. Petwo are island-born spirits, spirits who came out of the Revolution, born from men and women's misery. [These spirits were birthed] from the pain of being enslaved and put in bondage. Their attributes, the food they eat, the way they dress, the words they say are all very reflective of the era of the island in which they came from. So, it's interesting and odd, I think, for people to find out that the way the spirits are served in the South of Haiti is not how they do it in the North. Or the ason, which is so predominant in Port-au-Prince, is unheard of in Saint-Marc. People make general statements about Haiti and say "Vodou is all the same." It's just not. It's totally different depending on where you go in the island and who the African population was there. That [population] dictates how Vodou became the practice. The same thing, I'd have to assume, is what happened for Santería and for Candomblé, Macumba, all these different practices. They are the result of the African nations who were enslaved in those areas of the world and the religious practices that they brought with them and remembered.

Q: All right. Is there anything that I have not asked you about that you think people really need to know?

A: People need to know the gift that Vodou gave the world—a gift that nobody has ever recognized. I talk about this all the time. Vodou is a religion in which people looked at what made them similar rather than different. You know, on any given plantation, there may have been four hundred Africans who came from many different areas of Africa.

We have to remember that the West Africa kings were fighting for land and bodies to work that land. They had been at war for three centuries when the Portuguese arrive. The Portuguese went to the kings and negotiated for prisoners of war. The slaves brought across the Atlantic Ocean came from the prison camps of the Kongo kings. Those prison populations were made up of very different nations of conquered African peoples. They may have been blood enemies back in Africa. They didn't have a shared language. They did not worship the same way. Their gods were different. Yet, in the crucible of plantation era Haiti, they recognized that in order to survive, they would have to get along. Instead of looking at what made them different, they looked at what made them the same.

They created a religion that all of them could use to better their lives. I think that is an *astounding* achievement that never gets talked about. It gets glossed over in all of the academic talk about "Are these real possessions?" and "What about the chickens?" All of the set dressing, if you will, blinds people to the truth of what's happening. A Vodou service is a celebration about what makes us the same. In a Vodou service, when we praise God, we are really praising His diversity in making us unique. That's what helped us survive. That's how we managed to get out of bondage. Vodou is the religion that built a nation. How astounding is that? How amazing is it that a group of men and women defeated Napoleon's army and create a sovereign nation that still stands to this day?

Regardless of its problems or its poverty, there is one thing that unites all Haitians on the ground: that they *are* Haitian. When you talk to them and you ask, "What's the greatest thing about being here?" they say, "It's Haiti! That's the greatest thing." That is because every school kid knows the story: that a bunch of slaves defeated Napoleon and raised themselves up to be recognized by the rest of the world. And they did it by looking at what united them rather than what divided them. I say to my students is, "You could take a lesson from this. Instead of fighting amongst yourselves about who's got the fanciest iPod, think about what you have in common with one another, because that's what birthed a sovereign nation." I mean it blew me away when I recognized it. I said to my husband, "I need to be a part of this. I need to experience this. I need to be in this energy, this vortex of joy of being unique." Mama Lola has this saying, "If you're in you're in. But if you're out, you're out." What she's referring to is the initiation rites of kanzo. Once I became kanzo, I was in for life.

You know, I'm just—I'm a nèg. That's the other part. My Papa Lerine—last summer when I was in Haiti—I said "OK Papa your Blan says goodbye." He said "You're not blan. You're nèg." Nèg literally means a "black man" or "black woman," but it also implies that you're a sister and a brother and a member of the family. This sense of inclusiveness is what I want people to know. That in comparison to this country [the USA], where racism is still so dominant, this little island figured it out 200 years ago. They realized "Now, look what we can achieve if we all decide we are closer to each other than apart." I think that's an amazing gift that no other religion can claim.

My teaching example is this: "If a priest, a Muslim cleric, and a Jewish rabbi got together, could they make a religion or a religious practice that would honor all three sides equally?" Everybody always laughs and says no. And my response is always, "Well, that's what Vodou did." Vodou took four hundred and one diverse religious practices and wove them into a cohesive whole. Two hundred and fifty years later, it's still going strong. Now, if that's not magic, I don't know what is.

Source: Reprinted with permission of Mambo Patricia Scheu (Vye Zo Komande LaMenfo), 2013.

Documents from the Congress of Santa Barbara

The Congress of Santa Barbara, or KOSANBA as it is commonly known, came into existence in 1997. Part scholarly society, part cultural and political action group, it supports academic examinations of Vodou, attacks derogatory and stereotypical views of the faith, and works for the betterment of the people of Haiti. Since its founding, it has held numerous conferences to promote these goals and has produced several influential collections of essays. Following is its founding document, the Congress of Santa Barbara Declaration. In it, the organization summarizes its basic outlook and goals.

In addition to KOSANBA's publishing activities, it has been quite successful in the realm of cultural politics. One of its more visible achievements has been to convince the Library of Congress to change its subject heading from Voodooism *to* Vodou *in reference to the Haitian religion. A statement released by the organization to announce the victory follows the "Declaration."*

Congress of Santa Barbara Declaration

Thirteen Haitian Scholars met in April 1997, at the University of California, Santa Barbara for a colloquium on Haitian Vodou, The Spirit and The Reality: Vodou and Haiti. At the end of the conference, these scholars decided to institutionalize their efforts through a new association under the name, the Congress of Santa Barbara.

Imbued by a sense of collective wisdom and aware of the long, difficult and constant struggles and crises undergone by their homeland, the Founders—and others who might join them—pledged to create a space where scholarship on Vodou can be augmented. Cognizant of the meaning and the implications of this historic reunion where Haitian scholars seized the initiative, the Congress proposes to have an impact on Haitian cultural politics as well as on other measures and policies that affect the Republic of Haiti.

The presence, role and importance of Vodou in Haitian history, society and culture are inarguable, and recognizably a part of the national ethos. The impact of the religion qua spiritual and intellectual disciplines on popular national institutions, human and gender relations, the family, the plastic arts, philosophy and ethics, oral and written literature, language, sacred and popular music, science and technology, and the healing arts, is indisputable. It is the belief of the Congress that Vodou plays and shall continue to play a major role in the grand scheme of Haitian development and in the socio-economic, political, and cultural arenas. Development, when real and successful, always comes from the modernization of ancestral traditions, anchored in the rich cultural expressions of a nation.

The Founders of the Congress of Santa Barbara invite all scholars and interested parties who subscribe to its goals and objectives, to join it in the defense and illustration of this potomitan of the Haitian cultural heritage that is such an integral part of the country's future.

Source: "Declaration," Center for Black Studies Research: The Congress of Santa Barbara, 2014 <http://www.research.ucsb.edu/cbs/projects/haiti/kosanba/declaration.html> (June 23, 2014).

U.S. Library of Congress Changes Subject Heading from "Voodooism" to "Vodou," 2012

December 20, 2012 — For years, practitioners and scholars of Haitian Vodou have challenged misrepresentations of the religion and opposed the spelling "voodoo." A group of Haiti- and internationally-based scholars and scholar-practitioners came together last year to work jointly towards these ends. The Congress of Santa Barbara (KOSANBA), the Scholarly Association for the Study of Haitian Vodou, joined this effort and is very pleased to announce on behalf of the group that the initiative has already seen historic results.

In April 2012 the group petitioned the United States Library of Congress to change its primary subject heading for the religion from "Voodooism" to "Vodou." Subject headings are the categories assigned to books to indicate their subject matter. Earlier this fall, the Library of Congress notified the group that upon reviewing the submitted materials it had "found the documentation of the scholars' and practitioners' arguments that 'voodoo' is pejorative to be compelling" and decided to revise the subject heading to "Vodou."

The Library of Congress announced this revision in October 2012, making the statement: "PSD [Policy and Standards Division] was petitioned by a group of scholars and practitioners of vodou to change the spelling of the heading Voodooism. They successfully argued that vodou is the more accurate spelling, and that the spelling 'voodoo' has become pejorative. The base heading was revised to Vodou on this list, and all other uses of the word 'voodoo' in references and scope notes have also been revised." (http://www.loc.gov/aba/pcc/saco/cpsoed/psd-121015.html)

This change is now reflected on the Library of Congress Authorities site: http:/authorities.loc.gov/. Henceforth, books focusing on the religion and cataloged using Library of Congress Subject Headings will no longer be classified under "Voodooism" but will be assigned the heading "Vodou."

Source: Patrick Bellegarde-Smith and Kate Ramsey, "U.S. Library of Congress Changes Subject Heading from 'Voodooism' to 'Vodou'," University of Florida Digital Archives: Vodou Archive 2004–2013. <http://ufdcimages.uflib.ufl.edu/AA/00/01/34/43/00001/Recognition_of_the_Spelling_Vodou_by_the_U.S._Library_of_Congress.pdf> (July 15, 2014).

Bibliography

General Works on Mississippi Valley Voodoo

Anderson, Stacey. 2014. "Voodoo Is Rebounding in New Orleans After Hurricane Katrina." *Newsweek* (August 25). Accessed on December 9, 2014: http://www.newsweek.com/2014/09/05/voodoo-rebounding-new-orleans-after-hurricane-katrina-266340.html.

Antippas, A. P. 1988. *A Brief History of Voodoo: Slavery & the Survival of the African Gods.* New Orleans: Marie Laveau's House of Voodoo.

Bodin, Ron. 1990. *Voodoo: Past and Present.* Lafayette, LA: University of Southwestern Louisiana.

Fortier, Alcee. 1888. "Customs and Superstitions in Louisiana." *The Journal of American Folklore* 1 (July–September): 136–410.

"Husbands and Lovers Are Voodoo Sage's Specialty." 1902. *New Orleans Times-Democrat* (October 29): 10.

"Idolatry and Quackery." 1820. *Louisiana Gazette* (August 16): 2.

Mulira, Jessie Gaston. 1990. "The Case of Voodoo in New Orleans." In *Africanisms in American Culture*, edited by Joseph E. Holloway, 34–68. Blacks in the Diaspora Series, edited by Darlene Clark Hine, John McCluskey, Jr., and David Barry Gaspar. Bloomington, IN: Indiana University Press.

Roberts, Kodi. In press. *Voodoo and The Promise of Power: The Racial, Gender & Economic Politics of Religion in New Orleans, 1881–1940.* Baton Rouge, LA: Louisiana State University Press.

Saxon, Lyle. 1927. "Voodoo." *The New Republic* (March 23): 135–139.

Tallant, Robert. 1946 [1998]. *Voodoo in New Orleans.* New York: Macmillan; reprint, Gretna, LA: Pelican.

Touchstone, Blake. 1972. "Voodoo in New Orleans." *Louisiana History* 13: 371–386.

"Tribulations des Voudous." 1863. *L'Union* (August 1): 1.

"The Virgin of the Voudous." *Weekly Delta*, August 12, 1850, 354.

"A Voodoo Festival near New Orleans." 1897. *The Journal of American Folklore* 10 (January–March): 76.

"The Voudou Case Disposed Of." 1863. *Daily Picayune* (August 2): 3.

"Voudou Superstition." 1871. *Daily Picayune* (June 25): 5.

Warner, Charles Dudley. 1887. "A Voudoo Dance." *Harper's Weekly Magazine* 31(1592) (June 25): 454–455.

Williams, Marie B. 1875. "A Night with the Voudous." *Appleton's Journal: A Magazine of General Literature* 13: 404–405.

General Works on Haitian Vodou

Ackermann, Hans-Wolfgang, and Jeanine Gauthier. 1991. "The Ways and Nature of the Zombi." *Journal of American Folklore* 104: 466–494.

Ackermann, Hans-Wolfgang, Maryse Gautier, and Michel-Ange Momplaisir. 2011. *Les Esprits du Vodou Haïtien*. Coconut Creek, FL: Educa Vision, Inc.

Beaubrun, Mimerose P. 2013. *Nan Domi: An Initiate's Journey into Haitian Vodou*. San Francisco: City Lights Books.

Bellegarde-Smith, Patrick and Claudine Michel, eds. 2006. *Haitian Vodou: Spirit, Myth, Reality*. Bloomington, IN: University of Indiana Press.

Bellegarde-Smith, Patrick, LeGrace Benson, and Claudine Michel. 2013. "KOSANBA: A Scholarly Association for the Study of Haitian Vodou." Center for Black Studies Research: The Congress of Santa Barbara. Accessed on April 15, 2013: http://www.research.ucsb.edu/cbs/projects/haiti/kosanba/index.html.

Bellegarde-Smith, Patrick and Claudine Michel. 2006. *Vodou in Haitian Life and Culture: Invisible Powers*. New York: Palgrave MacMillan.

Casseus, Jules. 2013. *Toward a Contextual Haitian Theology*. Port-au-Prince, Haiti: Media-Texte.

Cosentino, Donald L., ed. 1995. *Sacred Arts of Haitian Vodou*. Los Angeles: University of California Fowler Museum of Cultural History.

Courlander, Harold. 1960. *The Drum and the Hoe: Life and Lore of the Haitian People*. Berkeley, CA: University of California Press.

Courlander, Harold. 1955. *The Loa of Haiti: New World African Deities*. Havana: Sociedad Económica de Amigos del País.

Dayan, Joan. 1998. *Haiti, History, and the Gods*. Berkeley, CA: University of California Press.

Deren, Maya. 1953. *Divine Horsemen: The Living Gods of Haiti*. London and New York: Thames and Hudson.

Desmangles, Leslie G. 1992. *Faces of the Gods: Vodou and Roman Catholicism in Haiti*. Chapel Hill, NC: University of North Carolina Press.

Dorsainvil, J. C. 1931. *Vodou et Névrose*. Port-au-Prince, Haiti: La Presse.

Dorsainvil, J. C. 1937. *Vodou et Magie: Psychologie Haïtienne*. Port-au-Prince, Haiti: Imprimerie Nemours Telhomme.

Dorsainvil, J. C. 1924. *Une Explication Philologique du Vaudou*. Port-au-Prince, Haiti: V. Pierre-Noel.

Galembo, Phyllis. 1998. *Vodou: Visions and Voices of Haiti*. Berkeley, CA: Ten Speed Press.

Geggus, David. 1991. "Haitian Voodoo in the Eighteenth Century: Language, Culture, Resistance." *Jahrbuch für Geschichte von Staat, Wirtschaft und Gesellschaft Lateinamerikas* 28: 21–51.

Gilles, Jerry and Yvrose Gilles. 2009. *Remembrance: Roots, Rituals, and Reverence in Vodou*. Davie, FL: Bookmanlit.

Gorov, Lynda. 1990. "The War on Voodoo." *Mother Jones* (June) 12.

Hebblethwaite, Benjamin. 2012. *Vodou Songs in Haitian Creole and English*. Philadelphia: Temple University Press.

Herskovits, Melville J. 1937a. *Life in a Haitian Valley*. New York: Alfred A. Knopf.

Herskovits, Melville J. 1937b. "African Gods and Catholic Saints in New World Negro Belief." *American Anthropologist* 39: 635–643.

Heusch, Luc de. 1989. "Kongo in Haiti." *Man*, New Series, 24: 290–303.

Houlberg, Marilyn. 1996. "Sirens and Snakes: Water Spirits in the Arts of Haitian Vodou." *African Arts* 29(2): 30–35, 101.

Hurbon, Laennec. 2002. *Dieu dans le Vaudou haitien*. Paris: Maisonneuve et Larose.

Hurbon, Laënnec. 1995. *Voodoo: Truth and Fantasy*. London: Thames and Hudson.

Hurston, Zora Neale. 1990. *Tell My Horse: Voodoo and Life in Haiti and Jamaica*. With a Foreword by Ishmael Reed and Afterword by Henry Louis Gates, Jr. New York: Harper and Row.

Laguerre, Michael S. 1989. *Voodoo and Politics in Haiti*. New York: St. Martins.

Loederer, Richard A. 1936. *Voodoo Fire in Haiti*. Translated by New York: Doubleday.
Long, Carolyn Morrow. 2006. "New Orleans Voudou and Haitian Vodou." In *Revolutionary Freedoms: A History of Survival, Strength and Immigration in Haiti*, edited by Cécile Accilien, Jessica Adams, and Elmide Méléance, 105–112. Illustrated by Ulrick Jean-Pierre. Coconut Creek, FL: Caribbean Studies Press.
Marcelin, Milo. 1936. *Mythologie Vodou (Rite Arada)*. Vol.1. Port-au-Prince, Haiti: Les Éditions Haitiennes.
Métraux, Alfred. 1972. *Voodoo in Haiti*. Translated by Hugo Charteris and with an Introduction by Sidney W. Mintz. New York: Schocken.
Michel, Claudine. 1995. *Aspects Educatifs et Moraux du Vodou Haïtien*. Port-au-Prince, Haiti: Le Natal.
Michel, Claudine, and Patrick Bellegarde-Smith. 2001. "Women's Moral and Spiritual Leadership in Haitian Vodou: The Voice of Mama Lola and Karen McCarthy Brown." *Journal of Feminist Studies in Religion* 17(2) (Fall): 61–87.
Michel, Claudine, and Patrick Bellegarde-Smith, eds. 2006a. *Haitian Vodou: Spirit, Myth, and Reality*. Bloomington, IN: Indiana University Press.
Michel, Claudine, and Patrick Bellegarde-Smith, eds. 2006b. *Vodou in Haitian Life and Culture: Invisible Powers*. New York: Palgrave Macmillan.
Newell, William W. 1888. "Myths of Voodoo Worship and Child Sacrifice in Hayti." *The Journal of American Folk-Lore* 1: 16–30.
Newell, William W. 1889. "Reports of Voodoo Worship in Hayti and Louisiana." *Journal of American Folk-Lore* 2: 41–47.
Pluchon, Pierre. 1987. *Vaudou, Sorciers, Empoissoneurs: De Saint-Domingue à Haïti*. Paris: Karthala.
Price-Mars, Jean. 1928. *Ainsi Parla l'Oncle. Essais d'éthnographie*. New York: Parapsychology Foundation Inc.
Price-Mars, Jean. 1983. *So Spoke the Uncle*. Boulder, CO: Lynne Rienner Publishers.
Ramsey, Kate. 2011. *Vodou and the Power in Haiti: The Spirits and the Law*. Chicago: University of Chicago Press.
Rigaud, Milo. 1985 [1969]. *Secrets of Voodoo*. Translated by Robert B. Cross. New York: Arco; reprint, San Francisco: City Lights.
Saint-Louis. 2000. *Le Vodou Haïtien: Reflet d'une Société Bloquée*. Paris: L'Harmattan.
Scheu, Patricia (Mambo Vye Zo Komande LaMenfo). 2011. *Serving the Spirits: The Religion of Vodou*. Philadelphia: Published by author.
Seabrook, William B. 1929. *The Magic Island*. New York: Harcourt, Brace.
Simons, Marlise. 1983. "Power of Voodoo, Preached by Sorbonne Scientist." *New York Times*, December 15, A2.
Simpson, George Eaton. 1940. "The Vodun Service in Northern Haiti." *The American Anthropologist* 42(2) (April–June): 236–254.
Siuda, Tamara L. (Mambo Chita Tann). 2012. *Haitian Vodou: An Introduction to Haiti's Indigenous Spiritual Tradition*. Woodbury, MN: Llewellyn.
Tivnan, E. 1979. "The Voodoo That New Yorkers Do." *New York Times Magazine* 182 (December 2): 182–192.

General Works on Conjure, Hoodoo, and Related Topics

Anderson, Jeffrey E. 2005. *Conjure in African American Society*. Baton Rouge, LA: Louisiana State University Press.
Anderson, Jeffrey E. 2008. *Hoodoo, Voodoo, and Conjure: A Handbook*. Greenwood Folklore Handbooks. Westport, CT: Greenwood Press.

Bacon, A. M. 1895. "Conjuring and Conjure-Doctors." *Southern Workman* 24: 193–194, 209–211.
Bass, Ruth. 1930. "Mojo: The Strange Magic That Works in the South Today." *Scribner's Magazine* 87: 83–90.
Bass, Ruth. 1935. "The Little Man." *Scribner's Magazine* 97: 120–123.
Bell, Michael E. 1980. "Pattern, Structure, and Logic in Afro-American Hoodoo Performance." PhD dissertation, Indiana University.
Bims, Hamilton. 1976. "Would You *Believe* It . . . Superstition Lives!" *Ebony* (July): 118–122.
Boyle, Virginia Frazier. 1900 [1972]. *Devil Tales*. With illustrations by A. B. Frost; reprint, Freeport, NY: Books for Libraries Press.
Brown, David H. 1990. "Conjure/Doctors: An Exploration of a Black Discourse in America, Antebellum to 1940." *Folklore Forum* 23: 3–45.
Chireau, Yvonne. 1997. "Conjure and Christianity in the Nineteenth Century: Religious Elements in African American Magic." *Religion and American Culture: A Journal of Interpretation* 7: 225–246.
Chireau, Yvonne. 2003. *Black Magic: Religion and the African American Conjuring Tradition*. Berkeley, CA: University of California Press.
Clayton, Edward T. 1951. "The Truth about Voodoo." *Ebony* (April): 54–61.
Courlander, Harold. 1976. *A Treasury of Afro-American Folklore: The Oral Literature, Traditions, Recollections, Legends, Tales, Songs, Religious Beliefs, Customs, Sayings, and Humor of Peoples of African Descent in the Americas*. New York: Crown Publishers.
Dana, Marvin. 1908. "Voodoo: Its Effect on the Negro Race." *The Metropolitan Magazine* 28: 529–538.
Davis, Daniel Webster. 1898. "Conjuration." *Southern Workman* 27: 251–252.
Davis, Rod. 1999. *American Voudou: Journey into a Hidden World*. Denton, TX: University of North Texas Press.
Handy, M. P. 1872. "Witchcraft Among the Negroes." *Appleton's Journal: A Magazine of General Literature* 8: 666–667.
Haskell, Joseph A. 1891. "Sacrificial Offerings among North Carolina Negroes." *Journal of American Folk-lore* 4: 267–269.
Haskins, James. 1990. *Voodoo and Hoodoo: The Craft as Revealed by Traditional Practitioners*. New ed. Lanham, MD: Scarborough House.
Hazzard-Donald, Katrina. 2013. *Mojo Workin': The Old African American Hoodoo System*. Urbana, IL: University of Illinois Press.
Herron, Leonora. 1891. "Conjuring and Conjure Doctors." *Southern Workman* 24: 117–118.
Hurston, Zora Neale. 1931. "Hoodoo in America." *Journal of American Folklore* 44: 317–417.
Hurston, Zora Neale. 1995. *Folklore, Memoirs, and other Writings*, selected and annotated Cheryl A. Wall. The Library of America. New York: Literary Classics of the United States, Inc.
Hyatt, Harry Middleton. 1970–1978. *Hoodoo-Conjuration-Witchcraft-Rootwork*. 5 vols. Memoirs of the Alma Egan Hyatt Foundation. Hannibal, MO: Western.
Kulii, Elon Ali. 1982. "A Look at Hoodoo in Three Urban Areas of Indiana: Folklore and Change." PhD dissertation, Indiana University.
Lea, M. S. 1927. "Two-head Doctors." *The American Mercury* 12: 236–240.
Long, Carolyn Morrow. 1997. "John the Conqueror: From Root-Charm to Commercial Product." *Pharmacy in History* 39: 47–53.
Long, Carolyn Morrow. 2001. *Spiritual Merchants: Religion, Magic, and Commerce*. Knoxville, TN: University of Tennessee Press.

Long, Carolyn Morrow. 2014. "The Cracker Jack: A Hoodoo Drugstore in the 'Cradle of Jazz'." *Louisiana Cultural Vistas* (Spring): 64–75.

Lucky Mojo Curio Company. 1994–2014. Accessed on February 21, 2014: http://www.luckymojo.com.

McMillan, Timothy J. 1994. "Black Magic: Witchcraft, Race, and Resistance in Colonial New England." *Journal of Black Studies* 25: 99–117.

Owen, Mary Alicia. 1892. "Among the Voodoos." In *The International Folk-lore Congress 1891: Papers and Transactions*, 230–248. London: David Nutt.

Owen, Mary Alicia. 1893 [2003]. *Old Rabbit, the Voodoo and Other Sorcerers*. With an Introduction by Charles Godfrey Leland. With Illustrations by Juliette A. Owen and Louis Wain. London: T. Fisher Unwin; reprint, Whitefish, MT: Kessinger Publishing.

Park, S. M. 1889. "Voodooism in Tennessee." *The Atlantic Monthly* 64: 376–380.

Pendleton, Louis. 1890. "Notes on Negro Folk-Lore and Witchcraft in the South." *Journal of American Folk-Lore* 3: 201–207.

Pinckney, Roger. 2000. *Blue Roots: African-American Folk Magic of the Gullah People*. St. Paul, MN: Llewellyn.

Prahlad, Anand ed. 2006. *The Greenwood Encyclopedia of African American Folklore*. 3 vols. Westport, CT: Greenwood Press.

Puckett, Newbell Niles. 1926 [1968]. *Folk Beliefs of the Southern Negro*. Patterson Smith Reprint Series in Criminology, Law Enforcement, and Social Problems, no. 22. Chapel Hill, NC: University of North Carolina Press; reprint, Montclair, NJ: Patterson Smith.

R., L., G., and A. 1878. "Conjure Doctors in the South." *The Southern Workman* 7: 30–31.

Snow, Loudell F. 1979. "Mail Order Magic: The Commercial Exploitation of Folk Belief." *Journal of the American Folklore Institute* 16: 44–73.

"Some Conjure Doctors We Have Heard Of." 1897. *Southern Workman* 26: 37–38.

Steiner, Roland. 1901a. "Braziel Robinson Possessed of Two Spirits." *Journal of American Folk-Lore* 14: 226–228.

Steiner, Roland. 1901b. "Observations on the Practice of Conjuring in Georgia." *Journal of American Folk-Lore* 14: 173–180.

Tyler, Varro E. 1991. "The Elusive History of High John the Conqueror Root." *Pharmacy in History* 33: 164–166.

Whitten, Norman E. 1962. "Contemporary Patterns of Malign Occultism among Negroes in North Carolina." *Journal of American Folklore* 75: 310–325.

Wicker, Christine. 2005. *Not in Kansas Anymore: A Curious Tale of How Magic is Transforming America*. New York: HarperCollins.

General Works on Other African Diasporic Religions

Baer, Hans A. 2001. *The Black Spiritual Movement: A Religious Response to Racism*. 2nd ed. Knoxville, TN: University of Tennessee Press.

Bascom, William. 1969. *Ifá Divination: Communication between the Gods and Men in West Africa*. Bloomington, IN: Indiana University Press.

Bellegarde-Smith, Patrick, ed. 2005. *Fragments of Bone: Neo-African Religions in a New World*. Urbana, IL: University of Illinois Press.

Berry, Jason. 1995. *The Spirit of Black Hawk: A Mystery of Africans and Indians*. Jackson, MS: University Press of Mississippi.

Brandon, George. 1993. *Santeria from Africa to the New World: The Dead Sell Memories*. Bloomington, IN: Indiana University Press.

Braude, Ann. 2001. *Radical Spirits: Spiritualism and Women's Rights in Nineteenth-Century America*. Bloomington, IN: Indiana University Press.

Brown, David H. 2003. *Santería Enthroned: Art, Ritual, and Innovation in an Afro-Cuban Religion*. Chicago: University of Chicago Press.

Carneiro, Edison. 1961. *Candomblés da Bahia*. Rio de Janeiro, Brazil: Conquista.

Clark, Mary Ann. 2005. *Where Men are Wives and Women Rule: Santería Ritual Practices and Their Gender Implications*. Gainesville, FL: University of Florida Press.

Clark, Mary Ann. 2007. *Santería: Correcting the Myths and Uncovering the Realities of a Growing Religion*. Westport, CT: Praeger Publishers.

Clark, Mary Ann. 2014. "Spiritual is Universal: Development of Black Spiritualist Churches." In *Esotericism in African American Religious Experience: "There Is a Mystery"*, edited by Stephen C. Finley, Margarita Simon Guillory, and Hugh R. Page, Jr. Leiden, 86–101. The Netherlands: Brill.

Cohen, Emma. 2008. "What is Spirit Possession? Defining, Comparing, and Explaining Two Possession Forms." *Ethnos* 73(1): 101–126.

Cox, Robert S. 2003. *Body and Soul: A Sympathetic History of American Spiritualism*. Charlottesville, VA: University of Virginia Press.

Curry, Mary Cuthrell. 1997. *Making the Gods in New York: The Yoruba Religion in the African American Community*. New York: Garland Pub.

Daniel, Yvonne. 2005. *Dancing Wisdom: Embodied Knowledge in Haitian Vodou, Cuban Yoruba, and Bahian Candomblé*. Urbana, IL: University of Illinois Press.

Dodson, Jualynne E. and José Millet Batista. 2008. *Sacred Spaces and Religious Traditions in Oriente Cuba*. Albuquerque: University of New Mexico Press.

Du Bois, William Edward Burghardt. 1900. "The Religion of the American Negro." *New World* 9: 614–625.

Edmonds, Ennis B., and Michelle A. Gonzalez. 2010. *Caribbean Religious History: An Introduction*. New York: New York University Press.

Fanthorpe, R. Lionel and Patricia. 2008. *Mysteries and Secrets of Voodoo, Santeria, and Obeah*. Toronto: Dundurn Press.

Frey, Sylvia R., and Betty Wood. 1998. *Come Shouting to Zion: African-American Protestantism in the American South and British Caribbean to 1830*. Chapel Hill, NC: University of North Carolina Press.

Grimm, Fred. 1981. "Ritual Sacrifices Turn Miami River Red." *The Miami Herald,* May 30, 1B–2B.

Huber, Leonard Victor. 1982. *Clasped Hands: Symbolism in New Orleans Cemeteries*. Lafayette, LA: Center for Louisiana Studies.

Jacobs, Claude F., and Andrew J. Kaslow. 1991. *The Spiritual Churches of New Orleans: Origins, Beliefs, and Rituals of an African-American Religion*. Knoxville, TN: University of Tennessee Press.

Jones, Mitchell. "Possession in Haitian Voodoo and Pentecostalism: A Cross-Cultural Analysis." *Open Anthropology Cooperative*. April 16, 2010. http://openanthcoop.ning.com/profiles/blogs/possession-in-haitian-voodoo\.

Kardec, Allan. 2005. *The Spirits' Book*. New York: Cosmos Classics.

Kennedy, Stetson. 1940. "Ñañigo in Florida." *Southern Folklore Quarterly* 4: 153–156.

Kremser, Manfred. 2000. *Ay Bobo: Afro-Karibische Religionen, African-Caribbean religions, Band 2*. Vienna, Austria: WUV-Universitätsverlag.

Landes, Ruth. 1994. *The City of Women*. Albuquerque: University of New Mexico Press.

Leonard, Todd Jay. 2005. *Talking to the Other Side: A History of Modern Spiritualism and Mediumship*. New York: iUniverse, Inc.

MacRobert, Iain. 1997. "The Black Roots of Pentecostalism." In *African-American Religion: Interpretive Essays in History and Culture*, ed. Timothy E. Fulop and Albert J. Raboteau, 295–309. New York and London: Routledge.

Mason, Michael Atwood. 2002. *Living Santería: Rituals and Experiences in an Afro-Cuban Religion*. Washington and London: Smithsonian Institution Press.

McMickle, Marvin Andrew. 2002. *An Encyclopedia of African American Christian Heritage*. Valley Forge, PA: Judson Press.

Millet, José. 1996. *El Espiritismo Varientes Cubanas*. Santiago de Cuba, Cuba: Editorial Oriente.

Murphy, Joseph M. 1993. *Santería: African Spirits in America*. With new Preface. Boston: Beacon Press.

Murphy, Joseph M. 1994. *Working the Spirit: Ceremonies of the African Diaspora*. Boston: Beacon Press.

Murrell, Nathaniel S. 2010. *Afro-Caribbean Religions: An Introduction to Their Historical, Cultural, and Sacred Traditions*. Philadelphia: Temple University Press.

Olmos, Margarite Fernández, and Lizbeth Paravisini-Gebert, eds. 1997. *Sacred Possessions: Vodou, Santería, Obeah, and the Caribbean*. Piscataway, NJ: Rutgers University Press.

Olmos, Margarite Fernández, and Lizbeth Paravisini-Gebert. 2003. *Creole Religions of the Caribbean: An Introduction from Vodou and Santería to Obeah and Espiritismo*. New York: New York University Press.

Parés, Luis Nicolau. 2006. "Shango in Afro-Brazilian Religion: 'Aristocracy' and 'Syncretic' Interactions." *Religioni e Società* 54: 20–39.

Raboteau, Albert J. 1978. *Slave Religion: The "Invisible Institution" in the Antebellum South*. Oxford and New York: Oxford University Press.

"The Religious Life of the Negro Slave." 1863. *Harper's New Monthly Magazine* 27: 479–485, 676–682, 816–825.

Román, Reinaldo L. 2007. *Governing Spirits: Religion, Miracles, and Spectacles in Cuba and Puerto Rico, 1898–1956*. Chapel Hill, NC: University of North Carolina Press.

Simpson, George Easton. 1978. *Black Religions in the New World*. New York: Columbia University Press.

Synan, Vinson. 1997. *The Holiness-Pentecostal Tradition: Charismatic Movements in the Twentieth Century*. 2nd ed. Grand Rapids, MI: William B. Eerdmans.

Tishken, Joel E. 2009. *Sàngó in Africa and the African Diaspora*. Bloomington, IN: Indiana University Press.

Vega, Marta Moreno. 2000. *The Altar of My Soul: The Living Traditions of Santería*. New York: One World, Ballantine Publishing Group.

Wacker, Grant. 2001. *Heaven Below: Early Pentecostals and American Culture*. Cambridge, MA: Harvard University Press.

Weisberg, Barbara. 2004. *Talking to the Dead: Kate and Maggie Fox and the Rise of Spiritualism*. New York: HarperCollins.

Wendel, Johan. 2003. *Santería Healing: A Journey into the Afro-Cuban World of Divinities, Spirits, and Sorcery*. Gainesville, FL: University Press of Florida.

Wetli, Charles V., and Rafael Martinez. 1983. "Brujeria: Manifestations of Palo Mayombe in South Florida." *Journal of the Florida Medical Association* 70: 629–634.

Williams, Joseph J. 2011. *Voodoo and Obeahs: Phases of West India Witchcraft*. New ed. Calgary, Canada: Theophania.

Young, Jason R. 2011. *Rituals of Resistance: African Atlantic Religion in Kongo and the Lowcounty South in the Era of Slavery*. Baton Rouge, LA: Louisiana State University Press.

Biographical Works

Bell, Michael E. 1979. "Harry Middleton Hyatt's Quest for the Essence of Human Spirit." *Journal of the Folklore Institute* 1(1–2): 1–27.

Bibbs, Susheel. 1998. *Heritage of Power: Marie Laveau—Mary Ellen Pleasant*. Revised edition. San Francisco: MEP.

Boyd, Valerie. 2003. *Wrapped in Rainbows: The Life of Zora Neale Hurston*. New York: Scribner.

Brown, Karen McCarthy. 2001. *Mama Lola: A Vodou Priestess in Brooklyn*. Updated and expanded ed. Berkeley, CA: University of California Press.

Burns, Khephra. 1992. "The Queen of Voodoo." *Essence* 23 (May): 80.

Colby, Vineta. 1953. "Robert Tallant." *Wilson Library Bulletin* 27 (April): 594.

"Death of Marie Laveau." 1881. *Daily Picayune* (May 17): 8.

Fandrich, Ina Johanna. 2005. *The Mysterious Voodoo Queen, Marie Laveaux: A Study of Powerful Female Leadership in Nineteenth-Century New Orleans*. Studies in African American History and Culture. New York: Routledge.

Gandolfo, Charles M. 1992. *Marie Laveau of New Orleans, the Great Voodoo Queen*. New Orleans: New Orleans Historical Voodoo Museum.

Hearn, Lafcadio. 1885. "The Last of the Voudoos." *Harper's Weekly Magazine* 29: 726–727.

Hurston, Zora Neale. 1942. *Dust Tracks on a Road*. New York: Lippincott.

Jaffe, Nina. 1997. *A Voice for the People: The Life and Work of Harold Courlander*. New York: Henry Holt and Company.

Johnson, F. Roy. 1963. *The Fabled Doctor Jim Jordan: A Story of Conjure*. Murfreesboro, TN: Johnson.

Joseph, Celucien L. 2012. "The Religious Philosophy of Jean Price-Mars." *Journal of Black Studies* 43(6) (September): 620–645.

Kaplan, Carla, ed. 2003. *Zora Neale Hurston: A Life in Letters*. New York: Anchor Books. Hurston to Langston Hughs, October 15, 1928, p. 127.

Lacey, Marc. 2008. "A U.S. Trained Entrepreneur Becomes Voodoo's Pope," *New York Times*, April 5, A7.

Long, Carolyn Morrow. 2006. *A New Orleans Voudou Priestess: The Legend and Reality of Marie Laveau*. Gainesville, FL: University Press of Florida.

McTeer, James Edwin. 1970. *High Sheriff of the Low Country*. With an Introduction by William L. Rhodes, Jr. Columbia, SC: JEM Company.

McTeer, James Edwin. 1976. *Fifty Years as a Low Country Witch Doctor*. Beaufort, SC: Beaufort Book Company.

Olson, Greg. 2012. *Voodoo Priests, Noble Savages, and Ozark Gypsies: The Life of Folklorist Mary Alicia Owen*. Columbia, MO: University of Missouri Press.

Peterson, Tracey. 1969. "The Witch of Franklin." *Southern Folklore Quarterly* 33: 297–312.

Rhodes, Jewell Parker. 1983. "Marie Laveau, Voodoo Queen." *Ms.* 28: 28–31.

"A Sainted Woman." 1881. *Democrat* (June 18): 2.

Seabrook, William B. 1942. *No Hiding Place: An Autobiography*. Philadelphia: J. B. Lippincott.

Sweet, James H. 2011. *Domingoes Álvares, African Healing, and the Intellectual History of the Atlantic World*. Chapel Hill, NC: University of North Carolina Press.

Trevigne, Barbara. 2010. "Ball of Confusion." *New Orleans Genesis* 48(192) (October): 319–323.

Turner, Arlin. 1956. *George Washington Cable: A Biography*. Durham, NC: Duke University Press.

Walker, Alice, ed. 1979. *I Love Myself When I Am Laughing and Then Again When I Am Looking Mean and Impressive: A Zora Neale Hurston Reader*. With an Introduction by Mary Helen Washington. New York: The Feminist Press at CUNY.

Ward, Martha. 2004. *Voodoo Queen: The Spirited Lives of Marie Laveau*. Jackson, MS: University Press of Mississippi.

Winslow, David J. 1969. "Bishop E. E. Everett and Some Aspects of Occultism and Folk Religion in Negro Philadelphia." *Keystone Folklore Quarterly* 14: 59–80.

Wirkus, Faustin. 1931. *The White King of La Gonave*. New York: Garden City.

Wolf, John Quincy. 1969. "Aunt Caroline Dye: The Gypsy in the 'Saint Louis Blues'." *Southern Folklore Quarterly* 33: 339–346.

Archaeological Studies of African Diasporic Practices

Brown, Kenneth L., and Doreen C. Cooper. 1990. "Structural Continuity in an African-American Slave and Tenant Community." *Historical Archaeology* 24: 7–19.

Fennell, Christopher C. 2000. "Conjuring Boundaries: Inferring Past Identities from Religious Artifacts." *International Journal of Historical Archaeology* 4: 281–313.

Ferguson, Leland G. 1980. "Looking for the 'Afro' in Colono-Indian Pottery." In *Archaeological Perspectives on Ethnicity in America*, edited by R. L. Schulyer, 14–28. Amityville, NY: Baywood.

Ferguson, Leland G. 1999. "'The Cross is a Magic Sign': Marks on Eighteenth-Century Bowls from South Carolina." In *"I, Too, Am America": Archaeological Studies of African-American Life*, edited by Theresa A. Singleton, 116–131. Charlottesville, VA: University Press of Virginia.

Galke, Laura J. 2000. "Did the Gods of Africa Die? A Re-examination of a Carroll House Crystal Assemblage." *North American Archaeologist* 21: 19–33.

Klingelhofer, Eric. 1987. "Aspects of Early Afro-American Material Culture: Artifacts from the Slave Quarters at Garrison Plantation, Maryland." *Historical Archaeology* 21: 112–119.

Leone, Mark P., and Gladys-Marie Fry. 1999. "Conjuring in the Big House Kitchen: An Interpretation of African American Belief Systems Based on the Uses of Archaeology and Folklore Sources." *Journal of American Folklore* 112: 372–403.

Orser, Charles E., Jr. 1994. "The Archaeology of African-American Slave Religion in the Antebellum South." *Cambridge Archeological Review Journal* 4: 33–45.

Patten, M. Drake. 1992. "Mankala and Minkisi: Possible Evidence of African-American Folk Beliefs and Practices." *African-American Archaeology* 6: 5–7.

Stine, Linda France, Melanie A. Cabak, and Mark D. Groover. 1996. "Blue Beads as African-American Cultural Symbols." *Historical Archaeology* 30: 49–75.

Wilkie, Laurie A. 1995. "Magic and Empowerment on the Plantation: An Archaeological Consideration of African-American World View." *Southeastern Archaeology* 14: 136–148.

Medical and Psychological Studies of African Diasporic Practices

Baer, Hans. 1982. "Toward a Systematic Typology of Black Folk Healers." *Phylon* 43: 327–343.

Brown, Jeremy. 1995. "Vital Signs: A Deadly Specter." *Discover Magazine* (September): 48–51.

Cannon, Walter B. 1942 [1957]. "Voodoo Death." *American Anthropologist* 44; reprinted in *Psychosomatic Medicine* 19: 182–190.

Colligan, Douglas. 1976. "Extreme Psychic Trauma is the Power Behind Voodoo Death." *Science Digest* (August): 44–48.

Conklin, Edmund S. 1919. "Superstitious Belief and Practice among College Students." *The American Journal of Psychology* 30: 83–102.

Davis, Wade. 1986. *The Serpent and the Rainbow: A Harvard Scientist's Astonishing Journey into the Secret Societies of Haitian Voodoo, Zombis, and Magic.* New York: Simon and Schuster.

Davis, Wade. 1988. *Passages of Darkness: The Ethnobiology of the Haitian Zombie.* Chapel Hill, NC: University of North Carolina Press.

Eastwell, Harry D. 1982. "Voodoo Death and the Mechanism for Dispatch of the Dying in East Arnhem, Australia." *American Anthropologist* 84: 5–18.

Fett, Sharla. 2002. *Working Cures: Healing, Health, and Power on Southern Slave Plantations.* Chapel Hill, NC: University of North Carolina Press.

Fontenot, Wonda L. 1994. *Secret Doctors: Ethnomedicine of African Americans.* Westport and London: Bergin & Garvey.

Hall, Arthur L., and Bourne, Peter G. 1973. "Indigenous Therapists in a Southern Black Urban Community." *Archives of General Psychiatry* 28: 137–142.

Hand, Wayland. 1966. "Plugging, Nailing, Wedging, and Kindred Folk Medical Practices." In *Folklore & Society: Essays in Honor of Benjamin A. Botkin*, ed. Bruce Jackson, 63–75. Hatboro, PA: Folklore Associates.

Harris, Marvin. 1984. "Death by Voodoo." *Psychology Today*, August, 16–17.

Jordan, Wilbert C. 1975. "Voodoo Medicine." In *Textbook of Black-Related Diseases*, edited by Richard Allen Williams. New York: McGraw-Hill Book Company.

Kimball, Chase Patterson. 1979. "A Case of Pseudocyesis Caused by 'Roots'." *American Journal of Obstetric Gynecology* 107: 801–803.

Maduro, Renaldo J. 1975. "Hoodoo Possession in San Francisco: Notes on Therapeutic Aspects of Regression." *Ethos* 3: 425–447.

Michaelson, Mike. 1972. "Can a 'Root Doctor' Actually Put a Hex On?" *Today's Health* (March): 38–41, 58, 60.

Mitchell, Faith. 1999. *Hoodoo Medicine: Gullah Herbal Remedies.* Columbia, SC: Summerhouse Press.

Moerman, Daniel E. 1979. "Anthropology of Symbolic Healing." *Current Anthropology* 20: 59–80.

Neal, James C. 1891. "Legalized Crime in Florida." In *Proceedings of the Florida Medical Association: Session of 1891*, 42–50. Jacksonville, FL: Times-Union.

"The Negro Cesar's Cure for Poison." 1792. *The Massachusetts Magazine* 4: 103–104.

Saphir, J. Robin, Arnold Gold, James Giambrone, and James F. Holland. 1967. "Voodoo Poisoning in Buffalo, NY." *The Journal of the American Medical Association* 202: 437–438.

Snow, Loudell F. 1978. "Sorcerers, Saints, and Charlatans: Black Folk Healers in Urban America." *Culture, Medicine and Psychiatry* 2: 69–106.

Straight, William M. 1983. "Throw Downs, Fixin, Rooting and Hexing." *The Journal of the Florida Medical Association, Inc.* 70: 635–641.

Tinling, David C. 1967. "Voodoo, Root Work, and Medicine." *Psychosomatic Medicine* 5: 483–490.

"Voodoo Kills by Despair." 1955. *Science News Letter* 67: 294.

Watson, Wilburn H., ed. 1984. *Black Folk Medicine: The Therapeutic Significance of Faith and Trust.* New Brunswick and London: Transaction.

Webb, Julie Yvonne. 1971. "Superstitious Influence—Voodoo in Particular—Affecting Health Practices in a Selected Population in Southern Louisiana." New Orleans: By the author.

Wintrob, Ronald M. 1973. "The Influence of Others: Witchcraft and Rootwork as Explanations of Behavior Disturbances." *Journal of Nervous and Mental Disease* 156: 318–326.

African Diasporic Magic and Religion as Crime or Deception

Berendt, John. 1994. *Midnight in the Garden of Good and Evil: A Savannah Story.* New York: Random House.
Catterall, Helen Tunnicliff, ed. 1926 [1968]. *Judicial Cases Concerning American Slavery and the Negro.* 5 vols. New York: Negro Universities Press; reprint.
Humes, Edward. 1991. *Buried Secrets: A True Story of Murder, Black Magic, and Drug-Running on the U.S Border.* New York: Penguin.
"Magazine: Jackson Resorts to Voodoo." 2003. MSNBC Website. Accessed on March 11, 2003: http://www.msnbc.com/news/880422.asp.
McCall, George J. 1963. "Symbiosis: The Case of Hoodoo and the Numbers Racket." *Social Problems* 10: 361–371.
"Md. Woman Facing Murder Charges Again." *The Washington Post*, January 5, 2002, B1.
Porteous, Laura L. 1934. "The Gri-gri Case." *Louisiana Historical Quarterly* 17: 48–63.
"'Root Doctor' Held in Murder of His Former Wife." *Jet*, June 1, 1987, 29.
"Special Judge Hears Case: Two Blacks Face Murder Charges in Voodoo Scheme." *Jet*, July 17, 1989, 52–53.
White, Jaclyn Weldon. 1999. *Whisper to the Black Candle: Voodoo, Murder, and the Case of Anjette Lyles.* Macon, GA: Mercer University Press.
Writers of the New Orleans Press. 1885. *Historical Sketch Book and Guide to New Orleans and Environs.* New York: Will H. Coleman.

Culture and African Diasporic Faiths

Anderson, Jeffrey E. 2011. "Voodoo in Black and White." In *Southern Character: Essays in Honor of Bertram Wyatt-Brown*, edited by Lisa Tendrich Frank and Daniel Kilbride, 143–159. Gainesville, FL: University Press of Florida.
Assélin, Charles. 1980. "Voodoo Myths in Haitian Literature." *Comparative Literature Studies* 17(4): 391–398.
Averill, Gage. 1997. *A Day For the Hunter, A Day For the Prey: Popular Music and Power in Haiti.* Chicago: University of Chicago Press.
Averill, Gage. n.d. *Alan Lomax's Recordings in Haiti.* Liner notes. Harte Recordings, LLC.
Baker, Houston A., Jr. 1991. *Workings of the Spirit: The Poetics of Afro-American Women's Writing.* Chicago: University of Chicago Press.
Bell, Caryn Cossé. 1997. *Revolution, Romanticism, and the Afro-Creole Protest Tradition in Louisiana, 1718–1868.* Baton Rouge, LA: Louisiana State University Press.
Blair, Jayson. 2002. "X-ray Vision Is Needed to Find Black Superheroes." *The New York Times*, May 5, 4.16.
Brown, Karen McCarthy. 1996. "Altars Happen." *African Arts* Vol. 29(2), Special Issue: Arts of Vodou (Spring): 67.
Cable, George Washington. 1886a. "Creole Slave Songs." With illustrations by E. W. Kemble. *The Century Magazine* 31: 807–828.
Cable, George Washington. 1886b. "The Dance in Place Congo." With illustrations by E. W. Kemble. *The Century Magazine* 31: 517–532.
Cable, George Washington. 1891. *The Grandissimes: A Story of Creole Life.* New York: Charles Scribner's Sons.
Chesnutt, Charles W. 1969. *The Conjure Woman.* With an Introduction by Robert M. Farnsworth. Ann Arbor, MI: University of Michigan Press.

Clar, Mimi. 1960. "Folk Belief and Custom in the Blues." *Western Folklore* 19: 173–189.
Cosentino, Donald J. 1996. "On Looking at a Vodou Altar." *African Arts* Vol. 29(2), Special Issue: Arts of Vodou (Spring): 67–70.
Courlander, Harold. 1973. *Haiti Singing*. New York: Cooper Square Publishers.
Donaldson, Gary A. 1984. "A Window on Slave Culture: Dances at Congo Square in New Orleans, 1800–1862." *Journal of Negro History* 69: 63–72.
Evans, Freddi Williams. 2011. *Congo Square: African Roots in New Orleans*. With a foreword by J. H. Kwabena 'Neketia. Lafayette, LA: University of Louisiana at Lafayette.
Férère, Nancy Turnie. 2005. *Vèvè: L'Art Rituel du Vodou Haitien/Ritual Art of Haitian Vodou/Arte Ritual del Vodu Haitiano*. With an Introduction by Gerard Alphonse Férère. Boca Raton, FL: ReMe Art Publishing.
Fortier, Alcée. 2011. *Louisiana Folktales: Lupin, Bouki, and Other Creole Stories in French Dialect and English Translation*. With an Introduction by Russell Desmond. Lafayette, LA: University of Louisiana at Lafayette Press.
Gates, Henry Louis. 1989. *The Signifying Monkey: A Theory of Afro-American Literary Criticism*. New York: Oxford University Press.
Gordon, Michelle Y. 2012. "'Midnight Scenes and Orgies': Public Narratives in New Orleans and Nineteenth Century Discourses of White Supremacy." *American Quarterly* 64(4) (December): 767–786.
Hurston, Zora Neale. 1939. *Moses, Man of the Mountain*. Philadelphia: J. B. Lippincott.
Jacob, Frank, ed. 2013. *Secret Societies: Studies in Culture, Society and History*. Würzburg, Germany: Königshausen and Neumann.
Jaskoski, Helen. 1974. "Power Unequal to Man: The Significance of Conjure in Works by Five Afro-American Authors." *Southern Folklore Quarterly* 38: 91–108.
Josephson, Nancy. 2007. *Spirits in Sequins: Vodou Flags of Haiti*. Atglen, PA: Schiffer Publishing.
Joyce, John. 1995. *Congo Square in New Orleans*. New Orleans: Louisiana Landmarks Society.
Kershaw, Andy. 2002. *The Rough Guide to Haiti*. World Music Network RGNET 1067.
Largey, Michael. 2006. *Vodou Nation: Haitian Art, Music, and Cultural Nationalism*. Chicago: University of Chicago Press.
Lindroth, James. 1996. "Images of Subversion: Ishmael Reed and the Hoodoo Trickster." *African American Review* 30: 185–196.
Mangione, Jerre. 1972. *The Dream and the Deal: The Federal Writers' Project, 1935–1943*. Boston: Little, Brown.
McAlister, Elizabeth. 2002. *Rara! Vodou, Power, and Performance in Haiti and Its Diaspora*. Berkeley, CA: University of California Press.
McAlister, Elizabeth, David Yih, Gerdes Fleurant, and Gage Averill. n.d. Liner notes. Various Artists. *Rhythms of Rapture: Sacred Musics of Haitian Vodou*. Shanachie LC 5762.
Mohammed, Patricia. 2005. "The Sign of the Loa." *Small Axe* 18 (September). Accessed on November 6, 2014: http://smallaxe.net/18.
Morrison, Toni. 1974. *Sula*. New York: Knopf.
Munro, Martin. 2013. *Exile and Post-1946 Haitian Literature: Alexis, Depestre, Ollivier, Danticat*. Liverpool, UK: Liverpool University Press.
Penkower, Monty Noam. 1977. *The Federal Writers' Project: A Study in Government Patronage of the Arts*. Urbana, IL: University of Illinois Press.
Pitkin, Helen. 1904. *An Angel by Brevet: A Story of Modern New Orleans*. Philadelphia and London: J. B. Lippincott Company.
Polk, Patrick Arthur. 1997. *Haitian Vodou Flags*. Jackson, MS: University Press of Mississippi.

Price-Mars, Jean. 1929. *Une Etape de l'Evolution Haïtienne: Etude de Socio-Psychologie*. Port-au-Prince, Haiti: Imprimerie "La Presse."

Pryse, Marjorie and Hortense J. Spillers, ed. 1985. *Conjuring: Black Women, Fiction, and Literary Tradition*. Bloomington, IN: Indiana University Press.

Reed, Ishmael. 1972a. *Conjure: Selected Poems, 1963–1970*. Amherst, MA: University of Massachusetts Press.

Reed, Ishmael. 1972b. *Mumbo Jumbo*. Garden City, NJ: Doubleday.

Rhodes, Jewell Parker. 1993. *Voodoo Dreams: A Novel of Marie Laveau*. New York: Picador USA.

Rhodes, Jewell Parker. 2005. *Voodoo Season: A Marie Laveau Mystery*. New York: Atria.

Rodman, Selden. 1988. *Where Art is Joy: Haitian Art: The First Forty Years*. New York: Ruggles de Latour.

Rodriguez, Domingo Aragú. 1995. *Los Instrumentos de Percusion*. Havana: Editorial Música Mundana.

Rushton, Cory J., and Christopher M. Moreman, ed. 2011a. *Race, Oppression and the Zombie: Essays on Cross-Cultural Appropriations of the Caribbean Tradition*. Jefferson, NC: McFarland.

Rushton, Cory J., and Christopher M. Moreman, eds. 2011b. *Zombies are Us: Essays on the Humanity of the Walking Dead*. Jefferson, NC: McFarland.

Russell, Candice. 2013. *Masterpieces of Haitian Art: Seven Decades of Unique Visual Heritage*. Atglen, PA: Schiffer Publishing.

Schroeder, Patricia R. 2002. "Rootwork: Arthur Flowers, Zora Neale Hurston, and the 'Literaery Hoodoo' Tradition." *African American Review* 36: 263–272.

Smith, Theophus H. 1994. *Conjuring Culture: Biblical Formations of Black America*. New York and Oxford: Oxford University Press.

Tallant, Robert. 1956 [2000]. *The Voodoo Queen*. New York: Putnam; reprint, Gretna, LA: Pelican.

Tsuzuki, Kyoichi. 1990. *Sam Doyle*. Books Nippan.

Tucker, Lindsey. 1994. "Recovering the Conjure Woman: Texts and Contexts in Gloria Naylor's *Mama Day*." *African American Review* 28: 173–188

Wilcken, Lois. 1992.*The Drums of Vodou*. Tempe, AZ: White Cliffs Media.

Wilson, Edmund. 1954. "Voodoo in Literature." *Tomorrow* 3.1 (Autumn).

Wilson, Judith. 1991. "Down to the Crossroads: The Art of Alison Saar." *Callaloo* 14: 107–123.

Yates, Irene. 1946. "Conjures and Cures in the Novels of Julia Peterkin." *Southern Folklore Quarterly* 10: 137–149.

Relevant Works on Haitian, African American, and African Diasporic History

Abbott, Elizabeth. 1988. *Haiti: An Insider's History of the Rise and Fall of the Duvaliers*. New York: Simon and Schuster.

Andrews, William L., and Henry Louis Gates, Jr., eds. 2000. *Slave Narratives*. Library of America Series, no.114. New York: Literary Classics of the United States, Inc.

Arthur, Charles, and Michael Dash, eds. 1999. *A Haitian Anthology: Libète*. Princeton, NJ: Markus Wiener Publishers.

Baker, T. Lindsay, and Julie P. Baker, eds. 1996. *The WPA Oklahoma Slave Narratives*. Norman, OK: University of Oklahoma Press.

Balutansky, Kathleen M., and Sourieau, Marie-Agnes, eds. 1998. *Caribbean Creolization: Reflections on the Cultural Dynamics of Language, Literature, and Identity*. Gainesville, FL: University Press of Florida.

Bastide, Roger. 1971. *African Civilisations in the New World.* Trans. by Peter Green, with a foreword by Geoffrey Parrinder. New York: Harper and Row.

Bellegarde-Smith, Patrick. 2004. *Haiti: The Breached Citadel.* 2nd ed. Toronto: Canadian Scholars' Press.

Bernard, Diederich, and Al Burt. 2006. *Papa Doc and the Tontons Macoutes.* Princeton, NJ: Wiener.

Bibb, Henry. 1850. *Narrative of the Life and Adventures of Henry Bibb, an American Slave.* 3rd ed. With an Introduction by Lucius C. Matlack. New York: Privately printed.

Blackburn, Robin. 1998. *Making of New World Slavery: From the Baroque to the Modern, 1492–1800.* New York: Verso.

Blassingame, John. 1979. *The Slave Community: Plantation Life in the Antebellum South.* 2nd ed. New York and Oxford: Oxford University Press.

Botkin, B. A., ed. 1945. *Lay My Burden Down: A Folk History of Slavery.* Athens, GA: University of Georgia Press.

Branch, Taylor. 1988. *Parting the Waters: America in the King Years, 1954–1963.* New York: Simon and Schuster.

Bremer, Thomas, ed. 2001. *History and Histories in the Caribbean.* Frankfurt am Main, Germany: Vervuert.

Brown, William Wells. 1850. *Narrative of the Life of William Wells Brown, an American Slave.* London: Charles Gilpin.

Brown, William Wells. 1880 [1968]. *My Southern Home: Or, the South and Its People.* A. G. Brown and Company; reprint, Upper Saddle River, NJ: The Gregg Press.

Bruce, Philip A. 1889. *The Plantation Negro as a Freedman: Observations on His Character, Condition, and Prospects in Virginia.* New York and London: G. P. Putnam's Sons.

Bulmer-Thomas, Victor. 2012. *The Economic History of the Caribbean since the Napoleonic Wars.* Cambridge, UK: Cambridge University Press.

Chambers, Douglas B. 2005. *Murder at Montpelier: Igbo Africans in Virginia.* Jackson, MS: University Press of Mississippi.

Chaudenson, Robert. 2001. *Creolization of Language and Culture.* New York: Routledge.

Central Intelligence Agency. 2014. "The World Fact Book: Haiti." Accessed on December 10, 2014: https://www.cia.gov/library/publications/the-world-factbook/geos/ha.html.

Cooksey, Susan, Robin Poynor, and Hein Vanhee, eds. 2013. *In Kongo Across the Waters.* Gainesville, FL: University of Florida Press.

Cooper, Anna Julia. 1988. *Slavery and the French Revolutionists, 1788–1805.* Translated by Freance Richardson Keller. Lewiston, NY: Mellen Press.

Dalmas, Antoine. 1814. *Histoire de la Révolution de Saint-Domingue: Depuis le Commencement des Troubles, jusqu'à la Prise de Jérémie et du Môle S. Nicolas par les Anglais; suivie d'un Mémoire sur le Rétablissement de cette Colonie.* Paris: Mame frères.

Dessens, Nathalie. 2007. *From Saint-Domingue to New Orleans: Migration and Influences.* Gainesville, FL: University Press of Florida.

Diouf, Sylviane A. 1998. *Servants of Allah: African Muslims Enslaved in the Americas.* New York: New York University Press.

Douglass, Frederick. 1995. *Narrative of the Life of Frederick Douglass.* With an introduction by William Lloyd Garrison, a letter from Wendell Phillips, and a new introductory note. New York: Dover.

Du Pratz, Le Page. 1763. *The History of Louisiana or of the Western Parts of Virginia and Carolina.* 2 vols. Translation. London: Becket and De Hondt.

Dubois, Laurent. 2004. *A Colony of Citizens: Revolution and Slave Emancipation in the French Caribbean, 1787–1804.* Chapel Hill, NC: University of North Carolina Press.

Dubois, Laurent. 2012. *Haiti: The Aftershocks of History*. New York: Metropolitan Books.
Dupuy, Alex. 2007. *The Prophet and the Power: Jean-Bertrand Aristide, the International Community, and Haiti*. Lanham, MD: Rowman and Littlefield.
Ferguson, James. 1988. *Papa Doc, Baby Doc: Haiti and the Duvaliers*. Oxford, UK: Blackwell.
Fick, Carolyn E. 1990. *The Making of Haiti: The Saint Domingue Revolution from Below*. Knoxville, TN: The University of Tennessee Press.
Garrigus, John D. 2011. *Before Haiti: Race and Citizenship in French Saint-Domingue*. Oxford, UK: Palgrave Macmillan.
Gaspar, David Barry, and Darlene Clark Hine. 1996. *More Than Chattel: Black Women and Slavery in the Americas*. Bloomington, IN: Indiana University Press.
Geggus, David. 2001a. "The French Slave Trade: An Overview." *The William and Mary Quarterly*. Third Series, 58, New Perspectives on the Transatlantic Slave Trade (January): 119–138.
Geggus, David. 2001b. *The Impact of the Haitian Revolution in the Atlantic World*. Columbia, SC: University of South Carolina Press.
Geggus, David. 2002. *Haitian Revolutionary Studies*. Bloomington, IN: Indiana University Press.
Gehman, Mary, and Lloyd Dennis. 1994. *The Free People of Color of New Orleans: An Introduction*. New Orleans: Margaret Media.
Georgia Writers' Project. 1940 [1986]. *Drums and Shadows: Survival Studies among the Georgia Coastal Negroes*. Reprint Athens, GA: University of Georgia Press.
Giraldo, Alexander. 2014. "Obeah: The Ultimate Resistance." Slave Resistance: A Caribbean Study. Accessed on July 1, 2014:http://scholar.library.miami.edu/slaves/Religion/religion.html.
Gomez, Michael A. 1998. *Exchanging Our Country Marks: The Transformation of African Identities in the Colonial and Antebellum South*. Chapel Hill, NC: University of North Carolina Press.
Gomez, Michael A. 2005. *Reversing Sail: A History of the African Diaspora*. Cambridge, UK: Cambridge University Press.
Gordon, Leah. 2011. "Took my heart to a Vodou priest, I said, 'What can you do Papa?' It's all screwed up…." In *Haiti Rising: Haitian History, Culture and the Earthquake of 2010*, edited by Martin Munro, 183–185. Kingston, Jamaica: University of the West Indies Press.
Greene, Anne. 1993. *The Catholic Church in Haiti: Political and Social Change*. East Lansing, MI: Michigan State University Press.
Grossman, James R. 1989. *Land of Hope: Chicago, Black Southerners, and the Great Migration*. Chicago: University of Chicago Press.
Gundaker, Grey. 1998. *Signs of Diaspora, Diaspora of Signs: Literacies, Creolization, and Vernacular Practice in African America*. New York: Oxford University Press.
Hall, Gwendolyn Midlo. 1992. *Africans in Colonial Louisiana: The Development of Afro-Creole Culture in the Eighteenth Century*. Baton Rouge, LA: Louisiana State University Press.
Hall, Gwendolyn Midlo. 2005. *Slavery and African Ethnicities in the Americas: Restoring the Links*. Chapel Hill, NC: University of North Carolina Press.
Herskovits, Melville J. 1990. *The Myth of the Negro Past*. With a new introduction by Sidney W. Mintz. Boston: Beacon Press.
Heywood, Linda M., ed. 2002. *Central Africans and Cultural Transformations in the American Diaspora*. Cambridge, UK: Cambridge University Press.
Higginbotham, Evelyn Brooks. 1993. *Righteous Discontent: The Women's Movement in the Black Baptist Church, 1880–1920*. Cambridge, MA: Harvard University Press.

Higman, B. W. 1984. *Slaves Populations of the British Caribbean, 1807–1834*. Baltimore: Johns Hopkins University Press.

Hirsch, Arnold, and Joseph Logsdon, ed. 1992. *Creole New Orleans: Race and Americanization*. Baton Rouge, LA: Louisiana State University Press.

Holloway, Joseph E., ed. 2005. *Africanisms in American Culture*. 2nd ed. Bloomington, IN: Indiana University Press.

Huggins, Nathan Irvin. 1971. *Harlem Renaissance*. London, Oxford, and New York: Oxford University Press.

Hughes, Louis. 1897. *Thirty Years a Slave: From Bondage to Freedom*. Milwaukee: South Side Printing Company.

Hutchinson, George. 1995. *The Harlem Renaissance in Black and White*. Cambridge, MA: Harvard University Press.

Janzen, John M. 1982. *Lemba, 1650–1932: A Drum of Affliction in Africa and the New World*. New York: Garland.

Jones, Jacqueline. 1995. *Labor of Love, Labor of Sorrow: Black Women, Work, and the Family from Slavery to the Present*. New York: Vintage.

Joseph, Celucien L. 2013. *Haitian Modernity and Liberative Interruptions: Disourse on Race, Religion, and Freedom*. Lanham: University Press of America, Inc.

Joyner, Charles. 1984. *Down by the Riverside: A South Carolina Slave Community*. Chicago: University of Chicago Press.

Juang, Richard M., and Noelle Morrissette, eds. 2008. *Africa and the Americas: Culture, Politics, and History*. Santa Barbara, CA: ABC-CLIO.

Katz, Jonathan M. 2013. *The Big Truck that Went By: How the World Came to Save Haiti and Left Behind a Disaster*. New York: Palgrave Macmillan.

Kein, Sybil, ed. 2000. *Creole: The History and Legacy of Louisiana's Free People of Color*. Baton Rouge, LA: Louisiana State University Press.

Kelley, Robin D. G. 1993. "'We Are Not What We Seem': Rethinking Black Working-Class Opposition in the Jim Crow South." *The Journal of American History* 80: 75–111.

Klein, Herbert S. 1999. *The Atlantic Slave Trade*. Cambridge, UK: Cambridge University Press.

Korstad, Robert, and Nelson Lichtenstein. 1988. "Opportunities Found and Lost: Labor, Radicals, and the Early Civil Rights Movement." *Journal of American History* 75: 786–811.

Kramer, Victor A. and Robert A. Russ, eds. 1997. *Harlem Renaissance Re-examined: A Revised and Expanded Edition*. Troy, NY: Whitston.

Landers, Jane. 1999. *Black Society in Spanish Florida*. With a Foreword by Peter H. Wood. Urbana, IL: University of Illinois Press.

Levine, Lawrence W. 1977. *Black Culture and Black Consciousness: Afro-American Thought from Slavery to Freedom*. New York: Oxford University Press.

Lovejoy, Paul E. 1983. *Transformations in Slavery: A History of Slavery in Africa*. Cambridge, UK: Cambridge University Press.

McKinney, Louise. 2006. *New Orleans: A Cultural History*. New York and Oxford: Oxford University Press.

Mishkin, Tracy. 1998. *The Harlem and Irish Renaissances: Language, Identity, and Representation*. With a Foreword by George Bornstein. Gainesville and Tallahassee, FL: University of Florida Press.

Moreau de Saint-Méry, Médéric-Louis-Élie. 1797. *Description Topographique, Physique, Civile, Politique et Historique de la Partie Française de l'Isle de Saint-Domingue*. 2 vols. Philadelphia.

Moreau de Saint-Méry, Médéric-Louis-Élie, and Ivor D. Spencer. 1985. *A Civilization That Perished: The Last Years of White Colonial Rule in Haiti.* Lanham, MD: University Press of America.

Morgan, Philip D. 1998. *Slave Counterpoint: Black Culture in the Eighteenth-Century Chesapeake and Low Country.* Chapel Hill, NC: University of North Carolina Press.

Müller, Gesine. 2012. *Die Koloniale Karibik. Transferprozesse in Hispanophonen und Frankophonen Literaturen.* Berlin: De Gruyter.

Mullins, Paul R. 1999. *Race and Affluence: An Archaeology of African American and Consumer Culture.* New York: Kluwer Academic/Plenum.

Ojo, Olatunji and Nadine Hunt, eds. 2012. *Slavery in Africa and the Caribbean: A History of Enslavement and Identity since the Eighteenth Century.* London: I. B. Tauris.

Ott, Thomas O. 1973. *The Haitian Revolution, 1789–1804.* Knoxville, TN: University of Tennessee Press.

Owen, Nicholas. 1930. *Journal of a Slave Dealer: A View of Some Remarkable Axcedents in the Life of Nics. Owen on the Coast of Africa and America from the Year 1746 to the Year 1757.* Edited and with and Introduction by Eveline Martin. London: George Routledge and Sons, Ltd..

Paul, Emmanuel Casséus. 1962. *Panorama du Folklore Haïtien: Présence Africaine en Haïti.* Port-au-Prince, Haiti: Impr. De l'État.

Perdue, Charles, Thomas Barden, and Robert Phillips. 1976. *Weevils in the Wheat: Interviews with Virginia Ex-slaves.* Charlottesville, VA: University Press of Virginia.

Pollitzer, William S. 1999. *The Gullah People and Their African Heritage.* With a Foreword by David Moltke-Hansen. Athens, GA: University of Georgia Press.

Postma, Johannes. 2003. *The Atlantic Slave Trade.* Westport, CT: Greenwood Press.

Price, Richard. 1996. *Maroon Societies: Rebel Slave Communities in the Americas.* 3rd ed. Baltimore: Johns Hopkins University Press.

Rawick, George P., ed. 1972–78. *The American Slave: A Composite Autobiography.* Westport, CT: Greenwood.

Rediker, Marcus. 2007. *The Slave Ship.* New York: Penguin.

Reinhardt, Catherine A. 2006. *Claims to Memory: Beyond Slavery and Emancipation in the French Caribbean.* New York: Berghahn Books.

Renda, Mary A. 2001. *Taking Haiti: Military Occupation and the Culture of U.S. Imperialsim, 1915–1940.* Chapel Hill, NC: University of North Carolina Press.

Rodriguez, Junius P. 2007. *Encyclopedia of Slave Resistance and Rebellion.* 2 vols. Westport, CT: Greenwood Press.

Saxon, Lyle. 1928 [2004]. *Fabulous New Orleans.* New York: Century; reprint, Gretna, LA: Pelican Publishing.

Shaw, Rosalind, and Charles Stewart. 1994. *Syncretism/Anti-Syncretism: The Politics of Religious Synthesis.* London: Routledge.

Smalley, Eugene V. 1887. "Sugar-Making in Louisiana." *The Century* 35: 100–120.

Smith, Katherine. 2010. "Gede Rising: Haiti in the Age of Vagabondaj." PhD dissertation, University of California Los Angeles.

St. John, Spenser. 1884. *Hayti or the Black Republic.* London: Smith, Elder, and Company.

Stepick, Alex, and Dale Frederick Swartz. 1982. *Haitian Refugees in the U.S.* London: Minority Rights Group.

Stewart, Charles. 2007. *Creolization: History, Ethnography, Theory.* Walnut Creek, CA: Left Coast Press.

Stoyer, Jacob. 1898. *My Life in the South.* 4th ed. Salem, MA: Newcomb and Gauss.

Sublette, Ned. 2008. *The World That Made New Orleans: From Spanish Silver to Congo Square.* Chicago: Lawrence Hill Books.

Suttles, William C., Jr. 1971. "African Religious Survivals as Factors in American Slave Revolts." *Journal of Negro History* 56: 97–104.
Sweet, Frank W. 2005. *Legal History of the Color Line: The Rise and Triumph of the One-Drop Rule*. Palm Coast, FL: Backintyme.
Sweet, James H. 2003. *Recreating Africa: Culture, Kinship, and Religion in the African-Portuguese World, 1441–1770*. Chapel Hill, NC: University of North Carolina Press.
Thornton, John. 1993. "'I Am the Subject of the King of Congo': African Political Ideology and the Haitian Revolution." *Journal of World History* 4(2) (Fall): 181–214.
Thornton, John. 1998. *Africa and Africans in the Making of the Atlantic World, 1400–1800*. Cambridge, UK: Cambridge University Press.
Valdman, Albert, et al. 2010. *Dictionary of Louisiana French as Spoken in Cajun, Creole, and American Indian Communities*. Jackson, MS: University Press of Mississippi.
Waligora-Davis, Nicole A. 2011. *Sanctuary: African Americans and Empire*. Oxford: Oxford University Press.
Woolford, Ellen, and Washabaugh, William, eds. 1983. *The Social Context of Creolization*. Ann Arbor, MI: Karoma Publishers, Inc.
Young, A. S. "Doc." 1953. "Are Creoles Negroes?" *JET Magazine*, June 25, 12–15.

African History, Traditional Religion, and Folklore

Afigbo, A. E. 1981. *Ropes of Sand: Studies in Igbo History and Culture*. Ibadan, Nigeria: University Press Limited.
Apter, Andrew. 1987. "The Historiography of Yoruba Myth and Ritual." *History in Africa* 14: 1–25.
Awe, Bolanle. 1974. "Praise Poems as Historical Data: The Example of the Yoruba Oríkì." *Journal of the International African Institute* 44(4) (October): 331–349.
Barnes, Sandra T., ed. 1989. *Africa's Ogun: Old World and New*. African Systems of Thought Series. Bloomington, IN: Indiana University Press.
Belcher, Stephen. 2005. *African Myths of Origin*. London: Penguin.
Blier, Suzanne Preston. 1995. *African Vodun: Art, Psychology, and Power*. Chicago and London: University of Chicago Press.
Bowen, T. J. 1857. *Adventures and Missionary Labors in Several Countried in the Interior of Africa, from 1849 to 1856*. Charleston, SC: Southern Baptist Publication Society.
Brown, Charles S., and Yvonne R. Chappelle. 1977. "African Religions and the Quest for Afro-American Heritage." In *African Religions: A Symposium*, ed. Newell S. Booth, Jr., 241–254. New York, London, and Lagos: NOK.
Burton, Richard F. 1864. *A Mission to Gelele, King of Dahome*. London: Tinsley Brothers.
Courlander, Harold. 1975. *A Treasury of African Folklore: The Oral Literature, Traditions, Myths, Legends, Epics, Tales, Recollections, Wisdom, Sayings, and Humor of Africa*. New York: Crown.
Ellis, A. B. 1883. *The Land of Fetish*. London: Chapman and Hall.
Ellis, A. B. 1887. *The Tshi-Speaking Peoples of the Gold Coast of West Africa: Their Religion, Manners, Customs, Laws, Language, Etc*. London: Chapman and Hall.
Ellis, A. B. 1890. *The Ewe-Speaking Peoples of the Slave Coast of West Africa: Their Religion, Manners, Customs, Laws, Languages, &c*. London: Chapman and Hall.
Ellis, A. B. 1891. "On Vŏdu Worship." *The Popular Science Monthly* 38: 651–663.
Ellis, A. B. 1964. *The Yoruba-Speaking Peoples of the Slave Coast of West Africa: Their Religion, Manners, Customs, Laws, Language, Etc*. Chicago: Benin Press, Ltd.
Falola, Toyin, and Matt D. Childs, eds. 2005. *The Yoruba Diaspora in the Atlantic World*. Bloomington, IN: Indiana University Press.

Farrow, Stephen S. 1926 [1996]. *Faith, Fancies and Fetich, Or Yoruba Paganism: Being an Account of the Religious Beliefs of the West African Blacks, Particularly of the Yoruba Tribes of Southern Nigeria*. Society for Promoting Christian Knowledge; reprint Athelia Henrietta Press.

Folk-Lore and Ethnology. 1893. *Southern Workman* 22: 180–181.

Harris, Joseph E. 1987. *Africans and Their History*. Revised ed. New York: Penguin GroUniversity Press.

Haskins, James and Joann Biondi. 1995. *From Afar to Zulu: A Dictionary of African Cultures*. New York: Walker and Company.

Herskovits, Melville J. 1938. *Dahomey: An Ancient West African Kingdom*. 2 vols. New York: J. J. Augustin.

Hilton, Anne. 1982. *The Kingdom of Kongo*. Oxford: Oxford University Press.

Hutton, Catherine. 1819–1821. *The Tour of Africa: Containing a Concise Account of All the Countries in that Quarter of the Globe Hitherto Visited by Europeans*. London: Baldwin, Cradock, and Joy.

Isichei, Elizabeth. 1976. *A History of the Igbo People*. London: Macmillan Press.

Janzen, John M., and Wyatt MacGaffey, eds. 1974. *An Anthology of Kongo Religion*. Lawrence, KS: University of Kansas Press.

Kingsley, Mary. 1982. *Travels in West Africa: Congo Français, Corisco and Cameroons*. 5th ed. With an Introduction by Elizabeth Claridge. London: Virago Press.

Law, Robin. 1976. "Early Yoruba Historiography." *History in Africa* 3: 69–89.

Law, Robin. 2004. *Ouidah: The Social History of a West African Slaving 'Port', 1727–1892*. Athens, OH: Ohio University Press.

Lloyd, P. C. 1955. "The Yoruba Lineage." *Journal of the International African Institute* 25(3) (July): 235–251.

MacGaffey, Wyatt. 1986. *Religion and Society in Central Africa: The BaKongo of Central Zaire*. Chicago and London: The University of Chicago Press.

MacGaffey, Wyatt, Michael D. Harris, Sylvia H. Williams, and David C. Driskell. 1993. *Astonishment and Power: The Eyes of Understanding: Kongo Minkisi: The Art of Renée Stout*. Washington, DC: Smithsonian Institution Press.

Okediji, Moyo. 1997. "Art of the Yoruba." *Art Institute of Chicago Museum Studies* 23(2), African Art at The Art Institute of Chicago: 164–181, 198.

Oliver, Roland and J. D. Fage. 1988. *A Short History of Africa*. 6th ed. London: Penguin Group.

Olupona, Jacob K., ed. 2000. *African Spirituality: Forms, Meanings and Expressions*. With a Foreword by Charles Long. New York: Crossroad.

Opoku, Kofi Asare. 1978. *West African Traditional Religion*. Accra, London, et al.: FEP International Private Limited.

Parrinder, E. G. 1962. *African Traditional Religion*. London: S. P. C. K.

Parrinder, Geoffrey. 1961. *West African Religion: A Study of the Beliefs and Practices of Akan, Ewe, Yoruba, Ibo, and Kindred Peoples*. 2nd ed. With a Foreword by Edwin Smith. London: Epworth Press.

Peel, J. D. Y. 2000. *Religious Encounter and the Making of the Yoruba*. Bloomington, IN: Indiana University Press.

Rosenthal, Judy. 1998. *Possession, Ecstasy, and Law in Ewe Voodoo*. Charlottesville and London: University Press of Virginia.

Spring, Christopher. 1993. *African Arms and Armor*. Washington DC: Smithsonian Institute Press.

Sundermeier, Theo. 1998. *The Individual and Community in African Traditional Religions*. Hamburg, Germany: Lit Verlag.

Thompson, Robert Farris. 1983. *Flash of the Spirit: African and Afro-American Art and Philosophy*. New York: Random House.

Thompson, Robert Farris. 1993. *Face of the Gods: Art and Altars of Africa and the African Americas*. New York: The Museum of African Art.

Thornton, John. 1983. *The Kingdom of Kongo: Civil War and Transition, 1641–1718*. Madison, WI: University of Wisconsin Press.

Thornton, John. 1984. "The Development of an African Catholic Church in the Kingdom of Kongo, 1491–1750." *Journal of African History* 25(2): 147–167.

Uchendu, V. C. 1965. *The Igbo of Southeastern Nigeria*. New York: Holt, Rinehart and Winston.

Umeh, John Anenechukwu. 1997, 1999. *After God is Dibia: Igbo Cosmology, Divination and Sacred Science in Nigeria*. 2 vols. London: Karnak House.

Some Prominent How-To Vodou, Voodoo, Hoodoo, and Conjure Books

Alvarado, Denise. 2011. *The Voodoo Hoodoo Spellbook*. Forward by Doktor Snake. San Francisco: Red Wheel/Weiser.

Aunt Sally's Policy Players' Dream Book. 1889. New York: H. J. Wehman; reprint, Los Angeles: Indio Products, Inc.

Best, Michael R., and Frank H. Brightman. 1973. *The Book of Secrets of Albertus Magnus of the Virtues of Herbs, Stones and Certain Beasts--Also a Book of the Marvels of the World*. Studies in Tudor and Stuart Literature series, edited by F. H. Mares and A. T. Brissenden, vol. 2. Oxford and New York: Oxford UP.

Black, S. Jason, and Christopher S. Hyatt. 1995. *Urban Voodoo: A Beginner's Guide to Afro-Caribbean Magic*. Tempe, AZ: New Falcon.

Canizares, Raul. 2001. *The Life and Works of Marie Laveau: Gris-gris, Cleansings, Charms, Hexes*. Plainview, NY: Original.

Claremont, Lewis de. 1966. *Legends of Incense, Herb & Oil Magic*. Revised ed. Arlington, TX: Dorene.

DeLaurence, Lauren William. 1902. *The Great Book of Magical Art, Hindu Magic, and East Indian Occultism*. Kansas City, MO: Neeland Media.

Filan, Kenaz. 2006. *The Haitian Vodou Handbook: Protocols for Riding with the Lwa*. Rochester, VT: Destiny Books.

Gamache, Henri. 1998. *The Master Book of Candle Burning*. Revised ed. Plainview, NY: Original.

Gandolfo, Charles M. n. d. *Voodoo Vé-Vé's and Talismans and How to Use Them*. New Orleans: New Orleans Historical Voodoo Museum.

Guigard, Mercedes Foucard. 2006. *Répertoire Pratique des Loa du Vodou Haïtien - Practical Directory of the Loa of Haitian Vodou*. Port-au-Prince, Haiti: Reme Art Publishing.

Hohman, John George. 1855. *Pow-Wows, or Long Lost Friend: A Collection of Mysterious and Invaluable Arts and Remedies for Man As Well As Animals—With Many Proofs*. Reprint. New York: Fulton Religious Supply.

Jim, Papa, and James e Sickafus. 1985. *Papa Jim Magical Herb Book*. 2nd ed. San Antonio: Papa Jim II, Inc.

Lampe, H. U. 1982. *Famous Voodoo Rituals & Spells: A Voodoo Handbook*. New ed. Minneapolis: Marlar.

Laveau, Marie [pseudonym]. 1991. *Original Black and White Magic*. Los Angeles: International Imports.

Malbrough, Ray T. 1986. *Charms, Spells, and Formulas: For the Making and Use of Gris-Gris, Herb Candles, Doll Magick, Incenses, Oils and Powders . . . To Gain Love, Protection, Prosperity, Luck, and Prophetic Dreams.* Llewellyn's Practical Magick Series. St. Paul, MN: Llewellyn.

Rucker, Herman. 1938. *Black Herman's Secrets of Magic, Mystery, and Legerdemain.* New York: Dorene.

Selig, Godfrey A. 1982. *The Secrets of the Psalms.* New ed. Arlington, TX: Dorene.

The Sixth and Seventh Books of Moses, or Moses' Magical Spirit Art. 1950. New ed. Arlington, TX: Dorene.

Snake, Doktor. 2000. *Doktor Snake's Voodoo Spellbook: Spells, Curses and Folk Magic for All Your Needs.* New York: St. Martin's Press.

Sonny Boy Blue Book Guide to Success Power. 2000. 6th ed. Birmingham: By the author, 1715 3rd Avenue N.

Turlington, Shannon R. 2002. *The Complete Idiot's Guide® to Voodoo.* Indianapolis: Alpha.

Yronwode, Catherine. 2002. *Hoodoo Herb and Root Magic: A Materia Magica of African-American Conjure and Traditional Formulary Giving the Spiritual Uses of Natural Herbs, Roots, Minerals, and Zoological Curios.* Forestville, CA: Lucky Mojo Curio Company.

About the Editor and Contributors

Editor

Jeffrey E. Anderson is Dr. William R. Hammond Professor of Liberal Arts at the University of Louisiana at Monroe. He is the author of *Conjure in African American Society* (2005), *Hoodoo, Voodoo, and Conjure: A Handbook* (2008), and numerous articles on related topics.

Contributors

N. Lynn Anderson studied history and sociology at Samford University. She is currently an independent scholar and works with her husband, Jeffrey E. Anderson, in his research on hoodoo, Voodoo, and related subjects.

Eoghan Craig Ballard received his MA (1995) and PhD (2005) in Folklore and Folklife from the University of Pennsylvania, where he also worked for fifteen years. His specialties include Gaelic culture and Afro-Cuban religions. His doctoral fieldwork concerned Congo religion in Cuba. His experiential approach to research led him to initiations in the Afro-Cuban Quimbisa, and in the Cuban form of Haitian Vodou (Vodú). He currently is researching the influence of Freemasonry in Afro-Caribbean religions and Umbanda as a research associate of the Roosevelt Center, a nonprofit focusing on Fraternalism and Civil Society.

Patrick R. Bigsby received his MA in Journalism (2010) from the University of Southern California. He is currently pursuing both a PhD in Journalism and a JD from the University of Iowa. He has been published in a variety of newspapers, magazines, and journals and is an accomplished musician.

Matthew R. Blaylock received his BS in Business Administration from the University of North Carolina Chapel Hill in 2005. He later majored in history at the University of North Carolina Asheville and then received an MA in American History from Western Carolina University in 2011. Matt is currently working on his PhD in American History at UTK. His main historical interests include social and cultural history with an emphasis on the American South.

Joshua Clegg Caffery is a Visiting Lecturer in Folklore at Indiana University, Bloomington, and was the Alan Lomax Fellow in Folklife Studies at the John W. Kluge Center of the Library of Congress from 2013 to 2014. In addition to his academic career, he was a 2010 Grammy Nominee for his work on Feufollet's *En Couleurs*. Among his notable publications is *Traditional Music in Coastal Louisiana: The 1934*

Lomax Recordings (2013). He is currently working on a second book, *In the Creole Twilight*.

John Cappucci received his doctorate from Carleton University in Ottawa, Canada. He teaches at the University of Windsor and offers several online courses for Algonquin College.

Mary Ann Clark is an independent scholar who teaches at Yavapai College in Prescott, Arizona. She has published widely about the Afro-Cuban religion of Santería and its sister traditions. Her most recent work includes *Then We'll Sing a New Song: African Influences on America's Religious Landscape*, a fascinating examination of how African religions have shaped beliefs and practices in the contemporary United States, and "Spirit is Universal: Development of Black Spiritualist Churches" in *Esotericism in African American Religious Experience*, which explores a new transdisciplinary enterprise focused on the esoteric lore and practices in Africa and the African Diaspora.

Louise Fenton is a Senior Lecturer in Contextual Studies at the University of Wolverhampton. Her research focuses primarily on representations of witchcraft, Voodoo, and zombis in film, literature, and other art forms. She coauthored with Lawrence Zeegen the second edition of *The Fundamentals of Illustration* (2012).

Matthew J. Forss is an independent ethnomusicology researcher, writer, author, and reviewer based in Omro, Wisconsin. He holds an MFA in creative writing from Goddard College-Plainfield, Vermont. He is published in *Ethnomusicology* and *Songlines*. He has published articles with Golson Media, Facts On File, Greenwood Press, Oxford University Press, and ABC-CLIO. Since 2000, he has been writing world music reviews for Edmonton-based Inside World Music.com. Since 2007, he has worked with ReviewYou.com as a contract music reviewer and biographer in multiple genres. He has nearly 5,000 recordings from every country in the world and continues to actively acquire more recordings.

Jonathan Foster is an Instructor of History at Great Basin College. He earned his PhD from the University of Nevada, Las Vegas, in 2009. His dissertation was entitled "Stigma Cities: Dystopian Urban Identities in the United States West and South in the Twentieth Century." He is the author of numerous scholarly articles, book reviews, and other publications.

Richard B. Freeman is a cultural and visual anthropologist and librarian with the University of Florida, who specializes in research on political activism in Latin America and visual anthropology. This all began because of his love of photography and travel. In 2012, he was introduced to Professor Ben Hebblethwaite, whose passion is the Kreyòl language and Vodou religion. Once introduced, Freeman worked with Hebblethwaite, making trips to Little Haiti in Miami and to Haiti to do video work and take photographs of Vodou ceremonies.

LaShawn Harris is an Assistant Professor of History at Michigan State University. Her scholarly articles have appeared in *Black Women, Gender & Families*, *Journal of*

African American History, *Journal for the Study of Radicalism*, and the *Journal of Social History*.

Kevin Hogg teaches English and Social Studies at Mount Baker Secondary School in Cranbrook, British Columbia. He holds an MA in English Literature from Carleton University and focuses his research on world religions and baseball history.

Ronald Jackson II is a PhD student at Michigan State University.

Frank Jacob is an Assistant Professor at the City University of New York, Queensborough Community College. Jacob studied Modern History, Ancient History, and Japanese Studies at the University of Würzburg, where he earned his MA in 2010. Two years later, he received his PhD at the University of Erlangen-Nürnberg. He has taught at the universities of Düsseldorf, Erlangen-Nürnberg, and Würzburg. He is the author of *Japanism, Pan-Asianism, and Terrorism: A Short History of the Amur Society (the Black Dragons), 1901–1945* (2014) and two other books in German about secret societies.

Adam Jortner is an Associate Professor of History at Auburn University. Among his many publications is *The Gods of Prophetstown: The Battle of Tippecanoe and the Holy War for the American Frontier* (2011).

Celucien L. Joseph, PhD (University of Texas at Dallas) is an Assistant Professor of English at Indian River State College. His most recent book is *Haitian Modernity and Liberative Interruptions: Discourse on Race, Religion, and Freedom* (University Press of America, 2014).

Helen Lock recently retired from the University of Louisiana at Monroe. She earned her PhD from the University of Virginia and is the author of *A Case of Mis-Taken Identity: Detective Undercurrents in Recent African American Fiction* (1994).

Carolyn Morrow Long is an independent scholar and a leading researcher in the fields of Voodoo, hoodoo, and New Orleans culture. In addition to several articles, she has published three books: *Spiritual Merchants: Religion, Magic, and Commerce* (2001), *A New Orleans Voudou Priestess: The Legend and Reality of Marie Laveau* (2006), and *Madame Lalaurie, Mistress of the Haunted House* (2012).

Wyatt MacGaffey is Professor of Anthropology, Emeritus, at Haverford College. He has published extensively on the social organization, religion, art, and history of Central Africa. His most recent work has been on the political history of northern Ghana.

Sandra Marshall is an independent scholar who received her MA in History from the University of Louisiana at Monroe (2014).

Tina N. Mullone is Associate Professor of Dance at the University of Louisiana at Monroe. She sits on the South Regional Board of the American College Dance Association. Additionally, she continues her professional dance career as Associate Guest Artist with Contemporary Dance/Fort Worth, a member of the Beckles

Dancing Company, and an independent artist. Ms. Mullone received her BA in Art History from the University of Oklahoma and her MFA in Dance from Texas Christian University. She is a strong advocate for arts and education.

Salvador Jimenez Murguia is Associate Professor of Sociology at Akita International University and Paul Orfalea Center Fellow in Global Studies at the University of California, Santa Barbara. His current research interests include visions, apparitions, and spirit possession. His work has appeared in over a dozen edited volumes, as well as in a host of journals including the *American Behavioral Scientist, ESSACHESS – Journal for Communication Studies*, the *Journal for the Scientific Study of Religion*, and *Preturnature*. He is working on four books including one under contract with Intellect Press titled *Epic Fails!: Crystal Pepsi, Mullets, and the Icons of Unpopular Culture*.

Arua Oko Omaka earned his PhD in history from McMaster University, Canada. He is currently a sessional faculty at University of Toronto, Scarborough, Canada. His research interests include African history, conflict resolution and peace-building, genocide, counterinsurgency, and human rights. His articles have appeared in learned journals such as *Canadian Journal of History, Journal of Retracing Africa, Oral History Association of Australia*, and *Journal of Intelligence, Security and Propaganda*.

Urszula Pruchniewska is a PhD student in media and communication at Temple University, Philadelphia, Pennsylvania. She was born in Poland, grew up in South Africa and New Zealand, and moved to the United States for graduate study. She has worked in various communication-related roles for eight years and has a BA in media and communication, as well as a BS in psychology. Her research interests lie at the crossroads of gender, sexuality, visual communication, and popular culture.

Christian Remse is a managing editor and independent scholar, who received his PhD from Bowling Green State University, Ohio. His research focus includes cultural politics, politics of representation, and postmodernism with special attention to Vodou, horror, and gothic texts. Apart from presenting at international conferences, Christian Remse has published in *Caribbeing: Comparing Caribbean Literatures and Cultures, The Projector: Film and Media Journal,* and the *Encyclopedia of Slavery in the Americas* (forthcoming).

Tom Riser is an independent scholar who received his MA from the University of Louisiana at Monroe. His research interests include Spiritualism, Spiritual Churches, and Mississippi Valley Voodoo.

Kodi Roberts is an Assistant Professor of History at Louisiana State University. He is currently preparing a book manuscript entitled *The Promise of Power: The Racial, Gender, & Economic Politics of Voodoo in New Orleans, 1889–1940*.

Phoenix Savage, a native of Philadelphia, Pennsylvania, is Assistant Professor of Art at Tougaloo College. Savage is widely known for her cultural writings that appear in the *Encyclopedia of Slavery and Resistance*, the *Encyclopedia of the Blues*, and the *Encyclopedia of Mississippi*. Her most recent publications are two books of illustrated histories using vintage black-and-white images: *African Americans of Jackson* (2008) and *African Americans of New Orleans* (2010). Phoenix Savage holds an MFA in sculpture and maintains an active exhibition schedule.

Patricia Scheu (Manbo Vye Zo Komande LaMenfo) is an independent scholar, author, and Manbo Asogwe of Haitian Vodou. In 2003, she was ordained as a priest of Vodou in Jacmel, Haiti, and returned to the United States to raise La Sosyete du Marche, Inc., a 501c3 Vodou church in southeastern Pennsylvania. LaMenfo works to demonstrate the theurgy and grace of Haitian Vodou through annual trips to Haiti and continuous scholarly study on the liturgy, music, and history of Haitian Vodou. She can be reached via the sosyete's website at www.sosyetedumarche.com.

Angela Watkins defended her dissertation in June 2014, earning a PhD in English from the University of Iowa. Her dissertation, entitled "Mambos, Priestesses, and Goddesses: Spiritual Healing Through Vodou in Black Women's Narratives of Haiti and New Orleans," examines the practice of Vodou as depicted through fiction by women writers of color, arguing that it is an integral African spiritual tradition.

Linda S. Watts is Professor of American Studies, School of Interdisciplinary Arts and Sciences, and Campus-Level Point-of-Contact for Assessment of Student Learning at the University of Washington, Bothell.

Jason R. Young is an Associate Professor of History at the State University of New York (SUNY), Buffalo. He is the author *Rituals of Resistance* (2007) and the co-editor, with Edward J. Blum, of *The Souls of W.E.B. Du Bois: New Essays and Reflections* (2009). He is currently conducting research toward his next book project, *'To Make the Slave Anew': Art, History and the Politics of Authenticity*.

Index

Bold page numbers indicate main encyclopedia articles.
Italicized page numbers indicate photographs.

African, The (Courlander), 60
African traditional religion. *See names of specific African spirits*; Vodu, West African
Agaja, 68
Agassu/Agoussou, **1**, 2
Agwe Ta'Woyo, **2–3**; feast day, colors, and offerings, 3; in lwa hierarchy, 167; as sea spirit, 71, 97, 151; services, 3. *See also* Ulrich, Saint
Ainsi Parla l'Oncle (Mars), 160, 243–44
Aizan-Veleteke, **3–4**
Alexander, Jim, **4–5**, 226, 307
Alexis, Jacques Stéphen, 161
Altars, **6–7**, 12, 71; on Haitian tombs, 49; Mississippi Valley Voodoo and, 49, 113; in openings, 221; swords on, 282. *See also* Paket Kongo; Simbi
American Voudou: Journey into a Hidden World (Davis), 292
"Among the Voodoos" (Owen), 344–50, 379
Ancestral spirits, **7–9**; Haitian Voudou and, 7–9, 167, 301. *See also names of specific spirits*
Anderson, Leafy, 159–60, 213, 277, 278. *See also* Spiritual Churches
Angel by Brevet, An: A Story of Modern New Orleans (Pitkin), 1, 29, 52, 110, 162, 171, 353, 367–78
Angel Heart (film), 89, 105
Another Good Loving Blues (Flowers), 163
Anthony, Saint (of Padua): Legba and, 157
Antisuperstition campaigns, 158–59; Anti-Superstition Oath and, 11. *See also* Anti-Vodou campaigns
Anti-Vodou campaigns, **10–11**, 158–59
Art, Haitian, 11, 12–15; American occupation and, 13; papier-mâché and sculpture, 14; political climate and, 13–14; sacred, 11–12. *See also* Art, Vodou/Voodoo in; Artists, Haitian
Art, Vodou/Voodoo in, **11–15**; Catholic iconography and, 11, 14; lwa and, 12–15. *See also* Altars; Art, Haitian; Artists, Haitian; Drapo; Vèvè
Artists, Haitian, 12–14; first generation of, 12; Saint-Soleil, 13; second and third generations of, 13. *See also names of specific Haitian artists*; Art, Haitian; Art, Vodou/Voodoo in
Asbury, Herbert: *The French Quarter,* 75
Asiento, 26
Asogwe, 15–16
Ason, **15–16**, 85, *332, 333, 334*; laplas and, 150; music and, 193, 194
Aspects Educatifs et Moraux du Vodou Haitien (Michel), 183
Aunt Sally's Policy Players Dream Book, 35
Ayida Wedo, **16–17**, 69; Catholic association, 70; feast days, 70
Azaka, **17–18**; avatars, 17; feast day and colors, 18; offerings, 18, *335*; praise name, 17. *See also* Isidore, Saint

Baby Doc. *See* Duvalier, Jean-Claude
Bak d'Agwe, 2
Baka, 168
Barbara, Saint: Chango and, 52
Baron LaCroix, 19
Baron Samedi, **19–20**, 49, 90; dance and, 72; death/dying and, 19; feast day, 20; film portrayals of, 104; healing and, 20; infertility and, 20; Kanzo initiatory rites and, 20; offerings, 20; vèvè, 20. *See also* Expedite, Saint; Martin, Saint (de Porres)
Baron Simitye, 19

Barra, Pierrot, 14
Bathing, ritual (Haiti), 329
Bayou St. Jean, **20–21**. *See also* Saint John's Eve
Beauvoir, Max Gesner, **22–23**; as Ati of Haiti, 23, 203; Bode Nasyonal and, 22; G.E.R.T. and, 22; Peristyle de Mariani and Temple of Yehwe and, 22, 23. *See also* National Confederation of Haitian Vodou
Bienville, Jean-Baptiste Le Moyne Sieur de, 21, 61, 211
Bellegarde-Smith, Patrick, **23–24**; *Haiti: The Breached Citadel*, 24; as KOSANBA editor, 56; literary importance of, 34
Benoit, Rigaud, 12, 13
Bight of Benin, **24–27**; trans-Atlantic slave trade and, 25–26, 124. *See also* Slavery and slave trade
Bight of Biafra, 24–25, 26
Black, S. Jason: *Urban Voodoo*, 210
Black Bagdad (film), 89
Black cat bone, **27–28**, 58, 186; hoodoo and, 126
Black Church of Simon Mpadi and, 144
Black Code. *See* Code Noir
Black Hawk, 130, 213, 277. *See also* Michael, Saint
Black Herman's Secrets of Magic, Mystery, and Legerdemain (Rucker), 35
Black Moon (film), 102
Blanc Dani, **28–29**, 68, 232, 306, 308; Fon and Ewe origins of, 271. *See also* Danbala; Michael, Saint
Blancour, Gerald, 161
Blaxploitation films, Vodou/Voodoo and, 104
Bois Caïman, 36–37, 38, 118, 120
Bòkò, **30–31**, 226; in Haitian fiction, 31; as harmful, 30; meanings of, 30; perceptions of Vodou and, 31; secret societies and, 30; zombification and, 73, 88
Bondye, **32–33**, 46, 96; gwo-bon-anj as part of, 276
Books, **33–35**; dream interpretation, 35, 174; self-help magic, 174; Vodou/Voodoo/hoodoo how-to manuals and spell books, 34–35, 114; Vodou/Voodoo scholarly works, 34. *See also authors and titles of specific books*; Literature, Vodou/Voodoo in
Boukman, Dutty, **35–38**; description of, 119–20; as maroon, 180. *See also* Bois Caïman; Haitian Revolution
Boukman Eksperyans, 196
Brazil: ason use in, 16; religious practices in, 43; slave trade and, 25–26; Yoruba culture in, 25–26. *See also* Candomblé; Espiritismo; Umbanda
Breton, Andre, 161
Brown, Karen McCarthy, 34, **38–39**; *Mama Lola*, 38–39
Brown, William Wells, 127, 343; *Clotel, or the President's Daughter*, 162; *My Southern Home*, 162, 343
Burial rites: Haitian Vodou, 7–8; Igbo, 8
Business: hoodoo as, 184–86; Spiritual Churches as, 185. *See also* Drugstores, hoodoo; Hoodoo and Voodoo/Vodou businesses, modern; Laveau, Marie; Tourism, Voudou/Voodoo

Cable, George Washington, **41**, 222; "Creole Slave Songs," 29, 41, 233; "The Dance in Place Congo," 41; *The Grandissimes*, 1, 41, 111, 162, 222; New Orleans tourism and, 292
Caesar, Julius P., 187
Candles, **42**; Catholicism and Vodou/Voodoo use of, 42, 113; Haitian Vodou altars and, 6, 42, 71. *See also specific types of Vodou/Voodoo*; Conjure; Hoodoo
Candomblé, **43–45**; Catholicism and, 43, 45; Chango and, 52; creolization and, 64; de Angola, de Caboclõ, de Congo, and de Male, 43–44; drumbeats, 45; Jejé, 43; offerings, 45; Ogun and, 100; ritual vestments, 45; spirits and deities, 44–45; Teirreros, 43; Yoruba and, 300. *See also* Brazil
Cannibalism and human sacrifice, films depicting, 89, 102, 103. *See also titles of specific films*
Carpentier, Alejo: *The Kingdom of This World*, 161; writing style, 161
Casey Jones, Joe Féraille and, 100–101
Casimir, Lumane, 196

Cassaise, Marie, 14
Castellanos, Henry: *New Orleans as It Was,* 5
Catholic Church: anti-vodou campaigns, 10–11; Code Noir and, 158. *See also specific saints*; Catholicism, Vodou/Voodoo and; Saints; Saints, spirits and deities syncretized with
Catholicism, Vodou/Voodoo and, **46–48**; creolization and, 64; emblems and iconography, 46; feast days, 47; Haiti and, 46–47; prayers and rituals, 46. *See also specific spirits, deities, and saints*; Altars; Candles; Saints; Saints, spirits and deities syncretized with; Vodou, Haitian; Voodoo, Mississippi Valley; Voodoo, New Orleans
Celestine, Oscar "Papa," 195
Cemeteries, **49–50**; Campo Santo of St. Roch's, 191; Haitian, 49; Haitian tombs and, 49; lwa and spirits associated with, 49; St. Louis Cemeteries of New Orleans, 50, 90. *See also* Baron Samedi
Center d'Art (Haiti), 13
Ceremonies, **50–51**; annual Voodoo, 51; calling lwa during, 167; drummers in, *334*; mambos and oungans in, *333, 334*; offerings in, 239; of Vodou Church in Haiti, 298–99; Vodou death rituals, 51; Vodou initiation, 51. *See also names of specific spirits and deities*; Initiations; Lave Tèt; Lwa; Maryaj Lwa (Marriage to Lwa); Openings; Parterre; Possession; St. John's Eve
Chamani, Miriam, 210
Chango, **52**. *See also* Barbara, Saint; Jeremy, Saint; John, Saint; Peter, Saint
Charlo, **52–53**, 171
Chesnutt, Charles W.: *The Conjure Woman,* 163
Child's Play (film), 105
Chireau, Yvonne, 34
Clotel, or the President's Daughter (Brown), 162
Code Noir, **53–54**, 158; Catholic iconography and Vodou rites under, 255; free blacks and, 54; Napoleon and, 54; religious intolerance and, 53; Roman Catholicism and, 158; slaves and, 47, 50, 53–54, 61, 201, 272; white colonists and, 54
Colbert, Jean Baptiste, 53
Comedians, The (film), 104
Comedians, The (Greene, novel), 103–4
Complete Fortune Teller and Dream Book (Russell), 35
Condé, Maryse: *I, Tituba, Black Witch of Salem,* 161
Congo Square, 29, **55–56**; as slave gathering place, 55; voodoo ceremonies in, 21
Congress of Santa Barbara (KOSANBA), 23–24, **56**, 390–92; documents, 391–92; *See also* Bellegarde-Smith, Patrick; Michel, Claudine
Conjure, **57–58**; business of, 185; candles and, 42; Catholicism and, 42; charms, 27, 57, 58; commercialization of, 174; herbal remedies and powders, 57; hoodoo and, 125; slaves and, 172–73; spells, 57; Voodoo and, 164. *See also* Black cat bone; Drugstores, hoodoo; Graveyard dirt; Gris-gris; Hand; High John the Conqueror Root; Hoodoo; Magic; Mojo; Rootwork; Voodoo, Mississippi Valley; Voodoo, New Orleans; Worker
Conjure Woman, The (Chesnutt), 163
Conjurers, 173, 174. *See also* Workers
Contagion, principle of, 126–27, 171
Corner Drugstore (Vicksburg), 84
Cosmogram, **59**, 314–15
Count Zero (Gibson), 164
Courlander, Harold, 34, **59–60**; *The African,* 60; *The Drum and the Hoe,* 60
Cracker Jack Drugstore (New Orleans), 83, 84, 186
"Creole Slave Songs" (Cable), 29, 41, 233
Creoles, Louisiana, **60–63**, 211; Cajun cuisine, 64; Cane River area, 60, 62; language spoken by, 111; New Orleans area, 60–62; zydeco music, 64
Creolization, **63–64**, 158; Mississippi Valley Voodoo and, 309
Crime, Voodoo and, 158; dispensing herbal/magical remedies, 159; fraud allegations, 159, 212; prostitution allegations, 290. *See also* Legislation against Vodou/Voodoo; Obeah; Toledano, Betsy; Voodoo, New Orleans

cross, 6, 19; on altars, 6; divination and, 77; physical gesture of, 6; in West Central Africa, 315. *See also specific spirits*; Artists, Haitian; Baron Samedi; Cosmogram; Legba; Vèvès
Cross marks, 155, 174
Crossroads, 6; ancestral spirits and, 9; creole societies and, 64; devil and, 136; divination and, 77; as literary metaphor, 163, 164; as location of Vodou rites, 301. *See also* Baron Samedi; Legba; Papa Gede; Papa Legba
Cultural politics, **65–66**
Curse of Simba, The (film), 103
Curses: on film, 103; Hoodoo, 128; in literature, 162; placing, 174; removing, 94, 129, 173. *See also* Fixing; Healing

Da, 29; as python, 246, 274, 306. *See also* Danbala
Dahomey, **67–69**; ason use in, 15; human sacrifice in, 67; slave trade, 25. *See also* Azaka; Bight of Benin; Fon; Slavery and slave trade
Dalmas, Antoine: *Histoire de la Révolution de Saint-Domingue,* 120
Damballah (Wideman), 164
Danbala, **69–70**, 167–168; Aaron and, 168; feast day and offerings, 70; fertility and, 97; Haiti and, 306, 308; in lwa hierarchy, 167; outdoor shrine to, 332; snakes and, 46, 274; West Central Africa and, 17. *See also* Blanc Dani; Patrick, Saint
"Dance in Place Congo, The" (Cable), 41
Dances, **71–72**; animal sacrifice and, 72; bamboula, 55; banda, 72; calinda, 55; drums and, 72; Ibo, 229; Kongo, 229; krabiye, 157; Legba and, 157; mayi, 157; release of spirits and, 71; ritual, 72; yanvalou, 157. *See also* Drums
Dangbe, 69
Danticat, Edwidge, 161; *Krik? Krak!,* 161
Davis, Andrew Jackson: Spiritualism and, 279, 280
Davis, Rod: *American Voudou,* 292
Davis, Wade, **73**; *The Serpent and the Rainbow,* 73, 105, 324; zombification and, 73, 88, 198, 324

Dawn's Revenge (Sledge), 162–163
de Claremont, Lewis: *Legends of Incense, Herb, and Oil Magic,* 35
Death, **73–74**; African/African Diasporic view of, 49. *See also* Baron Samedi; Cemeteries
Dechoukaj, 23
Dédé, Sanité, **74–75**
Défazi (Frankétienne), 161
Dejean, Yves, 286
DeLaurence, Scott, and Company, 187
Denmark Vesey Conspiracy, 272–73
Depestre, René, 161
Deren, Maya, 34, 164; *Divine Horsemen,* 164
Description Topographique, Physique, Civile...(Moreau de Saint-Méry), 33, 192, 274
Desmangles, Leslie, 34, **75–76**; *The Faces of the Gods,* 75–76, 275
Dessalines, Jean-Jacques, 118, 121
Devil's Daughter, The (film), 102
Diab, 168
d'Iberville, Pierre Le Moyne, 21
Dillon, Catherine: "Voodoo" manuscript, 99, 285, 308–9
Disembodied, The (film), 103
Divination, **76–78**; card reading, 76–77; object dropping/throwing, 76, 77; pendulum use, 76, 77–78; uses for, 76. *See also* Curses; Healing
Divine Horsemen: The Voodoo Gods of Haiti (Deren), 164
Dixie Drugstore (New Orleans), 83, 84, 186
Djouba nanchon, 17, 202; colors, 18; lwa, 202
Doctor John. *See* Montanée, Jean; Rebennack, Malcolm John, Jr.
Dolls, **78–79**, 90, 171; in film, 102–3, 104, 105; in Haitian art, 14; Ibeji, 294; lwa, 79
Dorsainvil, Justin Chrysostome (J. C.), **79–80**; *Une Explication Philologique du Vodou,* 79; *Psychologie Haitienne: Vodou et Magie,* 79; *Vodou et Nevrose,* 79, 80
Dr. Buzzard, 187, 249
Dr. Jim, 206
Drapo, 12, **80–81**; artists/makers, 80–81; history of, 80; images, 80
Dreyer, Edward: *Gumbo Ya-Ya,* 99, 285

Drugstores, hoodoo, **81–84**; pharmacies as, 186, 293, 318; proliferation of, 114. *See also names of specific hoodoo drugstores*
Drum and the Hoe: Life and Lore of the Haitian People, The (Courlander), 60
Drums, **84–85**, *336*; in ceremony, *334*; dance and, 72; greeting the, *333*; instruments associated with, 85; Petwo battery, 85; Racine Lakay group, *336*; Rada battery, 85; Santería and, 257. *See also* Ason; Dances; Music, Haitian Vodou and
du Pratz, Le Page, 33; *Histoire de la Louisiane,* 33, 265, 339–40
Duppies, 324
Durand, Oswald, 160
Duvalier, François: Catholic Church in Haiti and, 48; Haitian art scene and, 13; rule of terror under, 261; support of Biafra, 27; United States support of, 138; Vodou and, 48, 65
Duvalier, Jean-Claude: Haitian art scene and, 13–14; overthrow of, 138; rule of terror under, 261
Dye, Caroline, 188, 195, 249

Element Encyclopedia of 1000 Spells (Illes), 209
Ellis, Alfred Burdon, **87**, 304; *The Tsi-Speaking Peoples . . .,* 87; *The Yoruba-Speaking Peoples . . .,* 87
Entertainment, Voodoo as, **88–91**; film, 89–90, 102–6; music, 90, 193–96, 353–59. *See also specific films and film genres*; Art, Vodou/Voodoo in; Film, Vodou/Voodoo in; Literature, Vodou/Voodoo in; Tourism, Voudou/Voodoo
Espiritismo, **92–94**; Brazilian, 92–93; Cientifico, Cruzado, Cuban, and de Cordón, 93–94; countries practiced in, 92; major tenets of, 92. *See also* Kardec, Allan
Estimé, Léon Dumarsais, 11
Eve's Bayou (film), 105–6
Ewe, **95–96**; Haitian Vodou and, 96, 167; Louisiana and, 96; Rada spirits and, 96; Rosenthal's spirit possession studies of, 249–50; slave trade and, 95; zan bibi, 111

Ewi-Speaking Peoples of the Slave Coast of West Africa, The (Ellis), 87
Exil, Levoy, 13
Expedite, Saint: Baron Samedi and, 20
Explication Philologique du Vodou, Une (Dorsainvil), 79
Ezili, **97–98**, 177; Africa and, 25; avatars, 97; Binah and, 97; colors, offerings, and symbol, 98; Danbala and, 70; fertility and, 168; Lasiren and, 150; in lwa hierarchy, 167; Maryaj Lwa and, 182; Nibo and, 108; Virgin Mary and, 98, 168

Face of Marble, The (film), 102
Face of the Gods: Art and Altars of Africa and the African Americas (Thompson), 288
Faces of the Gods, The: Vodou and Roman Catholicism in Haiti (Desmangles), 75–76, 275
Fatiman, Cecile, 36, 120
Federal Writers' Project, **99–100**; accounts of openings, 136, 233, 378–79; flying slave stories recorded by, 110; Laura "Lala" Hopkins interview, 129–30. *See also* Louisiana Writer's Project
Félix, Lafortune, 13
Felix, Oscar "Nom," 226, 233, 234, 379
Féraille, Joe, **100–101**. *See also* Ogou
Fido (film), 89
Filan, Kenaz: *New Orleans Voodoo Handbook,* 34
Film, Vodou/Voodoo in, 88–90, **102–6**; blaxploitation films, 104; cannibalism/human sacrifice films, 89, 102, 103; 1980s to 2000s, 105–6; 1930s to 1970s, 102–4; romantic and erotic films, 90; sex films, 89–90; zombi films, 88–89, 102–5. *See also titles of specific films*
Fixing, 172, 174
Flash of the Spirit: African and Afro-American Art and Philosophy (Thompson), 28–29, 288
Fleming, Ian: *Live and Let Die,* 104
Flowers, Arthur: *Another Good Loving Blues,* 163
Folk Beliefs of the Southern Negro (Puckett), 34

Fon, 67, 95; Ayida Wedo and, 16; beginnings of Vodou and, 167; Da and, 29, 246; Gede and, 107; pythons and, 246; Rada rite and, 194
Fortier, Alcée: *Louisiana Folk-Tales,* 111
Foula, 196
Fox sisters, Spiritualism and, 279, 280
Frankétienne: *Défazi,* 161
French Quarter, The (Asbury), 75
French Quarter (New Orleans), 55, 91, 214
Fu-kiau, André, 59

Gads, 19
Gamache, Henri: *Master Book of Candle Burning,* 35, 42; popularization of candle use, 4, 232
Gates, Henry Louis, Jr.: *The Signifying Monkey,* 164, 232
Gede, **107–9;** altars, 6; Brazil and, 107; card reading and, 77; death and, 6, 49, 74, 97; fertility and, 74; gazolin drinking and, 108; Haiti and, 107; in lwa hierarchy, 167; Masaka, 49, 107; Nibo, 19, 107, 108; origins, 306; Oussou, 108; Ti Malis, 107; wisdom of, 168; Zaranye, 107. *See also* Baron Samedi; Papa Gede
Georgia Writer's Project, 112
Ghost Breakers, The (film), 102
Gibson, William: *Count Zero,* 164
Ginen, **109–10;** lwa, 167; music and, 193. *See also* Legba
Glassman, Sallie Ann, 210, 237
God. *See* Bondye
Goofer dust, 174; hoodoo and, 126
Gordon, Michelle Y., 162
Gouverneurs de la Rosée (Romaine), 161
Gran Ezili, 97
Grand Zombi, **110–11,** 308, 324; Confederate cause and, 273; Marie Laveau and, 239; West African origins, 271
Grandfather Rattlesnake, 28, 274, 308
Grandissimes, The: A Story of Creole Life (Cable), 1, 41, 111, 162, 222
Graveyard dirt, 58, **112,** 174, 248. *See also* Goofer dust
Great Migration, 81, 187
Greene, Graham: *The Comedians,* 103–4
Grimoires, 35, 288. *See also* 'Tit Albert

Gris-gris, 90, **113–14,** 173; in Africa, 302; Mississippi Valley slaves and, 265; Mississippi Valley Voodoo and, 110, 307
Groupe d'Etudes et de Recherches Traditionelles (G.E.R.T.), 22
Gruber, Michael: *Tropic of Night,* 164
Gu, 304
Guesdesine, 19
Gumbo Ya-Ya: A Collection of Louisiana Folk Tales (Dreyer, Saxon & Tallant), 99, 285

Haiti, **115;** anti-vodou campaigns, 10–11; Catholicism in, 115; earthquake of 2010, 37, 90, 138–39; as French colony of Saint-Domingue, 115; Igbo culture and, 26–27; slavery and, 115; Vodou practitioners, 115. *See also* Art, Haitian; Artists, Haitian; Haiti, United States interventionism and; Haitian Revolution; Vodou, Haitian; Vodou Church in Haiti
Haiti: The Breached Citadel (Bellegarde-Smith), 24
Haiti, United States interventionism and, 88, **137–39;** earthquake of 2010 and, 138–39; Haitian Revolution and, 137; 1986 coup d'etat, 138; 1915–1934 military control of, 137–38; second occupation, 138; Vodou religion and, 207
Haitian Diaspora, 6, 116, 184
Haitian immigration. *See* United States, Haitian immigration to
Haitian Massacre of 1804, 118
Haitian Revolution, 38, 115, **118–21,** 261; beginnings, 196; drapo and, 80; lakou and, 147; maroons and, 180; Ogou and, 168; revolt versus, 36; Vodou and, 47, 65, 158, 273. *See also* Boukman, Dutty; Haitian Immigration to the United States
Haitian Vodou: An Introduction to Haiti's Indigenous Spiritual Tradition (Siuda), 34
Haitian Vodou: Spirit, Myth, and Reality (Michel), 184
Hand, **121–22,** 174
Hayti; or the Black Republic (St. John), 33, 34, 88, 281, 286, 360–66
Healing, **122–23;** magic and, 123, 174; New Orleans and, 123; Paket Kongo

and, 231; payment for, 123; problems treated, 122; treatment forms, 122–23; Vodou/Voodoo and, 122–23

Hearn, Lafcadio, 190–91; "The Last of the Voudoos," 190

Herskovits, Melville J., 34

High John the Conqueror, 126, 174, 187, 189; conjure and, 58; in scrubs, 259

Histoire de la Louisiane (du Pratz), 33, 265, 339–40

Histoire de la Révolution de Saint-Domingue (Dalmas), 120

Historic Voodoo Museum (New Orleans), 91, 185, 291, 292

Hoodoo, **124–28**; African roots of, 96; Bible in, 126, 174; as business, 185–86; candles and perfumes in, 42, 126, 174; Catholicism and, 42; charms, 27, 112, 126; common practices, 124; conjure and, 57, 58, 172, 309; curses, 128; feeding spirits in, 166; fortunetelling and spell casting, 172; gris-gris as synonym of, 113; intended results from, 124; mass-produced products for, 128, 186–87; paying spirits, 31; practitioners, 125–26; principle of contagion, 126–27, 171; principle of similarity, 126, 171; Protestantism and, 48; racism and, 10, 127; scholarly attention to, 127; in *The Skeleton Key*, 106; slaves and slavery and, 272; Vodou/Voodoo and, 116, 125, 172, 287, 298. *See also* Conjure; Drugstores, hoodoo; Graveyard dirt; Hand; Hoodoo and Voodoo/Vodou businesses, modern; "Hoodoo Opening Ceremony"; Hopkins, Laura "Lala"; Magic; Mojo

Hoodoo and Voodoo/Vodou businesses, modern, **184–88**; botanikas, 184; products sold, 186; retail spiritual and supernatural shops, 185–86. *See also names of specific stores and companies*; Drugstores, hoodoo; New Orleans; Tourism, Voudou/Voodoo

Hoodoo-Conjuration-Witchcraft-Rootwork (Hyatt), 112, 132, 203

Hoodoo doctor, 172, 173

Hoodoo drugstores. *See* Drugstores, hoodoo

Hoodoo for Voodoo (film), 89

Hoodoo Herb and Root Magic: A Materia Magica . . . (Yronwode), 249

"Hoodoo in America" (Hurston), 34, 127, 131, 295

Hoodoo Medicine: Gullah Herbal Remedies (Mitchell), 249

"Hoodoo Opening Ceremony," 379–80

"Hoodoo Rootwork Correspondence Course," 128

Hopkins, Laura "Lala," **129–30**; openings for FWP writers and, 129, 234

Hurston, Zora Neale, 64, **130–31**, 163, 379; hoodoo in writings of, 34, 127, 128, 131, 295; influence of, 99; Marie Laveau and, 154; "Hoodoo in America," 34, 127, 131, 295; *Mules and Men,* 5, 28, 34, 82, 131, 249, 292; New Orleans research, 82, 309; New Orleans tourism and writings of, 292; questionable reliability of, 131; on rootwork versus hoodoo, 249; short stories, 131; *Tell My Horse,* 34, 131, 163, 292; *Their Eyes Were Watching God,* 130, 131; in Voodoo initiations, 136, 251, 274, 317

Hyatt, Christopher, 210; *Urban Voodoo* (with Black), 210

Hyatt, Harry Middleton, 121, **132–33**; *Hoodoo-Conjuration-Witchcraft-Rootwork,* 112, 132, 203

Hyppolite, Hector, 12, 13

I, Tituba, Black Witch of Salem (Condé), 161

I Walked with a Zombie (film), 88, 102–3

Ibo: animal sacrifice and, 251; lwa, 167

Icart, Brun, 22

Ifá, **135**. *See also* Bòkò

Igbo, new yam feast of, 178–79

Illes, Judika: *Element Encyclopedia of 1000 Spells,* 209

Immigration. *See* United States, Haitian immigration to

Indian Jim. *See* Alexander, Jim

Indio Products, 187

Initiations, **136**; gaining powers from, 173; Haitian, 51, 136; procession of initiates, 335; Voodoo, 136; Zora Neale Hurston and, 136, 251, 274, 317. *See also* Kanzo; Lave Tèt; Maryaj Lwa (Marriage to Lwa); Openings; Pris de Je

Isidore, Saint: Azaka Mede and, 18
Islam: Candomblé de Male and, 44; in Ghana, 305; Haitian Vodou and, 265; Muslim slaves in North America, 264; in Senegambia, 263; Vodu and, 305

James, Saint (the Elder), 283
James, Saint (the Greater): Ogou Feray and, 220
Jazz, 55; Papa Legba and, 232
Jazz des Jeunes, 196
Jean-Claude, Martha, 196
Jeremy, Saint: Chango and, 52
John, Saint, 253, 254; Chango and, 52
John the Conqueror Root. *See* High John the Conqueror Root
Jordan, Jim, 249
Judaism, Code Noir and, 53

Kalbas kouran, 15. *See also* Ason
Kanzo, 136, **141–42**, 226; ason and, 16; initiatory rites, 20, 141, 153; laplas ceremonies, 150; mambo and, 176; seclusion and pris de je during rites of, 245. *See also* Lave Tèt
Kardec, Allan, 92–93. *See also* Espiritismo
Kennedy, Stetson: *Palmetto Country*, 99
Keystone Laboratories (Memphis), 187
King Alexander, 307
King and the Zombie, The (film), 88
King of the Zombies (film), 102
Kingdom of This World, The (Carpentier), 161
Kings, Voodoo, 307
Konesans, **142**; mambos and, 176, 177; oungans and, 225–26
Kongo, **142–44**; Amicale of André Matsoua, 144; ancestor reverence, 314; Catholicism and, 241–42, 313, 315–16; Church of Christ on Earth and, 144; churches, 144; cosmogram and, 59, 314–15; Kimbanguist movement in, 144; kings, 143; lwa/spirits, 167, 314; minkisi, 144; music and Haitian Vodou and, 194; power of the dead and, 249; slave trade and, 143; tradition of renewal, 314. *See also* Simbi; West Central Africa
Kowalski, Marie Thérèse Alourdes Macena Margaux, 38

Kreyòl, **145**, 286, 300; music and, 193, 196. *See also* Music, Haitian Vodou and
Krik? Krak! (Danticat), 161

L. W. DeLaurence Company, 187
La Marassa, 167. *See also* Marasa
Laferrière, Dany, 161
Lafontaine, Charles. *See* Alexander, Jim
Lake Pontchartrain. *See* St. John's Eve
Lakou, 43, **147–48**; Badjo, Soukri Danach, and Souvenance, 147–148; Haitian Revolution and, 147; rise of Vodou and, 147, 300
Langaj, **148–49**
Laplas, **149–50**; oungan as, 225; responsibilities, 150, 282
Lasiren, **150–51**; lwa associated with, 151; in lwa hierarchy, 167; offerings, music, and symbols, 151. *See also* Agwe; Ezili
Last Days of Louisiana Red, The (Reed), 190
"Last of the Voudoos, The" (Hearn), 190
Lave Tèt, 50–51, **152–53**; in kanzo initiation, 136, 141, 152, 153, 226; mambo and, 176; reason for, 152
Laveau, Marie, 62, **153–55**, 249, 307; as businesswoman, 185, 187; Catholicism of, 62, 308; charitable and civil rights work, 53, 154; death of, 350–53; deification of, 74; demythologizing of, 166; Doctor Jim and, 5; Doctor John and, 190; in fiction, 162; as head of New Orleans Voodoo, 154; healing work, 122–23; impact on New Orleans, 153, 154–55; Laura Hopkins and, 129; Native Americans and, 293; parterre and services held by, 233, 234; pet snake, 110; possible Native American heritage, 206; rehearsals, 51; rumors about, 252; as spirit called upon, 308; spirit possession of, 239; tomb of as tourist spot, 50, 90, 155, 185; voodoo ceremonies led by, 21, 239; Voodoo popularized by, 64
Laws against Vodou/Voodoo. *See* Legislation against Vodou/Voodoo
Lazarus, Saint: Legba and, 157
Lébat. *See* Legba
Legba, 68, 97, **155–57**; African roots, 96; altar, 6, 157; avatars, 156; card reading

divination and, 77; colors, symbols, and offerings, 156–157; dances, 157; feast days, 157; fertility/sexuality and, 304; in openings, 220. *See also* Papa Legba; Anthony, Saint (of Padua); Lazarus, Saint; Peter, Saint; Roch, Saint
Legba's Crossing: Narratology in the African Atlantic (Russell), 164
Legends of Incense, Herb, and Oil Magic (de Claremont), 35
Legislation against Vodou/Voodoo, **158–60**, 161; licensing laws, 159; New Orleans City laws, 159. *See also* Anti-Vodou Campaigns; Code Noir; Crime, Voodoo and; Obeah
Lescot, Antoine Louis Léocardie Élie, 11
Lewis, Rockford, 187, 213–14
Lhérisson, Justin, 160
Liautaud, Georges, 14
Life and Works of Marie Laveau, The, 35, 83
Life in the Forests of the Far East (St. John), 281
Literature, Vodou/Voodoo in, **160–64**; African-American literature and literary criticism, 163–64; Anglophone folk magic in literature, 161–62; Haitian literature, 31, 160–61; Haitian writers in exile, 161; New Orleans Voodoo culture literature, 162–63, 212; tourist/tourism-related, 292. *See also names of specific authors and titles of books*; Books
Live and Let Die (film), 89, 104
Live and Let Die (Fleming, novel), 104
Loa. *See* Lwa
Loederer, Richard A., 34, 89, **165**; New Orleans tourism and writings of, 292
Loko, 3
Long, Carolyn Morrow, 53, 154, **165–66**, 233, 287, 291; Hurston's reliability and, 131; *A New Orleans Voudou Priestess*, 165, 166, 309, 350; *Spiritual Merchants*, 165, 166, 295
Louis XIV, Code Noir and, 53, 201
Louisiana. *See* New Orleans; Voodoo, Mississippi Valley; Voodoo, New Orleans
Louisiana Creole, 145
Louisiana Folk-Tales (Fortier), 111
Louisiana Writer's Project: Catherine Dillon and, 285, 308–9; interviews, 5, 82, 213, 289; participation in openings, 221, 317; Robert Tallant and, 285. *See also* Federal Writers' Project; *Voodoo in New Orleans* (Tallant)
Louis-Philippe, 54
L'Ouverture, Toussaint, 119, 120–21; negative view of Vodou, 159
Lucius, Albertus Parvus, 288
Luck ball, 121, 189, 345. *See also* Mojo
Lucky Mojo Curio Company, 128, 187
Lwa, 32, **166–68**, 239; cemeteries and, 49; common pantheons/nanchons, 167; feeding, 166; Haitian art and, 12–15; hierarchy, 167–168; mounting by 18, 97, 167, 239, 240, 327; Vodou Church in Haiti and, 298. *See also names of specific lwa*; Maryaj Lwa (Marriage to Lwa); Music, Haitian Vodou and; Nanchons; Saints, spirits and deities syncretized with

Macouloumba, Jean, **171**, 308
Macumba Love (film), 89
Magic, **171–74**; effectiveness, 172, 174; intended results, 173; New Orleans magical items, 173–74. *See also* Conjure; Hand; Hoodoo; Mojo
Magic Island, The (Seabrook), 34, 88, 89, 102, 163, 260, 286
Major League (film), 105
Makandal, François, 36, 119, **175–76**, 180, 273
Malé Revolt of 1835, 44
Mama Lola: A Vodou Priestess in Brooklyn (Brown), 38–39
Maman Brijit, 49
Mambo, **176–78**; asogwe and su pwen ranks, 176–77; ason use, 15, 16, 77; bòkò versus, 30; charitable acts/community service, 177–78; divination and, 76, 77; drapo design, 80; during ceremony, *333, 334*; as healers, 177; as prayer leaders and temple heads, 76; sosyete position and role of, 225, 298, 301; training abroad, 65–66; vèvè and, 297. *See also* Kanzo; Konesans; Lave tèt; Scheu, Patricia; Siuda, Tamara
Mambo Chita Tann. *See* Siuda, Tamara

Mambo Vye Zo Komande LaMenfo. *See* Scheu, Patricia
Manje-yanm (Eating of the Yams), 26, **178–79**; Ahajioku Lecture and, 179. *See also* Igbo
Mansa Musa, 263
Marasa, 293, 294; in spirit hierarchy, 202, 248
Marcelin, Frédéric, 160
Mardi Gras, 48, 64
Marie Laveau (Prose), 162, 190
Marie Laveau's House of Voodoo (New Orleans), 91, 185, 292
Maroons, 119, **179–81**; Hispaniola communities, 179–80; Palmares community in Brazil, 179; Southern U.S. communities, 122, 180, 181; Spanish attacks on, 181; Voodoo/Vodou and, 122, 180. *See also* Boukman, Dutty; Haiti Revolution; Makandal
Marshall, Paule, 164; *Praisesong for the Widow*, 164
Martin, Saint (de Porres): Baron Samedi and, 20
Mary Magdalene in Sepulchre, 20
Maryaj Lwa (Marriage to Lwa), 51, 136, **182**
Master Book of Candle Burning (Gamache), 35, 42
Mawu, 303–4
Mawu-Lisa: first soul sɛ and, 276; as male and female, 16–17, 303
Mediums, 279; fake, 280
Memphis Jug Band, 195
Métraux, Alfred, **182–83**; on Catholicism and Haitian Vodou, 316; description of wangas, 311; Haiti Bureau of Ethnology and, 183; Kreyòl language and, 145; on miracle of Our Lady of Mount Carmel, 236; UN Declaration of Human Rights and, 183; *Voodoo in Haiti*, 183, 226; as Voodoo scholar, 34, 60; as witness to spirit possession, 1; zombification and, 88
Michael, Saint, 283; Black Hawk and, 206; Blanc Dani and, 28, 308
Michel, Claudine, **183–84**; *Aspects Educatifs et Moraux du Vodou Haitien*, 184; *Haitian Vodou*, 184; *Journal of Haitian Studies*, 184; as Voudou scholar, 34, 302. *See also* Congress of Santa Barbara (KOSANBA)
Midnight in the Garden of Good and Evil (film), 105, 106
Miller's Dixie Hills Pharmacy (Atlanta), 84
Mississippi Valley. *See* New Orleans; Voodoo, Mississippi Valley; Voodoo, New Orleans
Missouri. *See* Voodoo, Missouri
Mitchell, Faith: *Hoodoo Medicine*, 249
Mojo, **189**; bags, 113, 189; conjure and hoodoo and, 189; multiple souls and, 275; types, 189. *See also* Conjure; Hand; Hoodoo; Luck ball; Tobie
Mojo Hand: An Orphic Tale (Phillips), 163
Monsieur d'Embarrass, 74, 308
Montanée, Jean, **190–91**, 307; facial scarification/tattoos, 265; fraud charges, 159; wealth, 188
Moreau de Saint-Méry, Médéric Louis-Élie, 41, 148, **192–93**
Morency, Wesner, 298
Morganfield, McKinley "Muddy Waters," 27
Morrison, Toni: hoodoo in writings of, 128
Morts, Les, 167
Moses, A Man of the Mountain (Seabrook), 163
Mounting, lwa, 167; Azaka, 18; Ezili, 97; possession and, 239, 240
Mules and Men (Hurston), 5, 28, 34, 82, 131, 249, 292
Mumbo Jumbo (Reed), 163, 232
Music, Haitian Vodou and, 90, **193–96**; Bizango secret societies, 194; Kongo-Petwo, 194; popular music and, 195–96; Rada, 194; rara celebration and, 194–95; rhythms, 194; roots music, 196. *See also names of specific musicians*; Dances; Drums; Music, Mississippi Valley Voodoo; Songs
Music, Mississippi Valley Voodoo, 64, 353–59. *See also names of specific musicians*; Dances; Drums; Music, Haitian Vodou and; Songs

My Southern Home: The South and Its People (Brown), 162, 343
Myalism, **197–99;** Christian element, 198; communal dances, 197; Pukkumina and, 199; resistance to slavery and, 198; spirit possessions and trance states and, 198; Vodou and, 198; Zion Revivalism and, 199
Mysteres, Les, 167

Nago nanchon, 202; lwa, 167, 201
Nanchons, 167, **201–2**, 235; major and minor groups, 201. *See also specific nanchons and lwa*
Napoleon (Napoleone di Buonaparté): Code Noir and, 54; Haitian governance and, 121; Louisiana sale by, 62
Narcisse, Clairvius, 73
Nation Sack, **203**
National Confederation of Haitian Vodou, **203–4**
Native Americans: African Americans and, 204; in New Orleans area, 20–21, 61; religion of deemed "superstition" by whites, 207; slavery and, 269; as suppliers to Marie Laveau, 293. *See also* Voodoo, Native American influences on
Native Baptist movement, 199
New Age and Neopaganism, Voodoo/Vodou and, 173, 185, **207–10;** Celtic Druidism and Wicca, 208, 209; how-to texts, 208–9; self-spirituality, 207–8
New Orleans, **211–14;** cemeteries, 50; free people of color in, 61; French founding of, 21, 211; Haitian Vodou in, 310; hoodoo drugstores, 82–83, 186, 210; literature from and about, 212–13; *plaçage* and, 61; tourist attractions, 34, 55, 91, 185, 210; Voodoo economy, 293. *See also specific New Orleans tourist attractions, locales, and businesses*; Blanc Dani; Creoles, Louisiana; Laveau, Marie; Louisiana Writer's Project; Spiritual Churches; Tourism, Voudou/Voodoo; Voodoo, New Orleans
New Orleans as It Was (Castellanos), 5
New Orleans Pharmacy Museum, 82
New Orleans Voodoo Handbook (Filan), 34

New Orleans Voodoo Spiritual Temple, 186
New Orleans Voudou Priestess, A (Long), 165, 166, 309, 350
Night of the Living Dead (film), 104
"Night with the Voudous, A" (Williams), 74–75
Not in Kansas Anymore: A Curious Tale of How Magic Is Transforming America (Wicker), 292
Nzambi a Mpungu, **215**, 316, 324

Obeah, **217–19;** legislation against, 217; Myalism and, 197, 199; Protestantism and, 218
Obin, Philomé, 12, 13
Ogou, **219–20;** African roots of, 96; avatars, 97; Badagris and, 2, 108; Balindjo and, 2; drapo and, 81; feast day, colors, and drink of, 220; Haitian Revolution and, 168; Lasiren and, 151; in lwa hierarchy, 167; marriage and, 182; Maryaj Lwa and, 182; possession by, 220; swords and, 282; war, iron, and steel and, 71. *See also* Féraille, Joe; James, Saint (the Greater)
Ogun: Haitian Revolution and, 219; Joe Féraille and, 100–101. *See also* Ogou
Okwara, Eleya, 8–9
"Old Rabbit, the Voodoo and Other Sorcerers" (Owen), 189
Ollivier, Émile, 161
On Stranger Tides (Powers), 164
One-drop (binary) rule, 62
Openings, 51, **220–21;** black cat, 129, 221; St. Peter, 129; uncrossing, 129. *See also* Hopkins, Laura "Lala"
Orchestre el Saieh, 196
Orgy of the Dead (film), 88
Ossange/Assonquer, **222**, 308; African roots, 223; Vodou version of, 222. *See also* St. Paul
Ouanga (film), 102
Ounfò, **223–24**, 298; interior, *332*; potomitan and peristyle, 156, 223, 224, *330, 332*; saint images, *332*; versus sosyete, 223. *See also* Altars; Vèvè

Oungan, **225–26**; during ceremony, 334; Fon and, 299; process to become, 225–26; sosyete position and role of, 298, 301; vèvè and, 297. *See also* laplas

Oungenikon, 225, **227–28**. *See also* Drums; Music, Haitian Vodou and

Ounsi, 225, **228–29**; ranks, 228

Our Lady of the Immaculate Conception, 70

Owen, Mary Alicia, **229**; "Among the Voodoos," 344–50, 379; Missouri Voodoo and, 342–43; "Old Rabbit, the Voodoo and Other Sorcerers," 189

Oxford Shadows (film), 90

Page, Thomas Nelson: *Red Rock,* 161

Paket Kongo, 12, **231**; as wangas, 12

Palmetto Country (Kennedy), 99

Papa Doc. *See* Duvalier, François

Papa Gede, 49, 108

Papa LaBas, **231–32**, 367. *See also* Legba; Papa Legba

Papa Legba, 155–57; African roots of, 231; crossroads and, 49; 1920s jazz and, 232. *See also* Legba; Papa LaBas

Papa Loko Attisou, 16, 108; mambos and, 177

Parterre, 51, **232–34**; recurring elements, 233. *See* also Voodoo, New Orleans

Passé en blanc (passing for white), 62

Patrick, Saint: Danbala and, 29, 46, 70, 168, 255

Paul, Saint: Assonquer and, 222, 308

Peristyle de Mariani, 22; attack on, 23; reinstatement of, 23

Peter, Saint: Chango and, 52; Legba and, 157, 220, 232, 234, 239, 255, 353

Peters, DeWitt, 12, 13

Petwo, 6, **235–36**; altars, 6; animal sacrifice, 251; Haitian Revolution and lwa, 235; Kongo Vodou rituals and, 235; lwa, 167; magic and, 30; music and Haitian Vodou and, 194; rites, 70. *See also* Ogou

Phillips, J. J.: *Mojo Hand,* 163

Pierre, André, 13

Pierre-Louis, Prosper, 13

Pilgrimages, **236–38**; Annual Custom, 237; Catholic, 237; New Orleans, 237; Vodou, 236

Pitkin, Helen: *An Angel by Brevet,* 1, 29, 52, 110, 162, 171, 353, 367–78

Plague of the Zombies, The (film), 88, 104

Politics of respectability, 127–28

Possession, **238–40**; African traditional religions and, 238; Christian Pentecostalism and, 240; dancing and, 71; faking, 240; Myalism and, 198; New Orleans Voodoo and, 277–78; Spiritual Churches and, 277, 278; Spiritualism and, 277; symptom intensity, 240; in Vodou, 238; in Voodoo, 238. *See also* Mounting, lwa

Possession, Ecstasy, and Law in Ewe Voodoo (Rosenthal), 250

Potomitan, 156, 223, 224, *330, 332. See also* Legba; Ounfò

Powers, Tim: *On Stranger Tides,* 164

Practitioners, Vodou/Voodoo: law enforcement persecution of, 66; legal prosecution of, 66, 339; moral life perspective of, 76. *See also names of specific Vodou/Voodoo practitioners*

Praisesong for the Widow (Marshall), 164

Predator 2 (film), 105

Prèt Savann, **241–43**; education/training, 242; responsibilities, 242–43; Virgin of Mount Carmel annual prayer service and, 242

Price-Mars, Jean, **243–44**; Haitian ethnology and, 243; Vodou literature, 244; as Vodou scholar, 34

Pris de Je, 136, **245**

Prose, Francine: *Marie Laveau,* 162, 190

Psychologie Haitienne: Vodou et Magie (Dorsainvil), 79

Puckett, Newbell Niles: *Folk Beliefs of the Southern Negro,* 34

Pukkumina, Myalism and, 199

Pythons, **245–46**; African peoples and, 28, 245–46; as sacred, 274. *See also* Da; Danbala; Snakes

Queen, Voodoo, 130; as priestesses, 307; snakes and, 28. *See also* Laveau, Marie

Rabbit's foot, 57, 173

Racism, Vodou/Voodoo and, 10, 127, 211

Rada, 6, **247–48**; altars, 6, 247; Ewe and, 96, 247; Fon and, 247; Haitian Vodou music and, 193–94; lwa, 167, 201, 247–48; most important deities, 68, 235; order in service, 201–2; parades, 16; rites, 70; slave beliefs and, 271; versus Petwo, 236, 248; Yoruba and, 247. *See also* Ayida Wedo; Drums; Ogou

Rainey, Gertrude "Ma," 27

Rara celebration: Haitian Vodou music in, 194–95; Rara bands, 195, 331; transvestites in, *331*

Rara Machine, 196

Raymond, Saint, 255

Re-Africanization, 45; of Voodoo, 65

Rebennack, Malcolm John, Jr., 195

Red Rock: A Chronicle of Reconstruction (Page), 161

Reed, Ishmael, 163; hoodoo in writings of, 128; *The Last Days of Louisiana Red,* 190; *Mumbo Jumbo,* 163, 232

Reincarnation, African belief in, 8–9

Resident Evil film series, 88

Revenge of the Zombie (film), 88

Reverend Zombie's House of Voodoo (New Orleans), 91, 185, 291

Rhodes, Jewell Parker, 162, 190

Rhys, Jean: *Wide Sargasso Sea,* 161

Rigaud, Milo, 183; *Secrets of Voodoo,* 34, 222

Rita, Saint, 255

Robinson, Braziel, 275, 276

Roch, Saint; Legba and, 157, 232

Rodman, Selden, 13

Romaine, Jacques: *Gouverneurs de la Rosée,* 161

Romantic and erotic films, Vodou/Voodoo and, 90

Root, 248. *See also* Rootwork; Rootworkers

Roots music (*mizik rasin*), 196

Rootwork, 172, **248–49**; in Georgia and South Carolina, 57. *See also* Conjure; Graveyard dirt; Gris-gris; Hoodoo

Rootworkers, 173, 248

Rosenthal, Judy, **249–50**; boundaries of Vodu and, 303; on origin of hoodoo as term, 124; *Possession, Ecstasy, and Law in Ewe Voodoo,* 250

Rucker, Herman: *Black Herman's Secrets of Magic, Mystery, and Legerdemain,* 35

Russell, Chloe: *Complete Fortune Teller and Dream Book,* 35

Russell, Heather: *Legba's Crossing,* 164

Ryswick, Treaty of (1697), 115, 119

Saba-yo, 196

Sacrifice, Vodou/Voodoo and, **251–52**; animal, 251, *331*; human, 251–52. *See also specific spirit and deities*; Cannibalism and human sacrifice, films depicting; St. John, Spenser

Saint John's Eve, **253–54**; New Orleans and, 253–54, 308; New Orleans tourism and, 291; spirit possession and, 238–39; Voodoo ceremonies on, 5, 21, 29, 51, 233, 238–39; Voodoo queens and, 130, 254

Saints, 65, 168, **254–55**; feast days of, 47; images of in Vodou/Voodoo ceremonies, 46, 65, 113, 254–55. *See also names of specific saints*; Catholicism, Vodou/Voodoo and; Saints, spirits and deities syncretized with; Vodou, Haitian; Voodoo, Mississippi Valley; Voodoo, New Orleans

Saints, spirits and deities syncretized with: Agwe with St. Ulrich, 3; Assonquer with St. Paul, 222, 308; Azaka Mede with St. Isidore, 18; Baron Samedi with St. Expedite and St. Martin de Porres, 20; Black Hawk with St. Michael, 206; Blanc Dani with St. Michael, 28, 308; Chango with St. Barbara, St. Jeremy, St. John, and St. Peter, 52; Danbala with St. Patrick, 29, 46, 70, 168, 255; Legba with St. Anthony of Padua, St. Lazarus, St. Peter, and St. Roch, 157, 220, 232, 234, 239, 255, 353; Ogou Feray with St. James the Greater, 220

Santería, **256–58**; blood offerings, 258; Chango and, 52; Church of Babalu Aye, 256; creolization and, 64; divination, 257–58; drums in, 257; healing in, 258; initiations, 256–57; Ogun and, 100, 101; orisha/gods, 256; Oyotunje Village, 256; priestly initiation, 257; versus Vodou, 219; Yoruba and, 300

Saxon, Lyle, 285; *Gumbo Ya-Ya*, 99, 285
Scheu, Patricia, 34, 381; interview, 381–90; *Serving the Spirits*, 34, 50, 381
Scream Blacula Scream (film), 104
Scrubs, **259**
Sea Bat, The (film), 102
Seabrook, William Buehler, **260**; *The Magic Island*, 34, 88, 89, 102, 163, 260, 286; *Moses, A Man of the Mountain*, 163; New Orleans tourism and, 292
Secret societies, **260–62**, 302–3; Bizango, 14, 194, 261, 302; Chanpwel, 302; criminal nature of, 262; in Duvalier era, 261; Ewe and, 96; Haitian, 260–62; organizational structure, 261; Sect Wouje, 302; as social networks, 260. *See also* Music, Haitian Vodou and; zobops
Secrets of Voodoo (Rigaud), 34, 222
Senegambia, **262–65**; ethnicities, 263; Islam in, 263; lwa, 265; slave trade, 96, 263–64
Serpent and the Rainbow, The (Davis, book), 73, 105, 324
Serpent and the Rainbow, The (film), 73, 105
Serving the Spirits (Scheu), 34, 50, 381
Sex films, Vodou/Voodoo and, 89–90
Shaun of the Dead (film), 89
Signifying Monkey, The: A Theory of African-American Literary Criticism (Gates), 164, 232
Silibo Nouvavou, 2
Simbi, **266–67**; altars, 267; avatars, 266–67; feast day and offerings, 267; Magi and, 266
Similarity, principle of, 126, 171
Simonis, Léonel, 14
Sinvil, Michel, 14
Siuda, Tamara, 34, 210; *Haitian Vodou*, 34
Sixth and Seventh Books of Moses, The, 35, 83, 186, **267–68**; Kabbalah and, 267
Slave Coast: Bight of Benin as, 25; Togo, Ghana, and Dahomey (Benin) as, 26
Slavery and slave trade, 25–26, **268–73**; in Africa, 268, 269; African attitudes toward, 269; Catholicism and, 50; Dohomey, 269; hoodoo and, 272; Kongo, 269; Louisiana/Mississippi Valley, 271, 272; Native Americans and, 269; Ouidah, 25; Oyo, 25; place and nature of, 271; Saint-Domingue/Haiti, 270, 271, 272; Senegambia, 96, 263–64; slave ports, 25; treatment of slaves, 272; West Africa, 269; Yoruba, 320. *See also* Asiento, the; Bight of Benin; Bight of Biafra; Code Noir; Slaves, flying
Slaves, flying, 110
Sledge, L. D.: *Dawn's Revenge*, 162–63
Snakes, **273–75**; African Vodu and, 245–46, 271; Haitian Vodou and, 273; Simbi, **266–67**; Voodoo and, 274. *See also* Danbala; Pythons; Patrick, Saint: Danbala and
Sobo, 97
Société Linto, shrine of, *332*
"Song of the Voudous on Congo Square," 357–59
Songs: "Call Me Baptist", 356; "I Am Walking on a Pin," 355; "I Will Wander in the Desert," 353–55; "St. Peter, St. Peter, Open the Door," 357; "Voodoo Eyes," 90; "The Voodoo Man," 90; "Voodoo Voodoo," 90; "We Are Going to Die in This Lake," 357. *See also* Music, Haitian Vodou and; Music, Mississippi Valley Voodoo
Sosyete, 149, 224; community service, 301; hierarchy, 301; versus ounfò, 222
Soulouque, Faustin-Élie, 10
Souls, **275–76**; African and Haitian Vodou beliefs, 275–76; Christian beliefs, 276; Native American beliefs, 276
Spirit guides, Spiritualism and, 280
Spiritual Churches, 213–14, **277–78**; Black Hawk spirit and, 130, 206, 277; as businesses, 184; early 20th-century New Orleans, 48, 277; Eternal Life Spiritual Church, 277; female leadership of, 278; minister training program, 278; Mississippi Valley Voodoo concepts and practices in, 160, 298, 309–10; spirit possession and, 278; spiritual supply shops and, 186; workers learning from, 318. *See also* Anderson, Leafy
Spiritual Merchants: Religion, Magic, and Commerce (Long), 165, 166, 295
Spiritual supply shops: candles in, 164; decline of individual conjure workers and, 58; disclaimer labels and, 159; Jim Jordan

and, 186; Native American suppliers and, 293; online presence of, 128
Spiritualism, **279–80**; afterlife and hell in, 280; beliefs, 279; fake mediums and, 280; mediums in, 279; possession and, 277; scientific community challenges to, 280; spirit guides and spirit manifestations and, 280
St. John, Spenser, **281–82**; *Hayti; or the Black Republic,* 33, 34, 88, 281, 286, 360–66; *Life in the Forests of the Far East,* 281; misconceptions about Vodou from, 33–34, 165, 252, 281, 359–60
St. Louis Cemeteries of New Orleans, 50; walking tour, 90
Stanley Drug Company (Houston), 83–84
Sugar Hill (film), 104
Summerland, 280
Swedenborg, Emanuel: Spiritualism and, 279
Sweet, James, 123
Swords, 282–83; images of saints with, 282; as ritual objects, 282; as symbols of power and authority, 282; Vodouist with symbolic, 329. See also Laplas
Syncretism, 158, **283–84**. See also specific religions, spirits, and deities; Creolization; Saints, spirits and deities syncretized with

Tacky's Rebellion, Obeah and, 218
Tale of the Voodoo Prostitute, The, (film), 90
Tallant, Robert, **285–86**, 309; as Federal Writers' Project employee, 379; *Gumbo Ya-Ya,* 99, 285; negative and sexual stereotypes of Voodoo and, 166, 292, 309; on human sacrifice in Louisiana, 252; *Voodoo in New Orleans,* 252, 260, 286, 287, 292, 309; *Voodoo Queen,* 99, 162, 190, 285
Tell My Horse: Voodoo and Life in Haiti and Jamaica (Hurston), 34, 131, 163, 292
Temple of Yehwe, 22, 23
Terminology, Vodou/Voodoo, **286–87**; different words with same meaning, 287; multiple spellings of Vodou and Voodoo, 286–87; Voodoo versus hoodoo, 287

Their Eyes Were Watching God (Hurston), 130, 131
Thompson, Robert Farris, 16, 17, **288**; cosmogram and, 59; *Face of the Gods,* 288; *Flash of the Spirit,* 28–29, 288; on Vodou dances, 72
Tissaint, Yosephat, 14
'Tit Albert, 34–35, 186, **288–89**
Toby: for gambling, 83; hand and, 121; mojo and, 187. See also Hand; Luck ball; Mojo
Toledano, Betsy, **289–91**; police harassment and arrest of, 159; as Voudou priestess, 4, 190, 307
Tourism, Voudou/Voodoo, 90–91, **291–93**; Haiti, 90, 291; Haiti tourist literature, 292; impact of, 292–93; New Orleans, 34, 55, 90, 91, 185, 210, 291; New Orleans tourist literature, 292; U.S. tourist literature, 292. See also specific Voodoo-related New Orleans tourist attractions; New Orleans
Trick doctors, 173
Tricking, 57, 172
Trinidad Orisha: Chango and, 52; creolization and, 64
Tropic of Night (Gruber), 164
Tsi-Speaking Peoples of the Gold Coast of West Africa, The (Ellis), 87
Turlington, Shannon R.: *Complete Idiot's Guide® to Voodoo,* 34
Twain, Mark, 162; *Adventures of Huckleberry Finn,* 162
28 Days Later (film), 88
28 Weeks Later (film), 88
Twins, **293–94**; Da, 16; La Marassa/Marasa, 167, 202, 248, 293, 294; Yoruba and, 294
Two Head, **294–95**; conjurers, 294; hoodoo doctors/doctors, 173, 294

Ulrich, Saint: Agwe and, 3
Umbanda, 92–93
United States, Haitian immigration to, **116–17**; economic and political conditions and, 117; Haitian Revolution and, 116, 339; states and regions settled, 116
Urban Voodoo (Black & Hyatt), 210

Valmor Company (Chicago), 187
Vériquité, 4, 96, 308, 367
Vèvè, **297**, *330*; as sacred art, 11–12; of Baron Samedi, 20; drawing, 297; evoking spirits with, 297; mambo creator of, 297; in openings, 71, 167, 220; origins of iconography, 297; in ounfò, 223, 224; oungan creator of, 297; in *The Serpent and the Rainbow* film, 105
Virgin Mary: Ezili and, 168; female lwa and, 255
Vodou, Haitian, **299–303**; American practitioners, 298; ancestral spirits in, 7–9, 167, 301; art, 11–15; candles in, 42; card reading in, 77; Catholic Church neglect and, 300; Catholicism and, 42, 46–47, 300, 315–16; Chango in, 52; Christianity and, 48, 50; civil rights and, 53; concept of death in, 73–74; creolization and, 64; cultural misappropriation of, 66; cultural politics and, 65–66; dancing in, 71–72; dolls in, 79; Ewe and, 299; Fon and, 299; God in, 32–33; Ibo and, 299; Kongolese contribution to, 299; lakou system and, 300; locations of practice, 301; monotheism versus polytheism in, 33; morality in, 301; object dropping/throwing, 76, 77; Ogun in, 100; prêt savann, 47; re-Africanization of, 214, 255; snakes in, 246; strains, 302; temple/urban versus rural, 301–2; twins and, 293–94; versus Hoodoo, 172. *See also names of specific spirits and deities;* Bondye; Catholicism, Vodou/Voodoo and; Cemeteries; Ceremonies; Kongo; Lwa; Maryaj Lwa (Marriage to Lwa); Sosyete; Vodou Church in Haiti; West Central Africa
Vodou Church in Haiti, **298–99**; ceremony, 298; possession and, 298. *See also names of specific spirits and deities;* Vodou, Haitian
Vodou et Nevrose (Dorsainvil), 79, 80
Vodu, West African, 167, 172, 272, **303–6**; afterlife in, 304; charms, 304–5; Christianity and, 305; deities and spirits, 303–4; human sacrifice in, 252; Islam and, 305; multiple souls in, 276, 304; possession in, 304; as pure Vodou/Voodoo, 282. *See also names of specific West African spirits, peoples, kingdoms, and regions*
Voodoo, Mississippi Valley, 171, **306–10**; altars, 308; animal sacrifice in, 251; books about, 34, 41; candles in, 42, 308; Catholicism and, 42, 47, 62, 113; Christianity and, 48, 159–60; civil rights and, 53; clergy, 307; conjure and, 57, 58; creolization and, 308; criminalization of, 211; cultural politics and, 65–66; death in, 73–74; difficulty studying, 286; end of, 298, 309; feeding spirits in, 166; Haiti and, 116; Haitian Vodou versus, 307; hoodoo and, 172, 307; initiations and openings, 308; local culture and, 48, 164; ministers, 307; origination of, 68; parterre in, 232–33; paying spirits, 31; Protestant churches and, 48; rituals, 308; Senegambians and, 265; songs, 353–59; spirits, 307–8; tenacity of, 98; versus conjure/rootwork, 307; white practitioners of, 208. *See also names of specific spirits and deities;* Catholicism, Vodou/Voodoo and; Dédé, Sanité; Gris-gris; Laveau, Marie; New Orleans; Snakes; Voodoo, New Orleans; wangateur/wangateuse
Voodoo, Missouri, 272, 308, 342–50; Grandfather Rattlesnake and, 28, 274; multiple souls in, 275; spirits, 308
Voodoo, Native American influences on, **204–7**; ancestor worship, 205; arrowheads, magical bags, and medicinal herbs, 206; dolls and conjure stones, 206; fear of serpents, 205; multiple souls and supernatural justice spiritual assumptions, 205; spirit summoning through rituals and ceremonies, 205; witchcraft, 205
Voodoo, New Orleans, 185, 211–12, 309; American Civil War and, 318; ceremony locations, 20, 21; criminalization of, 213; "Death of Marie Laveau" (*Daily Picayune,* 1881), 350–52; early descriptions, 339–42; end of, 298;

"Idolatry and Quackery" (*Louisiana Gazette,* 1820), 340; local culture and, 48; openings, 221; parterre in, 232–33; re-Africanization and, 214; "A Sainted Woman" (*Democrat,* 1881), 352–53; saints in, 213, 255; snakes in, 246; spirits, 231, 232, 308; "The Virgin of the Voudous" (*Weekly Delta,* 1850), 340–41; "The Voudou Case Disposed of (*Daily Picayune,* 1863), 341–42. *See also* Grand Zombi; Healing; Laveau, Marie; Macouloumba, Jean; Ossange/Assonquer; Tourism, Vodou/Voodoo; Voodoo, Mississippi Valley

Voodoo Academy 2 (film), 90
Voodoo and Obeahs (Williams), 197
Voodoo Authentica of New Orleans Cultural Center and Collection, 185, 214; Voodoofest, 291
Voodoo dolls. *See* Dolls
Voodoo Dreams: A Novel of Marie Laveau (Rhodes), 162, 190
Voodoo Dreams (film), 90
Voodoo Fest (New Orleans), 291
Voodoo Fire in Haiti (film), 89
Voodoo Fire in Haiti (Loederer, book), 34, 89, 165, 260, 286
Voodoo for Two (film), 90
Voodoo in Haiti (Métraux), 183, 226
Voodoo in New Orleans (Tallant), 252, 260, 286, 287, 292, 308; characters/subjects in, 285; misinformation in, 285, 309
Voodoo Island (film), 103
Voodoo Lagoon (film), 90
Voodoo Love and the Curse of Jean Lafitte's Treasure (film), 90
Voodoo Magnian, 29, 96. *See also* Blanc Dani
Voodoo Man (film), 102
Voodoo Possession (film), 89
Voodoo Queen: The Spirited Lives of Marie Laveau (Ward), 154, 309, 312
Voodoo Queen, The (Tallant), 99, 162, 190, 285
Voodoo Tiger (film), 89, 103
Voodoo Woman (film), 88, 103
Voodoofest (New Orleans), 185
Voodoos, 287

Walker, Alice: hoodoo in writings of, 128
Wanga, **311**; Baron Samedi and, 19; Bòkò use of, 30; as negative, 113, 173; Paket Kongo as, 12
Wangateur/wangateuse, 31, 226, 311
Wangol nanchon: lwa, 167
Ward, Martha, 309, **311–12**; *Voodoo Queen: The Spirited Lives of Marie Laveau*, 154, 309, 312
Water, Haitian Vodou altars and, 6
Weekend at Bernie's II (film), 105
Werewolves, 324
West Africa. *See* Vodou, West African; West Central Africa
West Central Africa, **313–16**; ancestor reverence in, 314; Catholicism in, 313, 315–16; chiefs, 314; Christian saints and Kongo spirits and, 313; healers, 314; prophets, 314; ritual objects, 314; spirits, 314; tradition of renewal, 314–15; Vodou and, 313, 315–16; witchcraft and witches and, 314. *See also* Cosmogram; Kongo; Wanga
Wheatley, Phillis, 264
White King of La Gonave, The (Wirkus), 10, 89
White Zombie (film), 88, 89, 102
Wicker, Christine: *Not in Kansas Anymore,* 292
Wide Sargasso Sea (Rhys), 161
Wideman, John Edgar: *Damballah,* 164
Williams, Joseph J., 197
Williams, Marie B.: "A Night with the Voudous," 74–75
Wirkus, Faustin E., 89; *The White King of La Gonave,* 10, 89
Worker, **317–18**; conjure and, 58; fees, 317; scrubs and, 259; services provided by, 317; training, 317–18
World War Z (film), 88

Yoruba, **319–20**; art, 320; Brazil and, 25–26; creation, origin, and migration stories, 319–20; Ifa in, 320; oral histories (oríkì) and praise poems, 319; raids on Dahomey by, 67; religion, 320; slave trade, 25, 320; twins and, 294; Vodou and, 167; waves of migration, 320

Yoruba-Speaking Peoples of the Slave Coast of West Africa, The (Ellis), 87
Yronwode, Catherine: *Hoodoo Herb and Root Magic*, 249

zinzin, 113, 173
Zion Revivalism, Myalism and, 199
zobops, 30. *See also* Secret societies
Zombi, **323–24**; African roots of, 323; astral, 323, 324; bòkò creation of, 30; cadaver, 323, 324; Creole French and, 111; history, 323–24; as Hollywood creation, 323; in Mississippi Valley/New Orleans Voodoo, 324; Myalism and, 198; offensive soul as, 49; popular misconceptions of, 323; types of, 323–24; Vodou and, 323. *See also* Bòkò; Grand Zombi; Zombi films; zombification
Zombi films, 88–89, 102–5. *See also titles of specific zombi films*
Zombieland (film), 89
Zombies of Mora Tau (film), 88
Zombies on Broadway (film), 103
zombification: Alfred Métraux and, 88; Bizango and, 14; Clairvius Narcisse case, 73; Wade Davis and, 73, 88, 198, 324. *See also titles of specific zombi films*; Zombi films
zydeco, 64

www.ingramcontent.com/pod-product-compliance
Lightning Source LLC
Chambersburg PA
CBHW060504300426
44112CB00017B/2545